International Securities
Volume II

The International Library of Critical Writings in Financial Economics

Series Editor: Richard Roll
    Allstate Professor of Economics
    The Anderson School at UCLA, USA

This major series presents by field outstanding selections of the most important articles across the entire spectrum of financial economics – one of the fastest growing areas in business schools and economics departments. Each collection has been prepared by a leading specialist who has written an authoritative introduction to the literature.

1. The Theory of Corporate Finance (Volumes I and II)
   Michael J. Brennan
2. Futures Markets (Volumes I, II and III)
   A.G. Malliaris
3. Market Efficiency: Stock Market Behaviour in Theory and Practice (Volumes I and II)
   Andrew W. Lo
4. Microstructure: The Organization of Trading and Short Term Price Behavior (Volumes I and II)
   Hans R. Stoll
5. The Debt Market (Volumes I, II and III)
   Stephen A. Ross
6. Options Markets (Volumes I, II and III)
   George M. Constantinides and A.G. Malliaris
7. Empirical Corporate Finance (Volumes I, II, III and IV)
   Michael J. Brennan
8. Continuous Time Finance
   Stephen M. Schaefer
9. International Securities (Volumes I and II)
   George C. Philippatos and Gregory Koutmos

Future titles will include:

Behavioral Finance
Harold M. Shefrin

Financial Forecasting
Roy Batchelor and Pami Dua

Emerging Markets

Asset Pricing Theory and Tests
Robert Grauer

International Capital Markets
Rene M. Stulz and Andrew Karolyi

Foreign Exchange Markets

Wherever possible, the articles in these volumes have been reproduced as originally published using facsimile reproduction, inclusive of footnotes and pagination to facilitate ease of reference.

For a list of all Edward Elgar published titles visit our site on the World Wide Web at
http://www.e-elgar.co.uk

International Securities
Volume II

Edited by

George C. Philippatos

*Distinguished Chaired Professor of Banking and Finance
University of Tennessee, USA*

and

Gregory Koutmos

*Professor of Finance
Fairfield University, USA*

THE INTERNATIONAL LIBRARY OF CRITICAL WRITINGS IN FINANCIAL ECONOMICS

An Elgar Reference Collection
Cheltenham, UK • Northampton, MA, USA

© George C. Philippatos and Gregory Koutmos 2001. For copyright of individual articles, please refer to the Acknowledgements.

All rights reserved. No part of this publication may be reproduced, stored in a retrieval system, or transmitted in any form or by any means, electronic, mechanical, photocopying, recording, or otherwise without the prior permission of the publisher.

Published by
Edward Elgar Publishing Limited
Glensanda House
Montpellier Parade
Cheltenham
Glos GL50 1UA
UK

Edward Elgar Publishing, Inc.
136 West Street
Suite 202
Northampton
Massachusetts 01060
USA

A catalogue record for this book is available from the British Library.

Library of Congress Cataloguing in Publication Data

International securities / edited by George C. Philippatos and Gregory Koutmos.
    p. cm. — (International library of critical writings in financial economics; 9) (An Elgar reference collection)
    Includes bibliographical references and index.
    1. Stock exchanges. 2. Securities. 3. Investments, Foreign. 4. International finance. I. Philippatos, George C. II. Koutmos, Gregory, 1955– III. Series. IV. Series: An Elgar reference collection

HG4551 .I547 2001
332.63'2—dc21   2001023858

ISBN   1 84064 275 0 (2 volume set)

Printed and bound in Great Britain
by Bookcraft (Bath) Ltd., Somerset

Contents

Acknowledgements ix
A preface by the editors to both volumes appears in Volume I
Introduction George Philippatos and Gregory Koutmos xiii

PART I   GLOBALIZATION OF FINANCIAL MARKETS

1. Peter A. Abken (1991), 'Globalization of Stock, Futures, and Options Markets', *Federal Reserve Bank of Atlanta Economic Review*, **76** (4), July/August, 1–22   3
2. G.C. Philippatos, A. Christofi and P. Christofi (1983), 'The Inter-Temporal Stability of International Stock Market Relationships: Another View', *Financial Management*, **12** (4), Winter, 63–9   25
3. Steven L. Heston, K. Geert Rouwenhorst and Roberto E. Wessels (1995), 'The Structure of International Stock Returns and the Integration of Capital Markets', *Journal of Empirical Finance*, **2** (3), September, 173–97   32
4. Gregory Koutmos (1996), 'Modeling the Dynamic Interdependence of Major European Stock Markets', *Journal of Business Finance and Accounting*, **23** (7), September, 975–88   57
5. François Longin and Bruno Solnik (1995), 'Is the Correlation in International Equity Returns Constant: 1960–1990?', *Journal of International Money and Finance*, **14** (1), February, 3–26   71
6. Bala Arshanapalli and John Doukas (1993), 'International Stock Market Linkages: Evidence from the Pre- and Post-October 1987 Period', *Journal of Banking and Finance*, **17** (1), February, 193–208   95
7. Philippe Jorion and William N. Goetzmann (1999), 'Global Stock Markets in the Twentieth Century', *Journal of Finance*, **LIV** (3), June, 953–80   111
8. M. Wayne Marr, John L. Trimble and Raj Varma (1991), 'On the Integration of International Capital Markets: Evidence from Euroequity Offerings', *Financial Management*, **20** (4), Winter, 11–21   139

PART II   INTERACTIONS OF FINANCIAL MARKETS AND PRICE DYNAMICS

9. George C. Philippatos, Efi Pilarinu and A.G. Malliaris (1993), 'Chaotic Behavior in Prices of European Equity Markets: A Comparative Analysis of Major Economic Regions', *Journal of Multinational Financial Management*, **3** (3/4), 5–24   153

	10.	Gregory Koutmos and G. Geoffrey Booth (1995), 'Asymmetric Volatility Transmission in International Stock Markets', *Journal of International Money and Finance*, **14** (6), December, 747–62	173
	11.	Johan Knif and Seppo Pynnönen (1999), 'Local and Global Price Memory of International Stock Markets', *Journal of International Financial Markets, Institutions and Money*, **9** (2), April, 129–47	189
	12.	Gregory Koutmos (1997), 'Feedback Trading and the Autocorrelation Pattern of Stock Returns: Further Empirical Evidence', *Journal of International Money and Finance*, **16** (4), August, 625–36	208
	13.	Robert F. Engle and Raul Susmel (1993), 'Common Volatility in International Equity Markets', *Journal of Business and Economic Statistics*, **11** (2), April, 167–76	220

PART III EMERGING MARKETS

14. John Mullin (1993), 'Emerging Equity Markets in the Global Economy', *Federal Reserve Bank of New York Quarterly Review*, **18** (2), Summer, 54–83 — 233
15. Gregory Koutmos (1997), 'Do Emerging and Developed Stock Markets Behave Alike? Evidence from Six Pacific Basin Stock Markets', *Journal of International Financial Markets, Institutions and Money*, **7** (3), October, 221–34 — 263
16. Gregory Koutmos (1999), 'Asymmetric Price and Volatility Adjustments in Emerging Asian Stock Markets', *Journal of Business Finance and Accounting*, **26** (1/2), January/March, 83–101 — 277
17. Richard A. DeFusco, John M. Geppert and George P. Tsetsekos (1996), 'Long-Run Diversification Potential in Emerging Stock Markets', *Financial Review*, **31** (2), May, 343–63 — 296
18. Claude B. Erb, Campbell R. Harvey and Tadas E. Viskanta (1999), 'New Perspectives on Emerging Market Bonds', *Journal of Portfolio Management*, **23** (2), Winter, 83–92 — 317
19. Geert Bekaert and Michael S. Urias (1999), 'Is There a Free Lunch in Emerging Market Equities?', *Journal of Portfolio Management*, **25** (3), Spring, 83–95 — 327
20. Vihang Errunza, Lemma W. Senbet and Ked Hogan (1998), 'The Pricing of Country Funds from Emerging Markets: Theory and Evidence', *International Journal of Theoretical and Applied Finance*, **1** (1), 111–43 — 340

PART IV INTERNATIONAL DERIVATIVE SECURITIES

21. Tribhuvan N. Puri and George C. Philippatos (1993), 'Equilibrium Pricing Functions of Foreign Exchange Forward, Futures, and Option Contracts', *Advances in Futures and Options Research*, **6**, 217–35 — 375
22. Darrell Duffie (1999), 'Credit Swap Valuation', *Financial Analysts Journal*, **55** (1), January/February, 73–87 — 394

	23. Lixin Wu, Yue Kuen Kwok and Hong Yu (1999), 'Asian Options with the American Early Exercise Feature', *International Journal of Theoretical and Applied Finance*, **2** (1), 101–11	409
	24. Ajay Dravid, Matthew Richardson and Tong-sheng Sun (1994), 'The Pricing of Dollar-Denominated Yen/DM Warrants', *Journal of International Money and Finance*, **13** (5), October, 517–36	420
	25. Merton H. Miller (1995), 'Do We Really Need More Regulation of Financial Derivatives?', *Pacific-Basin Finance Journal*, **3** (2–3), July, 147–58	440

PART V EUROPEAN MONETARY UNION AND IMPLICATIONS FOR FINANCIAL MARKETS

	26. Stan Beckers (1999), 'Investment Implications of a Single European Capital Market', *Journal of Portfolio Management*, **25** (3), Spring, 9–17	455
	27. Anil K. Kashyap and Jeremy C. Stein (1997), 'The Role of Banks in Monetary Policy: A Survey with Implications for the European Monetary Union', *Economic Perspectives*, Federal Reserve Bank of Chicago, **XXI** (5), September/October, 2–18	464
	28. Daniel Gros (1998), 'EMU and Capital Markets: Big Bang or Glacier?', *International Finance*, **1** (1), October, 3–34	481

PART VI INTERNATIONAL FINANCIAL CRISES

	29. George C. Philippatos and K.G. Viswanathan (1991), 'Brazilian Debt Crisis and Financial Markets: An Analysis of Major Economic Events Leading to the Brazilian Debt Moratorium', *Applied Financial Economics*, **1** (4), December, 223–34	515
	30. Richard Roll (1988), 'The International Crash of October 1987', *Financial Analysts Journal*, **44** (5), September–October, 19–35	527
	31. Merton H. Miller (1998), 'The Current Southeast Asia Financial Crisis', *Pacific-Basin Finance Journal*, **6** (3–4), August, 225–33	544
	32. Steven B. Kamin (1999), 'The Current International Financial Crisis: How Much is New?', *Journal of International Money and Finance*, **18** (4), August, 501–14	553
	33. Joseph E. Stiglitz (1999), 'Reforming the Global Economic Architecture: Lessons from Recent Crises', *Journal of Finance*, **54** (4), August, 1508–21	567

Name Index   581

Acknowledgements

The editors and publishers wish to thank the authors and the following publishers who have kindly given permission for the use of copyright material.

American Statistical Association for article: Robert F. Engle and Raul Susmel (1993), 'Common Volatility in International Equity Markets', *Journal of Business and Economic Statistics*, **11** (2), April, 167–76.

Association for Investment Management and Research for articles: Richard Roll (1988), 'The International Crash of October 1987', *Financial Analysts Journal*, **44** (5), September–October, 19–35; Darrell Duffie (1999), 'Credit Swap Valuation', *Financial Analysts Journal*, **55** (1), January/February, 73–87.

Blackwell Publishers, Inc. for articles: Philippe Jorion and William N. Goetzmann (1999), 'Global Stock Markets in the Twentieth Century', *Journal of Finance*, **LIV** (3), June, 953–80; Joseph F. Stiglitz (1999), 'Reforming the Global Economic Architecture: Lessons from Recent Crises', *Journal of Finance*, **54** (4), August, 1508–21.

Blackwell Publishers Ltd for articles: Gregory Koutmos (1996), 'Modeling the Dynamic Interdependence of Major European Stock Markets', *Journal of Business Finance and Accounting*, **23** (7), September, 975–88; Daniel Gros (1998), 'EMU and Capital Markets: Big Bang or Glacier?', *International Finance*, **1** (1), October, 3–34; Gregory Koutmos (1999), 'Asymmetric Price and Volatility Adjustments in Emerging Asian Stock Markets', *Journal of Business Finance and Accounting*, **26** (1/2), January/March, 83–101.

Eastern Finance Association for article: Richard A. DeFusco, John M. Geppert and George P. Tsetsekos (1996), 'Long-Run Diversification Potential in Emerging Stock Markets', *Financial Review*, **31** (2), May, 343–63.

Elsevier Science for articles: Bala Arshanapalli and John Doukas (1993), 'International Stock Market Linkages: Evidence from the Pre- and Post-October 1987 Period', *Journal of Banking and Finance*, **17** (1), February, 193–208; Ajay Dravid, Matthew Richardson and Tong-sheng Sun (1994), 'The Pricing of Dollar-Denominated Yen/DM Warrants', *Journal of International Money and Finance*, **13** (5), October, 517–36; François Longin and Bruno Solnik (1995), 'Is the Correlation in International Equity Returns Constant: 1960–1990?', *Journal of International Money and Finance*, **14** (1), February, 3–26; Merton H. Miller (1995), 'Do We Really Need More Regulation of Financial Derivatives?', *Pacific-Basin Finance Journal*, **3** (2–3), July, 147–58; Steven L. Heston, K. Geert Rouwenhorst and Roberto E. Wessels (1995), 'The Structure of International Stock Returns and the Integration of Capital Markets', *Journal of Empirical Finance*, **2** (3), September, 173–97; Gregory Koutmos and G. Geoffrey Booth (1995),

'Asymmetric Volatility Transmission in International Stock Markets', *Journal of International Money and Finance*, **14** (6), December, 747–62; Gregory Koutmos (1997), 'Feedback Trading and the Autocorrelation Pattern of Stock Returns: Further Empirical Evidence', *Journal of International Money and Finance*, **16** (4), August, 625–36; Gregory Koutmos (1997), 'Do Emerging and Developed Stock Markets Behave Alike? Evidence from Six Pacific Basin Stock Markets', *Journal of International Financial Markets, Institutions and Money*, **7** (3), October, 221–34; Merton H. Miller (1998), 'The Current Southeast Asia Financial Crisis', *Pacific-Basin Finance Journal*, **6** (3–4), August, 225–33; Johan Knif and Seppo Pynnönen (1999), 'Local and Global Price Memory of International Stock Markets', *Journal of International Financial Markets, Institutions and Money*, **9** (2), April, 129–47; Steven B. Kamin (1999), 'The Current International Financial Crisis: How Much is New?', *Journal of International Money and Finance*, **18** (4), August, 501–14.

Federal Reserve Bank of Atlanta for article: Peter A. Abken (1991), 'Globalization of Stock, Futures, and Options Markets', *Federal Reserve Bank of Atlanta Economic Review*, **76** (4), July/August, 1–22.

Federal Reserve Bank of Chicago for article: Anil K. Kashyap and Jeremy C. Stein (1997), 'The Role of Banks in Monetary Policy: A Survey with Implications for the European Monetary Union', *Economic Perspectives*, **XXI** (5), September/October, 2–18.

Federal Reserve Bank of New York for article: John Mullin (1993), 'Emerging Equity Markets in the Global Economy', *Federal Reserve Bank of New York Quarterly Review*, **18** (2), Summer, 54–83.

Financial Management Association International for articles: G.C. Philippatos, A. Christofi and P. Christofi (1983), 'The Inter-Temporal Stability of International Stock Market Relationships: Another View', *Financial Management*, **12** (4), Winter, 63–9; M. Wayne Marr, John L. Trimble and Raj Varma (1991), 'On the Integration of International Capital Markets: Evidence from Euroequity Offerings', *Financial Management*, **20** (4), Winter, 11–21.

Haworth Press, Inc. for article: George C. Philippatos, Efi Pilarinu and A.G. Malliaris (1993), 'Chaotic Behavior in Prices of European Equity Markets: A Comparative Analysis of Major Economic Regions', *Journal of Multinational Financial Management*, **3** (3/4), 5–24.

Institutional Investor, Inc. for articles: Claude B. Erb, Campbell R. Harvey and Tadas E. Viskanta (1999), 'New Perspectives on Emerging Market Bonds', *Journal of Portfolio Management*, **23** (2), Winter, 83–92; Stan Beckers (1999), 'Investment Implications of a Single European Capital Market', *Journal of Portfolio Management*, **25** (3), Spring, 9–17; Geert Bekaert and Michael S. Urias (1999), 'Is There a Free Lunch in Emerging Market Equities?', *Journal of Portfolio Management*, **25** (3), Spring, 83–95.

JAI Press Inc. for article: Tribhuvan N. Puri and George C. Philippatos (1993), 'Equilibrium Pricing Functions of Foreign Exchange Forward, Futures, and Option Contracts', *Advances in Futures and Options Research*, **6**, 217–35.

Taylor and Francis Ltd (http://www.tandf.co.uk/journals) for article: George C. Philippatos and K.G. Viswanathan (1991), 'Brazilian Debt Crisis and Financial Markets: An Analysis of Major Economic Events Leading to the Brazilian Debt Moratorium', *Applied Financial Economics*, **1** (4), December, 223–34.

World Scientific Publishing Co. Pte. Ltd for articles: Vihang Errunza, Lemma W. Senbet and Ked Hogan (1998), 'The Pricing of Country Funds from Emerging Markets: Theory and Evidence', *International Journal of Theoretical and Applied Finance*, **1** (1), 111–43; Lixin Wu, Yue Kuen Kwok and Hong Yu (1999), 'Asian Options with the American Early Exercise Feature', *International Journal of Theoretical and Applied Finance*, **2** (1), 101–11.

Every effort has been made to trace all the copyright holders but if any have been inadvertently overlooked the publishers will be pleased to make the necessary arrangement at the first opportunity.

In addition the publishers wish to thank the Library of the London School of Economics and Political Science and the Library of Indiana University at Bloomington, USA, for their assistance in obtaining these articles.

To Liana, Toula, Crito, Dimitris, Alex, Yanni and Ian. They all know the reasons that reason cannot know.

Introduction to Volume II

George Philippatos and Gregory Koutmos

Globalization of Financial Markets

The increased volume of international transactions in all sorts of financial instruments is an unmistakable sign of the globalization of financial markets. Abken's paper examines how trading systems in stocks, futures and options contribute to the globalization process. Philippatos, Christofi and Christofi investigate the coherence of several stock exchanges using principal component analysis. Heston, Rouwenhorst and Wessels test for integration of European stock markets and the US stock market by examining the pricing of country indices and comparing the prices of factor risks across countries. The test supports the hypothesis that markets are integrated since risk premia are identical across markets. Koutmos provides evidence on European stock market integration on the basis of multidirectional price and volatility linkages across markets. The paper by Longin and Solnik investigates the behavior of cross market correlations. Their evidence points to an increase in international correlations over the past thirty years, suggesting that the process of globalization has been intensifying. Using cointegration analysis, Arshanapalli and Doukas find that cointegrating relationships have changed in the period following the October 1987 market crash.

Interactions of Financial Markets and Price Dynamics

Recent empirical findings suggest that the random walk model is not a very useful framework for the analysis of the returns of speculative assets, especially for high frequency data. There is evidence of nonlinear structure in the returns that cannot be captured by the random walk model. Recent research has focused on uncovering non-linear dependencies using techniques adapted from complex systems theory which includes chaotic processes. The paper by Philippatos, Pilarinu and Malliaris applies such techniques to analyze the behavior of international stock markets. The nonlinear dependencies detected appear to be similar across stock market indices, supporting the hypothesis of integrated national markets.

Nonlinear linkages and interactions across the three major markets of US, Japan and UK are studied in the paper by Koutmos and Booth via a multivariate Exponential Garch model. It is found that news in a given market influences the volatility of the other markets asymmetrically in the sense that the influence is more pronounced when the news is bad. Using cointegration techniques, Knif and Pynnönen investigate lead-lag relationships in international stock markets and find that the US market is the most influential, affecting all other markets.

The study by Koutmos finds that the autocorrelation of stock returns is linked to the level of volatility. This linkage produces an intriguing asymmetric predictability in stock returns in the sense that returns are more predictable during periods of low volatility. This could be the manifestation of positive feedback trading strategies followed by some investors.

In another paper Engle and Susmel introduce an interesting new technique that can be used to test for common volatility across markets.

Emerging Markets

Emerging markets have become very attractive for both institutional and individual international investors. This attractiveness is justified on the grounds that emerging markets have considerable growth potential and at the same time offer additional diversification benefits due to their low correlation with the developed markets. The paper by Mullin investigates the return performance of emerging markets and it evaluates the degree of integration of emerging and developed markets. He finds that emerging markets are more integrated than commonly thought. Similarly, Koutmos reports that, at least in a statistical sense, the behavior of emerging market returns exhibits a striking resemblance to that of developed market returns. The second paper by Koutmos documents an asymmetric pattern of price and volatility adjustment to news for several emerging stock markets. DeFusco, Geppert and Tsetsekos find no evidence of cointegration between developed and emerging markets. This, in turn, suggests that investing in emerging markets can produce substantial diversification benefits.

Erb, Harvey and Viskanta examine the role of emerging bond markets in global investment portfolios. The authors suggest that the high return in these markets is just compensation for higher risk. Bekaert and Urias argue that caution should be exercised when evaluating the diversification potential in emerging markets. Rather than using market indices, the authors argue that investment vehicles such as closed-end mutual funds, open-end mutual funds and ADRs should be used.

International Derivative Securities

The markets for financial futures, options and interest rate and currency swaps are becoming increasingly important for global investors. These instruments can be used to hedge risks or take positions on the future direction of the market. They are very liquid and have very low transactions fees compared to the spot market.

The paper by Puri and Philippatos studies the equilibrium prices of foreign exchange forward, futures and options contracts in continuous time within a general equilibrium framework. The authors establish that the value of a forward contract can be found by discounting the terminal value of the contract using a random rate of return and subsequently taking the expected value. Duffie provides a framework for the valuation of credit swaps, Wu, Kwok and Yu for the valuation of Asian options and Dravid, Richardson and Sun for the valuation of dollar denominated yen/DM warrants. Finally, Miller's paper deals with the issue of regulating financial derivatives.

European Monetary Union and Implications for Financial Markets

The single most important development for financial markets in the last decade is the European Monetary Union (EMU) and the accompanying Euro which went into effect in January 1999. The changes caused by EMU will in some cases be protracted and in other cases instantaneous. The paper by Beckers documents higher correlations among European equity markets and it predicts significant reduction in the opportunities of active managers to add value. The paper by Kashyap and Stein and the paper by Gros investigate the macroeconomic effects of EMU.

International Financial Crises

Currency collapses and stock market crashes are recurrent phenomena. The readings in this section concentrate on recent financial crises. The paper by Philippatos and Viswanathan analyzes the Brazilian debt crisis and its impact on the value of US bank equities. Roll provides an extensive analysis and evaluation of the international crash of October 1987. The papers by Miller and Kamin deal with the recent Asian financial crisis. Finally, Stiglitz considers policy and reform issues for the purpose of inhibiting future financial crises.

Acknowledgements

It is a pleasure to acknowledge the assistance given us by the staff of Edward Elgar Publishing Limited, Cheltenham, UK; especially the encouragement, friendliness and professionalism of Edward Elgar, Ben Booth and Clare Arnold. Special thanks are due to the Series Editor, Professor Richard Roll and to our colleagues, A. Said Ouandlous and Patrick Truett, who helped us locate and classify several important papers that appear in these two volumes.

Part I
Globalization of Financial Markets

[1]
Globalization of Stock, Futures, and Options Markets

Peter A. Abken

The author is a senior economist in the financial section of the Atlanta Fed's research department. He would especially like to thank Jim Shapiro of the New York Stock Exchange and Bruce Phelps of the Chicago Board of Trade for helpful comments. However, any errors are the author's responsibility.

Of the trendy buzzwords to emerge from the 1980s, "globalization" surely ranks high on the list of overused words in the business lexicon, but not without good reason. The word has become associated with financial markets' growing interconnections, facilitated largely by advances in communications and computer technology. Capital moves across national borders primarily as investment flows and secondarily as international trade financing. In dollar terms, global financial transactions today stand at a historically high multiple of world trade volume (John G. Heimann 1989). Record trade imbalances, however, have also contributed to financial interdependence, the most prominent example being the net current account surplus of Japan, leading to large overseas investments of the surplus, and the net deficit of the United States, necessitating borrowing from abroad.

Financial transactions' increasing volume and their decreasing costs have put strong competitive pressures on financial institutions to change the ways in which they intermediate credit and other financial flows. The financial industry has turned to automated securities trading, which is transforming and displacing the face-to-face and mouth-to-telephone methods of making financial transactions and strengthening the globalization or internationalization of securities markets in the process. Automation of trading encompasses a number of innovations that have improved the efficiency of making financial transactions. The technologies range from quotation and communications systems that facilitate traditional trading methods to so-called screen trading systems that supplant them. Their operation can be confined to one organized financial exchange, as the New York Stock Exchange's SuperDot system is, or can link many organized exchanges, as the Chicago Mercantile Exchange's Globex system does. For convenience in this discussion of the gradual automation of securities trading, these innovations will be referred to generically as automated trading systems.

This article examines currently running and proposed automated systems for many of the world's principal organized exchanges for common stock, futures, and option contracts. These exchanges are voluntary associations of members who come together to trade securities in auction markets, paying for the right to trade on an exchange—they buy a "seat" on the exchange. They generally trade for their own accounts and for outside customers. In contrast, participants in over-the-counter (OTC) markets, who are geographically dispersed, are brought together by telephone and computer lines. Over-the-counter trades go through dealers, who quote prices to buy and sell. The National Association of Securities Dealers (NASD) is one of several important OTC markets for common stocks in the United States that will be discussed below.

The article concludes with a section on market performance and regulation that takes a broader perspective on globalization. The perceived impact of globalization is closely tied to one's view of market efficiency. Integrating markets through electronic trading may reduce the magnitude of certain kinds of price shocks that propagate across markets because of a lack of information about the sources of such shocks. If markets are efficient, twenty-four-hour trading has the potential to reduce such market volatility. On the other hand, some market observers and participants, believing that markets are inefficient and excessively volatile, have proposed measures to curb speculative activity and the volatility they believe it engenders. The continuing reduction in transactions costs through technological innovation may only exacerbate market volatility. The final section considers this debate.

The Growth of International Securities Trading

Since the 1980s, securities markets of all kinds have been developing rapidly around the world. The volume of equity and bond market transactions has grown steadily, and both American purchases and sales of foreign securities and foreign purchases and sales of U.S. securities have been expanding, as Table 1 shows. A useful indicator of market activity, the growth in transactions volume coincided with increases in volatility of most financial markets, which has been attributed to causes ranging from deregulation of financial markets, fiscal and trade imbalances, and so forth, to out-and-out irrationality and a gambling-casino mentality among traders. Some economists have recommended taxing securities transactions to alleviate the apparently unnecessary volatility.[1] On the other hand, there are substantive reasons for expecting that transactions volume will increase as uncertainty about "fundamentals" rises. For one thing, trading securities is necessary to adjust portfolios optimally in response to changing expected securities' payoffs.[2] In addition, volatility is a prime factor motivating financial risk management, which has spawned a variety of derivative instrument markets. Options and futures markets, for example, deal in contracts that are valued on the basis of stock, bond, and other primary securities prices. A discussion of the growth of primary and derivative securities markets follows.

Equities. Table 1 shows international equity market transactions, comparing activity for selected countries and regions in 1980 with 1990. The sum of purchases and sales, referred to here as transactions volume, measures the total transactions in equity markets by foreigners in U.S. stock markets and by Americans in foreign stock markets.[3] The dollar volume of transactions in 1980 and in 1990 was greater for foreigners transacting in U.S. markets than for Americans dealing in foreign markets. However, the overall margin of foreign volume over domestic volume diminished from 321 percent in 1980 to 43 percent in 1990.[4] The absolute levels of dollar purchases and sales have increased markedly, well in excess of the dollar's inflation rate and twice as fast as the growth of transactions volume on domestic exchanges during this period (Joseph A. Grundfest 1990, 349).

The compound annual growth rate for foreign transactions volume in U.S. securities was 17 percent, while the growth rate for U.S. transactions volume in foreign securities was 30 percent. Japanese transactions in U.S. stock markets grew at a 41 percent compound annual rate, faster than those of all other countries or regions. Japan's percentage share of the international transactions volume has correspondingly risen from 2.5 percent to 16 percent over the decade. The United Kingdom accounts for nearly half the 1990 European volume, up substantially from 1980. Much of its transactions volume probably stems from Middle Eastern and other non-United Kingdom buying and selling of U.S. stocks that occurs through London's markets, which are the preeminent financial

Table 1
Transactions Volume in Stocks

	Foreign Transactions in U.S. Securities				U.S. Transactions in Foreign Securities			
	Purchases[a]	Sales[a]	Aggregate Purchases and Sales[a]	Percentage Share of Market	Purchases[a]	Sales[a]	Aggregate Purchases and Sales[a]	Percentage Share of Market

1990

France	5.82	7.01	12.83	3.55	6.05	5.90	11.95	4.72
Germany	5.90	6.27	12.17	3.37	6.69	7.45	14.14	5.58
United Kingdom	44.94	48.07	93.01	25.74	44.80	45.52	90.32	35.64
Total Europe	84.95	93.53	178.47	49.39	74.53	78.40	152.94	60.36
Japan	27.47	30.38	57.85	16.01	30.89	31.52	62.41	24.63
Canada	19.52	18.63	38.14	10.56	4.78	4.92	9.70	3.83
Total Worldwide	173.04	188.34	361.37	100.00	122.49	130.89	253.38	100.00

1980

France	2.73	2.24	4.97	6.60	0.47	0.67	1.14	6.36
Germany	2.75	2.56	5.30	7.05	0.24	0.22	0.46	2.57
United Kingdom	7.44	4.94	12.38	16.44	1.38	1.36	2.75	15.38
Total Europe	24.62	21.55	46.16	61.32	3.16	3.62	6.78	37.97
Japan	0.87	1.03	1.90	2.52	0.93	1.77	2.70	15.10
Canada	6.35	5.48	11.83	15.71	3.02	3.66	6.68	37.43
Total Worldwide	40.32	34.96	75.28	100.00	7.89	9.97	17.85	100.00

Compound Annual Growth Rate, 1980-90
(percent)

	Foreign	U.S.
France	9.95	26.53
Germany	8.66	40.88
United Kingdom	22.35	41.81
Total Europe	14.48	36.56
Japan	40.73	36.92
Canada	12.42	3.80
Total Worldwide	16.98	30.38

[a] *In billions of U.S. dollars.*
Source: Derived by the Federal Reserve Bank of Atlanta from U.S. Department of the Treasury, *U.S. Treasury Bulletin* (Winter 1991), Table CM-V-5; (Winter 1981), Table CM-VI-10.

markets in Europe. From 1980 to 1990, both the United Kingdom and Japan were responsible for net inflows (cumulative excess of purchases over sales) into U.S. equity markets of about 17 billion dollars each.

U.S. transactions volume in foreign equities also grew markedly during the decade, almost twice as fast as foreign volume. This growth rate reflects the low 1980 level of U.S. purchases and sales of foreign stocks relative to foreign participation in U.S. markets. The transactions volume shares in the United Kingdom and Japan realized significant increases from 1980 to 1990, as did the corresponding compound annual growth rates. Though the share of overall volume was still relatively low in 1990, the growth rate for German stock market participation by U.S. investors was about as rapid as the rates for the United Kingdom and Japan.

Chart 1 gives another view of world equity trading, showing the dollar trading volume in major world equity markets. Clearly, the New York and Tokyo markets surpass other world markets. Each of these will be discussed further in connection with automated trading systems.

Bonds. The dollar transactions volume for bonds was approximately ten times as large as that for stocks in 1990; they were roughly comparable a decade earlier. The domestic and foreign bonds included in Table 2 exclude short-term bonds with remaining times to maturity of less than one year. Although there is considerable trading in these short-term securities, much of that trading includes government intervention in foreign exchange markets, leading in turn to sizable purchases and sales of short-term government securities such as U.S. Treasury bills. Long-term securities better gauge the growth in private cross-border capital movements. The securities included in U.S. market transactions are marketable Treasury and federally sponsored agency bonds as well as corporate bonds.

Almost all bonds are traded over-the-counter, though some are traded on organized exchanges. Somewhat less than 10 percent of all U.S. corporate bonds are traded on organized exchanges (Jack Clark Francis 1991, 87). As seen in Table 2, most foreign transactions in U.S. bond markets are in government bonds. Although the bond market is primarily

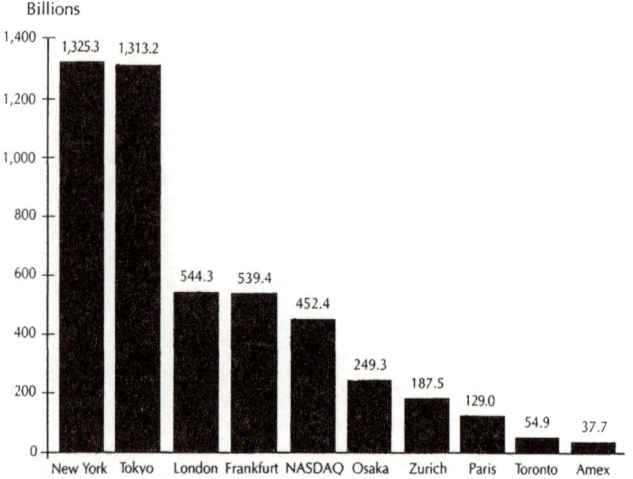

Chart 1
Dollar Trading Volume in Major World Equity Markets in 1990[a]

[a] Annual trading volume is the sum of each issue's daily share volume multiplied by its closing price and aggregated over all issues and trading days in the year.
Source: NASDAQ (1991).

Table 2
Transactions Volume in Long-Term Bonds[a]

	Foreign Transactions in U.S. Securities				U.S. Transactions in Foreign Securities			
	Purchases[b]	Sales[b]	Aggregate Purchases and Sales[b]	Percentage Share of Market	Purchases[b]	Sales[b]	Aggregate Purchases and Sales[b]	Percentage Share of Market
1990									
France	13.47	12.78	26.24	0.68	14.67	15.50	30.17	4.65
Germany	45.31	39.87	85.18	2.21	15.91	18.23	34.14	5.26
United Kingdom	564.62	555.67	1,120.29	29.08	113.95	114.16	228.10	35.12
Total Europe	804.32	773.85	1,578.17	40.97	185.46	189.78	375.25	57.77
Japan	731.08	744.96	1,476.04	38.32	36.71	43.50	80.21	12.35
Canada	66.81	69.46	136.26	3.54	54.48	56.91	111.39	17.15
Total Worldwide	1,945.19	1,906.80	3,851.99	100.00	313.58	335.93	649.50	100.00
1980									
France	0.71	0.45	1.16	0.94	0.66	0.62	1.28	3.64
Germany	2.54	5.21	7.75	6.31	0.45	0.43	0.88	2.50
United Kingdom	22.36	20.15	42.51	34.60	6.07	6.16	12.23	34.97
Total Europe	30.29	30.37	60.65	49.37	9.09	9.59	18.68	53.39
Japan	2.59	4.21	6.81	5.54	1.35	2.65	4.00	11.44
Canada	0.96	2.39	3.35	2.73	2.20	2.42	4.63	13.22
Total Worldwide	66.61	56.25	122.86	100.00	17.07	17.92	34.98	100.00

Compound Annual Growth Rate, 1980-90
(percent)

	Foreign	U.S.
France	36.66	37.22
Germany	27.09	44.24
United Kingdom	38.70	33.99
Total Europe	38.53	34.99
Japan	71.24	34.96
Canada	44.86	37.46
Total Worldwide	41.13	33.93

[a] Bonds having maturities of one year or greater.
[b] In billions of U.S. dollars.
Source: Derived by the Federal Reserve Bank of Atlanta from U.S. Department of the Treasury, *U.S. Treasury Bulletin* (Winter 1991), Table CM-V-5; (Winter 1981), Table CM-VI-10.

over-the-counter (and thus not the point of interest in this discussion), the growing number of international transactions in bonds has stimulated derivative securities markets worldwide. Increasingly, derivative securities trade in one country on underlying securities originating in another. Several examples—including the futures contracts on U.S. Treasury bonds that trade on the Tokyo Stock Exchange (TSE) and the German government bond futures that trade at the London International Financial Futures Exchange (LIFFE, pronounced "life")—will be discussed below.

The picture of globalization that emerged from the earlier consideration of equities trading comes into even sharper relief when cross-border bond trading is examined. Aside from the greater magnitude of dollar transactions volume mentioned earlier, the most striking feature is the uniformly high growth rates across countries and regions from 1980 to 1990. Equity market growth rates, particularly for French and German involvement in U.S. markets, do not show this evenness. All but one compound annual growth rate exceeds 30 percent. The transactions volume of Japanese investors in U.S. markets increased 71 percent annually! Similar to the equity data, the Japanese share in transactions volume rose over the decade from 5.5 percent to 38 percent, while the European share declined from 49 percent to 41 percent. U.S. investor participation in foreign bond markets mirrored the increased foreign activity in U.S. markets.

Futures and Options. Exchange-traded futures contracts have a long and—to some—notorious history. Commodity futures originated at the Chicago Board of Trade (CBOT) in the 1860s (see Chicago Board of Trade 1985, 1-4). Not until 1972 were the first financial futures introduced at the Chicago Mercantile Exchange (CME, or the "Merc"). The development of these currency futures reflected the anticipated hedging needs stemming from the decision allowing the dollar and other major currencies to float against one another rather than to be maintained at fixed parities. At the time agricultural contracts accounted for 97 percent of the CME's volume (William J. Brodsky 1990). Many new financial futures and options soon followed. The CBOT established the Chicago Board Options Exchange (CBOE) in 1973 to trade options on listed stocks; they created the Ginnie Mae futures contract in 1975.[5] The CME countered with its Treasury bill futures contract in 1976; the CBOT, with its Treasury bond futures contract in 1977. The latter is the most heavily traded futures contract in the world today.

In the early 1980s, these exchanges developed futures and options contracts on equity indexes, such as the Standard and Poor's (S&P) 500 futures (CME) and S&P 100 options contracts (CBOE). At the time of the market crash of October 1987, the S&P 500 futures achieved a notoriety in the minds of many investors and stock exchange members that lingers to this day. While a number of factors had contributed to the crash, the use of index futures in conjunction with so-called program trading, which uses the automated order-routing system at the New York Stock Exchange, was widely blamed. (This subject will be considered further in a later section.) In any case, many exchanges, including the New York Stock Exchange, greatly expanded capacity through automation to handle future surges in volume.

While volume in other futures contracts has remained generally flat during the 1980s, financial futures volume has grown steadily (see Robert W. Kolb 1991, 23). For example, by 1989 financial futures volume made up 91 percent of the CME's volume, with only the remaining 9 percent accounted for by commodity futures. At all U.S. futures exchanges in 1972, the total annual volume of futures trading measured by the number of contracts traded was 18.3 million. In 1990 this volume had risen to 276.5 million contracts, a compound annual growth rate of 16.3 percent. Though the U.S. exchanges are the world's most established, foreign futures markets are rapidly making inroads in the share of trading volume. For instance, since the opening of the London International Financial Futures Exchange in 1982, thirty options and futures exchanges have opened outside the United States (Brodsky 1991).

The U.S. exchanges are still dominant in the world, but, as Table 3 shows, foreign options and futures markets that emerged in the 1980s are also well represented in the top-twenty ranks. In particular, the Osaka Securities Exchange's Nikkei 225 index futures contract and Tokyo International Financial Futures Exchange's Euroyen contract surged in volume during 1990.

Automation of Equity Markets

Individual stock exchanges everywhere have adopted some degree of automation, reflecting the exigencies of competitive pressures from domestic as well as foreign exchanges. Derivative securities markets have aggressively employed the new technologies to

Table 3
Most Heavily Traded Futures and Options Contracts

Rank 1990	Rank 1989	Contract[a]	Exchanges[b]	Contract Volume 1990	Contract Volume 1989
1	1	T-bond (f)	CBOT	75,499,000	70,303,000
2	2	S&P 100 (o)	CBOE	58,845,000	58,371,000
3	3	Eurodollar (f)	CME	34,694,000	40,818,000
4	4	T-bond (o)	CBOT	27,315,000	20,784,000
5	5	Crude oil (f)	Nymex	23,687,000	20,535,000
6	6	Japanese government bond (f)	TSE	16,307,000	18,942,000
7	7	Notionnel government bond (f)	MATIF	15,996,000	15,005,000
8	30	Euroyen (f)	TIFFE	14,414,000	4,495,000
9	25	Nikkei 225 (f)	Osaka	13,589,000	5,443,000
10	8	S&P 500 (f)	CME	12,139,000	10,560,000
11	18	S&P 500 (o)	CBOE	12,089,000	6,274,000
12	11	Corn (f)	CBOT	11,423,000	9,271,000
13	10	Soybeans (f)	CBOT	10,302,000	9,635,000
14	9	Gold (f)	Comex	9,730,000	9,999,000
15	26	German bond (f)	LIFFE	9,582,000	5,330,000
16	17	Nikkei 225 (o)	Osaka	9,186,000	6,610,000
17	12	Deutsche Mark (f)	CME	9,169,000	8,186,000
18	16	Short Sterling (f)	LIFFE	8,355,000	7,131,000
19	13	Yen (f)	CME	7,437,000	7,824,000
20	15	Notionnel government bond (o)	MATIF	7,410,000	7,177,000

[a] (f) = futures contract; (o) = options contract.
[b] Nymex is the New York Mercantile Exchange; Comex is the Commodities Exchange (New York); other exchanges are described in the text.
Source: *Futures and Options World: 1991 Annual Worldwide Directory and Review* (Surrey, England: Metal Bulletin Journals Ltd., 1991), 9. Data used by permission of the publisher.

---

link exchanges. The discussion below considers the movement toward automated trading in equity markets and derivative markets.

New York Stock Exchange. U.S. equity markets are the largest and most liquid in the world. The biggest domestic exchange, the New York Stock Exchange (NYSE), is facing mounting competitive pressures from regional domestic exchanges and from foreign stock exchanges. The heart of the New York Stock Exchange is its specialists, charged by the exchange to maintain "fair and orderly" markets in the individual listed stocks assigned to them. The New York Stock Exchange is organized as a continuous two-sided auction market, with the specialist acting as auctioneer for incoming orders to buy or sell a particular stock. The specialist conducts an auction in the sense that he or she continually adjusts a stock's price to balance supply and demand throughout the trading day. She at times may also need to take the buy or sell side to keep prices from fluctuating too greatly. Overall about 10 percent of share purchases and 10 percent of sales on the NYSE result in specialists' staking their own capital in the trade (New York Stock Exchange 1991a, 17). This role is part of their obligation to the exchange in performing the specialist's function.

Also, the specialist has access to the computerized limit-order book, which displays orders to buy or sell if the market price reaches a specified level. Because of their knowledge, specialists have an informational advantage over traders off the exchange floor.[6] Although they may profit from their inventory position, exchange rules constrain trading for their own accounts. On every trade the specialist also receives the difference between the sale price (the ask) and the purchase price (the bid). Other market participants are willing to incur these costs in order to gain the liquidity specialists provide. However, the specialist's role is being questioned with increasing frequency: How important is it? Is the provision of liquidity worth the price?

Since the rise of institutional trading in the 1960s, the so-called upstairs market has developed, partly insulating the specialists from having to take positions in large blocks of 10,000 or more shares. Such blocks sent directly to the specialists may cause too much price fluctuation and be too risky for them to handle. Instead, block positioners match buyers and sellers and may also take positions in blocks themselves. Blocks are then sent to the specialist post for execution. Because of economies of scale, low commission rates are charged for block transactions. During the latter half of the 1980s, about half the NYSE's volume was accounted for by institutional block trading (NASDAQ 1991, 39). Preferring new, automated mechanisms that are even cheaper, institutional investors are beginning to dispense altogether with using the exchange.

More efficient handling of trading volume led to the development of the NYSE's automated routing system in 1976 called the Super Designated Order Turnaround System (SuperDot). SuperDot routes market orders of less than 2,099 shares to the specialist (or to a floor broker) for rapid execution, usually in less than a minute.[7] The system can also route large orders to the specialist. SuperDot is frequently used by program traders dealing in whole portfolios of stocks; they route lists of stocks through the system to appropriate specialists. The system handles market orders of as many as 30,099 shares and limit orders of as many as 99,999 shares of individual stocks, although the specialists are not obligated to execute these orders as rapidly as the New York Stock Exchange requires for smaller ones. Odd-lot orders of less than 100 shares are executed automatically by SuperDot at the prevailing price quote. About 75 percent of daily NYSE orders are processed through the system (New York Stock Exchange 1991a, 21).

Regionals. Regional exchanges have developed their own versions of automated order-routing and execution systems for small trades. The Midwest Stock Exchange (MSE), Pacific Stock Exchange (PSE), Philadelphia Stock Exchange (PHLX), and Boston Stock Exchange (BSE) use systems named MAX, SCOREX, PACE, and BEACON, respectively.[8] The Cincinnati Stock Exchange (CSE) is in fact an over-the-counter market with competing market makers. All trades on the CSE pass through the National Securities Trading System (NSTS), which is an order-matching system akin to the NASDAQ system to be discussed shortly (U.S. Securities and Exchange Commission 1991, 23-26).

The Securities Act amendments of 1975 mandated the Securities and Exchange Commission (SEC) to establish a national market system with the objectives of increasing competition among market makers at different exchanges and strengthening links among different exchanges (see Francis 1991, 132-33). One major change was that negotiated commissions replaced fixed commissions on securities sales and purchases. Another consequence of the act was the establishment of the "Consolidated Tape," which continuously lists the trades at seven stock exchanges and two over-the-counter markets (NASD and Instinet). Since 1978 the regional exchanges, the American Stock Exchange (Amex), NASD, and NYSE have been linked by the Intermarket Trading System (ITS), which enables a broker or specialist at one exchange to send orders to buy or sell at another exchange showing a better price.

Most of the stocks traded via the ITS communication system are NYSE-listed stocks, and a much smaller number traded are Amex-listed and regionally listed stocks. At the broker's or specialist's discretion, orders are routed to the exchange showing the best bid or offer. Once a small order is received, the BEACON, MAX, and SCOREX systems "expose" it to the specialist for fifteen seconds during which he or she may better the bid or offer price; otherwise, the order is automatically executed at the specialist's quoted bid or offer. (PACE automatically executes all small orders.) The Amex has an order-routing system called Post Execution Reporting (PER) that is very similar to the NYSE's SuperDot. Amex members can send orders for as many as 2,000 shares directly to the specialist using the system and receive an execution report for the trades (U.S. Congress 1990b, 49-50).

The regional exchanges and Amex have only a small slice of the trading-volume pie. Table 4 shows where they stand in relation to the NYSE and NASD, viewed both in terms of share volume and in terms of dollar volumes.

NASDAQ. National Association of Securities Dealers runs a telecommunications network called NASDAQ, for NASD Automated Quotations. In this over-the-counter market NASD dealers compete with one another in making bids and offers on stocks.[9] These OTC securities tend to be smaller capitalization stocks that do not meet exchange listing requirements; only a subset of them are also listed on organized exchanges.[10] To buy or sell a stock, an investor

Table 4
U.S. Equity Markets: 1990 Share and Dollar Volumes

	Share Volume		Dollar Volume	
	Millions	Percent	Millions	Percent
NASDAQ	33,380	39.2	$ 452,430	21.8
NASDAQ/OTC Trading in Listed Securities	2,589	3.0	86,494	4.2
Amex	3,329	3.9	37,715	1.8
Regionals (BSE, CSE, MSE, PSE, and PHLX)	6,208	7.3	178,139	8.5
NYSE	39,665	46.6	1,325,332	63.7
Totals	85,171	100.0	$2,080,110	100.0

Source: NASDAQ (1991).

calls a dealer, who checks NASDAQ to find the best quotation from competing dealers in a particular stock at the lowest cost (that is, lowest bid-ask spread and commission). Unlike stock exchange specialists, dealers are not obligated to provide liquidity through their own position-taking. The OTC market instead relies on interdealer competition.

About 13 percent of OTC transactions are handled by NASD's Small Order Execution System (SOES), in operation since 1985. Public buy or sell orders of as many as 1,000 shares go through SOES to the dealer offering the best price quote. However, if there are currently better price quotes on NASDAQ outside SOES, that dealer is required to fill the order at the better price.[11] In 1990 SOES added the capacity to automatically execute matching limit orders entered into the system.

Another NASDAQ system is SelectNet, which allows NASDAQ members to send buy or sell securities orders to other system members' terminals. SelectNet enables market makers to accept and execute orders partially or fully as well as to conduct price and quantity negotiations. System users are therefore not anonymous. NASDAQ securities orders must be for more than 1,000 shares.[12]

NASDAQ leads other domestic exchanges, most notably the New York Stock Exchange, in the indirect trading of foreign equities. This indirect trading is through American Depository Receipts (ADRs). Foreign corporations have American commercial or investment banks buy their equity shares and place them in a trust account, against which ADR certificates are issued. These certificates are negotiable and can be traded on exchanges and through NASDAQ. Investors find ADRs convenient because their purchase and sale and the distribution of dividend payments are entirely in dollars, not foreign currency. Foreign-currency denominated cash dividends are converted into dollars by the trustee, usually a commercial bank, and are passed on to the American Depository Receipts holders. The foreign corporation benefits by not having to comply with the SEC's disclosure requirements and other regulations enforced for domestic corporations (see Francis 1991, 62, 806-7).

In 1990 NASDAQ reached new records in ADR trading with a trading volume of 2.2 billion shares of eighty-seven ADR issues. In comparison, the NYSE had a 1.4 billion share volume for sixty-two ADR issues. NASDAQ dollar volume was 21 billion, while the dollar volume in foreign securities directly listed on NASDAQ was 7 billion.[13] NASDAQ is expanding in 1991 to offer an international quotation network based in the United Kingdom called NASDAQ International.

Instinet. NASDAQ dealers earn their livelihood from the difference in price between what they will pay for stock and their selling price, the bid-ask spread.

That spread has come under pressure to narrow because of an electronic order-execution system called Instinet, owned by Reuters Holdings PLC. Instinet is a screen trading system in that it enables subscribers to trade anonymously. These participants include not only OTC broker-dealers but also institutional investors. For example, NASDAQ dealers can trade with other NASDAQ dealers on Instinet to adjust their inventory of stocks. These trades can be accomplished within the bid-ask spread quoted on NASDAQ so that NASDAQ quotes would be unaffected. Institutional investors have also been trading actively on Instinet at much lower spreads than through NASDAQ dealers or exchange specialists. To stay competitive, dealers have had to cut their spreads.[14]

Most Instinet trades involve OTC and listed U.S. stocks, but an increasing number are in British, French, German, and other European stocks as well. The system, on-line an average of fourteen hours per day, can remain operational almost around-the-clock during periods of heavy trading.[15]

Anonymity is important to traders because a trader's identity can reveal how often and how much he or she is buying or selling, information that could move prices against the trader. For example, traders usually avoid selling large orders at once because doing so may prompt a stock's price to be bid down rapidly in the process of making the trade, on the assumption that some bad news is behind the sale. In that scenario, known as adverse selection risk, large orders will be put on the market in smaller blocks. Instinet allows traders to poll each other almost instantaneously on a prospective trade. They can send anonymous messages over the system to particular traders to negotiate quantity or price. They can see all of the bids and offers on particular stocks at a given time on the Instinet "book."

Madoff Investment Securities. This firm has set itself up in direct competition with NYSE specialists. Madoff makes a market in 350 of the S&P 500 stocks by attracting mainly retail trades from brokers, paying them a penny per share for orders. These orders are executed at prices that match the best quoted on any exchange, as reported through ITS. Madoff operates through the Cincinnati Stock Exchange's National Securities Trading System, which is essentially an over-the-counter market. Because of low overhead costs, his commission costs are much lower than for trades carried out on an exchange floor. According to a recent estimate, this firm alone generates 2 percent of the daily trading volume in NYSE listed stocks (Barbara Howard 1991, 16; William E. Sheeline 1990, 122).

Crossing Networks. To reduce transactions costs, many institutional investors have turned to so-called crossing networks, such as Instinet's The Crossing Network and Posit (Portfolio System for Institutional Trading) of Jefferies & Company, a registered broker-dealer. Many institutional investors deal in indexed equity portfolios—for example, a portfolio mimicking the S&P 500 index. These "passive" portfolio managers are not concerned about the precise timing of trade executions for individual stocks making up an index. For institutional investors seeking to trade in whole portfolios of stocks, crossing networks offer a low-cost alternative to transactions on organized stock exchanges.

The Crossing Network allows whole portfolios of stock to be bought or sold at primary markets' closing prices (for example, NYSE closing prices) and the mean of the bid-ask OTC prices. Because the trades are based on the closing price, and hence passive, there is no "market impact" on the trades themselves—that is, large buy and sell orders are matched or crossed at that price, unaffected by the unfavorable price movement such a trade might ordinarily produce. The price does not adjust to balance supply and demand, so some orders will go unmatched in a single after-hours session.

Posit is a crossing network that operates during trading hours as well as off-hours. Portfolio trades can be executed at the primary markets' opening, at prespecified times of day after the opening, or at closing prices. This system has many options that users can select; their choices affect the cost of their trades. For example, trades not matched through Posit's computer can be canceled, held for matching at a later time, sent to the primary markets for execution, or "price-guaranteed" by Jefferies (that is, Jefferies takes the other side of the trade). These alternatives entail different commission costs. The amount of information about a prospective trade, like the size of the order or identity of the investor, may be revealed or hidden from other system users (U.S. Securities and Exchange Commission 1991, 83-86).

Overseas Trading. The NYSE is also affected by the movement of institutional program trades overseas, particularly to London's over-the-counter market. A common transaction involves a stock-index futures purchase or sale on a U.S. futures exchange with a subsequent exchange-for-physicals (EFP) transaction to unwind the futures position.[16] For example, a portfolio manager who wishes to buy an S&P 500-

indexed portfolio could buy the underlying stocks on the New York Stock Exchange or alternatively buy S&P 500 contracts on the Chicago Mercantile Exchange. In the latter case, the long futures position could then be offset through an EFP over the counter in London by finding a trader (or traders) short the S&P 500 futures who holds the underlying stock portfolio. The cash prices and futures price for the EFP transaction would be determined by negotiation but typically reflect the underlying stocks' closing prices on the New York Stock Exchange, Amex, and OTC markets as well as the futures on the transaction date. The parties have traded stocks outside of the NYSE and have closed out their futures positions off the Chicago Mercantile Exchange exchange floor, saving commissions and market impact costs.[17] Similar over-the-counter program transactions also occur that do not involve index futures.

About 10 to 15 million NYSE shares currently trade after-hours in London every day (Kevin G. Salwen and Craig Torres 1991, C1). This exodus from the exchange floor was spurred in part by a postcrash NYSE rule requiring immediate display of program trades' price and volume.

SPAworks. A new system operated by R. Steven Wunsch takes after-hours trading a step further. He has designed a system, SPAworks, to trade stocks in an after-hours call market, which involves a single-price auction. This institutional arrangement was actually prevalent in the nineteenth century before the advent of continuous auction markets, and many relatively illiquid international exchanges still rely on it (see below). SPAworks has been operational since April 1991.

The system works by allowing buy and sell orders to accumulate after the NYSE closes at 4:00 P.M. (U.S. Securities and Exchange Commission 1991, 73-77; Wunsch 1991). At a predetermined time before the next day's opening, a single computerized auction of each individual stock would be held, whereby trades would be consummated at the price resulting in the largest volume of trade. Participants entering bids above or below the auction price are able to execute their trades at the auction price. Other orders go unmatched. This system saves the cost of paying for the immediate liquidity provided on the exchange floor.

Off-Hours Trading. In response to the inroads these outside trading systems have made, the NYSE announced in May 1991 that it would institute two after-hours sessions. "Crossing Session I" runs from 4:15 until 5:00 P.M. and allows investors to buy and sell at the 4:00 P.M. closing price. Once submitted by NYSE members through SuperDot, single-sided orders are matched against others based on the times they were submitted. Matched single-sided orders and paired (prearranged) orders are then executed through SuperDot at 5:00 P.M. "Crossing Session II," which operates from 4:00 to 5:15 P.M., specifically accommodates program traders. After the close New York Stock Exchange member firms place paired orders for programs that contain at least fifteen NYSE-listed stocks having a one-million-dollar market value or more. These coupled orders are executed as soon as they are received by the system. To make the new sessions attractive to program traders, the NYSE has granted a

Physical marketplaces (the trading floors) are becoming obsolete, while "virtual" marketplaces—networks of computers and computer terminals—are emerging as the "site" for transactions.

nine-month exemption from being required to report price and volume information for individual program trades. Only the aggregate volume and dollar value of program trades are disseminated at 5:15 P.M. Single-sided and coupled order volume are each reported separately for Crossing Session I, beginning at 5:00 P.M. (Salwen and Torres 1991, C1; U.S. Securities and Exchange Commission 1991, 36-39; New York Stock Exchange 1991b, 1-5).

Foreign Equity Markets. Many foreign stock markets are considerably less liquid than U.S. stock markets, and their institutional arrangements reflect this fact. The Austrian and Norwegian stock markets simply hold a single daily call auction. Others use a mixed system of call auctions at some times of day and continuous trading at other times. Mixed auctions are prevalent in Belgium, Denmark, France, Italy, Spain, Sweden, and Switzerland.[18] The Australian, British, Canadian, French, and Japanese markets have automated trading systems. Four of the major automated exchanges are relatively well developed.

The Toronto Stock Exchange uses the Computer Assisted Trading System (CATS), which functions as an electronic auction for less actively traded stocks and is being updated to handle more active stocks. Broker-dealers using the system can choose to have their trades executed by either a specialist or computer. CATS currently handles about 75 percent of trades on the exchange, a small volume compared with that of major American exchanges (Hansell 1989, 93; U.S. Congress 1990b, 63; Howard 1991, 15). CATS also displays the best five buy and sell limit orders along with the name of the broker making the order (Hansell 1989, 93; Howard 1991, 15).

The Paris Bourse (stock exchange) relies on a licensed version of CATS, which is also under consideration for use at exchanges in Madrid, Brussels, and Sao Paulo (Hansell 1989, 93, 98; Ian Domowitz 1990, 170). The system used by the French exchange is named CAC, for Cotation Assistée Continu. This exchange, overshadowed by the London market, is much less liquid. In fact, exchange member firms hold a single daily auction in stocks complemented by forward trading in listed stocks using both continuous trading and call auctions in forward contracts (Richard Roll 1988, 29).

The London International Stock Exchange is a dealer market very similar in operation to NASDAQ. The ISE is the most active world market in foreign (non-United Kingdom) stock trading, which makes up slightly more than half of the exchange's volume. The average daily foreign issue volume was 1.3 billion pounds sterling per day in 1990. ISE members have benefited from the migration of some U.S. program trading. The ISE's analog to the NASDAQ quote-display system is the Stock Exchange Automated Quotation System (SEAQ); small orders of fewer than 5,000 shares are automatically executed on the Stock Automated Exchange Facility (SAEF).

The Tokyo Stock Exchange (TSE) has a system similar to Toronto's CATS. Its Computer Assisted Order Routing and Execution System (CORES) now handles all but 150 of the exchange's most actively traded issues; however, the TSE is moving toward a fully automated system. Instead of specialists, the exchange has a group of overseers, called *saitori*, who use computer screens to monitor the trades arranged by the computer and by floor traders and to approve the prices. The saitori can also allow CORES to generate trades automatically within a specified price range. In addition, they act as human circuit breakers on the exchange floor when trading becomes too volatile; they have the authority to suspend trading briefly (Hansell 1989, 97).

Futures and Options Markets

Like prices of exchange-traded stocks, futures prices are established through an auction system, but one with no counterpart to the single individual, the specialist, making a market in a stock. Instead, futures prices are determined by an auction known as the open-outcry system. Exchange members—floor traders—congregate at designated trading pits and shout bids and offers at each other or use hand signals to indicate trading intentions. Exchange officials record the price and amount of each transaction. Effective in providing liquidity, this system is also subject to error and even abuse.[19]

As discussed above, international competition is forcing efficiency-enhancing automation. Many new overseas exchanges are fully or partially automated and trade many of the same contracts as American exchanges, although their volume levels are usually much lower. Systems emerging on futures and options markets harbinger the internationalization soon to come. In particular, the Chicago Mercantile Exchange's Globex (Global Exchange) system is being designed to handle volumes that exceed current open-outcry volume levels at peak trading times.

Globex. Globex, expected to be operable in early 1992, will automate *and link* participating exchanges. To date, the Chicago Board of Trade and Marché à Terme des Instruments Financiers (MATIF), the French financial futures market, are members of Globex. Other exchanges in the Far East are considering joining Globex, including Australia's Sydney Futures Exchange (SFE) and possibly Japan's Osaka Securities Exchange, or OSE (Ginger Szala and Amy Rosenbaum 1990, 44). Globex will operate after-hours, beginning at 6 P.M. Chicago time, when Japanese markets open.

The genesis of Globex lay in efforts to extend the futures trading day. In 1984 the CME established a relationship with the newly founded Singapore International Monetary Exchange (SIMEX), a relationship based mainly on mutual advantages gained from trading compatible Eurodollar and foreign currency futures contracts. The two exchanges set up a mutual offset permitting contracts opened on one exchange to be closed on the other and vice versa. This link effectively lengthened the trading day almost to twenty-four hours, helping the Chicago exchange to secure a foothold in booming East Asian financial markets. SIMEX enjoyed the benefits of the additional liquidity generated by the infusion of Chicago-based trades. Also catering to growing interest from abroad, the Merc's Chicago rival, the Chicago Board of Trade, instituted nighttime trading of its Treasury bond futures contracts in April 1987. However, this insomniac trading, as one observer termed it, and the CME's mutual offset arrangement were regarded as stopgap measures ("Futures Markets" 1988). More efficient and less error-prone electronic trading seems inevitable; the Chicago Board of Trade joined with the Chicago Mercantile Exchange as a Globex partner in 1990. Up to that point the CBOT had been developing its own after-hours system, called Aurora, that would electronically emulate open-outcry trading. (See the discussion below of LIFFE's Automated Pit Trading for a similar system).

The mechanical heart of Globex is a network of computer screens. The system is a joint venture of the "partner exchanges" (CME, CBOT, and MATIF) and Reuters Holdings PLC, which already has a large presence in over-the-counter spot foreign exchange markets. The Reuters network of computer terminals in banks and brokerage firms numbers about 180,000 worldwide. The CME emphasizes that trading via Globex is an alternate method of placing an order on its exchange or on partner exchanges (Brodsky 1990, 621). Because the exchanges do not view Globex as a new kind of futures exchange, they argue that regulatory approval of the system (particularly in Japan) should be straightforward.

Globex automatically matches and executes orders entered into the system. The system first checks the credit standing of the member firm initiating a transaction and then matches orders based on the time an order was submitted and its price. Unlike standard open-outcry trading, Globex does not allow for orders to be executed at the prevailing market price (that is, there can be no market orders); all orders must be good-until-canceled limit orders (the order stays on the book until it is executed or canceled).[20]

Trades are confirmed at participants' screens, prices and quantities are reported through the system, trades are cleared, and buyers' and sellers' accounts are adjusted. Traders on Globex deal anonymously with one another, an important consideration for most participants, as mentioned earlier. However, Globex, like other automated systems, does produce a so-called electronic audit trail, which is regarded as an improvement over the open-outcry system's less accurate recording procedures. Electronic monitoring is expected to give traders more confidence in the trading process and makes the regulator's job easier.

Although trading has not yet begun on Globex, its relative performance compared with the open-outcry auction has been assessed by Domowitz (1991). Using simulated trading experiments, he finds that Globex is the more efficient trading mechanism according to a number of measures. Globex tends to result in lower price volatility and greater market liquidity, and the differences become more pronounced as the size of the market increases.

In contrast, Merton H. Miller (1990) argues that screen trading systems, especially of the order-matching type like Globex, put traders (market makers) at a disadvantage because they cannot observe the order flow on a screen as they can from the trading pit. Traders with more current information can take advantage of previously posted traders' price quotes. For this reason Miller does not believe that electronic systems will ever attract sufficient competing market-maker participation to match the liquidity of the most active trading pits. To date, most screen trading systems have been used at low-volume exchanges or for low-volume contracts. Validation of Miller's or Domowitz's predictions will have to await actual trading through Globex as well as more extensive deployment of other screen trading systems.

Domestic Options Markets. A number of automated trading systems have been introduced to facilitate options trading. The most significant of these is the Chicago Board Options Exchange's Retail Automatic Execution System (RAES), which has been in operation since 1985. The system now handles both index options, including the heavily traded S&P 100 index option, and all CBOE equity options (on individual stocks). About 3.5 percent of contract volume is currently executed through RAES (U.S. Securities and Exchange Commission 1991, 19). The Amex uses a system called AUTO-EX for market and limit orders of as many as twenty equity contracts. The system is designed for use of Amex member firms and exchange specialists. In addition, the Amex has a mutual-offset link with the European Options Exchange in Amsterdam for the stock index options contract on the Amex's Major Market Index, or MMI (U.S. Congress 1990b, 96). The Pacific Stock Exchange has a similar system for equity options called POETS (Pacific Options Exchange Trading System). The Philadelphia Stock Exchange uses AUTOM (Automated Options Market System) for equity options. The NYSE's SuperDot also routes orders for trades on its equity and equity-index options.

Delta Government Securities, a screen-based system for trading options on U.S. Treasury bills, notes, and bonds, is operated jointly by RMJ Securities and RMJ Options, which are a registered clearing agency and registered broker-dealer, respectively. Delta always stands as the intermediary between buyer and seller using the system. It effectively operates like an electronic options exchange, issuing any options traded through the system (U.S. Securities and Exchange Commission 1991, 89).

Foreign Derivatives Markets. There is stiff competition among European futures exchanges. Marché à Terme des Instruments Financiers vies with the London International Financial Futures Exchange primarily over the three-month Euro-deutsche mark futures (a futures on the three-month rate on interbank deutsche mark-denominated deposits). MATIF, Europe's most active futures exchange, joined Globex in November 1989 and plans to list its government bond future (the Notionnel) and its short-term interest-rate future (on PIBOR—Paris Interbank Offered Rate) on the system. Part of the motivation behind MATIF's Globex membership was to boost foreign participation on the exchange and lessen London's advantage of having the offices of almost 600 international banks and brokerage firms (Janet Lewis 1990, 130).

The fact that LIFFE also offers a futures contract on the long-term German government bond, the Bund, in part spurred the creation of the first German futures market, the Deutsche Terminbörse (DTB) in 1990. A consortium of fifty-three institutions, mostly large banks, belong to the DTB. The exchange offers futures contracts to compete with LIFFE's as well as stock options on German firms (Lewis 1990, 130).

The Frankfurt-based exchange is organized as a computer network that matches and processes all trades electronically. The automated trading system employed is based on a similar system used by the Swiss Options and Financial Futures Exchange (SOFFEX), also an entirely automated order-matching system that allows member firms to be market makers, quoting bids and offers. Trades are entered anonymously, so large trades can be anonymously negotiated over the system (Hansell 1989, 93). Five fully automated futures and options exchanges now operate worldwide, as seen in Table 5.

LIFFE has a partially automated system, called Automated Pit Trading (APT), that mimics actual pit-trading (London International Financial Futures Exchange 1991). The after-hours system operates from 4:30 to 6:00 P.M. local time, with access restricted to LIFFE members. APT is not driven by quote-making dealers but by traders who post bids and offers for specified quantities. By the touch of a computer key, any trader can instantaneously accept bids and offers that appear on the screen. This system is the analog of the open-outcry method, in which bids and offers of floor traders are valid for "as long as the breath is warm." Because the futures exchanges deal in a limited set of futures contracts, liquidity is concentrated and rapid interactions between traders can be emulated on a screen. LIFFE expanded the system in 1990 to include a central limit-order book that enables purchases and sales of futures contracts if the market price reaches the posted limit price.

In Japan financial futures were banned until 1985. Regulators and legislators have gradually been deregulating and expanding their financial and derivative markets, and the Japanese have become very active in developing futures exchanges. Japanese firms are eager to use the new contracts. They may now deal directly in securities on foreign exchanges, and foreign brokerage firms may be members of Japanese futures exchanges (see Szala and Rosenbaum 1990, 42).

The first Japanese contracts were ten- and twenty-year yen bond futures, introduced on the Tokyo Stock Exchange in 1985. As of December 1989 the TSE offered U.S. Treasury bond futures equivalent to those of the CBOT. The Japanese Ministry of Finance, however, requires higher margins to be posted against Tokyo Stock Exchange futures contracts than does the Chicago Board of Trade for comparable positions. The higher margin levels apply even for Japanese firms taking positions in CBOT contracts, so these firms have little incentive to look abroad (Szala and Rosenbaum 1990, 42).

The TSE bond contracts, now the sixth most heavily traded future in the world (see Table 3), can all be traded through CORES. The TSE stock-index future on TOPIX (Tokyo Stock Price Index) is fully automated on CORES. Fully automated trading of a three-month Euroyen contract is conducted on the new Tokyo International Financial Futures Exchange (TIFFE), which competes against SIMEX in Singapore. SIMEX is still dominant in a number of contracts, including yen-U.S. dollar futures and Eurodollar futures, but it lags in Euroyen. Unlike TIFFE, SIMEX is a traditional open-outcry exchange.

The Nikkei 225 futures, the highest-volume Japanese index futures contract, trades at the Osaka Securities Exchange (OSE). The CME has acquired the rights to offer a Nikkei 225 contract on its exchange, though it would prefer to link up with the OSE through Globex (Szala and Rosenbaum 1990,

Table 5
Automated Trading Systems

System Operator	System
Equities	
American Stock Exchange	Post Execution Reporting
Amsterdam Stock Exchange	System based on MSE's MAX
Australian Association of Stock Exchanges	Stock Exchange Automated Trading (SEAT)
Boston Stock Exchange	BSE Automated Communication and Order Routing Network (BEACON)
Cincinnati Stock Exchange	National Securities Trading System (NSTS)
Instinet Corporation	Instinet The Crossing Network
Jefferies & Company, Inc.	Portfolio System for Institutional Trading (Posit)
London International Stock Exchange	Stock Automated Exchange Facility (SAEF)
Midwest Stock Exchange	Midwest Automated Execution (MAX)
National Association of Securities Dealers	Small Order Execution Service (SOES) SelectNet Private Offerings, Resales, and Trading through Automated Linkages (PORTAL)
New York Stock Exchange	Designated Order Turnaround system (SuperDot) Crossing Sessions I and II
Pacific Stock Exchange	Securities Communication Order Routing and Execution System (SCOREX)
Paris Bourse	Cotation Assistée en Continu (CAC)
Philadelphia Stock Exchange	Philadelphia Automated Communication and Execution System (PACE)
Tokyo Stock Exchange	Computer Assisted Order Routing and Execution System (CORES)
Toronto Stock Exchange	Computer Assisted Trading System (CATS)
Wunsch Auction Systems, Inc.	SPAworks
Futures and Options	
American Stock Exchange (equity options)	AUTO-EX
Chicago Board Options Exchange	Retail Automated Exchange System (RAES)
Chicago Board of Trade	Globex
Chicago Mercantile Exchange	Globex
Deutsche Terminbörse	Fully automated, integrated clearing
Irish Futures and Options Exchange	Fully automated, ATS-2
London International Financial Futures Exchange	Automated Pit Trading (APT)

(table continues)

Table 5 (continued)

System Operator	System
Futures and Options	
London Traded Options Market	Associated with LIFFE
Marché à Terme des Instruments Financiers	Globex
New York Stock Exchange	SuperDot
New Zealand Futures and Options Exchange	Fully automated ATS system
Pacific Stock Exchange	Pacific Options Exchange Trading System (POETS)
Philadelphia Stock Exchange	Automated Options Market System (AUTOM)
Stockholm Option Market	Integrated clearing facilities based on electronic trading and telephone brokering
Sydney Futures Exchange	Sydney Computerized Overnight Market (SYCOM)
Swiss Options and Financial Futures Exchange	Fully automated; integrated clearing
Tokyo Stock Exchange	Derivative markets fully automated CORES-F

Sources: U.S. Securities and Exchange Commission (1991); Angrist (1991); U.S. Congress (1990b); Kang and Lawton (1990); Rosenbaum (1990); Hansell (1989).

44). The CME's first overtures to the Ministry of Finance, one of the chief regulators of Japanese exchanges, were made in August 1988 and are still ongoing. The CBOT now lists a Japanese stock-index futures on the TOPIX and several Japanese government bond futures and options.

Market Performance and Regulatory Issues

Regulation of securities markets in the United States is generally intended to ensure that securities trading is conducted openly and based on publicly available information. The Securities Act of 1933 and Securities Exchange Act of 1934 mandated extensive registration and disclosure requirements for firms issuing securities to the public. However, recent policy discussions have shifted regulators' sights to safeguarding the performance and stability of financial markets.

The Brady Commission's recommendations in the wake of the 1987 crash stand out as the most sweeping proposals for changing the ways financial markets operate and for reorganizing their regulators' responsibilities.[21] To the Brady Commission and to a large number of market observers, the crash was prima facie evidence that private financial markets can fail—spectacularly. Concerns about the flow of information and the ability of participants to act on it superseded traditional questions about fairness and honesty in the marketplace.[22] The crash underscored the potential systemic risk of market failure as trading disruptions spread from one market to another. The problems can engulf the banking system as credit demands mount, for example, because of timing differences between the receipt and disbursement of funds by clearinghouses, straining liquidity and threatening widespread defaults.[23]

An important policy challenge is determining the appropriate mix of government and private-market actions to lessen the risk of securities market failure. It is feared that the electronic globalization of financial exchanges might contribute to systemic risks. The 1987 crash broadened the concerns, touching off a debate about whether a crash in one country's markets can trigger shocks beyond domestic boundaries to other countries' markets. The desirability and feasibility of international regulatory cooperation to contain such potential problems is an open question just beginning to be addressed (see Grundfest 1990; Paul Guy 1990; and U.S. Congress 1990a).

A survey of international regulatory issues is beyond the scope of this article. Rather, the following discussion focuses on the interconnections between markets and proposals to manage the international transmission of volatility. The basic issue to be considered has to do with the source of volatility and arguments for and against counteracting it. Since the stock market crash of October 1987, and even earlier in the decade, regulators and other market observers have become concerned about market volatility and cross-market spillovers.

The increasing prevalence of cross-border trading as well as the opening of new exchanges and deepening of existing ones would seem to imply that world financial markets are becoming unified. However, the evidence of such merging is not clear-cut. In fact, the Brady Commission concluded that through 1987 correlations of price movements from different world markets provide no evidence of closer links: "The correlations between the market in the U.S. and the markets in Germany and Japan appear to form totally random series. . . . [T]here is no evidence to suggest that the association is any closer today than it was a decade ago" (Nicolas F. Brady et al. 1988, II-6). Roll (1988) has observed that the only month in the 1980s in which all major world markets moved together was October 1987.

A number of recent academic papers address the question of world financial market integration. Using a sophisticated model of global equity market equilibrium (an international capital asset pricing model with time-varying moments), Campbell R. Harvey (1991) found evidence of a lack of integration, particularly for Japanese markets with the rest of the world. The basic object of study is the reward-to-risk ratio on equities required by investors. In a world of integrated markets, the reward-to-risk ratio would be the same in every equity market. In fact, this ratio turned out to be twice as large in Japanese markets as in U.S. markets.

In other words, Japanese investors require expected returns on stocks to be double the magnitude expected by U.S. investors. Complete integration across markets would equalize differences in the reward-to-risk ratio across countries because otherwise, for example, U.S. investors would skew their portfolios toward Japanese equities offering better trade-offs between return and risk than domestic equities. Increased U.S. purchases of Japanese stocks would bid up their prices and bid down U.S. stock prices, driving Japanese expected returns down and U.S. expected returns up. There are many subtleties and qualifications in this analysis, but the preponderance of evidence is against the simple hypothesis that world markets have become integrated.

The empirical work of David Neumark, P.A. Tinsley, and Suzanne Tosini reveals that price movements for U.S. stocks listed on New York, Tokyo, and London exchanges are more highly correlated during periods of high volatility than during times of low volatility because "only larger price changes pierce the transaction cost barriers between markets" (1991, 160). These authors noted that ordinarily the stock price volatility for this group of U.S. stocks (which are contained in the Dow Jones Industrial Average) is three times greater during New York trading hours than during London or Tokyo trading hours. In their view, this phenomenon occurs because the largest share of news relevant to the determination of the stock prices is disseminated during New York trading hours. This pattern was disrupted in the aftermath of the October 1987 crash when, in the authors' judgment, news was more globally dispersed and had mostly to do with "the volatile behavior of other investors" (176).

Yasushi Hamao, Ronald W. Masulis, and Victor Ng (1990) conducted another detailed study of intermarket linkages focusing on what they term price "volatility spillovers" among the New York, London, and Tokyo stock markets. For a subperiod that excludes the 1987 crash, they found that, while there was no significant transmission of volatility from Tokyo to either London or New York, the latter two cities' volatility did spill over to trading in Tokyo. When the post-1987 period is included, evidence indicates that all three markets were shocked by "volatility surprises," although Tokyo markets still did not affect New York's.

Mervyn A. King and Sushil Wadhwani (1990) have examined the market events surrounding October 1987 and offer a hypothesis about the worldwide scope of the market crash. To investigate the conundrum of what change in market fundamentals could explain a 23 percent drop in the Dow and similar gigantic declines in other markets around the globe, the authors developed a model in which rational traders in one market have less information about stocks than traders in the home market and must infer information partly from stock price movements abroad. This situation leads to the possibility of price movement "contagion" from one market to another, which will be particularly severe during periods of high market volatility. A sharp decline in a foreign price index is a (noisy) signal of bad news, some of which home market traders may not know from other sources. While the authors' hypothesis does not shed light on the "news" that triggered the October 1987 crash, it does explain why the crash was so uniform around the world despite important differences in markets and economic circumstances.

Gerard Gennotte and Hayne Leland (1990) have also developed a model in which rational traders' lack of information can precipitate a crash. Their concern is with informationless trading associated with hedging strategies like portfolio insurance. Formal portfolio insurance techniques systematically increase exposure to the market as stock prices rise and reduce it as stock prices fall (by shifting a portfolio's mix between index stocks and bonds or by adjusting the size of a short index futures hedge against a stock index portfolio). Although portfolio insurance-related selling is strictly passive, responding to declining stock prices, it could be mistaken for selling based on adverse information, and other traders look to prices and price changes as a way to glean information that they may lack. If nonpassive traders knew that they were taking the buy side of an informationless trade, they would more likely be willing to do so and would thereby supply liquidity to the market.

Gennotte and Leland's model shows how unobserved hedging programs, though only a small proportion of total trading, can destabilize a market. The disturbance may then propagate to other world markets. Their recommendation is that informationless trades should be preannounced and that "[e]lectronic 'open books' should be a seriously considered reform [to show the buy and sell order flow], and other forms of market organization (such as single-price auctions) should be examined" (1990, 1016). Some recent institutional developments are consistent with the authors' recommendations. Toronto's Computer Assisted Trading System displays limit orders to system users, and Wunsch's after-hours single-price auctions help concentrate market liquidity.

The King and Wadhwani and Gennotte and Leland models explain how trading itself can generate intermarket volatility. Joseph E. Stiglitz (1989) and Lawrence H. Summers and Victoria P. Summers (1989), go further by asserting that financial markets are excessively volatile because of irrational traders' speculative activity. Decreasing transactions costs owing to technological innovation and derivative markets promotes this speculation. These authors recommend a transactions tax to "throw sand into the gears" of financial markets (Tobin 1984, cited in Summers and Summers 1989, 263). Each securities purchase or sale would be subject to a "small" tax—for example, 0.5 percent of the stock price. In fact, many governments around the world impose stock transaction taxes, although the trend abroad is toward eliminating such taxes (see Roll 1989, table 4).

The gradual unification of world financial markets and continuing improvement in information flows will probably reduce the information asymmetry that produces contagion effects. However, in the view of those advocating transactions taxes these developments would just exacerbate irrational trading. At the core of their argument is the belief that financial markets are inefficient—that is, asset prices do not reflect "fundamentals." A growing list of so-called market anomalies seems to contradict efficient-markets theory. The apparent excess volatility analyzed by Robert J. Shiller (1989) stands as a challenge to efficient-markets proponents. Nevertheless, the theory is only being challenged, not overturned. Transactions taxes and other remedies for supposed excess trading and excess volatility have been proposed and sometimes implemented with little regard for their efficacy or possible adverse consequences.

Trading halts or circuit breakers, margin requirements, and price limits are also suggested as means of controlling trading. Of all these devices, margin requirements have been the most extensively studied and debated. In essence this work concludes that adjustments to margin requirements have no significant impact on stock market volatility (see David A. Hsieh and Miller 1990). Using data from twenty-three stock markets, Roll (1989) undertook a cross-market study of the effects of transactions taxes, margin requirements, and price limits on market volatility and found that none effectively reduce volatility.

Circuit breakers shut down an entire market temporarily to give participants a "time-out," mainly to avoid a panic selling spree. Both the New York Stock Exchange and Chicago Mercantile Exchange have instituted such circuit breakers (see Franklin R. Edwards 1988, 1989), although evidence is lacking concerning their usefulness. As Gennotte and Leland (1990) point out, the weekend of October 17-18, 1987, was an extended trading halt for the market declines of the previous week, but participants were not inclined to stage a market reversal the following Monday. It is not at all obvious that circuit breakers stabilize prices. To the contrary, they could induce traders to sell earlier and in larger quantities, fearing that a trading-halt price limit will soon be reached. This movement could destabilize prices. Sanford J. Grossman (1990) has argued persuasively that market equilibrium would be restored more quickly without halting trading. Rather than attempting to suppress mispricings, Grossman concludes that the market would be better served by being informed of them, whether they arise from panic or any other source, because better-informed traders would recognize such occurrences as profit opportunities and thus reverse the price movements.

Conclusion

The globalization of financial markets simultaneously fragments traditional financial transactions marketplaces and integrates them via electronic means. Physical marketplaces (the trading floors) are becoming obsolete, while "virtual" marketplaces—networks of computers and computer terminals—are emerging as the "site" for transactions. The new technology is diminishing the role for human participants in the market mechanism. Stock-exchange specialists are being displaced by the new systems, which by and large are designed to handle the demands of institutional investors, who increasingly dominate transactions. Futures and options floor traders also face having their jobs coded into computer algorithms, which automatically match orders and clear trades or emulate open-outcry trading itself.

International capital flows and the trading volume associated with them have been expanding over time. The internationalization of financial markets implies that investment portfolios are becoming more homogenized and creates a demand for worldwide twenty-four-hour trading. Derivative markets also benefit from this trend as multinational corporations need financial services around the clock for hedging and other reasons.

The competitive forces propelling changes in financial markets also compel changes in regulatory oversight of these markets.[24] Technology helps minimize some problems—for example, by making it possible to establish accurate audit trails of trades and thereby discouraging certain kinds of trading abuses—while it creates others, such as business being drawn to markets with the most lenient regulatory standards. Nevertheless, financial marketplaces are perhaps closest to the textbook paradigm of voluntary exchanges for mutual benefit of transacting parties. Competition among the world's financial exchanges as well as among their regulators is likely to be the most efficient way to elicit the best mechanisms for conducting and regulating transactions.

More problematic is the nature of trading and volatility associated with it. Does trading itself generate volatility that interferes with consumption, investment, and other economic decisions, in turn lowering social welfare? This article has given an overview of new automated trading systems and communications networks that are integrating markets. The technology discussed improves market mechanisms and information flows, but it may have the negative side effect of promoting "excess" trading. If markets are efficient, volatility per se is generally regarded as a neutral characteristic of markets. Derivative markets will continue developing to allow any desired degree of hedging against volatility. Only if markets are inefficient can a case can be made for curtailing volatility, but the evidence is ambiguous regarding market inefficiency. Even less clear is the efficacy of measures proposed to safeguard markets against volatility.

Notes

1. See Summers and Summers (1989) and the discussion of their proposal below.
2. Frequent trading will be necessary when the number of securities available to "complete markets" is smaller than the number of future "states." See Huang and Litzenberger (1988, chapter 7). This situation will be all the more likely if financial markets are incomplete. However, theory does not give an indication of how much trading is appropriate to allocate wealth over time efficiently.
3. The difference between purchases and sales represents the net capital flow, which is less relevant in considering the growth of securities trading and market liquidity.
4. $321\% = [(75.28/17.85) - 1] * 100$ and $43\% = [(361.37/253.38) - 1] * 100$.
5. See Smith (1991). Ginnie Mae stands for Government National Mortgage Association, a government-chartered agency that makes a secondary market in home mortgages and enhances the liquidity of that market by securitizing individual mortgages into "pass-through" certificates. The futures was on this underlying security.
6. The NYSE is in the process of instituting "A Look at the Book" program that permits public subscribers to the service to view the limit orders for 50 of the 2,370 NYSE-listed stocks. This service will be available through vendors and will show the limit-order book at three fixed times during the trading day. Currently, only the specialists and other NYSE members, such as floor brokers, on the exchange floor have access to the specialists' books.
7. Market orders specify quantity for trade at the current price. Limit orders specify price and quantity.
8. The meanings of the acronyms are given in Table 5.
9. The bid price is the price for which a dealer is willing to buy a stock, and the offer is the price for which he or she is willing to sell the stock.
10. See Bodie, Kane, and Marcus (1989) or Francis (1991) for further institutional details about organized exchanges and OTC markets and such details as listing requirements.
11. This account of SOES is based on Domowitz (1990).
12. See U.S. Securities and Exchange Commission (1991, 69); another NASDAQ system described in this source is PORTAL (Private Offerings, Resales, and Trading through Automated Linkages), which is used in the secondary market for privately placed equity and debt. See note 24 below for further description.
13. See NASDAQ (1991, 14-15). Because of differences in accounting conventions, the NASDAQ figures are inflated compared with the NYSE figures.
14. See Hansell (1989, 102). The amount of institutional participation in NASDAQ stocks as measured by the volume of block trading has been about 43 percent in recent years. See NASDAQ (1991).
15. Instinet-sponsored section in *Institutional Investor* (January 1991).
16. See Kolb (1991, 17-18) for a general discussion of EFP transactions and Miller (1990) for EFPs in connection with the CME's S&P 500 stock-index futures contract.
17. The futures exchange, however, would collect an additional fee for allowing the off-exchange or ex-pit EFP. The Commodity Exchange Act prohibits noncompetitive and prearranged transactions in futures, with the exception of EFPs. See Behof (1990, 2).
18. See Roll (1988, 29). Roll notes that the Spanish market trades groups of stocks continuously for ten minutes at a time. This article contains much interesting information about foreign stock markets.
19. See Kolb (1991, 59-61) for a succinct account of the FBI undercover sting operation at the CME and CBOT, which began in early 1987 and resulted in indictments against forty-seven traders in January 1989.
20. Information on Globex came from 1991 CME promotional literature. Domowitz (1990) provides a detailed description and analysis of the Globex trading algorithm as well as those for two other trading systems.
21. The Brady Commission's basic recommendations were: (1) to have one agency be the overarching regulator of U.S. financial markets; (2) to have a unification of clearing systems of financial exchanges and OTC markets; (3) to have "consistent" margin requirements across different exchanges; (4) to institute coordinated "circuit breakers" across exchanges; and (5) to improve information systems to monitor trading activity in related markets.
22. The Securities and Exchange Act of 1934 authorized the Federal Reserve Board to established initial and maintenance margins to prevent excessive leveraging of securities purchases on securities exchanges. (In practice, the Board has set only minimum initial margin levels.) Part of the rationale for control over margins was to limit massive selling off of leveraged positions during market downturns.
23. See Brady et al. (1988, especially 51-52). Despite the potential dangers, no defaults occurred in the clearinghouse system during October 1987.
24. The SEC's April 1990 approval of Rule 144A is an instance of a change in regulatory standards that reflect changes in the nature of financial transactions. This rule simplifies the SEC's disclosure requirements for private placement issuers (see Chu 1991). Foreign corporations are now able to raise capital in U.S. markets without having to meet the SEC's stringent financial disclosure requirements as long as transactions are limited to large institutional investors. British financial authorities have instituted a similar relaxation of regulations for institutional investors (see Grundfest 1990).

NASDAQ's new PORTAL system is used for communicating bids and offers on privately placed securities traded under the provisions of Rule 144A.

References

Angrist, Stanley W. "Futures Trade on Screens—Except in U.S." *Wall Street Journal*, May 21, 1991, C1, C14.

Behof, John P. "Globex: A Global Automated Transaction System for Futures and Options." Study by the Federal Reserve Bank of Chicago, June 1990.

Bodie, Zvi, Alex Kane, and Alan J. Marcus. *Investments*. Homewood, Ill.: Irwin, 1989.

Brady, Nicholas F., James C. Cotting, Robert G. Kirby, John R. Opel, and Howard M. Stein. *Report of the Presidential Task Force on Market Mechanisms*. Submitted to the President of the United States, the Secretary of the Treasury, and the Chairman of the Federal Reserve Board, January 1988.

Brodsky, William J. "Futures in the Nineties: Confronting Globalization." In *Proceedings from a Conference on Bank Structure and Competition*, 615-23. Federal Reserve Bank of Chicago, 1990.

———. "The Future Is Now." *Institutional Investor* 25 (January 1991): 7.

Chicago Board of Trade. *Commodity Trading Manual*. CBOT, 1985.

Chu, Franklin J. "The U.S. Private Market for Foreign Securities." *The Bankers Magazine* 174 (January/February 1991): 55-60.

Domowitz, Ian. "The Mechanics of Automated Trade Execution Systems." *Journal of Financial Intermediation* 1 (1990): 167-94.

———. "Equally Open and Competitive: Regulatory Approval of Automated Trade Execution in the Futures Markets." Center for the Study of Futures Markets Working Paper #214, forthcoming 1991.

Edwards, Franklin R. "Studies of the 1987 Stock Market Crash: Review and Appraisal." *Journal of Financial Services Research* 1 (1988): 231-51.

———. "Regulatory Reform of Securities and Futures Markets: Two Years after the Crash." Center for the Study of Futures Markets Working Paper #189, June 1989.

Francis, Jack Clark. *Investments: Analysis and Management*. 5th ed. New York: McGraw-Hill, Inc., 1991.

"Futures Markets Will Let Their Fingers Do the Dealing." *The Economist*, March 19, 1988, 77-78.

Gennotte, Gerard, and Hayne Leland. "Market Liquidity, Hedging, and Crashes." *American Economic Review* 80 (1990): 999-1021.

Grossman, Sanford J. "Institutional Investing and New Trading Technologies." In *Market Volatility and Investor Confidence: Report to the Board of Directors of the New York Stock Exchange, Inc.*, G2-1-17. June 7, 1990.

Grundfest, Joseph A. "Internationalization of the World's Securities Markets: Economic Causes and Regulatory Consequences." *Journal of Financial Services Research* 4 (1990): 349-78.

Guy, Paul. "IOSCO Moves Ahead." *FIA Review* (May/June 1990): 8-10.

Hamao, Yasushi, Ronald W. Masulis, and Victor Ng. "Correlations in Price Changes and Volatility across International Stock Markets." *Review of Financial Studies* 3 (1990): 281-307.

Hansell, Saul. "The Wild, Wired World of Electronic Exchanges." *Institutional Investor* (September 1989): 91ff.

Harvey, Campbell R. "The World Price of Covariance Risk." *Journal of Finance* 46 (1991): 111-57.

Heimann, John G. *Globalization of the Securities Markets*. Statement in hearings before the Senate Subcommittee on Securities of the Committee on Banking, Housing, and Urban Affairs. June 14, 1989, 76.

Howard, Barbara. "The Trade: Technology Aims to Take the Final Step." *Institutional Investor* 25 (January 1991): 15-16.

Hsieh, David A., and Merton H. Miller. "Margin Regulation and Stock Market Volatility." *Journal of Finance* 45 (1990): 3-29.

Huang, Chi-fu, and Robert H. Litzenberger. *Foundations for Financial Economics*. New York: North-Holland, 1988.

Kang, Jane C., and John C. Lawton. "Automated Futures Trading Systems." *FIA Review* (May/June 1990): 6-7.

King, Mervyn A., and Sushil Wadhwani. "Transmission of Volatility between Stock Markets." *Review of Financial Studies* 3 (1990): 5-33.

Kolb, Robert W. *Understanding Futures Markets*. 3d ed. Miami: Kolb Publishing Company, 1991.

Lewis, Janet. "The Euro-Futures War." *Institutional Investor* 24 (March 1990): 129ff.

London International Financial Futures Exchange. *APT Information Package*. 1991.

Miller, Merton H. "International Competitiveness of U.S. Futures Exchanges." *Journal of Financial Services Research* 4 (1990): 387-408.

NASDAQ. *Fact Book 1991*. 1991.

Neumark, David, P.A. Tinsley, and Suzanne Tosini. "After-Hours Stock Prices and Post-Crash Hangovers." *Journal of Finance* 46 (1991): 159-78.

New York Stock Exchange. *Fact Book 1991*. 1991a.

New York Stock Exchange. *Off-Hours Trading*. Brochure. 1991b.

Roll, Richard. "The International Crash of October 1987." *Financial Analysts Journal* 44 (September/October 1988): 19-35.

———. "Price Volatility, International Market Links, and Their Implications for Regulatory Policies." *Journal of Financial Services Research* 3 (1989): 211-46.

Rosenbaum, Amy. "Scouting Automation: What's the Competition Like?" *Futures* 19 (April 1990): 52-54.

Salwen, Kevin G., and Craig Torres. "Big Board After-Hours Trading May Lead to a Two-Tiered Market." *Wall Street Journal*, June 13, 1991, C1, C17.

Sheeline, William E. "Who Needs the Stock Exchange?" *Fortune*, November 19, 1990, 119ff.

Shiller, Robert J. *Market Volatility.* Cambridge, Mass.: MIT Press, 1989.

Smith, Stephen D. "Analyzing Risk and Return for Mortgage-Backed Securities." Federal Reserve Bank of Atlanta *Economic Review* 76 (January/February 1991): 2-11.

Stiglitz, Joseph E. "Using Tax Policy to Curb Speculative Short-Term Trading." *Journal of Financial Services Research* 3 (1989): 101-15.

Summers, Lawrence H., and Victoria P. Summers. "When Financial Markets Work Too Well: A Cautious Case for a Securities Transactions Tax." *Journal of Financial Services Research* 3 (1989): 261-86.

Szala, Ginger, and Amy Rosenbaum. "Deregulation in Japan May Have Different Meaning." *Futures* 19 (February 1990): 42-44.

Tobin, James. "On the Efficiency of the Financial System." *Lloyds Bank Review,* no. 153 (July 1984): 1-15.

U.S. Congress. Office of Technology Assessment. *Trading Around the Clock: Global Securities Markets and Information Technology—Background Paper.* OTA-BP-CIT-66. Washington, D.C.: U.S. Government Printing Office, July 1990a.

_____. *Electronic Bulls and Bears: U.S. Securities Markets and Information Technology.* OTA-CIT-469. Washington, D.C.: U.S. Government Printing Office, September 1990b.

U.S. Securities and Exchange Commission. *Questionnaire of the Working Party on Regulation of Secondary Markets.* May 29, 1991.

Wunsch, R. Steven. "Single-Price Auctions." *Institutional Investor* 25 (January 1991): 20.

The Inter-Temporal Stability of International Stock Market Relationships: Another View

G. C. Philippatos, A. Christofi, and P. Christofi

G. C. Philippatos is Professor of Banking and Finance, A. Christofi is Assistant Professor of International Finance, and P. Christofi is instructor in Management Science at, respectively, The University of Tennessee, The University of Maryland, and The Pennsylvania State University.

■ Recent research interest in the existence of conditions for meaningful *ex ante* international diversification has focused on the "sufficient" condition that deals with the inter-temporal stability of the correlations matrix among the national stock exchanges involved. The presence of such stability, along with the fulfillment of the "necessary" condition ($\rho < 1$), facilitates the selection of an *ex ante* optimal investment strategy without resorting to costly forecasting or naive equi-proportional funds allocation policies. Unfortunately, however, most studies on the subject [11, 17, 18, 19, 25, 26], while meritorious, have also confounded the central issue of stationarity by employing different methodologies, separate sample countries, dissimilar sample periods, and variable differencing intervals. Hence, we are confronted with conflicting results that support equally eloquently either stationarity or randomness in the inter-temporal relationships among national stock markets.

For example, Panton, Lessig, and Joy [19], employed cluster analysis to investigate "discernible co-movement structure . . ." and test for stability over time. The authors studied twelve stock market indices containing a subsample of the fourteen industrial countries[1] and Australia, utilizing weekly data over a ten-year period (1963–1972). The basic results of this study, as they relate to our present research, support the existence of strong stability for one-year and three-

---

This research constitutes a seriously enlarged study of an earlier version that was also presented at the 1982 FMA Meetings. We wish to thank the discussants as well as two *Journal* reviewers that contributed to the present, expanded and improved version.

[1] The term "industrial countries" is commonly used in international economics to refer to the fourteen developed countries whose economies are highly integrated through trade, capital movements and homogeneous economic objectives. They account for more than 90 percent of the total trade flows among the 24 OECD countries. In addition, most of these countries are characterized by active stock exchanges. These countries, also utilized in our present study, are as follows: Austria, Belgium, Canada, Denmark, France, Germany, Italy, Japan, the Netherlands, Norway, Sweden, Switzerland, the United Kingdom, and the United States.

year period relationships. Along similar lines, Watson [26] employed standard correlation analysis to test for inter-temporal stability, utilizing eight monthly indices — namely, Australia, Denmark, Germany, Japan, New Zealand, South Africa, the United Kingdom, and the United States over an eight-year period (1970–1977). Watson computed the inter-country correlation coefficients over one-year, two-year and four-year periods and found support for the presence of stationarity for the annual intercountry correlations over the entire horizon as well as between the two four-year subperiods.

However, the existence of inter-temporal stability is not universally supported by researchers. For example, in an earlier research Makridakis and Wheelwright [17] employed both standard correlation and principal components analyses in a study of fourteen indices (including three from the U.S.). The authors utilized daily data over a thirty-two month period (1/5/68–9/7/70) containing 2 "bull" markets separated by a "bear" market in a multivariate framework that included international, national, and political events. The relevant results did not provide support for the stability of inter-temporal relationships among the national stock market indices studied. Along similar lines, Hilliard [11] employed spectral analysis, utilizing daily data from a subset of eight of the fourteen industrial countries for a nine-month period (7/7/73–4/30/74), and found no significant leads or lags among the indices considered. Finally, in a very recent study published in this *Journal*, Maldonado and Saunders [18] employed Box-Jenkins techniques and non-parametric runs tests to investigate the presence of sensitivity to both sample period and investment horizon. The authors utilized monthly indices from a five-country subset of the fourteen industrial countries for a 22-year period (1957–1978), and concluded that for periods longer than two quarters ". . . the inter-country correlations are generally unstable . . . (and) . . . it is not possible to reject the hypothesis that correlations follow a random walk" [18, p. 62].[2]

The stability of inter-temporal relationships among various national stock markets serves as the foundation of the research focused on the benefits of international diversification and/or the comovement of equity prices. Thus, any serious questions raised about the stability of the international correlations matrix deserve a thorough study and a prompt response. However, it should be noted at this juncture that serious questions about the stability of inter-temporal relationships among national stock market indices must be investigated within a framework that allows for generalization of the results beyond that found in [18] and some of the other previous studies. First, one must recognize the presence of different exchange rate regimes and allow investors to adjust their expectations rather than restrict them to the extrapolation of historical data drawn from the fixed into the flexible exchange period. Such change in exchange rate regimes is likely to produce shifts in the underlying structure of the correlations matrix and, indeed, evidence of such a phenomenon has been reported in [10].[3] Second, utilization of the full-covariance model requires that the entire correlations matrix be analyzed rather than only the part relating the U.S. to other countries. In the case of Maldonado and Saunders [18], who studied five countries utilizing the full-covariance E-V model, the analysis should be carried on $(N^2-N)/2 = 10$ correlations rather than the four correlations explored by the authors. Third, the investment horizons tested must extend beyond the one-to-two years limitation imposed in [18], as we have reviewed evidence that such extensions yield patterns of stationarity and may also legitimately represent holding periods by international financial investors.[4] Fourth, the analysis of stationarity patterns requires that the full sample of fourteen industrial countries be examined rather than the smaller subsample of five countries studied in [18]. As the selection of the five countries is judgmental, it also restricts the generality of inferences drawn from the available data base. Finally, one must recognize that the proper utilization of Box-Jenkins techniques to identify possible patterns among correlations requires that the minimum sample size be much larger than that employed by Maldonado and Saunders [18] in order to draw valid, generalizable inferences. In the words of Box and Jenkins, "If possible at least 50 and preferably 100 observations or more should be used" [3, p. 18].

In light of the above, we propose to report the results

---

[2]Due to space limitations we do not review other recent studies that concentrated primarily on the "necessary" condition for *ex ante* gains from international diversification, such as Ripley [21], Haney and Lloyd [10], and Watson [25]. Moreover, we refer the reader to [10, 15, 18, 21] and other studies for reviews of the general literature on the analytics and/or the *ex post* gains from international diversification.

[3]Changes in the underlying structure of the correlations matrix necessitate a shift in the emphasis of the "sufficient" condition from inter-temporal stability to inter-temporal predictability, as stressed in the testing methodologies employed by [11] and [17]. Under these conditions the formation of future expectations may follow a Bayesian process, as described by Vasicek [24] and applied in [20].

[4]Empirical support for long-term investment horizons can be found in [22]. For a thorough investigation of the impact of the investment horizon on asset prices under conditions of uncertainty, the reader is also referred to Levhari and Levy [14].

of our research on the inter-temporal stability of the relationships among the national stock exchanges of the fourteen industrial countries for the period covering January 1959 to December 1978. Our study replicates the methodology in [18], but is also augmented by the utilization of the multivariate analyses found in [17] and [21], as well as the stability tests employed in [26]. In addition, our study concentrates on intermediate-term stability rather than the short-term stability considered in [18] and, except for a special runs-test discussed later, it covers the period 1959–1978, rather than 1957–1978 reported in [18]. Hence, the results could be viewed as complements and extensions of previous research. Finally, our research is designed to reflect the changes in the exchange rate regimes during the sample period. Thus, arguments about the appropriateness of one method versus the other can be pushed safely into the background, while we pursue the substantive question of stability[5] in the inter-temporal relationships among the national stock market indices of the fourteen industrial countries.

The results of our research are in line with those reported by Panton, Lessig, and Joy [19]. That is, the hypothesis of stable structure in the sample considered cannot be rejected for an investment horizon longer than two years, while for shorter-period investment horizons the evidence is not clear. The study is presented in four sections. Part II briefly discusses the data and methodology, while Part III analyzes the empirical results. Finally, Part IV summarizes the conclusions and attempts to explain some of the reasons for the discrepancies in the inferences drawn from our results and those reported in [18].

II. Data and Methodology

The sample studied consists of monthly common stock market averages of the fourteen industrial countries (Austria, Belgium, Canada, Denmark, France, Germany, Italy, Japan, the Netherlands, Norway, Sweden, Switzerland, the U.K., and the U.S.A.), covering the twenty-year period from January 1959 to December 1978. For each country we obtained the values of the industrial share price indices and the exchange rates, as recorded in the IMF International Financial Statistics Tapes.[6]

Let us define the dollar value of one foreign stock market unit at the end of period t, adjusted for exchange rate movements (unhedged), as

$$\widetilde{VI}_{it} = \widetilde{I}_{it}/\widetilde{X}_{it} \qquad (1)$$

and the monthly return relative for each country as

$$\widetilde{R}_{it} = \frac{\widetilde{VI}_{it}}{\widetilde{VI}_{it-1}} = \frac{\widetilde{I}_{it}/\widetilde{X}_{it}}{\widetilde{I}_{it-1}/\widetilde{X}_{it-1}}, \qquad (2)$$

where $\widetilde{I}_{it}$ = industrial share price index level for country i at time t;[7]

$\widetilde{X}_{it}$ = exchange rate expressed in units of country i currency per U.S. dollar at time t;

~: denotes random variables.

III. Empirical Results

In line with the methodology developed above, we applied both parametric and non-parametric tests to the results obtained from the sample of fourteen countries.[8]

A. Methodological Replication Tests

As a first step, we replicated the tests for annual and biennial correlation coefficients of the U.S. with each of the other thirteen countries — including the four studied in [18]. The resulting correlation coefficients from our study for the countries also considered by Maldonado and Saunders were consistently lower than those reported in [18]. Nevertheless, our results for the annual correlation coefficients are the same with those found by Levy and Sarnat [15].

The second step was the replication of the Box-

---

[5]The topic of beta stationarity has been the subject of many earlier studies dealing with the formation of expectations via the CAPM. The works of Blume [1, 2], Brenner and Smidt [4], Levy [16], and Sharpe and Cooper [23] are considered to be among the pioneering studies in this area. For a detailed review of these researches and an alternative methodology, see Eubank and Zumwalt [6]. More recently, Garbade and Rentzler [8] proposed a test for beta stationarity using a variable parameter regression (VPR), as opposed to the random coefficient model (RCM) utilized by Fabozzi and Francis [7].

[6]The period after 1970 was considered as the period of flexible exchange rates, since some currencies began floating before the March 1973 date of the official change. For example, the Canadian dollar floated June 1, 1970, while Germany and the Netherlands let their currencies float on May 10, 1971. Similarly, the U.S. suspended the convertibility of the dollar into gold and other reserve assets.

[7]As is common with most aggregate indices, dividends are not generally included in their computation. This exclusion results in the understatement of rates of return. However, the exclusion of transaction costs also overstates the rates of return, thus providing a balancing effect.

[8]Due to space limitations, many of the tests performed and their results are not presented here. However, they are available from the authors upon request. Moreover, it should be noted here that a market model equivalent was also used with Capital International Index (CIP) serving as the world index. The results of this experiment also pointed to stability in the structure of the international equity market returns. However, caution should be exercised in deriving conclusions from the application of the market model, since the world index, like many of its domestic counterparts, covers only a portion (not necessarily representative) of the market value of each national stock exchange.

Jenkins tests on the annual and biennial correlations of the U.S. with the other thirteen industrial countries. These tests corroborated the results of Maldonado and Saunders [18] on randomness. However, as we have stressed throughout this study, the proper application of Box-Jenkins requires a minimum number of observations that were not available in [18] and can hardly be considered truly sufficient in our study. The third step involved the reconstruction of the non-parametric runs tests on the annual correlations. When the tests were run on our data base (1/1959 to 12/1978) it was found that the Z-statistic accepts randomness in seven out of thirteen cases. However, when the tests were run for the period 2/1957 to 12/1978, which was employed in [18], the Z-statistic accepts randomness in only three out of thirteen cases (France, the Netherlands, and Canada). These results may be interpreted in one of the following two ways: (a) the shortening of the time period in our study by two years reduced the power of the test (fewer degrees of freedom); or (b) the move toward full currency convertibility in 1958 had serious implications for international capital market stability.[9]

The final step in the replication process encompassed an examination of the correlation coefficients over two equal sub-periods as performed in [18]. In our case the first subperiod was characterized by the fixed exchange rates environment (1963–1970) while the second equal subperiod evolved within the regime of flexible exchange rates (1971–1978). The results of this test indicated that only two out of thirteen coefficients in the second subperiod differ significantly from those in the first subperiod at the 0.05 level.[10]

The generality of the aforementioned three sets of tests replicating the methodology in [18] was limited by the fact that these tests were restricted to the unidimensional pairwise relations of the U.S. with the markets of the other countries rather than the entire correlation matrix required by the use of the full-covariance model. Consequently, the fidelity of replication notwithstanding, any inferences drawn would suffer from the same restrictions as the tests. The only way to overcome such strictures is to use the entire correlation matrix in the tests for structural stability of inter-temporal relationships among national stock market indices. In this spirit, we utilized an additional procedure — also employed by Watson [26] with related research — that requires the computation of inter-country correlation coefficients over four- and five-year subperiods, covering the entire horizon 1959–1978. The results indicated that only about one percent of the sample correlations were significantly different from the previous sub-period at the 0.05 level. Hence, the inference that must be drawn from these results is that the inter-country correlation coefficients, in general, did not change significantly from one sub-period to the next over the twenty-year horizon of this study.

B. Principal Components Analysis Tests

As an alternative test for the stability of the international stock market relationships, we applied the methodology of principal components analysis also utilized by earlier researchers on this topic [17, 21]. This method is a special case of Factor Analysis that is highly useful in the analysis of many time series and the search for patterns of movement common to several series.[11] Clearly, this approach is superior to many of the bivariate statistical techniques used earlier, in that it explores the interrelationships among a set of variables caused by common "factors," mostly economic in nature. Each factor (or principal component) is a linear combination of the original variables. The coefficients of the original variables used to construct factors are often called loadings or eigenvectors. The proportion of the variation explained by each principal component is the sum of the squared loadings (known alternately as eigenvalue, latent root, or characteristic root) divided by the number of variables. The product of the square root of the eigenvalue and the eigenvectors of the respective principal component, often called component correlations, indicates the relationship (correlation) between the factor and the original variables.

Exhibit 1 shows the results of the principal components analysis utilizing the entire 240 monthly observations.[12] As can be readily observed, the first component accounts for about 38 percent of the total variation

---

[9]The authors wish to thank an anonymous referee of this *Journal* for pointing out the second interpretation.

[10]Maldonado and Saunders [18] considered two slightly different sub-periods (1957–1967 and 1968–1978) and concluded that "In three cases out of four . . . there is a statistically significant change over the two sub-periods" [18, p. 60]. In order to make our analysis compatible with that of Maldonado and Saunders, we also considered the sub-periods 1959–1968 and 1969–1978, but the results were generally the same with those of the 1963–1970 and 1971–1978 sub-periods.

[11]For a detailed discussion on the technique of principal components analysis the interested reader is referred to [5, 9, 12, 13], or any standard textbook on multivariate data analysis. Also, for an application of this method on interrelationships among national stock market indices, see [17] and [21].

[12]It was necessary for the data to be expressed in logarithmic form so as to remove first-order serial correlation, which might have given rise to spurious inferences about the causes of common movement.

Exhibit 1. Principal Component Analysis (1/1959–12/1978)

	Eigenvectors					Component First	Correlation Second
USA	0.28801	−0.51187	0.03621	0.04896	−0.01897	.667*	−.586*
Austria	0.23937	0.44322	−0.03961	−0.07844	−0.03364	.554*	.507*
Belgium	0.32811	0.02029	−0.22464	−0.25876	−0.02728	.760*	.023
Denmark	0.18083	0.36367	0.56704	−0.06260	−0.12383	.419*	.416*
France	0.21160	0.10345	−0.02371	0.71400	0.16684	.490*	.118
Germany	0.28068	0.21572	−0.18804	0.24893	0.19446	.650*	.247*
Italy	0.25319	0.19915	−0.30686	−0.21142	0.16472	.586*	.228*
Netherlands	0.34881	0.07574	0.01944	0.02366	−0.05316	.808*	.087
Norway	0.25404	0.03955	−0.22294	−0.34060	−0.41036	.588*	.045
Sweden	0.23086	0.03102	0.41055	0.18608	−0.52857	.535*	.036
Switzerland	0.32441	0.00824	−0.23626	0.12424	0.06678	.751*	.009
UK	0.25251	−0.30881	0.16180	−0.21044	0.05665	.585*	−.354*
Canada	0.29390	−0.45629	0.04186	0.12063	−0.01339	.681*	−.522*
Japan	0.19198	0.00953	0.43894	−0.28042	0.65665	.445*	.011
Eigenvalues:	5.3650	1.3106	1.0994	.8895	.8182		
% Variance Explained:	38.32	9.36	7.85	6.35	5.84		

*Significant at the 1 percent level.

in the 14 variables (country indices) and more than 50 percent of the variation explained by the first five factors. It is also evident from Exhibit 1 that each national stock market index is relatively highly correlated with the first principal component, the correlations ranging from .4 to .8.[13] As a matter of simple interpretation, there appears to be one common factor that influences the movements of the original variables — a clustering that may well be accounted for by international capital flows for diversification purposes.

Although the contribution of at least the next two factors in explaining the total variation was statistically significant,[14] one-half of the component correlations of these factors were insignificant. But when the significant loadings of these two factors are combined with the first factor loadings, some interesting patterns emerge. First, five distinct clusters are formed that are invariant with exchange rates. One links the United States, United Kingdom, and Canada, while the other four clusters are associated with Austria, Germany, Sweden, and Japan. Second, although at least five more factor loadings appear to be significant, their patterns seem to vary with either the exchange rates or some other time series.

In an effort to investigate the consistency in the linkage among the national stock market indices covered by this study through a common factor, we then applied the method of principal components analysis on two equal sub-periods of the entire horizon (1959–1978). Exhibits 2 and 3 present the results for the first and second sub-periods, respectively. It is evident from these two Exhibits that the common factor identified earlier still persists during the two sub-periods. Although the first component correlations of Exhibit 1 represent the average of those shown in Exhibits 2 and 3, their similarity is striking. Thus, we can safely conclude that the national stock market indices of the fourteen industrial countries are interrelated through a common factor whose effect appears to be consistent over time.[15]

IV. Summary and Conclusions

We have now come full circle and can state safely that the results obtained from our study support the hypothesis of a stable structure in the inter-temporal relationships among national stock market indices of the industrialized world for intermediate-term investment horizons. In effect our tests on the correlation coefficients support strongly the hypothesis of non-randomness and point to the existence of international economic factors that contribute to the stability of the inter-temporal relationships. Moreover, when we replicated the methodology employed in [18] with our

---

[13] In assessing the significance of the component correlation coefficients, we applied the critical values (standard errors) for the Pearson product-moment correlation coefficients as explained in [13, pp. 413–431].

[14] Bartlett's χ^2, as explained in [5, 9, 12, 13], was greater than the critical value appearing in the χ^2-Table. This suggests inclusion of additional factors in our analysis.

[15] The principal components analysis was carried out also for smaller sub-periods and the results were very similar, especially those of the five-year sub-periods.

Exhibit 2. Principal Component Analysis (1/1959–12/1968)

	Eigenvectors					Component First	Correlation Second
USA	0.34058	−0.32231	−0.25478	0.14151	−0.35615	.734*	−.377*
Austria	0.19963	0.34168	0.27242	0.25560	−0.54890	.430*	.400*
Belgium	0.32261	0.03726	−0.06540	−0.09043	0.17345	.695*	.044
Denmark	0.09486	−0.09789	0.73619	−0.38188	−0.13280	.205†	−.114
France	0.26759	0.21670	−0.21178	0.01429	0.19317	.577*	.253*
Germany	0.26810	0.34178	−0.06760	−0.22914	0.07291	.578*	.400*
Italy	0.24939	0.36455	0.15887	−0.21286	0.08516	.538*	.426*
Netherlands	0.35926	−0.06836	−0.08385	−0.13803	0.07851	.775*	−.080
Norway	0.24463	0.15275	0.16494	0.26465	0.19795	.527*	.179†
Sweden	0.22954	−0.35313	0.23035	−0.10933	0.10506	.495*	−.413*
Switzerland	0.33676	0.18579	−0.20841	−0.06706	0.02377	.726*	.217†
UK	0.21084	−0.42791	0.05909	−0.08053	0.38855	.455*	−.500*
Canada	0.33706	−0.31817	−0.06503	0.13460	−0.39364	.727*	−.372*
Japan	0.11101	0.01293	0.31861	0.72971	0.33375	.239*	.015
Eigenvalues:	4.6476	1.3677	1.1223	1.0667	.9291		
% Variance Explained:	33.20	9.77	8.02	7.62	6.64		

*Significant at the 1 percent level.
†Significant at the 5 percent level.

Exhibit 3. Principal Component Analysis (1/1969–12/1978)

	Eigenvectors					Component First	Correlation Second
USA	0.25587	−0.50532	0.15040	−0.04538	0.11386	.634*	−.603*
Austria	0.26611	0.45338	−0.15137	−0.02000	0.11081	.659*	.541*
Belgium	0.31940	−0.03020	−0.33919	−0.16207	−0.04189	.791*	−.036
Denmark	0.20233	0.38233	0.40715	−0.13311	0.18229	.501*	.457*
France	0.18292	0.09452	0.14267	0.78043	−0.45774	.453*	.113
Germany	0.32305	0.20238	−0.00432	−0.08994	−0.25789	.800*	.242*
Italy	0.24227	0.04229	−0.40846	−0.10320	−0.21664	.600*	.050
Netherlands	0.33996	0.14618	0.03889	−0.08338	0.00151	.842*	.175†
Norway	0.24008	−0.07484	−0.44383	0.17301	0.48150	.595*	−.089
Sweden	0.22293	0.11706	0.29412	0.27291	0.55074	.552*	.140
Switzerland	0.32298	−0.03888	−0.10128	0.08555	−0.12403	.800*	−.046
UK	0.25215	−0.29964	0.09401	−0.19338	−0.16225	.625*	−.358*
Canada	0.26378	−0.45644	0.13947	0.18050	0.09212	.654*	−.545*
Japan	0.25273	−0.00510	0.40358	−0.37026	−0.17734	.626*	−.006
Eigenvalues:	6.1390	1.4258	1.1305	.8959	.7685		
% Variance Explained:	43.85	10.18	8.08	6.40	5.49		

*Significant at the 1 percent level.
†Significant at the 5 percent level.

sample, in order to test for short-term structure, the results were far from clear, as they exhibited high sample sensitivity and yielded confounding outcomes.

In view of the above, we must conclude that our results cannot be reconciled with those of Maldonado and Saunders [18]. As we have demonstrated clearly in this research, their inferences are limited by the methodologies and the sample employed and cannot be generalized easily. To wit, the analysis of a small part of the correlation matrix coupled with the small sample of five countries is apparently not representative of market behavior in the industrialized world. Moreover, the utilization of Box-Jenkins techniques was not warranted with the few observations available in [18]. Finally, the inclusion of the years 1957 and 1958 in [18] — a period when most European countries moved toward full currency convertibility — simply compounded the difficulties of interpretation by obscuring the nature of the relationships during the subsequent years.

Hence, having employed a wide variety of standard statistical methods on a large sample of industrialized countries, we must agree with the inferences drawn in earlier studies by Panton, Lessig and Joy [19], Watson [25, 26], and others [10, 15, 21]. There indeed exist both structure and stability of such structure in the inter-temporal relationships among the national stock market indices of the industrialized world. Hence, the results of earlier studies on *ex ante* gains from international diversification cannot be questioned on the grounds that the sufficient conditions are not met.

References

1. M. E. Blume, "On the Assessments of Risk," *Journal of Finance* (March 1971), pp. 1–10.
2. M. E. Blume, "Betas and Their Regression Tendencies," *Journal of Finance* (June 1975), pp. 785–796.
3. G. E. P. Box and G. M. Jenkins, *Time Series Analysis, Forecasting and Control*. San Francisco, Holden-Day, Inc., 1976.
4. M. Brenner and S. Smidt, "A Simple Model of Non-Stationarity of Systematic Risk," *Journal of Finance* (September 1977), pp. 1081–1092.
5. William W. Cooley and Paul R. Lohnes, *Multivariate Data Analysis*. New York, John Wiley & Sons, Inc., 1971.
6. A. E. Eubank, Jr. and K. Zumwalt, "How to Determine the Stability of Beta Values," *Journal of Portfolio Management* (Winter 1979), pp. 22–26.
7. F. J. Fabozzi and J. C. Francis, "Beta as a Random Coefficient," *Journal of Financial and Quantitative Analysis* (March 1978), pp. 101–116.
8. Kenneth Garbade and Joel Rentzler, "Testing the Hypothesis of Beta Stationarity," *International Economic Review* (October 1981), pp. 577–587.
9. Paul E. Green, *Analyzing Multivariate Data*. Hinsdale, Illinois, Dryden Press, 1978.
10. R. L. Haney, Jr. and W. P. Lloyd, "An Examination of the Stability of the Inter-Temporal Relationships Among National Stock Market Indices," *Nebraska Journal of Economics and Business* (May 1978), pp. 55–65.
11. Jimmy E. Hilliard, "The Relationship Between Equity Indices on World Exchanges," *Journal of Finance* (March 1979), pp. 103–114.
12. Richard A. Johnson and Dean W. Wichern, *Applied Multivariate Statistical Analysis*. Englewood Cliffs, NJ, Prentice Hall, Inc., 1983.
13. A. Koutsoyiannis, *Theory of Econometrics*, 2nd ed. New York, Barnes & Noble, 1977.
14. D. Levhari and H. Levy, "The Capital Asset Pricing Model and the Investment Horizon," *Review of Economics and Statistics* (February 1977), pp. 92–104.
15. Haim Levy and Marshall Sarnat, "Exchange Rate Risk and the Optimal Diversification of Foreign Currency Holdings," *Journal of Money Credit and Banking* (November 1978), pp. 453–463.
16. R. A. Levy, "On the Short-Term Stationarity of Beta Coefficients," *Financial Analysts Journal* (November/December 1971), pp. 55–62.
17. Spyros G. Makridakis and Steven C. Wheelwright, "An Analysis of the Interrelationships Among the Major World Stock Exchanges," *Journal of Business Finance and Accounting* (Summer 1974), pp. 195–215.
18. R. Maldonado and A. Saunders, "International Portfolio Diversification and the Inter-Temporal Stability of International Stock Market Relationships, 1957–78," *Financial Management* (Autumn 1981), pp. 54–63.
19. D. B. Panton, V. P. Lessig, and O. M. Joy, "Comovement of International Equity Markets: A Taxonomic Approach," *Journal of Financial and Quantitative Analysis* (September 1976), pp. 415–432.
20. G. C. Philippatos and A. C. Christofi, "U.S. Portfolio Investment in the Industrialized World: 1959–1978," *Review of Business and Economic Research* (forthcoming).
21. D. M. Ripley, "Systematic Elements in the Linkage of National Stock Market Indices," *Review of Economics and Statistics* (August 1973), pp. 356–361.
22. R. L. Roenfeldt, G. L. Griepentrog, and C. C. Pflaum, "Further Evidence on the Stationarity of Beta Coefficients," *Journal of Financial and Quantitative Analysis* (March 1978), pp. 117–121.
23. W. F. Sharpe and G. M. Cooper, "Risk-Return Classes of New York Stock Exchange Common Stocks, 1931–1967," *Financial Analysts Journal* (March/April 1972), pp. 46–54 and 81.
24. O. A. Vasicek, "A Note Using Cross-Sectional Information in Bayesian Estimation of Security Beta," *Journal of Finance* (December 1973), pp. 1233–1239.
25. J. Watson, "A Study of Possible Gains from International Investment," *Journal of Business Finance and Accounting* (Summer 1978), pp. 195–205.
26. J. Watson, "The Stationarity of Inter-Country Correlation Coefficients: A Note," *Journal of Business Finance and Accounting* (Summer 1980), pp. 297–303.

The structure of international stock returns and the integration of capital markets

Steven L. Heston [a,*], K. Geert Rouwenhorst [b], Roberto E. Wessels [c]

[a] *John M. Olin School of Business, Washington University, Campus Box 1133, One Brookings Drive, St. Louis, MO 63130-4899, USA*
[b] *School of Management, Yale University, 135 Prospect Street, New Haven, CT 06511, USA*
[c] *ARCAS-Wessels Roll Ross, USA*

Received 1 November 1991; revised 1 January 1995

Abstract

This paper investigates the structure of international stock returns in Europe and the U.S., and examines whether international capital markets are integrated. Using data on 6000 firms in the U.S. and twelve European countries from 1978 to 1990, we find evidence that countries share multiple risk factors. We test whether capital markets are integrated by examining the pricing of country indices and comparing the prices of factor risk across countries. Our tests support the hypothesis that capital markets in our sample are internationally integrated in the sense that the rewards for risks are identical across countries. However, we find a widespread size effect that is uncorrelated across countries. This finding provides international evidence against the joint hypotheses of our pricing model and the hypothesis that capital markets for large firms are integrated with the markets for small firms.

JEL classification: G15; G12

Keywords: Capital market integration; International equity markets; Factor models

---

[*] Corresponding author

0927-5398/95/$09.50 © 1995 Elsevier Science B.V. All rights reserved
SSDI 0927-5398(95)00002-X

1. Introduction

This paper investigates the covariance structure of international stock returns in 12 European countries and the U.S., and examines whether their capital markets are integrated. The correlations among international stock returns are of particular interest to portfolio managers who use international diversification to reduce risk. While most previous research has examined the correlations among aggregate indices [1], this paper characterizes these correlations at a disaggregate level by studying the pervasive sources of variation of returns within and across national markets.

Two equity markets are said to be integrated if the reward for various investment risks is the same in each market. If these rewards were different, a portfolio manager could increase expected return without altering risk by shifting investment to those countries with the higher return. For a corporate financial manager capital market integration matters because it is central to the independence of investment and financing decisions. In particular, if capital markets are segmented, the cost of capital and corresponding value of an investment will generally depend on the market in which the project is financed.

In theory, it is possible to test for capital market integration by examining the returns on two perfectly correlated portfolios of securities from different countries. If financial capital is free to flow across national boundaries, arbitrage should equalize the prices of financial assets with identical payoffs. As a practical matter however, it is very difficult to construct highly correlated portfolios across countries, because of the presence of idiosyncratic and country specific sources of return variation. Consequently, all tests of capital market integration rely on a pricing model to indicate which portion of the variation in portfolio returns commands a risk premium.

Most international pricing models used in empirical studies explain the unconditional means of asset returns in terms of their sensitivities to systematic risk factors [exceptions include Bekaert and Hodrick (1992), Campbell and Hamao (1992), Ferson and Harvey (1993) and Harvey (1991), Harvey (1994) who in addition address the predictability of returns]. Early studies of international capital market integration use a single risk factor as a proxy for the market portfolio in the capital asset pricing model. Solnik (1974) does not reject the integration of 8 European countries with the U.S.A., and Stehle (1977) does not reject the proper pricing of the U.S. market based on a world market portfolio. In more recent work, Errunza and Losq (1985) find limited power when testing for integration of 9 less developed countries with this approach. However, Jorion and Schwartz (1985) reject the integration of U.S. and Canadian capital markets.

---

[1] Exceptions include Cho, Eun and Senbet (1986), Gultekin, Gultekin, and Penati (1989), and Korajczyk and Viallet (1989).

Other international asset pricing studies have used consumption as the sole risk factor. In contrast to the results of Hansen and Singleton (1982) with U.S. securities, Wheatley (1988) does not reject a consumption-based model with 17 country indices in addition the U.S. index. Obstfeld (1986) also fails to reject a consumption-based international asset pricing model. Braun et al. (1993) find that incorporating habit persistence and durability of consumption improves the fit of a consumption-based model with data from 6 countries.

Finally, some empirical studies use disaggregate stock returns to construct benchmark portfolio returns that capture multiple sources of systematic risk. In contrast to single factor studies, the studies of Cho et al. (1986), Gultekin et al. (1989), and Korajczyk and Viallet (1989) provide some evidence against integration of U.S. capital markets with those of Japan, France, and the United Kingdom. While it is possible that the use of multiple risk factors makes tests of integration more powerful by explaining more of the cross-sectional variation in stock returns, the evidence is mixed. Gultekin, Gultekin, and Penati (1989) and Korajczyk and Viallet (1989) interpret temporal patterns of rejections in earlier sample periods as evidence that markets have grown more integrated over time. Bansal et al. (1993) find that nonlinear factor pricing improves the fit of a (conditional) international pricing model to returns on four country indices.

The present study uses this disaggregate approach to examine the integration of capital markets in the U.S. and 12 European countries. Our sample consists of return data on over 4000 U.S. and 1800 European stocks over the comparatively recent period 1978–1990. In this respect, it is the first comprehensive study of a sample of stock returns from the U.S. and many European countries. In addition, this study covers a reasonably long modern period that is free of earlier restrictions on capital flows.

Our findings can be summarized as follows. We first show that international equity markets share multiple factors, which suggests the economic interdependence of Europe and the United States. This first finding is consistent with the prespecified factor results of Ferson and Harvey (1994). We find more common risk factors among securities within a country than across countries. This reflects in part the economic specialization of countries into certain industries, as emphasized by Roll (1992), as well as the existence of country specific factors related to political and institutional structure as emphasized by Heston and Rouwenhorst (1994).

Next, we study the question of capital market integration using three different unconditional tests. In our first test, we measure the performance of country indices relative to a set of benchmark portfolios estimated from the full sample of over 6000 securities from the United States and 12 European countries. We find that most equally-weighted country index returns are properly priced by a set of full-sample risk factors. This does not necessarily imply that capital markets are fully integrated in the sense that risks are priced equally across countries. It may be that in the construction of country portfolios overpricing of some risk factors cancels out underpricing of other risk factors. Therefore, in our second test, we examine whether the major individual sources of risk in each country are priced correctly by the European and the full-sample factors. These tests generally fail to reject that capital markets are integrated internationally. In our third test we compare the pricing of large firms versus small firms across countries. In nearly every country, larger firms appear to enjoy a lower cost of capital that is not explained by exposure to systematic risk. Because these 'size effects' are largely uncorrelated across countries, small stocks appear to offer a return that is not commensurate with their diversifiable risks. This provides international evidence against the joint hypotheses of our pricing model and the integration of capital markets for large and small firms.

The outline of the paper is as follows: section 2 describes our method of constructing benchmark portfolios, followed by a description of the data in section 3. Section 4 provides an empirical analysis of the structure of international stock returns and the results of our tests of capital market integration. The final section presents some concluding remarks.

2. Estimating pervasive factors with incomplete international data

Testing whether risk is priced uniformly across countries requires an international pricing model. In our empirical implementation we assume that excess returns measured in a common currency follow a k-factor structure. To estimate these factors, we begin with an $N \times T$ matrix R of excess returns on N assets over T time periods measured in U.S. dollars.[2] We follow common practice in the finance literature and calculate these excess returns by subtracting from the individual stock returns the return on a one month U.S. Treasury bill. These excess returns are costless payoffs which can be decomposed into k systematic influences that affect many firms, and unsystematic disturbances which only affect individual stocks:

$$R = BF' + \epsilon, \qquad (1)$$

where B is $N \times k$ matrix of factor sensitivities ('asset betas'), F is the $T \times k$ matrix $[f_1, f_2, ... f_k]$ of factor realizations plus risk premiums, and ϵ is a $N \times T$ matrix of disturbances. The excess return on asset i is the i-th row of R:

$$R_i = b_i F' + \epsilon_i. \qquad (2)$$

Conceptually, the factors, F, are returns on k unobserved, perfectly diversified

---

[2] In international applications there is the issue in which currency numeraire these excess returns are measured. Solnik (1983) showed that the choice of risk free rate and currency numeraire is irrelevant as long as forward currency contracts obey the same model as the excess returns.

portfolios. Note that Eq. (2) assumes an exact linear pricing relationship, which is equivalent to the statement that the k factor portfolios span the mean variance efficient frontier.[3] The observations on individual excess returns can be thought of as vectors of length T, drawn from a cross-sectional population of assets. We will consider sampling from an infinite pool of assets, and take expectations across assets (holding T fixed). We further assume that $E[b_i \epsilon'_i] = 0$ and that $E[\epsilon_i \epsilon'_i] = \sigma^2 I_T$ is diagonal and proportional to the identity matrix. The first assumption says that on any given day high beta stocks will not outperform low beta stocks *after* adjusting for market movements. It corresponds to the approximate factor structure of Chamberlain (1983), which allows asset disturbances to have (limited) cross-sectional correlation. The diagonality assumption states that on average (across firms) the disturbances are uncorrelated *over time*. This approach allows returns to be autocorrelated through factor risk premiums, but not through the idiosyncratic components. Under these assumptions, Connor and Korajczyk (1986) show that (up to rotational indeterminacy) a consistent estimate of the factors is given by the eigenvectors of a cross-product matrix $\hat{\Omega}$:

$$\hat{\Omega}\hat{F} = \hat{F}\hat{\Lambda}, \qquad (3)$$

where $\hat{\Lambda}$ is a diagonal matrix of eigenvalues and the cross-product matrix is given by:

$$\hat{\Omega} = R'R/N. \qquad (4)$$

In empirical implementations we do not always have a T-period return history for each security. We therefore employ the same estimator for the factors as in Eq. (3), but modify the definition of $\hat{\Omega}$ in Eq. (4) to accommodate missing data:

$$\hat{\Omega}(s,t) = \Sigma_{i=\text{available}} R_{is} R'_{it} / N(s,t), \qquad (5)$$

where $N(s,t)$ is the number of available returns on both dates s and t.[4] This method of factor extraction has two convenient properties. First, the factors are nested within models, so that the factors of a five factor model correspond to the first 5 factors of a 10 or 15 factor model. Second, as shown by Connor and Uhlaner (1989) and discussed in the appendix, the factor estimates have the interpretation of 'replicating' portfolios. This portfolio interpretation provides the basis for our tests of capital market integration. Since the factors are actually

---

[3] Shanken (1982), Shanken (1985) emphasizes the role of these assumptions in tests of asset pricing models. Exact linear pricing is a strong assumption in this context, but it can emerge from equilibrium models as in Connor (1984).

[4] Missing data must not be systematically correlated with the elements of B or ϵ. Otherwise, our censored sample may not conform to the factor model of the complete population. Given this assumption, consistent estimation of the factors requires only enough cross-sectional independence to guarantee that the sample moments in $\hat{\Omega}$ converge to their population values across assets.

portfolios, the unconditional risk premium associated with a factor can be measured by the mean excess return on a portfolio.

In tests of asset pricing models, it is common practice to use out-of-sample measurements to estimate portfolio means (e.g., Fama and MacBeth (1973), Roll and Ross (1980)). In particular, it is possible that estimation errors in individual security betas are correlated with their means. Since the factor estimates are beta-weighted portfolios, this biases the factor means.[5] Fama and MacBeth (1973) avoided this small sample bias by using separate subperiods to estimate betas and portfolio means. This procedure has the drawback that it reduces the number of time periods available for measurement, which is an important consideration when the number of time series observations is relatively small. The portfolio interpretation of the factor estimates however enables one to estimate factors using data from every other time period, and then reconstruct the factors over the whole period. First, we use odd periods to estimate the factors, and then reconstruct the factor mimicking portfolios over even periods. Next, we use the covariance information from even periods to construct factors over the odd periods.[6] The resulting factors have the advantage that the reconstructed factor portfolios in a particular period are not biased by the average returns of firms in that same period.

In our empirical work we will extract factors based on estimates of $\hat{\Omega}$ for individual countries, as well as for the world. An important issue is the appropriate number of factors to extract. Since our factor estimates are nested, this issue reduces to whether we have extracted 'enough' factors to span the mean variance efficient frontier. For the pricing relationship to have empirical content, we limit ourselves to 5, 10, and 15 factor specifications. The eigenvector decomposition chooses the factors to maximize the explained cross-sectional variation in excess returns. If one believes that the finite factor model is merely an approximation to an infinite set of factors, then we are at least choosing the 'largest' factors. Absent other important economic considerations, these ones are the most likely to be associated with risk premiums. Although there are formal tests for the number of factors based on testing the equality of eigenvalues, we avoid these for several reasons. Likelihood ratio tests have restrictive parametric assumptions and sometimes produce extreme rejections.[7] Instead, we use canonical correlations to heuristically assess the practical significance of various factors. This approach gauges the significance of factors by our ability to reproduce them in distinct

---

[5] Shanken (1992) showed that the means and betas will not be correlated in the standard linear regression framework. Our methodology departs from this framework because the factors are not exogenous variables, but are produced by a factor analysis procedure.

[6] The details of the procedure are in the appendix.

[7] For example, Trzcinka (1986) easily rejects 20 factors with U.S. stock data, and it is not clear whether such rejections are economically meaningful.

subsets of data. These estimates appear in section 4 after a brief description of the data in section 3.

3. Data description

The source of the European data is ARCAS-Wessels Roll Ross. The database contains information on monthly returns for 1863 firms from 12 European countries over the 13 year period from 1978 through 1990 (156 time series observations). The selection of the stocks is based on the firms included in the European country indices compiled by Morgan Stanley Capital International (MSCI) and Financial Times (FT)-Actuaries World Indices. All stocks in the indices are included in the database except those that have restrictions which prohibit ownership by international investors. However, if a stock was deleted from an index but continued to trade, it was kept in the database. For some of the MSCI stocks in the database, historical returns were collected for firms that were added to the indices after 1978. [8] In addition firms were selected to cover at least 70 per cent of the total capitalization of each national market. [9] Stocks listed on multiple international exchanges are included in the subsample of the country it is assigned to by MSCI and FT-Actuaries. If a company is listed on multiple national exchanges, the quotations are taken from the largest exchange. Foreign exchange rates were collected from the Financial Times. One month U.S. T-bill rates were obtained from Ibbotson Associates (1992).

We appended the European data to the monthly CRSP data on United States firms listed on the NYSE and AMEX. Table 1 presents the distribution of securities across countries. The United States dominates the sample contributing about 70 per cent of all securities. The predominance of U.S. firms in our sample makes it easier to replicate the risks of U.S. firms using factors from the whole sample, and correspondingly more difficult to replicate the risks of European firms. U.S. and European firms constitute about 70% of the MSCI world index market value. Our sample omits the remaining 30% of MSCI world index value (mostly Japanese firms) and omits emerging market firms which equal about 8% of MSCI world index value (Harvey (1994)). Therefore, the risk factors that we estimate do not encompass all risk factors in world equity markets. The analysis will be limited to the examination of financial integration of the risk factors that affect U.S. and European firms.

---

[8] Collecting a return history for securities after they are included in the MSCI country indices potentially introduces a selection bias in our sample. We compared the performance of our country indices against those of MSCI and found the differences to be extremely small.

[9] An exception is the UK for which we cover slightly less than 70 per cent of the total capitalization.

Table 1
Sample Description.
The first panel gives information about the number of securities in each of the countries that are in our sample. The next columns give the mean and the standard deviation of the continuously compounded monthly return in US dollars on the EW and VW market in each of the countries. The currency return is the average continuously compounded monthly rate of change of the dollar price of a unit of foreign currency. Returns are expressed as per cent per year, and reported monthly standard deviations are roughly annualized by dividing by the square root of 12. The second panel gives the correlation matrix of the dollar returns on the EW markets

Country	# of assets	EW return ($) mean	EW return ($) std	VW return ($) mean	VW return ($) std	Currency return ($/FX) mean	Currency return ($/FX) std
United States	4490	13.8	19.7	13.8	16.7		
Netherlands	160	17.7	19.8	16.6	18.1	2.3	12.4
France	332	20.0	24.5	17.0	25.6	−0.6	11.9
United Kingdom	461	21.2	21.4	17.5	21.3	0.1	11.9
Germany	210	14.7	18.9	12.4	21.5	2.6	12.4
Belgium	110	17.0	19.4	15.2	19.9	0.5	12.4
Italy	181	21.2	24.6	19.6	26.7	−2.0	10.5
Sweden	88	21.7	21.2	17.7	22.2	−1.4	9.8
Switzerland	121	11.3	20.1	10.5	19.9	3.5	13.9
Spain	71	21.0	26.7	16.4	23.8	−1.2	10.4
Denmark	46	17.8	20.4	16.3	18.9	0.0	11.6
Norway	44	25.6	37.1	16.3	27.2	−1.0	9.6
Austria	39	17.1	22.6	14.5	24.1	2.9	11.9
Europe	1863	20.0	17.0				
World	6353	16.6	16.7				

Correlation matrix of dollar returns on EW indices 1978–1990

	Neth	Fr	UK	Ger	Be	It	Swe	Swi	Sp	Den	Nor	Aus	Eur	World	
United States	0.39	0.37	0.51	0.25	0.32	0.29	0.37	0.44	0.28	0.19	0.20	0.13	0.49	0.95	US
Netherlands		0.56	0.51	0.72	0.64	0.47	0.47	0.74	0.47	0.54	0.23	0.45	0.77	0.58	Neth
France			0.48	0.64	0.67	0.47	0.38	0.60	0.43	0.41	0.19	0.46	0.80	0.57	Fr
United Kingdom				0.53	0.54	0.44	0.48	0.63	0.49	0.42	0.38	0.32	0.83	0.69	UK
Germany					0.72	0.49	0.42	0.80	0.44	0.55	0.23	0.63	0.82	0.50	Ger
Belgium						0.42	0.40	0.69	0.47	0.47	0.18	0.47	0.78	0.53	Be
Italy							0.40	0.49	0.35	0.35	0.20	0.30	0.65	0.46	It
Sweden								0.52	0.37	0.28	0.27	0.31	0.58	0.50	Swe
Switzerland									0.46	0.55	0.28	0.51	0.84	0.65	Swi
Spain										0.32	0.17	0.29	0.60	0.44	Sp
Denmark											0.21	0.34	0.58	0.36	Den
Norway												0.19	0.37	0.28	Nor
Austria													0.55	0.31	Aus
Europe														0.75	Eur

Source: European data ARCAS –Wessels Roll Ross.; US data CRSP; currencies Financial Times.

During the period 1978-1990, European markets (in dollars) on average outperformed the U.S. market, with the exception of Switzerland and Germany, even though the dollar return in both markets was 'helped' by a strong appreciation of their respective currencies against the dollar. One of the questions we will address is whether Germany and Switzerland simply experienced a bad decade, or whether there are risk based explanations for this seemingly poor performance. The second panel of Table 1 presents a correlation matrix of the dollar returns on the national equally-weighted indices constructed from the securities in our sample. Most correlations are well below unity, which illustrates the potential benefits of international diversification.

4. Empirical results

4.1. Individual country factor analysis and common factors

Our first task is to characterize the covariance structure of international stock returns by examining the relative importance of the local factors in each country. The next step will be to examine the extent to which these factors are shared by countries so that we can test whether capital markets are integrated. For each country, we computed the eigenvalues of the cross $T \times T$ product matrix of excess returns in measured in dollars in excess of the U.S. T-Bill rate. These eigenvalues measure the contributions of the corresponding local factors to explaining the cross-sectional variation of returns on firms in that country. We also extracted factors for the combined subsample of European and U.S. firms, which we will refer to as the 'world'. Because the size of the eigenvalues indicates their contribution to explaining the variation in excess returns, we sorted the eigenvalues from largest to smallest. For each country, the ratio of the largest and the second largest eigenvalues, l_2 / l_1, is given in Table 2. For most countries the first eigenvalue strongly dominates the second. The next columns show that the factor corresponding to the largest eigenvalue is highly correlated with the equally-weighted market in every country. In the cases of Norway and Europe, the second largest factor is also correlated with the equally-weighted index. In all cases, the equally-weighted index is almost perfectly correlated with a linear combination of the first two factors. [10]

---

[10] Since the factors are constructed to be orthogonal over the sample period, they are approximately uncorrelated. Hence the correlations in Table 2 have the approximate interpretation of partial correlations. The multiple correlation of the excess return on the Norwegian equally-weighted market index with the first two Norwegian factors is approximately equal to $(0.899^2 + 0.424^2)^{1/2} = 0.994$, and the multiple correlation of the excess return on the European equally-weighted market index with the first two European factors is approximately equal to $(0.658^2 + 0.735^2)^{1/2} = 0.987$.

Table 2
Summary statistics for dominant factors.
Relative size of the largest two eigenvalues, l_2/l_1, and the correlations of the corresponding two factors with the excess return on the equally weighted market in each country. The individual country factors are expressed in U.S. dollars in excess of the U.S. T-Bill rate

Country	l_2/l_1	$\rho(f_j, R_{ew})$	
		$j=1$	$j=2$
United States	0.140	0.998	0.003
Netherlands	0.366	0.995	0.067
France	0.073	0.998	0.002
United Kingdom	0.060	0.999	0.007
Germany	0.094	0.999	0.029
Belgium	0.667	0.986	0.168
Italy	0.126	0.998	0.024
Sweden	0.209	0.996	0.055
Switzerland	0.249	0.998	0.038
Spain	0.120	0.995	0.052
Denmark	0.165	0.995	0.011
Norway	0.022	0.899	0.424
Austria	0.142	0.996	0.022
Europe	0.794	0.658	0.735
World	0.395	0.995	0.012

l_2/l_1: ratio of second largest and largest eigenvalues.
$\rho(f_j, R_{ew})$: correlation between the jth factor and the excess return on the EW market.

Table 3 reports the homoskedastic t-statistics for the factor means of the first 15 U.S., European, and world factors. Because the factors can be interpreted as (beta-weighted) excess portfolio returns, the question of whether a factor is priced therefore reduces to a test of the unconditional mean excess return on a factor portfolio. The pricing of these risks across countries is the central issue in capital market integration. For Europe, only the first factor has a significant t-statistic, and for the U.S. and the World, only factors corresponding to some of the smaller eigenvalues are significant. [11] In general, there is not strong evidence that the individual factor means are nonzero. This illustrates that pervasive sources of variation do not necessarily command a nonzero unconditional risk premium. [12]

---

[11] Because the factors are asymptotically orthogonal, the t-statistics are independent under the null hypothesis that the means are zero. The factors are not exactly orthogonal because of the final realignment in the Fama MacBeth procedure described in the appendix. However, the correlations among them are small.

[12] It is still quite possible that the risk factors command a nonzero conditional risk premium; see Ferson and Harvey (1991). A significant factor mean indicates that the unconditional mean-variance efficient frontier is not spanned by other factors alone. This might pose a complication in a sequential test procedure for the number of significant factors by simply inspecting the factor means.

Table 3
Testing the significance of factor risk premia.
The first 15 rows show (absolute values of) t-statistics which test whether factor means (extracted from returns in dollars over the US risk free rate) are zero. We do not present percentage returns because the factors are costless portfolios. Since the factors are chosen to be asymptotically orthogonal, the t-statistics are independent under the null hypothesis that the means are zero. The subsequent rows show χ^2 statistics that jointly test whether the means of the first, second, or third group of 5 factors are zero

Factor	U.S.	Europe	World
1	1.29	2.60 **	1.89
2	1.75	1.60	0.86
3	0.77	0.26	1.97
4	0.70	0.08	1.18
5	3.70 **	1.35	0.24
6	0.67	0.35	0.41
7	0.11	0.48	3.44 **
8	0.81	0.43	2.12 **
9	0.37	1.69	0.53
10	2.12 **	1.03	1.94
11	0.84	0.78	0.57
12	0.26	1.46	0.36
13	1.44	0.16	0.25
14	0.26	0.05	0.81
15	0.97	0.15	1.40
1–5	19.2	10.3	9.1
(p-value)	(0.002)	(0.068)	(0.103)
6–10	24.7	5.2	21.4
(p-value)	(0.0002)	(0.396)	(0.0007)
11–15	3.9	2.7	3.4
(p-value)	(0.557)	(0.746)	(0.639)

** significant at 5 per cent level.

On the other hand, the joint test strongly rejects the hypotheses that the means are zero on factors 1–5 and factors 6–10 in the U.S., and on factors 6–10 in the World. Our later tests examine the *equality* of these risk premiums across countries. These tests may have more power, because differences in means of correlated portfolios are often easier to estimate than the individual means.

Having estimated the local factors for the individual countries, we can ask whether countries share factors, or whether these pervasive sources of variation are unique to that country. If countries share many industries and are subject to the same economic risks, they should have many factors in common. But if countries specialize in certain industries, or implement economic policies which insulate these sectors from global economic forces, there would be more factors within individual countries than common factors among them. Although one could directly examine the industrial composition of countries (Roll (1992), Heston and

Rouwenhorst (1994)), industry classifications are sometimes coarse and difficult to measure. The advantage of the factor approach is that it has the flexibility to capture broader economic comovements that transcend industrial classifications. The existence of common factors does not address to the question of whether markets are integrated or not. It is only a heuristic method for examining economic interdependence. This is important for subsequent analysis of capital market integration, because it is not meaningful to test whether risks are priced equally in two countries unless they share common sources of risk.

Because we may have obtained a different rotation of the factors in each of the countries, we estimated the canonical correlations between sets of individual country factors. The first canonical correlation between two sets of factors is the maximum correlation between linear combinations of the two sets (See Theil (1971) for a discussion). Subsequent canonical correlations maximize the correlation subject to using linear combinations which are uncorrelated with the previously chosen ones. Given two groups of k factors, we test the significance of the $(k-d)$ smallest canonical correlations between them using a likelihood ratio statistic:

$$-2N\log(L) = -N\sum_{j=d+1}^{k}\log(1-r_j^2), \qquad (6)$$

where r_j is the j-th canonical correlation. Under the assumption of conditional homoskedasticity, this statistic has an asymptotic χ^2 distribution with $(k-d)^2$ degrees of freedom (see Seber (1984), page 266).

We also compare factors extracted from different securities in the *same* country. This provides a benchmark for comparing the number of factors across countries. In addition, it gives an idea of the robustness of the factor estimation procedure.[13] For this purpose we split the firms in each country into two subsamples ('odd' and 'even'), extracted the factors from both subsamples, and compute the canonical correlations between the two sets of factors. The diagonal elements in Table 4 report the number of nonzero canonical correlations between the odd and even subsamples for each of the countries. The first diagonal element indicates that for the U.S. it was possible to replicate twelve factors assuming a fifteen factor model. In other words, it is possible to find twelve orthogonal portfolios of U.S. stocks that have nonzero correlations with twelve disjoint portfolios. Because of the limited amount of data, it is sometimes more difficult to replicate the factors for the smaller countries.

The off-diagonal elements present the number of nonzero canonical correlations between the local country factors. The off-diagonal elements are generally larger than unity and seldom equal to zero. The U.S. has six factors in common with the

---

[13] Elton and Gruber (1988) follow a similar strategy.

Table 4
International common factors.
Number of significant canonical correlations (p-value < 0.05) calculated from the first 15 factors estimated for each individual country. The factors are extracted from dollar returns in excess of U.S. T-Bill rate

	US	Neth	Fr	UK	Ger	Be	It	Swe	Swi	Sp	Den	Nor	Aus	Eur	W	
United States	12	3	4	6	4	1	1	5	5	4	1	2	2	3	12	US
Netherlands		4	2	3	3	2	2	1	3	1	5	2	1	8	5	Neth
France			7	3	5	2	2	2	4	4	1	1	3	8	7	Fr
United Kingdom				8	2	2	1	3	4	2	4	3	1	7	7	UK
Germany					7	3	1	3	5	3	2	2	4	6	5	Ger
Belgium						4	2	1	4	2	1	2	1	6	2	Be
Italy							7	2	1	1	2	1	0	5	2	It
Sweden								7	1	1	1	2	0	3	4	Swe
Switzerland									11	2	2	3	3	7	6	Swi
Spain										6	1	1	1	6	5	Sp
Denmark											7	1	1	5	1	Den
Norway												9	1	5	4	Nor
Austria													9	4	3	Aus
Europe														13	10	Eur
World															11	W

UK, five with Switzerland, and four with France, Germany, Spain, and Sweden.[14] The important conclusion from Table 4 is that countries do indeed share multiple factors.

We view the canonical correlation test as a compelling heuristic illustration that countries share multiple factors, but caution against overinterpreting the entries in Table 4 for several reasons. As pointed out before, it does not provide evidence about the economic significance of these factors. In particular, a significant canonical correlation between two sets of factors does not imply that these factors command a risk premium, or that these risk premiums are equal across countries. We will turn to this question in our discussion of capital market integration. In addition, it is difficult to attach a precise interpretation to the actual number of significant canonical correlations. For example, is the number of 3 significant canonical correlations between the U.K. and the Netherlands to be considered large or small? The answer is not obvious, because our power to discover factors depends on the number of securities and distribution of factors within a country. To answer this question we bootstrapped the numbers in Table 4 for the European countries by randomly allocating securities to artificial 'country portfolios', and computed the number of significant canonical correlations between the factors estimated from these randomly constructed country portfolios. We repeated this exercise 100 times and compared the actual number of significant canonical correlations in Table 4 against the bootstrapped distribution. With the exception of the 5 canonical correlations between the Netherlands and Denmark, the actual number of significant correlations between all European countries lies in the left hand 5 percent tail of the bootstrapped distribution. This can be interpreted as a rejection of the hypothesis that the factor loadings are identically distributed across countries. Thus, while Table 4 suggests that countries share multiple factors, they share fewer factors than can be expected based on a random allocation of securities into portfolios.

Finally, Table 4 does not report the absolute size of the (significant) canonical correlations. The size of the canonical correlation indicates how well it is possible to replicate the factors of country i using securities (factors) of country j. Whereas the first canonical correlation between the factors of a country with itself is often (very close to) unity, the first canonical correlation across countries is often no

---

[14] These results were not qualitatively different if we measured the returns in local currency in excess of the local risk free rate. These excess returns differ approximately from excess returns in dollars by the return on a forward contract, which is the same for all securities of that country. Currency conversion will introduce at most one extra factor per country relative to our previous analysis of hedged returns, depending on the extent to which currency risks are spanned by the factors extracted from stock returns. Unreported findings suggest that exchange rate risk, the difference between hedged and unhedged returns, does not usually introduce an extra factor. This explains why the results of Korajczyk and Viallet (1989) and Cho, Eun, and Senbet (1986) were insensitive to the choice of numeraire.

larger than 0.60. This means that it is easy to replicate the German factor portfolios from disjoint subsamples of German securities, but very difficult to use German or U.S. stocks to replicate the Swiss factor portfolios, which indicates the presence of large country specific components of return variation. [15]

4.2. Capital market integration

Having demonstrated that countries share multiple factors, we turn to the question of capital market integration and the pricing of factor risks across countries. As discussed earlier, we can only test capital market integration under the joint hypothesis of an international asset pricing model. Our empirical pricing model uses the benchmark portfolios as exact proxies for underlying factors which span the mean-variance efficient frontier. [16] If world factors span the mean-variance efficient frontier, then they must correctly price all assets. Our first test of capital market integration examines whether or not country index returns are priced correctly by world factors.

The pricing model (1) implies that expected excess returns obey a linear pricing relationship with respect to k factors, i.e. that the mean-variance efficient frontier is spanned by the first k factors. In other words, expected excess returns should be zero after adjusting for k-factor risk. This can be tested with a t-test against zero of the intercept in a time series regression of excess returns on a portfolio of country i on the world factors:

$$R_{i,t} - r_{f,t} = a_i + b_{1i}f_{1,t} + b_{2i}f_{2,t} + \ldots + b_{ki}f_{k,t} + e_{i,t}, \qquad (7)$$

where $f_{i,t}$ is the realization of the i-th factor in period t.

Table 5 presents the intercepts for the excess return on the equally-weighted (EW) market (left panel) and the value-weighted (VW) market (right panel). For the equally-weighted markets of Germany and Switzerland, the two markets that performed poorest over the sample period, we reject that the intercept is zero at the 5% level. The exact F-test of Gibbons et al. (1989), however, does not reject the joint hypothesis that the intercepts of all countries are zero. [17] The individual country rejections are the same for the value-weighted markets, but we additionally reject the joint hypothesis that all intercepts are zero for the 10 and 15 factor

---

[15] Heston and Rouwenhorst (1994) present evidence of large country effects after correcting country index returns for their industry composition. Our factor analytic approach is more flexible and can potentially capture sources of return variation other than industry composition, such as size, dividend yield, and coordination of macroeconomic policies. Nevertheless we find that the first canonical correlation between sets of factors extracted from different countries is well below unity.

[16] Alternatively, Shanken (1987) shows how to test explicit bounds on the correlation between our benchmark portfolios and some portfolio on the mean-variance efficient frontier.

[17] The homoskedastic and asymptotic heteroskedasticity consistent χ^2 tests of White (1980) produce qualitatively similar results.

Table 5
World capital market integration.
This table shows the intercept and R^2 from a regression of the dollar excess return on the EW market (left panel) and VW market (right panel) in excess of the US risk free rate in country i on the first k world factors. The constant term has been approximately converted to percent per year. Standard errors are in parentheses. The F-statistic at the bottom of each column tests the joint restriction that all intercepts in that column are zero

	$k=5$		$k=10$		$k=15$		$k=5$		$k=10$		$k=15$	
	$a_i \times 1200$	R^2	$a_i \times 1200$	R^2	$a_i \times 1200$	R^2	$a_i \times 1200$	R^2	$a_i \times 1200$	R^2	$a_i \times 1200$	R^2
United States	−0.26 (0.42)	0.994	0.67 (0.39)	0.996	0.65 (0.39)	0.996	−0.71 (1.49)	0.904	−1.45 (1.43)	0.926	−2.10 (1.44)	0.931
Netherlands	−1.37 (3.59)	0.623	−0.76 (3.28)	0.736	−1.19 (3.37)	0.747	−0.23 (3.15)	0.647	−0.59 (2.85)	0.758	−1.56 (2.93)	0.767
France	−1.50 (3.87)	0.713	1.83 (2.45)	0.904	1.50 (2.45)	0.912	−4.57 (4.12)	0.696	−2.42 (2.81)	0.882	−2.76 (2.85)	0.889
United Kingdom	4.26 (2.91)	0.788	1.72 (1.91)	0.924	1.38 (1.99)	0.924	0.80 (2.90)	0.787	−1.45 (2.30)	0.888	−2.25 (2.36)	0.892
Germany	−4.10 (2.96)	0.714	−5.28** (2.66)	0.807	−5.61** (2.73)	0.814	−7.42** (3.61)	0.670	−9.39** (3.26)	0.774	−10.07** (3.32)	0.786
Belgium	−1.91 (3.45)	0.642	−0.26 (3.65)	0.665	−0.74 (3.71)	0.685	−3.59 (3.70)	0.608	−2.64 (3.93)	0.630	−3.15 (4.01)	0.650
Italy	4.18 (5.39)	0.449	−1.57 (4.66)	0.656	−1.23 (4.07)	0.761	2.48 (6.14)	0.407	−3.87 (5.43)	0.611	−3.35 (4.97)	0.703
Sweden	6.49 (5.05)	0.345	5.97 (5.34)	0.387	5.32 (5.47)	0.414	1.75 (5.16)	0.364	1.58 (5.41)	0.415	0.85 (5.53)	0.441
Switzerland	−7.59** (3.32)	0.676	−7.64** (3.32)	0.729	−6.87** (3.43)	0.735	−8.03** (3.55)	0.627	−9.62** (3.53)	0.692	−8.98** (3.66)	0.698
Spain	2.85 (6.21)	0.396	9.12 (5.80)	0.559	13.05** (5.11)	0.687	−0.53 (5.63)	0.366	4.80 (5.49)	0.496	7.56 (5.20)	0.588
Denmark	2.76 (4.94)	0.354	1.55 (5.08)	0.428	−0.28 (5.23)	0.445	1.92 (4.67)	0.318	0.66 (4.83)	0.390	−1.36 (4.97)	0.411
Norway	14.46 (12.83)	0.333	24.12 (13.77)	0.357	24.87 (14.35)	0.362	1.54 (5.86)	0.448	8.50 (5.94)	0.526	7.97 (6.07)	0.548
Austria	1.72 (5.54)	0.328	3.23 (5.78)	0.388	3.61 (5.99)	0.399	−0.85 (5.92)	0.336	−0.63 (6.28)	0.374	0.58 (6.52)	0.383
F-statistic	0.97		1.46		1.52		0.94		1.79		2.23	
(p-value)	(0.487)		(0.141)		(0.118)		(0.510)		(0.050)		(0.011)	

models. The R^2's show the extent to which one can replicate the risks of one country with securities from the others. The model has a good deal of explanatory power for the larger countries; the 15-factor R^2 is over 90% for the U.S., France, and United Kingdom regressions. The R^2's from the 5-factor value-weighted regressions are higher than the corresponding R^2's of Ferson and Harvey (1994) using 8 predetermined factors. This is not surprising, since the factor estimation maximizes the explained cross-sectional variation in individual security returns. The R^2 is somewhat lower for some of the smaller countries. In the case of Spain, for example, the 15 world factors explain respectively 69 and 59 percent of the variance of the equally-and value-weighted country indices. This is not caused by *firm* specific idiosyncratic risk, because the Spanish index consists of 71 securities with firms in each of the 7 major industry categories as defined by the FT-Actuaries. Our 15 factor 'world' model has enough flexibility to capture this many industry influences. The relatively low R^2 indicates a large component of return variation in Spain that is not captured by the world factors. This might occur because Spain contributes only slightly more than one per cent of the 6353 securities in the full sample, whereas the U.S., for example, contributes roughly two thirds of the total number of securities in the sample. Eliminating the U.S. securities from the data sample increased our ability to uncover factors that are important for some of the smaller European countries. [18]

At this point, the tests of capital market integration in Table 5 allow different economic interpretations. Out of 13 countries, only Germany and Switzerland had rejections both equally-weighted and value-weighted indices. Yet the overall F-statistic for all countries rejects the joint hypotheses of capital market integration and a 10-factor or 15-factor asset pricing model. One might be able to improve the fit of the regressions for the individual countries, and enhance power by increasing the dimension of the factor model. But an overly large factor model might essentially use additional factors as dummy variable proxies for individual country mispricing. Thus, an overly large factor model would not be relevant to capital market integration, because it would not focus on risk premia for factors that countries *share*. Instead, Stulz (1981) emphasizes the importance of testing asset pricing models against relevant alternatives. Wheatley (1988) expresses a similar conclusion after failing to reject a consumption-based model with data on 17 international stock market indices –'one significant way to raise the power of

---

[18] We also performed tests of integration of European capital markets, by regressing the excess country returns on the European factors. The resulting R^2's are higher than the corresponding R^2's in Table 5. Apparently, it is somewhat easier to replicate European country indices with European factors than with world factors. In the European factor tests, the only individual country rejections we found are for the equally-weighted and value-weighted indices of Switzerland (for $k = 5$, 10 and 15 as in Table 5) and for the equally-weighted market of the Netherlands (for $k = 10$ and 15). For $k = 10$ and 15, however, the joint test of capital market integration of European markets rejects at the 5% level for both equally-weighted and value-weighted indices.

Table 6
Factor test of capital market integration.
This table lists the F-statistic and associated p-values of the joint restriction that the intercepts of regressing the first 5 domestic factors of each country on the first k ($k = 5,10,15$) world factors are zero. The combined F-statistic test the joint restriction that all of the intercepts from regressing the first 5 domestic factors on world factors are zero.

	$k = 5$		$k = 10$		$k = 15$	
	F-stat	p-val	F-stat	p-val	F-stat	p-val
United States	3.14	0.010	0.63	0.679	1.01	0.415
Netherlands	0.18	0.970	0.48	0.790	0.73	0.603
France	1.21	0.305	0.88	0.498	1.07	0.379
United Kingdom	2.02	0.079	2.15	0.063	2.16	0.062
Germany	1.59	0.167	2.07	0.073	2.30	0.048
Belgium	1.00	0.422	0.80	0.548	0.92	0.471
Italy	0.97	0.440	1.12	0.352	1.23	0.297
Sweden	1.83	0.110	1.43	0.217	1.84	0.110
Switzerland	1.78	0.120	1.30	0.269	1.28	0.274
Spain	1.05	0.393	1.20	0.311	2.52	0.032
Denmark	1.01	0.415	0.96	0.445	0.97	0.438
Norway	0.77	0.569	1.56	0.177	1.86	0.105
Austria	2.31	0.047	2.90	0.016	2.00	0.082
Combined	1.18	0.230	1.04	0.434	1.10	0.343

these tests would be to include in them only foreign equities for which there are a priori grounds to believe that effective [capital] barriers... exist.' In particular, it is conceivable that capital market barriers exist, but do not systematically increase or decrease the returns on all firms in any given country. In this case, tests with market indices will have little or no power in identifying capital market segmentation. Therefore, we shall examine two alternative hypotheses to diagnose the form of market segmentation.

Our first alternative hypothesis is that some types of systematic risks are priced differently in different countries. Due to simultaneous overpricing and underpricing of risks within a country however, a market index may appear to be correctly priced even though individual risks in that country are misprised relative to other countries. Hence, the next test of capital market integration focuses directly on the question of whether risks are priced equally across markets. Theoretically, this question is not dependent on a particular pricing model but is a statement of the Law of One Price: identical investments must have the same price in different countries. As mentioned in our discussion of the canonical correlation, we can in practice never perfectly reconstruct a factor from one country with securities from other countries. Therefore, we must rely on a pricing model to ensure that differences in reconstructed factors are diversifiable and hence unpriced. We can test for the equality of risk premiums by estimating the factor portfolios for each individual country, and regressing the excess returns of these factor portfolios on the world factors. The regression finds the portfolio of world factors that is the closest substitute for the local factor portfolio by maximizing the correlation between them. The intercept measures the difference in mean return of these two substitutes; the intercepts of these regressions will be zero if the prices of risk are equal across countries. Because it might be difficult to obtain a good estimate of large factor models for the smaller countries, we regressed only the first five factor portfolios from each country on the first k world factors ($k = 5,10,15$). Table 6 gives the F-statistics and the associated p-values for a joint test of the 5 restrictions that these five local factor portfolios are priced correctly by the first k world factors. For the U.S., we reject the hypothesis that the first 5 U.S. factors are correctly priced by the first 5 world factors, but do not reject this hypothesis for 10 or 15 world factors. We also find rejections in Austria for the 5 and 10 factor models, and in Spain for the 15 factor model. [19] Given the large number of tests in this table, it is almost inevitable that we find some rejections purely by chance. The joint test of correct pricing of the first five local factors in all countries does not reject. Recall from Table 5 that a few countries, such as Germany and Switzerland, had abnormally low returns when measured against an international pricing model. But there is little evidence in Table 6 that the major German and Swiss *factors* were misprised the by world factors. Overall, the rejections of equality of risk premia do not correspond to the pattern of misprising of individual countries.

Our second alternative hypothesis to capital market integration concerns the role of firm size in surmounting capital market barriers. If informational or institutional barriers to international capital have a fixed component, then large firms can obtain a lower cost of capital than small firms. While financial theory does not yet explain the nature of these barriers, this capital market segmentation hypothesis is consistent with the size effect found in the United States by Banz (1981) and in Japan by Kato and Shallheim (1985). It is also consistent with results of Korajczyk and Viallet (1989) for France and the United Kingdom. It is not known whether this anomaly is compensation for systematic risk found in a few countries, or whether it is an inefficiency found in many stock markets. But we note the striking pattern in Table 5 that the 15-factor risk-adjusted returns (the intercepts a_i) of the equally-weighted country indices are uniformly higher than the corresponding value-weighted returns.

Given the large number of countries under consideration, we formed one size-based zero investment portfolio for each country by subtracting its value-weighted return from its equally-weighted index return. Table 7 presents joint tests of our pricing model and world capital market integration based on these size portfolios. Using a 15-factor model, the size effect is positive in every country,

---

[19] We repeated this experiment for pricing relative to European factors, and found rejections only for Austria.

Table 7
Size-based test of capital market integration.
This table shows the results of regressing the difference between the equally-weighted and value-weighted country index returns, measured in U.S. dollars, on 15 factors estimated from the full sample of firms (world factors). The first two columns give the intercept multiplied by 1200, and the standard error of the intercept. ** indicates coefficient significant at 5 per cent level. The next columns give the correlations between the residuals of the individual country regressions

	$a_i \times 1200$	std error	Size effect correlation											
			US	Neth	Fr	UK	Ger	Be	It	Swe	Swi	Sp	Den	Nor
United States	2.76	1.38 **												
Netherlands	0.36	3.06	0.23											
France	4.27	1.48 **	0.16	0.22										
United Kingdom	3.63	1.37 **	0.11	0.33	0.24									
Germany	4.46	1.68 **	0.09	0.21	0.15	0.01								
Belgium	2.41	1.44	−0.15	0.13	0.10	0.06	0.01							
Italy	2.12	2.23	−0.02	0.13	0.12	0.17	−0.01	0.09						
Sweden	4.46	1.65 **	0.09	0.11	0.02	0.17	0.00	0.03	0.01					
Switzerland	2.11	1.44	0.21	0.08	0.24	0.18	0.24	−0.02	0.13	0.12				
Spain	5.49	2.44 **	−0.05	0.07	−0.03	−0.08	0.05	−0.11	0.07	0.21	0.14			
Denmark	1.08	1.87	−0.06	0.00	0.00	0.04	0.06	0.03	0.03	0.01	0.09	−0.01		
Norway	16.90	12.57	0.14	−0.03	−0.03	0.03	0.04	0.03	−0.10	0.01	−0.07	0.07	0.01	
Austria	3.03	2.00	−0.05	0.00	−0.07	0.00	0.18	−0.01	0.03	0.00	0.04	0.08	0.06	0.06

F-statistic = 3.12.
p-value < 0.001.

and is significant at the 5% level in 6 of the 13 countries. These include the largest countries, the U.S., France, the United Kingdom, and Germany, in addition to Sweden and Spain. [20] Of these countries, only the German indices and the Spanish equally-weighted index were associated with statistically significant misprising according to the world 15-factor model. These size-based tests achieve higher power by differencing out the country specific effects which dominate the equity indices. Note that there is not a significant size effect for Switzerland, which appeared to be misprised by the world factor model. Thus, the size effect does not correspond to misprising of securities in all individual countries. An F-test of the joint significance of the size effects across countries provides evidence against the null hypothesis. Similar rejections were found for this joint hypothesis in case of the 5-and 10-world factor models ($F = 2.57$ and 2.85 respectively). The power increase is particularly notable since the 5-factor model did not reject the joint hypothesis of integration of value-weighted or equally-weighted market indices in Table 5.

Since these size-based tests of capital market integration require the joint hypothesis of our pricing model, it is possible that size is a proxy for some omitted risk factor. If this explanation is correct, then we would expect these risks to be correlated across countries in an integrated world capital market. Otherwise, investors can be compensated for risks that do not seem to have a systematic covariance with world capital markets. To diagnose this possibility, Table 7 displays the correlations among the residuals of the regressions of the size based portfolios on the 15 world factors. These correlations are generally quite small, and many are actually negative. Thus, they would add little risk to the portfolio of a geographically diversified investor. Therefore, these size effects provide widespread international evidence of pricing segmentation in capital markets for small and large firms or the existence of country specific premiums for size risks that are uncorrelated across countries.

5. Conclusions

This paper characterizes the covariance structure of U.S. and 12 European stock markets and examines whether capital markets are integrated. Canonical correlation analysis shows that international equity markets share multiple common factors. These risk factors are not identically distributed across countries, and there are large country specific sources of return variation.

Our tests of capital market integration examine the pricing of equity indices by world risk factors, and the equality of unconditional risk premiums across countries. Our results support both the hypothesis that most equally-weighted market

---

[20] The five and ten factor models gave similar results, but did not reject in the cases of the U.S. or Spain; the ten factor model also rejected for Austria.

indices are correctly priced by factors estimated from the full sample of firms, and the hypothesis that rewards for various factor risks are identical across countries. Although a few countries, such as Germany and Switzerland, had abnormally low returns when measured against an international pricing model, we found that the rewards for factor risk in these countries matched those in the rest of the world. Overall, the rejections of capital market integration do not indicate any systematic pattern of misprising of individual countries, and in this sense markets appear integrated. However, both the European and full sample factor models are affected by a size anomaly whereby value-weighted market indices appear overpriced relative to equally-weighted indices. Since these size effects are largely uncorrelated across countries, they are difficult to explain with covariance-based international asset pricing models.

Acknowledgements

We acknowledge comments by the referee and by Jon Ingersoll, John Long, Jay Shanken, the participants in the 1991 F.C.L.S. session at the National Bureau of Economic Research, the European Finance Association, and seminar participants at the Erasmus University Rotterdam, MIT, Northwestern University, the University of Rochester, and Yale University. The authors are responsible for any errors or omissions.

Appendix A

Modified Fama-MacBeth procedure

In accordance with the procedures of Fama and MacBeth (1973) and Roll and Ross (1980), this section shows how to estimate the factor risk premiums 'out-of-sample'. Unlike the previous techniques, this methodology avoids throwing away any of the time series data. With complete data, the factor estimates in Eq. (3) are 'beta-weighted' portfolios

$$\hat{F}' = \hat{\Lambda}^{-1}\hat{B}'R/N, \tag{A1}$$

where the betas are given by ordinary least squares regression:

$$\hat{B}' = (\hat{F}'\hat{F})^{-1}\hat{F}'R'. \tag{A2}$$

We use this relationship to first estimate the factors with data from even periods, and beta estimated for the even periods using (A2). These beta estimates can be used to construct factors over odd periods, using (A1). Next, we can estimate the factors and betas using odd period information, and construct factor estimates for the even periods. After doing this, we can 'zipper' the factors together to obtain estimates which are not affected by any in-sample biases in means.

The only complication in this procedure involves potentially different rotations of the factor estimates in the odd and the even periods. In particular, the factor estimates in Eq. (3) sequentially maximize the explained cross-sectional variance. In samples which include October 1987, the first factor tends to be an equally-weighted portfolio. But in other samples, it may contain size-based firms or other systematic risks. In order to 'zipper' the even and odd factor estimates together, we must first put them in the same 'order'. This order is completely arbitrary, so we rotate the odd and even factor estimates into the same alignment by projecting them onto the full sample factor estimates with an OLS regression. This does not change the span of the factors, it merely assures that the first factor estimates over even periods corresponds to the first factor estimated over odd periods. The reconstructed 'zippered' factors are highly correlated with the full sample factor estimates; they have the interpretation in Eq. (A1) of beta-weighted portfolios where the betas are slightly different in even and odd periods.

References

Bansal, Ravi, David A. Hsieh, and S. Viswanathan, 1993, A New Approach to International Asset Pricing, Journal of Finance, 48, 1719–1747.

Bekaert, Geert and Robert J. Hodrick, 1992, Characterizing Predictable Components in Excess Returns on Equity and Foreign Exchange Markets, Journal of Finance, 47, 467–509.

Braun, Phillip A., George M. Constantinides, and Wayne E. Ferson, 1993, Time Nonseparability in Aggregate Consumption: International Evidence, European Economic Review, 37, 897–920.

Campbell, John Y., and Yasushi Hamao, 1992, Predictable stock returns in the United States and Japan: A study of long-term capital market integration, Journal of Finance, 47, 43–70.

Cho, D.C., C.S. Eun, and L.W. Senbet, 1986, International Arbitrage Pricing Theory: An Empirical Investigation, Journal of Finance, 41, 313–329.

Connor, Gregory, 1984, A Unified Beta Pricing Theory, Journal of Economic Theory, 34, 13–31.

Connor, Gregory and Robert A. Korajczyk, 1986, Performance Measurement With the Arbitrage Pricing Theory: A New Framework for Analysis, Journal of Financial Economics, 15, 373–394.

Connor, Gregory, and Robert Uhlaner, 1989, A Synthesis of Two Approaches to Factor Estimation, Working Paper, University of California at Berkeley.

Chamberlain, Gary, 1983, Asset Pricing in Multiperiod Securities Markets, Econometrica, 56, 1283–1300.

Elton, Edwin, J., and Martin J. Gruber, 1988, A Multi-index Risk Model of the Japanese Stock Market, Japan and the World Economy, 1, 21–44.

Errunza, Vihang and Etienne Losq, 1985, International Asset Pricing under Mild Segmentation: Theory and Test, Journal of Finance, 40, 105–124.

Fama, Eugene and J. MacBeth, 1973, Risk, Return and Equilibrium: Empirical Tests, Journal of Political Economy, 81, 607–636.

Ferson, Wayne E. and Campbell R. Harvey, 1991, The Variation of Economic Risk Premiums, Journal of Political Economy, 99, 385–415.

Ferson, Wayne E. and Campbell R. Harvey, 1993, The Risk and Predictability of International Equity Returns, Review of Financial Studies, 6, 527–566.

Ferson, Wayne E. and Campbell R. Harvey, 1994, Sources of Risk and Returns in Global Equity Markets, Journal of Banking and Finance, 18, 775–803.

Gibbons, Michael R., Stephen A. Ross, and Jay Shanken, 1989, A Test of the Efficiency of a Given Portfolio, Econometrica, 57, 1121–1152.

Gultekin, N. Bulent, M.N. Gultekin and A. Penati, 1989, Capital controls and international capital market segmentation: The evidence from the Japanese and American stock markets, Journal of Finance 44, 849–869.

Hansen, Lars P. and Kenneth Singleton, 1982, Generalized Instrumental Variable Estimation of Nonlinear Rational Expectations Models, Econometrica, 50, 1269–1286.

Harvey, Campbell R., 1991, The World Price of Covariance Risk, Journal of Finance 46, 111–157.

Harvey, Campbell R., 1994, Predictable Risk and Returns in Emerging Markets, working paper, Duke University Fuqua School of Business.

Heston, Steven L., and K. Geert Rouwenhorst, 1994, Does Industrial Structure Explain the Benefits of International Diversification?, Journal of Financial Economics, 36, 1–27.

Ibbotson Associates, 1992, SBBI Yearbook, Chicago 1992.

Jorion, Philippe and Eduardo Schwartz, 1985, Integration Versus Segmentation in the Canadian Stock Market, Journal of Finance, 41, 603–614.

Kato, Kiyoshi and James S. Shallheim, 1985, Seasonal and Size Anomalies in the Japanese Stock Market, Journal of Financial and Quantitative Analysis, 20, 243–260.

Korajczyk, Robert A. and Claude J. Viallet, 1989, An Empirical Investigation of International Asset Pricing, Review of Financial Studies, 2, 553–585.

Roll, Richard, 1992, Industrial Structure and the Comparative behavior of International Stock Market Indices, Journal of Finance, 47, 3–41.

Roll, Richard, and Stephen A. Ross, 1980, An Empirical Examination of the Arbitrage Pricing Theory, Journal of Finance, 35, 1073–1103.

Seber, G.A.F., 1984, Multivariate Observations, John Wiley and Sons, New York.

Shanken, Jay, 1982, The Arbitrage Pricing Theory: Is it Testable?, Journal of Finance, 37, 1129–1140.

Shanken, Jay, 1985, Multibeta CAPM or Equilibrium-APT? A Reply to Dybvig and Ross, Journal of Finance, 40, 1189–1196.

Shanken, Jay, 1987, Multivariate Proxies and Asset Pricing Relations: Living with the Roll Critique, Journal of Financial Economics, 18, 91–110.

Shanken, Jay, 1992, On the Estimation of Beta-Pricing Models, Review of Financial Studies 5, 1–33.

Solnik, Bruno, 1974, The International Pricing of Risk: An empirical investigation of the world capital structure, Journal of Finance 29, 48–54.

Solnik, Bruno, 1983, International Arbitrage Pricing Theory. Journal of Finance, 38, 449–457.

Stehle, Richard, 1977, An empirical test of the alternative hypotheses of national and international pricing of risky assets, Journal of Finance, 32, 493–502.

Stulz, Rene M., 1981, On the Effects of Barriers to International Investment, Journal of Finance, 36, 923–934.

Theil, Henri, 1971, Principles of Econometrics, John Wiley and Sons, New York.

Trzcinka, Charles A., 1986, On the Number of Factors in the Arbitrage Pricing Model, Journal of Finance, 41, 347–368.

Wheatley, Simon, 1988, Some Tests of International Equity Integration, Journal of Financial Economics, 21, 177–212.

White, Halbert, 1980, A Heteroskedasticity-Consistent Covariance Matrix Estimator and a Direct Test for Heteroskedasticity, Econometrica, 48, 817–838.

[4]

MODELING THE DYNAMIC INTERDEPENDENCE OF MAJOR EUROPEAN STOCK MARKETS

GREGORY KOUTMOS*

INTRODUCTION

The growing globalization of financial markets has been accompanied by a growing body of empirical research attempting to describe and quantify the ways in which financial markets within and across countries interact. Better understanding of the nature of cross market linkages and interactions could be of help to investors and policy makers alike. With respect to policy, aspects of market interaction that promote efficiency could, in principle, be facilitated whereas, those with undesirable side effects could be controlled. Likewise, investment and hedging strategies could be more effective if the nature of market interactions were better understood. The extant literature provides convincing evidence that financial markets do influence each other. For example, Koch and Koch (1991) provide evidence on the evolution of contemporaneous and lead/lag relationships among eight national stock markets. They suggest that regional interdependencies have grown over time. Becker, Finnerty, and Gupta (1990) show that information generated in the US stock market could be used to trade profitably in Japan, contrary to the market efficiency hypothesis. However, when transaction costs and transfer taxes are included into the analysis, excess profits vanish. Eun and Shim (1989) document that markets around the globe respond to innovations in a way that is consistent with the notion of informationally efficient international stock markets. King and Wadhwani (1990) use a rational expectations model with asymmetric information to test for 'contagion effects' i.e., the notion that valuation mistakes in one market can be transmitted to other markets.[1]

More recent papers extend the scope of market interaction to include second moment linkages. This extension allows testing of the hypothesis that information generated in a given market at time t is useful in terms of predicting the conditional mean and variance in another market at time $t+1$. Hamao, Masulis and Ng (1990) examine first and second moment interdependencies in the three major stock markets (New York, Tokyo, and London) using univariate GARCH models. For the period after the October 1987 worldwide stock market crash, they find that innovations coming from

---

* The author is Associate Professor of Finance at Fairfield University. (Paper received July 1994, revised and accepted April 1995))

Address for correspondence: Gregory Koutmos, School of Business, Fairfield University, Fairfield, CT 064307524, USA.

New York and London are influencing volatility in both Tokyo and London. Lin, Engle, and Ito (1991) use a signal extraction model with GARCH processes to study the interaction of the US and the Japanese stock markets. Their findings suggest that mean and volatility interactions are generally reciprocal, in the sense that the two markets influence each other. Theodossiou and Lee (1993) examine mean and volatility interactions in five major stock exchanges.

This paper contributes to the ongoing debate on first and second moment stock market interactions. The markets under investigation are the four major European stock markets namely, those of England, France, Germany and Italy. It can be said that research interest in the European stock markets has not been as strong as the interest shown by international investors. The flow of equity capital into the European stock markets, in recent years, has been far greater than that received by the US and Japan (see Drummen and Zimmermann, 1992).

The majority of papers dealing with the European stock markets use univariate ARCH type models to characterize the short term dynamics of individual markets e.g., Poon and Taylor (1992) and Sentana and Wadhwani (1992) for the London market, Booth et al. (1992) for the Helsinki market, De Jong, Kemma and Kloek (1992) for the Dutch market and Corhay and Rad (1994) for a group of five major European stock markets. These studies document, among other things, significant departures from normality and volatility clustering i.e., conditional heteroskedasticity. Due to their univariate approach however, they do not deal with the nature of interdependence and interaction across markets i.e., whether innovations in a given market are informative with respect to the conditional mean and variances in other markets. The same can be said about studies that use multivariate analysis to test for cointegration of European stock markets e.g., Abbott and Chow (1993).[2]

This paper provides new evidence on the lead/lag relationships and volatility interactions of major European stock markets. It also contributes to methodology by extending the univariate EGARCH model, suggested by Nelson (1991), into a multivariate framework. This extension has obvious advantages. First, market interactions can be investigated and analysed in a one-step estimation procedure thus, eliminating the need to use estimated regressors.[3] Second, the hypothesis that innovations within and across markets influence volatility asymmetrically can be explicitly tested. The asymmetric impact of past innovations on current stock return volatility is well known e.g., Black (1976), Christie (1982), Nelson (1991), Poon and Taylor (1992), Koutmos (1992) and Cheung and Ng (1992), among others. This phenomenon has been attributed to the so-called 'leverage effect' whereby negative stock returns automatically produce a higher debt to equity ratio and hence higher volatility. What is not known is whether volatility interactions across markets are themselves asymmetric or, to put it differently,

© Blackwell Publishers Ltd 1996

whether innovations in one market affect volatility in other markets in an asymmetric fashion.

The remainder of this paper is organized as follows: The next section presents the multivariate VAR-EGARCH model. The third section describes the data and presents preliminary empirical findings. The fourth section presents the major findings based on the VAR-EGARCH model and discusses the implications. The final section offers a summary and concluding remarks.

THE MULTIVARIATE VAR-EGARCH MODEL

Let $R_{i,t}$ be the percentage return at time t for market i where, $i = 1, 2, 3, 4$ (1=France, 2=Germany, 3=Italy and 4=UK), Ω_{t-1} the σ-field generated by all the information available at time $t-1$, $\mu_{i,t}$ and $\sigma_{i,t}^2$ the conditional mean and the conditional variance respectively, $\sigma_{i,j,t}$ the conditional covariance between markets i and j, $\epsilon_{i,t}$ the innovation at time t (i.e., $\epsilon_{i,t} = R_{i,t} - \mu_{i,t}$) and $z_{i,t}$ the standardized innovation (i.e., $z_{i,t} = \epsilon_{i,t}/\sigma_{i,t}$). The multivariate VAR-EGARCH model can then be written as follows:

$$R_{i,t} = \beta_{i,0} + \sum_{j=1}^{4} \beta_{i,j} R_{j,t-1} + \epsilon_{i,t} \quad \text{for } i,j = 1,2,3,4, \quad (1)$$

$$\sigma_{i,t}^2 = \exp\{\alpha_{i,0} + \sum_{j=1}^{4} \alpha_{i,j} f_j(z_{j,t-1}) + \gamma_i \ln(\sigma_{i,t-1}^2)\} \quad \text{for } i,j = 1,2,3,4, \quad (2)$$

$$f_j(z_{j,t-1}) = (|z_{j,t-1}| - E(|z_{j,t-1}|) + \delta_j z_{j,t-1}) \quad \text{for } j = 1,2,3,4, \quad (3)$$

$$\sigma_{i,j,t} = \rho_{i,j} \sigma_{i,t} \sigma_{j,t} \quad \text{for } i,j = 1,2,3,4 \text{ and } i \neq j. \quad (4)$$

Equation (1) describes the returns of the four markets as a vector autoregression (VAR) where, the conditional mean in each market is a function of past own returns as well as cross-market past returns. Lead/lag relationships are captured by coefficients $\beta_{i,j}$, for $i \neq j$. A significant $\beta_{i,j}$ coefficient would imply that market i leads market j or, equivalently, current returns in market j can be used to predict future returns in market i. Related studies allow for volatility feedbacks (i.e., ARCH-M effects) and day of the week effects in the specification of the conditional means. Since the focus of this paper is on mean and volatility interactions among markets these effects are ignored. Furthermore, Theodossiou and Lee (1995) find no evidence of volatility feedbacks in European stock returns.

The conditional variance of the returns in each market, given by (2), is an exponential function of past own as well as cross-market standardized innovations. The particular functional form of $f_j(z_{j,t-1})$ is given in (3). As can be seen, $f(.)$ is an asymmetric function of past standardized innovations. For $z_{j,t-1} < 0$ the slope of $f(.)$ is equal to $-1+\delta_j$ whereas, for $z_{j,t-1} > 0$ the slope

© Blackwell Publishers Ltd 1996

becomes $1+\delta_j$. Thus, equation (3) permits standardized own and cross-market innovations to influence the conditional variance in each market asymmetrically. More intuitively, the term $(|z_{j,t-1}| - E|z_{j,t-1}|)$ measures the magnitude effect. Assuming $\alpha_{i,j}$ is positive, the impact of $z_{j,t-1}$ on $\sigma_{i,t}^2$ will be positive (negative) if the magnitude of $z_{j,t-1}$ is greater (smaller) than its expected value $E|z_{i,t-1}|$.[4] Similarly, the term $\delta_j z_{j,t-1}$ measures the sign effect. Depending on the sign of the coefficient and the sign of the innovation, the sign effect may be reinforcing, or, partially offsetting the magnitude effect. For example, stock market declines in market j ($z_{j,t-1} < 0$) will be followed by higher volatility than stock market advances ($z_{j,t-1} > 0$) if δ_j is negative. Such a response would be consistent with the leverage effect whereby, market declines produce a higher aggregate debt to equity ratio and hence higher volatility. The relative importance of the asymmetry or, leverage effect, can be measured by the ratio $|-1+\delta_j|/(1+\delta_j)$. Volatility interactions or, spillovers, across markets are measured by $\alpha_{i,j}$ for $i,j = 1, 2, 3, 4$ and $i \neq j$. A significant positive $\alpha_{i,j}$ coupled with a negative δ_j implies that negative innovations in market j have a higher impact on the volatility of market i than positive innovations, i.e., the volatility transmission mechanism is asymmetric.

The persistence of volatility implied by equation (2) is measured by γ_i. The unconditional variance is finite if $\gamma_i < 1$ (see Nelson, 1991). If $\gamma_i = 1$, then the unconditional variance does not exist and the conditional variance follows an integrated process of order one. As noted by Hsieh (1989) the exponential specification is less likely to produce integrated variances.

The contemporaneous relationship between the returns of the four markets is captured by the conditional covariance specification, given by (4). This specification implies that the correlation of the returns of markets i and j is constant or, what amounts to the same thing, the covariance is proportional to the product of the standard deviations. This assumption greatly simplifies estimation of the model and it is a plausible one for many applications e.g., Bollerslev (1990). Even with this simplification the number of parameters to be estimated is fifty four. Assuming normality, the log likelihood for the multivariate VAR-EGARCH model can be written as

$$L(\Theta) = -0.5(NT)\ln(2\pi) - 0.5 \sum_{t=1}^{T}(\ln|S_t| + \epsilon_t' S_t^{-1} \epsilon_t), \qquad (6)$$

where N is number of equations (four in this case), T is number of observations, Θ is the 54×1 parameter vector to be estimated, $\epsilon_t' = [\epsilon_{1,t}, \epsilon_{2,t}, \epsilon_{3,t}, \epsilon_{4,t}]$ is the 1×4 vector of innovations at time t, S_t is the 4×4 time varying conditional variance-covariance matrix with diagonal elements given by equation (2) for $i = 1, 2, 3, 4$ and cross diagonal elements given by equation (4) for $i,j = 1, 2, 3, 4$ and $i \neq j$. The log-likelihood function is highly nonlinear in Θ and therefore, numerical maximization techniques have to be used. We use the Berndt, Hall, Hall, and Hausman (1974) algorithm, which utilizes numerical derivatives to maximize $L(\Theta)$.

© Blackwell Publishers Ltd 1996

INTERDEPENDENCE OF EUROPEAN STOCK MARKETS

DATA AND PRELIMINARY FINDINGS

Data used in this paper are the daily figures for the aggregate stock price indices of the UK (FT 500 Share Index), France (CAC General), Germany (Commerzbank) and Italy (BCI General). Daily percentage returns are calculated as $100*\log(P_t/P_{t-1})$ where, P_t is the value of the index at t in terms of local currency. The data set extends from January 4, 1986 to December 31, 1991 for a total of 1,562 observations. All indices are value weighted and broadly based. The market capitalization of these four markets accounts for seventy percent of the total European market capitalization.

Table 1 reports summary statistics for the daily returns as well as statistics testing for normality and independence. The sample means for all three markets are statistically insignificant at the 5% level of significance. Measures for skewness and excess kurtosis indicate that all return series are negatively skewed and highly leptokurtic with respect to the normal distribution. Likewise, the Kolmogorov-Smirnov statistic rejects the null hypothesis that returns are normally distributed.[5] The Ljung-Box statistics (LB) for up to 12 lags, calculated for both the return and the squared return series, suggest the presence of significant linear and nonlinear dependencies respectively. The

Table 1

Preliminary Statistics

Statistics	France	Germany	Italy	UK
μ	0.0355	−0.0074	0.0063	0.0362
σ	1.1840	1.3380	1.2358	0.9621
S	−0.6017*	−0.4239*	−0.4479*	−2.4908*
K	8.0378*	4.9994*	6.1299*	26.9124*
D	0.0605*	0.0541*	0.1114*	0.0790*
LB(12) for R_t	46.0255*	20.1168	69.8693*	77.8747*
LB(12) for R_t^2	350.0904*	754.8429*	723.1341*	775.4200*

| | Correlation Matrix ||||
	France	Germany	Italy	UK
France	1.0000	0.3374	0.3170	0.25553
Germany		1.0000	0.2433	0.3634
Italy			1.0000	0.2338
UK				

Notes:
Stock returns are logarithmic percentage changes. Period Jan. 4, 1986 to Dec. 31, 1991 (1,562 days). μ = sample mean; σ = sample standard deviation; S = skewness; K = excess kurtosis; D = Kolmogorov-Smirnov test for normality (5% critical value is $1.36/\sqrt{T}$ where, T is number of observations); LB(n) is the Ljung-Box statistic for up to n lags (distributed as χ^2 with n degrees of freedom).
(*) Denotes significance at the 5% level.

© Blackwell Publishers Ltd 1996

source of linear dependencies may be attributed to nonsynchronous trading of the stocks that makeup each index e.g., Scholes and Williams (1977) and Lo and MacKinlay (1988) or, to time variation in short-term expected returns e.g., Fama and French (1988) and Conrad and Kaul (1988). Conrad and Kaul (1988) argue that, for US stock returns, autocorrelation is due to time varying expected returns rather than nonsynchronous trading. The model they use is consistent with an autoregressive process for the conditional mean. Nonlinear dependencies are most likely due to autoregressive conditional heteroskedasticity i.e., volatility clustering, as documented by several recent studies for both US and foreign stock returns (e.g., Nelson, 1991; Akgiray, 1989; and Booth et al., 1992, among others). It is interesting to note that the LB statistic for the squared returns is in all cases several times greater than that calculated for returns themselves. This is an indication that second moment (nonlinear) dependencies are far more significant than first moment dependencies.

The correlation structure of these European stock markets is probably the most important feature from the point of view of investors and portfolio managers. Hedging and diversification strategies invariably involve some measure of correlation (coherence). Most of the time sample correlation coefficients are used with the implicit assumption that the return series involved in the analysis are mean and variance stationary. Under this assumption conditional and unconditional estimates coincide. It will be seen later however, that unconditional estimates of pairwise correlations are significantly greater than conditional estimates thus, underestimating the potential for diversification. The unconditional correlation coefficients in Table 1 range from 0.3634, for Germany and the UK, to 0.2338 for Italy and the UK.

MAJOR EMPIRICAL FINDINGS

To assess the importance of market interdependence i.e., lead/lag relationships and volatility interactions, we first estimate a restricted version of the VAR-EGARCH model by setting all cross market coefficients equal to zero i.e., $\beta_{i,j} = \alpha_{i,j} = 0$ for $i,j = 1, 2, 3, 4$ and $i \neq j$. Note that this model is not equivalent to four univariate EGARCH models because contemporaneous correlations are allowed. It is more along the lines of Bollerslev (1990) with the exception that the conditional variances follow the EGARCH rather than the GARCH process. This will be the benchmark against which the full VAR-EGARCH model will be compared. The maximum likelihood estimates of the benchmark model are reported in Table 2. The autoregression coefficients, $\beta_{i,j}$, are statistically significant for France and Italy. Following Conrad and Kaul (1988) we interpret this as evidence of time varying expected returns.

© Blackwell Publishers Ltd 1996

INTERDEPENDENCE OF EUROPEAN STOCK MARKETS

Table 2

Maximum Likelihood Estimates of the Benchmark AR(1)-EGARCH

Mean: $R_{i,t} = \beta_{i,0} + \beta_{i,i} R_{i,t-1} + \epsilon_{i,t}$ for $i = 1, 2, 3, 4$

Variance: $\sigma_{i,t}^2 = \exp\{\alpha_{i,0} + \alpha_{i,i} f_i(z_{i,t-1}) + \gamma_i \ln(\sigma_{i,t-1}^2)\}$ for $i = 1, 2, 3, 4$

Covariance: $\sigma_{i,j,t} = \rho_{i,j} \sigma_{i,t} \sigma_{j,t}$ for $i, j = 1, 2, 3$ and $i \neq j$.

	France		Germany		Italy		UK
$\beta_{1,0}$	0.0477 (0.023)*	$\beta_{2,0}$	0.0209 (0.030)	$\beta_{3,0}$	0.0210 (0.024)	$\beta_{4,0}$	0.0679) (0.022)*
$\beta_{1,1}$	0.0878 (0.024)*	$\beta_{2,2}$	−0.0185 (0.025)	$\beta_{3,3}$	0.1718 (0.022)*	$\beta_{4,4}$	0.0299 (0.027)
$\alpha_{1,0}$	0.0184 (0.003)*	$\alpha_{2,0}$	0.0297 (0.005)*	$\alpha_{3,0}$	0.0162 (0.002)*	$\alpha_{4,0}$	−0.0253 (0.006)*
$\alpha_{1,1}$	0.1460 (0.015)*	$\alpha_{2,2}$	0.2011 (0.020)*	$\alpha_{3,3}$	0.1415 (0.011)*	$\alpha_{4,4}$	0.1900 (0.020)*
δ_1	−0.2966 (0.053)*	δ_2	−0.3618 (0.066)*	δ_3	−0.2067 (0.054)*	δ_4	−0.3599 (0.078)*
γ_1	0.9571 (0.007)*	γ_2	0.9350 (0.010)*	γ_3	0.9746 (0.004)*	γ_4	0.9001 (0.013)*

Correlation Matrix

	France	Germany	Italy	UK
France	1.0000	0.3161 (0.019)*	0.2352 (0.022)*	0.2317 (0.026)*
Germany		1.0000	0.2010 (0.022)*	0.2791 (0.021)*
Italy			1.0000	0.1734 (0.025)*
UK				1.0000

Model Diagnostics

	France	Germany	Italy	UK
$E(z_{i,t})$	−0.0106	−0.0089	−0.0109	−0.0207
$E(z_{i,t}^2)$	1.0009	1.0042	1.0010	1.0006
LB(12); $z_{i,t}$	15.5376	17.3472	23.2651*	24.3527*
LB(12); $z_{i,t}^2$	6.8237	5.3327	24.0076*	5.4954
D	0.0223	0.0676	0.0309	0.0653

Notes:
Numbers in parentheses are asymptotic standard errors. Stock returns are logarithmic percentage changes. Period: April 1, 1986 to Dec. 31, 1991 (1,562 days).
D = Kolmogorov-Smirnov testing for normality (5% critical value is $1.36/\sqrt{T}$ where, T is number of observations); LB(n) is the Ljung-Box statistic for up to n lags (distributed as χ^2 with n degrees of freedom). $z_{i,t}$ is the standardized residual for market i.
(*) Denotes significance at the 5% level.

© Blackwell Publishers Ltd 1996

Conditional heteroskedasticity is perhaps the single most important property describing the short term dynamics of all four stock markets. The conditional variance is a function of past innovations and past conditional variances. The relevant coefficients $\alpha_{i,i}$ and γ_i are statistically significant. The leverage effect, or, asymmetric impact of past innovations on current volatility, is significant in all instances lending support to the notion that volatility interactions across markets may also be asymmetric. The degree of asymmetry, on the basis of the estimated δ_i coefficients, is highest for Germany and the UK (negative innovations increase volatility approximately 2.13 times more than positive innovations), followed by France (approximately 1.84 times) and Italy (approximately 1.52 times). Volatility persistence, measured by γ_i, is in all cases high and very close to unity. A simple t-test however, rejects the hypothesis that the conditional variance in these markets are integrated. Thus, we are assured that the unconditional variances are finite.

The estimated conditional pairwise correlations are substantially lower than the unconditional estimates reported in Table 1. For example, the correlation between the returns of the UK and the German market is reduced from 0.3634 to 0.2791. A simple t-test suggests that the difference is statistically significant. Similar reductions can be observed for the rest of the correlation coefficients. Thus, failure to account for conditional heteroskedasticity leads to upward biased correlation estimates.

Diagnostics based on the standardized residuals show no serious evidence against the benchmark specification. For example, the estimated means and variances are zero and one respectively as expected. The LB statistic for twelve lags show that some dependence still persists in the standardized residuals of Italy and the UK. This may be due to the restriction imposed i.e., zero mean and variance interactions. Still the benchmark model is superior to any univariate modeling because it takes into account contemporaneous correlations across markets.

The maximum likelihood estimates of the full VAR-EGARCH model are reported in Table 3. Focusing on the parameters describing the conditional mean in each market, it can be seen that there are several significant multidirectional lead/lag relationships. For example, current returns in France are correlated with past returns in Germany and the UK. Similarly, returns in Germany are influenced by past returns in France and the UK. Italy is influenced by Germany and the UK. The latter is in turn influenced by France and Italy. The multidirectional nature of these relationships suggests that no market plays a major role as an information producer. All that can be said is that the UK market is the only market whose lagged returns influence significantly the conditional means of the remaining three markets. An important question that arises is to which extent these relationships can be exploited to generate abnormal profits? To put it differently, are these relationships economically significant? To answer this question one would

© Blackwell Publishers Ltd 1996

Table 3

Maximum Likelihood Estimates of the VAR-EGARCH

Mean: $R_{i,t} = \beta_{i,0} + \sum_{j=1}^{4} \beta_{i,j} R_{j,t-1} + \epsilon_{i,t}$ for $i, j = 1, 2, 3, 4$

Variance: $\sigma_{i,t}^2 = \exp\{\alpha_{i,0} + \sum_{j=1}^{4} \alpha_{i,j} f_j(z_{j,t-1}) + \gamma_i \ln(\sigma_{i,t-1}^2)\}$ for $i, j = 1, 2, 3, 4$

Covariance: $\sigma_{i,j,t} = \rho_{i,j} \sigma_{i,t} \sigma_{j,t}$ for $i, j = 1, 2, 3$ and $i \neq j$.

	France		Germany		Italy		UK
$\beta_{1,0}$	0.0417 (0.022)	$\beta_{2,0}$	0.0169 (0.030)	$\beta_{3,0}$	0.0210 (0.024)	$\beta_{4,0}$	0.0488 (0.021)*
$\beta_{1,1}$	−0.0126 (0.027)	$\beta_{2,1}$	−0.0719 (0.025)*	$\beta_{3,1}$	0.0174 (0.026)	$\beta_{4,1}$	−0.0622 (0.023)*
$\beta_{1,2}$	0.1054 (0.022)*	$\beta_{2,2}$	−0.0024 (0.027)	$\beta_{3,2}$	0.1009 (0.024)*	$\beta_{4,2}$	−0.0203 (0.021)
$\beta_{1,3}$	−0.0086 (0.023)	$\beta_{2,3}$	0.0073 (0.027)	$\beta_{3,3}$	0.1605 (0.026)*	$\beta_{4,3}$	0.0547 (0.021)*
$\beta_{1,4}$	0.3526 (0.029)*	$\beta_{2,4}$	0.2304 (0.035)*	$\beta_{3,4}$	0.1969 (0.032)*	$\beta_{4,4}$	0.1557 (0.028)*
$\alpha_{1,0}$	0.0202 (0.006)*	$\alpha_{2,0}$	0.0411 (0.006)*	$\alpha_{3,0}$	0.0227 (0.004)*	$\alpha_{4,0}$	−0.0353 (0.009)*
$\alpha_{1,1}$	0.2203 (0.021)*	$\alpha_{2,1}$	0.0306 (0.025)*	$\alpha_{3,1}$	0.0336 (0.018)*	$\alpha_{4,1}$	0.0712 (0.027)*
$\alpha_{1,2}$	0.1464 (0.026)*	$\alpha_{2,2}$	0.2392 (0.023)*	$\alpha_{3,2}$	0.1225 (0.022)*	$\alpha_{4,2}$	0.1890 (0.025)*
$\alpha_{1,3}$	0.0938 (0.017)*	$\alpha_{2,3}$	0.0782 (0.017)*	$\alpha_{3,3}$	0.1764 (0.017)*	$\alpha_{4,3}$	0.0143 (0.022)
$\alpha_{1,4}$	0.0582 (0.023)*	$\alpha_{2,4}$	0.0593 (0.027)*	$\alpha_{3,4}$	0.0091 (0.017)	$\alpha_{4,4}$	0.1426 (0.027)*
δ_1	−0.0597 (0.055)	δ_2	−0.2954 (0.054)*	δ_3	−0.2481 (0.065)*	δ_4	−0.2930 (0.143)*
γ_1	0.9169 (0.008)*	γ_2	0.9138 (0.011)*	γ_3	0.9411 (0.008)*	γ_4	0.8786 (0.016)*
R^2	0.0570		0.0122		0.0494		0.0136

	Correlation Matrix			
	France	Germany	Italy	UK
France	1.0000	0.2989 (0.022)*	0.1926 (0.023)*	0.2007 (0.025)*
Germany		1.0000	0.1691 (0.024)*	0.2672 (0.021)*
Italy			1.0000	0.1319 (0.027)*
UK				1.0000

© Blackwell Publishers Ltd 1996

Table 3 (Continued)

	France	Germany	Italy	UK
	Model Diagnostics			
$E(z_{i,t})$	−0.0119	−0.0112	−0.0200	−0.0077
$E(z_{i,t}^2)$	1.0010	1.0045	0.9993	1.0008
LB(12); $z_{i,t}$	15.3044	14.4638	13.2660	17.8877
LB(12); $z_{i,t}^2$	5.1603	4.4059	15.4948	7.7202
D	0.0454	0.0561	0.0243	0.0273

LB(12) for Cross Product of Standardized Residuals
LB($z_{1,2}$) = 3.8205 LB($z_{1,3}$) = 9.9883 LB($z_{1,4}$) = 9.1627 LB($z_{2,3}$) = 16.4407
LB($z_{2,4}$) = 9.2660 LB($z_{3,4}$) = 14.6427

Notes:
Numbers in parentheses are asymptotic standard errors. Stock returns are logarithmic percentage changes. Period: April 1, 1986 to Dec 31, 1991 (1,562 days).
D = Kolmogorov-Smirnov testing for normality (5% critical value is $1.32/\sqrt{T}$ where, T is number of observations); R^2 is the uncentred coefficient of determination. LB(n) is the Ljung-Box statistic for up to n lags (distributed as χ^2 with n degrees of freedom). $z_{i,t}$ is the standardized residual for market i. $z_{i,j}$ is the cross product of the standardized residuals i.e., $z_{i,t} z_{j,t}$ for i,j = 1, 2, 3, 4 and $i \neq j$.
(*) Denotes significance at the 5% level.

need detailed information concerning transactions costs as well as measures of foreign exchange risk. Table 3 reports uncentered R^2 statistics calculated as $R^2 = 1 - (\text{Var}(\epsilon_i)/\text{Var}(R_i))$, for i = 1, 2, 3, 4. These statistics range from 5.7%, for France, to 1.2% for Germany. Thus, the percentage of variation in returns that can be explained on the basis of past information is very small. If transactions costs and exchange rate risk are taken into account then we can safely conclude that the four markets are weak-form efficient.

Turning to second moment interdependencies (volatility interactions) it can be seen from Table 3 that they are equally extensive and reciprocal. In addition to own past innovations, the conditional variance in each market is also affected by past innovations generated in the other markets with minor exceptions i.e., Italy is not affected by UK innovations and the UK is not affected by Italy. Interestingly, the volatility transmission mechanism is mostly asymmetric with the exception of innovations originating in France. The coefficients measuring asymmetry, δ_i, are statistically significant for the remaining three markets. This finding supports the notion that both the size and the sign of the innovations are important determinants of the volatility transmission mechanism. The extent to which negative news (innovations) in one market increase volatility more than positive news in the other markets can be assessed using the estimated coefficients $\alpha_{i,j}$ and δ_j (see equations (2) and (3)). On the basis of these estimates we calculate the impact of a ±3% innovation in market i at time $t-1$ on the conditional variance of market j at time t assuming all other innovations are zero. The results of this exercise are given in Table 4. As expected, the impact of an innovation in market i is mostly felt within the same market. However, the volatility in the other markets is affected substantially. For example, a -3% (+3%) innovation in Germany at time $t-1$ increases volatility by 0.4521% (0.1926%) in France, by 0.3783% (0.1612%) in Italy and by 0.5836% (0.2486) in the UK at time t. On average, a negative innovation in a given market increases volatility within and across markets twice more than a positive innovation.

Comparing the estimates of the benchmark model to those of the unrestricted model (i.e., Tables 2 and 3 respectively), we can see that the degree of volatility persistence, γ_i, implied by the benchmark model is invariably higher. This is because the benchmark model does not take into account volatility interactions across markets. This is in agreement with Lastrapes (1989) who claims that the high degree of volatility persistence may be due to omitted variables. More importantly, the coherence (correlation structure) of the four markets implied by the VAR-EGARCH model is lower than that implied by the benchmark model. So that, accounting for conditional heteroskedasticity and interactions across markets substantially reduces the pairwise correlation coefficients. The implication is that sample correlation coefficients overstate the degree of relatedness and thus, understate the potential for diversification in these markets.

To test the joint significance of first and second moment interactions among the four European stock markets we use the likelihood ratio statistic calculated as $LR = 2*[L(\Theta_1)-L(\Theta_0)]$ where, $L(\Theta_1)$ and $L(\Theta_0)$ are the maximum log likelihood values obtained from the full VAR-EGARCH and the benchmark model respectively. This statistic is asymptotically chi-square distributed with degrees of freedom equal to the number of restrictions implied by the

Table 4

Impact of Symmetric Innovations on Volatility

Innovation at $t-1$ from:	% Δ of Volatility in France at t	% Δ of Volatility in Germany at t	% Δ of Volatility in Italy at t	% Δ of Volatility in UK at t
+3% France	0.4456	0.0619	0.0680	0.1440
−3% France	0.5245	0.0728	0.0800	0.1695
+3% Germany	0.1926	0.3147	0.1612	0.2486
−3% Germany	0.4521	0.7386	0.3783	0.5836
+3% Italy	0.1367	0.1140	0.1948	0.0208
−3% Italy	0.2763	0.2304	0.5197	0.0421
+3% UK	0.0770	0.0784	0.0120	0.1886
−3% UK	0.1793	0.1827	0.0280	0.4393

© Blackwell Publishers Ltd 1996

benchmark model (24 in this case).[6] The estimated value of the likelihood ratio statistic is 498.7576 thus rejecting the benchmark model at any level of significance. The presence of first and second moment interdependencies implies that European stock markets are integrated in the sense that news affecting asset pricing are not purely domestic in nature.

Residual based diagnostic tests show that the multivariate VAR-EGARCH model satisfactorily explains the interaction of the four stock markets. The Ljung-Box statistics show no evidence of either linear or nonlinear dependence in the standardized residuals.[7] The validity of the assumption of constant conditional correlations can be assessed by testing for serial correlation in the cross product of the standardized residuals. The Ljung-Box statistics up to 12 lags, reported in Table 3, show no evidence of serial correlation so that the constant correlation specification appears to be a reasonable parameterization of the variance-covariance structure of the four markets. Of some concern is the rejection of normality for the standardized residuals of France and Germany. Departures from normality imply that the standard errors may be understated. In most cases however, the coefficients are significant even at the one percent level. This is especially true for the coefficients describing the variance-covariance matrix.

SUMMARY AND CONCLUDING REMARKS

This paper investigates dynamic first and second moment interactions among the stock markets of the UK, France, Germany and Italy. These markets constitute seventy percent of total European equity market capitalization. Lead/lag relationships and volatility interactions are described by a multivariate VAR-EGARCH model. Unlike previous related studies, this paper explicitly accounts for potential asymmetries that may exist in the volatility transmission mechanism, i.e., the possibility that bad news (innovations) in market i have a greater impact on the volatility of the returns in market j. We find evidence of multidirectional lead/lag relationships (first moment interactions). We also document significant volatility or, second moment interactions. With one exception, the volatility transmission mechanism is asymmetric i.e., negative innovations in market i increase volatility in market j considerably more than positive innovations. These findings suggest that European stock markets are integrated in the sense that they react not only to local news but also to news originating in the other markets, especially when the news is adverse. An equally important finding, from a portfolio point of view, is the sensitivity of pairwise correlation estimates to different assumptions about the return generating process. Assuming stationary means and variances produces the highest correlation estimates. Explicit modeling of conditional heteroskedasticity and first and second moment interactions leads to much smaller correlation estimates.

© Blackwell Publishers Ltd 1996

Since these interactions are highly significant, failure to fully account for them tends to overstate the size of pairwise correlations and thus, to understate the potential for diversification.

NOTES

1. Several other studies provide empirical evidence on first-moment (mean) interactions among national stock markets e.g., Von Furstenberg and Jeon (1989), Becker, Finnerty and Tucker (1992), and Bennet and Kelleher (1988), among others.
2. Cointegration deals primarily with the existence of a stable long-run equilibrium among markets. It ignores however, short-term linkages and interactions.
3. Hamao, Masulis and Ng (1991) use estimated residuals obtained from univariate GARCH models to study volatility interactions in New York, Tokyo and London.
4. Assuming $\{z_{i,t}\}$ is a standard normal variate, the expected value of its absolute will be equal to $(2/\pi)^{1/2}$.
5. Hypothesis testing is based on the five percent level of significance throughout the paper.
6. The dimension of the parameter vector is 54×1 for the VAR-EGARCH model and 30×1 for the benchmark model.
7. Note that the return and the residual processes are conditionally heteroskedastic. The standardized residuals, however, are independent identically distributed.

REFERENCES

Abbott, A.B. and V.K. Chow (1993), 'Cointegration Among European Equity Markets', *Journal of Multinational Financial Management*, Vol. 2, No. 3/4, pp. 167–180.

Akgiray, V. (1989), 'Conditional Heteroskedasticity in Time Series of Stock Returns: Evidence and Forecasts', *Journal of Business*, Vol. 62, No. 1, 55–80.

Becker, K.G., J.E. Finnerty and M. Gupta (1990), 'The Intertemporal Relation Between the US and Japanese Stock Markets', *Journal of Finance*, Vol. 45, pp. 1297–1306.

—— —— and A.L. Tucker (1992), 'The Intraday Interdependence Between US and Japanese Equity Markets', *Journal of Financial Research*, Vol. 15, pp. 27–37.

Bennett, P. and J. Kelleher (1988), 'The International Transmission of Stock Price Disruption in October 1987', *Federal Reserve Bank of New York, Quarterly Review* (Summer), pp. 17–33.

Berndt, E.K., H.B. Hall, R.E. Hall and J.A. Hausman (1974), 'Estimation and Inference in Nonlinear Structural Models', *Annals of Economic and Social Management*, Vol. 4, pp. 653–666.

Black, F. (1976), 'Studies of Stock Market Volatility Changes', *Proceedings of the American Statistical Association, Business and Economics Studies Section*, pp. 177–181.

Bollerslev, T. (1990), 'Modelling the Coherence in Short-Run Nominal Exchange Rates: A Multivariate Generalized ARCH Model', *The Review of Economics and Statistics*, Vol. 72, pp. 498–505.

Booth, G.G., J. Hatem, I. Vitranen and P. Yli-Olli (1992), 'Stochastic Modeling of Security Returns: Evidence from the Helsinki Stock Exchange', *European Journal of Operational Research*, Vol. 56, pp. 98–106.

Cheung, Y.-W. and L.K. Ng (1992), 'Stock Price Dynamics and Firm Size: An Empirical Investigation', *Journal of Finance*, Vol. 47, pp. 1985–1997.

Christie, A.A. (1982), 'The Stochastic Behavior of Common Stock Variances: Value, Leverage and Interest Rate Effects', *Journal of Financial Economics*, Vol. 10, pp. 407–432.

Conrad, J. and G. Kaul (1988), 'Time Variation in Expected Returns', *Journal of Business*, Vol. 61, pp. 409–425.

Corhay, A. and A.R. Rad (1994), 'Statistical Properties of Daily Returns: Evidence from European Stock Markets', *Journal of Business Finance & Accounting*, Vol. 21, No. 2 (March), pp. 271–282.

© Blackwell Publishers Ltd 1996

DeJong, F., A. Kemma and T. Kloek (1992), 'A Contribution of Event Study Methodology with and Application to the Dutch Stock Market', *Journal of Banking and Finance*, Vol. 16, pp. 11–36.

Drummen, H. and H. Zimmerman (1992), 'The Structure of European Stock Returns', *Financial Analysts Journal* (July–August), pp. 15–26.

Eun, C.S. and S. Shim (1989), 'International Transmission of Stock Market Movements', *Journal of Financial and Quantitative Analysis*, Vol. 24, pp. 241–256.

Fama, E.F. and K.R. French (1988), 'Permanent and Temporary Components of Stock Prices', *Journal of Political Economy*, Vol. 96, pp. 246–273.

Hamao, Y.R., R.W. Masulis and V.K. Ng (1990), 'Correlation in Price Changes and Volatility Across International Stock Markets', *The Review of Financial Studies*, Vol. 3, pp. 281–307.

Harvey, A.C. (1981), *The Econometric Analysis of Time Series* (Oxford University Press).

Hsieh, D. (1989), 'Modeling Heteroskedasticity in Daily Foreign Exchange Rates', *Journal of Business and Economic Statistics*, Vol. 7, pp. 307–317.

King, M.A. and S. Wadhwani (1990), 'Transmission of Volatility Between Stock Markets', *The Review of Financial Studies*, pp. 3, 5–33.

Koch, P.D. and T.W. Koch (1991), 'Evolution in Dynamic Linkages Across Daily National Stock Indexes', *Journal of International Money and Finance*, Vol. 10, pp. 231–251.

Koutmos, G. (1992), 'Asymmetric Volatility and Risk Return Tradeoff in Foreign Stock Markets', *Journal of Multinational Financial Management*, Vol. 2, No. 2, pp. 27–43.

Lastrapes, W.D. (1989), 'Exchange Rate Volatility and US Monetary Policy: An ARCH Application', *Journal of Money Credit and Banking*, Vol. 21, pp. 66–77.

Lin, W.L., R.F. Engle and T. Ito (1991), 'Do Bulls and Bears Move Across Borders? International Transmission of Stock Returns and Volatility as the World Turns', *National Bureau of Economic Research*, Working Paper No. 3911.

Lo, A.W. and A.C. MacKinley (1988), 'Stock Market Prices Do Not Follow Random Walks', *Review of Financial Studies*, Vol. 1, pp. 41–66.

Nelson, D. (1991), 'Conditional Heteroskedasticity in Asset Returns: A New Approach', *Econometrica*, Vol. 59, pp. 347–370.

Poon, S-H. and S.J. Taylor (1992), 'Stock Returns and Volatility: An Empirical Study of the UK Stock Market', *Journal of Banking and Finance*, Vol. 16, pp. 37–59.

Scholes, M. and J. Williams (1977), 'Estimating Betas from Nonsynchronous Data', *Journal of Financial Economics*, Vol. 5, pp. 309–327.

Sentana, E. and S. Wadhwani (1992), 'Feedback Traders and Stock Return Autocorrelations: Evidence From a Century of Daily Data', *The Economic Journal*, Vol. 102, pp. 415–425.

Theodossiou, P. and U. Lee (1993), 'Mean and Volatility Spillovers Across Major National Stock Markets: Further Empirical Evidence', *Journal of Financial Research*, Vol. 16, pp. 337–350.

——— ——— (1995), 'Relationships Between Volatility and Expected Returns Across International Stock Markets', *Journal of Business Finance & Accounting*, Vol. 22, No. 2 (March), pp. 289–300.

Von Furstenberg, G.M. and B.N. Jeon (1989), 'International Stock Price Movements: Links and Messages', *Brookings Papers on Economic Activity*, Vol. 1, pp. 125–179.

Is the correlation in international equity returns constant: 1960–1990?

FRANÇOIS LONGIN

Department of Finance, ESSEC Graduate Business School, 95021 Cergy-Pontoise, Cedex, France

AND

BRUNO SOLNIK

Department of Finance and Economics, HEC-School of Management, 78351 Jouy-en-Josas, Cedex, France

> We study the correlation of monthly excess returns for seven major countries over the period 1960–90. We find that the international covariance and correlation matrices are unstable over time. A multivariate GARCH(1,1) model with constant conditional correlation helps to capture some of the evolution in the conditional covariance structure. However tests of specific deviations lead to a rejection of the hypothesis of a constant conditional correlation. An explicit modelling of the conditional correlation indicates an increase of the international correlation between markets over the past thirty years. We also find that the correlation rises in periods of high volatility. There is some preliminary evidence that economic variables such as the dividend yield and interest rates contain information about future volatility and correlation that is not contained in past returns alone. (JEL G15, F3).

The correlation matrix of international asset returns plays a special role in the finance literature. Since the seminal work of Levy and Sarnat (1970), Grubel and Fadner (1971), Lessard (1973) and Solnik (1974), international diversification of equity portfolios has been advocated on the basis of the low correlation between national stock markets. The covariance between national markets could change because the volatility of national markets evolves over time, but also because the interdependence across markets changes. Looking at the market correlation allows one to focus on the interdependence between markets. The covariance/correlation matrix is one of the inputs for the computation of a trading portfolio. Knowledge

---

* We have benefited from comments by Stefano Cavaglia, Bernard Dumas, Campbell Harvey, Evi Kaplanis, Ken Kroner, James Lothian (the Editor) Peter Pope and participants of the French Finance Association meetings and of the CEPR workshop on International Finance. The referee's comments and suggestions helped improve the article substantially. We are grateful to INQUIRE, FNEGE and Foundation HEC for financial support.

about its behavior, stability and predictability is then crucial. It is also of particular importance for testing international pricing theories as misspecification could lead to false conclusions.[1]

It is often stated that the progressive removal of impediments to international investment, as well as the growing political, economic and financial integration, affects international market linkages. This could lead to a progressive increase in the international correlation of financial markets reflecting the 'global finance' phenomenon. Kaplanis (1988) studied the stability of the correlation and covariance matrices of monthly returns of ten markets over a fifteen year period (1967–82). She compared matrices estimated over sub-periods of 46 months using Box (1949) and Jenrich (1970) tests. The null hypothesis that the correlation matrix is constant over two adjacent sub-periods could not be rejected at the 15 percent confidence level. The covariance matrix was much less stable (rejection at the 5 percent confidence level for most sub-periods). This result could be caused by changes in the conditional variances with constant international conditional correlations. Ratner (1992) also claimed that the international correlations remained constant over the period 1973–89. On the other hand, Koch and Koch (1991) looked at the correlation of eight markets using daily data for three separate years (1972, 1980 and 1987) and concluded from simple Chow tests that 'international markets have recently grown more interdependent'. Von Furstenberg and Jeon (1989) reached a similar conclusion using a VAR approach for four markets and a very short time period (1986–88). King, Sentana and Wadhwani (1992) claimed that this is only a transitory increase caused by the 1987 crash. Indeed, a question often raised is whether the international correlation increases in periods of high turbulence. The international correlation increases when global factors dominate domestic ones and affect all financial markets. The dominance of global factors tends to be associated with very volatile markets (the oil crises, the Gulf war, etc.). Using high-frequency data surrounding the crash of 1987, King and Wadhwani (1990) and Bertero and Mayer (1990) found that international correlation tends to increase during the stock market crisis.

Our objective is to test the hypothesis of a constant international conditional correlation, investigating various types of deviations. We explicitly model the conditional multivariate distribution of international asset returns and test for the existence of predictable time-variation in conditional correlation for the period 1960–90. Previous works have considered unconditional correlation computed over different sub-periods; here, we come up with an explicit model for conditional correlation. Previous studies have also looked at a fairly short history of monthly returns or focused on the recent period surrounding the crash of 1987. Here, we attempt to discover longer term phenomena by looking at monthly data for the seven major stock markets over the period 1960–90. This is a fairly original database which includes good-quality price indices and dividend yields over the total period. The data are described in Appendix A. The period covers several business and market cycles, with the steady growth of the sixties, the oil crises and the 1987 market crash.

A preliminary look at the data gives an indication of the stability of the correlation of markets. National stock markets have not been strongly correlated over the past thirty years. Table 1 reports the unconditional correlation of national

TABLE 1. Basic statistics.

	GE	FR	UK	SW	JA	CA	US
Mean	0.38	0.29	0.47	0.37	0.65	0.30	0.25
S.D.	5.16	5.87	6.19	5.15	4.97	4.81	4.36

	GE	FR	UK	SW	JA	CA	US
GE	1.00						
FR	0.45	1.00					
UK	0.34	0.42	1.00				
SW	0.60	0.51	0.45	1.00			
JA	0.24	0.26	0.25	0.29	1.00		
CA	0.30	0.42	0.48	0.46	0.27	1.00	
US	0.38	0.43	0.50	0.55	0.30	0.71	1.00

This table gives the mean and standard deviation of monthly excess returns (expressed in percentage monthly units) and the unconditional correlation matrix of national excess returns. The period is 1/1960–8/1990.

monthly excess returns estimated from 1960 to 1990. The lowest coefficient is 0.24 (Germany and Japan) and the highest is 0.71 (Canada and the USA). The average coefficient is around 0.5. The mean excess returns per month vary from 0.251 percent for the USA to 0.647 percent for Japan. The standard deviations are more similar across countries ranging from 4.36 percent per month for the USA to 6.19 percent per month for the UK.

To get a visual impression of the instability of the correlation across markets, we plotted the mean correlation of the US market with the other six markets in Figure 1. The correlations are estimated over a sliding window of five years. The correlation fluctuates over time. The inclusion of October 1987 in the calculation of the 5-year correlation leads to an increase in the correlation for a period of 5 years.

The global test for a constant unconditional correlation matrix performed by Kaplanis (1988) can be replicated on this longer time period. We estimate the unconditional correlation matrix for the seven countries over six sub-periods of five years and test for the equality of the correlation matrix over adjacent sub-periods as well as over non-adjacent sub-periods. The Jenrich test[2] of equality of two matrices calculated over different time periods, has an asymptotic chi-square distribution with 21 degrees of freedom for a seven by seven matrix.[3] A similar test can be applied to the covariance matrix although the number of degrees of freedom is now 28 since the diagonal elements can vary over time. The results are also reported in Table 2. The null hypothesis of a constant correlation matrix is rejected at the 15 percent confidence level in 10 out of 15 comparisons and at the 5 percent level in 5 out of 15 comparisons. The same test applied to the covariance matrix leads to a rejection of the hypothesis of a constant covariance matrix at the 1 percent level in all comparisons but one. These results confirm the findings by Kaplanis that the covariance matrix is less stable than the correlation matrix. However our p-values for the correlation

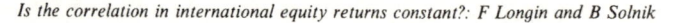

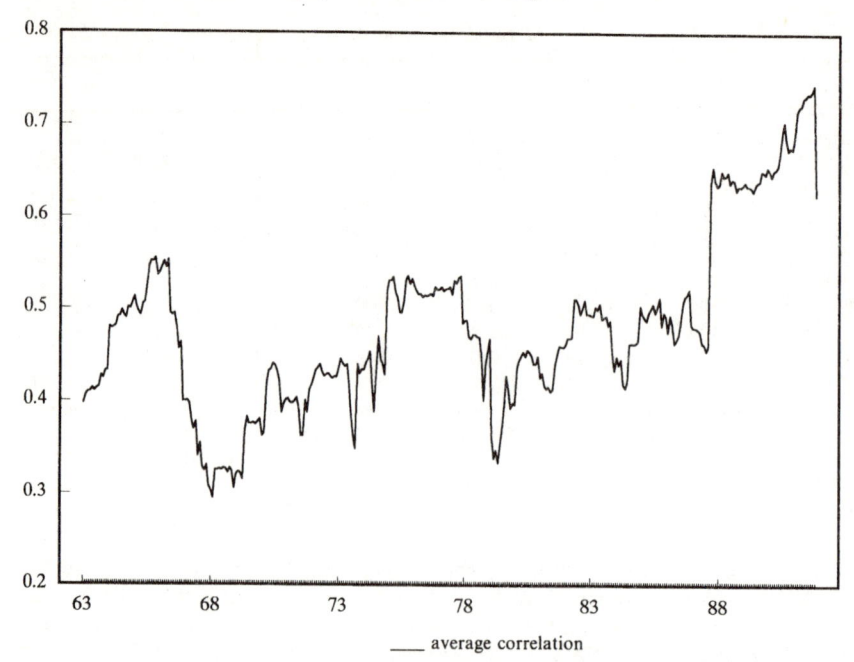

FIGURE 1. Correlation of the US stock market. This figure reports the (unweighted) average correlation of the US stock market with the other seven stock markets. The correlation is computed over sliding windows of four years, using local currency monthly total returns. The period is December 1959–91.

matrix are somewhat lower than hers; this could be explained by an increased instability in the eighties, since her data end in 1982.

What can explain this instability of the unconditional correlation matrix? A first alternative is that the conditional correlation remains constant over time but the market expected returns and variances vary over time. Indeed, we have extensive international evidence of predictable time-variations in the equity return distribution. Expected returns seem to depend worldwide on a set of information variables such as the dividend yield and various interest-rate-related variables.[4] The variance of returns has been shown to be heteroscedastic. The conditional variance of national equity markets has been modelled with good success using a univariate GARCH approach[5] for several national markets. A second alternative or, rather, additional explanation is that the interdependence of national equity markets is changing through time. Growing international integration could lead to a progressive increase in market correlation. Markets could be more highly correlated in periods of high volatility. The correlation could be higher when the markets go down, rather than up. The correlation could be higher in some periods of the business cycle, for example periods characterized by high levels of interest rates and dividend yields. These are some of the arguments often heard in financial circles.

TABLE 2. Test of the equality of the correlation and covariance matrices over time.

	Correlation matrix		Covariance matrix	
Periods compared	Test	p-value	Test	p-value
1960/65 to 1965/70	22.89	0.349	34.95	0.171
1965/70 to 1970/75	31.70	0.062	64.09	0.000
1970/75 to 1975/80	44.22	0.002	67.07	0.000
1975/80 to 1980/85	28.69	0.121	49.95	0.006
1980/85 to 1985/90	30.59	0.080	77.23	0.000
1960/65 to 1970/75	31.72	0.062	76.19	0.000
1960/65 to 1975/80	39.67	0.008	102.18	0.000
1960/65 to 1980/85	24.41	0.273	90.02	0.000
1960/65 to 1985/90	44.07	0.002	52.47	0.003
1965/70 to 1975/80	7.96	0.995	70.09	0.000
1965/70 to 1980/85	22.93	0.347	72.81	0.000
1965/70 to 1985/90	45.79	0.001	52.74	0.003
1970/75 to 1980/85	20.52	0.488	74.21	0.000
1970/75 to 1985/90	122.06	0.010	71.89	0.000
1975/80 to 1985/90	49.22	0.000	79.96	0.000

Correlation and covariance matrices of monthly national excess returns for seven countries are computed over periods of five years. We use the Jenrich test to test the equality of the correlation (and covariance) matrix over two periods. The rest is asymptotically distributed as a chi-square with 21 degrees of freedom for the correlation matrix and 28 degrees of freedom for the covariance matrix.

To test the assumption of a constant conditional correlation, we model the asset return dynamics explicitly using a bivariate GARCH model for each pair of markets. We also condition the first two moments of the distribution on a set of information variables observable at the start of the period used to calculate return, namely the dividend yield, the short- and long-term interest rates and a January seasonal. The parsimonious GARCH representation best fitted to our purpose is the GARCH constant-conditional-correlation model put forward in Bollerslev (1990). This specification has been extensively used to model international asset returns; it can be found in Ng (1991), Baillie and Bollerslev (1990) and Giovannini and Jorion (1989) among others. This will be our model of the null hypothesis of constant correlation and we will test different deviations from this model. To investigate whether the conditional correlation of markets becomes higher in turbulent periods, we develop a test on the conditional correlation inspired from the threshold GARCH models of Gouriéroux and Monfort (1992) and Engle and Ng (1993).

Looking at correlation alone one cannot reach conclusions with regard to market integration. In an asset pricing sense, markets can be fully integrated with or without correlation across asset returns. This paper focuses on the interdependence across markets and does not provide an asset pricing test of market integration.

The paper proceeds as follows. In Section I, we introduce our base model for the conditional multivariate asset process. This is a bivariate GARCH(1,1) model with information variables and constant conditional correlation. In Section II, we test various forms of deviations from constant conditional correlation. The findings are summarized in Section III.

I. Modelling the multivariate conditional return process

I.A. A multivariate conditional model

The multivariate process for asset returns can be written as:

$$R_t = m_{t-1} + e_t,$$
⟨1⟩
$$m_{t-1} = E(R_t | F_{t-1}),$$
$$e_t | F_{t-1} \sim N(0, H_t),$$

where R_t is a vector of asset excess returns (denoted R_t^i for country i), m_{t-1} is the vector of expected returns conditioned on the information set F_{t-1}, e_t is the vector of innovations or unexpected returns assumed to be conditionally normal with a conditional covariance matrix H_t. Elements of H_t are denoted $h_t^{i,j}$ for the off-diagonal terms and h_t^i for the diagonal terms (variances).

As mentioned in the introduction, there is extensive empirical evidence that expected returns depend on a set of information variables such as the dividend yield and various interest-rate related variables. The expected excess return for market i (its national risk premium) is conditioned on a set of information variables Z_{t-1}^i. We assume a linear relation between expected excess returns and the vector of information variables:

⟨2⟩
$$R_t^i = b^{i\prime} Z_{t-1}^i + e_t^i.$$

In line with some previous research (Harvey, 1991 and Solnik, 1993), we include in the information set of country i the national dividend yield, short-term and long-term interest rates as well as a January seasonal.[6] These variables are commonly used in models of the US market. We adopt the same national risk premium model for each country by using only domestic information variables. A 'better' risk premium model could certainly be found ex post but it would be the result of data mining.

We use a multivariate GARCH specification to model the time-variation in variances and also include the information variables discussed above. Several parsimonious multivariate GARCH specifications have been used in the literature. All these specifications are first-order processes denoted GARCH(1,1). To test the assumption of a constant conditional correlation across markets, we use as the null hypothesis the constant-conditional-correlation model proposed by Bollerslev (1990). We use excess equity returns in local currency. Because of interest rate parity (the forward currency basis is equal to the interest rate differential), this is equal to the currency-hedged excess return from any nationality viewpoint. This invariance to the numeraire used would not be preserved if the constant-conditional-correlation representation was written on unhedged returns.[7]

The variance term for each market is assumed to be a function of the past innovation and conditional variance of this market, as well as some national information variables. However the conditional correlation between the two markets is assumed to be constant over time:

$$\langle 3 \rangle \qquad h_t^i = a^i + b^i e_{t-1}^i e_{t-1}^i + c^i h_{t-1}^i + d^{i\prime} Z_{t-1}^i \text{ and } h_t^{i,us} = r^{i,us}\sqrt{h_t^i}\sqrt{h_t^{us}}.$$

The combination of equations $\langle 2 \rangle$ and $\langle 3 \rangle$ constitutes our base model with constant conditional correlation. We estimate this base model and then attempt to test for potential deviations from constant conditional correlation.

I.B. Estimation of the base model with constant conditional correlation

The conditional log-likelihood function at time t, $l_t(q)$, can be expressed as:

$$\langle 4 \rangle \qquad l_t(q) = -\frac{N}{2}\ln(2\pi) - \frac{N}{2}\ln|H_t| - \frac{1}{2}e_t' H_t e_t,$$

where q is the vector of all the parameters to be estimated and N the dimension of the model (the number of countries). Thus, the log-likelihood for the whole sample from time 1 to T, $L(q)$, is given by:

$$\langle 5 \rangle \qquad L(q) = \sum_{t=1}^{T} l_t(q).$$

This log-likelihood is maximized using the Berndt, Hall, Hall and Hausman (1974) algorithm[8]. A multivariate GARCH estimation with seven countries is not feasible for technical reasons as explained below. The full model would require the estimation of 98 coefficients (35 for the mean equations, 35 for the GARCH terms and the information variables in the conditional variances and 28 for the correlation coefficients). The large number of coefficients to be estimated makes the iteration process very long. Moreover the relatively small size of the database (368 observations) and the low frequency of the data (monthly observations) make the convergence of the iterative method very difficult especially if some of the coefficients are not strongly significant.[9] Hence we only conduct the estimations for country pairs. To simplify the exposition we focus on the correlation of the US market with foreign markets and hence estimate six bivariate GARCH processes. We had to estimate the GARCH models with a large number of parameters for each country pair: ten in the mean equations (five for each country), seven to model the GARCH process plus one term for each information variable in the conditional variance equation. This is very computer-time-consuming and leads to a convergence problem unless good starting values are found for the parameters. This is particularly true for the parameters in the variance equations. We use only the national dividend yield and short-term interest rate as information variables for each variance equation. This gives a total of 21 parameters to be estimated. A sufficient, but not necessary, condition for positive definitiveness of the covariance matrix is to constrain the coefficients of the information variables

TABLE 3. Estimation of the national risk premium models.

A. Return equations

	b_0	b_1	b_2	b_3	b_4	Lik
GE	0.015	2.21	−0.89	−2.74	0.014	1261.3
	(0.84)	(0.60)	(−0.43)	(−0.76)	(1.53)	
FR	0.001	5.46	1.22	−3.62	0.035	1209.9
	(0.00)	(1.84)	(0.74)	(−1.23)	(3.49)	
UK	−0.050	13.92	−2.58	2.14	0.017	1246.7
	(−4.30)	(5.14)	(−1.43)	(0.90)	(1.92)	
SW	0.013	6.94	−2.27	−4.55	0.023	1298.1
	(1.38)	(1.17)	(−1.41)	(−1.17)	(3.00)	
JA	0.012	1.22	−2.64	0.47	0.020	1255.4
	(0.90)	(0.51)	(−0.92)	(0.13)	(1.85)	
CA	−0.012	8.75	−1.24	−0.65	0.021	1406.6
	(−0.94)	(2.23)	(−0.68)	(−0.27)	(3.46)	
US	−0.021	15.16	−3.28	−0.87	0.009	
	(−2.20)	(3.69)	(−2.15)	(−0.42)	(1.49)	

B. Variance equations and correlation

	$a \cdot 10^3$	b	c	d_1	d_2	r
GE	0.705	0.130	0.740	−0.184	0.053	0.353
	(1.91)	(2.57)	(8.75)	(−1.92)	(1.66)	(8.39)
FR	0.558	0.086	0.657	0.009	0.037	0.407
	(1.00)	(1.38)	(2.35)	(0.11)	(0.68)	(8.54)
UK	0.199	0.118	0.630	−0.018	0.079	0.469
	(0.57)	(1.70)	(3.61)	(−0.22)	(1.76)	(11.4)
SW	0.193	0.010	0.975	−0.091	0.015	0.508
	(2.95)	(0.12)	(86.6)	(−4.46)	(4.28)	(15.3)
JA	−0.007	0.070	0.901	−0.002	0.016	0.297
	(−0.01)	(2.62)	(22.9)	(−0.17)	(1.07)	(5.43)
CA	−0.55	0.125	0.435	0.225	0.126	0.723
	(−1.18)	(2.28)	(1.80)	(1.20)	(1.98)	(28.5)
US	0.271	0.055	0.747	−0.044	0.035	
	(1.09)	(1.58)	(4.34)	(−0.64)	(1.16)	

Estimation of bivariate projections:

$$R_t^i = b_0^i + b_1^i \, DIV_{t-1}^i + b_2^i ST_{t-1}^i + b_3^i LT_{t-1}^i + b_4^i JAN_t + e_t^i \quad \langle 2 \rangle$$

$$h_t^i = a^i + b^i e_{t-1}^i e_{t-1}^i + c^i h_{t-1}^i + d^{i'} Z_{t-1}^i \quad \text{and} \quad h_t^{i,us} = r^{i,us} \sqrt{h_t^i} \sqrt{h_t^{us}} \quad \langle 3 \rangle$$

where R_t^i is the excess return for market i in period t, h_t^i is the conditional variance of market i, $h_t^{i,us}$ is the conditional covariance between market i and the US DIV_{t-1}^i, ST_{t-1}^i, LT_{t-1}^i and JAN_t are respectively the dividend yield, the short-term interest rate, the long-term interest rate of country i observed in $t-1$ and a January dummy that takes the value one if t is the month of January and zero otherwise. The t-statistics adjusted for heteroscedasticity are reported in parentheses. Lik is the value of the log-likelihood of the bivariate models. The period of estimation is 1/1960–8/1990. Estimation results for the USA are those obtained for the UK/US pair.

to be all positive as the variables are always positive. This is not satisfactory from an economic viewpoint as it would rule out the possibility of a negative influence of one of the variables on the variance or covariance. Negative coefficients could still lead to positive definitiveness of the covariance matrix over the sample space. In practice, we never encountered the problem of a negative conditional variance in our sample or for any plausible value of the information variables.

Results of the estimation are given in Table 3. The top panel gives the parameters of the mean equations. The bottom panel gives the parameters of the covariance equations. As mentioned above, these are the results of a bivariate estimation of the USA and a foreign country. The last line gives the results of the estimation of the USA derived from the UK/US estimation. The values for the USA derived from the other bivariate models are very similar.

The results for the conditional expected returns (Panel A) confirm previous findings. The coefficients of the dividend yield tend to be positive and the coefficients of the short-term interest rate tend to be negative; there is a positive January seasonal in all countries.

The coefficients for the variance equations (Panel B) show significant GARCH effects for many countries. The dividend yield tends to have mixed signs[10] in the variance equations. There is one negative coefficient for Switzerland, statistically significant at the 1 percent level. The interest rate has a positive coefficient in all variance equations. The coefficients have the same sign for each country, but their significance level is somewhat marginal. The fact that the conditional variance is predictably lower in periods of high dividend yields could have a plausible explanation: with high dividend yields, more of the current value of a firm is derived from near-term dividends, which can be regarded as more predictable than remote future dividends. The positive relation between volatility and interest rate levels is not surprising either. Inflationary periods lead to higher volatility in financial prices.

We test the significance of the various factors by estimating three nested models. The simplest model is the bivariate homoscedastic model with no information variables; it requires the estimation of only two unconditional mean terms and three covariance terms. Its computed likelihood function is referred to as Lik1. The second model is a bivariate homoscedastic model with information variables in the mean equation. Its computed likelihood function is referred to as Lik2. The base model is the bivariate GARCH(1,1) with information variables in the mean and variance equations and constant conditional correlation. The estimation of this base model is reported in Table 3 and the computed likelihood function is referred to as Lik3. The three specifications are nested, so we can perform likelihood-ratio tests (LR test hereafter).

The results reported in Table 4 indicate that both the modelling of the conditional expected return and variance are significant. The first section of Table 4 gives the value of the likelihood function of the simple bivariate homoscedastic model. The second section gives the value of the likelihood function of the bivariate homoscedastic model with information variables in the mean, as well as the p-value of the LR test against the null of the simple model. The hypothesis of a constant expected return is rejected at the 1 percent level in all cases. The third

TABLE 4. Likelihood ratio tests of bivariate GARCH specifications.

	1. Log-likelihood of bivariate homoscedastic					
Market	GE/US	FR/US	UK/US	SW/US	JA/US	CA/US
Lik1	1225.5	1186.9	1184.5	1264.4	1228.1	1355.6
	2. Bivariate conditional mean/homoscedastic					
Market	GE/US	FR/US	UK/US	SW/US	JA/US	CA/US
Lik2	1237.5	1200.2	1204.2	1282.2	1246.0	1368.9
p-value/model 1	0.002	0.001	0.000	0.000	0.000	0.001
			3. Base model			
Market	GE/US	FR/US	UK/US	SW/US	JA/US	CA/US
Lik3	1261.3	1209.9	1246.7	1298.1	1255.4	1406.6
p-value/model 1	0.000	0.000	0.000	0.000	0.000	0.000
p-value/model 2	0.000	0.013	0.000	0.001	0.016	0.000

section gives the value of the likelihood function of the base model as well as LR test against the alternative of the two homoscedastic models. Both simpler models are rejected. We see that the hypothesis of constant variances is rejected at the 5 percent level in all cases. It should be stressed that we estimate bivariate models of the US and foreign equity markets; the predictability in the conditional US expected return and variance affects the significance levels reported for each bivariate estimation.

We can test whether the estimated GARCH parametrization provides an adequate description of the heteroscedasticity by performing Ljung–Box portmanteau misspecification tests on the squared residuals as suggested by Li and McLeod (1983). This test is performed on the standardized squared residuals of country i, $e_t^i e_t^i / h_t^i$, obtained for the constant correlation specification. The Ljung–Box statistics with 20 lags ranges from 7 to 15 for the six country-pairs, while the 5 percent critical level is 31.44. We cannot reject the specification of variances at this confidence level for any country. A more direct test has been suggested by Bollerslev (1990). The GARCH parametrization assumes that all relevant past information F_{t-1} is reflected in the GARCH estimate of the variance H_{t-1}:

$$\langle 6 \rangle \qquad E(e_t^i \cdot e_t^j | F_{t-1}) = h_t^{i,j}.$$

This can be tested by including in the information set F_{t-1} past residuals and regressing $e_t^i e_t^i / h_t^i - 1$ on $1/h_t^i$, $e_{t-1}^i e_{t-1}^i / h_t^i, \ldots, e_{t-k}^i e_{t-k}^i \cdot 2/h_t^i$. Stopping at $k = 5$, we test whether the estimated regression coefficients are different from zero with a F-test. The 5 percent critical value for a F(6,361) is 2.13. The F-tests reported in Table 5 range from 0.28 for Canada to 1.61 for France and do not lead to a rejection of the constant correlation specification. A similar test is performed for the cross-product of residuals. We regress $e_t^i \cdot e_t^j / h_t^{i,j} - 1$ on $1/h_t^{i,j}$, $e_{t-1}^i \cdot e_{t-1}^j / h_t^{i,j}, \ldots, e_{t-5}^i \cdot e_{t-5}^j / h_t^{i,j}$ as well as $e_{t-1}^i e_{t-1}^i / h_t^{i,j}$ and $e_{t-1}^j e_{t-1}^j / h_t^{i,j}$. The 5 percent critical value for a F(8,359) is 1.97 and all F-tests fall below that value as seen in Table 5. Altogether, no evidence is found to reject our base model, using

Is the correlation in international equity returns constant?: F Longin and B Solnik

TABLE 5. Heteroscedasticity specification tests.

Squared residuals	GE	FR	UK	SW	JA	CA	US
F-test	0.571	1.611	1.374	0.469	0.896	0.283	0.518
p-value	(0.754)	(0.143)	(0.224)	(0.831)	(0.498)	(0.945)	(0.794)
Cross-product	GE/US	FR/US	UK/US	SW/US	JA/US	CA/US	
F-test	0.592	0.658	0.825	1.195	1.296	0.451	
p-value	(0.785)	(0.728)	(0.581)	(0.301)	(0.244)	(0.890)	

This table gives the results of heteroscedasticity specification tests as suggested in Bollersleu (1990). Standardized squared residuals and cross-product of residuals are regressed on lagged variables. The residuals are from the base model (a bivariate GARCH (1, 1) with constant conditional correlation). F-tests are reported with their *p*-values in parentheses.

standard heteroscedasticity tests. However, more powerful tests can be designed, by an explicit modelling of the deviations from our constant correlation base model.

II. Is the conditional correlation constant?

There are many reasons why the international market correlation should not remain constant over time. We examine three potential sources of deviation from our base model of constant conditional correlation: a time trend, the presence of threshold and asymmetry, and the influence of economic variables. Due to the large number of parameters to be estimated we have to study separately each cause of deviation from the base model.

II.A. A time trend

It is often stated that the progressive removal of impediments to international investment as well as the growing political, economic and financial integration affects international market linkages. More integrated economies could mean that national firms are more and more influenced by global factors. The extent of international activities by companies themselves is growing. Most companies can now be regarded as a diversified portfolio of international activities through their exports and through foreign implantation. Their stock price should behave like that of an internationally diversified portfolio and, hence, be more correlated with that of other firms worldwide. This could lead to a progressive increase in the international correlation of equity markets.

We use our long period of time to test this increase in correlation. There are no specific events (or too many of them) that should be used as cutoff points or structural breaks (the monthly frequency of our data would also limit the power of studies over short sub-periods). We use a simple test to detect a progressive increase in correlation over the past 30 years. We augment our base model to include a linear time-trend in the correlation specification and test the null hypothesis that this coefficient is zero. In other words, the covariance term of equation ⟨3⟩ is now written as:

⟨7⟩ $$h_t^{i,us} = (r_0^{i,us} + r_1^{i,us}t)\sqrt{h_t^i}\sqrt{h_t^{us}}.$$

To remove potential biases created by a structural increase in conditional variance, we also add a trend term in each variance equation. Needless to say, this specification is a simplistic modelling of the increase in correlation over time, and other specifications of the trend could have been used. In the absence of a formal model, our sole purpose is to test the existence of a trend. Estimation of the augmented model are reported in Table 6, where we only report the coefficients of the time trends. The coefficients for the variances are small and statistically insignificant. There is no secular increase in expected market volatility. The GARCH(1,1) specification seems to adequately capture the time evolution of the market variances and no additional time-trend needs to be added in the variance equation. The conclusion is quite different for the correlation, and hence the covariance, across markets. There is a positive time-trend in conditional correlation for all countries. The trend is statistically significant at the 5 percent level for four countries out of six. A similar conclusion is obtained if we estimate a GARCH model with a trend solely in the correlation but not in the variances. In other words, the international correlation seems to be increasing over time, even after the variance terms have been modelled with a GARCH parametrization. The average increase in correlation over 30 years is 0.36, or slightly more than 0.01 per year. Obviously such a constant linear trend is not consistent with the definition of a correlation coefficient. Other forms of trend could be modelled, but no theory exists of the exact form of this trend. We tried an exponential trend

TABLE 6. Time-trend in correlation.

Market	GE/US	FR/US	UK/US	SW/US	JA/US	CA/US
d^i	0.01	0.21	0.35	−0.00	0.01	0.07
	(0.44)	(0.98)	(1.75)	(−0.03)	(0.43)	(1.70)
d^{us}	0.17	0.15	0.20	0.17	0.23	0.10
	(1.03)	(0.96)	(1.06)	(0.96)	(1.05)	(1.52)
r_0	0.27	0.13	0.09	0.41	0.10	0.65
	(3.16)	(1.22)	(0.95)	(5.39)	(0.99)	(11.61)
r_1	0.20	0.49	0.76	0.25	0.38	0.16
	(1.55)	(3.15)	(6.13)	(2.40)	(2.33)	(1.82)
LR test	10.0	17.4	30.4	11.2	17.8	11.2
p-value	(0.019)	(0.001)	(0.000)	(0.011)	(0.001)	(0.011)

This table gives the estimates of the augmented model with time-trend. This model is similar to the base model with an additional time-trend in the variance equations (d^i for country i and d^{us} for the US) and in the correlation. The correlation is now estimated as:

$$h_t^{i,us} = (r_0^{i,us} + r_1^{i,us}t)\sqrt{h_t^i}\sqrt{h_t^{us}}$$ ⟨7⟩

T-statistics appear below the estimated coefficients. The likelihood ratio (p-value in parentheses) is a test of the augmented model against the base model.

of the form by modelling the correlation as follows:

$$\langle 8 \rangle \qquad h_t^{i,us} = (r^{i,us} + r^{i,us}(1 - e^{-at}))\sqrt{h_t^i}\sqrt{h_t^{us}}.$$

If a is positive, correlation varies from r at the beginning of the period to $r_0 + r_1(1 - e^{-aT})$ at the end of the period T; if the two bounds r_0 and $r_0 + r_1$ are between -1 and $+1$, then the correlation is always defined. To assure the convergence of the algorithm, a constraint can be imposed on r_0 and $r_0 + r_1$ such that the correlation is always defined. Empirically for the pair JA/US, we found a correlation increasing from -0.397 to 0.356 at an exponential rate 11.818.[11] For the other pairs of countries, the constraints were binding out of sample (GE/US and FR/US) or in sample (UK/US, SW/US and CA/US) with a negative value for the rate of convergence ($a < 0$). Such a result could be explained by a sharp increase in correlation at the end of the period (the eighties). The proposed simple econometric methodology (a linear time-trend) however satisfies our objective to test, and reject, the null hypothesis of a constant conditional correlation.

II.B. Threshold and asymmetry in the conditional correlation

International market linkages are due to common factors that affect all economies at the same time. It is often claimed that there are periods when international factors dominate purely domestic factors and vice versa.

The constant correlation GARCH model assumes that the conditional covariance, $h_t^{i,us}$, estimated from information available at time $t - 1$, is equal to a constant correlation times the product of the two conditional standard deviations $\sqrt{h_t^i}\sqrt{h_t^{us}}$ following a first order GARCH process. It is often claimed that the international correlation increases in periods of high market turbulence, when international factors dominate. For example, all markets went down together during the second oil shock of 1974 and in October 1987, and went up at the end of the Gulf War. This hypothesis can be tested by introducing a threshold in the constant correlation GARCH model. Threshold GARCH models have been extensively used in the univariate case but not in the multivariate case (see Appendix B for a discussion and results of the univariate asymmetric threshold GARCH model for the seven countries under study). To test the hypothesis of higher international correlation during turbulent periods, we introduce a threshold effect in our bivariate constant correlation GARCH specification. With this threshold on correlation, the covariance term of the GARCH specification can be written as:

$$\langle 9 \rangle \qquad h_t^{i,us} = (r_0^{i,us} + r_1^{i,us}S_{t-1})\sqrt{h_t^i}\sqrt{h_t^{us}},$$

where S_{t-1} is a dummy variable that takes the value 1 if the estimated conditional variance of the US market is greater than its unconditional value and 0 otherwise. The unconditional variance of innovations from the base model is taken as the exogenous threshold. In other words, the time-t international correlation is conditional on the time-t volatility of the US market; note that both the correlation and the US volatility are estimated using only information observable at time $t - 1$. The coefficient r_1 will be positive if the correlation increases when the conditional US variance is high; it will be zero if there is no threshold effect.

TABLE 7. Threshold in correlation.

	r_0	r_1	r	LR test (p-value)
GE/US	0.327	0.134	0.353	2.4
	(5.52)	(1.75)		(0.121)
FR/US	0.331	0.194	0.407	4.8
	(5.44)	(2.43)		(0.028)
UK/US	0.468	0.057	0.469	0.6
	(9.34)	(0.74)		(0.438)
SW/US	0.458	0.192	0.508	8.0
	(8.70)	(3.12)		(0.010)
JA/US	0.265	0.101	0.297	2.2
	(3.82)	(0.99)		(0.138)
CA/US	0.729	0.024	0.723	1.0
	(26.02)	(0.65)		(0.317)

The table gives the estimation of the bivariate GARCH(1,1) models with threshold correlation. The correlation is conditioned on the size of the US expected variance:

$$h_t^{i,us} = (r_0^{i,us} + r_1^{i,us} S_{t-1})\sqrt{h_t^i}\sqrt{h_t^{us}} \qquad (9)$$

The coefficient r is the estimate from the base model with constant correlation, as given in Table 3. The likelihood ratio test from the base model with constant correlation is indicated in the last column, with p-value in parentheses.

The results of the estimation of the threshold correlation specification are reported in Table 7. The estimated coefficient r_1 is positive for all countries and individually significant at the 5 percent confidence level in two cases. The magnitude of the coefficient is quite large in most cases. We can illustrate the results in the case of France. The constant correlation estimated was equal to 0.407; this compares with a constant term r_0 of 0.331 and a turbulence effect r_1 of 0.194. In other words the correlation is estimated to be equal to 0.331 in periods of low volatility and 0.525 in periods of high volatility. The average correlation in the six country-pairs was equal to 0.460 when using the constant correlation model. The average over all countries of the correlation r_0 is equal to 0.430 while the average turbulence effect r_1 is equal to 0.117. The correlation coefficient seems to increase by about 27 percent in periods of high turbulence.

We only introduced one exogenous threshold arbitrarily set at the unconditional variance. We would have liked to use several thresholds but were limited by the size of our database to get reliable statistical results. We also replicated these tests by conditioning the correlation on the conditional variance of the foreign market rather than that of the US market. The conclusions were quite similar and the results are not reported here.

We can say more about correlation by looking at asymmetry. In the previous threshold GARCH model, a positive or negative shock (e_{t-1}) observed at time $t-1$ has the same impact on correlation. It is interesting to test whether negative and positive shocks have a different impact on the conditional correlation. Rather than conditioning the correlation on the US market volatility (and hence indirectly on the absolute magnitude of e_{t-1}^{us}), we condition the correlation on both the sign and magnitude of past[12] shocks e_{t-1}^{us}. This threshold, asymmetric correlation GARCH specification can be written as:

$$h_t^{i,us} = (r_1^{i,us}S_{1,t-1} + r_2^{i,us}S_{2,t-1} + r_3^{i,us}S_{3,t-1} + r_4^{i,us}S_{4,t-1})\sqrt{h_t^i}\sqrt{h_t^{us}}, \quad \langle 10 \rangle$$

where $S_{k,t-1}$ are dummy variables that take the values:
$S_{1,t-1} = 1$ if e_{t-1}^{us} is less than $-\sigma^{us}$,
$S_{2,t-1} = 1$ if e_{t-1}^{us} is less than 0,
$S_{3,t-1} = 1$ if e_{t-1}^{us} is greater than 0,
$S_{4,t-1} = 1$ if e_{t-1}^{us} is greater than $+\sigma^{us}$,
and zero otherwise.

σ^{us} (the unconditional standard deviation of the innovations e^{us} from the base model), $-\sigma^{us}$ and zero are the exogenous thresholds used for the augmented model. Note that two dummy variables will be equal to one for large negative shocks ($S_{1,t-1}$ and $S_{2,t-1}$) and for large positive shocks ($S_{3,t-1}$ and $S_{4,t-1}$). This model allows one to capture asymmetry in the impact of shocks ($r_2 \neq r_3$) and different impacts for large and small shocks ($r_1 \neq 0$ and $r_4 \neq 0$). If the impact of small and large shocks are similar, we should find that the two coefficients r_1 and r_4 are equal to zero.

The results are reported in Table 8. The results confirm the previous findings. Several coefficients r_1 and r_4 are significantly positive, indicating that large shocks

TABLE 8. Asymmetry in correlation.

	r_1	r_2	r_3	r_4	LR test (p-value)
GE/US	0.307	0.313	0.327	0.304	10.2
	(2.95)	(5.10)	(3.76)	(2.33)	(0.016)
FR/US	0.165	0.365	0.309	0.345	6.2
	(1.59)	(5.92)	(3.73)	(2.92)	(0.102)
UK/US	0.005	0.489	0.452	0.117	0.6
	(0.05)	(8.34)	(6.64)	(0.91)	(0.896)
SW/US	0.282	0.468	0.544	−0.003	10.2
	(3.54)	(8.60)	(8.95)	(−0.36)	(0.016)
JA/US	−0.201	0.329	0.332	0.084	2.8
	(−1.20)	(3.82)	(4.67)	(0.46)	(0.423)
CA/US	−0.115	0.780	0.749	−0.099	4.8
	(−1.64)	(27.06)	(25.40)	(−1.29)	(0.187)

This table gives the estimation of a bivariate asymmetric correlation GARCH(1,1) where the correlation is modelled as:

$$h_t^{i,us} = (r_1^{i,us}S_{1,t-1} + r_2^{i,us}S_{2,t-1} + r_3^{i,us}S_{3,t-1} + r_4^{i,us}S_{4,t-1})\sqrt{h_t^i}\sqrt{h_t^{us}} \quad \langle 10 \rangle$$

The correlation is conditioned on the sign and size of past US shocks. No asymmetry corresponds to the case: $r_1 = r_4$ and $r_2 = r_3$. No threshold effect corresponds to the case: $r_1 = r_4 = 0$. The likelihood ratio test comparing the asymmetric model to the base model with constant correlation is indicated in the last column, with p-value in parentheses.

tend to increase the conditional correlation. However we have little evidence of asymmetry as the coefficients r_2 and r_3 are quite similar; furthermore we find no evidence that the coefficient r_1 is systematically greater than r_4. The correlation seems to increase in periods of high turbulence (following large positive or negative shocks) but is no more sensitive to negative than to positive shocks.[13]

II.C. Influence of information variables on correlation

We have seen that the information variables affect the conditional covariance matrix. Even with a constant correlation, the conditional covariance between two national markets is a function of the information variables, as each national conditional standard deviation is. For example, if all national variances increase in periods of high interest rates, the covariances will increase in parallel. The remaining question is whether the covariances will increase more (or less) than the variances. This can be investigated by testing an augmented model, identical to the base model but with the hypothesis that the conditional correlation itself is predictable based on past values of the information variables. Hence the covariance equation in model $\langle 3 \rangle$ is replaced by:

$$\langle 11 \rangle \qquad h_t^{i,us} = (r' + g_1^{i,us} DIV_{t-1}^{us} + g_2^{i,us} ST_{t-1}^{us}) \sqrt{h_t^i} \sqrt{h_t^{us}}.$$

The information set is supposed to be equal to the US dividend yield and interest rate. Estimates of the correlation parameters are given in Table 9. This table also gives a likelihood-ratio test of the augmented model against the base model. Several of the coefficients g's are significant at the 5 percent level but not at the 1 percent level. The p-values of the likelihood ratio tests show a rejection of the base model for half of the country-pairs at the 5 percent level. With one

TABLE 9. Information variables in correlation.

Market	GE/US	FR/US	UK/US	SW/US	JA/US	CA/US
r'	0.467	0.248	0.684	0.355	0.375	0.936
	(2.24)	(1.41)	(4.35)	(2.68)	(1.78)	(9.27)
g_1	−114.4	−8.47	−157.6	1.37	−147.7	−96.2
	(−1.32)	(−0.11)	(−2.16)	(0.02)	(−1.85)	(−2.17)
g_2	43.5	25.3	47.8	27.8	63.3	15.9
	(2.23)	(1.49)	(2.91)	(2.21)	(3.33)	(1.36)
LR test	0.0	0.2	7.6	9.6	8.6	5.6
p-value	(0.999)	(0.999)	(0.022)	(0.008)	(0.013)	(0.060)

This table gives the estimates of the augmented model with information variables (US dividend yield and US short-term interest rate) in the conditional correlation. The conditional correlation is now estimated as:

$$h_t^{i,us} = (r' + g_1^{i,us} DIV_{t-1}^{us} + g_2^{i,us} ST_{t-1}^{us}) \sqrt{h_t^i} \sqrt{h_t^{us}} \qquad \langle 11 \rangle$$

T-statistics appear below the estimated coefficients. The likelihood ratio (p-value in parentheses) is a test of the augmented model against the base model.

exception, the sign pattern is consistent. The conditional correlation is predicted to increase in periods of low dividend yield and high interest rates.

This result is consistent with the relation between conditional correlation and variance found in the previous section. For example, we found that the conditional variance increases with the level of interest rates and that the correlation increases in periods of high volatility. We confirm here that the conditional correlation is higher in periods of high interest rates.

III. Summary and conclusions

We studied the correlation of monthly excess returns for seven major countries over the period 1960-90. We find that the international covariance and correlation matrices are unstable over time. A multivariate GARCH(1,1) model with constant conditional correlation helps capture some of the evolution in the conditional covariance structure. We include information variables in the mean and variance equations. The volatility of markets changed somewhat over the period 1960-90 and the proposed GARCH model allows one to capture this evolution in variances. However tests of specific deviations lead to a rejection of the hypothesis of a constant conditional correlation. An explicit model of the conditional correlation indicates an increase in the international correlation between markets over the past 30 years. We also find that the correlation rises in periods when the conditional volatility of markets is large. There is some preliminary evidence that economic variables such as the dividend yield and interest rates contain information about future volatility and correlation that is not contained in past returns alone. However, further theoretical work is required to provide a satisfactory model. The effects are not of great magnitude but are often statistically significant.

Our results confirm and complete some previous findings mentioned in the introduction. These studies (e.g. Koch and Koch 1991, and Von Furstenberg and Jeon, 1989) typically computed correlation coefficients over short sub-periods, using high-frequency data, and then looked at their evolution over time. Here we explicitly model the multivariate asset return process and use a much longer time period. In their APT test of global market integration, King et al. (1992) briefly looked at changes in conditional correlation. They also explicitly model the conditional correlation, using monthly data over the period 1970-88. In both cases, a very parsimonious parametrization is used, but the models for the covariance and correlation are different. They assume that the national markets are correlated through common factors with constant factor loadings. In their factor model, the correlation can only increase over time if the variances of the common factor increase relative to the national residual variances. King et al. (1992) calculated the monthly conditional correlation and found only a modest (negligible) increase over time, without explicit significance test. A secular trend due to increased international market integration, or transitory changes due to business cycles, cannot be modelled[14] and tested. On the other hand, our parsimonious parametrization allows a direct test of the existence of a time trend and various influences in the conditional correlation. We do find evidence of predictable components in the time-variation of international correlation.

Some words of caution are in order. We are able to reject the hypothesis of constant international correlation but fall short of a full model. We test separately several deviations from a constant correlation model because the econometric methodology used does not allow us to include all of them in a single model. In our GARCH equation, we allowed the coefficients of the (positive) information variables to be negative. This means that the covariance matrix could lose its positive-definitiveness for some large values of the dividend yield. Negative coefficients could still lead to positive-definitiveness of the covariance matrix over the sample space. In practice, we never encountered the problem of a negative conditional variance in our sample or for any plausible value of the information variables and we felt that there was no economic rationale to rule out negative coefficients. The next step would be to describe the evolution in correlation over time by a richer model than the linear (or exponential) time-trend used in the hypothesis testing. Some form of event modelling would be more satisfactory if structural breaking points could be identified. Indicators such as the number of restrictions to free capital movements could also be used.

The methodology developed in this paper could be a useful basis for a more detailed study of the international integration of financial markets. However such conclusions cannot be reached by looking at the correlation alone and an international asset pricing model must be explicitly used. The methodology could also be applied to other areas of finance in which correlation is involved, such as the pricing of financial instruments like differential swaps or options on multiple assets.

Future research should also focus on the fundamental determinants of international correlation across equity markets. This correlation is likely to be affected by the industry mix of each national market as well as the correlation of the countries' business cycles.

Appendix A: Data description

The data on international financial markets vary greatly in terms of availability, quality and comparability. We have chosen to restrict the time period and the number of countries selected to insure good quality of the data. We get good month-end data for stock prices, as well as dividend yield, long- and short-term market interest rates used as instruments, for the seven major financial markets over the period January 1960 to August 1990. The countries are: France (FR), Germany (GE), Switzerland (SW), UK (UK), Japan (JA), Canada (CA) and the USA (US). These are the seven largest markets in terms of size and their combined stock market capitalization is more than 90 percent of that of the world. In many tables, these countries will be called by the letters indicated in parentheses.

Common stock returns: Month-end stock market indices calculated in local currency come from Morgan Stanley Capital International (MSCI). The MSCI sample covers around 65 percent of each market capitalization, with an attempt to stratify their sampling by industry breakdown so that each industry is represented in the national index in proportion to its national weight; hence the selection of individual companies is not solely based on their market capitalization. The data since 1970 is publicly available and widely used; the price indices from 1960 to 1969 were back-calculated by MSCI.[15] For each market we calculated a time-series of monthly excess returns in local currency. These are returns in excess of the risk-free rate of the country considered; the short-term interest rates used as risk-free rates are described below. We use returns in local currency to focus on the correlation across markets[16] rather than across currencies.

Dividend yield: The dividend yields are calculated in the usual fashion by averaging the dividend paid over the past twelve months. These data are published by MSCI since 1970. For the period 1960-69, we collected dividend yields from various sources. The major source is the OECD, but we also checked with local statistical publications for each country.

Long-term interest rates: We use the yield-to-maturity on long-term Government bonds. The maturity ranges from 5 to 15 years depending on the country. From 1971 on, we use bond yield indices calculated by Lombard Odier. These bond yields are calculated daily from a small sample of plain-vanilla, actively traded, long-term government bonds in each currency. While the number of bonds in each index is limited, the bond prices and yields are current. These indices have been published daily in the Wall Street Journal (Europe) since the early eighties. Prior to 1971, we use average long-term bond yields published by Morgan Guaranty. Free and active bond markets did not develop in many countries until the 1970s. Hence the quality of the yields prior to 1970 is less reliable for some of the countries under study.

Short-term interest rates: We use one-month Eurocurrency interest rates as risk-free rates. These are the only true market rates[17] for many countries and they are fully comparable. The data come from Morgan Guaranty and Lombard Odier for the period 1970-90 and from the OECD for the period 1960-70. An active Eurocurrency market did not exist prior to 1971 for most currencies. Hence we used domestic interest rates on instruments that were priced on a free money market. This means that these rates are not fully comparable across countries as these instruments differ in terms of characteristics and fiscal treatment. This is not a serious problem for our study as we never engage in the calculation of interest rate differentials or in international comparisons of interest rates.

Appendix B: Threshold and asymmetry in the expected variance

The traditional GARCH models have the property that the impact of the past shock e_{t-1} on the conditional variance (represented by the degree of persistence b) is independent of the sign and the size of the shock. For example a univariate GARCH(1,1) model has a conditional variance equation of the form:

$$\langle B1 \rangle \qquad h_t = a + be_{t-1}^2 + ch_{t-1}.$$

This specification imposes two constraints on the impact of past innovations, e_{t-1}, on the conditional variance h_t. First, negative and positive innovations have the same influence, only the absolute value of the shock matters. Second, the persistence of a shock is the same whatever the magnitude of the past shock; larger innovations create more volatility at a rate proportional to the square of the size of the innovation. These properties have been criticized and several extensions have been proposed for univariate GARCH specifications. There are many ways to introduce asymmetry (elasticity function of the sign of the shock) and thresholds (elasticity function of the magnitude of the past variance and of the shock) in univariate GARCH models. One approach is to specify a particular non-linear function of past shocks and variances (e.g. Nelson, 1991, Glosten *et al.*, 1993 and Hentschel, 1991). Another approach is to specify a piece-wise linear function with arbitrary threshold levels (Engle and Ng, 1993, Zakoïan, 1990, Rabemananjara and Zakoïan, 1991 and Gouriéroux and Monfort, 1992). Thresholds are exogenous to assure the efficiency of the estimators (see Friedman and Laibson, 1989 for an endogenous threshold). The basic idea is to allow different impact coefficients b for different signs and values of the past innovation e_{t-1}. An asymmetric, threshold GARCH(1,1) univariate specification that accounts for a differential impact of the past innovation, depending on its sign and magnitude, is:

⟨B2⟩
$$h_t = a' + b_1 S_{1,t-1}(e_{t-1}^2 - \sigma^2) + b_2 S_{2,t-1} e_{t-1}^2 + b_3 S_{3,t-1} e_{t-1}^2 + b_4 S_{4,t-1}(e_{t-1}^2 - \sigma^2) + c' h_{t-1}$$

where $S_{k,t-1}$ are dummy variables that take the values:
$S_{1,t-1} = 1$ if e_{t-1} is less than $-\sigma$,
$S_{2,t-1} = 1$ if e_{t-1} is less than 0,
$S_{3,t-1} = 1$ if e_{t-1} is greater than 0,
$S_{4,t-1} = 1$ if e_{t-1} is greater than σ,
and zero otherwise.

σ (the unconditional standard deviation of the innovations e from the GARCH model), $-\sigma$ and zero are the exogenous thresholds used in this threshold, asymmetric model. Note that two dummy variables will be equal to one for large positive or negative innovations. This model allows us to capture asymmetry in the impact of innovation ($b_2 \neq b_3$) and different impacts for large and small news ($b_1 \neq 0$ and $b_4 \neq 0$). If the impact of small and large innovations are similar, we should find that the two coefficients b_1 and b_4 are equal to zero; on the other side, it is often claimed that large shocks should have a shorter persistence than small shocks (b_1 and b_2 negative). Similarly, it is often stated (see Black, 1976, Nelson, 1990 and Campbell and Hentschel, 1992) that negative news should increase volatility more than positive news ($b_2 > b_3$). A sufficient condition for the positiveness[18] of the conditional variance is that $b_1 + b_2 > 0$ and $b_3 + b_4 > 0$.

The results of the estimation of the univariate threshold GARCH specification are given in Table 10. The mean equation includes the information variables as before, and only the

TABLE 10. Threshold and asymmetry in the conditional variance.

	b_1	b_2	b_3	b_4	b'	Lik	Lik'	LR test (p-value)
GE	−0.055	0.141	0.281	−0.260	0.105	588.3	584.5	7.6
	(−0.43)	(1.47)	(2.44)	(−1.95)	(3.19)			(0.055)
FR	−0.348	0.424	0.145	−0.129	0.139	535.6	530.1	11.0
	(−1.97)	(2.71)	(0.81)	(0.54)	(2.00)			(0.011)
UK	0.480	−0.051	0.398	−0.378	0.232	555.6	549.0	13.0
	(1.75)	(−0.37)	(2.82)	(−2.38)	(2.39)			(0.005)
SW	−0.085	0.066	0.209	−0.258	0.058	588.3	581.7	13.2
	(−1.34)	(1.21)	(3.94)	(−3.59)	(2.46)			(0.004)
JA	0.205	−0.128	0.187	−0.233	0.067	602.4	591.4	22.0
	(1.93)	(−1.34)	(2.29)	(−2.57)	(2.41)			(0.000)
CA	−0.131	0.146	0.165	−0.117	0.080	611.7	610.5	2.4
	(−1.05)	(1.45)	(1.52)	(−0.89)	(2.89)			(0.493)
US	−0.241	0.250	−0.032	0.135	0.058	649.3	643.4	11.8
	(−2.11)	(2.55)	(−0.45)	(2.11)	(2.12)			(0.008)

The table gives the estimation of the univariate GARCH(1,1) model with threshold, asymmetric conditional variance. The variance is conditioned on the sign and the size of the past innovation and on the past conditional variance. The coefficients b_k ($k = 1, 2, 3, 4$) capture the asymmetry in the conditional variance. b_1 and b_4 capture the size effect and b_2 and b_3 the sign effect. The t-statistics are reported in parentheses. No asymmetry corresponds to the case: $b_1 = b_4 = 0$ and $b_2 = b_3 = b'$. Lik and Lik' are the values of the log-likelihood function of the unconstrained and constrained GARCH(1,1) models. The likelihood ratio test (LR test) is indicated in the last column with the p-value in parentheses. The statistics of the test follows asymptotically a chi-square with 3 degrees of freedom.

estimated b coefficients are reported in the first four columns of the table. The next column recalls the single coefficient b' of the univariate GARCH without thresholds. The log-likelihood are reported for the threshold GARCH (Lik) and simple GARCH (Lik') specifications, as well as a likelihood ratio test between the two specifications (3 degrees of freedom). Significant threshold effects are found for a majority of the countries. Most authors found that negative news had a stronger impact on the volatility in the case of the US stock market. Our data for the USA confirm that finding ($b_2 > b_3$), but we cannot reach the same conclusion for other countries except France. On the other side, the coefficients for large shocks are negative in 11 out of 14 cases, providing evidence that large shocks have a smaller persistence than small shocks.

Notes

1. The use of a time-varying conditional covariance/correlation matrix can be found in studies based on international asset pricing models (see Engel and Rodrigues, 1989 and Chan et al., 1992 for example).
2. Kaplanis (1988) also used a stability test designed by Box (1949) for the covariance matrix. The results are quite similar. Both tests are asymptotically equivalent but their small-sample properties are not known. We conducted both types of tests on our data with similar conclusions and only reported the Jenrich test in Table 2.
3. Simulations conducted by Kaplanis showed that the length of the time period of 50 months is adequate for the asymptotic results. Tests of covariance stability, such as Jenrich's test, may lead to an incorrect rejection of the null if asset returns follow stable Paretian distributions (see Loretan and Phillips, 1994).
4. Some recent studies for the US market are Breen et al. (1989), Campbell (1987), Fama and French (1988), Ferson (1989), Ferson and Harvey (1991). Bekaert and Hodrick (1992) look at the stock markets and exchange rates of Japan, UK and Germany for the period 1/1981–12/1989; Campbell and Hamao (1992) look at Japan for the period 1/1970–3/1990; Cumby (1990) looks at Germany, UK and Japan for the period 1/1975–12/1987 using monthly observations of quarterly returns hence requiring an adjustment for overlapping; Cutler et al. (1991) look at 12 foreign stock and bond markets as well as their associated exchange rates with observations starting between 1/1960 and 7/1969, depending on the country, and ending in 1988; Harvey (1991) looks at 16 foreign stock markets for the period 1/1970–5/1989. Solnik (1993) looks at 7 foreign stock markets for the period 1/1971–8/1990.
5. A review of the literature can be found in Bollerslev et al. (1992).
6. Conditional volatility is not included in the risk premium equation since most studies have failed to discover a significant influence using monthly data (see for example Baillie and De Gennaro, 1990 and Sentana and Wadhwani, 1991). We got similar indications on our data.
7. For example, a constant-correlation GARCH model written on US dollar returns, i.e. using the US dollar as a base currency, would generally not give a constant-correlation GARCH model translated in another base currency.
8. We are grateful to Ken Kroner for providing us with a copy of his Fortran GARCH program.
9. GARCH effects for example tend to decrease by temporal aggregation as the distribution of returns tends toward normality (see Diebold, 1988).
10. This finding is consistent with previous research. For example, Attanasio (1991), Sentana and Wadhwani (1991), Glosten et al. (1989) included the dividend yield in univariate GARCH specifications with mixed results.
11. Parameters estimates are: $r = -0.397$ (-0.73), $r' = 0.753$ (1.41) and $a = 11.818$ (1.01) with Lik $= 1251.6$, LR test $= 8.0$ (p-value $= 0.018$).
12. It is not possible to condition on the future shock e_t and we cannot test whether the correlation is higher when the markets go up or go down.

13. The statistical significance of this phenomenon is rather low, so the conclusions are only tentative.
13. Economic variables do enter 'observable' factors, but again the assumption of constant b's imply that only changes in relative variance of these 'observable' factors can affect the correlation across markets.
15. We thank Morgan Stanley for making these data available to us for research purposes.
16. By interest rate parity the forward basis is equal to the short-term interest rate differential between the country of the asset and that of the investor. Hence the excess returns in local currency are (approximately) equal to the excess returns hedged against currency risk obtained by an investor of any nationality.
17. Remember that the volume of Eurodollar transactions is enormous and the LIBOR (London Interbank Offer Rate) has become the reference short-term dollar interest rate for borrowing in the USA. This is demonstrated by the fact that the Eurodollar futures contract has the largest transaction volume of all financial contracts in terms of underlying capital. A similar comment applies to other currencies.
18. We did not impose this constraint in our estimation and the sum turned out to be slightly negative in a couple of cases.

References

ATTANASIO, O.P., 'Risk, Time-varying Second Moments and Market Efficiency,' *Review of Economic Studies*, 1991, **58**: 479–494.

BABA, Y., R. ENGLE, D. KRAFT AND K. KRONER, 'Multivariate Simultaneous Generalized ARCH,' Working Paper, University of California, San Diego, 1989.

BAILLIE, R.T. AND T. BOLLERSLEV, 'A Multivariate Generalized ARCH Approach to Modelling Risk Premia in Forward Foreign Exchange Rate Markets,' *Journal of International Money and Finance*, September 1990, **9**: 309–324.

BAILLIE, R.T. AND R.P. DE GENNARO, 'Stocks Returns and Volatility,' *Journal of Financial Quantitative Analysis*, June 1990, **25**: 203–214.

BEKAERT, G. AND R.J. HODRICK, 'Characterizing Predictable Components in Excess Returns on Equity and Foreign Exchange Markets,' *Journal of Finance*, June 1992, **47**: 467–511.

BERNDT, E.K., B.H. HALL, R.E. HALL AND J.A. HAUSMAN, 'Estimation and Inference in Non-linear Structural Models,' *Annals of Economic and Social Measurement*, 1974, **69**: 542–547.

BERTERO, E. AND C. MAYER, 'Structure and Performance: Global Interdependence of Stock Markets around the Crash of October 1987,' *European Economic Review*, September 1990, **34**: 1155–1180.

BLACK, F., 'Studies in Stock Price Volatility Changes,' *Proceedings of the 1976 Business Meeting of the Business and Economic Statistics Section, American Statistical Association*, 1976: 177–181.

BOLLERSLEV, T., 'A Conditionally Heteroscedastic Time Series Model for Speculative Prices and Rates of Return,' *Review of Economics and Statistics*, August 1987, **69**: 542–547.

BOLLERSLEV, T., 'Modelling the Coherence in Short-run Nominal Exchange Rates: A Multivariate Generalized Approach,' *Review of Economics and Statistics*, August 1990, **72**: 498–505.

BOLLERSLEV, T., R.Y. CHOU AND K.F. KRONER, 'ARCH Modelling in Finance: A Review of the Theory and Empirical Evidence,' *Journal of Econometrics*, April/May 1992, **52**: 5–60.

BOX, G.E.P., 'A General Distribution Theory for a Class of Likelihood Criteria,' *Biometrika*, 1949, **36**: 317–346.

BREEN, W., L. GLOSTEN AND R. JAGANNATHAN, 'Economic Significance of Predictable Variations in Stock Index Returns,' *Journal of Finance*, December 1989, **44**: 1177–1190.

CAMPBELL, J.Y., 'Stock Returns and the Term Structure,' *Journal of Financial Econometrics*, June 1987, **18**: 373–399.

CAMPBELL, J.Y. AND Y. HAMAO, 'Predictable Stock Returns in the United States and Japan: A Study of Long-term Capital Market Integration,' *Journal of Finance*, March 1992, **47**: 43–69.

CAMPBELL, J.Y. AND L. HENTSCHEL, 'No News Is Good News,' *Journal of Financial Economics*, June 1992, **33**: 281–318.

CHAN, K.C., A.G. KAROLYI AND R. STULZ, 'Global Financial Markets and the Risk Premium on U.S. Equity,' *Journal of Financial Economics*, October 1992, **32**: 137–169.

CUMBY, R., 'Consumption Risk and International Equity Returns: Some Empirical Evidence,' *Journal of International Money and Finance*, June 1990, **9**: 182–192.

CUTLER, D.M., J.M. POTERBA AND L.H. SUMMERS, 'Speculative Dynamics,' *Review of Economic Studies*, 1991, **58**: 529–546.

DIEBOLD, F.X., 'Empirical Modelling Exchange Rate Dynamics,' Springer Verlag, New York, Heidelberg and Tokyo, *Lecture Notes in Economics and Mathematical Systems*, 1988, 303.

ENGEL, C. AND A.P. RODRIGUES, 'Test of International CAPM with Time-varying Covariances,' *Journal of Applied Econometrics*, 1989, **4**: 119–138.

ENGLE, R.F. AND V.K. NG, 'Measuring and Testing the Impact of News on Volatility,' *Journal of Finance*, 1993, **48**: 1749–1778.

FAMA, E.F. AND K.R. FRENCH, 'Permanent and Temporary Components of Stock Prices,' *Journal of Political Economy*, April 1988, **96**: 246–273.

FERSON, W.E., 'Changes in Expected Security Returns, Risk, and the Level of Interest Rates,' *Journal of Finance*, 1989, **44**: 1191–1218.

FERSON, W.E. AND C.R. HARVEY, 'The Variation of Economic Risk Premium,' *Journal of Political Economy*, April 1991, **99**: 385–415.

FRIEDMAN, B.M. AND D.I. LAIBSON, 'Economic Implications of Extraordinary Movements in Stock Prices,' *Brookings Papers on Economic Activity*, 1989, **2**: 137–172.

GIOVANNINI, A. AND P. JORION, 'The Time Variation of Risk and Return in the Foreign Exchange and Stock Markets,' *Journal of Finance*, June 1989, **44**: 307–326.

GLOSTEN, L.R., R. JAGANNATHAN AND D. RUNKLE, 'Relationship between the Expected Value and the Volatility of the Nominal Excess Return on Stocks,' *Journal of Finance*, 1993, **48**: 1779–1801.

GOURIÉROUX, C. AND A. MONFORT, 'Qualitative Threshold ARCH Models,' *Journal of Econometrics*, April/May 1992, **52**: 159–199.

GRUBEL, H.G. AND K. FADNER, 'The Interdependence of International Equity Markets,' *Journal of Finance*, 1971, **26**: 89–94.

HARVEY, C., 'The World Price of Covariance Risk,' *Journal of Finance*, March 1991, **46**: 111–158.

HENTSCHEL, L., 'The Absolute Value GARCH Model and the Volatility of U.S. Stock Returns,' Working Paper, Princeton University, 1991.

HODRICK, R.J., 'Risk, Uncertainty and Exchange Rates,' *Journal of Monetary Economics*, May 1989, **23**: 433–459.

JENRICH, J.I., 'An Asymptotic Chi-square Test for the Equality of Two Correlation Matrices,' *Journal of the American Statistical Association*, 1970, **65**: 904–912.

KAPLANIS, E.C., 'Stability and Forecasting of the Co-movement Measures of International Stock Market Return,' *Journal of International Money and Finance*, March 1988, **8**: 63–75.

KING, M., E. SENTANA AND S. WADHWANI, 'Volatility and Links between National Stock Markets,' Working Paper, 1992.

KING, M. AND S. WADHWANI, 'Transmission of Volatility between Stock Markets,' *Review of Financial Studies*, 1990, **3**: 5–33.

KOCH, P.D. AND T.W. KOCH, 'Evolution in Dynamic Linkages across National Stock Indexes,' *Journal of International Money and Finance*, June 1991, **10**: 231–251.

LESSARD, D.R., 'International Portfolio Diversification Multivariate Analysis for a Group of Latin American Countries,' *Journal of Finance*, 1973, **28**: 619–633.

LEVY, H. AND M. SARNAT, 'International Diversification of Investment Portfolios,' *American Economic Review*, 1970: 668–675.

LI, W.K. AND A.I. MCLEOD, 'Diagnostic Checking ARMA Time Series Models Using Squared Residual Correlations,' *Journal of Time Series Analysis*, 1983, **4**: 269–273.

LORETAN, M. AND P.C.B. PHILLIPS, 'Testing the Covariance Stationarity of Heavy-tailed Time

Series: An Overview of the Theory with Applications to Several Financial Datasets,' *Journal of Empirical Finance*, 1994, **2**: 211–248.
NELSON, D., 'Conditional Heteroscedasticity in Asset Returns: A New Approach,' *Econometrica*, March 1991, **59**: 347–370.
NG, L., 'Tests of the CAPM with Time-varying Covariances: A Multivariate GARCH Approach,' *Journal of Finance*, September 1991, **46**: 1507–1521.
POTERBA, J.M. AND L.H. SUMMERS, 'The Persistence of Volatility and Stock Market Fluctuations,' *American Economic Review*, December 1986, **76**: 1141–1151.
RABEMANANJARA, R. AND J.-M. ZAKOÏAN, 'TARCH Models and Asymmetries in Volatility,' *Journal of Applied Econometrics*, January–March 1991, **8**: 31–49.
RATNER, M., 'Portfolio Diversification and the Inter-temporal Stability of International Indices,' *Global Finance Journal*, 1992, **3**: 67–78.
SCHWERT, W.G., 'Why Does Stock Market Volatility Change over Time?,' *Journal of Finance*, December 1989, **44**: 1115–1153.
SENTANA, E. AND S. WADHWANI, 'Semi-parametric Estimation and the Predictability of Stock Market Returns: Lessons from Japan,' *Review of Economic Studies*, 1991, **58**: 547–564.
SOLNIK, B., 'Why not Diversify Internationally rather than Domestically?,' *Financial Analysts Journal*, July/August 1974, **30**: 48–54.
SOLNIK, B., 'The Performance of International Asset Allocation Strategies Using Conditioning Information,' *Journal of Empirical Finance*, 1993, **1**: 33–56.
VON FURSTENBERG, G.M. AND B.N. JEON, 'International Stock Prices Movements: Links and Messages,' *Brookings Papers on Economic Activity*, 1989, **1**: 125–179.
ZAKOÏAN, J.M. 'Threshold Heteroscedastic Models,' Working Paper, INSEE, 1990.

International stock market linkages: Evidence from the pre- and post-October 1987 period*

Bala Arshanapalli

Indiana University Northwest, Gary, IN 46408, USA

John Doukas

Old Dominion University, Norfolk, VA 23529, USA

Received December 1991, final version received June 1992

This paper uses recent developments in the theory of cointegration to provide new methods of testing the linkage and dynamic interactions among stock market movements. Our findings are in sharp contrast with previous research which discovered strong interdependence among national stock markets prior to October 1987. For the post-October 1987 period, however, our results show that the degree of international co-movements among stock price indices has increased substantially, with the Nikkei index the only exception. Furthermore, the US stock market is found to have a considerable impact on the French, German and UK markets in the post-crash period. We also find the response of the French, German and UK markets to US stock market innovations to be consistent with the view of cross-border informationally efficient stock markets. Finally, we find the Japanese equity market performance to have no links with both the US stock market and the stock markets in France, Germany and UK during the pre- and post-October crash period.

1. Introduction

The flow of international investment has been rapidly growing in recent years. This is frequently attributed to a number of different factors such as the relaxation of controls on capital movements and foreign exchange transactions, improvements in computer and communication technology that have lowered the cost of cross-border information flows and financial transactions, and expansion in the multinational operations of major corporations (whose shares are often listed on several stock exchanges) among others. This globalization of financial transactions has led some to claim that the 1987 behavior of national stock markets (prices) was influenced by

Correspondence to: Professor John Doukas, Finance Department, Graduate School of Business, Old Dominion University, Norfolk, VA 23529–0222, USA.

*The authors would like to thank an anonymous JBF referee for helpful comments.

0378-4266/93/$06.00 © 1993—Elsevier Science Publishers B.V. All rights reserved

international events more than ever. For instance, in its discussions of the 1987 fall in prices, the report by the Presidential Task Force on Market Mechanisms, better known as the Brady Commission report, notes that '(w)hat may have appeared strictly a "Wall Street" collapse was the result of the cumulative impact of several developments occurring simultaneously in several other financial centers'.[1] Roll's (1988) analysis of the worldwide decline in equity values during October 1987 suggests that the timing and magnitude of declines differed across markets around the world. Roll (1988) reports that the crash originated in Asia (excluding Japan), followed by Europe, then US and finally Japan. King and Wadhwani (1988), and Goodhart (1988), however, using hourly stock price data found strong cross-exchange linkages after the crash and argue that the October collapse originated in the US while the European capital markets experienced a similar decline with a time lag.

Studies on international stock market linkages may also provide new insights into the economic nature of the October 1987 crash phenomenon. Dwyer and Hafer (1988), using daily data for seven months before and after the October 1987 crash, show no evidence that the levels of stock price indices for the US, Japan, Germany and the UK are related. They report statistical evidence, however, that the changes in the stock price indices in these four markets are generally related. Similar results were obtained in earlier studies by Grubel (1968), Levy and Sarnat (1970), Aqmon (1972), Ripley (1973), Lessard (1976), Panton et al. (1976), and Hilliard (1979) using either correlation or variance–covariance or spectral analysis. The lack of interdependence across national stock markets has been presented as evidence supporting the benefits of international portfolio diversification. More recent studies, however, by Jaffe and Westerfield (1985), Schollhammer and Sand (1985), and Eun and Shim (1989) report a substantial amount of interdependence among national stock markets.

Studies testing for possible international stock market linkages have found conflicting evidence. The conflicting evidence leads naturally to the question: why are there differences in results? Solnik (1977), Kohlhagen (1983) and Khoury et al. (1987), among others, have pointed out some of the methodological problems associated with previous empirical studies that might explain the differences in results. It is not clear, then, what the high or low positive correlations in the rates of return imply about international equity market linkages. Meric and Meric (1989), analyzing the inter-temporal stability of the matrix of correlation coefficients among seventeen national stock markets, using Box's M statistical tests from 1973 to 1987, find that the longer the time period the greater the degree of stability among international stock market relationships. Maldonado and Saunders (1981), using monthly

---

[1] Presidential Task Force on Market Mechanism (1988), p. 2.

rates of return for US, Japan, Germany, Canada and UK from 1957 to 1978, show that the intertemporal relationships between correlation coefficients are unstable. In contrast, Philippatos et al. (1983) support the existence of intertemporal stability of international stock markets. Using principal components analysis on monthly rates of return for fourteen countries from 1959 to 1978, their results suggest that national market indices are interrelated over time through a common factor.

Schollhammer and Sand (1985) and Eun and Shim (1989) have shown, for several countries in the 1980s, that the levels of national stock price indices are non-stationary, However, the stationarity assumption is a requirement for models which examine the effectiveness of international portfolio diversification or models which examine the efficiency of international stock markets. In particular, the non-stationarity of international equity indices raises doubts about the consistency of the estimated standard errors of such models. In order to make the equity index series stationary, the normal econometric practice has been to take the first differences of the series [see, Schollhammer and Sand (1985) and Eun and Shim (1989)]. Unfortunately, first differencing imposes too many unit roots, and filters out potentially important information regarding long-run common trends among non-stationary stock indices.

Recent developments in the theory of cointegration by Engle and Granger (1987) provide new methods of testing international equity market linkages. Cointegration among a set of variables implies that even if they are non-stationary, they never drift far apart. In contrast, lack of cointegration suggests that such variables have no long-run link. We use this methodology to study how the different stock markets around the world are related. Engle and Granger (1987) have also shown that if two variables are cointegrated, then the variables follow a well specified error-correction model, where by 'well specified' it is meant that coefficient estimates, as well as the standard errors for the coefficients of the estimated equation(s) are consistent. The error-correction equation gives us a means of testing the dynamic interaction of national stock price movements.

In this paper, we study the linkages among stock prices in major world stock exchanges such as Germany, the United Kingdom, France, Japan and the United States, using daily closing data from January 1980 through May 1990. We also examine the relationship of stock price indices before and after the October crash. Finally, we investigate the impact of stock price movements in one market on another.

The remainder of the paper is organized as follows. Section 2 briefly discusses the statistical meaning of cointegration and error-correction model. Section 3 presents the data and methodology. In section 4 the results are presented and discussed. Section 5 provides a summary and concluding remarks.

2. Cointegration and the error-correction model

Cointegration is a relatively new statistical concept, introduced by Granger (1983), Granger and Weiss (1983), and Engle and Granger (1987). Cointegration is a property possessed by some non-stationary time series data. In general terms, two variables are said to be cointegrated when a linear combination of the two is stationary, even though each variable is non-stationary.[2] In contrast, lack of cointegration suggests that such variables have no long-run link; in principle, they can wander arbitrarily far away from each other. In terms of cross-border equity market efficiency, cointegration implies that national stock market indices are linked even if the stock market indices are non-stationary. We use this result to test cross-border equity market efficiency by determining if one national market index is cointegrated with the US stock market index.

More formally, consider the time series x_t. Following Granger (1983), x_t is considered integrated of order one if Dx_t has a stationary ARMA representation:

$$\alpha_i(L)Dx_t = \delta_i + \tau_i(L)\varepsilon_i, \tag{1}$$

where L is the lag operator, D is the difference operator, $\alpha_i(L)$ and $\tau_i(L)$ are polynomials in L with all roots outside the unit circle, δ_i is a drift parameter, and ε_i is a white noise stochastic input with $E(\varepsilon_i)=0$ and $Var(\varepsilon_i)=\sigma^2<\infty$. If x_t is integrated of order one, the level of the series is non-stationary in mean, whereas Dx_t is mean stationary. In particular, the level of x_t is expected to increase at a rate of δ_i. That is, the unconditional expectation $E(x_k)=x_0+\delta_i k$ and the unconditional variance around the expectation increases with k.

Consider two times series, say x_t and y_t. Assume that both x_t and y_t are non-stationary and integrated of order one, then the series are cointegrated so that $z_t = y_t - \bar{a}x_t$ has a stationary invertible ARMA representation. In other words, if two series are cointegrated, the unconditional expectation and variance of z_t are $E(z_t)=\delta_z$ and $Var(z_t)=\sigma^2<\infty$; that is, the level y_t is expected to fluctuate around $\bar{a}x_t$, and y_t and $\bar{a}x_t$ are not expected to drift apart in the long-run.

To illustrate the concept of cointegration in the context of this study, let x_t be the stock price index series of country i and y_t be the stock price index series of country j. If x_t and y_t are cointegrated then according to the Granger representation theorem [Granger (1969); Engle and Granger (1987)], there must exist an error-correction representation of the following form:

$$x_t - x_{t-1} = a_0 + a_1 z_{t-1} + B_1(L)(x_t - x_{t-1}) + B_2(L)(y_t - y_{t-1}) + e_{1t}, \tag{2a}$$

---

[2]Under these conditions, the regression error obtained from these variables is defined as stationary with well defined first and second movements.

$$y_t - y_{t-1} = a_2 + a_3 z_{t-1} + B_3(L)(x_t - x_{t-1}) + B_4(L)(y_t - y_{t-1}) + e_{2t}, \quad (2b)$$

where $B_1(L)$, $B_2(L)$, $B_3(L)$ and $B_4(L)$ are polynomials, L is the lagged operator, e_{1t} and e_{2t} are white noise error terms, and z_{t-1} is the lagged value of the error term from the following cointegration, or equilibrium, regression:

$$x_t = c + dy_t + z_t. \quad (3)$$

The error-correction model has the standard interpretation: the change in x_t is due to the immediate, short-run effect from the change in y_t and to last period's error, z_{t-1}, which represents the long-run adjustment to past disequilibrium. Hence, estimation of the error-correction equations is also expected to provide evidence about the long-run relationship and the nature of the adjustment process among national stock markets. Furthermore, the error-correction analysis is fundamental for testing the cross-border market efficiency hypothesis since it describes the long-run dynamic adjustment process between two stock exchange markets.

3. Data and methodology

3.1. Data

This study concentrates on the world's five largest stock exchanges: New York (Dow Jones Industrial Average – DJIA), Frankfurt (FAZ General Price Index – FAZ), London (FTSE 100 Price Index – FTSE100), Japan (Nikkei Stock Average 225 – Nikkei), and Paris (CAC General Price Index – CAC). Daily closing data for all five indices have been collected from the *Wall Street Journal* over the period beginning January 1980 and ending May 1990. The sample consists of 2,709 observations. When national stock exchanges were closed due to national holidays, bank holidays or severe weather conditions, the index level was assumed to remain the same as that on the previous trading day. The stock price performance across exchanges for the month of October 1987 is characterized as very unusual in the recent history of the stock market. To assure that the results are not being influenced by the stock price data of this period, two additional data sets are employed in this study: the pre-crash (January 1980–September 1987) and the post-crash (November 1987–May 1990). Since national stock markets are generally operating in different time zones with different opening and closing times, it is important to note that there is no trading overlap between the Tokyo stock exchange and the exchanges in Paris, Frankfurt and London, and between the New York stock exchange and the exchanges in Frankfurt, Paris and finally between the New York and Tokyo exchanges. There is, however, a half-an-hour overlap between London and New York stock exchanges (i.e., the London exchange closes half an hour after the NYSE has opened).

3.2. Methodology

Testing for cointegration involves four steps. First, determine the presence of units (order of integration) in each of the indices involved. This basically involves the Dickey–Fuller (DF) and the Augmented Dickey–Fuller (ADF) unit root type of analysis [see Dickey and Fuller (1979, 1981)]. The second state involves estimating the following cointegrating regression:

$$x_t = c + dy_t + z_t, \qquad (4)$$

where x_t (US stock market index) and y_t (foreign stock market index) are the national equity index series being tested for cointegration. In cointegration tests, the null hypothesis is non-cointegration (against the alternative of cointegration). Hence, a large test statistic rejects non-cointegration. Based on simulation, Engle and Yoo (1987) provide critical values for cointegration tests. Third, we test for the stationarity of the cointegrating regression error (z_t). That is, examine whether the estimated time series of the residuals from the cointegrating regression (4) has a unit root. This test is performed by estimating the following regression:

$$D\hat{z}_t = -p\hat{z}_{t-1} + e_t, \qquad (5)$$

where $\hat{z}_t$ is the estimated residual from eq. (4). This test involves the significance of the estimated $\hat{p}$ coefficient: if $\hat{p}$ is positive and signiicantly different from zero, the $\hat{Z}_t$ residuals from the equilibrium equation are stationary so the hypothesis of cointegration is 'accepted'.[3]

Finally, the next step involves the estimation of the error-correction model. If two variables (i.e., stock price indices) are cointegrated with a cointegrating vector d, then these variables can be expressed in an error-correction form as described in (2). The error-correction model shows the long-run dynamics of the adjustment process between two national market indices (variables). The significance and size of the error-correction terms a_1 or a_3 in (2) essentially captures the single-period response of the dependent variable to departures from equilibrium.[4]

---

[3]The augmented Dickey–Fuller test is similar to the DF test, but additional lags of $D\hat{z}_t$ are used to insure the residuals from the DF regression are serially uncorrelated.

[4]The cross-border equity market efficiency hypothesis test in the error-correction model is not subject to autocorrelation problems that plague tests in cointegrating regressions, and, therefore, a statistically significant coefficient in the error-correction term is a sufficient condition for the existence of an equilibrium relationship.

The optimal lag length of the error-correction equations is determined by estimating the following univariate process

$$I_{i,t} = C_0 + \sum_{k=1}^{m} C_k I_{i,t-k} + u_t, \qquad (6)$$

and employing Akaike's (1973) final prediction error (FPE) criterion. The lag length is allowed to vary and the FPE is calculated for each lag; the order with the lowest FPE is chosen as the optimal. To determine the lag length of the other stock market (I_j), the optimal lag length of the I_i is treated as given and I_j is introduced by estimating the following bivariate regression:

$$I_{i,t} = C_0 + \sum_{k=1}^{m} C_k I_{i,t-k} + \sum_{k=1}^{n} D_k I_{j,t-k} + u_t. \qquad (7)$$

The optimal lag is the one which yields the minimum FPE.

4. Empirical results

4.1. Unit root tests

Before testing for cointegration, the order of integration of the national indices must be determined. Tests for unit roots are performed using the Dickey–Fuller (DF) and the augmented Dickey–Fuller (ADF) tests. The null hypothesis is that the national stock indices have a unit root, against the alternative that they do not. The results of the unit root tests based on local currency units are presented in table 1. Panel A reports DF and ADF tests of stationarity for the entire period in the levels and first differences of the stock price indices about a non-zero mean. The critical values of the test statistics are tabulated in Engle and Yoo (1987). The reported results indicate the presence of a unit root in the levels of all indices (i.e., the null hypothesis cannot be rejected). However, there is no evidence to support the presence of a unit root in first differences of the stock price indices. The null hypothesis of a unit root in first differences is rejected for all five stock price index series. These results are broadly consistent with the hypothesis that the national stock index series are individually integrated of order one, $I(1)$.

In panels B and C of table 1, DF and ADF tests of stationarity for the pre- and post-crash periods are listed. The results indicate that the series are non-stationary in the levels but stationary in the first differences. In sum, the preceding analysis has provided reassuring new evidence that daily national stock market index series have a unit root (i.e., a stochastic trend in their univariate time-series representations) in the levels but their first differences are stationary.

Table 1

Unit root test statistics in stock exchange indices: January 1, 1980–May 17, 1990.

Country	Exchange index	DF[a] levels	DF differences	ADF[b] levels	ADF differences
Panel A: Entire period, N = 2,709					
France	CAC	0.186	−44.40*	0.180	−33.68* (1)[c]
Germany	FAZ	−0.323	−51.44*	−0.316	−22.97* (4)
Japan	Nikkei	−0.032	−50.25*	−0.061	−39.68* (1)
UK	FTSE100	−1.280	−49.64*	−1.279	−36.42* (1)
US	DJIA	−0.351	−51.44*	−0.377	−30.96* (2)
Panel B: Pre-October 1987, N = 2,025					
France	CAC	1.083	−43.46*	0.465	−28.18* (1)
Germany	FAZ	0.035	−43.51*	0.028	−23.08* (3)
Japan	Nikkei	0.161	−43.57*	−1.663	−22.69* (3)
UK	FTSE100	0.798	−36.41*	0.132	−31.70* (1)
US	DJIA	0.820	−41.58*	0.959	−30.19* (1)
Panel C: Post-October 1987, N = 663					
France	CAC	−0.731	−26.49*	0.594	−17.82* (1)
Germany	FAZ	−0.178	−26.22*	0.017	−14.03* (3)
Japan	Nikkei	−1.170	−23.18*	−1.663	−13.03* (3)
UK	FTSE100	−0.557	−24.38*	−1.205	−16.09* (2)
US	DJIA	−1.651	−22.97*	−0.691	−20.04* (1)

[a]DF denotes the Dickey–Fuller test.
[b]ADF denotes the augmented Dickey–Fuller test. The DF and ADF tests are based on the following regression:

$$Dx_t = a_0 + a_1 x_{t-1} + \sum_{j=1}^{m} b_j Dx_{t-j} + v_t,$$

where b_j equals zero for the DF tests, x_t denotes the stock market index and v_t the error term.
[c]For the ADF tests (in levels and differences) the number in parentheses denotes the minimum value of m required to achieve white noise errors, v_t.

The asterisk indicates statistical significance at the 5 percent level. Critical values for $N = 100, 250, \infty$ are −2.89, −2.88, −2.86, respectively, as reported in Engle and Yoo (1987).

4.2. Cointegration tests

Next we examine whether the national stock market index series are cointegrated. With the DJIA as the base index OLS estimation of the cointegrating regressions were performed to examine the stationarity of the residuals. Stationary residuals imply cointegration. Table 2 contains the results from the tests of cointegration. Several interesting observations emerge. First, the results from the entire sample show that the stock markets of France, Japan and UK appear to be cointegrated with the US stock market. However, the null hypothesis of no cointegration between the US and the German stock markets cannot be rejected. At the 5 percent level the critical value of the DF statistic is 3.37. The critical values of the DF

Table 2

Cointegration regressions: January 1, 1980–May 17, 1990.

Country	Constant	Coefficient of foreign index	R^2	D–W	DF
Panel A: Entire period, N = 2,709					
France	3.93	0.624	0.94	0.01	−3.46*
Germany	2.17	0.852	0.85	0.007	−2.23
Japan	0.88	0.671	0.95	0.02	−3.38*
UK	1.38	0.830	0.95	0.02	−3.51*
Panel B: Pre- and post-October cointegration regression results					
Pre-October 1987, N = 2,025					
France	4.18	0.571	0.90	0.01	1.80
Germany	2.93	0.710	0.86	0.008	−1.14
Japan	−0.30	0.800	0.94	0.02	−3.06
UK	−1.90	0.753	0.92	0.01	−2.79
Post-October 1987, N = 663					
France	4.64	0.515	0.91	0.09	−3.93*
Germany	3.93	0.602	0.89	0.09	−4.19*
Japan	0.14	0.737	0.76	0.04	−1.91
UK	−0.15	1.039	0.93	0.04	−3.71*

The asterisk indicates statistical significance at the 5 percent level. The critical value of the DF statistic at 5 percent level is 3.37 as reported in Engle and Yoo (1987).

Cointegration equation errors are used to perform the DF and ADF non-stationarity tests based on the following regressions:

$$D\hat{z}_t = \gamma \hat{z}_{t-1} + e_t,$$

$$D\hat{z}_t = \gamma \hat{z}_{t-1} + \sum_{i=1}^{m} \delta_i Dz_{t-i} + e_t,$$

where $D\hat{z}_t$ is the change in the error term from the cointegration equation and e_t is a random error. If γ is negative and significantly different from zero, the z residuals from the equilibrium equation are stationary so the hypothesis of cointegration is 'accepted'.

If z_t is a function of a higher order than a pure AR(1) process, the augmented DF tests is performed. In all the regressions reported in tables 2 and 3 we observe that the error series are white noise. Therefore no ADF tests are warranted.

statistics are tabulated in Engle and Yoo (1987). Second, for the pre-crash period none of the stock markets appear to be cointegrated with the US stock market at the 5 percent level. This results suggests that the link among stock prices in the five major stock exchanges has been very weak over the January 1980–September 1987 period. Furthermore, this result seems to be in sharp contrast with recent studies by Jaffe and Westerfield (1985), Schollhammer and Sand (1985), and Eun and Shim (1989), which report a substantial amount of interdependence among national stock markets for the pre-October 1987 period. Finally, for the post-crash period, we find the

French, German and UK stock markets to be cointegrated with the US stock market. The null hypothesis of no cointegration between Japan and US stock markets cannot be rejected. The reported DF statistic, −1.91, is well below its critical value, 3.37, at the 5 percent level. This result seems to suggest that the linkage between the Tokyo and New York market has been substantially reduced since the October crash. Therefore, the previous evidence in favor of cointegration between the two stock markets over the 1980–1990 period seems to be attributed to the strong cointegrating influence of the month of October 1987.[5]

Another interesting observation from table 2 relates to the behavior of US and German stock exchanges. While these two stock markets were found to be non-cointegrated over the January 1980–May 1990 period, the pre- and post-crash cointegration analysis shows that this result is mainly because the German and US stock markets were strongly non-cointegrated during the pre-crash period. Indeed, the sharp decline of the DF values in the pre-October period supports this view. On the other hand, the post-October result suggests that the degree of interdependence between the stock exchanges of US and Germany has increased substantially over the post-crash period. This is also true for the relationship between the US stock market and the stock markets of UK and France. The evidence suggests substantial interdependence between the US stock market and these two European stock markets over the post-crash period. The sharp increase of the DF values for France and UK during the post-October relative to the pre-October period explains why these two markets were found to be cointegrated with the US stock market during the entire sample period (1980–1990).

In general, these results indicate that the magnitude of interdependence between the US stock market and the stock markets in France, Germany and UK has increased since the crash of October 1987. Therefore, we find the linkage among these markets during the post-crash period to be consistent with the notion of cross-border market efficiency in the sense that these markets do not drift far apart, with the Tokyo stock market the only exception.[6]

We also examine whether the three major European stock markets are

---

[5]To verify the influence of the month of October 1987, we replicated the cointegration analysis for Japan by adding the month of October to the pre- and post-October samples. The results (not reported here, with DF values of −3.86 and −4.42 for the pre- and post-October period, respectively) indicate that the presence of strong cointegration forces during the month of October 1987 has influenced the entire sample results reported in panel A of table 2.

[6]It should be noted that the results presented here are all in local currency units. However, we have also repeated our empirical analysis using dollar-denominated stock market index series. Because both sets of results permit similar inferences in all cases our interpretation focuses primarily on local currency denominated index series. This is quite consistent with Dwyer and Hafer's (1988) study which shows that exchange rate fluctuations have little impact on their results.

Table 3

Cointegration regressions: January 1, 1980–May 17, 1990.

Country	Constant	Coefficient of foreign index	R^2	D–W	DF
Panel A: Entire period, N = 2,709					
France	4.75	0.892	0.91	0.004	−1.77
Germany	3.49	1.175	0.77	0.002	−1.28
UK	1.13	1.183	0.91	0.007	−2.46
Panel B: Pre- and post-October cointegration results					
Pre-October 1987, N = 2,025					
France	5.64	0.705	0.94	0.010	−1.53
Germany	4.14	0.873	0.88	0.010	−0.67
UK	2.85	0.926	0.95	0.020	−3.09
Post-October 1987, N = 663					
France	6.80	0.583	0.83	0.025	−1.93
Germany	6.44	0.611	0.66	0.014	−1.65
UK	1.66	1.138	0.79	0.034	−2.35

cointegrated with the Tokyo stock exchange. Using the Nikkei index as the base index, OLS estimation of the cointegrating regressions were conducted to investigate the stationarity of residuals. These cointegration results are reported in table 3. The null hypothesis of no cointegration between Japan and the stock markets in France, Germany and UK cannot be rejected. The listed DF statistics, for the 1980–1990 period, are substantially below the critical value of 3.37 at the 5 per cent level. The most interesting, perhaps, result reported in table 3 is the lack of cointegration between the Tokyo stock market and the three major European stock markets during the pre- and post-October period. This result is in sharp contrast with the evidence, reported in table 2, regarding the relationship between the US stock market and the stock markets in France, Germany and UK in the post-October period. The DF values for all three European stock exchanges listed in table 3 are not significant at any conventional level. The UK stock market, however, seems to be somewhat related to the one in Japan as the DF value for the London stock exchange exceeds its equivalents for the Paris and Frankfurt stock exchanges.

In sum, the evidence from the entire sample as well as the pre- and post-crash sample periods indicates that the Tokyo stock market is not cointegrated with the stock markets in France, Germany and UK. This implies that the three major European stock markets are not related to the Tokyo stock market. These results also imply that the performance of the Japanese stock market has no impression on the French, German and UK stock exchanges. An alternative interpretation of these results is that the Japanese market is not integrated with the French, German, UK and US stock markets. Another interesting implication of these results is that Japanese stocks offer an appealing choice for international portfolio diversification.

4.3. Error-correction tests

Having established that the stock markets in France, Germany and UK are cointegrated with the US stock market in the post-crash period, we next examine the interactions among these markets by estimating the error-correction equations (2a, 2b) using data from only the post-crash period (i.e., the last 663 observations).[7] We estimated the error-correction equations using Akaike's (1973) FPE criterion for the determination of the optimal lag structure of the error-correction equations. The error term, z_t, used in the error-correction regressions was obtained from the OLS estimation of the cointegration equations using the DJIA as the dependent variable. The results of the error-correction equations are reported in table 4.

The results indicate a substantial cross-exchange efficiency between the US market and the three major European markets in the post-October 1987 period. By construction, the error-correction term represents the degree to which stock markets are away from a long-run alignment. Note that the error-correction term is included in eqs. (2a) and (2b) in order to guarantee that the two markets (i.e., US and France, US and Germany, and US and UK) do not drift far apart. As previously noted by Engle and Granger (1987) and illustrated by the estimated error-correction models in table 4, a small value of z_{t-1} rather than a larger value is preferred in the sense that the disequilibrium error from the national cross-exchange relationships is not an important factor in the next period's change in the ith stock market. A large disequilibrium error, however, can be interpreted as a violation of weak form efficiency across national stock markets as it can be used to predict 'corrections' in future stock price index levels [see Granger (1986)]. The t-value of the coefficient of the error-correction term, z_{t-1}, appears to be almost indistinguishable from zero for the first pair of stock markets (i.e., New York and Paris). Despite that these two stock markets are tied together with a long-run relationship, this result implies that the equilibrium error cannot be used to predict next period's stock market price changes in either stock exchange. This result also suggests that the French and US stock exchange markets are efficient [see Granger (1986)]. Furthermore, the error-correction analysis for the French and US stock markets suggests that the US stock market innovations may be exogenous even though the two national stock markets are cointegrated.

---

[7]The error-correction tests can be performed on cointegrated time series only.

Table 4

Error-correction equations: Post-October period
November 1987–May 1990.

$$(x_t - x_{t-1}) = az_{t-1} + \sum_{i=1}^{m} b(y_t - y_{t-1})_{t-1}$$

$$+ \sum_{i=1}^{n} c(x_t - x_{t-1})_{t-1} + e_{1t}.$$

$$(y_t - y_{t-1}) = az_{t-1} + \sum_{i=1}^{m} b(y_t - y_{t-1})_{t-1}$$

$$+ \sum_{i=1}^{n} c(x_t - x_{t-1})_{t-1} + e_{2t}.$$

| | | F-statistics | |
Country	a	$\sum_{i=1}^{m} b$	$\sum_{i=1}^{n} c$
US	−0.023	1.25 (4)	
	(2.39*)		
France	0.009		136.04* (3)
	(1.01)		
US	−0.018	0.18 (2)	
	(1.75)		
Germany	0.016		39.20* (3)
	(1.47)		
US	−0.008	2.33 (1)	
	(−0.82)		
UK	0.007		5.47* (3)
	(0.91)		

The asterisk indicates significance at the 5 percent level. The joint significance of the indices is determined by the standard F-test. The DJIA index is denoted by x_t while y_t denotes the foreign index. The optimal lag length is given in parentheses following the F-statistics. The lag structure is determined by the final prediction error (FPE) criterion.

With respect to the second pair of stock markets (i.e., New York and Frankfurt), the results show that the error correction is not really significant with a t-statistic of 1.47, suggesting that the US stock market changes may have an impression on the German stock market. In this case again the results seem to be quite consistent with the view that the two markets are efficient in the sense that the error correction cannot be used to help predict stock market changes. Similar results were obtained from the final pair of stock market index series based on the New York and London stock exchanges in the post-October 1987 period. The t-value of the coefficient of the error-correction term is 0.91, essentially insignificant at any conventional level. This result is consistent with the notion of cross-border equity market efficiency between the US and UK stock exchanges, though far from strong evidence in its favor. The US stock market changes again seem to be exogenous.

Another interesting aspect of the error-correction analysis is that it yields information about the 'short-run' influence from the change in one market on the performance of another market. In all regressions reported in table 4, the results show that the US stock price index variable, $[\sum_{i=1}^{m}(x_t - x_{t-1})]$, exerts a substantial amount of influence on all three European markets. The results for the joint significance of the lagged indices show that the F-values for the US index are 136.04, 39.20 and 5.47 for France, Germany and UK, respectively (i.e., significant at the 5 percent level). In contrast, European 'short-run' stock market changes do not appear to have any significant impact on the US stock market. The F-values for the lagged European indices are 1.25, 0.18 and 2.33 for France, Germany and UK, respectively (i.e., insignificant at any conventional level). This result is inconsistent with the view that foreign stock market innovations have exerted substantial influence on the US market in the post-October 1987 period.

5. Summary and concluding remarks

We have used the theory of cointegration to examine the linkages and dynamic interactions among stock price indices in the major world stock exchanges. The data used in this study are daily closing stock market index time series, in local currency units, as reported in the *Wall Street Journal*. The sample consists of 2,709 observations and covers the period of January 1980 through May 1990. The evidence indicates that the degree of international co-movements in stock price indices has changed significantly since the crash of October 1987, with the Nikkei index the only exception. Specifically, for the pre-crash period we find that France, Germany and UK stock markets are not related to the US stock market. This result is not consistent with previous studies [see Jaffe and Westerfield (1985), Schollhammer and Sand (1985), and Eun and Shim (1989)], which report substantial interdependence among these stock markets. For the post-crash period, however, our results show that the three major European stock markets (i.e., France, Germany and UK) are indeed strongly linked (cointegrated) with the US stock market. Moreover, the error-correction analysis produced some interesting results with respect to the stock market interactions among the five major world stock exchanges. The US stock market is found to have a substantial impact on the French, German and UK markets in the post-crash period. Stock market innovations in any of the three European stock markets have no impact on the US stock market. In addition, we find no evidence of interdependence among stock price indices between US and Japan. Furthermore, the results show that the US and Japan stock markets have drifted far away from each other since the October crash. Finally, a similar result is obtained between Japan and the three European stock markets examined in this study. The pattern of interactions among France, Germany, UK, and Japan suggests that Japanese stock market innovations are unrelated to the performance of the major European stock markets. This result is consistent with the evidence in Harvey (1991) which shows that the Japanese stock market is not fully integrated with other world stock markets.[8]

[8] Tests of the conditional version of the Sharpe–Lintner capital asset pricing model conducted by Harvey (1991) show that the Japanese stock market is not fully integrated (i.e., the world price of risk is not the appropriate price of covariance risk for the Japanese stock returns) with other world stock markets.

References

Aqmon, T., 1972, The relations among equity markets: A study of share price co-movement in the United States, United Kingdom, Germany and Japan, Journal of Finance 27, Sept., 839–855.
Akaike, H., 1973, Information theory and the extension of the maximum likelihood principle, in: B.N. Petrov and F. Caski, eds., Second international symposium on information theory, Budapest.
Dickey, D.A. and W.A. Fuller, 1979, Distribution of the estimates for autoregressive time series with a unit root, Journal of the American Statistical Association 24, June, 427–31.
Dickey, D.A. and W.A. Fuller, 1981, Likelihood ratio statistics for autoregressive time series with a unit root, Econometrica 49, July, 1057–1072.
Dwyer, G.P. and R.W. Hafer, Are national stock markets linked?, Federal Reserve Bank of St. Louis, Review 39, Dec., 314.
Engle, R.F. and C.W.J. Granger, 1987, Cointegration and error-correction: Representation, estimation and testing, Econometrics 35, May, 143–159.
Eun, C.S. and S. Shim, 1989, International transmission of stock market movements, Journal of Financial and Quantitative Analysis 24, June, 241–256.
Goodhart, C.A.E., 1988, The international transmission of asset price volatility, in: Financial market volatility (Federal Reserve Bank of Kansas City, Kansas City), 79–121.
Granger, C.W.J., 1969, Investigating casual relations by econometric models and cross spectral methods, Econometrica 37, May, 424–438.
Granger, C.W.J., 1983, Forecasting white noise, in: Applied time series analysis of economic data (Bureau of the Census, Washington, DC).
Granger, C.W.J. and A.A. Weiss, 1983, Time series analysis of error-corrective models, in: Multivaria statistics (Academic Press, New York).
Grubel, H.G., 1970, Internationally diversified of investment portfolio's, American Economic Review 60, Sept., 668–675.
Harvey, C.R., 1991, The world price of covariance risk, Journal of Finance 46, Mar., 111–157.
Hilliard, J.E., 1979, The relationship between equity indices on world exchanges, Journal of Finance 34, Mar., 103–114.
Jaffe, J. and R. Westerfield, 1985, The weekend effect in common stock returns: The international evidence, Journal of Finance 40, Jun., 433–454.
Khoury, S.J., B. Dodin and H. Takada, 1987, Multiple time-series analysis of national stock markets and their structure: Some implications, in: S.J. Khoury and A. Ghosh, eds., Recent developments in international banking and finance (Lexington Books, Lexington), 169–186.

King, M. and S. Wadhwani, 1988, Transmission of volatility between stock markets, London School of Economics, Financial markets Working paper.

Kohlhagen, S., 1983, Overlapping national investment portfolios: Evidence and implications of international integration of secondary markets for financial assets, in: R.J. Hawkins and R.M. Levich, eds., Research in international business and finance, Vol. 3 (JAI Press, Greenwich, CT) 113–137.

Lessard, D.A., 1976, International diversification, Financial Analyst Journal 32, Feb., 32–38.

Levy, H. and M. Sarnat, 1970, International diversification of investment portfolios, American Economic Review 60, Sept., 668–675.

Maldonado, R. and A. Saunders, 1981, International portfolio diversification and the intertemporal stability of international stock market relationships, 1957–78, Financial Management, Autumn, 54–63.

Meric, I. and G. Meric, 1989, Potential gains from international portfolio diversification and inter-temporal stability and seasonality in international stock market relationships, Journal of Banking and Finance 13, 627–640.

Panton, D.B., V.P. Lessig and O.M. Joy, 1976, Co-movement of international equity markets: A taxonomic approach, Journal of Financial and Quantitative Analysis, Sept., 415–432.

Philippatos, G.C., A. Christofi and P. Christofi, 1983, The inter-temporal stability of international stock market relationships: Another view, Financial Management, Winter, 63–69.

Presidential Task Force on Market Mechanism, 1990, Report, Jan.

Ripley, D., 1973, Systematic elements in the linkage of national stock market indices, Review of Economics and Statistics 55, Aug., 356–361.

Roll, R.W., 1988, The international crash of October 1987, in: R. Kamphius, R. Kormendi and J.W.H. Watson, eds., Black Monday and the future of financial markets (Mid-American Institute), Oct., 35–70.

Schollhammer, H. and O. Sand, 1985, The interdependence among the stock markets of major European countries and the United States: An empirical investigation of interrelationships among national stock price movements, Management International Review 25, Jan., 17–26.

Solnik, B., 1977, Testing international asset pricing: Some pessimistic views, Journal of Finance 32, May, 503–512.

Global Stock Markets in the Twentieth Century

PHILIPPE JORION and WILLIAM N. GOETZMANN*

ABSTRACT

Long-term estimates of expected return on equities are typically derived from U.S. data only. There are reasons to suspect that these estimates are subject to survivorship, as the United States is arguably the most successful capitalist system in the world. We collect a database of capital appreciation indexes for 39 markets going back to the 1920s. For 1921 to 1996, U.S. equities had the highest real return of all countries, at 4.3 percent, versus a median of 0.8 percent for other countries. The high equity premium obtained for U.S. equities appears to be the exception rather than the rule.

IN A NOW-FAMOUS ARTICLE, Mehra and Prescott (1985) argue that standard general equilibrium models cannot explain the size of the risk premium on U.S. equities, which averages about 6 percent over the 1889–1978 period. They show that one would need a very large coefficient of risk aversion, largely in excess of the usual value of two, to generate such a premium. This unsettling result has sparked a flurry of theoretical research that explores alternative preference structures, including dropping the expected utility assumption and introducing habit formation.[1] Such efforts, however, come at the cost of losing the intuition of standard models.[2]

Rather than searching for preference structures that fit historical data, other explanations focus on the limitations of the data. Rietz (1988) proposes a solution to the puzzle that involves infrequently occurring "crashes." Assuming a crash where output falls by 50 (or 25) percent of its value with a

---

*Jorion is with the University of California at Irvine; Goetzmann is with the Yale School of Management. We thank seminar participants at the University of California at Los Angeles, Carnegie-Mellon, Indiana University, the London Business School, the Stockholm School of Economics, the University of Houston, the University of Michigan, the University of Notre Dame, the University of Southern California, the 1997 European Finance Association meetings, and the 1997 Western Finance Association meetings for useful comments. The referee and the editor, René Stulz, also provided valuable comments. Able research support was provided by Robin Brooks. George Bittlingmayer kindly provided a copy of the German data. This research received financial support from the Institute for Quantitative Research in Finance, for which we are grateful.

[1] See Epstein and Zin (1991) for nonadditive utility functions and Constantinides (1987) for habit formation. Bansal and Coleman (1996) suggest that liquidity services provided by cash partly explain why returns on cash are so low.

[2] Burnside and McCurdy (1992) provide a good review of the equity premium puzzle.

probability of 0.4 percent (or 1.4 percent), Rietz generates ex ante equity premiums consistent with those observed in the United States and risk aversion of five (or ten).

A related argument is advanced in Brown, Goetzmann, and Ross (1995), who claim that survival of the series imparts a bias to ex post returns. They show that an ex ante equity premium of zero can generate a high ex post positive premium by simply conditioning on the market surviving an absorbing lower bound over the course of a century.[3] The implication is that risk aversion cannot be inferred from the empirical analysis of historical data whose observation is conditional on survival. Although the Rietz (1988) argument leads to higher ex ante equity premiums, the survival argument points to biases in ex post premiums.

Unfortunately, these arguments are nearly impossible to sort out based on a century of U.S. equity data. Consider, for instance, a 0.4 percent annual probability of a large crash. We would then expect one crash to occur every 250 years. Even if we observed such a long sample series, our estimate of the crash probability would still be subject to enormous estimation error.

The only solution to this dilemma is to expand the sample by collecting additional cross-sectional data. In this paper, we reconstruct real capital appreciation series for equity markets in 39 countries over much of the twentieth century. We include not only those markets that survived, but also those markets that experienced both temporary and permanent interruptions. We use this new database to estimate the long-term returns to investing in global markets over the twentieth century.

The first part of our analysis treats each market separately. In effect, it takes all stock market histories as draws from one urn. Under these conditions, we show that the process of discarding markets with interruptions creates serious biases in the measurement of expected returns. Such an experiment assumes that all markets have the same statistical characteristics. This framework is valid when markets are segmented due, for instance, to capital controls. The assumption of constraints on such diversification is not unreasonable for the time period under study.

This paper provides the first comprehensive long-run estimates of return on equity capital across a broad range of markets. To date, virtually the only long-run evidence regarding equity rates of return is derived from the United States, for which we have continuous stock price history going back to 1802. We are able to augment the U.S. experience with a wide range of different global equity market histories.

We find striking evidence in support of the survival explanation for the equity risk premium. Over our sample period, the United States has the highest uninterrupted real rate of appreciation, at 4.3 percent annually. For other countries, the median real appreciation rate is approximately 0.8 per-

---

[3] A similar argument is advanced by Goetzmann and Jorion (1996). They argue that many so-called "emerging markets" are in fact "reemerging markets" as they have longer histories than commonly believed. Few analysts, however, bother to track the histories of markets that have disappeared.

cent. This strongly suggests that estimates of equity premiums obtained solely from the U.S. market are biased upward by survivorship. An alternative line of explanation is that of fundamentally different risk premiums. With segmented markets, risk premiums are determined by local market conditions. Thus differing expected returns could be due to different investor expectations about risk or to different risk aversion.

Beyond its potential value for shedding light on the equity premium puzzle, this global database allows a broad investigation into the behavior of equity markets over the very long run. We have been able to construct monthly real and dollar-valued capital appreciation indices for virtually all the equity markets that existed during the twentieth century. This enables us to examine markets in crisis and to compare the behavior of losing markets to the behavior of winning markets.

In the second part of the study, we construct a world market appreciation index in order to examine the potential experience of a diversified global investor. This allows us to analyze the benefits of international diversification, comparing return and risk measures across the U.S. and the global portfolios. We estimate the return that such an investor would have earned had it been possible to hold the world market from the early 1920s. Even though one could argue that few investors could have held globally diversified portfolios during these turbulent times, this is still an informative experiment as a guide for future investing.

This paper is organized as follows. Section I motivates the search for differences in return on capital. Section II describes the construction of the global market database. Section III compares the performance of global stock markets and discusses biases affecting the construction of a global stock market index. Section IV contains some concluding comments.

I. The Importance of Compound Growth

In September 1626, Pierre Minuit, the Governor of the West India Company, purchased Manhattan Island from the local Indians for the total sum of 60 guilders, or about 24 dollars. At first sight, this seems like the deal of the century.

Yet, slight differences in the time value of money over long horizons can result in vastly different conclusions. If one compounds this payment at a 5 percent rate of interest, it would have grown in 1995 to about 1.6 billion in current dollars, which seems expensive for 31 square miles of undeveloped land. Compounding at 3 percent, however, results in a much lower current price of $1.3 million—a thousandfold difference! This story shows that differences in rates of return on capital can lead to drastically different numbers when compounded over long horizons.

Our estimates of the rate of return on equity capital are typically based on a century of U.S. data, which reveals an equity premium of about 6 percent. As shown in this example, however, small differences in rates of return can have momentous implications over the long run. How much faith can we have in this number?

Not much, given the volatility of stock returns. Consider, for instance, a market that grows at a 6 percent annual rate with a standard deviation of 20 percent. The question is, how many years do we require to establish that growth is positive with statistical confidence? Using the standard t-test at the 5 percent level, we require that the statistic

$$t = \frac{\hat{\mu}}{\hat{\sigma}/\sqrt{N}} = \frac{0.06}{0.20/\sqrt{N}} \tag{1}$$

be greater than two. This requires N to be at least 44 years. In other words, we need approximately half a century of returns to be confident that this 6 percent equity premium is positive. If the expected return is 3 percent instead, we will need more than 178 years of data to establish statistical significance.

Another problem is that we have reasons to suspect that estimates of return on capital from the United States are affected by survival. At the beginning of the century, active stock markets existed in a number of countries, including Russia, France, Germany, Japan, and Argentina. All of these markets have been interrupted for a number of reasons, including political turmoil, war, and hyperinflation. Assuming there was some probability of disruption for the U.S. market, this probability is not reflected in the observed U.S. data. In turn, this will bias our estimates of the equity premium.

As small differences in estimates on equity capital have dramatic implications for long-term growth, we feel it is important to extend our knowledge of equity premiums to a large cross-sectional sample of long-term data.

II. A Global Stock Market Database

The standard data sources on international stock prices are *Morgan Stanley Capital International Perspectives* (MSCIP) for developed markets and the International Finance Corporation (IFC) for emerging markets. Both are relatively recent.

MSCIP started to construct equity indices in January 1970 for a sample of 19 markets from industrial (developed) countries. These indices are built using a uniform methodology and include income and currency effects. A similar approach was undertaken by the IFC, which in 1980 started to build indices for nine emerging markets, which were expanded to 26 by 1995.

Beyond these databases, unfortunately, there is little systematic information on the long-term performance of global stock markets. The United States is a rare exception, as monthly stock market indices have been constructed by Standard and Poor's and, prior to 1926, by Alfred Cowles (1939), going back into the 1870s.[4]

For the non-U.S. data, we must turn to a variety of sources. The first is the International Monetary Fund (IMF), which publishes monthly stock price indices as reported by the local authorities in its *International Financial Statistics* (IFS) publication. The published indices generally represent monthly averages, as opposed to the end-of-month MSCIP and IFC data, and do not include dividends.[5] The IMF also publishes price indices and exchange rates, which can be used to compute real returns and dollar returns. We use the Wholesale Price Index (WPI) to deflate nominal returns, whenever available. The WPI measure offers a number of advantages, in that the WPI indices generally have longer histories than consumer indices, are less affected by differences in domestic consumption patterns, and are more responsive to monetary disturbances than other inflation measures.[6]

One drawback of this dataset is that it does not allow us to measure directly the equity premium, usually defined as the difference between the total return on stocks minus the Treasury bill rate. Decomposing the total return on stocks (R_S) into capital return (CR_S) and income return (IR_S), and the Treasury bill rate (R_{TB}) into the inflation component and the real rate, we can write

$$\begin{aligned}\text{Equity Premium} &= R_S - R_{TB} \\ &= [CR_S + IR_S] - [\text{Inflation} + \text{Real Rate}] \\ &= [CR_S - \text{Inflation}] + [IR_S - \text{Real Rate}]. \end{aligned} \quad (2)$$

Our methodology measures the capital return in excess of inflation, which is the first bracketed term. To the extent that cross-sectional variations in the second bracketed term are small, this allows comparisons of equity premiums across countries. Some evidence on the quality of this approximation is presented later.

---

[4] For evidence on long-term U.S. data, see Wilson and Jones (1987), Schwert (1990), Siegel (1992) and Goetzmann and Ibbotson (1994). There is some long-term evidence from the U.K. markets; for instance, see Goetzmann (1993), DeLong and Grossman (1993), and Goetzmann and Jorion (1995). Parsons (1974), Mirowski (1981), and Neal (1987, 1990) provide data on the Amsterdam and London exchanges in the eighteenth century.

[5] Relative to more modern data, the IFS data suffer from two drawbacks: possible noncomparability in the construction of the series and use of monthly average instead of end-month price. The Cowles indices, the standard data source before 1926 for U.S. data, however, have similar drawbacks because prices are measured as the average of high and low values during the month.

[6] There are a few instances where we have to use Consumer Price Index data (e.g., post-1947 data for Belgium, France, New Zealand, Peru, and Israel). Because nominal prices in Germany were distorted during the hyperinflation period, we measure nominal prices for 1921–1923 in gold marks.

The first IFS publication was issued in 1948. Prior to the IMF, our source is the *Statistical Yearbooks* of the League of Nations (various issues), which include data on the capital appreciation of market indices in the period from 1929 through 1944. This collection effort was bridged by the United Nations' *Monthly Bulletin of Statistics* from 1945 to 1948. Finally, the *International Abstract of Economic Statistics* publications (ICES 1934, 1938) have stock market data going back to 1919.[7]

By connecting data from these sources, we are able to reconstruct histories for a number of stock markets going back to the early 1920s. This is a challenging effort, because of erratic data reporting.[8] The IMF, for example, provides a CD-ROM with data starting in 1957. Unfortunately, this database suffers from sample selection biases, as a number of markets that were followed in the 1960s are not contained in the CD-ROM. Data for these markets have to be collected from the IFS monthly publications. More recent emerging market data, when not available from the IFS publication, are available from the IFC database.

In order to minimize survivorship biases, we follow all markets that were reported by the League of Nation or the IMF at any point during the 1929 to 1970 period. After 1970, a flurry of new markets opened (or reopened). These emerging markets, however, have relatively short histories and are not included in the database as they have been already extensively analyzed. We obtain a total of 39 markets.[9] All in all, this involves a total of approximately 76,000 data points.

Whenever data sources do not overlap, we attempt to link series by comparing annual averages. This is the case for Austria, for instance, whose price history was interrupted by the Anschluss (German annexation) in April 1938. Fortunately, the United Nations' publications provide annual averages from 1946 on and going back to 1935; allowing us to reconstruct a long-term history for Austria, albeit with an 8-year gap during the war.

---

[7] Alfred Cowles, founder of the Cowles Commission for Research in Economics, was apparently the first scholar to document time-series data on global stock markets. We learned of the League of Nations data from the appendix to his 1939 publication which lists periodical sources for stock market data in 20 countries. A recent source of global stock market information which uses the League of Nations data, as well as information from other historical sources, is the Global Financial Markets database collected by Bryan Taylor, which we learned of after submission of this paper for publication. Taylor's database covers similar markets to ours; there are, however, some differences in the data sources and in particular during the breaks. For instance, we find the German stock price data collected by Gielen (1994) to be an excellent source for reconstruction of the German markets during the early part of the 20th century.

[8] The measurement of exchange rates also proves quite difficult. The League of Nations, for instance, reports rates in percentage of their 1929 gold parity value, from which current spot rates relative to the dollar have to be reconstructed. Many currencies also changed units or denomination during this century. Around World War II, trading in some currency pairs was either nonexistent or subject to heavy governmental control.

[9] The only market we deliberately omit is Lebanon, for which we cannot find inflation data.

Initially, we begin by collecting annual data. We find, however, that the monthly data create more precise estimates. In particular, we notice discrepancies between returns using monthly and annual data.[10] We also find that monthly data lead to cleaner linkages between various sources, which is particularly important as we sometimes have to patch series together. Finally, the monthly data allow us to perform event studies centered around specific dates.

Note that, despite all our efforts, this database is still not free from selection biases. The first type of bias occurs when backfilling of an index uses only stocks that are in existence at the end of the sample. In the case of Austria, for instance, even though the stock market has recovered, some companies may have fared badly or disappeared during the war. Therefore, a selection bias is induced if these companies are not included in the index.

The second type of remaining bias is much more serious. The UN–IMF data sources do not allow us to link gaps for six countries. In particular, there appears to be no link between stock market prices of Germany and Japan before and after the war in standard data sources. As these two countries did not fare well during these gaps, we can surmise that omitting the gaps misses important negative information. We attempt to correct for this by turning to other data sources for bridging these gaps.[11]

III. Empirical Analysis

A. Performance of Global Stock Markets

We calculate returns using three different numéraires: the local currency, a real price index, and the dollar. Because of wide differences in inflation across time and countries, we primarily focus on WPI-deflated returns. Returns in dollars as a common currency should give similar results over the long run if exchange rates move in line with inflation differentials—that is, if Purchasing Power Parity holds. Differences between real and dollar returns, however, may be induced when exchange rates are pegged by central banks at artificial levels, or when official exchange rates do not reflect the actual rates facing international investors.

---

[10] The difference can be particularly pronounced over short periods when the data are monthly or annual averages. As an illustration, comparing returns on the S&P index total returns series over 1926–1945, we find the annual growth to be 7.2 percent and 6.6 percent, respectively, for monthly and annual data.

[11] We have permanent gaps in the series for Chile, Germany, Japan, Peru, Portugal, and Argentina. The gap for Chile is filled using data from publications from the Chilean Central Bank. The gap for Germany is covered using data spliced by Gielen (1994). The gap for Japan is bridged using Bank of Japan (1966) data. The gap for Peru is filled using data received by the Lima stock exchange. To cover the gap for Portugal, we use information from the Portuguese Central Bank. Overall, Argentina is the only remaining country with a permanent break over July 1965 to December 1975, which is the first date for which we have data from the IFC. We have been unable to find data to bridge the gap.

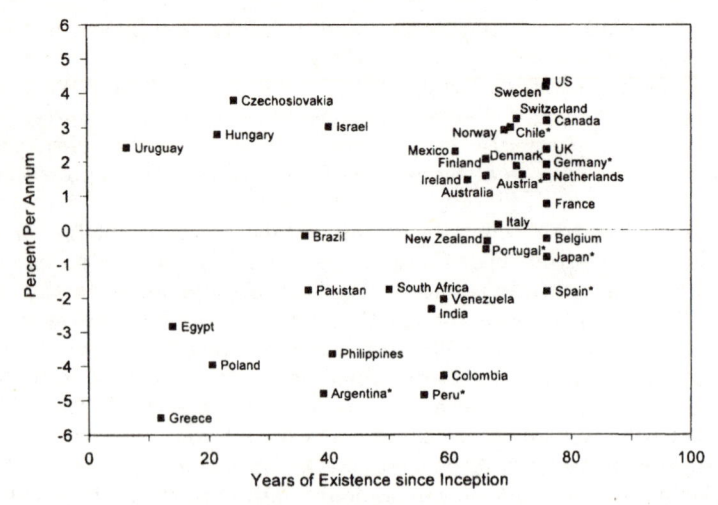

Figure 1. Real returns on global stock markets. The figure displays average real returns for 39 markets over the period 1921 to 1996. Markets are sorted by years of existence. The graph shows that markets with long histories typically have higher returns. An asterisk indicates that the market suffered a long-term break.

Table I presents geometric returns for 39 markets grouped by regions, compounded annually. These results are striking. Of the sample of 39 countries, real returns are the highest for the United States, at 4.32 percent per annum. There is no country with a higher return over the total period. Therefore, the high U.S. equity premium seems to be the exception rather than the rule.

These results are perhaps better visualized in Figure 1, which plots the compound return for each market against its observed "life" since 1921. Longer lives lead to more precise, less volatile, estimates of expected returns. Moving to the right of the figure, we observe that the U.S. market has the highest realized return of all markets.

At the bottom of Table I we show average and median returns for all countries, as well as for a group of countries for which we have data going to the 1920s. The median real returns for all 39 countries is 0.75 percent. By way of contrast, we also analyze countries with continuous histories going back to the 1920s; the median return for this group is also much higher, at 2.35 percent. These results strongly suggest that the 4.3 percent real capital appreciation return for the United States is highly unusual. As it is also one of the few series without any break, this high return could be ascribed to survival.

An alternative explanation is that the United States had a higher level of risk than any other market over the period. In perfectly integrated capital markets, a high equity premium can simply compensate for a high β. Of course, this is a difficult proposition to test directly because survivorship affects not only returns but also capital weights. Ex post, the most successful index will represent the largest share of the market.

Other high returns, however, are obtained in some cases. Over 1921 to 1996, Swedish equities displayed returns quite close to the 4.32 percent obtained in the United States, perhaps not surprisingly as Sweden also avoided major upheavals in this century. Higher returns are observed over more recent periods. For instance, Germany experienced a steep run-up in prices, 6 percent in real terms, over the period 1950 to 1996. But this high return must be offset against mediocre growth up to July 1944; additionally, during the five-year break in our series, German equities fell by 72 percent in real terms. As a result, the long-term growth of the German market is only 1.91 percent when evaluated over most of this century. The story is similar for Japan, where we observe a sharp difference between the postwar return of 5.52 percent and the prewar return of -0.34 percent. During the 1944 to 1949 break, the market fell by 95 percent in real terms.

Other markets that gapped, such as Portugal, Chile, and Peru, also did well recently, but not so well when going back further in time. These are typical "reemerging markets," whose recent performance appears to be, on the surface, nothing short of stellar. Our analysis shows that the performance of the same markets has also been mediocre at other times.

Table I also reports dollar returns. As expected, rankings for this column are very similar to those obtained with real returns.[12] In general, dollar returns for other currencies are slightly closer to U.S. returns than real returns. For example, the difference between U.S. equities and the median is 4.32 − 0.75 = 3.57 percent when measured in real terms; the difference is 6.95 − 4.68 = 2.27 percent in dollar terms. This discrepancy reflects the slight depreciation of the dollar, relative to its Purchasing Power Parity value, over the sample period.

In addition to geometric returns, which represent returns to a buy-and-hold strategy, it is also useful to consider arithmetic averages, which give equal weight to each observation interval. Table II presents conventional measures of annualized average (arithmetic) capital appreciation returns and standard deviations.[13] Data are presented in the local currency, in real terms, and in dollars. The table shows that the 16.2 percent volatility of the U.S. market is not particularly high when compared with other stock markets. Therefore the high return obtained in the United States does not seem to compensate for higher risk as measured by volatility (which would be the appropriate measure of risk under segmented capital markets).

---

[12] Uruguay and Czechoslovakia had higher returns than U.S. equities, but this was over shorter periods during which currencies were subject to controls; hence, these returns are not representative.

[13] Since price data are monthly averages, it should be noted that the reported standard deviations are lower than those from using month-end data. Additionally, averaging induces spurious positive autocorrelation in the return series.

Table I
Long-Term Performance of Global Equity Markets
(Compound Return in Percentage per Annum)

The table compares the long-term performance of global equity markets with annually compounded data. The sample period varies across country and is reported in the second column. Data for subperiods are reported within brackets. Percentage returns are measured in nominal terms in the local currency, in real terms—deflating by the Wholesale Price Index, and translated into U.S. dollars. The last column reports the inflation rate. * indicates a break in the series that has been bridged; + indicates a permanent discontinuity in the series.

Country	Period	Nominal Return	Real Return	Dollar Return	Inflation
United States	1/21–12/96	6.95	4.32	6.95	2.52
Canada	1/21–12/96	5.78	3.19	5.35	2.51
Austria*	1/25–12/96	5.64	1.62	5.00	3.95
Belgium	1/21–12/96	4.45	−0.26	3.51	4.73
Denmark	1/26–12/96	5.87	1.87	5.19	3.93
Finland	1/31–12/96	10.23	2.07	6.19	7.99
France	1/21–12/96	9.09	0.75	4.29	8.28
Germany*	21–96	4.43	1.91	5.81	2.47
Germany	1/21–7/44	[3.29]	[2.23]	[5.59]	[1.04]
Germany	1/50–12/96	[8.46]	[6.00]	[10.78]	[2.32]
Ireland	1/34–12/96	7.00	1.46	5.14	5.45
Italy	12/28–12/96	10.10	0.15	3.22	9.94
Netherlands	1/21–12/96	3.71	1.55	4.47	2.12
Norway	1/28–12/96	7.13	2.91	6.29	4.10
Portugal*	31–96	6.89	−0.58	3.78	7.51
Portugal	12/30–4/74	[5.21]	[1.16]	[4.96]	[4.00]
Portugal	3/77–12/96	[20.11]	[5.63]	[11.92]	[13.71]
Spain*	1/21–12/96	4.66	−1.82	1.53	6.61
Sweden	1/21–12/96	7.42	4.29	7.00	3.00
Switzerland	1/26–12/96	4.83	3.24	6.84	1.54
United Kingdom	1/21–12/96	6.30	2.35	5.20	3.86
Czechoslovakia	1/21–4/45	4.33	3.79	9.50	0.52
Greece	7/29–9/40	−2.12	−5.50	−8.08	3.58
Hungary	1/25–6/44	6.29	2.80	9.07	3.40
Poland	1/21–6/39	−7.00	−3.97	−4.30	−3.15
Romania	12/37–6/41	−5.36	−28.06	−14.64	31.55
Australia	1/31–12/96	7.06	1.58	6.29	5.39
New Zealand	1/31–12/96	5.69	−0.34	3.63	6.01
Japan*	21–96	7.33	−0.81	1.80	8.21
Japan	1/21–5/44	[1.23]	[−0.34]	[−1.83]	[1.58]
Japan	4/49–12/96	[8.30]	[5.52]	[10.90]	[2.63]
India	12/39–12/96	5.10	−2.33	0.80	7.60
Pakistan	7/60–12/96	7.79	−1.77	0.59	8.57
Philippines	7/54–12/96	5.95	−3.65	−0.30	9.96
Argentina+	47–65,75–96	87.48	−4.80	−1.43	96.92
Argentina	9/47–7/65	[−5.78]	[−25.09]	[−23.64]	[25.78]
Argentina	12/75–12/96	[236.29]	[16.71]	[22.43]	[188.15]
Brazil	2/61–12/96	142.34	−0.17	4.68	147.52
Mexico	12/34–12/96	20.13	2.30	6.12	17.43

Global Stock Markets

Table I—Continued

Country	Period	Nominal Return	Real Return	Dollar Return	Inflation
Chile*	27–96	37.12	2.99	6.38	33.16
Chile	1/27–3/71	[12.98]	[−5.37]	[−4.23]	[19.39]
Chile	1/74–12/96	[64.19]	[15.52]	[20.94]	[42.13]
Colombia	12/36–12/96	10.15	−4.29	−0.88	15.09
Peru*	41–96	45.29	−4.85	3.45	52.68
Peru	3/41–1/53	[2.03]	[−12.36]	[2.03]	[16.41]
Peru	1/57–12/77	[1.53]	[−9.88]	[−7.40]	[12.66]
Peru	12/88–12/96	[340.95]	[30.45]	[50.92]	[232.18]
Uruguay	3/38–11/44	6.70	2.42	10.01	4.19
Venezuela	12/37–12/96	9.67	−2.04	0.78	11.95
Egypt	7/50–9/62	−1.46	−2.84	−1.63	1.42
Israel	1/57–12/96	37.05	3.03	7.21	33.02
South Africa	1/47–12/96	6.13	−1.76	1.48	8.03
All 39 countries					
Mean			−0.47	3.11	
Median			0.75	4.68	
11 countries with continuous histories into the 1920s					
Mean			1.88	5.09	
Median			2.35	5.20	

The table also reports the results from standard statistical tests of significance of the real capital appreciation return premium. At the 99 percent level, we can only reject the hypothesis of a zero long-run appreciation return for the United States and Sweden. Over shorter periods, we observe significantly positive returns for Germany and Japan in the postwar period. When averaged with prewar data, however, these returns look less impressive.

B. The Effect of Dividend Omission

The previous section has revealed a striking result: long-term returns on the U.S. stock market appear to be greater than those of any other market during this century. One question that arises is whether this result could be due to the omission of dividends. To shed light on this issue, Table III presents performance numbers for markets for which we have dividend data.

Panel A reports data for the more recent MSCIP indices, which mainly cover industrial countries since 1971. The table displays compound real returns, with and without reinvestment of dividends. The difference due to the omission of dividends is shown in the third column. The fourth column reports the average level of inflation. Presumably, the results in the previous section could simply reflect a bias due to the omission of dividends. For this bias to be effective, other markets must systematically display a higher income component of return than the United States.

Table II
Return and Risk of Global Equity Markets
(Arithmetic Return in Percentage per Annum)

The table compares average stock returns and their standard deviations. Percentage returns are measured in nominal terms in the local currency, in real terms, deflating by the Wholesale Price Index, and translated into U.S. dollars. The arithmetic average return is obtained from the monthly average multiplied by 12; the standard deviation is annualized by multiplying the monthly volatility by the square root of 12. For series with breaks, (1), (2), (3) refer to different subperiods.

		Nominal Return		Real Return		Dollar Return	
Country	Period	Average	(Std.Dev.)	Average	(Std.Dev.)	Average	(Std.Dev.)
United States	1/21–12/96	8.09**	(16.20)	5.48**	(15.84)	8.09**	(16.20)
Canada	1/21–12/96	7.06**	(16.81)	4.54*	(16.65)	6.88**	(18.17)
Austria	1/25–12/96	6.77**	(18.92)	2.32	(19.49)	7.22**	(21.49)
Belgium	1/21–12/96	6.25**	(17.92)	1.49	(18.97)	5.77**	(21.80)
Denmark	1/26–12/96	6.43**	(12.04)	2.65	(12.69)	6.10**	(14.36)
Finland	1/31–12/96	10.74**	(16.56)	3.50	(17.07)	8.18**	(20.49)
France	1/21–12/96	11.19**	(21.57)	3.16	(21.25)	7.76**	(25.50)
Germany (1)	1/21–7/44	10.22	(40.24)	7.62	(34.26)	12.54	(40.49)
Germany (2)	1/50–12/96	9.35**	(15.50)	7.06**	(15.60)	11.75**	(17.19)
Ireland	1/34–12/96	7.88**	(14.85)	2.59	(15.02)	6.43**	(16.73)
Italy	12/28–12/96	12.62**	(26.01)	3.15	(25.66)	3.15	(25.66)
Netherlands	1/21–12/96	4.78**	(15.12)	2.78*	(14.80)	5.85**	(16.50)
Norway	1/28–12/96	8.49**	(17.90)	4.47*	(17.90)	7.97**	(19.33)
Portugal (1)	12/30–4/74	6.50**	(15.15)	2.34	(14.69)	7.40**	(15.03)
Portugal (2)	3/77–12/96	27.08**	(46.38)	14.69	(47.68)	20.42	(47.11)
Spain	1/21–12/96	6.77**	(18.92)	−0.51	(16.00)	2.44	(28.89)
Sweden	1/21–12/96	8.56**	(16.61)	5.60**	(16.65)	8.38**	(17.69)
Switzerland	1/26–12/96	5.83**	(14.79)	4.28*	(14.73)	7.91**	(15.97)
United Kingdom	1/21–12/96	7.25**	(15.43)	3.60*	(15.68)	6.66**	(17.57)
Czechoslovakia	1/21–4/45	5.04*	(12.53)	4.56	(12.84)	10.50**	(17.12)
Greece	7/29–9/40	−0.09	(21.77)	−3.44	(21.61)	−5.31	(25.50)
Hungary	1/25–6/44	9.34	(25.84)	6.20	(26.58)	11.99*	(26.02)
Poland	1/21–6/39	13.60	(71.20)	14.40	(65.69)	16.69	(71.54)
Romania	12/37–6/41	0.14	(33.31)	−27.30	(31.38)	−9.45	(35.06)
Australia	1/31–12/96	7.78**	(13.49)	2.57	(13.94)	7.68**	(18.06)
New Zealand	1/31–12/96	6.20**	(12.12)	0.55	(12.50)	4.98**	(15.97)
Japan (1)	1/21–5/44	2.72	(17.51)	0.89	(15.79)	−0.35	(17.40)
Japan (2)	4/49–12/96	9.79**	(18.78)	7.21**	(18.90)	12.61**	(20.97)
India	12/39–12/96	6.18**	(15.53)	−1.07	(16.13)	2.37	(17.46)
Pakistan	7/60–12/96	7.46**	(14.37)	−0.64	(15.23)	2.39	(17.50)
Philippines	7/54–12/96	10.62	(37.35)	1.21	(37.21)	5.30	(38.91)
Argentina (1)	9/47–7/65	−1.13	(31.91)	−23.32**	(32.73)	−18.17	(40.11)
Argentina (2)	12/75–12/96	179.34	(133.55)	49.68	(87.83)	57.85**	(93.68)
Brazil	2/61–12/96	110.69**	(68.22)	12.92	(51.93)	18.45*	(53.44)
Mexico	12/34–12/96	21.97**	(26.79)	5.37	(24.45)	10.46**	(29.09)
Chile (1)	1/27–3/71	14.51**	(22.45)	−3.91	(21.85)	−0.12	(28.64)
Chile (2)	12/73–12/96	57.19**	(40.34)	20.48**	(36.25)	25.94**	(38.59)
Colombia	12/36–12/96	11.66**	(21.56)	−2.32	(21.78)	1.67	(23.39)
Peru (1)	3/41–1/53	3.02	(12.90)	−12.08**	(14.15)	3.39	(16.58)
Peru (2)	1/57–12/77	1.89	(8.62)	−9.94**	(9.08)	−6.61*	(13.66)
Peru (3)	12/88–12/96	200.64**	(118.38)	55.55	(87.98)	71.95*	(87.18)
Uruguay	12/36–11/44	10.55	(28.98)	6.67	(29.66)	13.80	(29.63)
Venezuela	12/37–12/96	12.03**	(24.65)	0.88	(24.84)	4.85	(28.08)
Egypt	7/50–9/62	−0.83	(11.50)	−2.11	(12.54)	−0.19	(17.33)
Israel	1/57–12/96	35.18**	(26.07)	5.68	(22.96)	10.07*	(24.33)
South Africa	1/47–12/96	7.24**	(15.75)	−0.46	(15.89)	3.34	(18.87)

*, ** Significantly different from zero at the 5 and 1 percent levels, respectively.

Table III
Comparison of Real Returns with and without Dividends

The table compares stock returns with and without dividends. Returns are measured in real terms and are annually compounded. The top part reports Morgan Stanley Capital International Perspective (MSCIP) data; the bottom part presents long-term data, obtained from various sources.

Country		Compound Return with Dividend (% pa)	Compound Return without Dividend (% pa)	Difference due to Dividend	Inflation (% pa)
\multicolumn{6}{c}{Panel A: Markets Covered by MSCIP, 1970–1995}					
Australia		3.65	−0.71	4.36	6.79
Austria		4.89	2.07	2.82	2.75
Belgium		12.97	4.05	8.92	2.46
Canada		4.34	0.65	3.69	5.78
Denmark		6.54	2.71	3.83	5.62
France		4.45	−0.29	4.74	7.40
Germany		5.52	1.44	4.08	3.09
Italy		−0.26	−2.95	2.69	9.87
Japan		8.59	6.75	1.84	2.18
Netherlands		8.84	3.09	5.74	3.41
Norway		6.03	2.78	3.26	5.90
Spain		2.30	−4.00	6.31	8.40
Sweden		8.79	5.03	3.76	7.42
Switzerland		5.72	3.06	2.66	2.54
United Kingdom		6.39	1.23	5.16	8.35
United States		6.15	2.01	4.14	4.89
Average		5.93	1.68	4.25	5.43
\multicolumn{6}{c}{Panel B: Long-Term Markets}					
Denmark	1923–95	4.88	0.64	4.24	3.72
Germany	1924–95	4.83	1.21	3.63	2.47
Sweden	1926–95	7.13	3.30	3.83	3.64
Switzerland	1921–95	5.57	2.12	3.45	2.49
United Kingdom	1921–95	8.16	2.99	5.17	3.75
United States	1921–95	8.22	3.38	4.84	2.69
United States	1871–1920	5.43	0.27	5.16	0.59

Table III clearly shows that this is not the case. Over the 1970–1995 period, the dividend effect for the United States was 4.14 percent, which is quite close to the group average of 4.25 percent. Therefore, there is no indication that the high return obtained for U.S. equities in Table I is due to dividend bias. If anything, the bias is in the opposite direction. For example, Japanese equities, which by now constitute the largest market outside the United States, paid an income return of 1.84 percent over the past 25 years, which is much lower than that of U.S. equities.

Panel B of Table III reports the only long-term data with dividends that we are aware of.[14] To maintain comparability with the original data sources, we use the Consumer Price Index (CPI) to deflate returns, except for Denmark where the WPI is employed. Including dividends, the United States displays the highest real equity returns since 1921, at 8.22 percent. Britain, another long-term survivor, is a close second; other markets provide returns that are lower by 109 to 334 basis points. Another way to look at the data is to notice that the ranking of returns is essentially the same with and without dividends. Therefore, there is no evidence that the performance of U.S. equities is artificially high because of relatively low U.S. dividend payments.

C. Evidence on the Equity Premium Puzzle

The data we present thus far do not explicitly solve the equity premium puzzle, as theoretically formulated. Strictly speaking, the equity premium puzzle concerns the spread of expected total return on the market portfolio of equities over the return of a riskless security. Siegel (1994) points out that defaults on "riskless" government securities have often occurred in periods of global stress—which of course raises the question of what the riskless asset might actually be and whether the stylized, single economy, two-asset formulation of the equity premium puzzle is robust.

In the absence of a riskless asset that is immune to the crisis events imagined by Rietz (1988), it seems reasonable to substitute physical storage of goods (i.e., inflation rates for T-bill rates). In this case, using real returns as a proxy for the equity premium clearly supports the hypothesis that the ex post observed U.S. premium is higher because the United States was a winner. This evidence, in turn, is consistent with the "survival" hypothesis suggesting that the magnitude of ex post observed equity returns may be higher than their ex ante expectation.

Is there any evidence in the data supporting the Rietz (1988) hypothesis that the ex ante equity premium is as high as supposed? The issue is whether there was some probability of the U.S. market experiencing a large crash. In fact, this problem is akin to the "peso problem" in the foreign exchange market, where peso forward rates appeared to be biased forecasts of future spot rates over short sample periods, essentially because they account for a nonzero probability of devaluation that is not observed. More generally, peso problems can be interpreted as a failure of the paradigm of rational expectations econometrics, which requires that the ex post distribution of endogenous variables be a good approximation to the ex ante distribution that agents think may happen. The failure may not be that of the economic agent, but that of the econometrician, who only analyzes series with continuous

---

[14] Data sources are as follows: For the U.S. market, Ibbotson (1995) and prior to that, Cowles (1939); for the U.K., Barclays deZoete Wedd (1993); for Switzerland, Wydler (1989); for Sweden, Frenneberg and Hansson (1992); and for Denmark, Timmerman (1992). All of the data have been updated to 1995 using the MSCIP indices.

histories. Unusual events with a low probability of occurrence but severe effects on prices, such as wars or nationalizations, are not likely to be well represented in samples and may be totally omitted from survived series.

Our cross-sectional data provide evidence about major market crashes not present in U.S. data. We have, for example, 24 markets for which we have data in 1931. Of these, seven experienced no interruption (the United States, Canada, the United Kingdom, Australia, New Zealand, Sweden, and Switzerland), seven experienced a temporary suspension of trading (less than one year), and the remaining 10 markets suffered long-term closure. Even though these events are not independent, they indicate that market failure is not a remote possibility. Under the assumption that market risks are "priced" individually, rather than under the assumption of integration, the frequency of failure would provide clear justification for a peso problem explanation.

Although it is entirely possible that the magnitude of the observed equity premium is due both to survival bias and to the "pricing" of an infrequently occurring crash, it is difficult to believe that the ex ante premium for the United States should be higher than for other markets. The increased probability of a large crash may explain a higher average equity premium, but if past crash frequency is any indication of future crash probability, then the Rietz (1988) hypothesis would suggest that markets with more interruptions should have a higher equity premium. If we believe that the magnitude of the equity premiums for each country is related to the ex post historical real appreciation, then the opposite appears to be the case. Absent survival effects, the Rietz hypothesis is inconsistent with cross-sectional differences in historical global equity market returns. In the next section, we investigate the possibility that markets anticipate major crashes.

Table III provides additional evidence on the equity premium puzzle by comparing the performance of U.S. equities during the recent period with longer term, 1871–1920, Cowles data. The last line in the table shows that the high real capital return obtained since 1921 is much higher than that obtained in the preceding 50 years—3.38 percent during 1921–1995 against 0.27 percent during 1871–1920. Siegel (1992) also points out that the U.S. equity premium is particularly high during this century. Put differently, this large premium seems not only large in a cross-country comparison but also by historical standards. Siegel concludes that "investors in ... 1872 did not universally expect the United States to become the greatest economic power in the next century." If so, returns on U.S. equities this century cannot be viewed as representative of global stock markets.

D. Disappearance as an Event

To understand how risk premiums respond to the probability of major market crashes, we can examine the behavior of markets around interruptions. Sample selection of markets will create a bias if the performance of interrupted markets is systematically poor before the break. By the same token,

Table IV
Analysis of Stock Prices around Breaks

The table describes the behavior of stock prices measured in real terms around major breaks. It reports the break date, the return in the year previous to the break, the series restart date, and subsequent change, when available. Real returns are in excess of the Wholesale Price Index for the corresponding countries. * indicates that equities were effectively subject to price controls; + indicates that the subsequent change was obtained from alternative data sources.

Country	Break date	Previous year return	Series restart date	Subsequent change	Comment
Hungary	7/31	−0.222	9/32	0.125	Financial crisis, country in default
Germany	7/31	−0.316	4/32	−0.232	Credit crisis
Greece	10/31	−0.099	12/32	−0.581	Financial crisis, drought
Spain	7/36	−0.113	3/40	−0.147	Civil War
Austria	4/38	−0.179	12/46	0.941	Annexation by Germany
Czechoslovakia	10/38	−0.205	1/40	0.015	Session of land to Germany
Poland	7/39	0.169			Invaded by Germany (Sep 30)
Finland	12/39	−0.192	3/40	−0.101	Invaded by Soviets (Nov 30)
Denmark	4/40	−0.328	6/40	−0.084	Invaded by Germany (Apr 9)
Norway	4/40	−0.274	6/40	−0.154	Invaded by Germany (Apr 11)
Netherlands	5/40	−0.231	9/40	0.105	Invaded by Germany (May 10)
Belgium	5/40	−0.267	12/40	0.850	Invaded by Germany (May 10)
Switzerland	5/40	−0.193	7/40	−0.207	Mobilization
France	6/40	−0.122	4/41	0.824	Invaded by Germany (Jun 14)
Greece	10/40	−0.249	none		Invaded by Germany (Oct 28)
Romania	7/41	−0.396	none		Enters war
Czechoslovakia*	7/43	−0.141	none		War
Japan*	6/44	−0.211	4/49	−0.949+	War
Hungary*	7/44	−0.491	none		War
Belgium*	8/44	0.161	6/45	−0.145	War
Germany*	8/44	−0.013	1/50	−0.838+	Invaded by Allies (Sep 15)
Egypt	10/62	−0.126	none		Arab socialism
Argentina	8/65	−0.692	N/A		Widespread unrest, hyperinflation
Chile	4/71	−0.543	1/74	1.618+	State takes control of economy (Apr 4) Junta reverses policies (Sep 11, 73)
Portugal	4/74	−0.112	3/77	−0.860+	Takeover by leftist junta (Apr 27)

falling stock prices prior to a market break may be indicative of investor assessment of increasing probability that the market will fail.

To test this hypothesis, we adopt the event-study methodology by constructing an equally weighted index in which real returns are aligned on the interruption date. We identify a sample of 25 breaks for which the data series are clearly interrupted. Table IV identifies each of these events. Many are of a global nature, such as the Second World War, or the depression of the early 1930s. A number of events, however, are country-specific, involving a banking crisis or political turmoil.

Figure 2 plots the time-series of the portfolio value, starting one year before the break. It shows prices falling on average by 21 percent relative to their peak. The t-test based on the standard deviation of monthly changes in

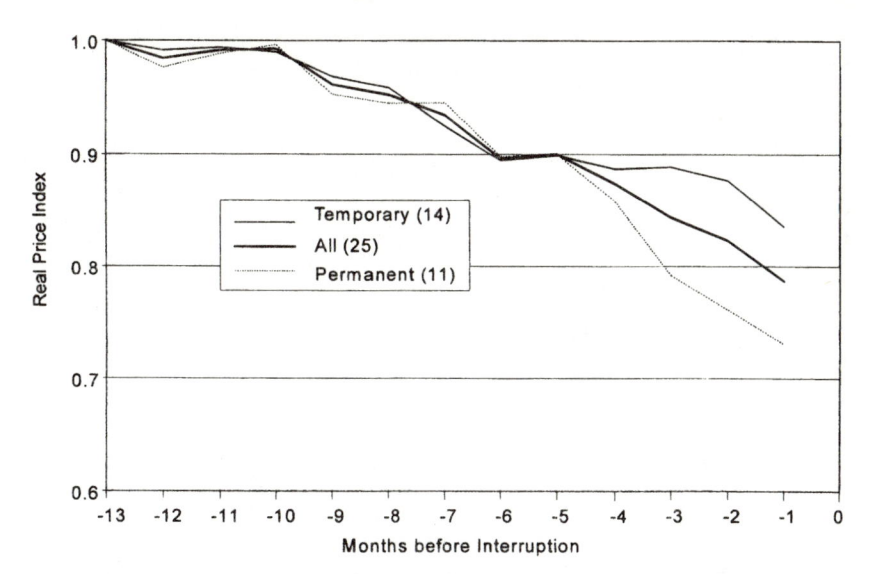

Figure 2. Real stock prices before interruption. The figure displays the performance of an equally weighted index where real returns are aligned on the interruption date. The total sample of 25 is further divided into a sample for which the interruption turns out to be temporary, and a sample for which the interruption is permanent.

the previous year is −4.95 for this number, which is highly significant. However large, this fall of 21 percent in real terms understates the true loss of value to equities. During World War II, in particular, prices were kept artificially high through price controls and do not represent transaction prices as liquidity dried up.[15]

Eventually, reality prevailed. Figure 3 compares the performance of markets sorted by country involvement during the war.[16] As the figure shows, the advent of the war led to a sharp fall of about 20 percent in the value of equities of Allied countries (including the United States, Canada, the United Kingdom, and Commonwealth countries) for the next two months. A similar fall was suffered by neutral countries (Sweden and Switzerland). The index

---

[15] In Germany, Italy, and German-occupied territories, dealing in shares was subject to strict controls, ranging from taxes on profits and capital gains to the rationing of purchases and to the compulsory declaration of securities holdings. In June 1942, for instance, the sale of German shares became prohibited unless they were first offered to the Reichsbank. The Reichsbank had the option to buy them at December 1941 prices in exchange for bonds that remained in the bank's possession. It is no wonder that this confiscatory system led to a sharp fall in trading activity. There were also rigid price controls in Japan during the war; see for instance Adams and Hoshii (1971). Therefore many of these price indices do not represent market-determined prices.

[16] The index for occupied countries includes Belgium, Czechoslovakia, France, Denmark, Finland, Germany, Hungary, Italy, Netherlands, and Norway.

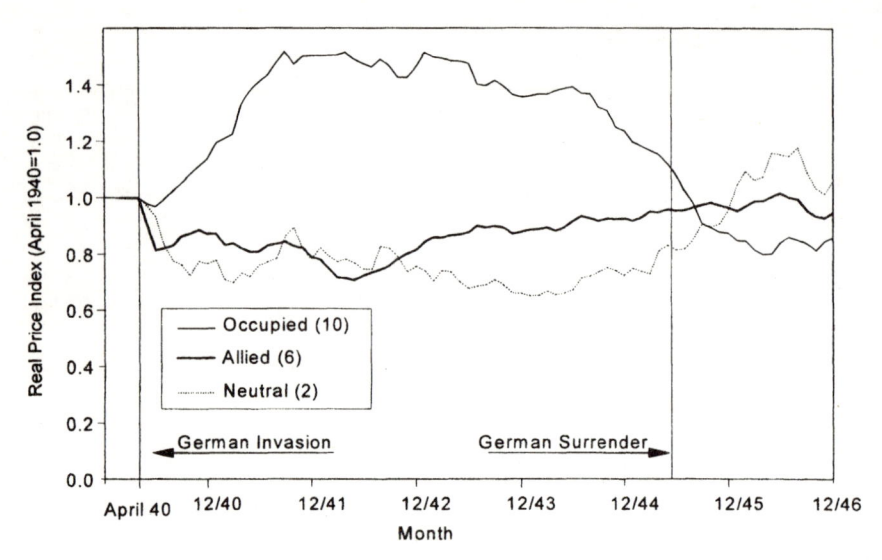

Figure 3. Real stock prices during World War II. The figure displays the performance of portfolios of equities measured in real terms during the war. The sample is divided into occupied, allied, and neutral countries.

for occupied countries, in contrast, registered steady gains, which were only wiped out later as stock prices started to reflect transaction prices and as inflation became apparent. Five years later, the index moved below that of Allied countries, as we would have expected. In reality, the index should have been even lower if we had accounted for those markets that disappeared in the process (such as Germany, Hungary, and Czechoslovakia.)

Table IV also details the performance around each individual break. All markets suffered a substantial drop before the break, reaching 69 percent for Argentina. One exception is Poland, which experienced a slight price increase, possibly because the series was stopped in July, three months before Poland was invaded, or because the advent of the war was unanticipated. As explained before, the price drops in Germany and occupied Europe are also unusual, for artificial reasons. In all other cases, the event creating the market closure was anticipated.

In eleven of these cases, the UN–IMF equity series are interrupted without restarting later (or there are no continuous series spanning the interruption). These cases include Germany, Japan, Eastern European countries taken over by the Soviet Union, Greece, Egypt, Chile, Argentina, and Portugal. Some of these were the result of a foreign occupation and widespread destruction due to war. In Egypt and Chile, the state took control of the economy. The Buenos Aires Stock Exchange, the oldest in Latin America, virtually disappeared as a result of inflation and interest rate policies in the late 1960s; reportedly, investors lost all interest in the market. These are precisely the situations where we would expect equities to fare most badly.

We have to turn to other data sources to bridge these "permanent" breaks. We find that, over the 1944–1949 break in Japan, equities fell by 95 percent in real terms.[17] For Germany, we find that equities fell by 84 percent in real terms over 1944–1950. Another example is the Portuguese stock market, which closed in April 1974 as a military junta took over the country, reopened in March 1977, then traded intermittently. The stock price series suffered a fall of 86 percent in real terms during the interruption in trading. In contrast, most of the loss for the Chilean stock market occurred before the interruption; the market recovered somewhat over the 1971–1974 break, as the military junta reversed the socialist policies of the Allende government.[18] Furthermore, these numbers probably underestimate the true loss in value by ignoring companies that failed during the interruption, as indices are backfilled from companies quoted before and after the break.

Going back to Figure 2, we have separated markets that were temporarily interrupted from those that disappeared, or "died," later. Markets that became extinct dropped by 27 percent the year before the break; markets that subsequently recovered dropped by only 16 percent before the break. To the extent that the event causing the break was anticipated, the market seems to have been able to gauge the gravity of unfolding events. Price declines before breaks are consistent with increasing demand for risk compensation for a catastrophic event.

E. A Global Stock Index

The global equity data provide a unique opportunity to construct a global equity index—an index that for the first time includes defunct as well as surviving countries and extends back 75 years. Because we have no data on market capitalization going back that far, we assign weights based on Gross Domestic Product (GDP). Annual GDP information is obtained from Mitchell (1992, 1993, 1995) and converted to U.S. dollars using annual averages. At the beginning of each decade, we construct a cross section of national GDPs, which are used to construct initial weights.

To minimize rebalancing, we adopt a portfolio value-weighted approach. Our global indices are therefore similar to market capitalization indices, except that the weights are reset to GDP weights at the beginning of each decade. A value-weighted scheme is more appropriate for measurement of investor returns when survival is an issue. As our analysis in the previous section demonstrates, markets that die tend to have less weight when they do so.

---

[17] The Bank of Japan (1966) estimates that the material damage due to World War II was to reduce national wealth from 253 to 189 billion yen, which is a fall of 64 billion yen (not accounting for human losses), or about $15 billion. For comparison purposes, the market value of equities in 1945 was about 40 billion yen.

[18] The market lost 54 percent in the year to April 1971 during the Allende ascent to power, but then increased by 62 percent later, which is only a partial recovery. Assuming a starting value of 100, the market fell to 46, then recovered to 1.62 times 46, or 74, ending with a net loss in value relative to the starting point.

The indices represent the return an investor would have earned had it been possible to hold the market since the 1920s. This is a hypothetical experiment, however, because it would have been difficult to maintain such a portfolio. Constraints on cross-border capital flows and on liquidation of equity positions were acute during crises—precisely the times when the ability to diversify is most beneficial. In this period, investors were sometimes involuntarily separated from their assets, due to expropriations or nationalizations. As a result, it is not clear whether, for example, a U.S. investor could have continued to hold German or Japanese equities during World War II.

Table V presents the GDP weights at three points in time: 1920, 1950, and 1990. The table reveals a number of interesting observations. The United States accounts for about one-half of the world's output until the 1950s; the proportion then declines to approximately 30 percent. This decline is due to faster growth in other countries such as Japan and Germany. Japan, in particular, zooms from 4 percent of world GDP to 16 percent over this period, even after dipping below 2 percent after the war.

The GDP-based weights can be compared to stock market capitalization-based weights, which are reported in the last column. We observe that the stock market capitalization percentages of the United States, the United Kingdom, Japan, and South Africa are generally greater than those of other countries. Continental Europe, for example, has a history of relying on bank lending rather than raising funds through capital issues. Overall, however, the GDP weights are roughly of the same order of magnitude as market weights.

Biases can be introduced in the measured performance in a number of ways. The first is backfilling, and the second is due to interruptions. There is not much the researcher can do about backfilling if the series are the only ones available. As for interruptions, the problem is that data before the interruption are commonly ignored. Interruptions can be of two types: temporary closure of an exchange, with the series starting again later, or permanent interruption of these series, with no information about the continuity of prices across the interruption.

We take two approaches to the construction of the global index:

(i) Our "survived markets" index includes all markets since the last interruption, which can be a temporary break or a permanent closure; only markets in existence at the end of the sample are considered. As of December 1996, we have a total of 32 markets; of which only 18 had continuous histories to December 1940, for instance.

(ii) Our "all markets" index extends the sample to all markets in existence in our sample, including returns before temporary and permanent closures. As of December 1940, this "comprehensive" series yields 29 markets, adding Austria, Belgium, and France (which suffered a temporary interruption of trading during World War II), Chile, Germany, Japan, Portugal, Uruguay, and three markets that suffered a permanent break during the war: Czechoslovakia, Hungary, and Romania.

Table V
Relative Importance of Economies
(Percentage Weights Based on U.S. Dollar Prices)

The table describes the percentage of each country in the total Gross Domestic Product (GDP) in 1920, 1950, and 1990. The last column shows the percentage weight based on stock market capitalization.

Country	GDP Weights 1920	GDP Weights 1950	GDP Weights 1990	Stock Market Capitalization 1995
United States	46.17%	51.52%	30.59%	41.03%
Canada	2.40%	3.16%	3.17%	2.16%
Austria	0.48%	0.47%	0.87%	0.24%
Belgium	0.73%	1.27%	1.09%	0.66%
Denmark	0.55%	0.56%	0.72%	0.37%
Finland	0.17%	0.42%	0.76%	0.26%
France	6.14%	5.19%	6.61%	3.27%
Germany	6.04%	4.19%	8.29%	3.75%
Ireland	0.42%	0.19%	0.24%	0.16%
Italy	1.67%	2.43%	6.07%	1.16%
Netherlands	0.98%	0.89%	1.57%	1.97%
Norway	0.56%	0.38%	0.59%	0.28%
Portugal	0.62%	0.25%	0.33%	0.12%
Spain	2.16%	0.82%	2.72%	0.99%
Sweden	1.22%	1.11%	1.26%	1.14%
Switzerland	0.84%	0.80%	1.25%	2.60%
United Kingdom	10.36%	6.57%	5.41%	8.77%
Czechoslovakia	0.52%	0.31%	0.25%	0.10%
Greece	0.33%	0.39%	0.37%	0.11%
Hungary	0.38%	0.71%	0.18%	0.02%
Poland	1.82%	0.35%	0.03%	
Romania		0.00%	0.21%	—
Australia	2.31%	1.07%	1.63%	1.59%
New Zealand	0.15%	0.35%	0.24%	0.21%
Japan	4.06%	1.96%	16.24%	23.19%
India	6.92%	3.54%	1.68%	0.82%
Pakistan		0.67%	0.22%	0.06%
Philippines		0.63%	0.24%	0.38%
Argentina	1.20%	0.90%	0.78%	0.24%
Brazil	0.75%	2.84%	2.66%	0.96%
Mexico	0.66%	0.85%	1.34%	0.59%
Chile	0.19%	0.75%	0.15%	0.48%
Colombia		0.72%	0.22%	0.12%
Peru		0.19%	0.20%	0.08%
Uruguay		0.18%	0.05%	0.00%
Venezuela		0.57%	0.27%	0.02%
Egypt		0.45%	0.31%	0.05%
Israel		0.24%	0.29%	0.24%
South Africa	1.03%	0.65%	0.56%	1.82%
Memorandum:				
GDP (millions)	$198,200	$556,500	$18,049,700	
Market cap (m)				$15,448,900

Table VI
Performance of Global Stock Index: 1921–1996
(Real Returns in Percentage per Annum)

The table displays the risk and return of real returns on stock market indices, measured in excess of the Wholesale Price Index inflation. Arithmetic return is obtained from the monthly average multiplied by twelve; risk is monthly volatility multiplied by the square root of twelve; Sharpe ratio is the ratio of monthly average to monthly volatility; geometric return uses annual compounding. Ending wealth reports the final value of $1 invested on December 1920 at the end of the sample. "Survived markets" series includes only markets in our sample in existence in 1996, taken since the last interruption (temporary or permanent). "All markets" series accounts for all markets in the sample, imputing a 75 percent loss in the month the series permanently disappears, or the actual loss spread over the period of the break.

Index	Arithmetic Return	Risk	Monthly Sharpe	Geometric Return	Ending Wealth
U.S. index	5.48	15.83	0.0999	4.32	27.3
Global index					
Survived markets	4.98	12.08	0.1190	4.33	27.3
All markets	4.59	11.05	0.1199	4.04	21.9
Non-U.S. index					
Survived markets	4.52	10.02	0.1301	4.09	22.2
All markets	3.84	9.96	0.1114	3.39	13.1

We expect the bias to decrease as we move from (i) to (ii). The difficult part, of course, is to estimate market losses during a permanent interruption such as war or nationalization. We have 11 occurrences of permanent breaks (or "deaths") out of our sample of 39 markets. For some of these, such as Germany, Japan, Portugal, we are able to trace the fall in value, which we evenly spread over the time period of the interruption. This smoothing preserves the geometric return, but induces an artificially low volatility and therefore increases the arithmetic return. We should note, however, that the same problem occurs when reported prices are controlled or do not represent transaction data. For the few remaining markets that suffered a permanent interruption, we assume that the market fell by 75 percent the following month.[19]

Table VI presents the performance of the various global stock indices. We focus on performance data first and discuss volatility later. Over the past 76 years, the U.S. stock market provided an arithmetic capital return of 5.48 percent, measured in real terms. Its geometric growth was 4.32 percent over this period. Figure 4 plots the performance of the U.S., global, and non-U.S. real capital growth indices (using the comprehensive series).

---

[19] The markets affected were Czechoslovakia, Egypt, Greece, Hungary, Poland, and Romania. The 75 percent imputed drop is in line with the fall in value of markets that suffered a severe breakdown. The arbitrariness of the charge is mitigated by the fact that all of these markets are relatively small.

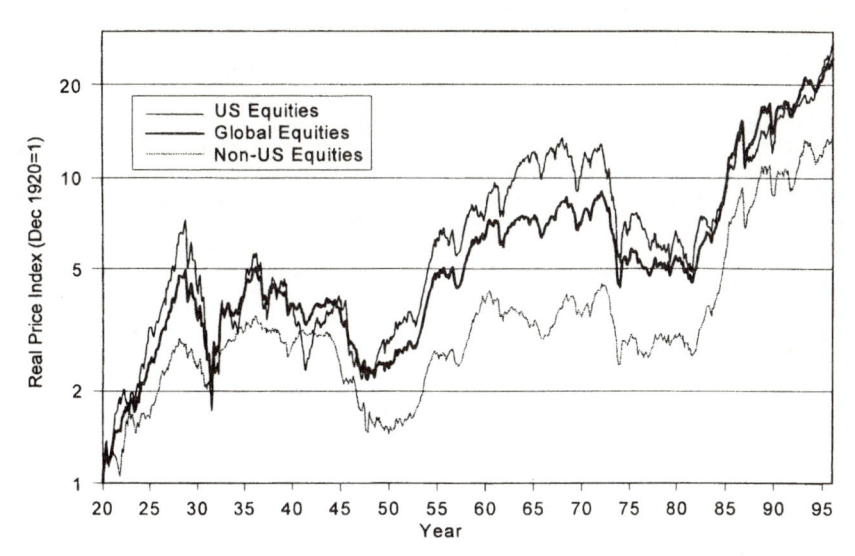

Figure 4. A Global Stock Market Index. The figure displays the performance of the U.S., global, and non-U.S. real capital growth indices. The latter indices are obtained using GDP weights and all existing markets, even if they fail later.

The differences in the performance of the global indices point to the importance of accounting for losing markets. The "survived markets" index has a compound return of 4.33 percent; it accounts only for markets in existence in 1996 and examined since their last break. The "all markets" index has a compound return of 4.04 percent; it accounts for all markets and attempts to interpolate returns over major breaks in the series. Going from the first to the second estimate should move us closer to a true, unbiased measure of long-term return.

At first sight, the difference between the long-term performance of the U.S. index and of the global comprehensive index appears to be small, at only 29 basis points. This result may appear puzzling in light of the evidence in Table I that all non-U.S. markets have lower long-term growth than the United States, often significantly so. One reason for the narrow difference lies in the temporal variation in weights. Consider the Japanese market, for instance. In the first half of the century, the performance of Japanese equities was mediocre. At that time the market carried a weight of less than 4 percent in the global index. In the second half of the century, however, Japanese equities outperformed U.S. equities, precisely at a time when their weight in the index was rising, reaching 16 percent in 1990. Another reason is the large weight in the U.S. market at the beginning of the century. Consider, for example, a $100 investment in global stocks starting in 1921. From the GDP weights in Table V, the amount to allocate to U.S. stocks was $46.17. Over the next 76 years, this amount grew to $1149, using the 4.32 percent

Table VII

Performance of Global Stock Index: 1921–1996

(Nominal Returns in U.S. Dollars, Percentage per Annum)

The table displays the risk and return of dollar returns on stock market indices, translated into U.S. dollars at the official rate. Arithmetic return is obtained from the monthly average multiplied by twelve; risk is monthly volatility multiplied by the square root of twelve; Sharpe ratio is the ratio of monthly average to monthly volatility; geometric return uses annual compounding. Ending wealth reports the final value of $1 invested on December 1920 at the end of the sample. "Survived markets" series includes only markets in our sample in existence in 1996, taken since the last interruption (temporary or permanent). "All markets" series accounts for all markets in the sample, imputing a 75 percent loss in the month the series permanently disappears, or the actual loss spread over the period of the break.

Index	Arithmetic Return	Risk	Monthly Sharpe	Geometric Return	Ending Wealth
U.S. index	8.04	16.19	0.1433	6.95	171.2
Global index					
Survived markets	7.98	13.34	0.1728	7.32	222.9
All markets	7.76	12.14	0.1845	7.25	211.2
Non-U.S. index					
Survived markets	7.53	12.17	0.1785	7.00	176.5
All markets	7.28	12.08	0.1740	6.75	146.2

U.S. growth rate. Let us make now an extreme assumption, which is that all of the money invested outside the United States is lost. Using the $1149-to-$100 ratio, the rate of growth is still 3.26 percent. The large initial size of the U.S. market therefore ensures that the growth on the global index must be within 100 basis points of the U.S. growth number.

The last column in Table VI shows that a difference of 29 basis points can be quite significant over 76 years. Assuming a dollar invested in the U.S. index and in the comprehensive global index, the investments would have grown to 27.3 and 21.9 in real terms, which is a substantial difference.

Table VI also shows that a non-U.S. stock market index, based on our "comprehensive" measure, has grown at the rate of 3.39 percent, which is a full 93 basis points below U.S. equities. If one ignores survivorship issues, however, the return of the non-U.S. index appears to be 4.09 percent. Survival bias therefore induces a difference of 70 basis points in this index, which is quite substantial when accumulated over 76 years.

Table VII presents similar data, measured in nominal U.S. dollars. Over 1921 to 1996, the compound capital return on U.S. equities was 6.95 percent. The return on the global survived index was 7.32 percent; the return on the global comprehensive index was 7.25 percent. Similarly, the average return on the non-U.S. index was 7.00 percent and 6.75 percent. Here the survival bias is on the order of 25 basis points.

As in Table I, we observe that the difference between U.S. and non-U.S. returns is smaller when returns are measured in dollars instead of in real terms. In fact, the return on the unbiased global index is now variation in weights and the real appreciation of most other currencies discussed previously. Also, the return on the value-weighted global index appears not too sensitive to the survivorship issue.

Tables VI and VII also provide estimates of the volatility of the various indices. Using real returns, the volatility of the U.S. index is 15.8 percent. All other indices display lower volatility. For instance, the volatility of the non-U.S. indices is about 10 percent, which is much lower than that of the U.S. market alone, reflecting the fact that the portfolio is spread over a greater number of markets, thus benefiting from imperfect correlations across markets. Next, the risk of our global indices is also driven by correlations. Over the 76 years, the correlation coefficient between returns on the U.S. index and on the comprehensive non-U.S. index is 0.460 in real terms and about the same, 0.452, in dollar terms.[20] As a result of lower volatility for foreign markets and a low correlation coefficient, the risk of the global portfolio is substantially lower than that of U.S. equities. The "comprehensive" global index, for example, displays a volatility of 11.05 percent. Based on these long-term series, the main benefit of going international appears to be risk reduction rather than increased returns.

Taking into account survivorship decreases returns slightly, but also decreases volatility. This is partly due to the (artificial) interpolation of returns when markets are closed, but also because of additional diversification resulting from the inclusion of more markets. We measure the trade-off between risk and return with the Sharpe ratio, defined as average monthly returns divided by their volatility. These are reported in the third columns of Tables VI and VII. With real returns, the Sharpe ratio of the global index is 0.1199, which is higher than that of U.S. equities at 0.0999. With dollar returns, the Sharpe ratio of the global indices is about 0.1845, also higher than that of U.S. equities, at 0.1433. These differences, however, are not statistically significant.[21]

Systematic differences in return can be attributed to two classes of explanations. The first is survivorship, an ex post explanation. The second is rational, ex ante, differences in risk profiles. For example, if markets can be viewed as integrated, a higher return for U.S. equities could be explained by the fact that the U.S. market has a higher world β. Indeed, over the 1921–1996 period, U.S. equities had the highest beta, with a value of 1.24. A regression of real returns on real betas reveals a correlation of 0.53, which is significantly positive.

---

[20] As for the measurement of volatilities, correlations may be too low because of the smoothing of the series during the breaks. However, the correlation with the survived series is very close, at 0.510 in real terms and 0.520 in dollars. This suggests that the bias is not large.

[21] Using the performance tests developed by Jobson and Korkie (1981).

Testing this proposition is not straightforward because estimation of β with respect to the world index depends on survival issues as well. Had the outcome of the Second World War been different, for example, the β of the United States on the world index would likely have been different. The regression is also afflicted by data and econometric problems. The variables are estimated over different periods and thus have quite different sampling variability. Additionally, the betas that include periods of price controls or infrequent trading are not reliable. Thus it seems difficult to disentangle the higher systematic risk explanation from survivorship to explain the high returns on U.S. equities.

To understand the momentous implications of differences in long-term rates of return reported here, consider the following experiment. First, let us record the current capitalization of non-U.S. equity markets, which was approximately $9,000 billion at the end of 1996. From Table VI, these markets have grown at an average rate of 3.39 percent, which is less than the 4.32 percent growth rate for the United States. Going back to 1921, this implies that the market capitalization of non-U.S. equities was $9,000 billion divided by $(1 + 3.39\%)^{76}$, which amounts to $714 billion in current dollars.

Next, assume that all markets have grown at the U.S. rate of growth. The market value of these equities would then be $714 billion times $(1 + 4.32\%)^{76}$, which amounts to $17,775 billion. In other words, the opportunity cost of growing at about 3.4 percent instead of the 4.3 percent U.S. rate is $8,775 billion in today's dollars. Foreign markets would be double their current size if they had grown only 1 percent faster than they did. Viewed in this context, survival biases of 70 basis points recorded in Table VI are quite significant.

IV. Conclusion

"Financial archaeology" involves digging through reams of financial data in search for answers. Sometimes this involves relying on poor quality data from which to draw inferences about markets in states of crisis. Even so, these data provide invaluable information to help understand long-term histories of capital markets. If one relies on historical data as the basis for estimates of long-term market growth, there is no reason to look at U.S. data only. This is why our paper paints a broad picture of the performance of global stock markets over more than 75 years of a turbulent century for financial markets.

The main lesson from our long-term data is that global capital markets have been systematically subject to dramatic changes over this century. Major disruptions have afflicted nearly all the markets in our sample, with the exception of a few such as the United States. Markets have been closed or suspended due to financial crises, wars, expropriations, or political upheaval.

No doubt this explains our finding that the 4.3 percent real capital appreciation return on U.S. stocks is rather exceptional, as other markets have typically had a median return of only 0.8 percent. These results suggest that the large equity premium obtained in the United States is at least partly to the result of conditioning estimates on the best performing market. This conditioning may also create time-variation in expected returns; for instance, we expect markets that have done well to exhibit more mean-reversion than others because periods of large losses must be followed by periods of upswings.[22]

This line of analysis treats each market separately. Another approach is to track the hypothetical performance of a diversified global investment. Interestingly, we find that the performance of a globally diversified portfolio is much closer to the performance of U.S. equities, averaging 4.0 percent. This is partly because markets with large capitalization at the beginning of the century performed well. This result also reflects the benefits of diversification, which spreads the risk of dramatic events over a large portfolio.

Whether similar disruptions will happen again is an open question. By now, however, it should be clear that if we fail to account for the "losers" as well as the "winners" in global equity markets, we are providing a biased view of history which ignores important information about actual investment risk.

REFERENCES

Adams, Thomas, and Iwao Hoshii, 1971, *A Financial History of the New Japan* (Kodansha, Tokyo, Japan).

Bank of Japan, 1966, *A Hundred Years of Statistics of Japanese Economy* (Bank of Japan, Tokyo, Japan).

Bansal, Ravi, and Wilbur Coleman, 1996, A monetary explanation of the equity premium, term premium, and risk-free rate puzzles, *Journal of Political Economy* 104, 1135–1171.

Barclays de Zoete Wedd, 1993, The BZW Equity Gilt Study: Investment in the London Stock Market since 1918 (Barclays deZoete Wedd, London, United Kingdom).

Brown, Stephen J., William Goetzmann, and Stephen Ross, 1995, Survival, *Journal of Finance* 50, 853–873.

Burnside, Craig, and Thomas McCurdy, 1992, The equity premium puzzle; in Peter Newman, Murray Milgate, and John Eatwell, eds.: *The New Palgrave Dictionary of Money and Finance* (Stockton Press, New York).

Constantinides, George, 1987, Habit formation: A resolution of the equity premium puzzle, *Journal of Political Economy* 98, 519–543.

Cowles, Alfred, 1939, *Common Stock Indices, 1871–1937* (Cowles Commission for Research in Economics, Monograph no. 3, Principia Press, Bloomington, Ind.).

Epstein, Larry, and Stanley Zin, 1991, Substitution, risk aversion and the temporal behaviour of consumption and asset returns: An empirical investigation, *Journal of Political Economy* 99, 263–286.

Frenneberg, Per, and Bjorn Hansson, 1992, Swedish stocks, bonds, bills, and inflation (1919–1990), *Applied Financial Economics* 2, 79–86.

Gielen, Gregor, 1994, *Konnen Aktienkurse Noch Steigen?* (Gabler, Wiesbaden, Germany).

Goetzmann, William N., 1993, Patterns in three centuries of stock market prices, *Journal of Business* 66, 249–270.

Goetzmann, William N., and Roger Ibbotson, 1994, An emerging market, the New York Stock Exchange 1816–1872, *Journal of Business* 68, 483–508.

---

[22] Goetzmann and Jorion (1995) also show that survival should induce other effects of interest, such as predictability based on dividend yields.

Goetzmann, William N., and Philippe Jorion, 1995, A longer look at dividend yields, *Journal of Business* 68, 483–508.

Goetzmann, William N., and Philippe Jorion, 1997, Re-emerging markets, {mimeo} University of California at Irvine.

Ibbotson, Roger, 1995, *Stocks, Bonds, Bills, and Inflation: 1995 Yearbook* (Ibbotson Associates, Chicago, Ill.).

International Conference of Economic Services, 1934, *International Abstract of Economic Statistics* (ICES, London, United Kingdom).

International Conference of Economic Services, 1938, *International Abstract of Economic Statistics* (International Statistical Institute, Permanent Office, The Hague, The Netherlands).

International Finance Corporation, 1995, *The IFC Indexes: Methodology, Definitions, and Practices* (International Finance Corporation, Washington, DC).

International Monetary Fund, various issues, *International Financial Statistics* (International Monetary Fund, Washington, D.C.).

Jobson, J. D., and B. Korkie, 1981, Performance hypothesis testing with the Sharpe and Treynor measures, *Journal of Finance* 36, 888–908.

League of Nations, various issues, *Statistical Yearbook* (League of Nations, Geneva, Switzerland).

Mehra, Rajnish, and Edward Prescott, 1985, The equity premium: A puzzle, *Journal of Monetary Economics* 15, 145–161.

Mehra, Rajnish, and Edward Prescott, 1988, The equity premium: A puzzle?, *Journal of Monetary Economics* 22, 133–136.

Mirowski, Philip, 1981, The risk (and retreat) of a market: English joint stock shares in the eighteenth century, *Journal of Economic History* 41, 559–577.

Mitchell, Brian, 1992, *International Historical Statistics: Europe, 1750–1988* (Stockton Press, New York).

Mitchell, Brian, 1993, *International Historical Statistics: The Americas, 1750–1988* (Stockton Press, New York).

Mitchell, Brian, 1995, *International Historical Statistics: Africa, Asia & Oceania, 1750–1988* (Stockton Press, New York).

Neal, Larry, 1987, The integration and efficiency of the London and Amsterdam stock markets in the eighteenth century, *Journal of Economic History* 47, 97–115.

Neal, Larry, 1990, *The Rise of Financial Capitalism: International Capital Markets in the Age of Reason* (Cambridge University Press, Cambridge, Mass.).

Parsons, Brian, 1974, The behavior of prices on the London stock market in the early eighteenth century, Ph.D. dissertation, University of Chicago.

Rietz, Thomas, 1988, The equity premium: A solution, *Journal of Monetary Economics* 22, 117–131.

Schwert, William, 1990, Indexes of U.S. stock prices from 1802 to 1987, *Journal of Business* 63, 399–426.

Siegel, Jeremy, 1992, The equity premium: Stock and bond returns since 1802, *Financial Analysts Journal* 48, 28–38.

Siegel, Jeremy, 1994, *Stocks for the Long Run* (Richard D. Irwin, New York).

Timmerman, Allan, 1992, Changes in Danish stock prices 1914–1990, *Nationalokonomisk Tidsskrift* 130, 473–482.

United Nations, various issues, *Monthly Bulletin of Statistics* (United Nations, New York).

Wilson, Jack, and Charles Jones, 1987, A comparison of annual common stock returns, *The Journal of Business* 60, 239–258.

Wydler, Daniel, 1989, Swiss stocks, bonds, and inflation: 1926–1987, *Journal of Portfolio Management* 15, 27–32.

International Finance Special Issue

On the Integration of International Capital Markets: Evidence From Euroequity Offerings

M. Wayne Marr, John L. Trimble, and Raj Varma

M. Wayne Marr is the First Union Professor of Banking at the College of Business Administration, Clemson University, Clemson, South Carolina. John L. Trimble is an Assistant Professor of Finance at the College of Business and Economics, Washington State University, Vancouver, Washington. Raj Varma is an Assistant Professor of Finance at the College of Business and Economics, University of Delaware, Newark, Delaware.

■ In recent years, new financial instruments have played an important role in dismantling barriers faced by foreign investors in United States securities[1] — and thus, in moving U.S. and foreign capital markets a step closer to being a single, integrated market. Among such securities are those issued under a specialized Securities and Exchange Commission (SEC) procedure, called the "targeted registered offering." As the name suggests, this offering procedure targets a clientele of foreign investors — in particular, those who find security-ownership registration unattractive.

Under this procedure, securities can be offered abroad as bearer instruments, called "targeted registered securities," which are exempt from U.S. withholding taxes, provided certain conditions are met. Among them, the targeted registered shares must be registered with offshore

---

We thank Jim Sprow, Sam Szewczyk, the seminar participants at Washington State University and two anonymous referees of this Journal for helpful comments. An earlier version of this paper was presented at the 1989 Financial Management Association meetings. Raj Varma gratefully acknowledges financial support from the University of Delaware, General University Research Program. John Trimble is grateful for research support from the University of Central Florida, where he was a visitor during the 1990-1991 academic year. Peter Dempsey and John Trach provided valuable research assistance.

[1]Tufano [31] describes 58 financial innovations in the period 1974-1986, many of them (including Euroequity) for international transactions. Mason [16] describes 115 financial innovations in international bond markets over a similar period.

financial institutions. And, they must be simultaneously issued with a registered offering of the same security domestically. U.S. government and government-agency bonds, corporate bonds and, recently, corporate stock have been issued under the targeted registered offering procedure. There is a hitch, however. Targeted registered securities revert, once and for all, to being standard registered instruments if resold to U.S. taxpayers.

Euroequity, the focus of this paper, is a recent financial innovation applying the targeted registered offering procedure to corporate stock. Euroequity is thus a registered new issue of stock by an American corporation that is sold simultaneously in two tranches; one tranche is sold to investors at home as standard registered shares and the other tranche is sold abroad as targeted registered shares.

This paper provides an empirical test of capital market integration using Euroequity. In perfectly integrated capital markets, whether a corporation chooses to issue Euroequity or domestic equity should not have a differential effect on the price of its stock. However, previous research by Stapleton and Subrahmanyam [25], Alexander, Eun and Janakiramanan [2], and Errunza and Losq [8] suggests that, if national capital markets are even partially segmented, firms choosing to list their stocks on foreign exchanges will dismantle some effective investment barriers, causing their stock prices to rise. Saudagaran [20] and Smith [22] suggest that such benefits will most likely be realized in offshore markets where the issuer has operations. Because of its similarity to international listings in removing barriers, one would therefore expect similar benefits to issuers from the sale of Euroequity.

We test capital market integration by comparing the two-day announcement returns of 32 Euroequity with 196 domestic-equity offerings by American corporations during the period 1985-1988. Our results are consistent with previous research which shows that stock prices decline following announcements of domestic-equity financing. We find, however, that, on the average, Euroequity offerings are much larger than domestic-equity offerings. After controlling for characteristics of firms choosing Euroequity financing, we find that the negative stock-price responses are proportionately smaller for Euroequity offers the larger the offshore tranche (expressed as a percentage of the total amount financed). These findings are consistent with the following hypothesis: During their infancy, new financial instruments that reduce previously effective barriers to investment across national borders enable firms to capitalize on beneficial financing opportunities in overseas markets.

The remainder of the paper is organized as follows. The first section describes the targeted registered offering procedure. Section II outlines the expected stock-price effects from issuing Euroequity by associating it with previous research on international listings. Section III describes the data and the results for stock-price responses to announcements of equity offerings. Section IV presents the test of capital market integration. The last section summarizes the study.

I. Targeted Registered Offering Procedure

A. Changes in U.S. Tax Laws and Regulations

The Tax Reform Act passed in July 1984 modified the procedures by which U.S. firms could issue securities for sale overseas to foreign investors.[2] Those procedures were further modified by temporary Treasury regulations in the same year. Before 1984, U.S. corporations had been able to issue bearer securities through an offshore finance subsidiary; the Tax Reform Act made it possible to do so directly. But the Act left in place withholding-tax and information-reporting requirements considered by the investment banking community to hinder the sale of U.S. securities overseas to foreign investors. The Act also did not alter the situation of U.S. government agencies, which by law could not issue bearer securities, and thus could not sell securities abroad to foreign investors who demanded anonymity. To ease these burdens, temporary Treasury regulations were instituted that remain in effect today. These regulations exempt an issuer of securities from the information-reporting and withholding-tax requirements of the Act, provided, the issuer certifies in writing that it has no actual knowledge that the investors to whom interest or dividend payments will be made are U.S. taxpayers.

B. Targeted Registered Offerings

Under the combined provisions of the Tax Reform Act and the temporary Treasury regulations, simultaneous offerings of securities to U.S. and foreign investors may be exempt from the withholding-tax and information-reporting requirements of existing law under certain conditions — for example, if the simultaneous offerings are registered with the SEC and if the foreign tranche complies with SEC requirements as to final placement with foreign investors. Targeted registered offerings fall under these

---

[2]Section I is based on Securities and Exchange Commission [22].

provisions. The foreign beneficial owner of such a security does not have to identify itself.

To be classified as a targeted registered offering, an issue must satisfy four conditions: the registered owner overseas must be a financial institution; interest coupons or dividends must be paid to the institution outside the U.S.; the issuer must certify that it has no actual knowledge that a U.S. taxpayer is the beneficial owner of the security; and the issuer and registered financial institutions must follow rather elaborate SEC certification procedures.

II. Expected Stock-Price Reactions

A. Euroequity Compared With International Listings

We assume that the motivations of corporations issuing Euroequity are similar to those for issuing government bonds under the targeted registered offering procedure. In particular, we assume that corporations wish to issue stock that is attractive to foreign investors desiring anonymity as well as to foreign investors for whom anonymity is not a factor.

To the extent that foreign investors desiring anonymity are affected, U.S. laws requiring registration of securities' ownership erect barriers that tend to segment U.S. and foreign capital markets; [1], [5], [12], [28], [29]. Segmentation generally has the effect of depressing security prices; [6], [7], [13], [23], [26], [31]. Consequently, segmentation creates an incentive for corporations to adopt mitigating policies that increase the diversification opportunities available to foreign investors, as Stapleton and Subrahmanyam [25] have observed.

Stapleton and Subrahmanyam [25] argue that a corporation can reduce obstacles to holding its stock for (and thereby increase the diversification opportunities of) foreign investors by listing its securities on foreign capital markets.[3] Euroequity also makes it easier for foreign investors to hold stock in U. S. corporations. Thus, Euroequity should increase diversification opportunities in much the same way as international listings.

Stonehill and Dullum [27], and Alexander, Eun and Janakiramanan [3] note several ways in which foreign investors may benefit from such an increase in their diversification opportunities. They may benefit because transactions costs are lower; because the foreign-listed stock is traded in their home currency (whereas Euroequity is denominated in dollars); because there may be reductions in information barriers if the foreign listing results in additional financial disclosure offshore; and, according to Smith [22], because they face lower monitoring costs owing to company operations being located nearer to them.[4] Accordingly, Solnik [24] notes that companies may also benefit in several ways: (i) reduction in the chance of a successful takeover; (ii) enlargement of their capital market and increased diversification of ownership; (iii) a higher profile in foreign markets, thus making it easier to sell debt nationally and internationally; and (iv) greater visibility of the company's name in foreign markets, which means good overseas advertising for its product brands.

B. The Comparative Advantage of Euroequity

However, in overseas markets, where large numbers of investors desire anonymity, foreign listings may not be an effective instrument for achieving these benefits. Registration of ownership is a barrier for such investors, as noted. A corporation can remove the barrier by listing its stock as a bearer instrument on foreign exchanges. But, the liquidity of such an instrument would suffer because secondary markets in U.S. securities overseas are typically satellite markets dependent on the dominant U.S. market; [24]. Since bearer stock cannot be legally sold to investors in the U.S., the satellite relationship needed for a liquid secondary market in the stock would not exist. Consequently, international listings do not effectively dismantle the registration barrier for foreign investors desiring anonymity.

On the other hand, since it is a bearer instrument with a liquid secondary market, Euroequity does dismantle the registration barrier. In addition, the legal structure of Euroequities may work to the advantage of issuers because of the following two constraints to financial arbitrage in secondary markets between its bearer and registered shares: (i) targeted registered shares can only be created under special SEC procedures; and (ii) a Euroequity share reverts to being a registered share, once and for all, if repatriated to the U.S. Consequently, if Euroequity actually removes effective barriers for foreign investors, American corporations planning to issue stock in the

---

[3] Other policies cited are foreign portfolio investment and direct foreign investment by corporations. For studies focusing on the latter, see Errunza and Senbet [10], [11].

[4] Saudagaran [20] presents evidence that, on average, firms with foreign operations choose to list their stock on foreign exchanges more often than other domestic firms.

Euroequity market may find that it enables them to capture beneficial financing opportunities.[5]

While Euroequity and foreign-listed issues are both instruments that dismantle barriers for foreign investors, each appeals to different interests. Bearer foreign-listed issues appeal to the privacy interests of many individual foreign investors; but, such issues lack broad appeal among foreign investors generally because secondary-market trading is limited to the exchanges where the stock is listed or to the existence of an active over-the-counter market. The breadth and depth of an over-the-counter market overseas in bearer foreign-listed shares is limited by the legal difficulty of reselling them in the U.S. market. Similar, but less severe, limitations hold for over-the-counter markets offshore in registered foreign-listed stock issued in the home currency of an overseas exchange. Of course, listing in the home currency is an advantage to foreign investors in the local market. Other things being equal, because of the greater likelihood of reselling dollar-denominated, registered, foreign-listed stock to American investors, offshore over-the-counter markets in such shares are broader and more liquid compared to international listings. Furthermore, listing fees (which can be substantial) are minimized with Euroequity. An American issuer may therefore achieve a broader (and possibly larger) placement of shares in foreign-investor portfolios with Euroequity than with international listings.

This suggests that corporations planning to issue equity may realize financing bargains in issuing a new security like Euroequity — particularly in its infancy — if it removes barriers for foreign investors while other barriers to financial arbitrage remain in place.[6] When equity financing bargains occur offshore, we would expect American corporations to sell as much stock as they could to foreign investors at "bargain" prices; and that such issues would continue until the bargains disappeared. Hence, we would expect to find that corporations issuing offshore realize a benefit that varies directly with the proportion of the stock issue they sell offshore.

C. Stock-Price Effects of International Listings

Alexander, Eun and Janakiramanan [3] examined the home-country behavior of the stock prices of foreign firms listing their stock on one of the U.S. exchanges. They found that the monthly returns of those firms declined following the month of the U.S. listing. This result was consistent with previous theoretical research by Stapleton and Subrahmanyam [25], and Alexander, Eun and Janakiramanan [2], which concluded that (expectations constant) expected returns will decline because prices rise following a new international listing. However, because exact announcement dates were unavailable to them, Alexander, Eun and Janakiramanan [3] were unable to examine price movement directly via stock-price reactions. Further, they did not compare the returns or the characteristics of firms choosing to issue offshore with comparable-risk firms choosing to issue domestically.

In summary, previous theoretical and empirical research suggests that corporations may be able to realize increases in their market value if they can issue securities that dismantle barriers for (and thereby increase the diversification opportunities of) foreign investors. We investigate this issue for Euroequity in its infancy, using the following hypothesis: New financial products that dismantle previously effective barriers to international investment permit firms to capitalize on beneficial financing opportunities in overseas markets.

III. Description of the Data

Common stock issues by nonfinancial firms during the period 1985 through 1988 were identified from two sources: (*i*) the Investment Dealers Digest *Directory of Corporate Financing,* and (*ii*) the Security Data Company's *New Issues of Corporate Securities.*

To be included in the study, an issue had to meet the following criteria:

(*i*) The issuing corporation's common stock was trading on the New York Stock Exchange or the American Stock Exchange during the announcement period.

(*ii*) At least 50 historical returns were available on the Center for Research in Security Prices' (CRSP) Daily Returns File for 61 trading days prior to the issue's announcement date.

(*iii*) There were no missing returns on the announcement date.

These selection criteria did not eliminate any of the original population of 32 Euroequity stock issues made by 30 different, mostly industrial, firms from 1985 through 1988. The comparison sample of domestic-equity offer-

---

[5]The realizable reduction in cost of equity, however, will not likely exceed the issuer's return on business investment. Thus, only firms planning to issue stock would act on financing opportunities in equity markets; see Kim and Stulz [14].

[6]Financing opportunities with Euroequity could also be reinforced by (or once the markets have adjusted to the new security, occur independently as a result of) an increase in demand offshore for dollar-denominated securities, which, for example, could be caused by depreciation in the value of the dollar vis-a-vis other currencies.

Exhibit 1. Issue, Issuer and Ownership Characteristics of U.S. Corporations Making 32 Euroequity and 196 Domestic-Equity Offerings From 1985 Through 1988[a]

Characteristic[b]	Euroequity Offerings Mean	Euroequity Offerings Median	Domestic-Equity Offerings Mean	Domestic-Equity Offerings Median
Offering and Issuer Characteristics:				
Offering size ($ millions)	204.38	121.85	67.38	39.35
Offshore tranche (%)[a]	22.89	20.00	0.00	0.00
Issuer's market value ($ billions)[c]	1784.11	1089.80	830.99	275.59
Ratio of issue size to market value	0.16	0.12	0.18	0.15
Ownership Characteristics:				
Management holdings (%)[d]	10.07	2.00	10.13	4.00
Institutional holdings (%)[e]	45.14	47.32	33.72	33.30
Large shareholder holdings (%)[f]	5.15	5.00	8.54	8.27

Notes:
[a] With Euroequity offerings, some of the issued shares (the domestic tranche) are sold to investors in the United States. The remainder (the offshore tranche) are sold to foreign investors overseas. With domestic-equity offerings, all shares are sold to investors in the United States.
[b] Issue characteristics were taken from Investment Dealers Digest *Directory of Corporate Financing* and Security Data Company's *New Issues of Corporate Securities.*
[c] Closing price of the issuer's common stock at the end of the month preceding the announcement date times the number of shares outstanding at that time, as reported in Standard and Poor's Stock Guide.
[d] The percentage of the corporation's outstanding stock held by directors, officers, and other insiders of the company, according to the most recently reported figure in an edition of Value Line preceding the announcement date.
[e] The percentage of the corporation's outstanding stock held by institutional investors, as reported in Standard and Poor's Stock Guide for the end of the month preceding the announcement date.
[f] The percentage of the corporation's outstanding stock held by investors owning 5% or more of the total number of shares, according to the most recently reported figure in an edition of Value Line preceding the announcement date.

ings resulting from these criteria consists of 196 common stock offerings made by 173 different corporations.

Exhibit 1 presents issue, issuer and ownership characteristics of Euroequity and domestic-equity offerings. As would be expected, larger firms favor Euroequities, and the average Euroequity issue is larger than the average domestic-equity issue, by a factor of more than three ($204.38 million compared to $67.38 million). The difference, moreover, is statistically significant at the one percent level. The offshore tranche represents only 22.89% of a Euroequity issue on average. As expected, the average Euroequity issuer is much larger — again, by a factor of three — than the average domestic-equity issuer. This difference is statistically significant at the ten percent level.

The ownership characteristics consist of the percentages of a company's outstanding shares held by managers, institutions and large investors. There appear to be significant differences in the holdings of Euroequities and domestic equities among different investor groups. Institutions held a larger average proportion of the shares of Euroequity issuers than shares of domestic-equity issuers, while the reverse was true with respect to large shareholders' positions.

IV. Stock-Price Responses to Common Stock Offerings

A. Statistical Procedure for Measuring Price Responses

The event-study method, according to the procedure outlined by Mikkelson and Partch [18], was used to examine stock-price responses to announcements of common stock issues. The announcement date (day 0) is defined as the earlier of either (*i*) the date the issue was announced in the *Wall Street Journal* or (*ii*) the trading date following the date on which the issue was registered with the SEC. Abnormal returns are measured by the difference between the two-day (day -1 and day 0) observed return and the corresponding two-day market-model expected return. For the latter, we use the CRSP equally weighted index of daily returns to measure the daily market portfolio return. The parameters of the market model were estimated from historical returns — day -200 through day -61 — before the announcement day of the stock issue.

B. Results of the Event Study

Exhibit 2 presents the average abnormal returns and cumulative average abnormal returns for the sample of Euroequity and domestic-equity issues. Selected daily av-

Exhibit 2. Domestic Market Percentage Average Abnormal Returns (AAR), Cumulative Average Abnormal Returns (CAR), Window Average Abnormal Returns (WAR), and *t*-statistics Associated With 32 Euroequity and 196 Domestic-Equity Offerings By U.S. Industrial Corporations From 1985 Through 1988[a]

Trading Day[b]	Euroequity Offerings AAR	Euroequity Offerings CAR	Domestic-Equity Offerings AAR	Domestic-Equity Offerings CAR
-60	0.128	0.128	0.184	0.184
-50	0.064	1.211	0.175	0.588
-40	0.178	4.175	0.149	0.577
-30	-0.341	4.100	0.140	1.362
-20	0.625	6.503	-0.046	1.901
-10	1.385	8.312	0.263	1.411
-9	-0.182	8.130	0.314	1.725
-8	0.048	8.177	-0.089	1.636
-7	-0.634	7.543	-0.160	1.476
-6	-0.462	7.081	0.190	1.666
-5	-0.106	6.975	-0.187	1.480
-4	-0.619	6.357	-0.297	1.182
-3	-0.941	5.416	-0.089	1.093
-2	-0.346	5.069	0.113	1.206
-1	-2.905	2.165	-1.653	-0.447
0	0.766	2.931	-0.711	-1.158
1	-0.125	2.806	-0.214	-1.371
2	-0.299	2.507	-0.152	-1.524
3	0.113	2.619	0.116	-1.408
4	0.531	3.150	-0.101	-1.508
5	-0.310	2.839	0.052	-1.456
6	-0.090	2.750	-0.121	-1.577
7	0.949	3.699	0.099	-1.478
8	0.226	3.925	-0.120	-1.598
9	0.349	4.274	-0.080	-1.678
10	-0.865	3.409	-0.101	-1.779
20	-0.349	2.515	-0.087	-3.520

Trading Day[b]	WAR	*t*-statistic	WAR	*t*-statistic
-60 to -2	5.069	2.020	1.206	1.570
-1 to 0	-2.138	-3.900	-2.364	-10.400
1 to 20	-0.416	-0.040	-2.363	-3.320

Notes:
[a] With Euroequity offerings, some shares are sold to investors in the United States, and the balance are sold offshore to foreign investors. With domestic-equity offerings, all shares are sold to investors in the United States.
[b] Day 0 is the earlier of (*i*) the registration of the offering with the Securities and Exchange Commission, and (*ii*) the first report of the offering in the *Wall Street Journal*.

erages of abnormal returns for each group are reported in the top portion of the exhibit from day -60 to day 20. The bottom portion of the exhibit reports window average abnormal returns for pre-announcement (day -60 to day -2), announcement (day -1 to day 0), and post-announcement (day 1 to day 20) periods.

The averages reported in the top portion of Exhibit 2 appear to indicate a run-up of stock prices prior to the announcement of either type of new stock offering. However, as the bottom portion of the exhibit shows, abnormal returns in the pre-announcement period are statistically significant at conventional levels of confidence only for Euroequities. In the announcement period, abnormal returns average -2.138% for Euroequities and -2.364% for domestic equities; both figures are significantly different from zero at conventional levels. The significance of the negative figures, moreover, is not due merely to extreme observations in the tail of the distribution. The proportion of negative observations, which is 0.75 for both domestic equities and Euroequities, is significantly greater than 50% in both cases (p-values of 0.001 and 0.000 for domestic equities and Euroequities) according to Wilcoxon's signed-ranks test. In the post-announcement period, abnormal returns for Euroequities are not significantly different from zero. But, for domestic equities, they are significantly negative at the same level as in the announcement period.

The negative announcement-period returns found for both types of issues are consistent with independent studies by Asquith and Mullins [4], Masulis and Korwar [17], and Mikkelson and Partch [18] of stock-price reactions to new equity issues in the U.S. domestic market. Furthermore, these negative returns are not significantly different from one another according to the standard differences-in-means test. This test is not, however, an appropriate test of capital market integration because it does not account for the substantially larger issue sizes and issuer capitalizations of Euroequities as compared to domestic equities. These differences strongly suggest that self-selection of Euroequities by large corporations may be affecting the test.

In the next section, we describe our test of capital market integration. In this test, we examine the differences between domestic-equity and Euroequity announcement returns after controlling for differences in issue and issuer characteristics and for the effects of self-selection bias.

V. Test of Capital Market Integration

As previously noted, American firms with overseas operations may be able to sell part of a planned new issue of stock more cheaply to foreign investors overseas than to investors in the U.S. If so, they should be more likely to choose Euroequity over domestic-equity offerings than would American firms without overseas operations — an effect that our sample of Euroequity offers should reflect.

A. Selection Bias

If our samples were random, a reasonable test of capital market integration would consist of the following: A cross-sectional regression of issue and issuer characteristics and the percentage of the issue sold offshore, tranche, regressed on announcement returns. Tranche, which is zero for domestic issues and positive for Euroequity issues, would serve as the test variable measuring whether, and the extent to which, Euroequity issuers on average have realized a lower cost of equity.

But, because there is a likely self-selection bias in the sample, unobserved variables in the regression may be correlated with announcement returns. This could cause a bias in the regression estimates, and thus invalidate our test.

Relevant unobserved variables exist with any regression involving market data. Ordinarily their differential effects between the "control" and "experimental" samples are eliminated by randomization. However, randomization is not possible when self-selection is a factor. When self-selection is present, the effects of variables which ordinarily would have been eliminated by randomization become significant determinants of the differential effects between the two groups. Included in the list of such variables are any characteristics of companies that are likely to appeal to foreign investors. Thus, if a barrier to foreign investors is lifted, stocks of American firms with an established name overseas (i.e., lower information costs) would be more appealing to foreign investors looking for diversification benefits than stocks of companies without such an established name. Similarly, if foreign investors located close to a company's overseas operations have better information, as Smith [22] argues, those firms would expect a larger reduction in cost of equity than firms without such operations, other things being the same.

If all such variables could be identified and measured, then we could control for the effects of self-selection by including those variables in our regression of announcement returns. Given the virtual impossibility of such a task, we must look to other methods.

B. Statistical Procedure Accounting for Selection Bias

The problem with the regression described above is that, owing to its potential dependence on particular characteristics of firms having a comparative advantage in issuing offshore, the tranche variable may actually be endogenous (because the percentage of a stock issued that is sold offshore will depend on the reduction in cost of equity — i.e., on the announcement return). We test, and simultaneously control, for potential selection bias in Euroequity offerings by using a standard econometric model that allows the dummy variable portion of the tranche variable (1 if Euroequity, 0 if domestic equity) to be endogenous and dependent on observed and unobserved variables. A fundamental idea in methods that attempt to control for selection bias is that, if unobserved variables materially affect a firm's financing decision, we can be assured that the firm's actual financing choices will reflect this. Such methods therefore aim to control for self-selection bias by developing a control variable based upon a comparison of actual choices. In our regression of announcement returns, for example, the control variable is based upon a probit regression of firms' choices between domestic-equity and Euroequity financing as a function of issue and issuer characteristics.

Maddala [15] discusses several estimation procedures from the literature which yield consistent parameter estimates for regressions involving selection bias. For our proposed regression, each of the procedures involves the following two steps in estimation: (*i*) estimate the probability of a firm choosing Euroequity (versus domestic-equity) financing with the dummy variable as the dependent variable; and (*ii*) include in the regression equation of announcement returns an instrumental variable calculated from the first step which controls for the self-selection bias.

One such instrument is based on standard regression assumptions and the assumption of a normal distribution for unobserved effects on the choice between domestic-equity and Euroequity offerings. In this case, the instrumental variable measuring selection bias is:[7]

$$W = \begin{cases} -\phi(\alpha X) / \Phi(\alpha X), & \text{for Euroequity issues} \\ \phi(\alpha X) / [1 - \Phi(\alpha X)], & \text{for domestic–equity issues} \end{cases} \quad (1)$$

where X is a vector of variables, with corresponding coefficients α, measuring characteristics of firms choosing between Euroequity and domestic-equity offerings; $\phi(.)$ and $\Phi(.)$ are the standard normal density and distribution functions. Ordinary least squares estimation will provide a consistent estimate of the coefficient for the instrumental variable W in our regression of announcement returns, according to Maddala [15].

We estimate a probit probability that a firm will choose to issue Euroequity. To account for differential characteristics between issuers of Euroequity and domestic equity, this probability is specified as a function of issue size and the size and ownership structure of the issuing firm. We know from Exhibit 1 that large firms were responsible for most Euroequity issues during our sample period. To account for different motivations in issuing offshore for large firms, we use two measures of size — the market value of its common stock (issuer's market value) and the dollar proceeds of the stock issue (issue size). More so than small firms, large firms are likely to have operations overseas, and may issue offshore primarily to finance those operations, rather than to capture financing bargains; if so, we would expect that issuer's market value would have a stronger effect in the probit regression than

issue size. On the other hand, firms may be searching for financing bargains; if so, they would want to capture as much of a likely short-lived bargain as they could by issuing as much as possible overseas. In this case, we would expect that issue size would have the stronger effect.

According to earlier arguments by Smith [22] and evidence by Saudagaran [20], foreign investors may have a comparative advantage in monitoring the performance of firms located close to them. Given a prevalence of impediments to international investment, it follows that, given such an advantage, foreign investors may value a nearby firm's stock more highly than distant domestic investors would. If these investors also desire anonymity, they would be likely investors in Euroequity. If so, firms with overseas plants whose stock is more highly valued overseas than it is domestically will have a greater incentive to issue Euroequity than other firms with overseas operations, other things being the same.

Because they too are better informed than investors on average, management, large shareholders and institutional investors ought to have similar investments abroad. Therefore, we expect that the percentages of institutional, management and large shareholder holdings will be positively correlated with the announcement returns of Euroequity issues.

However, these holdings will not likely be significant in the probit regression. If management, institutions and large shareholders are better informed than other investors on average, their informational advantage would hold whether or not the firm has foreign operations. Consequently, we expect these holdings to have no effect in the probit regression, and a positive effect in the announcement-returns regression.

To test capital market integration, we test the hypothesis that Euroequity issuers have been able to realize a lower cost of equity than they would have experienced had they issued domestic equity instead. For the test, we regress the following independent variables on the abnormal returns for domestic-equity and Euroequity issues: the firm's beta coefficient, the size and ownership structure variables, the selection bias variable W, and tranche (the percentage of the issue in the offshore).

The tranche variable tests capital market integration. By definition it is equal to zero for domestic-equity issues. A positive coefficient for the tranche variable suggests that the larger the fraction of shares issued offshore, the more subdued the domestic stock-price reaction to the announcement of a Euroequity issue. This effect, moreover, is measured net of the selection bias. A positive, signifi-

---

[7]W measures the expected bias (due to self-selection) in the residual of the announcement return regression; see Maddala [15, pp. 257-262].

Exhibit 3. Probit Regression of the Characteristics of the Representative Industrial Corporation Choosing Either a Euroequity Offering or an Identical Domestic-Equity Offering From January 1985 Through December 1988 (the Independent Variable is a Dummy Variable Taking the Value 1 in the Case of Euroequity Offerings and 0 in the Case of Domestic-Equity Offerings)

Independent Variable[a]	Coefficient	t-statistic	Sample Mean
Intercept	-1.616	-4.316	1.000
Beta	-0.272	-1.297	1.246
Issuer's market value ($ billions)	-0.006	-0.119	0.965
Institutional holdings (%)	0.011	1.823	35.319
Management holdings (%)	0.012	1.187	10.123
Large shareholder holdings (%)	-0.003	-0.279	8.064
Issue size ($ millions)	0.003	3.659	86.605

Notes:

[a]The independent variables are defined as follows: Beta is the coefficient for the CRSP equally weighted index of daily stock returns estimated from a market model regression of the corporation's daily stock returns on the index for the period from 200 to 61 trading days before the announcement date. Issuer's market value is the closing price of the issuer's common stock at the end of the month preceding the announcement date times the number of shares outstanding at that time, as reported in Standard and Poor's Stock Guide. Institutional holdings is the percentage of shares held by institutional investors, as reported in Standard and Poor's Stock Guide for the end of the month preceding the announcement date. Management holdings is the percentage of shares held by directors, officers, and other insiders of the company, according to the most recently reported figure in an edition of Value Line preceding the announcement date. Large shareholder holdings is the percentage of shares held by investors owning 5% or more of the total number of shares, as most recently reported in an edition of Value Line preceding the announcement date. Issue size is the dollar proceeds of the stock offering, as reported in Investment Dealers Digest *Directory of Corporate Financing* or Security Data Company's *New Issues of Corporate Securities*.

cant tranche variable would be inconsistent with capital market integration. It would suggest instead that Euroequity issuers have been able to lower their cost of equity in proportion to the amount of equity issued offshore.

C. Results of the Probit Analysis

The probit estimates appear in Exhibit 3. The coefficient for issue size is positive and is the dominant variable. The coefficient is highly significant — at the 0.01% level or better. The coefficient for the issuer's market value is not significant. These results are consistent with the hypothesis that issuers were motivated by the existence of financing bargains. The coefficient for the issuer's beta is not significant. The coefficient for institutional holdings is positive and significant (at the 5% level), contrary to expectations. The coefficients for management and large shareholder holdings are not significant at conventional levels, as expected.

D. Results of the Test of Capital Market Integration

Exhibit 4 presents a direct test of the integrated capital markets hypothesis. The coefficients for the issuer's beta, its market value and its management holdings are insignificant, as in the probit regression. The coefficient for issue size is also not significant, but it has a strong influence on the variable measuring the selection bias. The coefficient for that variable is significant at the 10% level.

The coefficient for institutional holdings is positive and significant (at the 5% level), as expected. The coefficient for large shareholder holdings (not significant in the probit regression) is positive and only marginally insignificant (11% level) in this regression. Finally, the coefficient for selection bias is positive and significant (at the 10% level), as expected.

The estimated coefficients for management and large shareholder holdings are inconsistent with the hypothesis that these characteristics differentiate between firms likely to lower their cost of equity by choosing Euroequity over domestic equity. In the case of large shareholders, however, the coefficient has the expected sign and is only marginally insignificant.

Finally, the coefficient of the variable that tests for capital market integration, tranche, is positive and significant at the 5% level. This result is inconsistent with the hypothesis that equity markets are integrated. It implies that Euroequity issuers experienced a smaller decrease in their market value than did comparable domestic-equity issuers. The decrease on the average was 0.57%, a figure computed by multiplying the coefficient for tranche in Exhibit 4 by the average value of tranche also reported in that exhibit (i.e., 0.178×0.03213).

VI. Conclusion

When they first appear, new U.S. financial instruments that remove previously effective barriers for foreign inves-

Exhibit 4. Cross-Sectional Test of the Integration of International Equity Markets Hypothesis (the Dependent Variable is the Abnormal Return for Days -1 and 0 Associated With the Announcement of a New Euroequity or Domestic-Equity Issue as Registered on Share Prices in the U.S. Market; the Sample Consists of 228 Equity Offerings Issued From January 1985 Through December 1988, of Which 32 are Euroequity Issues and the Remaining 196 are Domestic-Equity Issues)

Variable[a]	Coefficient	Test Statistic[b]	Sample Mean
Intercept	-4.008	-4.253	1.000
Beta	-0.084	-0.164	1.246
Issuer's market value ($ billions)	0.078	0.567	0.965
Institutional holdings (%)	0.070	1.957	35.319
Management holdings (%)	-0.017	-0.601	10.123
Large shareholder holdings (%)	0.045	1.615	8.064
Issue size ($ millions)	-0.004	-1.183	86.605
Tranche (%)	0.178	1.697	3.213
Selection bias (× 100)	0.002	2.687	0.004
Mean announcement return=-0.023	R^2=0.046	Adjusted R^2=0.012	

Notes:
[a]The independent variables are defined as follows: Beta is the coefficient for the CRSP equally weighted index of daily stock returns estimated from a market model regression of the corporation's daily stock returns on the index for the period from 200 to 61 trading days before the announcement date. Issuer's market value is the closing price of the issuer's common stock at the end of the month preceding the announcement date times the number of shares outstanding at that time, as reported in Standard and Poor's Stock Guide. Institutional holdings is the percentage of shares held by institutional investors, as reported in Standard and Poor's Stock Guide for the end of the month preceding the announcement date. Management holdings is percentage of shares held by directors, officers, and other insiders of the company, according to the most recently reported figure in an edition of Value Line preceding the announcement date. Large shareholder holdings is the percentage of shares held by investors owning 5% or more of the total number of shares, as most recently reported in an edition of Value Line preceding the announcement date. Issue size is the dollar proceeds of the stock offering, as reported in Investment Dealers Digest *Directory of Corporate Financing* or Security Data Company's *New Issues of Corporate Securities*. Tranche is the percentage of shares offered offshore to foreign investors. Selection bias is an instrumental variable that controls for the self-selection bias that may occur if Euroequity issuers actually have a comparative advantage in issuing offshore; selection bias is calculated according to Equation (1) of the text using the probit results from Exhibit 3.
[b]For all variables except selection bias (for which it is inappropriate), we report the standard *t*-test of significance. For selection bias, we report Hausman's specification test which has a chi-squared distribution with 1 degree of freedom. Hausman's test is described in Maddala [15].

tors net financing bargains for the U.S. corporations issuing them. Euroequity is a new financial instrument offering such an advantage for American firms having an investor following offshore. Euroequity is advantageous because it has greater appeal to foreign investors desiring anonymity than any previous security that U.S. corporations could have issued.

Our evidence is consistent with previous research which shows that stock prices decline on the announcement of domestic-equity offerings. But, after controlling for characteristics of firms choosing to finance with Euroequity, we find that the negative stock-price responses are proportionately smaller for Euroequity issues the larger the proportion of the issue financed offshore. These findings are consistent with the hypothesis that new financial instruments that reduce effective barriers to investment across national borders allow firms to capitalize on profitable financing opportunities in overseas markets.

References

1. M. Adler and B. Dumas, "International Portfolio Choice and Corporation Finance: A Synthesis," *Journal of Finance* (July 1983), pp. 925-984.
2. G. Alexander, C. Eun and S. Janakiramanan, "Asset Pricing and Dual Listing on Foreign Capital Markets: A Note," *Journal of Finance* (March 1987), pp. 151-158.
3. G. Alexander, C. Eun and S. Janakiramanan, "International Listings and Stock Returns: Some Empirical Evidence," *Journal of Financial and Quantitative Analysis* (June 1988), pp. 135-151.
4. P. Asquith, and D. Mullins, "Equity Issues and Offering Dilution," *Journal of Financial Economics* (June 1986), pp. 61-89.
5. F. Black, "International Capital Market Equilibrium with Investment Barriers," *Journal of Financial Economics* (December 1974), pp. 337-352.
6. C. Bonser-Neal, G. Brauer, R. Neal and S. Wheatley, "International Investment Restrictions and Closed-End Country Fund Prices," *Journal of Finance* (June 1990), pp. 523-547.

7. I. Cooper, and E. Kaplanis, "Costs to Crossborder Investment and International Equity Market Equilibrium," in *Recent Developments in Corporate Finance*, J. Edwards, J. Franks, C. Mayer and S. Schaefer (eds.), New York, NY, Cambridge University Press, 1986, pp. 209-240.
8. V. Errunza and E. Losq, "International Asset Pricing Under Mild Segmentation: Theory and Test," *Journal of Finance* (March 1985), pp. 105-124.
9. V. Errunza and E. Losq, "Capital Flow Controls, International Asset Pricing and Investors' Welfare: A Multi-Country Framework," *Journal of Finance* (September 1989), pp. 1025-1037.
10. V. Errunza and L. Senbet, "The Effects of International Operations on the Market Value of the Firm: Theory and Evidence," *Journal of Finance* (June 1981), pp. 401-417.
11. V. Errunza and L. Senbet, "International Corporate Diversification, Market Valuation and Size-Adjusted Evidence," *Journal of Finance* (July 1984), pp. 727-743.
12. C. Eun and S. Janakiramanan, "International Ownership Structure and Firm Value," unpublished manuscript, November 1990.
13. M. Gultekin, N. Gultekin and A. Penati, "Capital Controls and International Capital Market Segmentation: The Evidence from the Japanese and American Stock Markets," *Journal of Finance* (September 1989), pp. 849-869.
14. Y. Kim and R. Stulz, "The Eurobond Market and Corporate Financial Policy: A Test of the Clientele Hypothesis," *Journal of Financial Economics* (December 1988), pp. 189-205.
15. G. Maddala, *Limited Dependent and Qualitative Variables in Econometrics*, New York, NY, Cambridge University Press, 1986.
16. R. Mason, *Innovations in the Structures of International Securities*, London, Credit Suisse First Boston Research, 1986.
17. R. Masulis and A. Korwar, "Seasoned Equity Offerings: An Empirical Investigation," *Journal of Financial Economics* (June 1986), pp. 91-118.
18. W. Mikkelson and M. Partch, "Valuation Effects of Security Offerings and the Issuance Process," *Journal of Financial Economics* (June 1986), pp. 31-60.
19. S. Myers and N. Majluf, "Corporate Financing and Investment Decisions When Firms Have Information That Investors Do Not Have," *Journal of Financial Economics* (August 1984), pp. 187-221.
20. S. Saudagaran, "An Empirical Study of Selected Factors Influencing the Decision to List on Foreign Stock Exchanges," *Journal of International Business Studies* (March 1988), pp. 101-127.
21. Securities and Exchange Commission, *Internationalization of the Securities Markets*, Washington D.C., Division of Corporate Finance of the U.S. Securities and Exchange Commission, 1990, pp. III:54-III:58.
22. C. Smith, "Globalization of Financial Markets," unpublished manuscript, University of Rochester, 1990.
23. B. Solnik, "The International Pricing of Risk: An Empirical Investigation of the World Capital Market Structure," *Journal of Finance* (June 1974), pp. 365-378.
24. B. Solnik, *International Investments*, Reading, MA, Addison-Wesley, 1988, pp. iii, iv, 161, 162.
25. R. Stapleton and M. Subrahmanyam, "Market Imperfections, Capital Market Equilibrium and Corporation Finance," *Journal of Finance* (June 1977), pp. 307-321.
26. R. Stehle, "An Empirical Test of the Alternative Hypotheses of National and International Pricing of Risky Assets," *Journal of Finance* (June 1977), pp. 493-502.
27. A. Stonehill and K. Dullum, *Internationalizing the Cost of Capital*, New York, John Wiley and Sons, 1982.
28. R. Stulz, "On the Effects of Barriers to International Investment," *Journal of Finance* (September 1981), pp. 923-934.
29. M. Subrahmanyam, "On the Optimality of International Capital Market Integration," *Journal of Financial Economics* (June 1975), pp. 3-28.
30. P. Tufano, "Financial Innovation and First-Mover Advantages," *Journal of Financial Economics* (December 1989), pp. 213-240.
31. S. Wheatley, "Some Tests of International Equity Integration," *Journal of Financial Economics* (September 1989), pp. 177-212.

Part II
Interactions of Financial Markets and Price Dynamics

[9]
Chaotic Behavior in Prices of European Equity Markets: A Comparative Analysis of Major Economic Regions

George C. Philippatos
Efi Pilarinu
A. G. Malliaris

SUMMARY. Brock's Residual Test Theorem and the BDS statistical test are the dynamic tools employed in this paper for analyzing international stock market data. Raw and detrended weekly returns and index levels for eleven International Indices (European, North-American, and from the Far East and Pacific region) are analyzed in a non-parametric fashion. By utilizing non-linearity tests adapted from chaos theory evidence is presented supporting integrated equity markets.

I. INTRODUCTION

The primary purpose of this paper is to apply techniques adapted from chaos theory to analyze the behavior of international stock

---

George C. Philippatos is affiliated with the University of Tennessee, Knoxville, TN. Efi Pilarinu is associated with Salomon Brothers, New York, NY. A. G. Malliaris is affiliated with Loyola University of Chicago, Chicago, IL.

The authors thank J. Doukas, P. Theodossiou, G. Koutmos, and A. Shafie for constructive comments that helped to improve the contents of this paper.

[Haworth co-indexing entry note]: "Chaotic Behavior in Prices of European Equity Markets: A Comparative Analysis of Major Economic Regions." Philippatos, George C., Efi Pilarinu, and A. G. Malliaris. Co-published simultaneously in *Journal of Multinational Financial Management* (The Haworth Press, Inc.) Vol. 3, No. 3/4, 1993, pp. 5-24; and: *European Equity Markets and Corporate Financial Decisions* (ed: John Doukas, and Ike Mathur) The Haworth Press, Inc., 1993, pp. 5-24. Multiple copies of this article/chapter may be purchased from The Haworth Document Delivery Center [1-800-3-HAWORTH; 9:00 a.m. - 5:00 p.m. (EST)].

© 1993 by The Haworth Press, Inc. All rights reserved.

markets. The stochastic approach to modeling the complexity and the apparent randomness of financial markets constitutes at present the most popular methodology. However, there exist many stylized facts that have recently led the profession to reevaluate the use of the random walk framework and its companions (EMH). An informative collection of some of these disturbing phenomena can be found in Brock (1992). These puzzles have contributed to consideration of a new research methodology based on techniques adapted from complex systems theory, which includes chaotic processes.

Pathways that may lead to chaotic and erratic dynamics have been investigated by several authors. Benhabib and Day (1981) and Gaertner (1988), analyze consumer choice. Day (1983) and Dana and Montrucchio (1986), analyze a classical economic growth model and a dynamic oligopoly setting, respectively. Baumol and Benhabib (1989) and Shaffer (1991), consider models of firm behavior. Lorenz (1992) proves the existence of a strange attractor for a Kaldor type business cycle model. The Santa Fe Institute Volume (1988), presents collectively the work of scientists from various disciplines in discussing the issue of the *Economy as an Evolving Complex System*. Examples include households that heavily discount the future, incomplete markets, abandonment of the equilibrium assumption in favor of learning dynamics, complex and chaotic dynamics in tastes and technology, and other settings shown to lead to complex and random appearing behavior produced by deterministic mechanisms.

Recently, researchers have been investigating for the presence of non-linear dependencies hidden in the assumed IID residuals of various stochastic models. The key idea is that although standard statistical techniques may support a specific statistical specification, there may exist additional non-linear structure which these techniques cannot detect. Empirical research in Finance employing tools from chaos theory (correlation dimension estimates) examines whether there exists additional structure above and beyond that captured by fitting stochastic models to log transformed, detrended/deseasonalized stock return series. For example, Scheinkman and LeBaron (1989), have examined U.S. daily and weekly returns from the value weighted (VW) CRSP index but the dependencies detected do not seem to be captured from an ARCH type specification. Brock (1987) has examined subsets of the same data and also monthly returns of the value weighted (VW) and equally weighted (EW) NYSE index. Genotte and Marsh (1986), have examined subsets of the same monthly data and also adjusted for the January effect. Hsieh (1991), has examined weekly returns of various portfolios and indices, daily returns and 15-minute returns of the S&P500. Willey (1992), has tested for non-linear dependencies in the daily prices of the Standard & Poor's 100 Stock Index and the NASDAQ 100 Stock Index. Finally, Philippatos and Pilarinu (1994) have analyzed weekly stock prices from various International Indices.

All these studies have examined whether there exists predictability over and above stochastic financial stock return models (e.g., random walk, martingale, ARCH, GARCH).[1] Since it has been shown empirically by Fischer and Palasvirta (1990) and others that the various national markets are somewhat integrated and move more or less in tandem with the U.S. market, it is interesting to hypothesize that some of the major financial markets of the world exhibit similar chaotic dynamics. Hence, we test empirically for the presence of deterministic non-linearities in the markets of the following six European countries: United Kingdom, Belgium, Switzerland, France, Germany, and Italy. The results in the European Region are then compared empirically to the respective results from the North-American Region (Canada and U.S.), and from the Far Eastern and Pacific Rim Region (Australia and Japan), as well as the results from the World Index. It is found that the non-linear dependencies, quantified using techniques adapted from chaos theory, are similar across both the European indices and the non-European International Indices.

Specifically, in this paper some new techniques adapted from chaos theory are employed, since they appear more promising in revealing non-linear dependencies. These dependencies may lead to the re-evaluation of the asset price paradigm postulating that tomorrow's expected value is equal to today's actual price and thus readily admitting that no short run prediction can be accomplished. In fact, we examine indices of ten industrialized countries from Europe, North America, the Far East, and the Pacific region and the World index and investigate whether the spatial correlations are different across countries. More importantly we wish to address the issue of the appropriate choice of the single observable examined, when quantifying static or dynamic properties of a multidimensional complex system. Section II presents an informal and intuitive view of chaos theory. Section III discusses the methodology used. In Section IV, the results are presented and compared to previous research in the local Capital Markets. Section V deals with the implications of this work and future directions of research.

II. CHAOS AND RANDOMNESS

Illustrations of simple non-linear equations that exhibit rich behavioral variety have been presented across various disciplines (May (1974)). The interesting feature of such systems stems from the fact that the time series generated from a range of parameter values (the chaotic region) is virtually indistinguishable from a random series. Not only standard statistical tests but even frequency domain analysis cannot identify the underlying dependencies (Bunov and Weiss (1979)).

Malliaris and Philippatos (1991) have studied the discrete logistic map (a one-dimensional non-linear map) as a model for changes in prices and contrasted the time sequence with that produced from a random number generator. The two series not only appear indistinguishable, but standard statistical tests fail to detect the underlying differences. In the random case no dependencies exist and in the chaotic case each price is exactly determined from the previous price. It is thus important to understand the source of complex and random appearing behavior in a system. Time series generated from chaotic systems are capable of deceiving certain statistical tests. Randomness with a deterministic origin arises from the three properties that define chaotic behavior: (a) sensitivity to initial conditions, (b) transitivity, and (c) a dense set of periodic points. An intuitive and non-mathematical view of these properties reveals the difference of random and complex behavior with a deterministic origin versus a stochastic one.[2]

(a) *Sensitivity to initial conditions.* Since a chaotic map is a deterministic system it may be fully predictable. However, this is only true if one knows the initial value with complete accuracy. An inaccuracy of an infinitely small order in measuring the initial condition of the system, may grow exponentially as the system evolves in time. Indeed this property renders the system practically unpredictable even if the law of motion is known. The difference between a chaotic and a purely random process (which is also unpredictable) lies in what causes randomness. In the latter case it is due to statistical independence, but for chaotic systems it is due to the lack of infinitely accurate information coupled with sensitivity to initial conditions. In practical terms, this property allows for major effects to be caused by small imperceptible changes. It is a manifestation of the accumulated effect of the feedback (feed forward) non-linear mechanisms at work, since sensitivity to initial conditions cannot be present in a linear world.

(b) *Transitivity.* Chaotic prices may wander anywhere. They can sore up and plunge to zero.

(c) *The periodic chaotic prices are dense in the real numbers.* Chaotic maps may well resemble random and complex appearing processes, but structure is present. Each sequence of periodic points converges.

A very important property of certain chaotic maps is the existence of a "strange attractor." This is a compact set towards which trajectories from almost all initial conditions converge. In simple terms, it is a region that may contain more points than other regions. This set can be detected by examining a time series in increasing d-dimensional spaces, simply by coupling delayed values. For a random process all space is filled in any d-dimensional reconstruction. However, for a chaotic process not all space is filled and moreover, it may be the case that the attractor in d-dimensions has a non-integer dimension (fractal). In practice, it is possible to distinguish complexity and randomness due to random sampling from that resulting from simple causes (chaos). This is accomplished by observing the correlation behavior of a time series in higher dimensional spaces.[3] Our empirical interest is in discovering low dimensional chaos because as the dimension increases the chaotic process becomes indistinguishable from a purely random process.

III. METHODOLOGY

Correlation Dimension Invariant

The correlation dimension is a measure of the average local spatial correlation of the series. It can be used to distinguish random from

10   European Equity Markets and Corporate Financial Decisions

deterministic-chaotic series, simply because pure randomness has a completely different average local spatial correlation behavior than that of a random appearing, but truly chaotic system. The basis of this difference is the existence of strange attractors in chaotic systems. In simple terms, in a system that has a strange attractor as time evolves the system converges to a set (strange attractor). The importance of this property can be readily visualized if one embeds the scalar time series into higher dimensional spaces. The idea is as follows: Examine phase plots (i.e., plots of delayed values) at various dimensions. A completely random series will fill the space in all cases. In essence, any two, three, or higher dimensional plots of delayed values of a random series will not show any structure, by assumption. But a chaotic series reveals a completely different hidden structure, although a simple inspection of a chaotic time series makes it look indistinguishable from a random one.[4] The structure unfolds as one increases the dimensions of the delayed value vectors (plotted in the phase plots) and observes that less space is filled and essentially everything lies within a set that has a small dimension. Looked at from another point of view, the idea is that if one observes the near neighborhood behavior of the two series at increasing scales (resolution parameters), these neighborhoods will include more points at an increasing rate. However, for the chaotic series this increase moves at a decreasing rate that in fact saturates at some point.

The correlation dimension D quantifies the average spatial correlation. It is the average information gained by increased resolution, by taking into account conditional probabilities:[5]

$$D = \lim_{\varepsilon \to 0} \lim_{N \to \infty} \frac{\log C(\varepsilon)}{\log \varepsilon}$$

$$C(\varepsilon) = \frac{\{\# (x_i, x_j) : \|x_i - x_j\| < \varepsilon\}}{N^2}$$

Since the true law of motion governing the system under examination is unknown and the only available information is a single observable of the system, we employ the time delay method for reconstructing the phase space (Takens (1983)). Assume that the only available measurement is a single variable x_i, $i = 1, 2, \ldots, N$. There exists a diffeomorphism between the n-dimensional true generating process and the reconstructed d-histories, if $d < 2n + 1$. Thus, by "transforming" the single time series into vector series of various dimensions, we embed the reconstructed phase space into the true one:

$$x_i^d = (x_i, x_{i+\tau}, x_{i+2\tau}, \ldots, x_{i+(d-1)\tau}), \quad i = 1, 2, \ldots N - (d-1)\tau$$

Having created the d-histories by coupling τ delayed values, we then calculate the correlation integral $C^d(\varepsilon)$:

$$C(\varepsilon) = \frac{\{\# (x_i^d, x_j^d) : \|x_i^d - x_j^d\| < \varepsilon\}}{N_n^2}$$

As ε changes the number of points included in the correlation integral also change. If structure exists and not all the degrees of freedom are exploited by the system, then proportionally fewer new neighborhoods will be included as ε increases. For example, consider a three dimensional object embedded in a four dimensional space. For any increase in the resolution parameter, the increase in the points included in the correlation integral is only due to three out of four available directions. Grassberger and Procaccia (1983) have shown that there exists a scaling relationship between the correlation integral $C^d(\varepsilon)$ and the correlation dimension D as the resolution ε shrinks:

$$C^d(\varepsilon) \approx \varepsilon^D$$

In practice, since the true dimension (N) is unknown we study the behavior of the correlation integral $C^d(\varepsilon)$ for increasing embedding dimensions d. We estimate D^d for each embedding dimension value d:

$$D^d = \lim_{\varepsilon \to 0} \frac{\log C^d(\varepsilon)}{\log \varepsilon}$$

If as d increases so does D^d, then the system is viewed as being high dimensional. If D^d converges or saturates to some level D, then

12   European Equity Markets and Corporate Financial Decisions

D is the estimated correlation dimension. In practice, one can detect structure by inspecting the logarithmic plots of the correlation integral versus the resolution parameter at various embedding dimensions. If structure exists, these plots (known as Grassberger-Procaccia plots (GP), (1983)) will appear like parallel lines. If the series are completely random, the slopes will be equal to each embedding dimension.

Brock's Residual Test Theorem

Brock's Residual Test Theorem exploits an important property of chaotic dynamical systems. It is a direct application of the invariance to coordinate transformations of these systems. In other words, the two invariant measures, namely the correlation dimension and the Lyapunov exponents, of a time series should be the same as those of the residuals of the original series constructed from a linear time series model with a finite number of lags (Brock and Dechert (1986)). This theorem has been used in most financial applications, in order to detect additional structure above and beyond particular stochastic specifications. In fact, it is a clever way of distinguishing low dimension estimates that are due to the presence of near unit root processes from chaos.

In practice, by comparing the correlation dimension estimates of the original series and of the filtered series, one should reject a linear generating process if these values are the same. However, caution is required in such comparisons for two important reasons: (a) There does not exist a statistical test that enables us to distinguish between two correlation dimension estimates, and (b) There exists a considerable bias in the correlation dimension estimates of relatively small sample sizes as those typically employed in economic and financial studies[6] (Ramsey and Yuan (1989), Ramsey et al. (1990)).

BDS Statistical Test

The BDS statistic is a non-parametric test of non-linearity (Brock, Hsieh, and LeBaron (1991)). It tests the null hypothesis that a time series is Independently and Identically distributed (IID) against an unspecified alternative using a non-parametric technique.

Under the null hypothesis of an independently and identically distributed process, the correlation integral $C_m(\varepsilon,T)$ at any fixed embedding dimension m and resolution parameter ε and for a finite sample size T, converges with probability one to $(C_1(\varepsilon)^m)$. This limiting quantity is the correlation integral of a completely random series. For a random series, as the embedding dimension increases, so do the points included in an ε-sphere by a power law whose exponent is equal to the embedding dimension. This property leads to a statistical test for randomness. It is shown that the standardized difference of the correlation integral of a series from a completely random series $(D_m(\varepsilon,T))$, has a normal limiting distribution with mean zero and variance $b^2m(\varepsilon)$:

$$W_m(\varepsilon,T) = T^{1/2} * \frac{D_m(\varepsilon,T)}{b_m(\varepsilon,T)}$$

where $\quad D_m(\varepsilon,T) = C_m(\varepsilon,T) - [C_1(\varepsilon,T)]^m$

$$b_m(\varepsilon,T) = 4 * \left[K^m + 2 \sum_{j=1}^{m-1} K^{m-j} * C^{2j} + (m-1)^2 * C^{2m} - m^2 * K * C^{2m-2} \right]$$

where $C = C_1(\varepsilon,T)$ and

$$K = \frac{6}{T(T-1)(T-2)} * \sum_{t<s<r} I_\varepsilon(x_t,x_s) * I_\varepsilon(x_s,x_r)$$

$I_\varepsilon(x_t, x_s)$ is the indicator function that equals 1 if $\|x_t - x_s\| < \varepsilon$ and zero otherwise, where $\|.\|$ is the sup-norm.

The BDS statistic is the mathematical analog of comparing the GP plots of the original data with those of a scrambled counterpart. It essentially quantifies the difference of the correlation integral values at each embedding dimension m of the original series $(C_m(\varepsilon))$ with those of a completely random part, which scales as a power of the embedding dimension $(C_1(\varepsilon)^m)$.

IV. EMPIRICAL FINDINGS

The database (Table 1) consists of the 833 percentage weekly logarithmic price relatives[7] of ten International Indices from Europe, North America and the Far East of Industrialized Countries and of the World Index (Barrons National Business and Financial Weekly). The sample period is from January 16, 1976 to December 27, 1991. All indices are based on local currencies and are value weighted (i.e., weights proportional to their market capitalizations). The World Index is constructed from the ten International Indices as a value weighted portfolio based on the dollar value of GNP for each country.

Recall that the implementation of Brock's Residual test theorem requires a comparison of the correlation dimension behavior of the raw series and a detrended counterpart. Furthermore, although there exists no statistical test that quantifies the difference between the correlation dimension estimates of two series, the behavior of the actual observable of the system (i.e., prices) is compared to that of a transformed one (i.e., returns). In effect, the correlation dimension estimates and the BDS statistic are obtained for the following four different time series for each country:

TABLE 1. Stock Indices

Region	Country	Index
North America	Canada	TSE 300
	United States	S&P 500
Europe	United Kingdom	Financial Times Stock Exchange 100
	Belgium	Stock Index
	Switzerland	Swiss Bank Corporation
	France	Agefi
	Germany	Commerzbank
	Italy	M.I.N.
Far East and Pacific Region	Australia	All Ordinaries
	Japan	Topix

The original return series

Residuals of an OLS regression on the return series

Transformed index level series

Residuals of an OLS regression on the index level series.

Tables 2-6 show the results (i.e., correlation integral values, BDS statistic values) for embedding dimension values 2, 4, 6, 8 and for five resolution parameter values ranging from 0.50 to 1.50 multiples of the standard deviation of the data.[8]

BDS Statistic

The BDS statistic is high for all four series of each country (critical value of 1.96 with a 5% significance). Thus, the BDS test of price and return series of raw and filtered series seem to reject the IID hypothesis. However, if one compares the results between raw and filtered data it is evident that only price series and not returns exhibit a dramatic drop of the BDS test. For example, the analysis of the weekly data from the United Kingdom at an embedding dimension equal to 8 and a resolution parameter equal to 1.5 standard deviations shows:

BDS	Index levels	Returns
Raw	400.88	6.20
Filtered	18.71	6.32

Previous studies that analyze domestic stock markets have examined daily and weekly return series. These BDS values found in the present study for national markets are very different from those reported by Willey (1992) for two U.S. stock indices, the S&P100 and the NASDAQ100. Willey finds values significantly lower than the critical value of the BDS statistic for both raw and detrended series of the logged first difference values used. Thus the null of an IID process is retained. By comparing our results of the return series we can infer that the difference stems from the aggregation level examined (daily versus weekly).[9] However, the present results

16 *European Equity Markets and Corporate Financial Decisions*

TABLE 2. Correlation Integral Values and BDS Statistic for (a) United Kingdom and (b) Belgium

M	ε	Index Levels	BDS	Residuals of index levels	BDS	Returns	BDS	Residuals of Returns	BDS
(a)									
2	0.5	0.34953	142.2895	0.1515	8.6529	0.09127	1.8703	0.0912	1.8944
4	0.5	0.33745	412.4978	0.03311	14.6336	0.00925	3.7858	0.00921	3.7049
6	0.5	0.32804	1569.4685	0.00898	22.6495	0.001	4.6302	0.00099	4.4655
8	0.5	0.32013	7148.0919	0.00261	34.6994	0.00011	5.5262	0.0001	4.2967
2	0.75	0.44337	177.7483	0.29628	9.3958	0.1919	1.5494	0.19223	1.6851
4	0.75	0.43303	372.2178	0.11818	14.9177	0.04063	3.8577	0.04063	3.8118
6	0.75	0.42484	954.9433	0.05611	21.4314	0.00967	5.9761	0.00972	6.0286
8	0.75	0.41799	2857.8244	0.0285	30.3534	0.00251	8.0806	0.00253	8.1564
2	1	0.52414	196.2778	0.442	10.0061	0.31244	1.5705	0.31271	1.8149
4	1	0.51633	330.6326	0.24763	15.3706	0.10566	3.8061	0.10582	3.9326
6	1	0.50994	650.9538	0.15994	20.9269	0.03909	5.6740	0.03927	5.8307
8	1	0.50486	1458.8323	0.10969	27.7354	0.01538	7.2973	0.01543	7.4010
2	1.25	0.57581	186.5996	0.56643	9.7522	0.4398	1.7178	0.4405	2.0550
4	1.25	0.56881	278.3061	0.38051	14.4858	0.20533	3.8051	0.20596	3.9833
6	1.25	0.56368	472.9702	0.28405	18.5905	0.10201	5.3554	0.10258	5.5248
8	1.25	0.55966	899.6118	0.22337	23.0083	0.05258	6.4537	0.05295	6.6056
2	1.5	0.63623	133.7091	0.66538	8.8703	0.56094	1.9272	0.56118	2.2257
4	1.5	0.62733	174.6506	0.49801	13.0765	0.32879	3.8927	0.32903	4.0428
6	1.5	0.61994	252.5437	0.40141	16.0624	0.20133	5.2662	0.20171	5.4146
8	1.5	0.61369	400.8883	0.33597	18.7171	0.12674	6.2044	0.12698	6.3247
(b)									
2	0.5	0.36061	134.7723	0.28609	12.8682	0.11869	3.36917	0.1162	3.03201
4	0.5	0.35096	377.6721	0.14797	24.4488	0.01652	4.79822	0.01507	3.74476
6	0.5	0.34304	1378.9667	0.10013	46.2411	0.00257	6.00099	0.00225	5.20077
8	0.5	0.33624	6008.7512	0.07711	98.1732	0.00047	8.46797	0.0004	7.76859
2	0.75	0.46455	146.9046	0.42731	11.7609	0.23887	4.26843	0.23424	3.1294
4	0.75	0.45654	289.8383	0.26609	18.9247	0.0651	5.50278	0.06133	4.41659
6	0.75	0.44976	691.9357	0.19976	28.4753	0.01941	6.62904	0.01755	5.52131
8	0.75	0.44398	1914.7565	0.16654	45.3559	0.0064	8.44749	0.00549	7.0007
2	1	0.53113	170.9854	0.54445	11.6768	0.36689	4.84653	0.36439	3.21979
4	1	0.52582	284.4413	0.3776	16.0232	0.1499	6.02782	0.1466	4.89638
6	1	0.52106	551.7202	0.29899	21.1171	0.06619	7.19384	0.0638	6.17877
8	1	0.517	1215.5457	0.25559	28.4425	0.0313	8.70322	0.02979	7.66073
2	1.25	0.57853	168.8451	0.64022	12.4459	0.48923	5.20063	0.48756	3.23046
4	1.25	0.57289	250.8035	0.48473	15.1312	0.26062	6.38723	0.25642	4.93468
5	1.25	0.57042	320.8271	0.43621	16.4444	0.19385	6.77102	0.18988	5.47583
7	1.25	0.56614	576.4005	0.37358	19.9613	0.11223	7.87811	0.10804	6.50813
9	1.25	0.56237	1138.5051	0.33357	24.5258	0.06801	9.20531	0.06423	7.64901
2	1.5	0.63958	126.3754	0.7097	12.1855	0.59879	5.80872	0.59705	3.14201
4	1.5	0.6325	164.4213	0.57005	14.1781	0.38437	7.08995	0.37852	5.11376
6	1.5	0.62658	237.0304	0.48481	15.8367	0.25663	7.85322	0.25028	6.18198
8	1.5	0.62194	375.2754	0.43134	18.1190	0.17742	8.73775	0.17072	7.04836

TABLE 3. Correlation Integral Values and BDS Statistic for (a) Switzerland and (b) France

M	ε	Index Levels	BDS	Residuals of index levels	BDS	Returns	BDS	Residuals of Returns	BDS
(a)									
2	0.5	0.37689	102.8531	0.19721	12.1732	0.12495	6.4649	0.12342	5.6085
4	0.5	0.36233	261.5042	0.06306	20.0498	0.01965	8.5359	0.01927	8.0066
6	0.5	0.35066	849.7740	0.02538	33.5070	0.00368	11.6886	0.00345	10.4271
8	0.5	0.34094	3276.9096	0.01051	55.9121	0.00068	13.8755	0.00062	12.3827
2	0.75	0.44897	139.8323	0.34468	11.9078	0.24391	6.0594	0.24198	5.7029
4	0.75	0.43731	285.2078	0.16929	18.2292	0.07183	8.3823	0.07103	8.2155
6	0.75	0.42773	709.2088	0.10142	27.4958	0.02501	11.7184	0.02452	11.4260
8	0.75	0.41954	2052.0855	0.06374	40.8463	0.00915	15.0581	0.00904	14.9613
2	1	0.50297	178.1099	0.47933	11.4853	0.37019	6.0992	0.36819	5.7316
4	1	0.49065	312.3603	0.29881	17.0162	0.15791	8.1885	0.15672	8.0116
6	1	0.48222	647.5016	0.21775	23.6212	0.07672	10.9865	0.0754	10.6173
8	1	0.4751	1534.3571	0.16731	31.9279	0.03922	13.6081	0.03817	13.0687
2	1.25	0.5662	165.8033	0.59258	11.2747	0.49894	6.9297	0.4949	6.4575
4	1.25	0.55303	248.6523	0.42518	16.0527	0.27715	8.7295	0.27394	8.5651
6	1.25	0.54288	425.2325	0.34126	20.6249	0.16776	10.7963	0.16486	10.5839
8	1.25	0.53414	814.3343	0.28698	25.6368	0.10537	12.5334	0.10308	12.3089
2	1.5	0.63391	126.3799	0.68356	11.0910	0.60983	7.4664	0.60697	6.9911
4	1.5	0.61984	164.0890	0.53635	15.1697	0.40185	8.9122	0.39887	8.6475
6	1.5	0.60893	235.6737	0.45817	18.6455	0.28067	10.4614	0.27767	10.1778
8	1.5	0.6002	371.5333	0.40652	21.9402	0.20231	11.7561	0.19901	11.3751
(b)									
2	0.5	0.35132	125.0025	0.26428	15.6075	0.10314	4.4993	0.12249	3.57013
4	0.5	0.34121	361.6413	0.12285	26.0531	0.01187	4.65315	0.01631	3.34355
6	0.5	0.33333	1372.5552	0.0707	45.9314	0.00166	6.93042	0.00253	459255
8	0.5	0.32664	6227.9195	0.04312	86.7570	0.00025	9.16101	0.00042	5.694
2	0.75	0.46079	132.3467	0.41206	15.3329	0.21208	4.81668	0.2503	4.97629
4	0.75	0.45072	261.6756	0.26409	24.0203	0.04945	4.9905	0.06967	5.19951
6	0.75	0.44274	627.4124	0.20044	36.7662	0.01307	6.52775	0.02102	5.95041
8	0.75	0.43584	1744.1363	0.16135	58.8341	0.00379	8.44404	0.00698	7.37185
2	1	0.53231	149.5863	0.51829	14.2514	0.33406	4.90744	0.37667	5.47758
4	1	0.52523	246.3632	0.36968	20.5499	0.12101	5.23734	0.15638	6.01763
6	1	0.51968	472.5046	0.30437	28.3530	0.04789	6.47687	0.06973	6.92587
8	1	0.51468	1027.4024	0.26596	39.9308	0.01996	7.66447	0.03285	8.05027
2	1.25	0.58196	151.5834	0.59684	12.6662	0.45524	4.99207	0.50098	5.94916
4	1.25	0.57303	221.4746	0.4479	17.3006	0.22136	5.44429	0.26999	6.24946
6	1.25	0.5665	367.3392	0.37838	22.2826	0.11483	6.51418	0.15449	7.14527
8	1.25	0.56104	679.8461	0.33755	28.6581	0.06176	7.40653	0.09205	8.08106
2	1.5	0.64708	119.7243	0.65929	10.9830	0.56601	4.88432	0.60605	5.72204
4	1.5	0.63725	152.6766	0.51329	14.7652	0.33686	5.4188	0.38844	6.17596
6	1.5	0.62928	215.0439	0.44046	18.3343	0.20959	6.28565	0.26137	7.11767
8	1.5	0.62252	331.5061	0.39231	21.9002	0.13378	6.93408	0.18106	7.90053

TABLE 4. Correlation Integral Values and BDS Statistic for (a) Germany and (b) Italy

M	ε	Index Levels	BDS	Residuals of index levels	BDS	Returns	BDS	Residuals of Returns	BDS
(a)									
2	0.5	0.34608	135.8093	0.20378	15.2037	0.10344	6.54479	0.10231	6.51315
4	0.5	0.328	386.8586	0.07682	27.3901	0.01317	8.62825	0.01286	8.65672
6	0.5	0.31369	1441.6557	0.03703	51.9035	0.00191	10.9958	0.0018	10.6230
8	0.5	0.30187	6436.8829	0.01938	107.8070	0.00031	14.5980	0.00028	13.9469
2	0.75	0.44268	173.6088	0.35071	16.1395	0.21325	6.55167	0.21077	6.74641
4	0.75	0.4295	360.6907	0.19639	25.6049	0.05441	8.73911	0.05336	9.04262
6	0.75	0.41861	916.3282	0.13596	42.1102	0.01532	10.6561	0.01496	11.1073
8	0.75	0.40896	2711.9430	0.10235	74.1047	0.00478	13.8592	0.00456	14.1043
2	1	0.50684	227.0280	0.472	15.8958	0.33746	6.80058	0.33413	6.85221
4	1	0.49419	395.1699	0.31634	23.1559	0.13259	9.15899	0.13034	9.30803
6	1	0.48437	810.0234	0.24788	33.0805	0.05662	10.9718	0.0556	11.3175
8	1	0.47621	1897.6321	0.20903	49.3219	0.02593	13.4260	0.02536	13.8734
2	1.25	0.57072	189.1624	0.56707	15.2087	0.46172	7.2351	0.45796	7.0026
4	1.25	0.55784	281.5219	0.41908	21.1389	0.24315	10.0183	0.23897	9.82732
6	1.25	0.54663	476.3601	0.34973	27.6920	0.13842	12.0896	0.13446	11.8147
8	1.25	0.53685	902.0133	0.30901	36.7861	0.08297	14.3591	0.07936	13.9043
2	1.5	0.63208	134.9655	0.64731	14.4060	0.57533	7.54599	0.57205	7.17835
4	1.5	0.62043	176.7728	0.50652	18.9364	0.36562	10.1687	0.36167	9.96753
6	1.5	0.61038	256.3069	0.43473	23.1748	0.24591	11.8251	0.2427	11.7559
8	1.5	0.60133	407.9381	0.39142	28.3488	0.17204	13.4995	0.16883	13.3831
(b)									
2	0.5	0.38967	118.1428	0.24792	10.6870	0.12252	3.48499	0.12249	3.5701
4	0.5	0.37436	287.2782	0.10121	18.5261	0.0163	3.26786	0.01631	3.3436
6	0.5	0.36131	882.4280	0.05572	33.8001	0.00251	4.44437	0.00253	4.5926
8	0.5	0.3498	3202.6313	0.03381	64.7369	0.00039	4.90919	0.00042	5.6940
2	0.75	0.4701	153.9017	0.3983	11.3608	0.25119	5.10709	0.2503	4.9763
4	0.75	0.45976	296.7052	0.22403	16.9764	0.06985	5.16534	0.06967	5.1995
6	0.75	0.4511	688.4484	0.15697	26.1501	0.02115	5.9506	0.02102	5.9504
8	0.75	0.44314	1845.0238	0.12014	41.1349	0.00701	7.34163	0.00698	7.3719
2	1	0.51955	211.6555	0.5193	11.6045	0.37737	5.4544	0.37667	5.4776
4	1	0.51185	361.2259	0.34171	15.3764	0.15634	5.87251	0.15638	6.0176
6	1	0.50528	722.2126	0.25826	20.3277	0.06974	6.80499	0.06973	6.9259
8	1	0.49927	1643.8643	0.2117	27.5877	0.0329	7.94232	0.03285	8.0503
2	1.25	0.55823	210.6335	0.612	12.0955	0.5013	5.9273	0.50098	5.9492
4	1.25	0.54999	326.4808	0.44693	14.8595	0.26965	6.12587	0.26999	6.2495
6	1.25	0.54344	581.0165	0.35609	17.7246	0.15443	7.07501	0.15449	7.1453
8	1.25	0.53804	1163.4267	0.30261	21.8432	0.09214	8.03869	0.09205	8.0811
2	1.5	0.61252	158.6913	0.68717	12.9052	0.60695	5.7892	0.60605	5.7220
4	1.5	0.60137	216.6015	0.54045	14.9002	0.38892	6.12017	0.38844	6.1760
6	1.5	0.59238	330.3036	0.45059	16.6208	0.2622	7.11656	0.26137	7.1177
8	1.5	0.58464	556.4121	0.39156	18.9379	0.18198	7.92148	0.18106	7.9005

TABLE 5. Correlation Integral Values and BDS Statistic for (a) Canada and (b) United States

M	ε	Index Levels	BDS	Residuals of index levels	BDS	Returns	BDS	Residuals of Returns	BDS
(a)									
2	0.5	0.26508	715.6151	0.16668	6.66878	0.13776	3.83404	0.13545	3.48695
4	0.5	0.24747	3142.4688	0.04337	12.97701	0.02336	5.73899	0.02246	5.57991
6	0.5	0.23374	19580.1077	0.01583	24.11166	0.00439	6.98643	0.00406	6.65665
8	0.5	0.22191	149209.474	0.00776	54.61056	0.0008	7.29379	0.0007	6.6353
2	0.75	0.36961	523.0852	0.29378	5.93158	0.26308	4.32287	0.25982	3.66782
4	0.75	0.35484	1418.5990	0.11607	10.86721	0.08048	5.88999	0.07825	5.48027
6	0.75	0.34276	4980.3077	0.05678	16.7128	0.02695	7.09106	0.02576	6.69278
8	0.75	0.33223	20849.6570	0.03359	27.99887	0.00952	8.3551	0.00881	7.70136
2	1	0.46339	267.1342	0.41729	5.42344	0.39567	5.2861	0.39579	4.51817
4	1	0.44841	521.7622	0.2089	8.84756	0.17645	6.67909	0.17514	5.99576
6	1	0.4368	1231.3830	0.11737	11.5749	0.08308	7.41748	0.08212	6.81576
8	1	0.42684	3365.3171	0.07389	15.74827	0.04114	8.43521	0.04039	7.77709
2	1.25	0.56465	185.8130	0.53298	4.46016	0.52163	5.74554	0.52245	5.24036
4	1.25	0.54817	277.8109	0.31639	6.98849	0.29677	6.81803	0.2972	6.48276
6	1.25	0.53563	473.3419	0.20118	8.54516	0.17582	7.36006	0.17617	7.08292
8	1.25	0.52492	902.7569	0.13624	10.38453	0.10931	8.31368	0.10899	7.93881
2	1.5	0.68596	137.2288	0.63306	3.64354	0.62303	5.81457	0.62294	5.41831
4	1.5	0.67056	162.1309	0.42673	5.53165	0.41604	7.03802	0.41548	6.76417
6	1.5	0.65878	208.5907	0.29813	6.35569	0.28641	7.48901	0.28569	7.25104
8	1.5	0.64865	290.1335	0.21643	7.29735	0.20384	8.18779	0.20269	7.90941
(b)									
2	0.5	0.32621	146.5547	0.14155	11.4517	0.09275	4.4184	0.09255	4.3234
4	0.5	0.31517	471.5580	0.03269	20.7714	0.00911	3.9348	0.00903	3.7789
6	0.5	0.30691	2029.8368	0.0103	38.5680	0.00099	5.1241	0.00099	5.0967
8	0.5	0.29986	10510.1263	0.00392	81.6125	0.00013	7.8990	0.00013	8.0493
2	0.75	0.44414	139.2251	0.27607	11.5941	0.1934	4.5197	0.19289	4.3292
4	0.75	0.43333	288.5192	0.11314	19.7586	0.03993	4.5503	0.03967	4.4029
6	0.75	0.42504	730.7389	0.05739	31.1663	0.00858	4.7924	0.00851	4.7149
8	0.75	0.41818	2156.6149	0.03351	53.5035	0.00186	4.8466	0.00184	4.7361
2	1	0.52808	147.1702	0.41156	11.2753	0.3146	4.6781	0.3138	4.4448
4	1	0.51994	244.1053	0.22838	18.2189	0.10605	5.2029	0.10526	4.9868
6	1	0.51358	471.6673	0.14829	25.7391	0.03716	5.5943	0.03667	5.3746
8	1	0.50818	1034.6057	0.10704	37.9552	0.01327	5.8442	0.01302	5.6232
2	1.25	0.58744	150.4926	0.53064	10.9034	0.44038	4.6600	0.43939	4.3486
4	1.25	0.57999	217.9729	0.34804	16.4096	0.20485	5.1574	0.20355	4.8973
6	1.25	0.5741	356.7665	0.25434	21.0320	0.09786	5.3791	0.09695	5.1789
8	1.25	0.56922	650.5895	0.2022	27.7203	0.04784	5.6719	0.04729	5.5070
2	1.5	0.65156	123.1837	0.62978	10.3601	0.56059	5.0031	0.55951	4.6074
4	1.5	0.64071	155.7479	0.45826	14.6127	0.3288	5.5576	0.32701	5.2393
6	1.5	0.63312	216.6186	0.35766	17.3297	0.19684	5.7273	0.19514	5.4553
8	1.5	0.62746	329.1723	0.29691	20.9563	0.11979	5.9219	0.11838	5.6707

20 European Equity Markets and Corporate Financial Decisions

TABLE 6. Correlation Integral Values and BDS Statistic for (a) Australia and (b) Japan

M	ε	Index Levels	BDS	Residuals of index levels	BDS	Returns	BDS	Residuals of Returns	BDS
(a)									
2	0.5	0.32441	221.98045	0.26387	12.37628	0.11424	3.80586	0.1087	3.58537
4	0.5	0.3091	716.00974	0.1144	23.10215	0.01416	4.21288	0.01267	3.74322
6	0.5	0.29659	3092.5926	0.06768	43.37883	0.00203	6.17336	0.00163	4.85917
8	0.5	0.28574	16099.6106	0.04671	89.5645	0.00021	3.02381	0.00016	2.57096
2	0.75	0.44087	201.45878	0.43998	11.30787	0.23788	4.20812	0.22539	3.64904
4	0.75	0.42888	424.36987	0.2581	17.85313	0.06091	4.6619	0.05348	3.54664
6	0.75	0.419	1097.7116	0.18382	26.57669	0.01705	5.96649	0.01392	4.77177
8	0.75	0.41042	3314.12114	0.1428	39.3433	0.00491	6.76271	0.00358	4.9126
2	1	0.51837	196.48457	0.59271	9.99028	0.37943	4.59286	0.36167	4.0842
4	1	0.51062	335.97096	0.41248	14.26479	0.1521	4.8039	0.13692	4.0069
6	1	0.50437	673.78885	0.32218	18.68083	0.06533	5.98879	0.05575	5.17337
8	1	0.49892	1539.47218	0.26899	23.81945	0.02877	6.69943	0.0234	5.93344
2	1.25	0.57424	172.61848	0.71184	9.18568	0.51755	4.86743	0.49794	4.4804
4	1.25	0.56545	257.06349	0.55253	11.77956	0.27764	4.69481	0.25712	4.34834
6	1.25	0.55831	435.91252	0.45774	14.2338	0.15644	5.70303	0.13935	5.2524
8	1.25	0.55204	826.86337	0.39576	16.62997	0.09043	6.4082	0.07711	5.78516
2	1.5	0.63357	136.5053	0.79749	9.20049	0.64204	5.41786	0.62073	4.94577
4	1.5	0.62356	178.86462	0.6679	10.48083	0.42263	4.9906	0.39591	4.70358
6	1.5	0.6158	259.92647	0.58176	12.0577	0.28691	5.72898	0.26053	5.38581
8	1.5	0.60918	414.76238	0.5193	13.33468	0.19791	6.19506	0.17302	5.61372
(b)									
2	0.5	0.38265	99.2853	0.33333	17.7189	0.12764	4.8366	0.12769	4.7610
4	0.5	0.37382	252.8343	0.21778	33.5398	0.02126	8.3810	0.0213	8.3596
6	0.5	0.36675	822.3960	0.16372	60.0764	0.00423	11.9897	0.00422	11.8726
8	0.5	0.36115	3172.0605	0.12808	116.6000	0.00096	17.7468	0.00095	17.3835
2	0.75	0.47808	110.6025	0.45823	16.6995	0.25277	5.6279	0.25312	5.7390
4	0.75	0.47171	209.3109	0.34522	28.3451	0.07768	8.4008	0.0779	8.4731
6	0.75	0.46636	474.9036	0.30097	44.0538	0.0272	11.0589	0.02712	10.9802
8	0.75	0.46175	1242.7993	0.27648	72.1209	0.01015	14.0679	0.01011	13.9514
2	1	0.53541	128.0932	0.54619	14.7611	0.39007	6.4553	0.39063	6.5981
4	1	0.52923	209.1868	0.41504	21.9765	0.17644	8.7716	0.17653	8.7715
6	1	0.52433	396.6731	0.36658	30.8997	0.08776	10.8329	0.08749	10.7356
8	1	0.52021	852.2415	0.34432	44.2901	0.04627	13.1512	0.04592	12.9635
2	1.25	0.58474	132.2916	0.62796	12.5012	0.51917	7.4699	0.51993	7.7352
4	1.25	0.57753	192.4844	0.48606	17.2045	0.30338	9.6580	0.30372	9.7313
6	1.25	0.57157	317.2975	0.42189	22.0471	0.1894	11.2471	0.18953	11.2849
8	1.25	0.56667	583.5887	0.38978	28.3116	0.12305	12.8640	0.12297	12.8647
2	1.5	0.63666	116.7465	0.70131	10.8822	0.63048	8.2936	0.63144	8.6476
4	1.5	0.62934	152.5812	0.56571	14.6265	0.43754	10.5977	0.43784	10.6622
6	1.5	0.6236	220.7266	0.49391	17.6316	0.3177	11.7906	0.3174	11.7735
8	1.5	0.61855	350.3109	0.45106	20.8481	0.2373	12.9141	0.23662	12.8509

are in agreement with the findings of Hsieh (1991) who examines weekly returns of the S&P500 from 1962 to 1989. Overall, the BDS statistic leads to the conclusion that non-linearities exist at the weekly time-aggregation level and the index portfolio aggregation level and across all countries for all series examined.

Correlation Integral Values

All indices examined exhibit similar (approximately equal), correlation integral values at each embedding dimension and resolution parameter value. This consistency translates to identical dependencies across all countries and for all series examined. In other words, the average local spatial correlations, as measured by the correlation integral, are of the same type for all countries.

Values for the raw price series range from 0.3 to 0.6 as the resolution parameter increases. These values remain essentially constant as the embedding dimension increases for each given resolution parameter value. The detrended counterpart exhibits similar behavior, although the values decrease as the embedding dimension increases. Hence we conclude that these series pass the Residual Brock Test.

The raw return series lack the convergence present in the raw price levels. However, the return series pass the Brock Residual Test, since their detrended counterpart shows similar behavior. Willey (1992) focuses on U.S. market data and finds that only the S&P100 Index passes this test.

V. CONCLUSIONS

In summary, the dependencies at a weekly time aggregation level are very similar across all major stock indices of six European, two North American and two Far Eastern countries. The spatial characteristics of all series examined (prices and returns) are also similar. However, price series appear more relevant candidates for investigating further the existence of strange attractors. Evidence of low dimensional structure as a plausible alternative to modeling complex and random appearing weekly index levels cannot be inferred from the above analysis due to the scarcity of the data limitations (which induces a bias in the estimates of correlation dimensions). Based on Hsieh's (1991) findings, the evidence detected is not due to structural changes (non-stationarity). Furthermore, Brock, Dechert, and Scheinkman (Brock and Malliaris (1989)) have shown that GARCH processes generate zero bispectra, which are inconsistent with the evidence of non-zero bispectra of stock returns cited in bispectral analysis studies (Hinich and Patterson (1985, 1988)). In effect, although there exists no statistical test under the null of chaos, sophisticated stochastic non-stationary specifications do not seem sufficient for accounting for the observed variability. A comparison of the present results and those found by Willey (1992) indicates that the dependencies detected are more prominent and uniform across all countries at a weekly time-aggregation level rather than at a daily holding period. Furthermore, the similarity of the results across European and non-European indices supports the hypothesis of integrated national markets, at least in the sense that the price dynamics of the markets are similar.

ENDNOTES

1. Other studies have examined rates of return on silver and gold (Frank and Stengos (1989)), daily foreign exchange rates (Hsieh (1989)), and futures prices for commodities and for financial assets (Blank (1991)).

2. We offer a brief analysis to motivate the empirical test. A detailed presentation may be found in Pilarinu (1993) and Malliaris and Philippatos (1992).

3. Philippatos and Pilarinu (1993) analyze in detail the behavior of the exponential logistic map.

4. The structure in such series cannot even be detected by many standard statistical tests.

5. The correlation dimension is a lower bound to the information dimension, that is based on the unconditional probability distribution constructed by embedding the true space in a probability space through an invariant probability measure.

6. Usually less than 2,000 observations.

7. $R_t = 100 * (\log (P_t) - \log (P_{t-1}))$.

8. Due to space limitations Tables 2-6 present embedding dimensions 2,4,6,8. Detailed results for embedding dimensions from 2 to 10 are available from the authors upon request.

9. The authors have recently obtained a database with daily data for numerous world stock indices and are planning to investigate this issue further.

REFERENCES

Anderson, P., Arrow, K., and D. Pines. (1988), *The Economy as an Evolving Complex system*, Santa Fe Institute Studies in the Sciences and Complexity, Vol. V, Addison-Wesley Publishing Company.

Baumol, W. J. and J. Benhabib (1989), "Chaos: Significance, Mechanism and Economic Applications." *Journal of Economic Perspectives*, Vol. 3, No. 1.

Benhabib, J. and R. H. Day. (1981), "Rational Choice and Erratic Behavior." *Review of Economic Studies*, Vol. 48.

Blank, C. Steven (1991), "Chaos in Futures Markets? A Nonlinear Dynamical Analysis." *The Journal of Futures Markets*, Vol. 11, No. 6.

Brock, A. W. (1987), "Nonlinearity and Complex Dynamics in Economics and Finance." In the *Economy as an Evolving Complex System*, edited by P. W. Anderson, K. J. Arrow, and D. Pines. Addison-Wesley Publishing Company.

Brock, A. W. (1992), "Understanding Macroeconomic Series Using Complex Systems Theory." In the *Structural Change and Economic Dynamics*, edited M. Landesmann at Cambridge University, England.

Brock, W. A. and W. D. Dechert (1986), "Theorems on distinguishing Deterministic from Random Systems." In *Dynamic Econometric Modeling*, edited by W. A. Barnett, E. R. Berndt, H. White.

Brock, W. A. and W. D. Dechert (1989), "Statistical Inference Theory for Measures of Complexity in Chaos Theory and Nonlinear Science." In *Measures of Complexity and Chaos*, edited by N. B. Abraham, A. M. Alfonso, A. Passamante, and P. E. Rapp, NATO ASI Series.

Brock, W. A., D. Hsieh, and B. LeBaron (1991), *Nonlinear Dynamics, Chaos, and Instability: Statistical Theory and Economic Evidence*. MIT Press.

Brock, W. A. and A. Malliaris (1989), *Differential Equations, Stability, and Chaos in Dynamic Economics*. North-Holland.

Bunov, B. and G. Weiss (1979), "How Chaotic is Chaos? Chaotic and Other "Noisy" Dynamics in the Frequency Domain." *Mathematical Biosciences* 47.

Dana, R. A. and P. Montrucchio (1986), "Dynamic Complexity in Duopoly Games." *Journal of Economic Theory*, Vol. 40.

Day, R. H. (1983), "The Emergence of Chaos from Classical Economic Growth." *Quarterly Journal of Economics*, Vol. 98.

Fischer, K. P. and A. P. Palasvirta (1990), "High Road to a Global Marketplace: The International Transmission of the Stock Market Fluctuations." *The Financial Review*, Vol. 25.

Frank, M. and T. Stengos (1989), "Measuring the Strangeness of Gold and Silver Rates of Return." *Review of Economic Studies*, Vol. 40.

Gaertner, W. (1988), "Periodic and Aperiodic Consumer Behavior." Unpublished paper cited by Kesley D. in The Economics of Chaos or the Chaos of Economics. *Oxford Economic Papers*, Vol. 40.

Genotte, G. and T. Marsh (1986), Variations in Ex Ante Risk Premium on Capital Assets. University of California, Berkeley, Business School, Unpublished.

Grassberger, P. and I. Procaccia (1983), "Measuring the Strangeness of Strange Attractors." *Physica D*, Vol. 9.

Hinich, J. M. and D. M. Patterson (1985), "Evidence of Nonlinearity in Daily Stock Returns." *Journal of Business & Economic Statistics*, Vol. 3, No. 1.

Hinich, J. M. and D. M. Patterson (1988), "Evidence of Nonlinearity in the Trade-by-Trade Stock Market Return Generating Process." In the *Economic Complexity: Chaos, Sunspots, Bubbles and Nonlinearity*, edited by W. A. Barnett, J. Geweke, K. Shell.

Hsieh, A. D. (1989), "Testing for Nonlinear Dependence in Daily Foreign Exchange Rates." *Journal of Business*, Vol. 63, No. 3.

Hsieh, A. D. (1991), "Chaos and Nonlinear Dynamics: Application to Financial Markets." *The Journal of Finance*, Vol. XLVL, No. 5.

Lorenz, H. W. (1989), *Non Linear Dynamical Economics and Chaotic Motion*, Springer-Verlag.

Lorenz, H. W., "Strange Attractors in a Multisector Business Cycle Model." *Journal of Economic Behavior and Organization* (forthcoming).

Malliaris, G. A. and G. C. Philippatos (1992), "Random Walk vs. Chaotic Dynamics in Financial Economics." Proceedings of the Conference on Chaos in the Social Sciences, Springer-Verlag.

Martell, T. F. and G. C. Philippatos (1974), "Adaptation, Information, and Dependence in Commodity Markets." *Journal of Finance*, Vol. XXIX.

May, R. H. (1974), Biological Populations with Nonoverlapping Generations, Stable Points, Limit Cycles, and Chaos. *Science*, Vol. 186.

Philippatos, C. G. and E. Pilarinu (1994), "Instabilities and Chaotic Behavior of Stock Prices in International Capital Markets." *Managerial Finance* (forthcoming).

Philippatos, C. G. and C. J. Wilson (1972), "Entropy, Market Risk, and the Selection of Efficient Portfolios." *Applied Economics*, Vol. 4.

Pilarinu, E. (1993), "A Chaotic Approach to the Analysis of Financial Data." Ph.D. Dissertation, University of Tennessee, Knoxville.

Ramsey, J. B. and H. Yuan (1989), "Bias and Error Bars in Dimension Calculations and their Evaluation in Some Simple Models." *Physics Letters A*, Vol. 134, No. 5.

Ramsey, J. B., C. Sayers, and P. Rothman (1990), "The Statistical Properties of Dimension Calculations Using Small Data Sets: Some Economic Applications." *International Economic Review*, Vol. 31, No. 4.

Scheinkman, J. A. and B. LeBaron (1989), "Nonlinear Dynamics and Stock Returns." *Journal of Business*, Vol. 62, No. 3.

Shaffer, S. (1991), "Structural Shifts and the Volatility of Chaotic Markets." *Journal of Economic Behavior and Organization*, Vol. 15.

Takens, F. (1983), "Distinguishing Deterministic and Random Systems." In *Non Linear Dynamics and Turbulence*, G. Borenblatt, G. Iooss, and D. Joseph.

Willey, T. (1992), "Testing for Nonlinear Dependence in Daily Stock Indices." *Journal of Economics and Business*, Vol. 44.

Asymmetric volatility transmission in international stock markets

GREGORY KOUTMOS*

School of Business, Fairfield University, Fairfield, CT 06430 7524, USA

AND

G GEOFFREY BOOTH

Department of Finance, Louisiana State University, Baton Rouge, LA 70803, USA

> The transmission mechanism of price and volatility spillovers across the New York, Tokyo and London stock markets is investigated. The asymmetric impact of good news (market advances) and bad news (market declines) on volatility transmission is described by an extended multivariate Exponential Generalized Autoregressive Conditionally Heteroskedastic (EGARCH) model. Using daily open-to-close returns, we find strong evidence that volatility spillovers in a given market are much more pronounced when the news arriving from the last market to trade is bad. A before and after October 1987 crash analysis reveals that the linkages and interactions among the three markets have increased substantially in the post-crash era, suggesting that national markets have grown more interdependent. (JEL C15).

It is fairly well established that stock traders in a given market incorporate into their 'buy' and 'sell' decisions not only information generated domestically but also information produced by other stock markets. Such behavior is consistent with the efficient markets hypothesis, provided that news generated by international stock markets is relevant for the pricing of domestic securities. This is the result of the increased globalization of financial markets, brought about by the relatively free flow of goods and capital as well as the revolution in information technology. Understanding the ways in which stock markets interact permits investors to carry out hedging and trading strategies more successfully. Likewise, regulatory proposals can be properly evaluated when linkages and interactions across national stock markets are taken into account.

Most of the research effort so far has focused on the interdependence and interaction of major stock markets in terms of the conditional first moments of

---

*This paper was presented at the annual Financial Management Association Meeting in St. Louis, October 1994. We thank the discussant, Kenneth Kroner and two anonymous referees of this journal for their helpful comments and suggestions.

the distribution of returns. For example, Koch and Koch (1991) use a dynamic simultaneous equations model to investigate the evolution of contemporaneous and lead/lag relationships among eight national stock markets. Their results point to a growing regional interdependence over time and to an increasing influence of the Tokyo market at the expense of the New York market. Becket et al. (1990) use regression analysis to study the intertemporal relation of the US and the Japanese stock markets. Their results show that information generated in the US market could be used to trade profitably in Japan, contrary to the market efficiency hypothesis. However, when transaction costs and transfer taxes are included into the analysis, excess profits vanish. Eun and Shim (1989) study the transmission of stock market movements using VAR methods. They document dynamic responses to innovations that are generally consistent with the notion of informationally efficient international stock markets. King and Wadhwani (1990) provide support for the hypothesis of 'contagion' effects in the three major markets. In such a setting, 'mistakes' in one market can be transmitted to other markets.[1]

More recent research explores stock market interactions in terms of both first and second moments. The list of such studies is rapidly growing, but the following sample serves to illustrate the extant literature. To wit, Hamao et al. (1990) examine price spillovers (i.e. first-moment interdependencies) and volatility spillovers (i.e. second-moment interdependencies) in the three major stock markets (New York, Tokyo, and London) using univariate GARCH models. For the period after the October 1987 worldwide stock market crash, they find volatility spillovers from New York to Tokyo, London to Tokyo, and New York to London. In contrast, no such spillovers are found in the pre-crash period. Hamao et al. (1991) test for structural changes and non-stochastic time trends in the spillover mechanism. They find that the spillover effect from the Japanese market to the US market has increased steadily over time. Lin et al. (1991) use a signal extraction model with GARCH processes to study the interaction of the US and the Japanese stock markets. Their findings suggest that price and volatility spillovers are generally reciprocal, in the sense that the two markets influence each other. Theodossiou and Lee (1993), using a multivariate GARCH-M model, find that the US market is the major 'exporter' of volatility. Ng et al. (1991) provide evidence on volatility spillovers in the stock markets of the Pacific-Basin. Finally, Susmel and Engle (1994) examine price and volatility spillovers between New York and London using hourly returns. They conclude that these spillovers are, at best, small and of short duration.

Despite the extensive investigation of the linkages and interactions of major stock markets, no attempt has been made to investigate the possibility that the quantity of news (i.e. the size of an innovation), as well as the quality (i.e. the sign of an innovation) may be important determinants of the degree of volatility spillovers across markets.[2] Studies dealing with the US market, however, suggest that such a possibility is very likely. For example, Black (1976) finds that current returns and future volatility are negatively related. Christie (1982) finds that this negative relationships is to a large part due to the leverage effect, *i.e.* a reduction in stock prices automatically produces a higher debt to equity ratio and hence higher volatility.

Nelson (1991) develops the exponential GARCH model (EGARCH) in an attempt to capture the asymmetric impact of shocks on volatility. His findings confirm that, for the US market, negative innovations increase volatility more than positive ones. Cheung and Ng (1992) find a significant leverage effect in a sample of individual stocks that persists even after conditioning on past volume. In terms of foreign stocks markets, Koutmos (1992) finds a significant leverage effect in the stock returns of Canada, France and Japan, as do Poon and Taylor (1992) for the UK. The evidence that volatility in the US and other stock markets is responding asymmetrically to own past innovations suggests that volatility spillovers themselves may be asymmetric, in the sense that negative innovations in a given market produce a higher volatility spillover in the next market to trade, than do positive innovations of an equal magnitude.

This paper contributes to the ongoing debate about stock market interactions by providing new evidence on price and volatility spillovers across the three major stock markets, *i.e.* New York, Tokyo and London. Unlike most previous research in this area, this paper explicitly models potential asymmetrics that may exist in the volatility transmission mechanism. The method employed is a multivariate extension of Nelson's (1991) univariate EGARCH model. Modeling the returns of the three markets simultaneously has several advantages over the univariate approach that has been used so far. First, it eliminates the two-step procedure, thereby avoiding problems associated with estimated regressors. Second, it improves the efficiency and the power of the tests for cross market spillovers. Third, it is methodologically consistent with the notion that spillovers are essentially manifestations of the impact of global news on any given market. The multivariate EGARCH model is ideally suited to test the possibility of asymmetries in the volatility transmission mechanism because it allows own market and cross market innovations to exert an asymmetric impact on the volatility in a given market. In other words, news generated in one market is evaluated in terms of both size and sign by the next market to trade.

A competing model that also allows volatility to respond asymmetrically to innovations is the Quadratic GARCH model proposed by Engle (1990) and used by Campbell and Hentschel (1992). However, on the basis of several diagnostics, Engle and Ng (1993) find that the EGARCH model performs better than the Quadratic GARCH model because the latter tends to underpredict volatility associated with negative innovations. An additional advantage of the EGARCH model is that no parameter restrictions are required to insure positive variances at all times. This is important because Hamao *et al.* (1990) report that some of the coefficients in the conditional variance specification violate the non-negativity assumption.

The remainder of this paper is organized as follows: Section I discusses the methodology; Section II describes the data and analyzes the empirical findings for the entire sample period, as well as the pre-crash and the post-crash periods; Section III offers a summary and concluding remarks.

I. The multivariate EGARCH model

The New York and Tokyo stock markets open and close sequentially, as do the Tokyo and London markets. There is therefore, no overlap in the daily open-to-close returns of these two market pairs. Between New York and London, however, there is approximately a two hour overlap (*i.e.* late trading in London corresponds to early trading in New York). Nevertheless, to simplify the analysis we assume that all three markets open and close sequentially but we discuss possible biases resulting from the two-hour overlap between New York and London in Section III. Non-overlapping trading implies that the estimation of the means and variances in each market is conditional on own past information as well as information generated by the last two markets to close.

Let $R_{i,t}$ be the open-to-close return at time t for market i, ($i = 1,2,3$ where, $1 =$ New York, $2 =$ London and $3 =$ Tokyo), I_{t-1} the information set at time $t-1$, $\mu_{i,t}$ and $\sigma_{i,t}^2$ the conditional mean and the conditional variance respectively, $\sigma_{i,j,t}$ the conditional covariance, $\epsilon_{i,t}$ the innovation at time t (*i.e.* $\epsilon_{i,t} = R_{i,t} - \mu_{i,t}$) and $z_{i,t}$ the standardized innovation (*i.e.* $z_{i,t} = \epsilon_{i,t}/\sigma_{i,t}$). Then, the multivariate EGARCH model used to describe price and volatility spillovers across markets may be written as follows:

$$\langle 1 \rangle \quad R_{i,t} = \beta_{i,0} + \sum_{j=1}^{3} \beta_{i,j} \epsilon_{j,t-1} + \epsilon_{i,t}, \quad \text{for } i,j = 1,2,3;$$

$$\langle 2 \rangle \quad \sigma_{i,t}^2 = \exp\left\{\alpha_{i,0} + \sum_{j=1}^{3} \alpha_{i,j} f_j(z_{j,t-1}) + \gamma_i \ln(\sigma_{i,t-1}^2)\right\}, \text{ for } i,j = 1,2,3;$$

$$\langle 3 \rangle \quad f_j(z_{j,t-1}) = \left(|z_{j,t-1}| - E(|z_{j,t-1}|) + \delta_j z_{j,t-1}\right), \quad \text{for } j = 1,2,3;$$

$$\langle 4 \rangle \quad \sigma_{i,j,t} = \rho_{i,j} \sigma_{i,t} \sigma_{j,t}, \quad \text{for } i,j = 1,2,3 \text{ and } i \neq j.$$

The time subscripts in equations $\langle 1 \rangle$–$\langle 4 \rangle$ correspond directly to trading time but not necessarily to calendar time. For example, if $i =$ New York, the information set for traders in New York at the opening of the market in a given day includes past New York innovations as well as innovations from London and Tokyo during the same day. In terms of trading time all this is past information (*i.e.* part of the information set $I_{i,t-1}$). However, in terms of calender time innovations in Tokyo and London are contemporaneous.

Equation $\langle 1 \rangle$ describes the open-to-close returns of the three markets as a vector moving average (VMA), whereby the conditional mean in each market is influenced by own past innovations as well as innovations coming from the two markets to close. The term $\beta_{i,j} \epsilon_{j,t-1}$ for $i = j$ in $\langle 1 \rangle$ allows for autocorrelation in the returns due to non-synchronous trading (*e.g.* Hamao *et al.*, 1990; French *et al.*, 1987), even though the use of value weighted indices should minimize this problem.

Innovations in market j enter the information set of traders in market i. Take, for example, the Tokyo market, which opens after the closing of the New York and London markets. To the extent that innovations coming from these two markets are useful for the evaluation of domestic securities (*i.e.* reflect global information), they will be exploited by traders in Tokyo so that the domestic closing price incorporates its own as well as cross market information. The same can be said to be true of the other two markets. Coefficients $\beta_{i,j}$, for $i \neq j$, then measure the extent of price spillover across markets.

The conditional variance process given by $\langle 2 \rangle$ follows an extended EGARCH process that allows its own lagged standardized innovations as well as cross market standardized innovations to exert an asymmetric impact on the volatility of market i. Asymmetry is modeled by equation $\langle 3 \rangle$, with the partial derivatives being

$\langle 5 \rangle$
$$\partial f_j(z_{j,t})/\partial z_{j,t} = 1 + \delta_j \text{ for } z_j > 0 \text{ and,}$$
$$\partial f_j(z_{j,t})/\partial z_{j,t} = -1 + \delta_j \text{ for } z_j < 0.$$

Asymmetry is present if δ_j is negative and statistically significant. The term $|z_{j,t}| - E(|z_{j,t}|)$ measures the size effect and $\delta_j z_{j,t}$ measures the corresponding sign effect. If δ_j is negative, a negative $z_{j,t}$ tends to reinforce the size effect, whereas a positive $z_{j,t}$ tends to partially offset it. This phenomenon has been attributed to the aforementioned leverage effect. The relative importance of the asymmetry, or leverage effect, can be measured by the ratio $|-1 + \delta_j|/(1 + \delta)$. Volatility spillovers across markets are measured by $\alpha_{i,j}$ for $i,j = 1,2,3$ and $i \neq j$. A significant positive $\alpha_{i,j}$ coupled with a negative δ_j implies that negative innovations in market j have a higher impact on the volatility of market i than positive innovations, *i.e.* the volatility spillover mechanism is asymmetric.

The conditional covariance specification in $\langle 4 \rangle$ assumes constant correlation coefficients along the lines suggested in Bollerslev (1990). This assumption significantly reduces the number of parameters to be estimated. Its validity of course must be assessed empirically. Some caution should be exercised when interpreting these cross market correlation coefficients. This is because the returns are not contemporaneous in trading time. Thus, they cannot be interpreted as measuring contemporaneous relationships. Instead they should be interpreted as measuring intraday lead/lag relationships.

The persistence of volatility implied by equation $\langle 2 \rangle$ is measured by γ_i. The unconditional variance is finite if $\gamma_i < 1$ (see Nelson, 1991). If $\gamma_i = 1$, then the unconditional variance does not exist and the conditional variance follows an integrated process of order one. As noted by Hsieh (1989), the exponential specification is less likely to produce integrated variances.

Assuming the conditional joint distribution of the returns of the three markets is normal, the log likelihood for the multivariate EGARCH model can be written as

$\langle 6 \rangle$
$$L(\Theta) = -(1/2)(NT)\ln(2\pi) - (1/2) \sum_{t=1}^{T} \left(\ln|S_t| + \epsilon_t' S_t^{-1} \epsilon_t \right),$$

where N is the number of equations, T is the number of observations, Θ is the 33×1 parameter vector to be estimated, $\epsilon_t' = [\epsilon_{1,t} \; \epsilon_{2,t} \; \epsilon_{3,t}]$ is the 1×3 vector of innovations at time t, S_t is the 3×3 time varying conditional variance–covariance matrix with diagonal elements given by equation $\langle 2 \rangle$ for $i = 1,2,3$ and cross diagonal elements are given by equation $\langle 4 \rangle$ for $i,j = 1,2,3$ and $i \neq j$. The log-likelihood function is highly non-linear in Θ, and, therefore, numerical maximization techniques have to be used. We use the Berndt *et al.* (1974) algorithm, which utilizes numerical derivatives to maximize $L(\Theta)$.

II. Empirical findings

II.A. Data, preliminary statistics and univariate analysis

Data used in this paper are the daily opening and closing figures for the aggregate stock price indices of the US, UK and the Japanese stock markets. The indices used are the S&P 500 for the USA, obtained from Tick Data Inc., the Financial Times 100 Share Index (FTSE-100) for the UK, obtained from Commodity Systems Inc. (CSI) and the Nikkei 225 Stock Index for Japan also obtained from CSI. The S&P 500 and the FTSE-100 are value weighted indices representing approximately 76 and 70 percent of total market capitalization, respectively. The Nikkei 225 is a price weighted index and it represents approximately 52 percent of total market capitalization. Hamao *et al.* (1990) provide a useful description of these indices. The daily open-to-close returns for each index are the continuously compounded percentage returns calculated as $R_{i,t} = 100 * \log(P_{i,\text{close},t} / P_{i,\text{open},t})$. To assess the size of the bias introduced by the two-hour overlap between London and New York, we also calculate the noon-to-close return for the S&P 500. The period under examination extends from September 3, 1986 to December 1, 1993. The number of observations across markets is 1,700, which is less than the total number of observations because joint modeling of three markets requires matching returns.

Table 1 reports summary statistics for the daily returns of the three markets as well as statistics testing for normality and independence. The sample means for all three markets are not statistically different from zero. The measures for skewness and excess kurtosis show that all return series are negatively skewed and highly leptokurtic with respect to the normal distribution. Likewise, the Kolmogorov–Smirnov statistic rejects normality for each of the return series at the 5 percent level of significance, a level that is used throughout this paper. The Ljung–Box statistic for up to 12 lags, calculated for both the return and the squared return series, indicate the presence of significant linear and non-linear dependencies, respectively, in the returns of all three markets. Linear dependencies may be due either to non-synchronous trading of the stocks that make up each index (see Scholes and Williams, 1977; Lo and MacKinley, 1988) or to some form of market inefficiency. Non-linear dependencies may be due to autoregressive conditional heteroskedasticity, as documented by several recent studies for both US and foreign stock returns (*e.g.* Nelson, 1991; Akgiray, 1989; Booth *et al.*, 1992, among others).

We first estimate the model given by equations $\langle 1 \rangle$–$\langle 4 \rangle$ by restricting all cross-market coefficients, measuring price and volatility spillovers, as well as

TABLE 1. Preliminary statistics. Daily open-to-close stock returns.
Period: 9/3/86 to 12/01/93 (1,700 days).

	Tokyo	London	New York
Sample mean (μ)	−0.0387	0.0179	−0.0006
Standard deviation (σ)	1.3848	0.7332	1.0874
Skewness (S)	−0.5124*	−0.4407*	−5.9507*
Excess kurtosis (K)	16.7012*	5.3353*	115.9237*
Kolmogorov–Smirnov (D)	0.0456*	0.0906*	0.0626*
LB(12)	19.2985*	43.7211*	70.9938*
LB^2(12)	89.9047*	208.9816*	51.0496

* Denotes significance at the .05 level at least. All returns are expressed in percentages. The test statistic for skewness and excess kurtosis is the conventional t-statistic. LB(n) and LB^2(n) is the Ljung–Box statistic for returns and squared returns respectively distributed as χ^2 with n degrees of freedom. The critical value at the .05 level is 21.026 for 12 lags. The assumed density for the Kolomogorov–Smirnov statistic is the normal; sample critical value at the .05 level is 0.032.

the correlation coefficients to be zero. This restriction reduces the multivariate model to three univariate EGARCH models. The restricted model is used as the benchmark model, and its estimates are presented in Table 2. The moving average coefficients, $\beta_{i,i}$, are statistically significant for the Japanese and the UK markets, indicating that either non-synchronous trading or market inefficiency induces autocorrelation in the return series. For the US market $\beta_{i,i}$ is insignificant. Conditional heteroskedasticity is perhaps the single most important property describing the short-term dynamics of all three markets. The conditional variance is a function of past innovations and past conditional variances. The relevant coefficients $\alpha_{i,i}$ and γ_i are statistically significant. The leverage effect, or asymmetric impact of past innovations on current volatility, is significant in all instances lending support to our assertion that volatility spillovers may also be asymmetric. The degree of asymmetry, on the basis of the estimated δ_i coefficients, is highest for the Japanese market (negative innovations increase volatility approximately 4.34 times more than positive innovations), followed by the UK market (approximately 3.27 times) and the US market (approximately 2.14 times). Volatility persistence, measured by γ_i, is highest for New York, followed by London and Tokyo.[3] The hypothesis that the return series are homoskedastic (i.e. $\alpha_{i,i} = \delta_i = \gamma_i = 0$) is rejected at any sensible level of significance on the basis of the likelihood ratio test. The estimated Ljung–Box statistics for the standardized and the squared standardized residuals show that the benchmark EGARCH model successfully accounts for all linear and non-linear dependencies present in the return series. On the basis of the Kolmogorov–Smirnov statistic, the hypothesis of univariate normality is rejected for the US and the UK return series. Rejection of univariate normality, however, does not preclude multivariate normality of the joint distribution of returns.

Asymmetric volatility transmission: G Koutmos and G G Booth

TABLE 2. Results from benchmark EGARCH.
Full sample period: 9/3/86 to 12/01/93 (1,700 days).

	Tokyo		London		New York
$\beta_{3,0}$	00048 (0.0223)	$\beta_{2,0}$	0.0228 (0.0166)	$\beta_{1,0}$	−0.0011 (0.0213)
$\beta_{3,3}$	0.0549 (0.0244)*	$\beta_{2,2}$	−0.0855 (0.0284)*	$\beta_{1,1}$	0.0110 (0.0313)
$\alpha_{3,0}$	0.0301 (0.0072)*	$\alpha_{2,0}$	−0.0385 (0.0093)*	$\alpha_{1,0}$	0.0141 (0.0031)*
$\alpha_{3,3}$	0.3811 (0.0125)	$\alpha_{2,2}$	0.1526 (0.0176)*	$\alpha_{1,1}$	0.2305 (0.0208)*
δ_3	−0.6256 (0.0466)*	δ_2	−0.3637 (0.0973)*	δ_1	−0.5314 (0.0794)*
γ_3	0.9267 (0.0073)*	γ_2	0.9355 (0.0133)*	γ_1	0.9535 (0.0057)*

Log-likelihood = −6,624.12, LR(9) = 1,541.08* (H$_0$: $\alpha_{i,j} = \delta_i = \gamma_i = 0$ for $i = 1,2,3$.)

	Diagnostics on standardized residuals		
D	0.0296	0.0384*	0.0364*
LB(12)	18.4949	16.1858	12.3609
LB^2(12)	4.6693	10.4229	3.5153

* Denotes significance at the .05 level at least. Numbers in parentheses are standard errors. LR(9) is the likelihood ratio statistic distributed as $\chi^2_{(9)}$. The .05 critical value is 16.191. LB(n) is the Ljung–Box statistic for the standardized residuals distributed as $\chi^2_{(n)}$, (see Table 1 notes). LB^2(n) is the Ljung–Box statistic for the squared standardized residuals distributed as $\chi^2_{(n-j)}$, where j is number of own EGARCH parameters (two in this case); thus, the .05 critical value is 18.037 for 12 lags. D is the Kolmogorov–Smirnov statistic testing for normality. Sample critical value at the .05 level is 0.032.

II.B. Price and volatility spillovers

The maximum likelihood estimates of the multivariate model with no parameter restrictions are reported in Table 3. The full model considers both price and volatility spillovers from the last two markets to close to the next market to trade.[4] In terms of first moment interdependencies, there are significant price spillovers from New York to Tokyo as well as from Tokyo and New York to London. Despite the two hour overlap, there is no significant price spillover from London to New York. This is because the correlation coefficients $\rho_{1,2}$ accounts for most of the overlap effect. When we re-estimate the model using noon to close returns for the US market, the value of $\rho_{1,2}$ drops from 0.3748 to 0.1772. The rest of the coefficients, however, are not materially altered. Thus, the impact of the overlap is to almost double the correlation coefficient. Since the pairwise correlations are not the focus of our study, we continue the analysis using US open-to-close returns.[5]

Turning to second moment interdependencies (volatility spillovers), it can be seen from Table 3 that these are far more extensive and reciprocal. In addition to own past innovations, the conditional variance in each market is also affected by innovations coming from the last two markets to close. Thus, there are significant volatility spillovers from New York and London to Tokyo, from Tokyo and New York to London and from London and Tokyo to New York.[6] More importantly, the volatility transmission mechanism is asymmetric in all instances. The coefficients measuring asymmetry, δ_i are significant for all three

TABLE 3. Multivariate EGARCH model. Price and volatility spillovers. Full sample period: 9/3/86 to 12/01/93 (1,700 days).

From New York ($\beta_{3,1}$, $\alpha_{3,1}$) & London ($\beta_{3,2}$, $\alpha_{3,2}$) to Tokyo		From Tokyo ($\beta_{2,3}$, $\alpha_{2,3}$) & New York ($\beta_{2,1}$, $\alpha_{2,1}$) to London		From London ($\beta_{1,2}$, $\alpha_{1,2}$) & Tokyo ($\beta_{1,3}$, $\alpha_{1,3}$) to New York	
$\beta_{3,0}$	0.0695 (0.0104)*	$\beta_{2,0}$	0.0382 (0.0144)*	$\beta_{1,0}$	0.0249 (0.0182)
$\beta_{3,1}$	0.1519 (0.0249)*	$\beta_{2,1}$	−0.0400 (0.0184)*	$\beta_{1,1}$	0.0204 (0.0258)
$\beta_{3,2}$	0.0562 (0.0339)	$\beta_{2,2}$	−0.0815 (0.0249)*	$\beta_{1,2}$	−0.0529 (0.6724)
$\beta_{3,3}$	0.0422 (0.0247)*	$\beta_{2,3}$	−0.0858 (0.0358)*	$\beta_{1,3}$	0.0736 (0.0270)
$\alpha_{3,0}$	0.0605 (0.0042)*	$\alpha_{2,0}$	−0.0116 (0.0051)*	$\alpha_{1,0}$	0.0314 (0.0029)*
$\alpha_{3,1}$	0.0890 (0.0122)*	$\alpha_{2,1}$	0.0521 (0.0106)*	$\alpha_{1,1}$	0.1118 (0.0130)*
$\alpha_{3,2}$	0.0764 (0.0194)*	$\alpha_{2,2}$	0.0951 (0.0140)*	$\alpha_{1,2}$	0.1440 (0.0138)*
$\alpha_{3,3}$	0.2407 (0.0172)*	$\alpha_{2,3}$	0.0767 (0.0105)*	$\alpha_{1,3}$	0.0249 (0.0106)*
δ_3	−0.5121 (0.0557)*	δ_2	−0.2545 (0.0797)*	δ_1	−0.4447 (0.1077)*
γ_3	0.9676 (0.0050)*	γ_2	0.9756 (0.0049)*	γ_1	0.9834 (0.0047)*
Correlation coefficients					
$\rho_{1,3}$	0.0407 (0.0417)	$\rho_{2,3}$	0.2305 (0.0526)*	$\rho_{1,2}$	0.3748 (0.0498)*

Log-likelihood = −6,306.44, LR(15) = 636.36* (H_0; $\alpha_{i,j} = \delta_j = \gamma_j = \rho_{i,j} = 0$ for $i,j = 1,2,3$.)

Diagnostics on standardized and cross standardized residuals			
D	0.0296	0.0305	0.0248
LB(12)	12.8428	11.9184	7.1424
LB^2(12)	5.0891	12.5879	6.5658
LB^a(12)	8.2562	7.3230	8.4049

* Denotes significance at the .05 level at least. Numbers in parentheses are standard errors. LR(15) is the likelihood ratio statistic distributed at $\chi^2_{(15)}$. The .05 critical value is 24.996. LB(n) and LB^2(n) are the Ljung–Box statistics for the standardized and the squared standardized residuals respectively. LB^a(12) is the Ljung–Box Statistic for the cross product of the standardized residuals i.e. $z_{i,t}$ $z_{j,t}$. See also Table 1 and Table 2 notes.

markets. This finding confirms our assertion that both the size of the innovations are important determinants of volatility spillovers.

The extent to which negative news (innovations) in one market increase volatility more than positive news in the next market to trade can be assessed using the estimated coefficients. Thus, a negative innovation in (i) New York, (ii) London, (iii) Tokyo increases volatility in the other two markets by (i) 2.6, (ii) 1.68, (iii) 3.12 times more than a positive innovation.[7] The final impact of an innovation from market i on the conditional variance of market j is determined by the size of $\alpha_{i,j}$ and δ_j (see equations $\langle 2 \rangle$ and $\langle 3 \rangle$). On the basis of these estimates we calculate the impact of a $\pm 5\%$ innovation in market i on the conditional variance of market j assuming all other innovations are zero.[8] The results are given in Table 4. As expected, the impact of an innovation in market i is mostly felt in the next market to trade. The impact is still felt in the following market to open but it is typically reduced. For example, a -5% ($+5\%$) innovation in New York increases volatility by 0.6414% (0.2471%) in Tokyo and by 0.3763% (0.1446%) in London the next day. Similarly, a -5% ($+5\%$) innovation in Tokyo increases volatility by 0.5798% (0.1870%) in London and by 0.1882% (0.0607%) in New York the same day.

Comparing the estimates of the benchmark model to those of the unrestricted model (*i.e.* Tables 2 and 3, respectively), we can see that the degree of asymmetry implied by the benchmark model is invariably higher. This is because the benchmark model does not take into account volatility spillovers from the other markets. Also, the parameters measuring volatility persistence γ_i are much closer to unity than the estimates of the benchmark model. In fact, simple t-tests fail to reject the hypothesis that there is a unit root in the conditional variances of the three stock markets (*i.e.* $\gamma_i = 1$ for $i = 1,2,3$). Thus, current innovations remain important for all future forecasts of the conditional variance.

We use the likelihood ratio statistic to test the hypothesis that price and volatility spillovers from the last two markets to close to the next market to trade are jointly zero (*i.e.* the benchmark versus the unrestricted model). The null hypothesis is rejected at any plausible level of significance. The existence of first and second moment interdependencies points to the presence of a global marketplace, whereby news affecting asset pricing are not purely domes-

TABLE 4. Impact of innovations on volatility.

Innovations	%Δ in New York volatility	%Δ in London volatility	%Δ in Tokyo volatility
+5% New York		0.1446	0.2471
−5% New York		0.3763	0.6415
+5% London	0.5367		0.2848
−5% London	0.9032		0.4792
+5% Tokyo	0.0607	0.1870	
−5% Tokyo	0.1882	0.5798	

tic in nature but, to a considerable extent, international. In this respect our findings support the 'meteor shower hypothesis' of Engle *et al.* (1990) who find that in foreign exchange markets news follows a process like a meteor shower hitting the earth as it revolves. The impact of such a process is manifested in the form of volatility spillovers from one market to the next.

Residual based diagnostic tests show that the multivariate EGARCH model satisfactorily explains the interaction of the three major stock markets. The Ljung–Box statistics show no evidence of linear and non-linear dependence in the standardized residuals. The validity of the assumption of constant conditional correlations can be assessed by testing for serial correlation in the cross product of the standardized residuals. The Ljung–Box statistics up to 12 lags show no evidence of serial correlation. Moreover, on the basis of the Kolmogorov–Smirnov statistic, conditional multivariate normality is not rejected.

II.C. Pre- and post-crash analysis

Bollerslev *et al.* (1992) suggest that the asymmetric response of volatility to innovations may be the result of a few extreme observations such as those associated with the October 1987 crash. To investigate this possibility, as well as possible changes in the nature of price and volatility spillovers in the period following the 1987 crash, we estimate the unrestricted model for the pre- and post-crash periods.

The results for the unrestricted model for the pre-crash period are reported in Table 5. There is evidence of price spillovers from New York to Tokyo and London. There is also evidence of volatility spillovers from London to New York. These spillovers are symmetric since the coefficient measuring asymmetry for the London market is insignificant. There are no significant spillovers from Tokyo to either London or New York. Conditional volatility of the returns in New York and Tokyo respond asymmetrically to own past innovations but there is no evidence of asymmetric volatility transmission in any direction. These findings suggest that market interactions were limited in the pre-crash period with the New York market being the major producer of information. Nevertheless, these results should be interpreted carefully because of the small size of the pre-crash period.

The picture changes substantially when we look at the estimates of the model for the post-crash period, which are reported in Table 6. The interactions now are very similar to those documented for the entire period. In all three markets the leverage effect is significant. There are significant price spillovers from New York to Tokyo and London, from Tokyo to London and New York and from London to New York. In terms of second moment interactions, there are significant asymmetric volatility spillovers from New York to Tokyo, from London to New York, and from Tokyo to both London and New York.

A comparison of the results from the pre- and post-crash period reveals that national markets have grown more interdependent in the sense that information affecting asset prices has become more global in nature. The New York and London markets have become more sensitive to news originating in Tokyo

TABLE 5. Multivariate EGARCH model. Price and volatility spillovers. Pre-crash period: 9/3/86 to 9/3/87 (257 days).

From New York ($\beta_{3,1}$, $\alpha_{3,1}$) & London ($\beta_{3,2}$, $\alpha_{3,2}$) to Tokyo		From Tokyo ($\beta_{2,3}$, $\alpha_{2,3}$) & New York ($\beta_{2,1}$, $\alpha_{2,1}$) to London		From London ($\beta_{1,2}$, $\alpha_{1,2}$) & Tokyo ($\beta_{1,3}$, $\alpha_{1,3}$) to New York	
$\beta_{3,0}$	0.0959 (0.0650)	$\beta_{2,0}$	0.1051 (0.0458)*	$\beta_{1,0}$	0.0681 (0.0633)
$\beta_{3,1}$	0.2436 (0.0548)*	$\beta_{2,1}$	−0.0312 (0.0522)*	$\beta_{1,1}$	0.0906 (0.0573)
$\beta_{3,2}$	0.0897 (0.0918)	$\beta_{2,2}$	−0.0186 (0.0688)	$\beta_{1,2}$	−0.0157 (0.1858)
$\beta_{3,3}$	0.0627 (0.0711)	$\beta_{2,3}$	−0.1657 (0.2276)	$\beta_{1,3}$	0.1154 (0.1162)
$\alpha_{3,0}$	−0.0426 (0.0169)*	$\alpha_{2,0}$	−0.2296 (0.0340)*	$\alpha_{1,0}$	−0.0179 (0.0091)*
$\alpha_{3,1}$	0.0004 (0.0147)	$\alpha_{2,1}$	−0.0001 (0.0047)	$\alpha_{1,1}$	0.1241 (0.0465)*
$\alpha_{3,2}$	−0.0236 (0.0885)	$\alpha_{2,2}$	0.0674 (0.0314)*	$\alpha_{1,2}$	−0.0184 (0.0438)*
$\alpha_{3,3}$	0.1474 (0.0701)*	$\alpha_{2,3}$	−0.0023 (0.0169)	$\alpha_{1,3}$	−0.0479 (0.0344)
δ_3	−0.1107 (0.0538)*	δ_2	−0.2352 (0.7247)	δ_1	−0.5699 (0.2157)*
γ_3	−0.9287 (0.0339)*	γ_2	0.6553 (0.0498)*	γ_1	0.9703 (0.0117)*
Correlation coefficients					
$\rho_{1,3}$	−0.0554 (0.1479)	$\rho_{2,3}$	0.2518 (0.2722)	$\rho_{1,2}$	0.2948 (0.1558)
Diagnostics on standardized and cross standardized residuals					
D	0.0275		0.0413		0.0280
LB(12)	13.2479		8.2737		13.5966
LB²(12)	14.2138		17.5794		7.6513
LBª(12)	7.7435		8.2186		8.0665

* Denotes significance at the .05 level at least. Numbers in parentheses are standard errors. Sample critical value for D at the .05 level is 0.082. See also Table 3 notes.

in agreement with the findings of Hamao *et al.* (1991). Most striking is the finding that the volatility transmission mechanism is asymmetric in the sense the bad news (market declines) in one market has a greater impact on the volatility of the next market to trade.

III. Summary and concluding remarks

This paper investigates the dynamic interaction of the three major stock markets, *i.e.* Tokyo, London and New York. Price and volatility spillovers are

TABLE 6. Multivariate EGARCH model. Price and volatility spillovers.
Post-crash period: 11/2/87 to 12/01/93 (1,424 days).

From New York ($\beta_{3,1}$, $\alpha_{3,1}$) & London ($\beta_{3,2}$, $\alpha_{3,2}$) to Tokyo		From Tokyo ($\beta_{2,3}$, $\alpha_{2,3}$) & New York ($\beta_{2,1}$, $\alpha_{2,1}$) to London		From London ($\beta_{1,2}$, $\alpha_{1,2}$) & Tokyo ($\beta_{1,3}$, $\alpha_{1,3}$) to New York	
$\beta_{3,0}$	−0.0241 (0.0188)	$\beta_{2,0}$	0.0290 (0.1515)	$\beta_{1,0}$	0.0197 (0.0199)
$\beta_{3,1}$	0.1447 (0.0268)*	$\beta_{2,1}$	−0.0456 (0.0187)*	$\beta_{1,1}$	0.0235 (0.0249)
$\beta_{3,2}$	0.0244 (0.0371)	$\beta_{2,2}$	−0.0712 (0.0272)*	$\beta_{1,2}$	−0.2634 (0.1075)*
$\beta_{3,3}$	0.0382 (0.0289)	$\beta_{2,3}$	0.1222 (0.0329)*	$\beta_{1,3}$	0.0769 (0.0300)*
$\alpha_{3,0}$	0.0540 (0.0048)*	$\alpha_{2,0}$	−0.0092 (0.0032)*	$\alpha_{1,0}$	−0.0844 (0.0187)*
$\alpha_{3,1}$	0.0834 (0.0223)*	$\alpha_{2,1}$	0.0157 (0.0093)	$\alpha_{1,1}$	0.0402 (0.0107)*
$\alpha_{3,2}$	0.0051 (0.0197)	$\alpha_{2,2}$	0.0521 (0.0105)*	$\alpha_{1,2}$	0.0629 (0.0098)*
$\alpha_{3,3}$	0.2061 (0.0212)*	$\alpha_{2,3}$	0.0583 (0.0091)*	$\alpha_{1,3}$	0.0356 (0.0071)*
δ_3	−0.6336 (0.0707)*	δ_2	−0.4776 (0.1493)*	δ_1	−0.5301 (0.1791)*
γ_3	0.9728 (0.0046)*	γ_2	0.9851 (0.0036)*	γ_1	0.9927 (0.0051)*
Correlation coefficients					
$\rho_{1,3}$	0.0111 (0.0542)	$\rho_{2,3}$	−0.0951 (0.0577)	$\rho_{1,2}$	0.5182 (0.0637)*
Diagnostics on standardized and cross standardized residuals					
D	0.0309		0.0329		0.0244
LB(12)	14.9328		12.0051		7.8428
LB^2(12)	5.0891		12.5879		6.5658
LB^a(12)	8.2122		13.8560		9.6631

* Denotes significance at the .05 level at least. Numbers in parentheses are standard errors. Sample critical value for D at the .05 level is 0.035. See also Table 3 notes.

examined in the context of an extended multivariate Exponential Generalized Autoregressive Conditionally Heteroskedastic (EGARCH) model. Unlike previous related studies, this paper fully takes into account potential asymmetries that may exist in the volatility transmission mechanism, *i.e.* the possibility that bad news in a given market has a greater impact on the volatility of the returns in the next market to trade. We find evidence of price spillovers from New York to Tokyo and London, and from Tokyo to London. More extensive and reciprocal, however, are the second moment interactions. We document significant volatility spillovers from New York to London and Tokyo, from London to New York and Tokyo and from Tokyo to London and New York. In all instances the volatility transmission mechanism is asymmetric, *i.e.* negative innovations in a given market increase volatility in the next market to trade considerably more than positive innovations. These findings suggest that stock markets are sensitive to news originating in other markets, especially when the news is adverse. A pre- and post-crash analysis reveals that the stock markets in New York and London have become more sensitive to innovations originating in Tokyo.

Notes

1. Several other studies provide empirical evidence on first-moment (mean) interactions among national stock markets, *e.g.* Von Furstenberg and Jeon (1989), Becker *et al.* (1992), and Bennet and Kelleher (1988).
2. Susmel and Engle (1994) allow for a leverage effect in their univariate GARCH representation, but this effect is not linked to the volatility transmission mechanism. A related study by Kroner and Ng (1991) shows that bad news from portfolios of large firms spills over to portfolios of small firms, but not vice versa.
3. For the US market, the univariate results are very similar when noon-to-close returns are used.
4. 'Price spillover' is the impact of an innovation from market i on the conditional mean of market j, whereas 'volatility spillover' is the impact of an innovation from market i on the conditional variance of market j.
5. The results of the multivariate model that uses noon-to-close returns for the US are available from the authors upon request.
6. Related studies report fewer volatility spillovers across markets, *e.g.* Hamao *et al.* (1990, 1991) and Susmel and Engle (1994). Some of the differences can undoubtedly be attributed to different sample periods. This paper employs a much larger data set covering a six-year post-crash period. Differences can also be attributed to different methodologies since all of the aforementioned studies use univariate ARCH type models. Koch and Koch (1991) use a simultaneous equation approach but they do not examine volatility spillovers.
7. These figures also measure the differential impact of own past innovation on the current conditional variance of any given market.
8. From a theoretical point of view, an additional assumption is required namely that the persistence coefficients γ_i are unity. From Table 3 it can be seen that all persistence coefficients are very close to unity.

References

AKGIRAY, V., 'Conditional heteroskedasticity in time series of stock returns: evidence and forecasts,' *Journal of Business*, January 1989, **62**: 55–80.

BECKER, K.G., J.E. FINNERTY AND M. GUPTA, 'The intertemporal relation between the U.S. and Japanese stock markets,' *Journal of Finance*, September 1990, **45**: 1297–1306.

BECKER, K.G., J.E. FINNERTY AND A.L. TUCKER, 'The intraday interdependence between U.S. and Japanese equity markets,' *Journal of Financial Research*, Spring 1992, **15**: 27–37.

BENNETT, P. AND J. KELLEHER, 'The international transmission of stock price disruption in October 1987,' *Federal Reserve Bank of New York Quarterly Review*, Summer 1988, 17–33.

BERNDT, E.K., H.B. HALL, R.E. HALL AND J. A. HAUSMAN, 'Estimation and inference in nonlinear structural models,' *Annals of Economic and Social Measurement*, 1974, **4**: 653–666.
BLACK, F., 'Studies of stock market volatility changes,' *Proceedings of the American Statistical Association, Business and Economics Studies Section*, 1976, 177–181.
BOLLERSLEV, T., 'Modelling the coherence in short-run nominal exchange rates: a multivariate generalized ARCH model,' *The Review of Economics and Statistics*, August 1990, **72**: 498–505.
BOLLERSLEV, T., R.Y. CHOU AND K.F. KRONER, 'ARCH modeling in finance: a review of the theory and empirical evidence,' *Journal of Econometrics*, April/May 1992, **52**: 5–59.
BOOTH, G.G., J. HATEM, I. VITRANEN AND P. YLI-OLLI, 'Stochastic modeling of security returns: evidence from the Helsinki stock exchange,' *European Journal of Operational Research*, January 1992, **56**: 98–106.
CAMPBELL, J.Y. AND L. HENTSCHEL, 'No news is good news: an asymmetric model of changing volatility in stock returns,' *Journal of Financial Economics*, June 1992, **31**: 281–318.
CHEUNG, Y.-W. AND L.K. NG, 'Stock price dynamics and firm size: an empirical investigation,' *Journal of Finance*, December 1992, **47**: 1985–1997.
CHRISTIE, A.A., 'The stochastic behavior of common stock variances: value, leverage and interest rate effects,' *Journal of Financial Economics*, 1982, **10**: 407–432.
ENGLE, R.F., 'Discussion: stock volatility and the crash of '87,' *Review of Financial Studies*, 1990, **3**: 103–106.
ENGLE, R.F., T. ITO AND W.-L. LIN, 'Meteor showers or heat waves? Heteroskedastic intra-daily volatility in the foreign exchange market,' *Econometrica*, 1990, **58**: 525–542.
ENGLE, R.F. AND V.K. NG, 'Measuring and testing the impact of news on volatility,' *Journal of Finance*, December 1993, **48**: 1749–1778.
EUN, C.S. AND S. SHIM, 'International transmission of stock market movements', *Journal of Financial and Quantitative Analysis*, June 1989, **24**: 241–256.
FRENCH, K.R., G.W. SCHWERT AND R.F. STAMBAUGH, 'Expected stock returns and volatility,' *Journal of Financial Economics*, September 1987, **19**: 3–29.
HAMAO, Y.R., R.W. MASULIS AND V.K. NG, 'Correlation in price changes and volatility across international stock markets,' *The Review of Financial Studies*, 1990, **3**: 281–307.
HAMAO, Y.R., R.W. MASULIS AND V.K. NG, 'The effect of the 1987 stock crash on international financial integration,' in Ziemba, W.T., W. Bailey and Y.R. Hamao, eds, *Japanese Financial Market Research*, Elsevier Science Publishers B.V., 1991: 483–502.
HSIEH, D., 'Modeling heteroskedasticity in daily foreign exchange rates,' *Journal of Business and Economics Statistics*, July 1989, **7**: 307–317.
KING, M.A. AND S. WADHWANI, 'Transmission of volatility between stock markets,' *The Review of Financial Studies*, 1990, **3**: 5–33.
KOCH, P.D. AND T.W. KOCH, 'Evolution in dynamic linkages across daily national stock indexes,' *Journal of International Money and Finance*, June 1991, **10**: 231–251.
KOUTMOS, G., 'Asymmetric volatility and risk return tradeoff in foreign stock markets,' *Journal of Multinational Financial Management*, 1992, **2**: 27–43.
KRONER, K.F. AND V.K. NG, 'Modelling the time-varying comovement of asset returns,' Unpublished manuscript, Department of Economics, University of Arizona, 1991.
LIN, W.L., R.F. ENGLE AND T. ITO, 'Do bulls and bears move across borders? International transmission of stock returns and volatility as the world burns,' *National Bureau of Economic Research*, 1991, Working Paper No. 3911.
LO, ANDREW, W. AND A.C. MACKINLEY, 'Stock market prices do not follow random walks,' *Review of Financial Studies*, 1988, **1**: 41–66.

NELSON, D., 'Conditional heteroskedasticity in asset returns: a new approach,' *Econometrica*, March 1991, **59**: 347–370.

NG, V.K., P.R. CHANG AND R.Y. CHOU, 'An examination of the behavior of Pacific-Basin stock market volatility,' in Ghon, R. and R.P. Chang, eds, *Pacific-Basin Capital Markets Research*, Elsevier Science Publishers BV, 1991: 245–260.

POON, S-H. AND S.J. TAYLOR, 'Stock returns and volatility: an empirical study of the U.K. stock market,' *Journal of Banking and Finance*, February 1992, **16**: 37–59.

SCHOLES, M. AND J. WILLIAMS, 'Estimating betas from nonsynchronous data,' *Journal of Financial Economics*, 1977, **5**: 309–327.

SUSMEL, R. AND R.F. ENGLE, 'Hourly volatility spillovers between international equity markets,' *Journal of International Money and Finance*, February 1994, **13**: 3–25.

THEODOSSIOU, P. AND U. LEE, 'Mean and volatility spillovers across major national stock markets: further empirical evidence,' *Journal of Financial Research*, Winter 1993, **16**: 337–350.

VON FURSTENBERG, G.M. AND B.N. JEON, 'International stock price movements: links and messages,' *Brookings Papers on Economic Activity*, 1989, **1**: 125–179.

Local and global price memory of international stock markets

Johan Knif [a], Seppo Pynnönen [b],*

[a] *Hanken, Swedish School of Economics and Business Administration, P.O. Box 287, 65101 Vaasa, Finland*
[b] *Department of Mathematics and Statistics, University of Vaasa, P.O. Box 700, 65101 Vaasa, Finland*

Received 1 December 1997; accepted 1 November 1998

Abstract

The prime focus of this paper is on the impact of the world's leading markets (USA, Japan, Hong Kong, UK, France, Switzerland and Germany) on the returns of the small Nordic markets (Denmark, Finland, Norway and Sweden). The order and the degree of processing both 'local' and 'global' information are uncovered using a combination of cointegration analysis and structural VAR modeling utilizing daily index returns. The results indicate that the US price changes, conditioned on the same day changes on the other markets, have an impact on all other markets during the following day, including the US market itself. Price changes on the Asian–Pacific markets are completely absorbed in price changes in Europe and do not have any direct effect on US prices. Finally, a cointegration relationship between Sweden and Norway is found, which affects also Finland. © 1999 Elsevier Science B.V. All rights reserved.

Keywords: Short-term dynamics; Cointegration; Stock markets

JEL classification: G15; C32

1. Introduction

Since deregulation of financial markets began in the 1980s, there has been a growing interest towards the empirical study of the common behavior of interna-

* Corresponding author. Tel.: +358-6-3248259; fax: +358-6-3248557.
E-mail address: sjp@uwasa.fi (S. Pynnönen)

tional stock markets. Besides the advanced technology for worldwide information transmission and processing, the liberalization of capital movements, and the securitization of stock markets result in national markets that more rapidly react to new information from international sources.

Earlier studies suggest low relationships between markets (Grubel and Fadner 1971). More resent studies, however, indicate an increasing co-movement of major stock markets. Eun and Shim (1989) in their analysis of daily index returns on nine major capital markets find substantial interrelations between markets with the USA as the most influential. Kasa (1992) claims that there is a single common factor driving the stock markets of the US, UK, Germany, Canada and Japan. Forbes (1993) applies cointegration analysis for the banking sector and finds some degree of integration of the European stock markets. Engle et al. report on the existence of a cross-market dynamic effect of news on the short-run time path of volatility, such that news revealed during the open time of one market contribute to the return of the next market to open (Engle et al., 1990, 1992). Susmel and Engle (1994) continue this kind of analysis by using intra-day data and focusing on spillovers of volatility and mean between the New York and London stock markets, especially at the hours when both markets are open. They find that the volatility spillover is minimal and has a duration lasting for ~ 1 h. With the exception of two anomalies, they found no spillovers of mean during non-overlapping trading periods. Engle and Susmel (1993) investigate common volatility processes on international stock markets. Their data consist of weekly stock-index returns on 18 major stock markets. The results suggest a common time-varying volatility in certain groups of countries (one European and one Asian-Pacific). However, not many countries seem to share a common volatility structure, and if it exists, it is at most regional rather than global. Booth et al. (1995) find a single common factor generating volatilities on US, UK and Japanese stock-index futures markets. Karolyi (1995) investigates short-run dynamics in returns and volatility for the New York and Toronto stock exchanges on a daily basis. He finds that the inference about the magnitude and persistence of return innovations is heavily dependent on how the cross-market dynamics in volatility is modeled. Karolyi and Stulz (1996) analyze influences of the macro economic, industry, yen/dollar exchange rate, and broad-based stock market index effects on return correlations of NYSE-traded American depositor receipts and a matched-sample portfolio of US stocks on intra-day basis. They find that only large shocks to broad-based market indices positively influence both magnitude and persistence of return correlations, while changes in the other background variables have no measurable impact on the return correlations. The existence of common predictable components on regional stock markets is analyzed in Cheung et al. (1997). They report that only North American instrumental variables were able to predict excess returns in Europe and the Pacific.

Koutmos (1996) investigates dynamic first and second moment interaction among four major European stock markets; UK, France, Germany and Italy, using a multivariate VAR-EGARCH model. He finds evidence of multidirectional lead/lag relationships among returns as well as significant asymmetric volatility interaction, where negative innovations on one market increase the volatility on another market considerably more than positive innovations.

The above-listed papers are all concerned with large stock markets with the exception of Engle and Susmel (1993), where some small markets are included as well. Hietala (1989), Mathur and Subrahmanyam (1990) and Malkamäki (1993) focus on smaller markets by analyzing relationships between the US, UK, German and Nordic markets utilizing monthly data. The general finding is that the larger markets lead the smaller Nordic ones. Malkamäki (1993) also finds that Finnish markets are most strongly led by the German market contrary to what previously has been suggested, i.e. that the Stockholm Stock Exchange is the main leading market for the Helsinki Stock Exchange (Malkamäki et al. 1993; Bos et al. 1995; Knif et al. 1995; Martikainen et al. 1993). Knif et al. (1996) investigate the existence of a common autocorrelation feature in a long history of returns from Finnish and Swedish markets. They report evidence of common autocorrelation during the period before the Second World War and after the second oil crisis. Pynnönen et al. (1996), Pynnönen and Knif (1998) extend this analysis by investigating volatility and long-term relationships between the Finnish and the Swedish stock markets. Their results indicate some evidence for volatility lead-lag relations between the two markets. However, in spite of a very similar economic structure, no support for cointegration or fractional cointegration between the two Nordic stock markets was found. No material cross-market dynamics in means in the monthly data were found, either. Contemporaneous correlation between the markets increased, however, considerably in the course of time. This suggests that virtually all information from one market is absorbed into the returns on the other within the same month. Thus we may argue that a monthly level is much too high a level of time aggregation for an analysis of inter-market dynamics.

Following the approach of Eun and Shim (1989), this paper extends the literature in mainly three aspects. Firstly, by analyzing daily index returns, we try to empirically reveal possible short-term inter-market dynamics. Secondly, we look at the internationalization from a small market point of view. In particular, we intend to capture the short-term dynamic structure of these relatively small stock markets in relation to their dependence of information shocks on the major stock markets. Thirdly, in the analysis of daily close to close index returns, we explicitly model the mismatch in the open hours and the possible cointegration of some of the markets. Eun and Shim (1989) analyze the effects of the non-synchroneity in the trading hours by interpreting the contemporaneous residual correlations after fitting a VAR model to the index returns. We, however, deal with the problem explicitly by modeling the structure of different trading hours of the stock exchanges. In addition, as mentioned above, we start off with an analysis of the levels of the series in order to capture possible long-run relationships between the markets.

The remainder of the paper is organized as follows. The characteristics of the data are briefly described in Section 2. Methodological aspects concerning VAR analysis and relevant causality concepts are considered in Section 3. Section 4 reports the main empirical findings. Finally, conclusions and comments on further research are presented in Section 5.

2. Data of the study

The analysis utilizes daily close to close index returns from eleven markets including the stock exchanges in New York (Dow Jones Industrial Average 30), Tokyo (Nikkei 225 Index), Hong Kong (Hang Seng), London (FT 100), Frankfurt (DAX), Zurich (SI), Paris (CAC 40), Copenhagen (KFX), Stockholm (Veckans Affärer), Oslo (CSI) and Helsinki (HEX). The sample period starts on August 28, 1993 and ends August 8, 1996.[1] Fig. 1 illustrates the trading hours of the markets

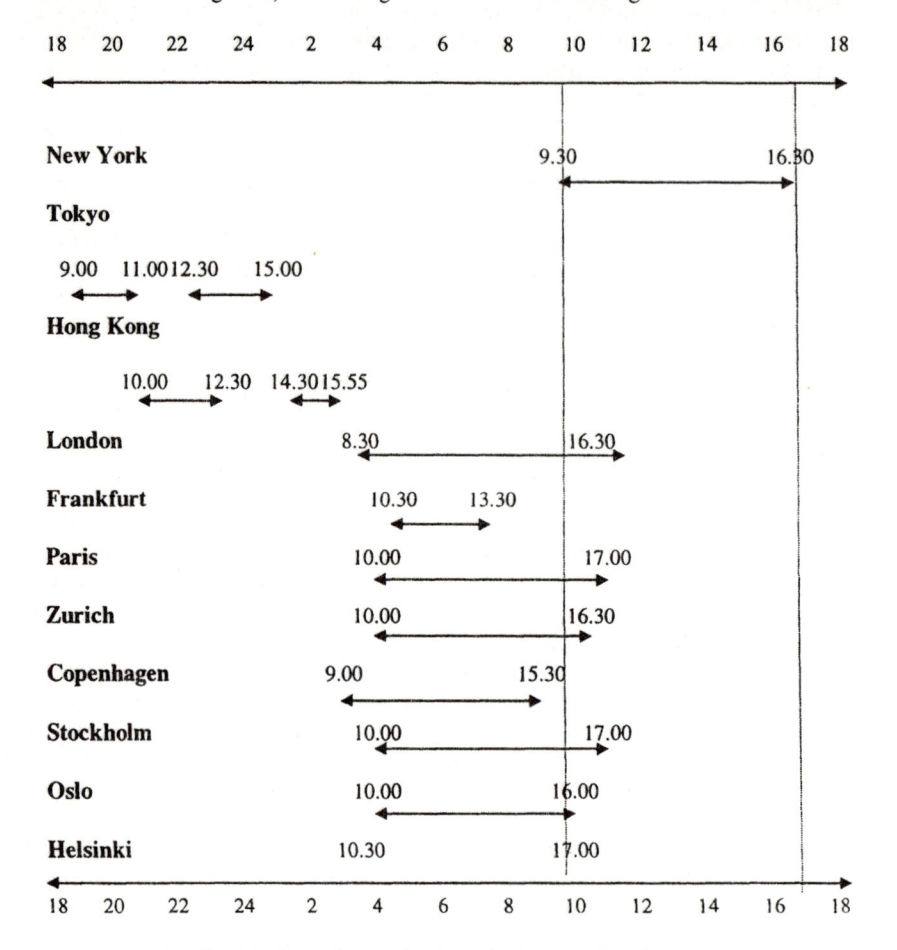

Fig. 1. Relative floor trading hours in eleven stock exchanges.

[1] Data is obtained from Startel Oy, Finland. Consequently, data are available only for Finnish working days. In cases of national holidays in other countries, the missing index value is replaced by the last trading day's value, which in terms of returns means zero-return.

Table 1
Descriptive statistics of daily stock index returns[a]

	FIN	SWE	NOR	DEN	UK	GER	FRA	SWZ	USA	JPN	HON
Mean	0.06	0.06	0.05	0.03	0.03	0.04	−0.01	0.05	0.06	0.00	0.06
Median	0.01	0.03	0.04	0.00	0.01	0.06	0.00	0.06	0.03	0.00	0.00
Standard deviation	1.21	0.96	0.83	0.76	0.75	0.92	1.04	0.77	0.65	1.25	1.58
Excess Kurtosis	3.30	1.53	2.47	0.99	1.38	0.99	0.17	4.86	2.12	5.78	3.95
Skewness	−0.45	0.08	−0.04	−0.22	−0.08	−0.36	0.02	−0.21	−0.55	0.44	−0.53
Minimum	−7.52	−3.45	−3.73	−3.07	−3.08	−4.08	−3.47	−3.97	−3.09	−5.76	−10.08
Maximum	4.86	4.88	4.66	2.24	3.10	3.22	3.19	5.19	2.00	8.32	5.71
Count	741	741	741	741	741	741	741	741	741	741	741

[a] Daily returns are calculated as log differences $r_t = 100 \times [\ln(P_t) - \ln(P_{t-1})]$, where P_t denotes the index value at day t. Data are obtained from Startel Oy, where data is available only for Finnish working days. National holidays in other countries occurring on Finnish working days are imputed as zero returns.

Table 2
Contemporaneous correlations between market returns[a]

	FIN	SWE	NOR	DEN	UK	GER	FRA	SWZ	USA	JPN	HON
FIN	1										
SWE	0.48	1									
NOR	0.43	0.54	1								
DEN	0.35	0.44	0.44	1							
UK	0.28	0.46	0.41	0.35	1						
GER	0.41	0.44	0.50	0.49	0.42	1					
FRA	0.28	0.45	0.39	0.33	0.60	0.48	1				
SWZ	0.31	0.46	0.47	0.41	0.42	0.50	0.44	1			
USA	0.11	0.26	0.13	0.09	0.26	0.11	0.24	0.12	1		
JPN	0.11	0.16	0.23	0.18	0.14	0.23	0.14	0.16	0.02	1	
HON	0.19	0.18	0.26	0.25	0.20	0.33	0.16	0.23	0.10	0.19	1

[a] Daily returns are calculated as log differences $r_t = 100 \times [\ln(P_t) - \ln(P_{t-1})]$, where P_t denotes the index value at day t. Data are obtained from Startel Oy, where data are available only for Finnish working days. National holidays in other countries occurring on Finnish working days are imputed as zero returns.

graphically. Note that New York has a 2-h overlap with London, a 1.5 h overlap with Paris, Stockholm and Zurich, and a 0.5 h overlap with Oslo and Helsinki, whereas Hong Kong and Tokyo do not overlap with New York or European stock exchanges.

Table 1 presents a descriptive summary of the individual index return distributions of the markets over the sample period. The returns are defined as

$$r_t = 100 \times [\ln(P_t) - \ln(P_{t-1})], \tag{1}$$

where P_t denotes the index value at day t. Generally, the sample period is characterized by a small positive mean return around 0.025% for the USA, Switzerland, Sweden, Finland, Norway and Hong Kong. The markets of Denmark, the UK and Germany returned between 0.011 and 0.017% whereas France and Japan report slightly negative average returns.

Table 2 shows the contemporaneous correlation coefficients between the markets, as they would look if the time zone differences were not accounted for. The correlations between the European markets are close to 0.40 indicating relatively high mutual dependence. The contemporaneous correlations of Asian-Pacific markets with European and US markets give preliminary evidence about the transmission of information from Japan and Hong Kong to other markets during the day. The same is true with the correlations of European markets with US. The low correlations of Asian-Pacific markets with US and higher correlations with some European markets suggest that Asian-Pacific market information is probably fully processed on European markets. Similarly the contemporaneous correlation coefficients of UK and France with US give preliminary indications that these are the primary markets that affect the US markets during the same day.

3. Methodological aspects

Vector autoregression (VAR) has proven to be a useful tool for the analysis of short-term dynamics of several economic time series. The basic VAR model is just a multivariate generalization of the univariate autoregressive (AR) model. Formally a VAR model can be written as

$$\Phi(L)y_t = e_t, \qquad (2)$$

where $\Phi(L) = I - \Phi_1 L - \Phi_2 L^2 - \cdots - \Phi_p L^p$ is a matrix polynomial of order p. The time series vector y_t is assumed to be centered for the sake of simplicity, e_t is a random vector of m variables, Φ_k is an $m \times m$ matrix ($k = 1, ..., p$), and L is the lag operator. It is assumed that all variables in the vector e_t are (weak) white noise processes that, however, can be contemporaneously correlated. Formally,

$$E(e_t) = 0, \quad \text{for all} \quad t$$

$$E(e_s e_t') = \begin{cases} \Sigma, & \text{if } s = t \\ 0, & s \neq t, \end{cases} \qquad (3)$$

where the prime denotes transpose. Because each part of Eq. (2) has the same explanatory variables, the coefficient matrices Φ_k can be efficiently estimated equation by equation with ordinary least squares (OLS). Only in the case where the differences of the equations are large and at the same time there is considerable contemporaneous correlation in the residuals will a more complicated estimation method, like the method of seemingly unrelated regressions (SUR), outperform OLS.

Although the main tool in this paper is VAR and related tools, we also briefly discuss the vector error correction (VEC) model in the next section to capture possible cointegration of the integrated stock indices. Furthermore, we study the response of one variable to shocks of other variables by employing impulse response analysis. In this study the impulse responses are orthogonalized utilizing the standard Cholesky decomposition.

4. Empirical results

In a VAR analysis of integrated series, as stock indexes typically are, an important first step is to analyze whether the series are cointegrated. If so, the long-run dynamics such as a common trend or adjusting dynamics towards that trend should be utilized by the model.

To confirm that the series are integrated we run augmented Dickey Fuller (ADF) and Phillips-Perron tests for the log-index series and corresponding first differences.

The test results indicated that in each case the first hypotheses that the series are integrated on levels is accepted in each case even at the 10% level with both tests, and rejected for the first differences at a lover level than 1%.[2] Hence, we can conclude with high confidence that all of the series are integrated of order one.

In order to analyze possible common trends we first test for cointegration with the Johansen's likelihood ratio (LR) test. The results reported in Appendix A suggest that there is only one cointegration relation between the series. This, however, does not imply that all of the series should be cointegrated.

The variables are ordered according to the market capitalization in ascending order, such that Norway is first. The standardized coefficients are the regression coefficients for a model with Norway as the dependent variable and the rest of the countries as the explanatory variables. The only statistically significant coefficient in this regression is that of Sweden and also perhaps of Great Britain. However, a further check, where Norway was excluded, exposed no cointegration between the remaining stock indexes. On the other hand, when Norway, Sweden and Great Britain were analyzed alone and in pairs, it was found that the British series is not cointegrated with the other two. Furthermore, a test of equality of the absolute values of the coefficients of Sweden and Norway in the cointegration equation (we have scaled the indexes such that at the starting date, August 28, 1993, the indexes have a value of 1000) accompanied with zero coefficients for the other countries, imposed 10 restrictions, and yielded a test statistic $\chi^2(10) = 17.3$ with a p-value equal to 0.07. Hence, the restrictions are borderly accepted, and further support the result that the relation is between Sweden and Norway.

In the analysis of short-term dynamics, the strong indication of cointegration between the Norwegian and Swedish series is modeled using a VEC approach, the general form of which is

$$\Delta y_t = \mu + \Pi y_{t-1} + \Gamma_1 \Delta y_{t-1} + \cdots + \Gamma_k \Delta y_{t-k} + e_t, \tag{4}$$

where in our case, $\Pi = \alpha \cdot \beta'$ is an 11×11 matrix, with the prime denoting transpose. The β-matrix contains the long-run equilibrium parameters, which here is simply an 11×1 matrix (vector) with ones of opposite signs for Sweden and Norway and zeros for the other series. The dimension of the α-matrix is here 11×1. It contains adjusting response coefficients on the discrepancies of the Swedish-Norwegian long-term equilibrium. Estimates with the associated t-values of the adjusting α-parameter are reported in the last table of Appendix A. The t-values indicate that in addition to Sweden and Norway, also Finnish stock returns react on the disequilibrium in the Swedish and Norwegian long-term trend such that if Swedish stocks are below the equilibrium, a positive return in the Finnish stock index is to be expected. The adjustment, however, is relatively low. For example, a disequilibrium of 10% would result in Norway and Sweden in a daily adjustment of 0.3%, and in Finland a daily adjustment of 0.5%.

---

[2] In order to save space, we have not given the tables here, however, they are available from the authors upon request.

Note that the statistical insignificance of the other α-estimates together with no cointegration relation indicates that the long-run relationship between Sweden and Norway affects only on the three Nordic countries, Finland, Sweden and Norway. A formal significance test of these coefficients accompanied with the above no-cointegration restriction imposes altogether 18 restrictions and yields a test statistic: $\chi^2(18) = 27.1$ with a p-value of 0.08, which is not significant at the usual 5% level.

The VAR part of the model reflects the short-term dynamics left after accounting for the specified long-run dynamics. In order to alleviate the problem with the non-synchroneity of trading hours, we introduce to the European equations as explanatory variables the same day returns of Japan and Hong Kong and to the US equation the European same day returns in addition to those of Japan and Hong Kong. The VAR model to be analyzed is of the form

$$\Delta y_t = \mu + \Pi_0 y_{t-1} + \Gamma_0 \Delta y_t + \Gamma_1 \Delta y_{t-1} + \cdots + \Gamma_k \Delta y_{t-k} + e_t, \tag{5}$$

where Π_0 contains the coefficient of the cointegration relationship between Sweden and Norway, and the reaction of the Finnish market on the temporary disequilibrium between Sweden and Norway. The symbol Γ_0 denotes a coefficient matrix which accounts for the same day effects in the manner described above. Technically, we proceed by using SUR on equations of the form

$$\Delta y_t^i = \mu_i + \alpha_i D_1 (y_{t-1}^{Nor} - y_{t-1}^{Swe}) + D_2(\gamma_0^{Jpn} \Delta y_t^{Jpn} + \gamma_0^{Hon} \Delta y_t^{Hon})$$

$$+ D_3(\gamma_0^{Gbr} \Delta y_t^{Gbr} + \cdots + \gamma_0^{Fin} \Delta y_t^{Fin}) + \sum_k \sum_j \gamma_{t-j}^k \Delta y_{t-j} + e_t^i \tag{6}$$

where i is running over the stock exchanges, $D_1 = 1$ for Finland, Norway and Sweden (i = Fin, Nor or Swe) and zero otherwise, $D_2 = 1$ for all others except Japan and Hong Kong and zero otherwise, and $D_3 = 1$ for the USA and zero otherwise.

Table 3 reports Akaike's information criterion (AIC), Schwarz's information criterion (SC) at different common lag lengths, the LR tests with associated p-values, and the LR difference. According to AIC, the best model has a lag length equal to one. SC suggests no lags, and the LR test a model with three lags. Nevertheless, the major drop in the test statistic occurs when moving from no lags

Table 3
Akaike's information criterion (AIC), Schwarz's information criterion (SC), and likelihood ratio (LR) values for VAR order estimation of Eq. (6)

Lag	Criterion			LR			
	AIC	SC	LR	p-value	Difference	df	
0	−4.47	−4.47	1005.7	0.000	NA	NA	
1	−4.77	−4.02	541.6	0.036	464.1	121	
2	−4.61	−3.10	418.1	0.024	123.5	121	
3	−4.47	−2.21	278.3	0.054	139.8	121	
4	−4.34	−1.31	134.9	0.183	143.4	121	
5	−4.19	−0.41	0	NA	134.9	121	

to the model with one lag. Other changes are not statistically significant. Hence, considering the above sources of information, we choose a lag length equal to one for our analysis.

Many of the VAR estimates of the full model are statistically insignificant. Therefore, we re-estimated the model after deleting the insignificant variables. The estimated parameters of the reduced model are reported in Appendix 2. The results indicate that there exists both locally and globally processed information that affect stock prices.

As the Asian-Pacific markets open, the changes of stock prices on these markets affect European markets during the same day. This is seen from the highly statistically significant same-day coefficients in all the European equations (except for Japan in the Finnish equation and Hong Kong in the Swedish equation). The insignificance of Japan and Hong Kong in the US equation, suggests that all US-relevant information born in the Asian-Pacific markets is already processed within the European markets. Note, however, that France and UK have direct effects on Japan and Hong Kong the next day, indicating that all information emerged in these two European markets, relevant to Asian-Pacific, are not processed in the USA in between.

The markets that most affect the US market the are the UK, France and, surprisingly, Sweden, but not Germany or Switzerland.[3]

New market information emerging in the USA is processed first in Japan and Hong Kong. However, these markets do not absorb all the relevant information because US returns still have a highly significant 1-day lag in the European equations. Furthermore, the 1-day lag is significant (negative coefficient) even in its own equation. This mean reverting behavior is an indication of local information. Note, however, that in a univariate unconditional analysis, US daily returns are not serially correlated. The local, country-specific, information is characteristic besides for the US, also for Germany, France and Denmark. Moreover, in Germany and France their cross-country previous day returns have also highly significant coefficients.

The index returns in Finland, Denmark, Norway and Sweden are not dependent on the historical returns of other European countries. Sweden and Norway have the earlier mentioned cointegration relation that affects also the Finnish market, whereas the Danish market is dependent only on its own previous day return.

In summary the empirical results indicate, in line with the findings of Engle and Susmel (1993), that there seem to be four different blocs of markets. Furthermore, as reported in many papers (Cheung et al., 1997), USA is the dominating market having an effect on all other markets around the world. The empirical results suggest even an existence of a slight 1-day recoiling effect on the US market itself after the elimination of the same-day effects of other markets. Asian-Pacific markets form another group with the characteristic that the USA and some European countries influence their price changes. The direct link from some European markets, bypassing the US, indicates that all relevant information born

---

[3] It must be noted that there is a 2-h overlap of Great Britain and Sweden with the US, and there is no overlap between Frankfurt and NYSE.

in European markets are not fully processed in the US, but some fraction is left over and directly affects the Asian-Pacific markets. The third group consists of Western European countries (France, Germany, Great Britain and Switzerland), where France and Germany are influencing the other two, and exerting a mutual effect with a 1-day lag. A fourth group consists of the Nordic countries, with Norway and Sweden having a long-term relationship that also affects the Finnish market. Denmark is neither related directly to the other Nordic markets nor to the other European markets.

Appendix C contains impulse responses, and Appendix 4 the corresponding variance decompositions calculated from the residual series of the full VAR model. Generally, shocks tend to influence primarily the own market behavior and are processed during the same day. Note that there is no instantaneous effect of the US onto other markets because of the time difference that has been taken into account already in the model building stage. The same is true for the US and European markets with respect to Japan and Hong Kong.

A closer investigation of Appendix C reveals that a unit shock in the UK market has the largest instantaneous effect on the other markets, especially France and Germany. Furthermore, it has a notable effect in Hong Kong the next day. This supports the earlier finding that some information born in European markets directly affect Asian-Pacific The US shocks affect virtually all markets, except its own. In the Nordic countries the effect of Sweden is dominating. This is partially due to the ordering of the series, but the Swedish shock affects also the next-day return at some magnitude, especially on the Finnish market. The main effect, however, occurs within the same day. Accordingly, the shocks are absorbed within 1-day, but in addition, given the relevance of ordering, there is evidence that the Swedish market leads, to some extent, the Finnish market by 1-day.

From the variance decompositions we conclude that, generally, most of the innovation variation emerges from each country's own market. The exceptions are France and to some extent Norway. In France, a considerable portion, $\sim 30\%$ of total variances are explained by the UK whereas in Norway, shocks from the UK, Germany and Sweden explain ~ 12, 8 and 7% of the variances, respectively.

5. Conclusions

This paper investigates lead-lag relationships between international stock markets by taking account of the different trading hours of stock exchanges. The main findings are that New York is evidently the most influential market affecting all other analyzed stock exchanges in Europe and in the Asian-Pacific. Information born in the USA is not processed completely within the Asian-Pacific markets. A considerable fraction affects directly the European stock exchanges as well. On the other hand, from the US point of view, all local information born in the Asian-Pacific seems to be absorbed completely by the European markets and affects US prices only through the changes in European prices. A fraction of the information born in Europe, more accurately in France and Great Britain, affects directly on Japan and Hong Kong exchanges even after being processed by the US markets. The Nordic bloc, consisting of small exchanges, seems to constitute a separate region, that is characterized by a cointegration relationship between Norway and Sweden. Of the Nordic markets, Finland, Norway and Sweden are sensitive to deviations from this long-run relation, but Denmark and the other European countries as well as the USA and Asian-Pacific markets are not.

Otherwise, the empirical results suggest that there exist two kinds of information being transferred across markets, local or region-specific and global or inter-region specific. Local information seems to be characteristic of Denmark, Germany, France and the USA. Taking account of the different trading hours, the local information is measured in terms of the residual autocorrelation in a stock index after controlling for the other stock markets' impacts. In France, Germany and the US, own previous day change tends to a have reverse (negative) impact on the own market the next day. In the smaller Danish market the change tends to be of the same sign (positive impact). Furthermore, the larger European stock exchanges seem to be interrelated such that France and Germany affect each other and they both have an effect on the London Stock exchange with a 1-day lag. The US (Dow Jones index), is related to the changes in Great Britain and France the same day and, surprisingly, to Swedish returns even with a 1-day lag. US returns, however, are not directly related to price changes in the Asian-Pacific region. Moreover, it is interesting to note that while the Dow Jones Industrial index for the New York stock exchange is not itself autocorrelated, it is negatively autocorrelated once the impacts of the other stock exchanges have been accounted for.

An impulse response analysis indicates that most of the new information is processed within 1-day. Shocks on a market have primarily a local effect. As a consequence, it seems that in order to gain a more accurate picture of the interrelations between markets, intra-day data should be used.

Acknowledgements

The authors are grateful for the comments of the anonymous referees and the editor, Ike Mathur, who made several suggestions to improve the paper. The authors wish to thank the Startel Oy for providing most of the daily index values data of the study. The authors also wish to thank John Rogers for checking the English of the paper. Financial support from Jenny and Antti Wihuri Foundation is gratefully acknowledged.

Appendix A. Johansen's cointegration test results

Johansen's LR test for cointegration of 11 national stock markets: USA, Great Britain, Germany, France, Switzerland, Japan, Hong Kong, Denmark, Sweden, Norway and Finland. Daily observations on the sample period September 1993–August 1996 are obtained from Startel Oy, where data are available only for Finnish working days. National holidays in other countries occurring on Finnish working days are imputed as previous day's index values (zero returns). Five lags were used in the VEC model for testing the number of the cointegration equations (CE).

Eigen-value	LR statistic	Critical value		No. CE(s)
		5%	1%	
0.068	282.5	277.7	293.4	None*
0.064	230.7	233.1	247.2	≤1
0.061	182.1	192.9	206.0	≤2
0.046	135.5	156.0	168.4	≤3
0.041	100.7	124.2	133.6	≤4
0.028	70.0	94.2	103.2	≤5
0.024	49.2	68.5	76.1	≤6
0.018	31.0	47.2	54.5	≤7
0.012	17.7	29.7	35.7	≤8
0.011	8.6	15.4	20.0	≤9
0.001	0.5	3.8	6.7	≤10

* Significant at 5% level.

Coefficients for the one statistically significant cointegration vector normalized for Norway.

	FIN	DEN	SWE	SWZ	HON	GER	GBR	FRA	JPN	USA	Const
Coefficient	0.12	−0.30	−1.24	−0.14	−0.14	0.30	0.56	0.10	0.03	0.03	−2.17
S.E.	0.10	0.16	0.26	0.17	0.10	0.18	0.23	0.12	0.05	0.15	

Short-term adjusting parameter estimation results for the cointegration analysis.

	Alpha	t-values
FIN	0.05	3.04
SWE	0.03	1.98
NOR	−0.03	−2.27
DEN	0.00	0.14
GBR	0.00	0.05
GER	0.02	1.71
FRA	0.00	−0.23
SWZ	−0.01	−1.11
USA	0.01	0.84
JPN	−0.01	−0.57
HON	0.01	0.25

Appendix B. Estimated model with non-significant coefficients deleted

	Finland	Sweden	Norway	Denmark	Great Britain	Germany	France	Switzerland	USA	Japan	Hong Kong
Constant	0.27 (0.00)	0.22 (0.00)	−0.10 (0.08)	0.01 (0.83)	0.01 (0.68)	0.02 (0.56)	−0.04 (0.34)	0.04 (0.17)	0.05 (0.03)	−0.02 (0.70)	0.01 (0.91)
$(N-S)_{t-1}$	4.22 (0.00)	3.22 (0.00)	−2.27 (0.01)								
FIN_{t-1}											
SWE_{t-1}	0.10 (0.01)								0.14 (0.00)		
NOR_{t-1}									0.07 (0.01)		
DEN_{t-1}				0.12 (0.00)							
GBR_{t-1}									0.18 (0.00)		0.46 (0.00)
GER_{t-1}					0.06 (0.02)	−0.16 (0.00)	0.10 (0.02)	0.05 (0.07)			
FRA_{t-1}					−0.09 (0.00)	0.18 (0.00)	−0.12 (0.00)		10.0 (0.00)	0.15 (0.00)	
SWZ_{t-1}											
USA_{t-1}	0.47 (0.00)	0.43 (0.00)	0.26 (0.00)	0.22 (0.00)	0.16 (0.00)	0.35 (0.00)	0.21 (0.00)	0.19 (0.00)	−0.13 (0.00)	0.29 (0.00)	0.59 (0.00)
JPN		0.07 (0.00)	0.05 (0.01)	0.07 (0.00)	0.05 (0.00)	0.09 (0.00)	0.09 (0.00)	0.06 (0.01)			
HON	0.08 (0.00)		0.08 (0.00)	0.08 (0.00)	0.07 (0.00)	0.12 (0.00)	0.07 (0.00)	0.07 (0.00)			
HON_{t-1}											
R^2	0.12	0.12	0.14	0.13	0.07	0.25	0.06	0.09	0.10	0.05	0.14
s	1.14	0.90	0.77	0.71	0.72	0.80	1.01	0.74	0.65	1.22	1.47

p values in parentheses.

Appendix C. Innovation responses

Days after	USA	GBR	GER	JPN	FRA	SWZ	HON	SWE	DEN	FIN	NOR
	Response to shock in USA										
0	0.63	0.00	0.00	0.00	0.00	0.00	0.00	0.00	0.00	0.00	0.00
1	−0.01	0.15	0.28	0.18	0.19	0.17	0.37	0.30	0.17	0.32	0.21
2	0.02	0.00	−0.01	0.03	0.00	0.01	0.05	−0.02	0.01	0.01	0.00
3	0.00	0.00	0.01	0.00	0.00	0.00	0.01	0.01	0.00	0.00	0.00
	Response to shock in GBR										
0	0.17	0.71	0.31	0.00	0.57	0.27	0.00	0.37	0.21	0.26	0.27
1	0.00	−0.01	0.19	0.16	0.00	0.05	0.44	0.07	0.11	0.18	0.10
2	0.01	0.01	−0.04	−0.01	0.02	0.01	−0.02	−0.02	−0.01	−0.02	−0.01
3	0.00	0.00	0.02	0.00	−0.01	0.00	0.01	0.00	0.00	0.01	0.00
	Response to shock in Germany										
0	0.01	0.00	0.73	0.00	0.27	0.24	0.00	0.18	0.22	0.26	0.23
1	0.01	0.03	−0.07	0.09	0.03	0.04	0.02	−0.02	0.05	−0.04	−0.01
2	−0.01	−0.01	0.02	−0.01	−0.01	−0.01	0.02	0.00	0.00	0.00	0.00
3	0.00	0.00	−0.01	0.00	0.00	0.00	−0.01	0.00	0.00	−0.01	0.00
	Response to shock in Japan										
0	0.00	0.08	0.13	1.21	0.12	0.08	0.17	0.09	0.08	0.05	0.13
1	0.04	0.00	-0.06	−0.04	0.04	−0.05	−0.03	−0.04	−0.04	−0.05	−0.04
2	0.00	0.01	0.04	0.01	0.01	0.01	0.02	0.02	0.01	0.02	0.02
3	0.00	0.00	−0.01	0.00	0.00	0.00	0.00	0.00	0.00	0.00	0.00
	Response to shock in France										
0	0.09	0.00	0.00	0.00	0.77	0.09	0.00	0.13	0.04	0.06	0.06
1	0.00	−0.01	0.19	0.13	−0.04	0.04	0.10	0.04	0.08	0.07	0.06
2	0.01	0.01	−0.05	0.00	0.02	0.00	−0.01	−0.01	0.00	−0.02	−0.01
3	0.00	0.00	0.02	0.00	−0.01	0.00	0.01	0.00	0.00	0.01	0.00
	Response to shock in Switzerland										
0	0.01	0.00	0.00	0.00	0.00	0.63	0.00	0.18	0.11	0.11	0.14
1	−0.02	−0.04	−0.02	0.00	−0.09	−0.04	0.05	−0.05	0.00	−0.03	−0.04
2	0.00	0.00	−0.03	−0.03	0.00	−0.01	0.04	0.01	−0.01	−0.02	−0.01
3	0.00	0.00	0.01	0.00	0.00	0.00	0.00	0.00	0.00	0.00	0.00
	Response to shock in Hong Kong										
0	0.06	0.12	0.17	0.00	0.12	0.12	1.45	0.08	0.11	0.11	0.12
1	−0.01	0.00	0.02	−0.02	−0.01	0.04	0.08	−0.04	−0.02	−0.02	0.00
2	−0.01	0.00	−0.01	−0.01	−0.01	0.00	0.00	−0.01	−0.01	−0.02	−0.01
3	0.00	0.00	0.00	0.00	0.00	0.00	0.00	0.00	0.00	0.00	0.00
	Response to shock in Sweden										
0	0.10	0.00	0.00	0.00	0.00	0.00	0.00	0.75	0.12	0.30	0.20
1	0.06	0.03	0.07	0.04	0.03	0.04	0.05	0.07	0.06	0.16	0.07

Appendix C. (Continued)

Days after	USA	GBR	GER	JPN	FRA	SWZ	HON	SWE	DEN	FIN	NOR
	Response to shock in USA										
2	0.01	0.02	0.02	0.03	0.02	0.02	0.04	0.03	0.02	0.04	0.02
3	0.00	0.00	0.00	0.00	0.00	0.00	0.01	0.00	0.00	0.01	0.00
	Response to shock in Denmark										
0	−0.03	0.00	0.00	0.00	0.00	0.00	0.00	0.00	0.61	0.08	0.08
1	−0.01	−0.01	−0.01	0.00	−0.03	−0.03	−0.01	−0.01	0.07	−0.02	−0.01
2	0.00	0.00	−0.01	−0.01	0.00	−0.01	−0.02	−0.01	0.00	−0.01	−0.01
3	0.00	0.00	0.00	0.00	0.00	0.00	0.00	0.00	0.00	0.00	0.00
	Response to shock in Finland										
0	−0.02	0.00	0.00	0.00	0.00	0.00	0.00	0.00	0.00	1.01	0.09
1	0.03	0.04	0.02	0.05	0.05	0.02	−0.03	0.07	0.02	0.08	0.04
2	0.00	0.00	0.03	0.02	0.00	0.00	0.03	0.02	0.01	0.03	0.02
3	0.00	0.00	0.00	0.00	0.00	0.00	0.00	0.00	0.00	0.00	0.00
	Response to shock in Norway										
0	−0.02	0.00	0.00	0.00	0.00	0.00	0.00	0.00	0.00	0.00	0.61
1	0.00	0.00	−0.04	0.06	0.01	0.00	−0.01	0.00	−0.02	−0.08	0.00
2	0.00	−0.01	0.00	−0.01	−0.01	−0.01	0.00	−0.01	−0.01	−0.01	0.00
3	0.00	0.00	0.00	0.00	0.00	0.00	0.00	0.00	0.00	0.00	0.00

Appendix D. Variance decompositions

Days ahead	S.E.	USA	GBR	GER	JPN	FRA	SWZ	HON	SWE	DEN	FIN	NOR
		Decomposition of variance for USA										
1	0.67	88.5	6.4	0.0	0.0	1.9	0.0	0.7	2.0	0.2	0.1	0.1
2	0.68	87.3	6.3	0.1	0.3	1.9	0.2	0.7	2.7	0.2	0.2	0.1
3	0.68	87.3	6.3	0.1	0.3	1.9	0.2	0.7	2.7	0.2	0.2	0.1
10	0.68	87.3	6.4	0.1	0.3	1.9	0.2	0.7	2.7	0.2	0.2	0.1
		Decomposition of variance for Great Britain										
1	0.73	0.0	96.1	0.0	1.1	0.0	0.0	2.8	0.0	0.0	0.0	0.0
2	0.75	3.8	91.4	0.2	1.0	0.0	0.4	2.7	0.2	0.0	0.3	0.0
3	0.75	3.8	91.3	0.2	1.0	0.1	0.4	2.7	0.2	0.0	0.3	0.0
10	0.75	3.8	91.3	0.2	1.0	0.1	0.4	2.7	0.2	0.0	0 3	0.0

Appendix D. (Continued)

Days ahead	S.E.	Decomposition of variance for USA										
		USA	GBR	GER	JPN	FRA	SWZ	HON	SWE	DEN	FIN	NOR
		Decomposition of variance for Germany										
1	0.82	0.0	14.3	79.0	2.4	0.0	0.0	4.3	0.0	0.0	0.0	0.0
2	0.92	9.3	15.8	63.9	2.3	4.3	0.1	3.5	0.5	0.0	0.1	0.2
3	0.92	9.2	15.9	63.3	2.4	4.5	0.1	3.5	0.6	0.0	0.2	0.2
10	0.92	9.2	15.9	63.3	2.4	4.6	0.1	3.5	0.6	0.0	0.2	0.2
		Decomposition of variance for Japan										
1	1.21	0.0	0.0	0.0	100.0	0.0	0.0	0.0	0.0	0.0	0.0	0.0
2	1.25	2.2	1.6	0.5	94.1	1.0	0.0	0.0	0.1	0.0	0.1	0.3
3	1.25	2.2	1.6	0.5	93.9	1.0	0.0	0.0	0.2	0.0	0.2	0.3
10	1.25	2.2	1.6	0.5	93.9	1.0	0.0	0.0	0.2	0.0	0.2	0.3
		Decomposition of variance for France										
1	1.01	0.0	31.8	7.3	1.4	58.0	0.0	1.5	0.0	0.0	0.0	0.0
2	1.03	3.4	30.3	7.0	1.5	55.2	0.8	1.4	0.1	0.1	0.2	0.0
3	1.03	3.3	30.2	7.0	1.5	55.2	0.8	1.4	0.1	0.1	0.2	0.0
10	1.04	3.3	30.2	7.0	1.5	55.2	0.8	1.4	0.1	0.1	0.2	0.0
		Decomposition of variance for Switzerland										
1	0.74	0.0	13.1	10.6	1.2	1.6	70.7	2.8	0.0	0.0	0.0	0.0
2	0.77	4.7	12.5	10.2	1.6	1.8	66.0	2.8	0.3	0.1	0.1	0.0
3	0.77	4.7	12.5	10.2	1.6	1.8	66.0	2.8	0.3	0.1	0.1	0.0
10	0.77	4.7	12.5	10.2	1.6	1.8	65.9	2.8	0.3	0.1	0.1	0.0
		Decomposition of variance for Hong Kong										
1	1.46	0.0	0.0	0.0	1.3	0.0	0.0	98.7	0.0	0.0	0.0	0.0
2	1.58	5.5	7.7	0.0	1.2	0.4	0.1	85.0	0.1	0.0	0.0	0.0
3	1.58	5.6	7.7	0.0	1.2	0.4	0.2	84.7	0.2	0.0	0.1	0.0
10	1.58	5.6	7.7	0.0	1.2	0.4	0.2	84.7	0.2	0.0	0.1	0.0
		Decomposition of variance for Sweden										
1	0.89	0.0	17.0	4.2	1.1	2.0	4.0	0.8	70.9	0.0	0.0	0.0
2	0.95	9.7	15.5	3.7	1.1	2.0	3.8	0.9	62.8	0.0	0.6	0.0
3	0.95	9.7	15.5	3.7	1.2	2.0	3.8	0.9	62.6	0.0	0.6	0.0
4	0.95	9.7	15.5	3.7	1.2	2.0	3.8	0.9	62.6	0.0	0.6	0.0
10	0.95	9.7	15.5	3.7	1.2	2.0	3.8	0.9	62.6	0.0	0.6	0.0
		Decomposition of variance for Denmark										
1	0.71	0.0	8.4	9.6	1.4	0.3	2.2	2.5	2.9	72.8	0.0	0.0
2	0.75	5.3	9.4	9.1	1.5	1.5	2.0	2.3	3.1	65.7	0.1	0.1
3	0.76	5.3	9.4	9.0	1.5	1.5	2.0	2.3	3.2	65.5	0.1	0.1
10	0.76	5.3	9.4	9.0	1.5	1.5	2.0	2.3	3.2	65.5	0.1	0.1

Appendix D. V(Continued)

Days ahead	S.E.	Decomposition of variance for USA										
		USA	GBR	GER	JPN	FRA	SWZ	HON	SWE	DEN	FIN	NOR
		Decomposition of variance for Finland										
1	1.13	0.0	5.3	5.1	0.2	0.3	0.9	0.9	7.3	0.5	79.5	0.0
2	1.21	7.1	6.9	4.6	0.3	0.6	0.8	0.8	8.2	0.5	69.8	0.4
3	1.21	7.0	6.9	4.5	0.4	0.6	0.9	0.8	8.3	0.5	69.6	0.4
10	1.21	7.0	6.9	4.5	0.4	0.6	0.9	0.8	8.3	0.5	69.6	0.4
		Decomposition of variance for Norway										
1	0.78	0.0	11.8	8.6	2.7	0.6	3.4	2.5	6.7	0.9	1.3	61.3
2	0.82	6.3	12.0	7.8	2.6	1.0	3.3	2.3	6.8	0.8	1.5	55.4
3	0.82	6.3	12.0	7.8	2.7	1.0	3.4	2.3	6.9	0.8	1.5	55.3
10	0.82	6.3	12.0	7.8	2.7	1.0	3.4	2.3	6.9	0.8	1.5	55.3

References

Booth, G.G., Chowdhury, M., Martikainen, T., 1995. Common volatility in major stock index furures markets. Proceedings of the University of Vaasa. Discussion Papers 184.

Bos, T., Fetherson, T.A., Martikainen, T., Perttunen, J., 1995. The international co-movements of Finnish stocks. Eur. J. Finance 1, 95–111.

Cheung, Y.-W., He, J., Ng, L.K., 1997. Common predictable components in regional stock markets. J. Bus. Econ. Stat. 15, 35–42.

Engle, R.F., Ito, T., Lin, W.-L., 1990. Meteor shower or heat waves? Intra-daily volatility in the foreign exchange market. Econometrica 58, 525–542.

Engle, R.F., Ito, T., Lin, W.L., 1992. Where does the meteor shower come from? The role of stochastic policy coordination. J. Int. Econ. 32, 221–240.

Engle, R.F., Susmel, R., 1993. Common volatility in informational equity markets. J. Bus. Econ. Stat. 11, 167–176.

Eun, C.S., Shim, S., 1989. International transmission of stock market movements. J. Financ. Quant. Anal. 24, 241–256.

Forbes, W.P., 1993. The integration of European stock markets: The case of the banks. J. Bus. Finance Account. 20, 427–439.

Grubel, H.G., Fadner, K, 1971. The interdependence of international equity markets. J. Finance 26, 89–94.

Hietala, P.T., 1989. Asset pricing in partially segmented markets. Evidence from the Finnish markets. J. Finance 44, 697–718.

Kasa, K., 1992. Common stochastic trends in international stock markets. J. Monetary Econ. 29, 95–124.

Karolyi, G.A., 1995. A multivariate GARCH model of international transmission of stock returns and volatility: The case of the United States and Canada. J. Bus. Econ. Stat. 13, 11–25.

Karolyi, G.A., Stulz, R.M., 1996. Why do markets move together? An investigation of U.S.-Japan return comovements. J. Finance 51 (3), 951–986.

Knif, J., Pynnönen, S., Luoma, M., 1995. An analysis of lead-lag structures using frequency domain approach: Empirical evidence from the Finnish and Swedish stock markets. Eur. J. Oper. Res. 81, 259–270.

Knif, J., Pynnönen, S., Luoma, M., 1996. Testing for autocorrelation features of two Scandinavian stock markets. Int. Rev. Financ. Anal. 5, 55–64.

Koutmos, G., 1996. Modeling the dynamic interdependence of returns in major European stock markets. J. Bus. Finance Account. 23, 975–988.

Mathur, I., Subrahmanyam, V., 1990. Interdependencies among the Nordic and US stock markets. J. Int. Financ. Markets 1, 91–114.

Malkamäki, M., 1993. Essays of conditional pricing of Finnish stocks. Bank of Finland B:48.

Malkamäki, M., Martikainen, T., Perttunen, J., Puttonen, V., 1993. On the causality and co-movements of Scandinavian stock market returns. Scand. J. Manag. 9, 67–76.

Martikainen, T., Virtanen, I., Yli-Olli, P., 1993. Integration of the Finnish stock market into the Swedish and US stock markets. Econ. Syst. Res. 5, 409–417.

Pynnönen, S., Knif, J., Luoma, M., 1996. A new look at the volatility information flows between stock markets; A case of two Nordic stock exchanges. J. Int. Financ. Markets Inst. Money 6, 69–92.

Pynnönen, S., Knif, J., 1998. Common long-term and short-term price memory in two Scandinavian stock markets. Appl. Financ. Econ. 8, 257–265.

Susmel, R., Engle, R.F., 1994. Hourly volatility spillovers between international equity markets. J. Int. Money Finance 13, 3–25.

Feedback trading and the autocorrelation pattern of stock returns: further empirical evidence

GREGORY KOUTMOS*

School of Business, Fairfield University, Fairfield, CT 06430-7524, USA

This paper examines the pattern of autocorrelation of stock returns in several foreign stock markets, assuming that some investors follow a positive feedback trading strategy. There is strong evidence that positive feedback trading induces negative autocorrelation in index stock returns even though the consensus is that high frequency index returns are positively autocorrelated. This sign reversal occurs during periods of rising stock return volatility. The range of autocorrelations is considerably large. Moreover, in most cases, positive feedback trading is more intense during market declines. These findings are in agreement with studies for the US stock market. (JEL G15). © 1997 Elsevier Science Ltd.

Index stock returns have been known to be positively autocorrelated at high frequencies (Cutler et al., 1991; Lo and MacKinlay, 1988; and Fama, 1965). Two reasons have been most frequently cited for this phenomenon: (a) microstructure biases caused by non-synchronous trading, e.g. Scholes and Williams (1977) and Lo and MacKinlay (1990); and (b) time-varying short-term expected returns or risk premia, e.g. Fama and French (1988) and Conrad and Kaul (1988). Non-synchronous trading can cause spurious autocorrelation in index stock returns because some of the stocks in the index do not trade very frequently. This type of autocorrelation does not imply that stock returns are predictable. On the other hand, autocorrelation induced by changes in expected returns or risk premia does imply predictability of returns. As noted by Fama and French (1988) and Fama (1991), predictability is compatible with the Market Efficiency Hypothesis in the context of modern intertemporal asset pricing models of the type of Lucas (1978) and Breeden (1979). Balvers et al.

---

*This paper was presented at the annual meetings of the Eastern Finance Association (1996), the Multinational Finance Society (1996) and the European Financial Management Association (1996).

(1990) present a general equilibrium model with no excess-profit opportunities but predictable stock returns, due to the predictability of aggregate output.

Non-synchronous trading and time variation in risk premia are expected to produce positive and time invariant autocorrelations. Recent research, however, suggests that the autocorrelation pattern of stock returns is more complex than commonly believed. LeBaron (1992) uses a GARCH model with an exponential time varying first order autocorrelation to describe the short run dynamics of several US stock index returns as well as individual stock returns. He reports significant non-linear first moment dependencies in the sense that autocorrelation and volatility are inversely related. Stating it differently, first order autocorrelations of stock price changes are higher during tranquil periods and lower during volatile periods. This evidence would appear to be consistent with the notion that non-synchronous trading is the cause of autocorrelation. Taking into account that high trading volume reduces the non-synchronous trading problem but increases volatility, it is plausible that volatility and autocorrelation are inversely related. This explanation, however, may not be entirely correct because this inverse relationship is also present in weekly returns, as well as, in individual stock returns, where non-synchronous trading is not a problem. Some authors suggest that autocorrelation may be caused by the interventions of the floor specialists in their attempts to maintain orderly markets or by the accumulation of news required by traders in order to enter a transaction (e.g. Cohen *et al.*, 1986). Cutler *et al.* (1991) argue that changing risk premia due to changing risk factors cannot explain the autocorrelation pattern in a large set of financial and real assets. Campbell *et al.* (1993) find that trading volume and stock return autocorrelation are inversely related for US stock returns. During high volume days autocorrelations turn negative. Such a relationship is consistent with their model where risk-averse market makers accommodate buying or selling pressure from liquidity or non-informational investors.

The role of positive feedback trading in the US stock market is investigated by Sentana and Wadhwani (1992). They find that during low volatility periods daily stock returns are positively autocorrelated but during high volatility periods they tend to be negatively autocorrelated. This sign reversal in stock return autocorrelation is consistent with the notion that some traders follow positive feedback strategies, i.e. they buy (sell) when the price rises (falls). Moreover, during volatile periods positive feedback traders exert a greater influence on price movements and the degree of autocorrelation and hence predictability rises. This does not necessarily imply excess-profits because the higher volatility (risk) makes it harder for rational risk-averse investors to exploit the predictable pattern of stock prices.

Despite the evidence on positive feedback trading in the US stock market, there has been no empirical work documenting a similar behavior in other stock markets. Is it possible that positive feedback trading is limited to the US market or is it shared with other national stock markets? Given the growing interdependence and integration of national stock markets (e.g. Longin and Solnik, 1995), one would expect that positive feedback trading is more widespread. This paper presents new evidence that this is indeed the case. For six stock markets analyzed there is evidence of positive feedback trading which in turn causes stock return autocorrelation to become negative. This reversal is much more pronounced during high volatility periods, suggesting that during these periods feedback traders have a greater influence on price. In several instances positive feedback trading is more intense during market declines than it is during market advances.

The rest of this paper is organized as follows. The next section outlines a feedback trading model and establishes the testable hypotheses. Section II presents and discusses the empirical findings. Section III concludes this paper.

I. Feedback trading and autocorrelation

Following Shiller (1984) and Sentana and Wadhwani (1992), it is assumed that traders consist of two heterogeneous groups. The demand for shares by the first group (smart money) is governed by risk-return considerations. Specifically, the first group will hold a fraction of shares of the market portfolio given by

$$\langle 1 \rangle \qquad Q_{1,t} = (E_{t-1}(R_t) - \alpha)/\theta\sigma_t^2,$$

where, $Q_{1,t}$ is the fraction of shares demanded by this group, R_t is the ex-post return at t, E_{t-1} is the expectation as of time $t-1$, α is the rate of return on a risk-free asset, σ_t^2 is the conditional variance (risk) at t and θ is a fixed coefficient. Assuming θ is positive, the product $\theta\sigma_t^2$ is the required risk premium at time t.[1] The second group of investors follow a positive feedback strategy, i.e. they buy (sell) after price increases (decreases). Thus, their demand function is given by

$$\langle 2 \rangle \qquad Q_{2,t} = \rho R_{t-1},$$

where, $\rho > 0$.[2] Positive feedback trading is not necessarily irrational or noise trading in the sense of De Long et al. (1990). It is consistent with portfolio insurance strategies and the use of stop-loss orders. Portfolio insurance is rational if risk aversion declines rapidly with wealth (e.g. Sentana and Wadhwani, 1992). In equilibrium all shares must be held, i.e. $Q_{1,t} + Q_{2,t} = 1$. It follows from $\langle 1 \rangle$ and $\langle 2 \rangle$ that

$$\langle 3 \rangle \qquad E_{t-1}(R_t) = \alpha + \theta\sigma_t^2 - \theta\rho\sigma_t^2 R_{t-1}.$$

The term $-\theta\rho\sigma_t^2 R_{t-1}$ in $\langle 3 \rangle$ implies that the presence of positive feedback trading will induce negative autocorrelation in returns. The higher the volatility the more negative the autocorrelation. As pointed out earlier, the higher predictability that arises because of feedback trading will not necessarily be exploited by the first group of investors because the risk is higher. It is easy to convert $\langle 3 \rangle$ into a regression equation with a stochastic error term by setting $R_t = E_{t-1}(R_t) + \epsilon_t$ and substituting into $\langle 3 \rangle$ to get:

$$\langle 3a \rangle \qquad R_t = \alpha + \theta\sigma_t^2 - \theta\rho\sigma_t^2 R_{t-1} + \epsilon_t.$$

As it is, $\langle 3a \rangle$ does not allow for a constant autocorrelation due to non-synchronous trading. Likewise, the possibility that positive feedback trading is more

627

Feedback trading: G Koutmos

intense during down markets cannot be tested in the framework of $\langle 3a \rangle$. To account for these two possibilities, the following empirical version of $\langle 3a \rangle$ is used in the estimation:

$$\langle 4 \rangle \qquad R_t = \alpha + \theta \sigma_t^2 + \left(\phi_0 + \phi_1 \sigma_t^2 \right) R_{t-1} + \phi_2 |R_{t-1}| + \epsilon_t.$$

The presence of positive feedback trading implies that ϕ_1 is negative and statistically significant. The possibility for asymmetry in the feedback mechanism is captured by the term $\phi_2 |R_{t-1}|$. If $\phi_2 > 0$ then, negative returns will be followed by more intense feedback trading. Thus, the coefficient on R_{t-1} is

$$\langle 5 \rangle \qquad \phi_0 + \phi_1 \sigma_t^2 + \phi_2 \text{ for } R_{t-1} \geq 0 \text{ and,}$$
$$\langle 6 \rangle \qquad \phi_0 + \phi_1 \sigma_t^2 - \phi_2 \text{ for } R_{t-1} < 0.$$

Numerous studies have shown that stock returns are conditionally heterokcedastic.[3] Consequently, the conditional variance of the returns is modeled as a GARCH (1,1) process given by

$$\langle 7 \rangle \qquad \sigma_t^2 = \alpha_0 + \alpha_1 \epsilon_{t-1}^2 + \beta \sigma_{t-1}^2$$

where, σ_t^2 is the conditional variance of the returns at time t, ϵ_t is the innovation at time t and α_0, α_1 and β are non-negative fixed parameters. The degree of volatility persistence is measured by $\alpha_1 + \beta$ and the unconditional variance, σ^2, is given by $\alpha_0/(1 - \alpha_1 - \beta)$. Existence of the unconditional variance requires that persistence is less than one (see Bollerslev, 1986). Several parametric specifications have been used in the literature for stock returns, the most common being the standard normal distribution (e.g. Engle, 1982; LeBaron, 1992). More often than not, the standardized residuals obtained from GARCH models that assume normality appear to be leptokurtic, thereby rendering standard t-tests unreliable. As such, distributions with flatter tails such as the student's t (e.g. Bollerslev, 1987; Baillie and Bollerslev, 1989; Akgiray and Booth, 1991) and the Generalized Error Distribution (GED) (e.g. Nelson, 1991; Booth *et al.*, 1992) have been suggested. In this paper we employ the GED. Its density function is given by

$$\langle 8 \rangle \qquad f(\mu_t, \sigma_t, \nu) = \nu/2 [\Gamma(3/\nu)]^{1/2} [\Gamma(1/\nu)]^{-3/2}$$
$$\times (1/\sigma_t) \exp\left\{ -[\Gamma(3/\nu)/\Gamma(1/\nu)]^{\nu/2} |\epsilon_t/\sigma_t|^\nu \right\},$$

where, $\Gamma(.)$ is the gamma function and ν is a scale parameter, or degrees of freedom to be estimated. For $\nu = 2$, the GED yields the normal distribution, while for $\nu = 1$ it yields the Laplace or double exponential distribution.

Given initial values for ϵ_t, and σ_t^2 the parameter vector $\Theta \equiv (\alpha, \theta, \phi_0, \phi_1, \phi_2, \alpha_0, \alpha_1, \beta, \nu)$ can be estimated by maximizing the log-likelihood over the sample period, which can be expressed as

$$\langle 9 \rangle \qquad L(\Theta) = \sum_{t=1}^{T} \log f(\mu_t, \sigma_t, \nu),$$

where, μ_t and σ_t are the conditional mean and the conditional standard deviation, respectively. Since the log-likelihood function is highly non-linear in the parameters, numerical maximization techniques are used to obtain estimates of the parameter vector. The method of estimation used in this paper is based on the Berndt *et al.* (1974) algorithm.

II. Data and empirical findings

II.A. Data and preliminary statistics

The data include daily figures for the stock price indexes of six industrialized countries, namely Australia, Belgium, Germany, Italy, Japan and the UK. All prices are in local currency and they do not include dividend payments. The data set extends from 4 January 1986 to 31 December 1991 for a total of 1562 observations. Daily returns for each country are calculated as the percent logarithmic difference in the daily stock price index, i.e. $R_t = 100*(\log P_t - \log P_{t-1})$. The names of the particular indexes used are given in Table 1.

Preliminary statistics for the daily returns are in Table 2. The statistics reported are the mean and the standard deviation, measures for skewness and kurtosis, the Kolmogorov–Smirnov D-statistic and the Ljung–Box statistic for 12 lags.[4] The skewness and kurtosis measures are highly significant indicating that none of the series is normally distributed.

Likewise, the D-statistics show significant departures from normality. Rejection of normality can be partially attributed to temporal dependencies in the moments of the series. It is common to test for such dependencies using the Ljung and Box portmanteau test (LB), e.g. Bollerslev *et al.* (1994). The LB statistic, using 12 lags, is significant for all return series, the only exception being the German market. This provides evidence of temporal dependencies in the first moment of the distribution of returns. It is not clear to which extent non-synchronous trading contributes to these dependencies. More importantly, the LB statistic is incapable of detecting any sign reversals in the autocorrelations due to positive feedback trading. All it provides is an indication that first moment dependencies are present. Evidence on higher order temporal dependencies is provided by the LB statistic when applied to the squared returns. It can be seen that for the squared returns this statistic is in general several times higher than the LB calculated for the returns suggesting that higher moment

TABLE 1. Stock market indexes for six industrialized countries

Country	Stock market index
Australia	All ordinary
Belgium	General
Germany	Commerzbank
Italy	BCI general
Japan	Tokyo Stock Exchange All Stock Index (Topix)
UK	Financial times 500 share index

Feedback trading: G Koutmos

TABLE 2. Sample statistics

	Australia	Belgium	Germany	Italy	Japan	UK
	Daily stock returns; 4 January 1986–31 December 1991 (1562 days)					
μ	0.0304	0.0425	−0.0081	0.0065	0.0309	0.0364
σ	1.2514	0.9765	1.3381	1.2362	1.2192	0.9623
S	−8.2508*	−0.3886*	−0.4228*	−0.4483*	−1.4608*	−2.4910*
K	181.7423*	31.3865*	5.0004*	6.1250*	23.3030*	26.9012*
D	0.1113*	0.1433*	0.0541*	0.1114*	0.0867*	0.0790*
LB(12)	137.2244*	158.0137*	20.3170	69.9107*	44.0712	77.7691*
LB^2(12)	41.8717*	697.7115*	754.5266*	722.6947*	164.6455*	774.9352*

*Significance at the 5% level at least.

μ, mean; σ, standard deviation; S, skewness; K, excess kurtosis; D, Kolmogorov–Smirnov statistic (5% critical value is $1.36/\sqrt{T}$, where T is sample size); LB(n) and LB^2(n) are the Ljung–Box statistics for R_t and R_t^2, respectively, distributed as χ^2 with n degrees of freedom where n is the number of lags.

temporal dependencies are more pronounced. This of course is an empirical regularity encountered in almost all financial time series, especially in high frequencies. What is not clear from these statistics is the extent to which the two types of dependencies are linked, i.e. whether volatility and autocorrelation are linked.

II.B. Empirical evidence on positive feedback trading

Table 3 reports the maximum likelihood estimates for the empirical version of the feedback model described by $\langle 4 \rangle$–$\langle 9 \rangle$. The coefficients describing the conditional variance process, α_0, α_1 and β, are highly significant in all cases. This in turn implies that current volatility is a function of last period's squared innovation and last period's volatility or, equivalently, the conditional variance is updated in the light of new information and the weight given to the last squared innovation is equal to α_1. The autoregressive nature of volatility is important in situations where forecasts of future volatility are needed. This is obviously true for the evaluation of derivative securities, such as options and options on futures, where ex-ante volatility measures are critical inputs. The GARCH-M effect (parameter θ) is insignificant for all markets in agreement with findings for the US stock market, e.g. Nelson (1991).

The parameters of interest in this paper are those governing the autocorrelation of the returns, i.e. ϕ_0, ϕ_1 and ϕ_2. The constant component of the autocorrelation, ϕ_0, is statistically significant in all six markets.[5] It is possible that the source of this type of autocorrelation is related to non-synchronous trading (e.g. Fisher, 1966; Scholes and Williams, 1977; Lo and MacKinlay, 1990) even though, time variation in ex-ante returns can cause autocorrelation in ex-post returns (e.g. Conrad and Kaul, 1988). Atchison *et al.* (1987) find that

TABLE 3. Maximum likelihood estimates of the feedback model daily stock returns; 4 January 1986 to 31 December 1991 (1562 days)

$$R_t = \alpha + \theta\sigma_t^2 + (\phi_0 + \phi_1\sigma_t^2)R_{t-1} + \phi_2|R_{t-1}| + \epsilon_t$$
$$\sigma_t^2 = \alpha_0 + \alpha_1\epsilon_{t-1}^2 + \beta\sigma_{t-1}^2$$

	Australia	Belgium	Germany	Italy	Japan	UK
α	0.0512	0.0045	0.0544	0.0123	0.0152	0.1241
	(0.029)	(0.006)	(0.046)	(0.027)	(0.024)	(0.047)*
θ	−0.0657	−0.0151	−0.0559	0.0015	−0.0249	−0.0995
	(0.030)	(0.012)	(0.036)	(0.025)	(0.025)	(0.071)
ϕ_0	0.1471	0.2229	0.1022	0.1801	0.1275	0.1310
	(0.025)*	(0.015)*	(0.035)*	(0.026)*	(0.025)*	(0.029)*
ϕ_1	−0.0276	−0.0118	−0.0160	−0.0254	−0.0165	−0.0297
	(0.004)*	(0.002)*	(0.005)*	(0.009)*	(0.006)*	(0.012)*
ϕ_2	0.1058	0.1349	0.1007	−0.0214	0.0942	0.0119
	(0.039)*	(0.017)*	(0.046)*	(0.030)	(0.035)*	(0.043)
α_0	0.1387	0.0302	0.0820	0.0263	0.0454	0.0590
	(0.033)*	(0.007)*	(0.021)*	(0.010)*	(0.013)*	(0.013)*
α_1	0.2166	0.1962	0.1319	0.0897	0.1560	0.0800
	(0.032)*	(0.036)*	(0.022)*	(0.018)*	(0.024)*	(0.019)*
β	0.6566	0.7865	0.8204	0.8942	0.8204	0.8392
	(0.052)*	(0.031)*	(0.027)*	(0.021)*	(0.025)*	(0.028)*
ν	1.0987	0.7466	1.3375	0.9818	1.0163	1.3623
	(0.038)*	(0.024)*	(0.042)*	(0.043)*	(0.032)*	(0.026)*
LR	11.5308*	32.6294*	12.6250*	8.5302*	17.5883*	7.0551*
Model diagnostics						
$E(\epsilon_t/\sigma_t)$	−0.0211	−0.0260	−0.0463	0.0102	−0.0244	−0.0288
$E[(\epsilon_t/\sigma_t)^2]$	1.0538	1.0192	1.0214	1.0099	1.0571	1.0447
LB(12)	17.6901	16.3257	9.6374	16.6466	17.4762	18.5562
LB^2(12)	3.5795	1.1376	5.1358	5.9505	3.4912	9.9282
D	0.0275	0.0150	0.0252	0.0257	0.0262	0.0261

*Significance at the 5% level. Parentheses include the standard errors for the estimates.
LR is the likelihood ratio statistic for H_0: $\phi_1 = \phi_2 = 0$. See also Table 2 notes.
D is the Kolmogorov–Smirnov statistic testing the GED with the estimated scale parameter ν.

for a value-weighted portfolio the theoretical autocorrelation due solely to non-synchronous trading is much lower to that observed empirically. For a portfolio of 260 US stocks they find the actual first order autocorrelation to be 0.1286 with a theoretically predicted autocorrelation due to non-synchronous trading being 0.0167.

As pointed out earlier, non-synchronous trading and/or time variation in ex-ante returns can cause positive autocorrelation in ex-post returns, at least in high frequency data. Positive feedback trading, on the other hand, causes negative autocorrelation which rises, in absolute terms, with the level of volatility. In this respect it is interesting to see that for all six markets ϕ_1 is negative and statistically significant. The implication is that positive feedback trading is an important determinant of short-term movements in these markets in agreement with the findings of Sentana and Wadhwani (1992) for the US stock market.

Thus, it appears that stock return dynamics are similar across national stock markets. This should not be surprising given the growing interdependence of stock markets around the world. The greater predictability (negative autocorrelation) that is induced by feedback traders, is unlikely to produce arbitrage opportunities for rational risk averse investors because volatility also rises. This is especially true if this type of investors have short holding horizons and are concerned about liquidating mispriced assets. The extent of mispricing is likely to increase during periods of higher volatility because it is then that positive feedback traders have a greater influence on price.

Another important issue raised in this paper is the possibility that positive feedback trading is more intense during market declines than it is during market advances. The coefficient that captures this asymmetry, ϕ_2, is positive and statistically significant for four out of the six markets examined. Specifically, for the stock markets of Australia, Belgium, Germany and Japan, feedback trading is more pronounced during down markets. A similar phenomenon is documented by Sentana and Wadhwani (1992) for the US market. It is not obvious why feedback traders should be more active during markets declines. One possibility is that a substantial amount of feedback trading is due to portfolio insurance strategies and the extensive use of stop-loss orders. Since these strategies lead to sell decisions during market declines it is natural to expect greater feedback activity during down markets. Margin trading could also be a contributing factor because during large market declines there is a greater likelihood that margin accounts will be liquidated. This raises the possibility that margin requirements can be used to curtail feedback trading and hence market volatility. Hardouvelis (1989) provides evidence that higher margin requirements lead to lower stock return volatility, whereas Hsieh and Miller (1990) and Schwert (1989) argue otherwise. Sentana and Wadhwani (1992) do not find any evidence that margin requirements in the US influence feedback trading. However, as they point out, for much of the period they examine margin credit was a small percentage of total market value. Obviously, further research is needed for more definite answers.

In the empirical literature the consensus is that high frequency stock returns are positively autocorrelated. However, when positive feedback trading is taken into account, the range of values that the first autocorrelation takes can be quite large. Table 4 provides the extreme values (i.e. minimum and maximum) and the average of the first order autocorrelation for the six markets. The minimum values range from -0.6304 (for Japan) to -0.1567 (for Italy), whereas the maximum values range from 0.3269 (for Belgium) to 0.1312 (for the UK).[6] On the basis of these findings it can be concluded that the autocorrelation of stock returns is quite unstable. It is inversely related to volatility taking on positive values during calm periods and negative values during volatile periods. Such an inverse relationship is also documented by LeBaron (1992) for US stock returns. An important difference however, is that

TABLE 4. Range of autocorrelations

Stock market	Minimum	Maximum	Average
Australia	−0.4433	0.2518	0.1434
Belgium	−0.4441	0.3269	0.2109
Germany	−0.3486	0.1942	0.0738
Italy	−0.1567	0.1456	0.1424
Japan	−0.6304	0.2169	0.1029
UK	−0.4801	0.1311	0.1070

Note: The calculations are based on $\langle 5 \rangle$ and $\langle 6 \rangle$.

in LeBaron's study there is no sign reversal i.e. the minimum value for autocorrelations is zero.

The joint significance of the feedback coefficients ϕ_1 and ϕ_2 is tested on the basis of the likelihood ratio test. The likelihood ratio statistic (LR) is calculated as $LR = -2[L_R - L_U]$, where L_R is the value of the log likelihood under the null hypothesis $H_0: \phi_1 = \phi_2 = 0$ and L_U is the log likelihood under the alternative. This statistic is distributed as χ^2 with degrees of freedom equal to the number of restrictions under the null hypothesis. The null hypothesis is rejected in all instances. The implication is that feedback trading is an important force behind short term stock price changes.

For all six markets the estimated degrees of freedom parameter, ν, is well below two, the value required for normality, and very close to unity suggesting that the empirical distributions of the returns are in all cases close to the double exponential or Laplace distribution. In fact conventional t-tests reject the hypothesis that $\nu = 2$ for all six markets at the conventional level. This confirms the earlier statement that departures from normality observed in the raw return series cannot be entirely attributed to temporal first and second moment dependencies.

In any empirical investigation, the validity of the results depends on the correct specification of the model. For ARCH-type models correct specification requires that: (a) the standardized residuals have zero mean and unit variance; (b) they are linearly and non-linearly independent; and (c) they obey the assumed distribution with the estimated scale parameter or degrees of freedom. As can be seen from Table 3, the means and variances of the standardized residuals fulfil the first requirement of zero mean and unit variance. Linear and non-linear independence is tested again by means of the Ljung–Box statistic. The calculated LB values show that up to twelve lags the standardized (ϵ_t/σ_t) and the squared standardized residuals $(\epsilon_t/\sigma_t)^2$ follow i.i.d. processes. Thus, the feedback model with errors following GARCH (1,1) processes successfully accounts for all linear and non-linear dependencies in the returns. The appropriateness of the density function used is tested on the basis of the Kolmogorov–Smirnov statistic D, where the null hypothesis now is that the estimated standardized residuals from each market follow the GED with the estimated degrees of freedom ν. In all instances the estimated D statistics are below their critical value so that the assumed density function is not rejected.

III. Conclusion

This paper has examined the autocorrelation pattern of the returns of six stock markets assuming that some traders follow positive feedback trading strategies. In all six markets it is found that feedback trading is an important factor of short-term movements in stock returns. The impact of feedback trading is to produce negative first order autocorrelation in stock returns, which becomes more negative as the level of volatility rises. The higher predictability in returns resulting from the actions of feedback traders is not necessarily producing exploitable opportunities for risk-averse rational traders because the level of risk rises simultaneously with the degree of predictability. Equivalently, during periods of high volatility, feedback traders exert a higher influence on price.

In four out of the six markets, feedback trading is more intense during market declines. This may be the result of margin trading which could lead to forced liquidations (depyramiding) during market declines. Another possibility is that feedback traders are mostly portfolio insurers and stop-loss order users. Since these strategies are more likely to translate into sell decisions during market declines it is plausible to expect more feedback trading during down markets.

The estimated time varying autocorrelations fluctuate considerable with the minimum estimated value being -0.6304 (for Japan) and the maximum estimated value being 0.3269 (for Belgium). The average autocorrelations are always positive. Model specification tests show that the feedback model along with time varying volatility describe the short term dynamics in these markets quite well.

Notes

1. Note that if all investors had the same demand function given by $\langle 1 \rangle$, then in equilibrium, $E_{t-1}(R_t) - \alpha = \theta \sigma_t^2$, which is the dynamic Capital Asset Pricing Model proposed by Merton (1973).
2. If $\rho < 0$ then there is negative feedback trading (see also Sentana and Wadhwani, 1992).
3. For an excellent survey of studies modeling stock returns as conditionally heteroscedastic processes see Bollerslev et al. (1992).
4. The Kolmogorov–Smirnov statistic is calculated as $D_n = \max |F_n(R) - F_0(R)|$, where F_n is the empirical cumulative distribution of R_t and $F_0(R)$ is the postulated theoretical distribution. The Ljung–Box statistic for n lags is calculated as

$$LB(n) = T(T+2) \sum_{j=1}^{n} \left(\rho_j^2 / T - j \right)$$

where ρ_j is the sample autocorrelation for j lags and T is the sample size.
5. For uniformity, the five percent level of significance is used throughout.
6. It should be pointed out that the mean, maximum and minimum autocorrelations are subject to estimation error since they are based on previously estimated time varying autocorrelations.

References

Akgiray, V. and Booth, G. G. (1991) Modeling the stochastic behavior of Canadian foreign exchange rates. *Journal of Multinational Financial Management* **1**, 43–71.

Atchison, A. D., Butler, K. C. and Simonds, R. R. (1987) Nonsynchronous security trading and market index autocorrelation. *Journal of Finance* **42**, 111–118.

Baillie, R. T. and Bollerslev, T. (1989) The message in daily exchange rates: a conditional variance tale. *Journal of Business and Economic Statistics* **7**, 297–305.

Balvers, R. J, Cosimano, T. F. and McDonald, B. (1990) Predicting stock returns in an efficient market. *The Journal of Finance* **45**, 1109–1128.

Berndt, E. K., Hall, H. B., Hall, R. E. and Hausman, J. A. (1974) Estimation and inference in nonlinear structural models. *Annals of Economic and Social Measurement* **4**, 653–666.

Bollerslev, T. (1986) Generalized autoregressive conditional heteroskedasticity. *Journal of Econometrics* **31**: 307–327.

Bollerslev, T. (1987) A conditional heteroskedastic time series model for speculative prices and rates of return. *Review of Economics and Statistics* **69**, 542–547.

Bollerslev, T., Chou, R. Y. and Kroner, K. F. (1992) ARCH modeling in finance: a review of the theory and empirical evidence. *Journal of Econometrics* **52**, 5–59.

Bollerslev, T., Engle, R. F. and Nelson, D. B. (1994) ARCH models. In *Handbook of Econometrics*, eds R. F. Engle and D. L. McFadden, Vol. IV, Chapter 49. Elsevier Science B.V.

Booth, G. G., Hatem, J., Vitranen, I. and Yli-olli, P. (1992) Stochastic modeling of security returns: evidence from the Helsinki stock exchange. *European Journal of Operational Research* **56**, 98–106.

Breeden, D. T. (1979) An intertemporal asset pricing model with stochastic consumption and investment opportunities. *Journal of Financial Economics* **7**, 265–296.

Campbell, J. Y., Grossman, S. J. and Wang, J. (1993) Trading volume and serial correlation in stock returns. *Quarterly Journal of Economics* **108**, 905–939.

Cohen, K. J., Maier, S. F., Schwartz, R. A. and Whitcomb, D. K. (1986) *The Microstructure of Securities Markets*. Prentice-Hall, Englewood Cliffs, NJ.

Conrad, J. and Kaul, G. (1988) Time-variation in expected returns. *Journal of Business* **61**, 409–425.

Cutler, D. M., Poterba, J. M. and Summers, L. H. (1991) Speculative dynamics. *Review of Economic Studies* **58**, 529–546.

De Long, B. J., Shleifer, A., Summers, L. H. and Waldman, R. J. (1990) Noise trader risk in financial markets. *Journal of Political Economy* **98**, 703–738.

Engle, R. F. (1982) Autoregressive conditional heteroskedasticity with estimates of the variance of UK inflation. *Econometrica* **50**, 987–1008.

Fama, E. F. (1965) The behavior of stock market prices. *Journal of Business* **38**, 34–105.

Fama, E. F. and French, K. R. (1988) Permanent and transitory components of stock prices. *Journal of Political Economy* **96**, 246–273.

Fama, E. F. (1991) Efficient capital markets: II. *The Journal of Finance* **46**, 1575–1617.

Fisher, L. (1966) Some new stock market indexes. *Journal of Business* **39**, 191–225.

Hardouvelis, G. A. (1989) Margin requirements volatility and the transitory component of stock prices. *American Economic Review* **79**, 736–762.

Hsieh, D. A. and Miller, M. H. (1990) Margin requirements and stock market volatility. *Journal of Finance* **44**, 3–29.

LeBaron, B. (1992) Some relations between volatility and serial correlations in stock market returns. *The Journal of Business* **65**, 199–219.

Lo, A. W. and MacKinlay, A. C. (1988) Stock market prices do not follow random walks: evidence from a simple specification test. *Review of Financial Studies* **1**, 41-66.

Lo, A. W. and MacKinlay, A. C. (1990) An econometric analysis of nonsynchronous trading. *Journal of Econometrics* **45**, 181-211.

Longin, F. and Solnik, B. (1995) Is the correlation in international equity returns constant: 1960-1990. *Journal of International Money and Finance* **14**, 3-26.

Lucas, R. E. (1978) Asset prices in an exchange economy. *Econometrica* **46**, 1429-1445.

Merton, R. C. (1973) An intertemporal capital asset pricing model. *Econometrica* **41**, 867-888.

Nelson, D. (1991) Conditional heteroskedasticity in asset returns: a new approach. *Econometrica* **59**, 347-370.

Scholes, M. and Williams, J. (1977) Estimating betas from nonsynchronous data. *Journal of Financial Economics* **5**, 309-327.

Schwert, G. W. (1989) Business cycles financial crises and stock volatility. *Carnegie-Rochester Conference Series on Public Policy* **31**, 83-126.

Shiller, R. J. (1984) Stock prices and social dynamics. *Brookings Papers on Economic Activity* **2**, 457-498.

Sentana, E. and Wadhwani, S. (1992) Feedback traders and stock return autocorrelations: evidence from a century of daily data. *The Economic Journal* **102**, 415-425.

Common Volatility in International Equity Markets

Robert F. Engle
Department of Economics, University of California at San Diego, La Jolla, CA 92093-0508

Raul Susmel
Department of Economics, University of South Florida, Tampa, FL 33620

> In this article, we take advantage of the time-varying structure of stock-returns variances to investigate whether two international stock markets share the same volatility process. We use a test recently developed by Engle and Kozicki. This test is also used to assess the validity of a one-factor autoregressive conditional heteroscedasticity model. We find that some international stock markets have the same time-varying volatility.
>
> KEY WORDS: ARCH; Common features; Factor model.

This article builds on the recent literature of stock-markets links. We investigate whether international stock markets have the same volatility process. The use of autoregressive conditional heteroscedasticity (ARCH) models to model volatility in financial data has been one of the most popular tools. It seems natural to use a multivariate framework, given the increasing integration between international financial markets, as pointed out by von Furstenberg and Jeon (1989). The problem of a multivariate ARCH approach to model volatility relies on the imposition of restriction to reduce the number of parameters of the model to be estimated—recall that with N series, $N(N + 1)/2$ processes, which characterize the variance covariance matrix, have to be estimated. Recent papers by Engle, Ng, and Rothschild (1990) and King, Sentana, and Wadhwami (1990) addressed this problem using a factor approach to model financial data. By allowing the existence of K factors, the numbers of processes is reduced to $K + N$. Therefore, choosing the number of factors, K, is crucial to achieve an adequate and parsimonious model. Engle et al. (1990) found a linear one-factor model for individual treasury bills, an attractive specification. King et al. (1990) proposed a factor model with four observable and two unobservable factors. They analyzed 16 major stock markets. They found that observable factors account for a very small proportion of the time variation in the covariances between stock markets. Changes in unobservable international components are the driving forces behind the correlation between these markets. In this article, we take advantage of the time-varying structure of stock returns' variances to test for common volatility. At the same time, we evaluate the validity of a one-factor ARCH model. We use a recent test proposed by Engle and Kozicki (1990) to test for common features. If two individual stock markets have a one-factor model representation for stock returns with a time-varying variance, we can form a linear combination that does not display a time-varying variance; that is, we eliminate the factor.

This article is related to the growing literature on stock-markets integration; for a recent survey of linkage of international stock markets, see Roll (1989). Recent works have focused their attention on analyzing how news from one international market influences other markets' volatility process (see Engle et al. 1990; Hamao, Masulis, and Ng 1990a, b; King and Wadhawami 1990). These works provide evidence of volatility spillovers between international stock markets. They also provide an international perspective to explain volatility. The majority of the studies explaining volatility are concentrated on the U.S. market. We focus on the major international stock markets of the world and investigate whether international stock markets have the same volatility process. We group these stock markets into three regions—North America, the Far East, and Europe. By grouping the data according to time zones, we look for common regional news factors. Regional factors have been mentioned to be the cause of the rejection of an international arbitrage pricing theory (APT) model.

The purpose of this article is twofold. We first test for a time-varying volatility process in international stock markets. Next, we investigate the relationship between these markets within and outside each region. Second, we address the issue of a common component driving the volatility in these international markets.

The article is organized as follows. In Section 1, a simple factor model with time-varying variances is presented. In Section 2, data analysis for the 18 series and preliminary results are shown. In Section 3, the testing procedure for common features and the empirical findings are described. In Section 4, conclusions are summarized.

1. A FACTOR MODEL WITH TIME-VARYING VARIANCE

To make this article as self-contained as possible, we give a brief explanation of a factor model for international stock markets.

The model begins by postulating that the returns on each of N assets are generated by this model:

$$r_t = m_t + \varepsilon_t \tag{1}$$

and

$$\varepsilon_t = Bf_t + v_t, \tag{2}$$

where r_t is the $N \times 1$ vector of observed returns, m_t is the $N \times 1$ vector of time-varying risk premia on the N assets, and ε_t is the $N \times 1$ vector of unexpected component of the returns. The unexpected component is decomposed into two parts—the idiosyncratic component, v_t, and the common component, Bf_t. B is a nonstochastic, full-column-rank $N \times k$ matrix of factor loadings and f_t is a $k \times 1$ vector of common factors.

It is also assumed that

$$E_{t-1}(f_t) = E_{t-1}(v_t) = 0 \tag{3}$$

and

$$E_{t-1}(f_t v_t') = 0, \quad E_{t-1}(f_t f_t') \\ = \Sigma_t, \quad E_{t-1}(v_t v_t') = \Omega_t, \tag{4}$$

where Σ_t is a $k \times k$ matrix and Ω_t is an $N \times N$ matrix. Both matrices are diagonal positive definite.

From the preceding assumptions, the conditional variance of the returns can be expressed as

$$V_{t-1}(r_t) = B\Sigma_t B' + \Omega_t. \tag{5}$$

This factor model with time-varying volatility is too general and, without restrictions, has too many parameters. In this case, there are time-varying processes for each of the $N \times (N + 1)/2$ different elements of the variance–covariance matrix of returns. Usual restrictions either set k equal to a small number or impose $\Omega_t = \Omega$. Under some additional assumptions, the preceding model can be converted to an APT model. In an APT model, the risk premium of an asset is a linear combination of the risk premia associated with the factors.

In this article, the simplest factor model is analyzed. This simple model, used successfully by Diebold and Nerlove (1989), imposes the restriction of one common factor ($k = 1$) and constant idiosyncratic variance ($\Omega_t = \Omega$). It is also assumed that the common factor follows an ARCH process. More general models have been proposed in the recent literature (see King et al. 1990); however, they are computationally expensive. Moreover, if the simple factor model ($k = 1$ and $\Omega_t = \Omega$) is the true model, more general models might lead to overparameterizations and inferences that are inefficient. Therefore, a way to test these factor models without going into the computationally cumbersome estimation of a more general model is desirable. In this article, we complete (1)–(5), by imposing

$$k = 1; \quad \Omega_t = \Omega. \tag{6}$$

The validity of this simple model is tested in this article. On inspection of (1)–(6), there is a portfolio of at least two series, that makes the conditional variance of this new portfolio constant. Therefore, by testing whether there is a portfolio that has a constant variance we are testing the validity of the simple model. Note that (6) allows for correlations between the series. In Section 3, we explain in detail the testing procedure.

2. DATA ANALYSIS

2.1 Univariate Statistics

The data used in this article consist of time series of weekly stock-market indexes, in dollar terms, of 18 of the major stock markets in the world. These data have been compiled by Morgan Stanley Capital International Perspective. The indexes have been constructed not to double count those stocks multiple-listed on foreign stock exchanges; they are value-weighted indexes, and they cover at least 80% of each country's stock-market capitalization. They cover the period from the first week of January 1980 to the first week of January 1990. These stock-market indexes are transformed into weekly (Thursday to Thursday) rates of return. U.S. returns have a correlation of .80 with the Standard and Poor's 500. By using weekly data, we expect to eliminate the problems of nonsynchronous trading and short-term correlations due to noise. As a final note, we should mention that each of these markets has different regulations, trading systems, and transaction costs; see Roll (1989) for a summary of the characteristics of each market.

Table 1 provides univariate statistics for the 18 countries in our sample, divided into time zones. First-order autocorrelations and Ljung–Box (LB) test statistics for serial correlation are also calculated.

The European markets show a negative skewness for all markets but Austria, Belgium, and Denmark, which have a small positive skewness coefficient. The unconditional distribution for all of the markets seems to be nonnormal. Moreover, there are small autocorrelations, and the LB statistic, with six lags, shows that they are significantly different from 0 (exceptions are Denmark, Spain, and the United Kingdom). There seems to be a negative relationship between capitalization of the market and the first-order autocorrelation coefficient rho.

The Far East markets show similar results. The unconditional distribution of weekly returns is clearly not normal, and again there is a negative skewness for all markets except Japan (which displays a nearly zero

Table 1. Univariate Statistics

Market	Mean	Std. dev.	Skew.	Kurt.	Rho(1)	LB(6)	Capitaliz. 1980	Capitaliz. 1988
A. European								
Austria	.24*	2.64	.53	1.47	.25	40.86*	2.0	8.9
Belgium	.23*	2.71	.08	3.88	.13	25.69*	10.0	58.9
Denmark	.31	2.76	.23	1.30	.12	10.08	5.4	30.2
France	.25	3.16	−.98	5.41	.16	19.04*	54.6	244.8
Germany	.24	2.81	−.18	1.89	.14	14.65*	71.7	251.8
Italy	.34*	3.73	−.82	5.49	.04	18.69*	25.3	135.4
Netherlands	.27*	2.61	−.72	4.13	.08	13.44*	86.2	113.6
Norway	.17	3.46	−.90	4.91	.18	27.68*	3.2	14.3
Spain	.21	3.24	−.76	8.76	.08	5.88	16.6	174.9
Sweden	.44*	2.92	−.50	2.86	.14	14.04*	12.9	100.1
Switzerland	.27	2.53	−.90	8.40	.16	16.67*	37.6	140.5
U.K.	.25	3.03	−1.07	7.29	.00	9.32	205.2	771.2
B. Far East								
Hong Kong	.17	4.97	−1.69	12.91	.15	18.30*	39.1	74.4
Japan	.46*	2.73	.05	0.94	.10	9.02	370.2	3.816.9
Singapore	.20	3.48	−2.32	17.93	.18	22.59*	36.8	47.4
Australia	.16	3.70	−2.07	15.55	.18	25.95*	59.7	183.5
C. North America								
Canada	.15	2.64	−.76	5.53	.16	29.43*	118.3	241.9
U.S.	.22*	2.25	−1.03	8.04	.05	12.68*	1,448.1	2,793.8
D. World								
Index	.28*	1.91	−1.09	8.36	.12	10.88	2,728.1	9,776.3

NOTE: Singapore also includes Malaysia. LB(6): Ljung–Box statistic with 6 lags; Capitaliz.: Market capitalization in billions of U.S. dollars, December 1980 and 1988.
* Significant at the 5% level.

skewness). Evidence of a small autocorrelation for all of the markets is shown, except for the biggest, the Japanese market.

The most analyzed markets, the American and the Canadian, show results similar to the preceding.

2.2 ARCH Tests

In Table 2 several ARCH tests are shown. These ARCH Lagrange multiplier tests have been calculated using two different information sets. The first ARCH test uses a univariate information set. Here, the returns are squared and used as an approximation to each country's volatility. Then, the own-squared returns are regressed against a constant and four lags. The statistic is obtained by multiplying the uncentered R^2 times the sample size. This statistic has a chi-squared distribution with 4 df. This test was developed by Engle (1982). The second ARCH test is similarly constructed, but it makes use of a multivariate information set. We use as regressors own-squared returns, as well as the squared returns of other countries. We regress each country's squared returns against this multivariate information set. For the European markets, we use squared returns lagged one period from the United Kingdom, France, Germany, and own-squared returns. For the Far East markets, we use squared returns from each market lagged one period. For the North American markets, we use squared returns from both Canada and the United States.

We call this multivariate test MARCH-1. Moreover, a similar test using extracontinental information is reported. For the European and the Far East markets, we add to the other variables the United States, and for the North American markets, we add the United Kingdom. We call this MARCHC-1. The same tests, but with two lags, are also calculated under the names MARCH-2 and MARCHC-2. The statistic has a chi-squared distribution with the degrees of freedom given by the number of regressors used.

In Europe, all of the markets except Belgium, Denmark, the Netherlands, Switzerland, and the United Kingdom show evidence of ARCH effects. The multivariate information ARCH tests give evidence of heteroscedasticity in all of the stock markets except Denmark and possibly the United Kingdom.

In the Far East, we observe evidence of ARCH effects using the multivariate information test. The univariate ARCH test gives a similar result except for Hong Kong.

In North America, Canada shows evidence of a time-varying variance, but the United States displays this characteristic only when the United Kingdom is used as regressor.

2.3 Correlation Analysis

Correlation analysis was frequently used in the initial literature of international stock-markets linkages. The

Table 2. ARCH Tests

Market	ARCH(4)	MARCH-1	MARCHC-1	MARCH-2	MARCHC-2
A. European
Austria	81.61*	61.36*	61.63*	61.36*	62.25*
Belgium	4.91	159.19*	174.64*	164.30*	178.72*
Denmark	3.33	4.15	8.05	7.09	11.30
France	28.81*	8.84	9.48*	16.63*	17.09*
Germany	41.22*	70.25*	84.57*	71.79*	87.33*
Italy	28.96*	37.33*	39.65*	40.04*	44.87*
Netherlands	2.93	5.13	17.81*	5.69	18.54*
Norway	57.84*	81.86*	106.03*	84.26*	106.46*
Spain	60.11*	301.24*	331.99*	307.37*	336.69*
Sweden	53.06*	140.68*	166.44*	147.76*	171.12*
Switzerland	1.08	4.88	17.74*	5.36	19.53*
U.K.	.33	4.02	10.11*	6.19	12.02
B. Far East
Hong Kong	6.31	202.49*	337.31*	340.76*	357.21*
Japan	15.94*	35.03*	38.52*	45.09*	46.65*
Singapore	144.61*	162.05*	202.49*	175.08*	176.16*
Australia	156.61*	155.66*	189.41*	166.27*	167.13*
C. North America
Canada	20.83*	17.66*	24.15*	30.81*	37.99*
U.S.	7.42	5.04	14.03*	6.52	15.80*

NOTE: ARCH(4): ARCH test with four lags for the own-squared returns. MARCH-1: ARCH test with a multivariate information set (own time zone); for the European markets, it also includes lagged U.K., Germany, France, and own lagged squared return; for the Far East markets, it also includes Hong Kong, Japan, Singapore, and Australia lagged squared returns; for the American markets, it also includes Canada and U.S. lagged squared returns. MARCHC-1: ARCH test with a bigger multivariate information set than in MARCH-1; for the European and Far East markets, it also includes U.S. lagged squared returns; for the American markets, it also includes lagged U.K. squared returns. MARCH-2: Same test as MARCH-1, but with two lags. MARCHC-2: Same test as MARCHC-1, but with two lags.
* Significant at the 5% level.

low correlation between returns of international stock markets was seen as an incentive to hold internationally diversified portfolios, as discussed by Grubel (1968), Levy and Sarnat (1970), and Agmon (1972). In Tables 3 and 4, the correlation matrix is calculated for the returns and the squared returns. The intuition behind the analysis of squared correlations is the same as the intuition behind ARCH. International markets might be uncorrelated in returns. They might not be independent, however, since it is possible that they are related through their volatilities. As Table 2A shows, correlations between the returns of European markets are

Table 3. Correlation Matrix for the Return Series

	Aus.	Aust.	Bel.	Can.	Den.	Fra.	Ger.	Hong Kong	Ita.	Jap.	Net.	Nor.	Sing.	Spa.	Swe.	Swit.	U.K.	U.S.
A. Europe market
Austria	1.0		.42		.32	.44	.52		.28		.31	.38		.31		.33	.23	.52	.29	.15
Belgium	.42		1.0		.34	.48	.46		.29		.39	.46		.42		.39	.28	.50	.32	.27
Denmark	.32		.34		1.0	.34	.39		.31		.36	.37		.32		.31	.29	.46	.33	.24
France	.44		.48		.34	1.0	.49		.31		.38	.49		.43		.37	.25	.51	.41	.30
Germany	.52		.46		.39	.49	1.0		.30		.41	.58		.41		.37	.37	.74	.44	.32
Italy	.28		.29		.31	.31	.30		1.0		.28	.33		.25		.30	.23	.33	.33	.19
Netherlands	.38		.46		.37	.49	.58		.33		.38	1.0		.55		.32	.35	.67	.64	.56
Norway	.31		.42		.32	.43	.41		.25		.29	.55		1.0		.33	.35	.53	.30	.39
Spain	.33		.39		.31	.37	.37		.30		.36	.32		.33		1.0	.25	.40	.37	.22
Sweden	.23		.28		.29	.25	.37		.23		.32	.35		.35		.25	1.0	.43	.32	.27
Switzerland	.52		.50		.46	.51	.74		.33		.48	.67		.53		.40	.43	1.0	.54	.45
U.K.	.29		.32		.33	.41	.44		.33		.36	.64		.30		.37	.32	.54	1.0	.46
B. Far East market
Hong Kong		.37						1.0		.27			.48				.26	.27
Japan		.36						.21		1.0			.21				.36	.28
Singapore		.47						.48		.26			1.0				.36	.36
Australia		1.0						.37		.36			.47				.44	.34
C. North America market
Canada				1.0						.25							.49	.71
U.S.				.71						.28							.46	1.0

NOTE: Singapore also includes Malaysia.

Table 4. Correlation Matrix for the Squared Returns

	Aus.	Aust.	Bel.	Can.	Den.	Fra.	Ger.	Hong Kong	Ita.	Jap.	Net.	Nor.	Sing.	Spa.	Swe.	Swit.	U.K.	U.S.
A. Europe market																		
Austria	1.0		.06	.11	.07	.36		.01	.14	.15	.15		.09	.12	.22	.18	.10
Belgium	.06		1.0	.09	.15	.39		.15	.13	.14	.37		.53	.42	.15	.12	.10
Denmark	.11		.09	1.0	.06	.24		.07	.20	.28	.27		.13	.24	.31	.33	.25
France	.07		.15	.06	1.0	.12		.27	.10	.15	.15		.11	.11	.13	.14	.13
Germany	.36		.39	.24	.12	1.0		.17	.40	.50	.60		.45	.57	.64	.52	.44
Italy	.01		.15	.07	.27	.17		1.0	.09	.11	.19		.17	.17	.11	.12	.16
Netherlands	.15		.14	.28	.15	.50		.11	.34	1.0	.68		.12	.45	.81	.80	.80
Norway	.31		.37	.27	.15	.60		.19	.33	.68	1.0		.45	.67	.73	.70	.67
Spain	.09		.53	.13	.11	.45		.17	.22	.12	.45		1.0	.55	.18	.17	.14
Sweden	.12		.42	.24	.11	.57		.17	.23	.45	.67		.55	1.0	.51	.48	.45
Switzerland	.22		.15	.31	.13	.64		.11	.41	.81	.73		.18	.51	1.0	.85	.82
U.K.	.18		.12	.33	.14	.52		.12	.37	.80	.70		.17	.48	.85	1.0	.70
B. Far East market																		
Hong Kong		.58						1.0		.11			.62				.12	.07
Japan		.36						.11		1.0			.32				.37	.34
Singapore		.91						.62		.32			1.0				.63	.62
Australia		1.0						.58		.36			.91				.68	.64
C. North America market																		
Canada				1.0						.77							.67	.77
U.S.				.77						.34							.79	1.0

NOTE: Singapore also includes Malaysia.

not very high. Here we see that only 11 out of 66 correlation coefficients are higher than .5, and only 3 are higher than .6. There are markets such as those in Denmark, Italy, Spain, and Sweden with nearly all correlations below .4. No country shows a correlation higher than .5 with Japan, and only one, the Netherlands, shows a correlation higher than .5 with the United States. As might be expected, since their economies are more related to each other, there is a pattern of higher correlation between neighboring countries. There are moderate correlations, around .5, between Switzerland, Germany, France, and Austria and between the Netherlands, Belgium, France, and Germany. These patterns are similar to the findings of Hilliard (1979) and Panton, Lessing, and Joy (1976). In Table 2B, it is observed that the correlation coefficients for the squared returns are in general lower, but there are 15 correlations higher than .5 and 9 higher than .6. Moreover, four countries have correlations higher than .67 with the U.S. market. It is worth noting that Austria, Denmark, France, and Italy display much lower correlations in squared returns than in mean returns. On the other hand, two clear groups appear that generally show higher correlations among their members in squared returns than in mean returns. The first group is formed by Germany, Belgium, Spain, Sweden, and Norway. The second group is formed by the United Kingdom, Switzerland, and the Netherlands. The former group is formed by countries (with the exception of Spain) that dramatically increase their ARCH effect when a multivariate information set is used, whereas the latter group is formed by countries in which univariate ARCH statistics are not significant. Moreover, the MARCH tests without the U.S. market are insignificant. Finally, as noted by Kendall and Stewart (1969), when correlations of squares are higher than correlation of levels, then it can be shown that the series are not multivariate normally distributed.

For the Far East markets, correlations for returns are moderate (the highest correlation is .48), but correlations for squared returns are in general higher. The exception to this rule is Japan. Again, there is a group formed by Australia, Hong Kong, and Singapore/Malaysia that increases the correlations among its members in squared returns. Some correlations in squared returns are much higher; for instance, the correlation coefficient between Singapore/Malaysia and Australia is .91. Furthermore, Australia and Singapore/Malaysia have a correlation higher than .6 with the United Kingdom and the United States.

Similar results hold for both the United States and Canada, where all the correlations of squared returns are higher than the correlations of the returns.

These findings are in agreement with what appears in the literature. International stock markets show small correlations in returns, but some stock markets are not independent because they are related through their second moments.

3. TESTING FOR COMMON ARCH FEATURES

As mentioned before, a common approach for modeling multivariate volatility entails using a factor model with the addition of a time-varying volatility. Many of these specifications use the ARCH process to model the conditional time-varying volatility. This model was proposed originally by Engle (1987) and used by Diebold and Nerlove (1989) and Engle et al. (1990). A related approach was used by King et al. (1990), in which the number of unobservable factors is equal to $k = 2$, and they also added four observable factors. They found that volatility was driven by the unobservable factors. A factor ARCH model imposes restrictions that reduce the number of parameters to be estimated in the covariance matrix. It is computationally expensive to estimate models that allow the number of factors to be large and allow general specifications of time-varying variances. Natural questions to ask are: How can we test for factor ARCH, and when is factor ARCH a valid model? A test for common features recently developed by Engle and Kozicki (1990) can be used to address these questions. Because this test is fairly new, we explain it with a simple model, based on the more general model of Section 1. This will be done in the next subsection.

3.1 ARCH as a Common Feature

The intuition behind the test is similar to the intuition behind cointegration. Suppose that we have two series showing ARCH effects. The test looks for a linear combination of the series that eliminates the ARCH effects. More formally, suppose that we have $y_t = w_t + e_{yt}$, $e_{yt}|I_{t-1} \sim D(0, \sigma_y^2)$, $w_t|I_{t-1} \sim D(0, h_w)$, and $h_{wt} = \alpha_{w0} + \alpha_{w1}w_{t-1}^2$, where σ_y^2 is a constant and h_{wt} is time varying and follows a simple ARCH(1) process (the usual restrictions for the ARCH process apply). I_{t-1} is the information set on which agents condition their decisions at time t that includes all past information. More complicated ARCH processes may be allowed. Note that the conditional errors need not be normally distributed.

The variance of y_t is equal to $V(y_t) = h_{wt} + \sigma_y^2$, which is clearly time varying. Suppose that we have another series, $x_t = \delta p_t + e_{xt}$, $e_{xt}|I_{t-1} \sim D(0, \sigma_x^2)$, $p_t|I_{t-1} \sim D(0, h_p)$, and $h_{pt} = \alpha_{p0} + \alpha_{p1}p_{t-1}^2$, where σ_x^2 is a constant and h_{pt} is time varying and follows an ARCH(1) process. Similarly, the variance of x_t is equal to $V(x_t) = h_{pt} + \sigma_x^2$, which is also time varying. Now, we ask if there is any linear combination of y_t and x_t that show no time-varying volatility. If we define $u_t = x_t + \tau y_t$, then the variance of u_t is $V(u_t) = \tau^2 h_{wt} + h_{pt} + \tau^2 \sigma_y^2 + \sigma_x^2$. If $w_t = p_t$ and $\tau = \delta$, then $u_t = \delta y_t - x_t$, which has a constant variance equal to $V(u_t) = \delta^2 \sigma_y^2 + \sigma_x^2$.

We should point out that if the idiosyncratic components also have a time-varying covariance matrix—that is, the second restriction in (6) does not hold—there is no linear combination of x_t and y_t that shows a constant variance.

In this example, y_t and x_t share a common feature, a common factor that displays a time-varying variance. In the notation of Section 1, we can express this bivariate system as

$$r_t = \begin{bmatrix} y_t \\ x_t \end{bmatrix} = Bf_t + v_t = \begin{bmatrix} 1 & 0 \\ 0 & \delta \end{bmatrix} w_t + \begin{bmatrix} e_{yt} \\ e_{xt} \end{bmatrix}, \quad (7)$$

where $m_t = 0$.

Suppose that there is another series, s_t, such that $s_t = \beta w_t + q_t + e_{st}$, $e_{st}|I_{t-1} \sim D(0, \sigma_s^2)$, $q_t|I_{t-1} \sim D(0, h_q)$, $h_{qt} = \alpha_{q0} + \alpha_{q1}q_{t-1}^2$, and $V_t(s_t) = \beta^2 h_{wt} + h_{qt} + \sigma_s^2$, where σ_s^2 is a constant and h_{qt} is time varying and follows an ARCH(1) process. Clearly, there is no linear combination of x_t and s_t that achieves a constant variance (besides the trivial case, $q_t = w_t$). In this case, the first restriction in (6) does not hold.

3.2 Common-Feature Test

This approach has two steps. First, we test both series for the ARCH feature. For this, an ARCH test, as described in Section 3, can be used. If ARCH effects are found in both series, then we proceed to test for common ARCH (factor ARCH). We try to find a portfolio of both series that displays no ARCH. If this happens, the bivariate system can be expressed as (7), where m_t can be different from 0 and the idiosyncratic noises can be correlated. Define a large information set Z_t, composed of $y_{t-1}^2, x_{t-1}^2, y_{t-2}^2, x_{t-2}^2, \ldots, y_{t-p}^2, x_{t-p}^2$, and lagged cross-products $y_{t-1}x_{t-1}, y_{t-2}x_{t-2}, \ldots, y_{t-p}x_{t-p}$. We can also include other lagged series such as s_t. Note that the usual ARCH test is just the $T*R^2$ from the regression of the squared series against own and possible lagged squared series. Therefore, we are going to minimize over the parameter τ a $T*R^2$. We obtain this $T*R^2$ from the regression of $y_t - \tau x_t$ on lagged y_t, lagged x_t, and the cross-product of y_t and x_t. We can generalize this test to portfolios composed of k variables; that is, more generally we look for a vector τ that minimizes a test of this form:

$$\min_\tau s(u) = T*R(\tau)^2$$

$$u(\tau) = y_t - x_t\tau$$

$$R^2 = u_t^2(\delta\tau)'Z_t(Z_t'Z_t)^{-1}Z_t'u_t^2(\delta)/\sigma^2, \quad (8)$$

where Z_t is the large information set defined before, y_t is $T \times 1$, x_t is a $T \times K$ vector, τ is $K \times 1$, K is the number of variables and σ^2 is a consistent estimator of the variance of u^2. The test proposed in (8) is a general method-of-moments-type test. We are trying to find a portfolio that is not correlated in the squares with any information included in Z_t. Engle and Kozicki (1990) showed that, under the assumptions of Hansen (1982), $\min_\tau s(u)$ follows a chi-squared distribution with the degrees of freedom given by the number of overidentifying restrictions (number of instruments included in the information set Z_t minus $K - 1$). To minimize (8) we use a grid search and then the International Mathematical and Statistical Libraries subroutine DUMINF.

In the next section, we apply this test procedure to all of the international stock markets in the sample.

3.3 Application

From the previous two sections we can extract two conclusions. First, using the results from Section 2, the univariate ARCH estimations display a high degree of similarities across international markets. Second, using the results from Section 1, the need for a multivariate model of volatility for some countries is clear.

The first step of the common feature test is to discover that each series has ARCH effects. In this case, we are interested in a common ARCH feature. As seen in Table 2, the ARCH feature is shown by all of the series with the exception of Denmark and possibly the United Kingdom. The use of the MARCH tests, with different lags, gives the idea that some markets need a different lag structure from others. In most of the markets, the feature is discovered using only one lag and the same time-zone information. In Europe, using the big three markets of the continent, only one lag is enough for the majority of the countries. In some markets the inclusion of the United States is irrelevant, but in others—for instance, the Netherlands and Switzerland—it is not. In the case of France, two lags are needed to discover the ARCH feature. In the Far East markets, we have similar results. Moreover, when two lags are used in the MARCH test, the inclusion of the United States as regressor in the test is irrelevant. In North America, the inclusion of the U.K. information is relevant to testing for an ARCH feature for the U.S. market.

Given the results of the squared correlations and the MARCH tests, there are two groups that are suspected of having similar volatility behavior, one in each continent. One is composed of Belgium, Germany, Norway, Sweden, and Spain. The second one is composed of Hong Kong, Singapore/Malaysia, and Australia. These groups share the same information, since both groups lie within the same time zone.

In the second step, we look for portfolios of each pair of variables in each time zone that does not display ARCH effects. Careful examination of the previous ARCH results is necessary. Otherwise, if a country shows no ARCH, when the test is minimized a weight of 0 will be given to the other countries included in the portfolio.

In Table 5, the results are displayed for all of the portfolios found that show no ARCH effects. The parameter that minimizes the linear combination of both series is shown in column 2. The third column shows the minimum $T*R^2$. The distribution of this test is chi-squared with 11 df because four lags of both series and cross-products are used as instruments.

European countries suspected of having similar volatility processes are mainly those shown in Table 5: Belgium, Germany, Norway, Sweden, and Spain seem to have a common feature. Spain is borderline when combined with Sweden and Germany. A portfolio formed by Belgium and −1.06 times Germany shows no time-varying volatility. Moreover, there is evidence of a constant variance for a portfolio formed by Belgium and −.70 times France and by Italy and −1.27 times Norway. It is worth pointing out that the no-ARCH portfolios show a hugely reduced value of the MARCH test—third column—when compared with the MARCH test for each series—fourth and fifth column.

In the Far East, Australia, Hong Kong, and Singapore/Malaysia, as suspected, show evidence of a common feature with time-varying variance. Two borderline cases are Japan and Singapore/Malaysia and Singapore/Malaysia and Australia. Again, the reduction of the MARCH test for the no-ARCH portfolio is huge when compared to the MARCH tests for the individual series.

In North America, we see an example of why the first step is necessary. The United States does not show ARCH effects when regressed against Canada and its own past. The minimization procedures gives a weight of −.10 to Canada and the portfolio is very similar to the United States. Therefore, the portfolio does not show any evidence of ARCH effects.

As a further check, we regress the no-ARCH portfolio—that is, the portfolio that does not show time-varying volatility, against the instruments that were so efficient in detecting ARCH in Table 2. A univariate ARCH(4) test is also run. The results are shown in Table 6. As a result, in Europe it is observed that the no-ARCH portfolios that include Spain, when regressed against a richer multivariate information set, show evidence of time-varying volatility. The same happens with the no-ARCH portfolios of Belgium and France and the no-ARCH portfolios of Italy and Norway. In

Table 5. Common Feature: Estimation

Market	Param	min-Test	MARCH-1	MARCH-2
A. European				
Belgium/France	−.70	10.21	20.98	37.69*
Belgium/Germany	−1.06	11.31	68.05*	44.69*
Belgium/Norway	−1.29	8.93	129.63*	63.61*
Belgium/Spain	−.46	6.11	13.51	69.71*
Belgium/Sweden	−.72	5.46	69.71*	62.31*
Germany/Norway	−1.04	13.74	61.87*	66.48*
Germany/Spain	−.30	20.02*	43.99*	172.01*
Germany/Sweden	−.89	15.57	53.74*	76.34*
Norway/Spain	−.41	14.45	63.37*	270.25*
Italy/Norway	−.82	9.89	45.84*	61.55*
Sweden/Norway	−1.27	13.58	65.37*	117.43*
Sweden/Spain	−.39	21.93*	62.24*	21.89*
B. Far East				
Japan/Singapore	−.32	19.99*	32.52*	162.37*
Singapore/Australia	−1.23	21.50*	171.45*	169.18*
Hong Kong/Australia	−2.00	11.03	307.03*	164.42*
Hong Kong/Singapore	−1.90	7.46	331.12*	169.51*
C. North America				
U.S./Canada	−.10	12.65	13.00	55.37*

NOTE: Singapore also includes Malaysia. Param: Parameter obtained that minimizes the ARCH test for a linear combination of both series. min-Test: Minimum test obtained for the linear combination, when using Param. MARCH-1: ARCH test for the first series—the normalized series—with a multivariate information set. This information set is given by four own lags, four lags of the other series, and cross-products. MARCHC-2: Same ARCH test as MARCH-1 but for the second series.
* Significant at the 5% level.

Table 6. Common Feature: ARCH Tests for Optimal Combination

Market	ARCH(4)	MARCH-1	MARCHC-1	MARCH-2	MARCHC-2
A. European					
Belgium/France	4.12	35.50*	38.03*	40.05*	45.29*
Belgium/Germany	3.89	5.66	5.67	11.06	11.39
Belgium/Norway	2.67	9.08	11.46	12.63	15.66
Belgium/Spain	4.78	12.10*	12.12	15.58	16.60
Belgium/Sweden	2.96	11.89	11.94	17.15	17.48
Germany/Norway	9.52*	4.17	4.18	5.31	5.47
Germany/Spain	15.36*	14.53*	15.94*	18.39*	22.08*
Germany/Sweden	6.17	10.99*	11.55*	17.23*	18.26
Norway/Spain	10.03*	18.30*	25.23*	21.46*	29.14*
Italy/Norway	3.13	18.56*	19.38*	27.67*	31.59*
Sweden/Norway	3.16	6.55	7.74	14.08	15.51
Sweden/Spain	13.03*	16.34*	18.24*	21.89*	23.88*
B. Far East					
Japan/Singapore	1.93*	28.03*	29.03*	34.73*	34.74*
Singapore/Australia	13.51*	4.85	4.90	11.02	12.47
Hong Kong/Australia	8.52	.76	5.91	2.33	7.17
Hong Kong/Singapore	2.61	5.61	10.84	7.67	17.95
C. North America					
U.S./Canada	7.70	4.41	12.92*	6.22	15.01*

NOTE: Singapore also includes Malaysia. ARCH(4): ARCH test with four lags for the own-squared returns. MARCH-1: ARCH test with a multivariate information set (own time zone). For the European markets, lagged U.K., Germany, France, and own-lagged squared return. For the Far East markets, lagged Hong Kong, Japan, Singapore, and Australia lagged-squared returns. For the American markets, Canada and U.S. lagged squared returns. MARCHC-1: ARCH test with a bigger multivariate information set than in MARCH-1. For the European and Far East markets, it also includes U.S. lagged squared returns. For the American markets, it also includes lagged U.K. squared returns. MARCH-2: Same test as MARCH-1 but with two lags. MARCHC-2: Same test as MARCHC-1 but with two lags.
* Significant at the 5% level.

the Far East, the no-ARCH portfolio composed of Japan and Singapore/Malaysia, when regressed against the bigger multivariate information set, shows evidence of ARCH effects. The no-ARCH portfolio formed by Singapore/Malaysia and Australia shows ARCH effects when the univariate test is run but none when the multivariate information is used. In North America, the MARCH tests reject the no-ARCH portfolio. This is not surprising, given the results in Table 2, since the no-ARCH portfolio is very similar to the U.S. series.

One possible explanation for the results in this section is that all of the stock returns are denominated in dollars. These returns obviously contain foreign-exchange-rate movements. Moreover, some of the series in which ARCH effects are eliminated are members of the European Monetary System, therefore, their exchange rates versus the dollar will have to stay close together. It may be that the common ARCH comes from the common dollar denomination of stock returns. To discriminate the dollar effect from the stock-market effect, we transform the returns into local currency returns, using exchange rates (Fridays average) from Citibase. Although our stock-market indexes are Thursday quotes, we take them as a good approximation. These data are not available for Spain, Austria, Malaysia/Singapore, and Hong Kong. The results for the rest of the sample in local currencies are very similar. The only exception is Germany and Sweden, with a borderline rejection. With that exception, we still find a common volatility feature in the group formed by Belgium, Germany, Norway, and Sweden. Moreover, the combination of Italy and Norway shows a minimum-MARCH test of 60.60, which is highly significant. Therefore, we do not consider the dollar denomination as a determinant of the results in this section.

Summarizing the findings, a common factor that has a time-varying volatility was found in Europe and in the Far East. The group in Europe that shows no ARCH when combined between its members is Belgium, Germany, Norway, and Sweden. Note that these countries are geographically close. The group in the Far East is composed of Australia, Hong Kong, and Singapore/Malaysia. There are no other portfolios that show no ARCH effects.

3.4 Is There a World Factor?

In this section, we test if the European factor and the Far East factor are the same. If the factor is the same for both regions, there must exist a linear combination of stock markets from both groups that displays no ARCH effects. In the European group, we also include Spain, which was a borderline case. In Table 7, we show all of the pairwise comparisons. In 10 out of 15 cases, the test suggests a common ARCH feature between both groups. As in the previous section, however, we perform more tests on the minimum no-ARCH portfolio. We regress the no-ARCH portfolio against France, Germany, and Japan lagged-one-period and own-series lagged squared returns. We call this test MARCH-W for world information. We also run ARCH(4) tests for the no-ARCH portfolios. The results are displayed in Table 7, columns 6 and 7. With

Table 7. Common Feature: Estimation

Market	Param	min-Test	MARCH-1	MARCH-2	MARCH-W	ARCH(4)
A. European						
Belgium/Hong Kong	−.28	2.80	12.85	11.50	9.77	2.79
Belgium/Australia	−.71	3.60	161.12*	160.66*	18.31*	1.08
Belgium/Singapore	−.50	7.67	157.31*	159.76*	6.39	5.27
Germany/Hong Kong	−.17	23.15*	50.62*	120.94*	9.16	11.51*
Germany/Australia	−.30	15.95	80.79*	163.05*	8.06	12.11*
Germany/Singapore	−.26	27.71*	73.87*	158.44*	9.62	13.77*
Norway/Hong Kong	−.26	14.38	69.42*	244.87*	11.90	1.99
Norway/Australia	−.44	11.53	85.06*	169.03*	13.28*	6.93
Norway/Singapore	−.40	19.06	77.97*	168.30*	11.99	11.62*
Sweden/Hong Kong	−.20	41.68*	88.98*	164.98*	11.91	21.20*
Sweden/Australia	−.70	27.50*	152.27*	162.55*	2.43	11.83*
Sweden/Singapore	−.39	13.84	127.51*	149.54*	5.01	12.39*
Hong Kong/Spain	.68	14.50	20.10	69.43*	114.04*	3.68
Spain/Australia	−1.30	24.30*	333.21*	161.67*	24.54*	14.09*
Spain/Singapore	1.31	18.27	298.91*	155.95*	19.99*	14.25*

NOTE: Singapore also includes Malaysia. Param: Parameter obtained that minimizes the ARCH test for a linear combination of both series. min-Test: Minimum test obtained for the linear combination, when using Param. MARCH-1: ARCH test for the first series—the normalized series—with a multivariate information set. This information set is given by four own lags, four lags of the other series, and cross-products. MARCHC-2: Same ARCH test as MARCH-1, but for the second series. MARCH-W: Multivariate ARCH test for the minimum no-ARCH portfolio. It uses as instruments lagged U.K., Germany, France, and Japan, as well as one-lagged squared returns of each individual series in the no-ARCH portfolio. ARCH(4): ARCH test with four-lagged own squared returns of the no-ARCH portfolio.
* Significant at the 5% level.

the exception of three cases, we reject the no-ARCH hypothesis. There seems to be evidence that the common factors are regional factors, not world factors. These results confirm that the dollar denomination of stock returns does not play a significant role, since the factors seem to be regional. With a different approach, Cho, Eun, and Senbet (1986) also suggested the existence of regional common factors.

3.5 Implications

In the simple setup of this article, we test a model with one factor and a constant idiosyncratic noise variance. It appears to be an attractive model for the countries in the groups mentioned previously. More general models might lead to overparameterizations. The usual finding in the factor ARCH literature is that with a few factors adequate representations are achieved. King et al. (1990) estimated a model that allows for more factors and time-varying variance for the idiosyncratic noise. They found that changes in the correlations between markets are driven primarily by movements in two unobservable factors. The existence of a second international factor is probably the reason we cannot find more no-ARCH portfolios. Additionally, we need to mention that another reason might be that the variance of the idiosyncratic noise, $\Omega_t = \Omega$, is also time varying. Given our methodology, both cases are indistinguishable.

4. CONCLUSIONS

In this article, we investigated volatility in international stock markets. First, we looked at univariate statistics and we fit univariate ARCH models to the 18 series. We observed some similarities in the 18 stock markets. We also observed that second moments might be related for some countries. Second, we implemented a common ARCH-feature test to international stock-market data. We investigated if a group of countries shows a similar time-varying volatility. We find two groups of countries with these characteristics. One group is composed of Belgium, Germany, Norway, and Sweden. The second group is composed of Australia, Hong Kong, and Singapore/Malaysia. For the countries in these two groups, an APT-type model with one regional factor with a time-varying variance might be appropriate.

[Received October 1991. Revised September 1992.]

REFERENCES

Agmon, T. (1972), "The Relations Among Equity Markets in the United States, United Kingdom, Germany and Japan," *Journal of Finance*, 28, 839–855.

———— (1987), "A Conditional Time Series Model for Speculative Prices and Rates of Returns," *Review of Economics and Statistics*, 69, 524–54.

Cho, D. C., Eun, C. S., and Senbet, L. W. (1986), "International Arbitrage Pricing Theory: An Empirical Investigation," *Journal of Finance*, 41, 313–329.

Diebold, F. X., and Nerlove, M. (1989), "The Dynamics of Exchange Rate Volatility: A Multivariate Latent Factor ARCH Model," *Journal of Applied Econometrics*, 4, 1–21.

Engle, R. F. (1982), "Autoregressive Conditional Heteroskedasticity With Estimates of the Variance of U.K.," *Econometrica*, 50, 987–1008.

———— (1987), "Multivariate GARCH With Factor Structures—Cointegration in Variance," working paper, University of California at San Diego, Dept. of Economics.

Engle, R. F., and Kozicki, S. (1990), "Testing for Common Features," working paper, University of California at San Diego, Dept. of Economics.

Engle, R. F., Ng, V., and Rothschild, M. (1990), "Asset Pricing With a Factor ARCH Covariance Structure: Empirical Estimates for Treasury Bills," *Journal of Econometrics*, 45, 213–239.

Grubel, H. (1968), "Internationally Diversified Portfolios: Welfare Gains and Capital Flows," *American Economic Review*, 58, 1299–1314.

Hamao, Y., Masulis, R., and Ng, V. (1990a), "Correlations in Price Changes and Volatility Across International Stock Markets," *The Review of Financial Studies*, 3, 281–308.

────── (1990b), "The Effect of the 1987 Stock Crash on International Financial Integration," unpublished manuscript, University of California at San Diego, Dept. of Economics.

Hansen, L. P. (1982), "Large Sample Properties of Generalized Method of Movements Estimators," *Econometrica*, 50, 1023–1054.

Hilliard, J. E. (1979), "The Relationship Between Equity Indices on World Exchanges," *Journal of Finance*, 34, 103–114.

Kendall, M. G., and Stuart, A. (1969), *The Advanced Theory of Statistics* (3rd ed.), New York: Hafner Press.

King, M., and Wadhwani, S. (1990), "Transmission of Volatility Between Stock Markets," *The Review of Financial Studies*, 3, 5–33.

King, M., Sentana, E., and Wadhwami, S. (1990), "Volatility and Links Between National Stock Markets," Working Paper 3357, National Bureau of Economic Research, Cambridge, MA.

Levy, J., and Sarnat, M. (1970), "International Diversification of Investment Portfolios," *American Economic Review*, 60, 668–675.

Panton, D. B., Lessing, V. P., and Joy, O. M. (1976), "Comovement of International Equity Markets: A Taxonomic Approach," *Journal of Financial and Quantitative Analysis*, 9, 433–454.

Roll, R. (1989), "Price Volatility, International Markets Links and Their Implications for Regulatory Policies," *Journal of Financial Services Research*, 3, 211–246.

Von Furstenberg, G. M., and Jeon, B. N. (1989), "International Stock Price Movements: Links and Messages," *Brookings Papers on Economic Activity*, I:1989, 125, 167.

Part III
Emerging Markets

[14]
Emerging Equity Markets in the Global Economy

by John Mullin

Developing-country equity markets have undergone great changes in recent years. International investors have purchased emerging-market equity shares at unprecedented rates, tripling the value of their emerging-market equity portfolios between 1989 and 1992. Greater foreign investment in emerging markets has tightened their price linkages to the international financial centers. Partly as a result of these changes, emerging markets have matured considerably, achieving increased market size and an increased capacity to support equity issuance.[1]

Much of the attraction of developing-economy equity markets derives from the outstanding return performances registered by many of these markets in recent years. Between 1976-92, annualized equity returns exceeded 20 percent in Argentina, Chile, Mexico, South Korea, and Thailand. Equity returns in Chile and Mexico soared to almost 50 percent per year during 1990-92.

This article seeks to explain these striking emerging-market return performances. It examines recent structural reforms and their effects on equity portfolio inflows in nine of the most highly capitalized emerging markets: Argentina, Brazil, Chile, Mexico, South Korea, Taiwan, Malaysia, Thailand, and India.[2] The article also charts broad trends in developing-country equity markets, giving attention to the integration of these markets with the global financial system, analyzing how these markets have become more like developed-country markets, and identifying the substantial differences that remain. Finally, the article evaluates the effects of increased integration on the potential diversification gains that these markets offer to international investors.

The analysis shows that across national markets, equity returns have borne a positive relationship to measures of economic performance, such as rates of export growth and dividend-per-share growth. Nevertheless, the extraordinary equity returns registered by several developing-country markets in recent years have exceeded levels that can be explained by measures of ex ante risk and ex post macroeconomic performance. Returns in these countries appear to reflect fundamental structural changes that have increased investor demand for developing-country equity shares.

Among these structural changes are measures designed to make it easier for international investors to buy and sell developing-country stocks. Officials in several developing countries have modified domestic accounting and underwriting regulations in successful efforts to make public equity offerings in the United States. In addition, market openings in Mexico, Brazil, and South Korea have clearly accelerated foreign equity portfolio investment in those markets.

Other structural changes contributing to the demand for emerging-market equity shares involve basic economic reforms. Far-reaching programs to stabilize exchange rates and prices have helped bring about the particularly large increases in equity portfolio inflows observed in some Latin American countries. Ambitious

---
[1] The International Finance Corporation considers all stock markets in developing countries to be "emerging." The World Bank defines developing countries as those with GNP per capita of less than $7,620 in 1990 (see International Finance Corporation, *Emerging Stock Markets Factbook*, 1992, p. 3).

[2] These countries represent the nine most highly capitalized markets tracked by the International Finance Corporation's Emerging Markets Data Base.

privatization programs in Argentina and Mexico have also increased equity portfolio inflows, both directly by increasing the supply of internationally marketable equity shares and indirectly by improving government fiscal balances and thereby promoting future macroeconomic stability.

Evidence of increased emerging-market integration with the global financial system is found in the joint movements of returns realized by investors in developing-country and developed-country equities. Historically, monthly return correlations between pairs of developed markets have most often exceeded those between emerging and developed markets. In recent years, however, monthly return correlations have tended to increase between developed markets and those developing-country markets that became more open to foreign investment during the past decade. Moreover, an examination of correlations at different frequencies reveals that many developing-country markets may have been even more closely integrated with the global financial system during the past decade than the monthly return correlations would suggest.

The article's review of trends in emerging markets suggests that structural changes and equity portfolio inflows have helped accelerate a decade-long movement toward greater stock market capitalization—that is, an increase in the value of emerging-market equity shares outstanding. By 1991, several emerging markets' ratios of capitalization to gross domestic product (GDP) had converged with those of the world's most mature equity markets. Rapid capitalization growth has been accompanied by a recent surge in developing-country equity issuance, which has been particularly pronounced in the rapidly growing economies of East Asia. Equity issuance in these countries has exceeded the post-World War II norm for Group of Seven (G-7) economies and has been roughly in line with the high rates of equity issuance experienced by the United States during the 1920s. These patterns of equity issuance support the hypothesis that equity issuance becomes a more important source of finance in the latter part of an economy's rapid-growth stage of economic development.

Although emerging equity markets have become more like developed-country markets in key ways, substantial differences remain. One important difference is that developing-economy equity markets generally lack breadth. In addition, many developing-country stock markets remain more volatile than their more developed counterparts. The evidence indicates that this return volatility tends to reflect the volatility of economic conditions, especially that of inflation rates and real exchange rate changes.

The final section of the article finds that the vast changes that have taken place in emerging markets over the past decade have important implications for international investors. Financial analysts often argue that developing-country stocks, though volatile, offer striking diversification benefits because their returns have historically been both impressive and relatively uncorrelated with developed-country equity returns. Because many developing markets have undergone important structural changes in recent years, however, the procedure of using historical return averages and correlations to calculate ex ante diversification strategies is particularly suspect.

Return performance: the allure of emerging equity markets

Much of the allure of developing-country equity markets stems from the outstanding return performances registered by many of these markets. For instance, the International Finance Corporation (IFC) total return indexes for Argentina and Chile both grew at annualized rates in excess of 30 percent between December 1975 and December 1992 (Chart 1).[3] During the same seventeen-year span, the IFC total return indexes for Mexico, South Korea, and Thailand increased at impressive annualized rates of 22 to 24 percent.

In comparison, developed-country return performances tended to be more modest. The world equity return index computed by Morgan Stanley Capital International (MSCI) grew at an annualized rate of 14 percent between December 1975 and December 1992.[4] During the same period, the New York Stock Exchange (NYSE) total return index computed by the Center for Research in Securities Prices (CRISP) appreciated at an annualized rate of 15 percent, while the MSCI Japan total return index appreciated at an annualized rate of 17 percent. Of the seven emerging markets for which sixteen years of IFC data are available, only Brazil's IFC index increased at a significantly lower rate (6 percent per year) than the return indexes of these developed-country markets.

Chart 1 also gives the cumulative annualized rates of return of the NYSE over consecutive sixteen-year intervals since 1802.[5] The exceptional nature of the recent return performances of the Argentine, Chilean, Mex-

---

[3]Throughout the paper, unless explicitly noted, returns are calculated in terms of U.S. dollars. Return indexes are constructed in such a manner that the percentage change of a market's return index equals the market's rate of return.

[4]The Morgan Stanley Capital International index is almost exclusively composed of developed-country stocks.

[5]Data for 1802-25 were compiled originally by the Cowles Commission and subsequently adjusted by William Schwert in "Indexes of United States Stock Prices, 1802-1987," *Journal of Business*, July 1990.

FRBNY Quarterly Review/Summer 1993   55

ican, Korean, Thai, and Taiwanese stock markets is underscored by the fact that annualized returns of the NYSE did not exceed 16 percent in any of these sixteen-year periods.

Both developing-country and developed-country returns have been somewhat mixed in recent years. During 1990-92, three of the four Latin American markets under consideration—Argentina, Chile, and Mexico—had phenomenal annualized returns of between 30 and 50 percent. In the same three-year period, however, Korea and Taiwan experienced asset price deflations. The experience of these two countries mirrored that of Japan, where the speculative stock market rally of 1987-89 set the stage for a subsequent period of asset price deflation. Japan's tumbling share prices caused the MSCI world index to decline during the period, even though returns were positive in the United States and Europe.[6]

Stock returns and macroeconomic performance

Buying developing-country equity shares is often likened to taking a stake in the growth prospects of a

[6]World returns, as measured by the MSCI index, would have been higher (and perhaps positive) during the period had Japan's market capitalization been adjusted downward to take into account the effects of cross-holdings. See Jack McDonald, "The Mochiai Effect: Japanese Corporate Cross-Holding," *Journal of Portfolio Management*, Fall 1989, pp. 90-94.

Chart 1
Annualized Equity Returns

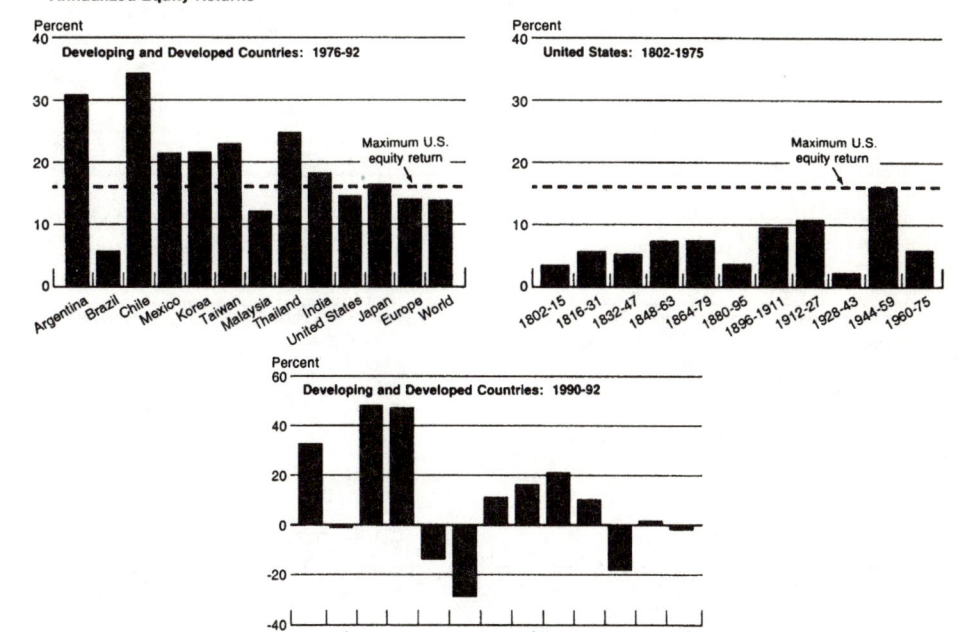

Sources: International Finance Corporation; Center for Research in Securities Prices; Morgan Stanley Capital International; William Schwert, "Indexes of United States Stock Prices, 1802-1987." *Journal of Business*, July 1990.

Notes: Grey-shaded bars represent developing countries. Data for Malaysia and Taiwan span 1985-92.

developing country. While ex ante or expected equity returns should reflect risk considerations, ex post or actual returns should also reflect an economy's realized macroeconomic performance. For this reason, it seems puzzling that cumulative equity returns in Argentina were greater between 1975 and 1991 than equity returns in Japan, Korea, and Thailand. After all, Argentine output growth was lethargic during the period, while the Japanese, Korean, and Thai economies boomed. Should we not expect to find a positive cross-country

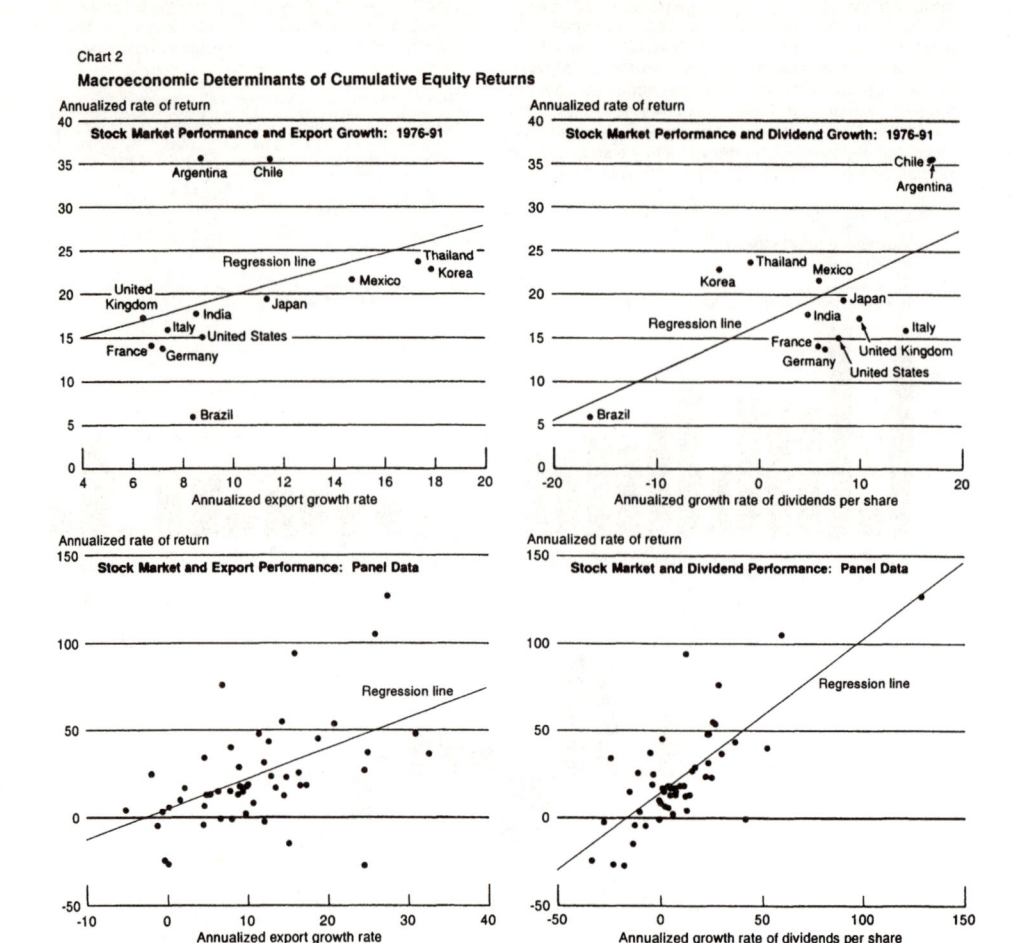

Chart 2
Macroeconomic Determinants of Cumulative Equity Returns

Sources: International Finance Corporation, Emerging Markets Data Base; Morgan Stanley Capital International; International Monetary Fund, International Financial Statistics; Bank for International Settlements.

correlation between cumulative equity returns and macroeconomic performance measures such as output and export growth rates? Should we not expect to see a negative relationship between equity returns and inflation? This section examines these questions and finds that cumulative equity returns are in fact correlated with various economic fundamentals. High returns among many developing countries stem partially from the robust growth that these economies have experienced over the past two decades. Nevertheless, the outstanding return performances registered by several of these countries surpass levels that can be explained by measures of ex ante risk and ex post performance. These return performances appear to reflect basic structural changes in the economies in question.

Returns and export and output growth rates
Consider first the relationship between equity returns and one important economic fundamental, export growth rates. A simple cross-country scatter diagram (Chart 2) provides only mixed support for the hypothesis that 1976-91 export growth rates and equity returns are positively related. While three export superstars (Korea, Thailand, and Mexico) had annualized stock returns of between 21 and 24 percent, two countries with much more modest export performances (Argentina and Chile) registered equity returns in excess of 35 percent.[7] The cross-country relationship appears much tighter, however, when three South American countries—Argentina, Brazil, and Chile—are excluded from the analysis.

[7]Exports are measured in U.S. dollars.

Table 1
Manufacturing's Share in the International Finance Corporation Index Relative to its Share in GDP

Country	(A) Share in IFC Index (Percent)	(B) Share in GDP (Percent)	(A)/(B)
Argentina	44	22	2.0
Brazil	52	39	1.3
Chile	23	21	1.1
Mexico	35	25	1.4
South Korea	35	31	1.1
Taiwan	41	34	1.2
Malaysia	22	27	0.8
Thailand	33	26	1.3
India	97	19	5.1

Sources: Capitalization data are International Finance Corporation estimates for end-1991; GDP composition data are Federal Reserve Bank of New York staff estimates for 1989.

Stronger support for the hypothesis arises from an alternative way of assessing the relationship between equity returns and export growth rates. A panel-data scatter diagram, constructed by breaking each country's experience into four-year periods, indicates that the relationship between annualized returns and export growth rates is fairly tight. Regression analysis confirms that the panel-data relationship is statistically significant, whether or not dummy variables are included to take into account time-period and regional effects.

Corresponding tests of the relationship between output growth and equity returns reveal no statistically significant relationship between these two measures of performance. The finding that the correlation between export performance and equity returns is greater than the correlation between output performance and equity returns is perhaps not surprising when one considers that, in general, the IFC indexes for the countries in question are disproportionately composed of stocks in the manufacturing (traded goods) sector (Table 1). Only in Malaysia does the share of manufacturing capitalization in the IFC index fall below the share of manufacturing output in GDP. In most countries, and particularly in Argentina and India, the share of manufacturing capitalization in the IFC index overstates the share of manufacturing in GDP.

Returns and growth rates of dividends per share
A fundamental that in theory should be closely related to equity performance is dividend-per-share growth.[8] A simple cross-country plot of equity returns against dividend-per-share growth in U.S. dollars indicates that dividend-per-share growth is positively correlated with equity returns. The countries with very high rates of dividend-per-share growth—Argentina and Chile—exhibit high rates of return, while Brazil, with a very low rate of dividend-per-share growth, experienced very low returns over 1976-91. This positive relationship between dividend-per-share and equity performance holds up in the panel-data diagram as well. Regression results indicate that 57 percent of the variation in equity returns can be explained by rates of dividend-per-share growth.

Returns and rates of inflation
The time-series evidence for the United States reveals a negative relationship between inflation and equity returns.[9] Surprisingly, perhaps, cross-country data indi-

[8]Merton Miller and Franco Modigliani, "Dividend Policy, Growth, and the Valuation of Shares," *Journal of Business*, vol. 34 (1961), pp. 411-33.

[9]See Nai-Fu Chen, Richard Roll, and Stephen Ross, "Economic Forces and the Stock Market," *Journal of Business*, vol. 59, no. 3 (1986), pp. 383-403. Strictly speaking, Chen, Roll, and Ross find a negative relationship between unexpected inflation and equity

cate no statistically significant relationship between equity returns and inflation rates. In part, this result reflects the very different equity performances of two high inflation countries: Brazil had very low annualized equity returns relative to other countries in the sample, while Argentina (with an even higher annualized rate of inflation) had extremely high equity returns (Chart 3). Like the cross-country data, the panel-data diagram does not indicate a negative relationship between equity returns and inflation.

Overall, the data support the hypothesis that ex post equity returns are related to economic performance. However, even a combination of measures of ex post performance and ex ante risk cannot adequately explain the outstanding equity returns registered by several emerging markets during the period of analysis. In a cross-country regression of mean annual returns against cumulative export growth rates, cumulative dividend-per-share growth rates, and a commonly used measure of risk (beta), the fitted regression errors tend to be positive among the developing countries and negative among the developed countries.[10] When a dummy variable for the developing economies is added to the equation, the dummy variable's estimated coefficient is positive and statistically significant (Table 2). A possible explanation of this finding is that high returns in several of the developing countries under examination reflect profound and largely unexpected changes in economic structure that have increased the demand for developing country stock and thereby increased share prices.

Structural reform and equity portfolio inflows

Structural reforms in developing countries have helped to accelerate foreign purchases of emerging-market stocks. This section highlights some of the more important changes that have made this trend possible, including market openings in developing countries, efforts by developing-country officials to obtain listings for emerging market companies on the world's major stock exchanges, and policies designed to stabilize exchange rates and prices.

Emerging market equity shares have historically been underrepresented in international investment portfolios. At the end of 1989, the combined market capitalization of the world's emerging equity markets amounted to more than 5 percent of world equity market capitalization. If international equity investors had held emerging

Footnote 9 continued
returns. Given the substantial cross-sectional variation in the present data set and the lengthy time period of each observation (sixteen years per observation for the simple scatter diagrams and four years per observation for the panel-data diagrams), I assume that actual inflation rates are adequate proxies for unanticipated inflation rates.

[10] Beta is defined as the ratio of (a) the covariance between an asset's excess return and the world excess return to (b) the variance of the world excess return. The beta used in this exercise is based on annual data. A discussion of beta and the distinction between betas based on annual data and betas based on monthly data is contained in Box 2.

Chart 3
Inflation and Cumulative Equity Returns

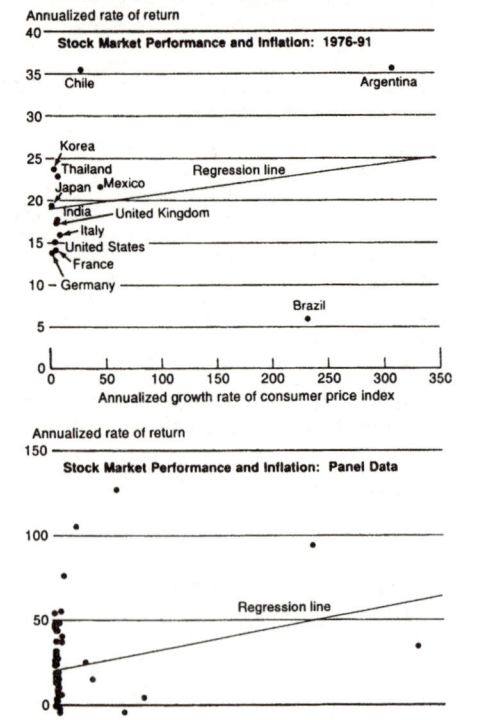

Sources: International Finance Corporation, Emerging Markets Data Base; Morgan Stanley Capital International; International Monetary Fund, International Financial Statistics.

market shares in proportion to the markets' world capitalization weights, they would have devoted 5 percent of their funds to emerging market equity shares. At the end of 1989, however, estimated foreign equity portfolio holdings of emerging market shares amounted to no more than $17 billion, or 0.2 percent, of the roughly $7 trillion in funds controlled by institutional investors in the major industrialized countries.[11]

Since 1989, a rapid acceleration of net foreign purchases of developing-country equity shares has significantly increased the share of emerging market equity holdings in international portfolios. The World Bank estimates that during 1990-92, cumulative foreign equity portfolio inflows into emerging markets amounted to $19.5 billion.[12]

Reliable estimates of equity portfolio inflows are difficult to assemble, largely because only a handful of developing countries have compiled data on direct foreign purchases of shares on their stock exchanges.

[11] See International Finance Corporation, *1991 Annual Report*, pp. 10-12; and World Institute of Development Economics Research of the United Nations University, "Foreign Portfolio Investment in Emerging Equity Markets," March 1990, pp. 12-13.

[12] See *1992-93 World Debt Tables*, vol. 1: Analysis and Summary Tables, p. 114. One reason that the World Bank estimate may be low is that it does not include Taiwan (although the IFC does include Taiwan in its emerging markets data base).

Table 2
Equations for Mean Annual Excess Return: 1976-91

Variable	Regression 1 Coefficient		Regression 2 Coefficient	
Constant term	−16.0	(15.1)	−17.8	(9.5)
Beta	13.2	(6.9)	13.5	(6.4)
Growth rate of dividends per share	1.0	(0.4)	1.0	(0.4)
Growth rate of exports	−2	(1.1)	—	—
Dummy variable to control for emerging markets	28.2	(8.7)	27.5	(6.7)
Statistics				
n	13		13	
R^2	.76		.76	
Adjusted R^2	.64		.68	

Notes: Standard errors are given in parentheses. Sample includes six developed countries (France, Germany, Italy, Japan, the United Kingdom, and the United States) and seven developing countries (Argentina, Brazil, Chile, Mexico, South Korea, Thailand, and India).

Data supplied by four developing countries, however, indicate that the World Bank estimate may understate the level of equity portfolio inflows into emerging markets over the past three years (Table 3). Brazil, Mexico, South Korea, and Taiwan have each experienced rapid accelerations of equity portfolio inflows since 1989. For this group alone, cumulative equity portfolio inflows amounted to $19.9 billion during 1990-92.

Equity portfolio inflows can be divided into three categories:

(a) international equity issuance, including both publicly offered and privately placed American depository receipts (ADRs);

(b) direct equity portfolio inflows: direct purchases in emerging stock markets by foreign institutions and individuals other than closed-end mutual funds;

(c) flows through country-specific and multicountry closed-end mutual funds.

International equity issuance

A notable feature of the recent increase in equity portfolio investment in developing countries has been a large increase in international equity market placements by developing-economy companies. The vast majority of these placements have taken the form of ADRs. An ADR is essentially a claim, issued by a U.S. depository institution, to an underlying share of stock in a foreign-based company. In what is essentially a custodial arrangement, the U.S. depository institution backs the ADR by holding shares of the underlying stock on behalf of the owner of the ADR. In exchange for a fee, the depository institution provides the service of converting dividend receipts denominated in a foreign currency into dollars and distributing them to ADR holders. Owners of ADRs are entitled at any time to redeem their ADRs for shares of the underlying stock. A particular advantage of the ADR instrument is that settlement of trades between U.S. investors can be handled by the depository institution without recourse to the home equity market of the non-U.S. company that issued the equity. In this way, the ADR mechanism avoids the risks and transaction costs associated with settlement and clearance in foreign markets.

Developing-country companies can place ADRs in the United States by two means. The first is a public ADR offering. To offer an ADR publicly in the United States, the company must obtain a listing on a U.S. exchange—the NYSE, AMEX, or NASDAQ. In several recent cases, developing-country officials have modified domestic accounting and underwriting regulations to help domestic companies obtain listings on United States exchanges and to make public equity placements in the United States. In the case of the May 1991 public offering of ADRs by Telemex (the Mexican telephone company), the U.S. Securities and Exchange Commission worked closely with Mexican officials to facilitate the offering, granting several technical exemptions to S.E.C. underwriting rules.[13]

Private placements have been a second means of issuing developing-country ADRs in international markets. During 1990-92, private ADR placements by developing-country companies were four times as numerous as public offerings.[14] Private ADR placements by developing-country companies received stimulus from the June 1990 adoption of Rule 144A by the U.S. Securities and Exchange Commission. Rule 144A exempts qualified institutional buyers—institutions that own and invest on a discretionary basis at least $100 million in securities—from a rule that previously required them to hold privately placed securities for two years before trading them.[15] The adoption of Rule 144A increased the liquidity of privately placed developing-country ADRs and thus enhanced the attractiveness of these securities.

Before 1990, international equity placements by developing country companies were quite rare. In 1990, Compania de Telefonos de Chile became the first Latin American company to list ADRs on the NYSE. The successful $1.2 billion Telemex offering of May 1991, however, marked a watershed for developing countries. International equity placements by developing-country companies increased from an estimated $1.2 billion in 1990 to an estimated $9 billion in 1992. As a result, the share of total international equity issuance attributable to developing-economy companies increased from an estimated 15 percent in 1990 to an estimated 40 percent during 1992.[16]

A breakdown of international depository receipt issuance for seven emerging markets is given in Table 3.

[13]See Edward Greene, "Cross-Border Equity Offerings: A Discussion of Some of the Critical Issues," Cleary, Gottlieb, Steen & Hamilton Working Paper, 1991.

[14]Citibank ADR data indicate that during 1990-92, there were thirty-eight private ADR placements by developing-country companies and only eight public offerings.

[15]See SEC Release No. 33-6862: "Resale of Restricted Securities; Changes in Method of Determining Holding Period of Restricted Securities Under Rules 144 and 145."

[16]IMF staff estimates of international equity issuance. Totals include Singapore, Hong Kong, and Israel. These countries' equity markets are categorized as developed, not emerging, by the IFC.

Table 3
Equity Portfolio Inflows: 1990-92
Millions of U.S. Dollars

	1990	1991	1992	1990-92
Total equity portfolio inflows				
Brazil	100	600	1,800	2,500
Mexico	1,300	6,300	6,000	13,600
South Korea	500	300	2,100	2,900
Taiwan	100	200	500	800
Total for four	2,000	7,500	10,500	19,900
American depository receipt placements				
Argentina	0	400	400	700
Brazil	0	0	100	100
Chile	100	0	100	200
Mexico	0	3,000	3,300	6,300
South Korea	0	200	200	400
Taiwan	0	0	500	500
India	0	0	200	200
Direct equity portfolio inflows				
Brazil	100	600	1,600	2,300
Mexico	1,100	3,200	2,700	7,000
South Korea	0	0	1,800	1,800
Taiwan	100	200	100	300

Sources: Citibank ADR Department; Federal Reserve Bank of New York staff estimates; author's communications with Bolsa Mexicana de Valores, Central Bank of Brazil, Korean Stock Exchange, and Taiwan Stock Exchange Corporation.
Notes: Equity portfolio inflows can be decomposed into three parts: (1) international placements, including ADR placements; (2) direct equity portfolio inflows; and (3) inflows through closed-end country funds. Components may not add to totals because of rounding.

Mexico has clearly been the dominant issuer of ADRs among developing countries, having raised $6.3 billion in international offerings during the past two years. Issuance of Telemex ADRs accounted for $2.4 billion of this total. By 1992, Telemex ADRs had become the most actively traded issue on the NYSE in terms of dollar volume. The dollar volume of trading in Telemex ADRs on the NYSE exceeded $23 billion during the year, compared with less than $16 billion for the second most actively traded ADR, the British pharmaceutical company Glaxo Holdings.[17]

Direct equity portfolio inflows
Direct foreign purchases of equity shares have accelerated dramatically in three of the four countries for which data are available (Table 3). In Mexico, Brazil, and South Korea, rapid increases in direct foreign share purchases largely reflect the dismantling of capital-account restrictions and other impediments to direct foreign share purchases.

In Mexico, the government implemented reforms in 1989 that permitted foreigners to purchase Mexican equities directly on the Bolsa (Table 4). At the same time, the Nafinsa Trust was established to allow foreigners to purchase "A" shares formerly restricted to Mexican nationals.[18] In the three years following these

[17]Bank of New York, "Depository Receipts: 1992 Market Review."

[18]"A" shares have full economic and corporate rights but can be directly owned only by Mexicans. Foreigners can own these indirectly by holding certificates of ordinary participation issued by a Mexican trust. The certificates convey full economic rights but no

Table 4
Liberalization of Restrictions on Foreign Access to Developing-Country Equity Markets

Country	Country Fund Admitted	Restrictions on Direct Equity Portfolio Purchases Liberalized	Repatriation Restrictions Liberalized	Recent Tax Rate Changes
Argentina	October 1991	July 1989. Prior approval of foreign portfolio investments is no longer required.	October 1991. Required three-year holding period prior to repatriation of capital is eliminated.	October 1991. Capital gains tax of 36% is removed.
Brazil	September 1987	May 1991. Foreign institutional investors are allowed to buy stocks directly	1991. Required ninety-day holding period is eliminated.	1991. Dividend tax and capital gains tax are lowered from 25% to 15%.
Chile	October 1989	Foreign investment remains highly regulated because the government wishes to discourage short-term capital inflows.	January 1992. Required holding period is lowered from three years to one year.	Little change. Capital gains tax of 35% is maintained to discourage large inflows.
Mexico	June 1981	1989. Foreigners are permitted to buy shares directly on Bolsa.	—	1990. Dividend tax of 40% is removed.
Korea	November 1981	January 1992. Market is opened to direct foreign purchases, with foreign ownership of listed companies limited to 10%.	—	—
Taiwan	Ocober 1983	December 1990. Market is opened but foreign involvement is regulated extensively.	Repatriation restrictions remain.	—
Malaysia	May 1987	Relatively few restrictions on direct equity portfolio inflows exist.	Capital and earnings may be freely repatriated.	1990. Dividend tax of 35% is removed.
Thailand	August 1985	April 1975: The Thai exchange has been open to foreign investment since its inception. However, ceilings on foreign ownership in individual stocks (25%-49%) have limited foreign inflows.	April 1991. Exchange control deregulation allows for easier repatriation of capital and earnings.	1991. Capital gains tax of 25% is removed.
India	July 1986	September 1992. Draft guidelines propose an easing of restrictions on foreign equity portfolio investment.	—	1991. Capital gains and dividend tax rates are lowered.

Sources: *Euromoney Guide to World Equity Markets*, 1992; International Finance Corporation, *Emerging Stock Markets Factbook*, various issues; International Monetary Fund, *Exchange Arrangements and Restrictions*, various issues; various country sources.

measures, cumulative direct foreign share purchases have amounted to $7 billion.

Two years after Mexico's market opening, Brazil followed suit. Before May 1991, foreigners could only purchase Brazilian equity shares through closed-end funds or Brazilian investment companies. Resolutions implemented in May 1991, however, allowed foreign institutional investors to buy stocks directly. In addition, dividend and capital gains tax rates on foreign equity holdings were lowered from 25 percent to 15 percent, and a ninety-day minimum time period for the repatriation of investments by foreigners was abolished. These liberalization measures contributed to an increase of direct foreign share purchases from $103 million in 1990 to $1.6 billion in 1992.

Argentina has also taken several steps in recent years to stimulate direct foreign equity purchases (Table 4). In 1989, the government eliminated the requirement that foreign portfolio investments receive prior approval. Two years later, the government lowered the capital gains tax rate applicable to foreigners from 36 percent to zero and eliminated a requirement that investors observe a three-year holding period before repatriating capital. Unfortunately, however, it is not possible to gauge the effects of these recent liberalization measures on direct equity portfolio inflows into Argentina because data on these flows are not presently available.

Recent liberalization attempts across the Pacific have had mixed results. The January 1992 opening of the Korean Stock Exchange induced a large flow of direct foreign purchases, which increased from zero in 1991 to $1.8 billion in 1992. Recent liberalization measures in Taiwan, however, have been partial and therefore less effective in stimulating direct equity portfolio inflows. Although the stock market was officially opened to direct foreign purchases in December 1990, remaining restrictions on access and the repatriation of cash dividends and capital gains discouraged potential investors. Direct foreign share purchases accelerated in 1991 following Taiwan's market opening, but not to the extent that foreign purchases accelerated in Mexico, Brazil, or South Korea following those countries' market openings.

Whereas Korea and Taiwan have only recently made efforts to open their equity markets to direct foreign purchases, Thailand and Malaysia have maintained open equity markets since the mid-1980s. The relatively liberal policies of Thailand and Malaysia are reflected in

Footnote 18 continued
voting rights. Mexican "B" shares convey the same rights as "A" shares but can be owned by foreigners as well as Mexicans. "N" and "L" shares can also be owned by foreigners, but "N" shares convey no voting rights and "L" shares convey only very limited corporate rights.

data on foreign ownership presented in Table 5, which gives the percentages of equity owned by foreigners in three markets: Thailand, Malaysia, and Mexico. Whereas foreign ownership of Mexican stock did not come close to 20 percent until 1991, foreign ownership of stock in Thailand and Malaysia exceeded 20 percent at least several years earlier. These data indicate that the Thai and Malaysian markets have been fairly well integrated with the global financial system for some time.

The evidence given in Table 4 indicates that by 1992, most of the developing countries under consideration had taken steps to encourage direct equity portfolio inflows. Five countries—Mexico, Brazil, Taiwan, South Korea, and Argentina—have taken these steps quite recently, while two countries—Thailand and Malaysia—maintained relatively open markets throughout the latter half of the 1980s. In contrast, two countries—Chile and India—stand out as having taken few steps in recent years to dismantle restrictions that discourage direct equity portfolio inflows.

Equity portfolio inflows through closed-end funds
A large number of closed-end funds specializing in developing-country equity shares were established during the 1980s. The IFC promoted the establishment of these funds by advising developing countries on legal and regulatory frameworks and by underwriting and investing capital in these funds. Since 1984, when the IFC helped establish the Korea Fund, the IFC has assisted in bringing twenty-five funds to the international market.

During the mid-1980s, closed-end country funds were the primary and in some cases only available channel through which international portfolio investors purchased emerging market equity shares. Developing-country closed-end fund issuance peaked, however, in

Table 5
Foreign Equity Portfolio Ownership
Percent

	Thailand	Malaysia	Mexico
1985	20	—	—
1986	22	—	—
1987	27	28	—
1988	12	27	—
1989	12	27	4
1990	19	25	12
1991	17	22	19
1992	19	—	21

Sources: Stock Exchange of Thailand, the Kuala Lumpur Stock Exchange, and the Bolsa Mexicana de Valores.

1990 at $3.4 billion and then declined to $1.2 billion in 1991.[19] This decline stands in sharp contrast to the rapid rise of international placements and direct equity portfolio inflows during the same period. Apparently, the availability of these new means of acquiring developing-country equity shares dampened the demand for closed-end fund shares.

[19]IMF staff estimates.

Latin American reform and equity portfolio investment
The acceleration of equity portfolio inflows into Latin America derives only in part from innovations that have made it easier for foreigners to buy shares of the region's companies. The trend also owes much to the adoption of fundamental reforms in several of the region's economies. In 1987, following the lead of Chile, Mexico embarked on a stabilization program that has substantially reduced the government budget deficit

---

Box 1: United States Equity Portfolio Investment in Developing Countries

Treasury International Capital data indicate that United States net portfolio purchases of developing-country stocks reached record levels in recent years. According to Table CM-V-5 of the *Treasury Bulletin*, net equity portfolio inflows from the United States into nine of the most highly capitalized developing-country equity markets increased to a cumulative $8.5 billion during 1990-92 from a cumulative $791 million during 1987-89 (see table).

Most of this dramatic increase is attributable to an increase in U.S. net purchases of Mexican and Brazilian equity shares. During 1990-92, according to Treasury data, cumulative U.S. net purchases of Mexican stock amounted to $5.8 billion and cumulative U.S. net purchases of Brazilian stock amounted to $1.4 billion.

A comparison of the Treasury data with data provided by the central banks of Mexico and Brazil indicates that the U.S. share of total equity portfolio inflows into each of the two countries has been substantial in recent years. The $5.8 billion Treasury figure for U.S. net purchases of Mexican stock during 1990-92 equals 42 percent of the £13.6 billion in foreign net portfolio purchases of Mexican stock reported by the central bank of Mexico for the same period. In the case of Brazil, the $1.4 billion Treasury figure for U.S. stock purchases equals 56 percent of the $2.5 billion figure for foreign net portfolio purchases of Brazilian stock reported by the central bank of Brazil.

Net Portfolio Equity Inflows from the United States
Millions of U.S. Dollars

	Cumulative Inflows					
	1984-86	1987-89	1990-92	1990	1991	1992
Argentina	7	−40	73	−3	64	12
Brazil	9	515	1,415	22	326	1,067
Chile	8	92	116	97	−74	93
Mexico	37	38	5,761	918	2,078	2,765
India	2	0	2	−1	3	0
Korea	64	−1	435	−31	0	466
Thailand	18	161	331	41	89	201
Malaysia	12	79	348	138	−25	235
Taiwan	10	−53	46	−6	38	14
Total	167	791	8,515	1,175	2,499	4,841

U.S. Share of Total Portfolio Equity Inflows: 1990-92
Percent

Brazil	56
Mexico	42
South Korea	14
Taiwan	5

Sources: Treasury Bulletin, Table CM-V-5, various issues; country sources.

while stabilizing the exchange rate and reducing the domestic rate of inflation. The government also undertook an ambitious privatization program that contributed to increased equity portfolio inflows directly by expanding the supply of internationally marketable equity shares, such as Telemex, and indirectly by widening the scope of the private sector in Mexico. In addition, prospects for a North American Free Trade Agreement between the United States, Canada, and Mexico boosted confidence in the sustainability of economic growth in Mexico and thereby stimulated portfolio investment. The successful completion of a Brady Plan debt reduction agreement between the country and its commercial bank creditors in March 1990 also increased confidence.

The Argentine government followed suit, embarking on an ambitious program in 1990 to divest itself of long-held industries. The government balanced its fiscal accounts and, in April 1991, pegged the peso to the dollar in order to reduce domestic inflation. As in Mexico, the successful completion of a commercial bank debt-restructuring agreement under the Brady Plan has buoyed investor confidence in the country.

Although equity inflows in recent years have typically come on the heels of significant changes in government policy, this has not always been the case. Brazil experienced large equity portfolio inflows in 1992 despite continuing high inflation and fiscal incoherence. To a certain extent, these flows reflect the liberalization of Brazilian restrictions on direct equity portfolio inflows. However, the flows also reflect investors' belief, in early 1992, that the prospects were fairly good for an improvement in Brazil's situation. By early 1992, the country had restructured its Paris Club debt, signed a stand-by agreement with the International Monetary Fund, and appeared to be moving toward a Brady Plan agreement with its commercial bank creditors. During the first half of 1992, direct equity portfolio inflows into Brazil amounted to $1.4 billion. As prospects for financial improvement dimmed in the summer of 1992, however, inflows dropped to $344 million during the second half of 1992.

Equity market integration and rate of return correlations
Structural changes that have encouraged equity portfolio flows into emerging markets have helped integrate these markets with the global financial system. As this process has unfolded, developing-country equity markets have assumed many of the behavioral traits of their more developed counterparts. A key trait of developed-economy equity markets is that their returns tend to move together; that is, when returns are higher than average on the NYSE, returns tend to be higher than average on the London Stock Exchange.[20] Also noteworthy is that the return correlations of developed-country equity markets tend to increase during periods in which world equity markets are particularly volatile.[21] The analysis in this section shows that in recent years developing-economy equity markets have increasingly exhibited each of these two traits: developing-country stock returns have become more closely correlated with the returns of the world's developed stock markets, and developing-country return correlations have tended to peak during periods of high world return volatility.

The analysis in this section also suggests that monthly return correlations may understate the actual degree of interconnectedness between developing-country and developed-country equity markets. Annual return correlations indicate that developed and developing markets may be more closely tied than is commonly thought.

Evolution of monthly return correlations
In recent years, equity returns in those developing countries that have opened their markets to foreign portfolio investment have become more closely correlated with the returns of developed nations. In seven of the nine developing-country markets under consideration, monthly return correlations with the MSCI world index were greater during 1990-92 than during 1985-89 (Chart 4). Five of these seven countries (Argentina, Brazil, Mexico, Korea, and Taiwan) have taken substantial steps in recent years to remove impediments to equity portfolio inflows, while two of the seven (Malaysia and Thailand) have maintained relatively open equity markets since the mid-1980s. In fact, only in India and Chile—two countries that have continued to maintain relatively tight restrictions on foreign investment—were correlation coefficients lower during 1990-92 than during 1985-89.

Evidence of a somewhat longer term trend toward behavioral convergence is found in an examination of monthly return correlations during periods in which world equity markets have displayed large price swings, that is, during periods in which rates of return have been highly volatile. Among developed-country equity markets, return correlations tend to increase during these periods of high return volatility. Rate-of-return evidence indicates that during the latter 1980s, this pattern became more prevalent among developing-country markets as well. Chart 5 plots (a) the two-year rolling correlations between four emerging markets'

---
[20]See Bruno Solnik, *International Investments* (Addison-Wesley, 1988).

[21]See Paul Bennett and Jeanette Kelleher, "The International Transmission of Stock Price Disruption in October 1987," Federal Reserve Bank of New York *Quarterly Review*, Summer 1988, pp. 17-33.

monthly excess returns and the world monthly excess return and (b) the two-year rolling standard deviation of the world excess return.[22] The plots indicate that since 1986, world return volatility peaked twice. These two peaks are associated with the two largest post-1986 world stock market declines, the crash of October 1987 and the large decline of August 1990, the latter precipitated by large increases in international petroleum prices following Iraq's invasion of Kuwait. Similar declines hit seven of the nine emerging markets under consideration—Argentina, Brazil, Chile, Mexico, Thailand, Malaysia, and Taiwan—in October 1987 and August 1990. Consequently, the relationship between (a) correlation with world equity returns and (b) world return volatility was positive and statistically significant in each of these seven countries during the post-1986 period. The two countries in which the relationship was not statistically significant during the post-1986 period were Korea—whose equity market was not opened to direct foreign purchases until January 1992—and India—whose equity market remains closed to direct foreign purchases. In contrast, during the pre-1986

[22]An asset's excess return equals its return minus the return on a risk-free asset. As a practical matter, excess return correlations differ very little from return correlations during the period of analysis for the countries under examination. At each point in time, the twelve-month rolling correlation (standard deviation) equals the correlation (standard deviation) over the twelve-month period prior to and including the current month.

Chart 4
Changing Correlations between Developing-Country and World Monthly Returns

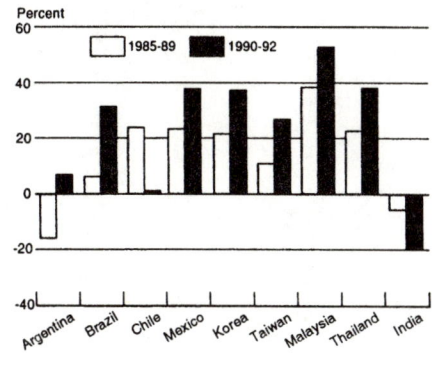

Source: International Finance Corporation, Emerging Markets Data Base.

Chart 5
Emerging-Market Return Correlations and World Return Volatility

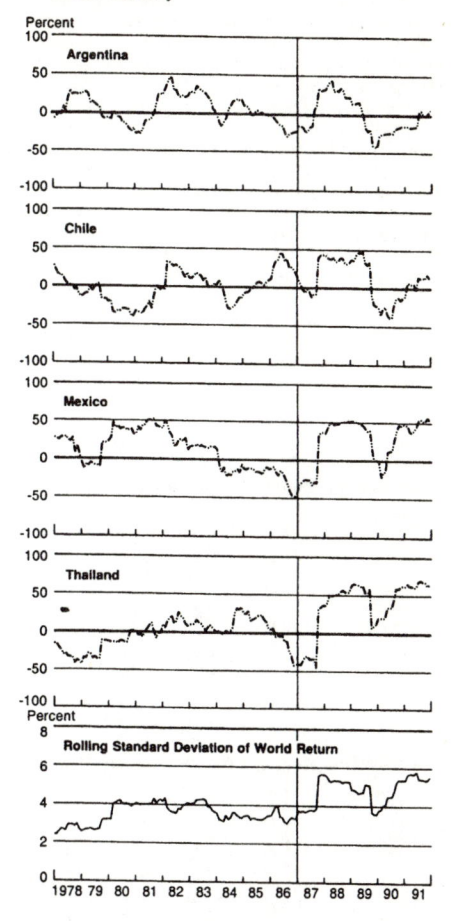

Sources: International Finance Corporation, Emerging Markets Data Base; Morgan Stanley Capital International.

Notes: Dashed lines represent rolling correlation between country returns and world returns. Line separating 1986 and 1987 represents a structural break.

period, the relationship was statistically significant in only two countries out of the group of nine: Mexico and Thailand.

Structural changes in developing countries have promoted recent changes in the behavior of monthly return correlations between developed and emerging markets. During the latter 1980s, when many impediments to foreign equity portfolio inflows were eliminated by developing-country governments, international investors were increasingly able to shift between developed- and developing-country equity shares. Emerging market equity returns consequently became more sensitive to the shifts in international investor sentiment that affected developed-country equity returns. Correlations between developing-country and developed-country monthly returns therefore increased, and events that sharply affected developed-country returns began to affect developing-country returns in a similar way.[23]

[23]Of course, it can be argued that capital market integration need not imply high correlations (see Vihang R. Errunza, "Emerging Markets: Some New Issues," *Journal of Portfolio Management*, forthcoming). On the NYSE, for example, a wide range of correlations are observed between pairs of stocks. Nevertheless,

A comparison of monthly and yearly correlations and covariances

An examination of return correlations based on annual data reveals that the emerging markets under consideration may be more integrated with the global financial system than is indicated by return correlations based on monthly data. A comparison of the top panel with the bottom panel of Table 6 reveals that the (six) coefficients of excess-return correlation between the MSCI world index, Japan, the United States, and Europe do not vary significantly when the statistics are computed using monthly instead of yearly excess-return data. In contrast, among the emerging markets, yearly and monthly excess-return correlations can differ significantly. For instance, the yearly coefficient of excess-return correlation between Argentina and the NYSE is 62 percent, whereas the monthly coefficient of excess-return correlation is only 4 percent. For the seven

Footnote 23 continued
the average correlation between pairs of common stocks on the integrated U.S. exchange is about 40 percent, which is much higher than most estimates of the average correlation between emerging market indexes and, say, the MSCI world index.

Table 6
Correlation Matrix of Yearly Excess Returns: 1976-91

	Argentina	Brazil	Chile	Mexico	India	Korea	Thailand	World	Japan	NYSE	Europe
Argentina	1.00										
Brazil	**0.33**	1.00									
Chile	**0.43**	-0.09	1.00								
Mexico	0.31	**0.36**	**0.44**	1.00							
India	0.20	**0.37**	0.17	0.07	1.00						
Korea	-0.01	0.09	0.27	0.18	0.17	1.00					
Thailand	-0.01	0.08	0.35	0.31	-0.23	**0.46**	1.00				
World	**0.22**	0.34	**0.41**	0.44	**0.35**	0.32	0.27	1.00			
Japan	-0.06	0.07	**0.33**	0.31	0.14	**0.64**	0.33	*0.78*	1.00		
NYSE	**0.62**	**0.46**	0.34	0.33	**0.33**	-0.14	0.08	*0.73*	*0.21*	1.00	
Europe	0.02	0.28	**0.36**	0.44	**0.56**	0.24	0.37	*0.78*	*0.52*	*0.49*	1.00

Correlation Matrix of Monthly Excess Returns: 1976-91

	Argentina	Brazil	Chile	Mexico	India	Korea	Thailand	World	Japan	NYSE	Europe
Argentina	1.00										
Brazil	-0.04	1.00									
Chile	**0.10**	0.00	1.00								
Mexico	0.13	-0.03	0.13	1.00							
India	0.14	-0.05	0.04	0.01	1.00						
Korea	-0.10	-0.00	0.05	0.11	0.02	1.00					
Thailand	-0.01	-0.01	0.11	0.26	0.05	**0.02**	1.00				
World	-0.03	0.10	**0.06**	0.25	**0.05**	0.26	0.23	1.00			
Japan	-0.04	0.06	**0.08**	0.11	0.02	**0.26**	0.17	*0.72*	1.00		
NYSE	**0.04**	**0.06**	0.04	0.29	**0.02**	0.20	0.14	*0.80*	*0.25*	1.00	
Europe	-0.03	0.11	**0.08**	0.21	**0.16**	0.19	0.28	*0.81*	*0.53*	*0.55*	1.00

Notes: Boldface type highlights those two-country couplets whose yearly return correlations exceed their monthly return correlations by at least 25 percentage points. Italicized type highlights those couplets composed exclusively of developed countries.

emerging markets included in the matrix, yearly excess-return correlations with the MSCI world index range between 22 percent and 44 percent. In contrast, the corresponding monthly excess-return correlations range between −3 percent and 26 percent.

The differences between these estimates of monthly correlations and yearly correlations point to the association of current returns in one market with past or future returns in another market. Significant impediments to capital mobility existed in most of the developing countries under consideration during the 1976-91 period. Restrictions on equity portfolio flows, including repatriation restrictions, undoubtedly dampened the monthly return correlations between these markets and the NYSE. In addition, poor liquidity in some of these markets made it difficult for investors to buy or sell stock quickly in response to changes in the economic environment. Many of these impediments to capital mobility were permeable over time, however, and investors were ultimately able to shift between foreign and domestic equity shares. Consequently, events that affected NYSE returns immediately tended to affect developing-country returns with a lag. This sort of lag structure tended to increase correlations between developing-country and developed-country returns at frequencies lower than one month.[24]

A statistical analysis of the difference between monthly and yearly return covariances provides additional evidence of the association between emerging markets' current returns and other countries' past or future returns (Box 2). This evidence implies that monthly return correlations have tended to understate the long-run interrelatedness of emerging markets and their more developed counterparts.

As impediments to capital mobility are increasingly reduced and emerging markets become more liquid, events that previously affected developing-country returns either before or after affecting developed-country returns will increasingly affect developing- and developed-country returns contemporaneously. This observation suggests that monthly return correlations between developed and developing countries may continue to rise in the future.

Convergence of stock market capitalization values
The same innovations that have promoted the integration of developing-country stock markets with the global financial system have encouraged a convergence of developing-country and developed-country ratios of stock market wealth to GDP. Market openings have tended to increase market capitalization, defined as the market value of outstanding equity shares listed on a country's stock exchanges, by increasing the demand for developing-country equity shares and thereby encouraging share price increases. Privatization programs and international equity placements have also contributed to the trend by increasing the supply of developing-country equity shares.

Emerging-market capitalization growth over the past decade has been striking. The combined capitalization of the largest nine emerging stock markets tracked by the IFC increased 761 percent between 1981 and 1991, from $64 billion to $551 billion (Table 7). Equity market capitalization in these nine markets grew twice as quickly during the period as equity market capitalization among the Group of Seven (G-7) countries, which increased 336 percent.

Market capitalization has also grown rapidly in relation to GDP in the emerging markets under examination. Between 1981 and 1991, the ratio of market capitalization to GDP more than doubled in all of the nine emerging markets except Brazil. Emerging equity markets were not unique in this respect, however; capitalization ratios also increased markedly in many of the G-7 economies, especially in the United Kingdom and Japan. Nevertheless, by 1991 capitalization ratios among the nine emerging markets had substantially converged towards those of their more developed counterparts. Malaysia's ratio (127 percent) exceeded those of all G-7 countries, while Chile's ratio (93 percent) was similar to the ratios of the United Kingdom (99 percent) and Japan (93 percent), and Taiwan's ratio equaled that of the United States (74 percent). By the end of 1991 within the group of developing and developed countries under examination, there appeared to be little correlation between market capitalization ratios and measures of economic development such as per capita income levels.

The historical rarity of such high capitalization ratios among developing countries is underlined by Goldsmith's 1985 data on two centuries of market capitalization ratios for the G-7 countries and for India and Mexico.[25] These data (Table 8) reveal that it is fairly unusual for countries' capitalization ratios to exceed 50 percent. The United States and the United Kingdom are notable exceptions because of the long-standing "thickness" of their securities markets in general and their equity markets in particular. In the bank-based economies of Germany, Italy, and Japan, however, capitalization ratios have historically hovered at levels below 50

---

[24]The existence of nonsynchronous trading is another potential explanation for the disparity between monthly and yearly correlations. Since developing-country stocks do not necessarily trade every day, monthly price data are not always based on end-of-month observations. This problem, which leads to underestimation of return correlations, becomes more modest as the frequency of observations becomes smaller.

[25]Raymond Goldsmith, *Comparative National Balance Sheets* (University of Chicago Press, 1985).

Box 2: Monthly and Yearly Correlations and Covariances

The linkages between one market's current returns and other markets' past and future returns are known as lead and lag effects. This box examines whether these lead and lag effects are more important among emerging markets than among three of the world's most highly developed and integrated markets: the NYSE, Japan, and the United Kingdom. Statistical theory holds that a comparison of monthly and yearly *covariances* provides more information relevant to this question than a comparison of monthly and yearly *correlations*. Yearly return covariances can be decomposed as follows:

$$cov(X_t, Y_t) = 12 \cdot cov(x_t, y_t) + \sum_{k=1}^{11}(12-k) \cdot cov(x_t, y_{t+k}) + \sum_{k=1}^{11}(12-k) \cdot cov(y_t, x_{t+k}),$$

where X_t and Y_t denote year-t returns in the respective markets and x_t and y_t denote month-t returns in the same markets.[†] This equation indicates that the covariance of yearly returns equals twelve times the covariance of monthly returns (the first term on the right-hand side) plus the sum of lead and lag effects (the second and third terms on the right hand side). Consequently, the yearly covariance exceeds twelve times the monthly covariance if and only if the sum of lead and lag effects is positive.

The following statistic, therefore, is a reasonable point estimate of the relative size of the sum of lead and lag effects between countries x and y:

$$\frac{\frac{1}{15}\sum_{t=1}^{16}(X_t - \bar{X})(Y_t - \bar{Y}) - \frac{12}{191}\sum_{t=1}^{192}(x_t - \bar{x})(y_t - \bar{y})}{\frac{1}{15}\sum_{t=1}^{16}(X_t - \bar{X})(Y_t - \bar{Y})}$$

The first term of the numerator is an estimate of the annual covariance (based on 16 annual observations spanning 1976-91), while the second term is twelve times an estimate of the monthly covariance (based on 192 monthly observations over the same period). The expected value of the statistic is zero under the null hypothesis that lead and lag effects sum to zero. Alternatively, the expected value of the statistic is positive under the hypothesis that the sum of lead and lag effects is positive.

On average, this statistic is much higher for two-country couplets involving emerging markets than for cou-

plets composed exclusively of the world's most developed equity markets. The mean of the statistic over forty-nine couplets that include emerging markets is 66.3 percent, with a standard error of 10.1 percent.[‡] The implied t-statistic of greater than 6 means that, for the group of emerging markets under consideration, the sum of lead and lag effects is significantly greater than zero for the 1976-91 period. In contrast, the mean of the statistic over the three couplets exclusively involving the NYSE, Japan, and the United Kingdom is 1.5 percent with a standard error of 8.5 percent, which implies that the mean for these three couplets is not significantly different from zero in a statistical sense. The difference between the emerging-market mean and the three-couplet mean is 64.8 percent, or more than thirteen times the standard error of the difference between the means. This result indicates that lead and lag effects play a larger role in emerging markets than in the most highly integrated of world equity markets.

These results also indicate that monthly return covariances tend to understate the substantial interrelatedness of developing-country and developed-country equity markets over the longer intervals that matter to many investors. The question then arises, Which measure of developing-country covariance risk is reflected in expected equity returns: a measure based on monthly time intervals or one based on yearly intervals?

Monthly and yearly correlations and the CAPM
According to the Capital Asset Pricing Model (CAPM), the ratio of the expected excess return of asset i to the expected excess return of the world portfolio should equal stock i's riskiness as measured by its "beta" with respect to the market portfolio. Stock i's beta is defined as:

$$\rho_{i,w}\frac{\sigma_i}{\sigma_w},$$

where rho denotes the correlation between asset i's excess return and the world excess return and sigma denotes standard deviation. The CAPM implies that asset i's expected excess return must reflect the risk associated with asset i's volatility or standard deviation. In addition, the model implies that assets that are more highly correlated with the world portfolio must offer higher expected returns. The reason is that assets that are highly correlated with the world index do not provide

[†] This relationship is derived under the assumption that returns equal log differences of total return indexes.

[‡] The 42 couplets include (7 x 6)/2 = 21 combinations involving emerging markets exclusively plus (7 x 4) couplets involving the emerging markets and Japan, Europe, the NYSE, and the MSCI world index. The (approximate) standard error of the mean of the statistic is obtained by dividing the standard deviation of the point estimate over the couplets by the square root of the number of couplets.

Box 2: Monthly and Yearly Correlations and Covariances *(Continued)*

the diversification benefits of assets that are relatively uncorrelated with the world index.

Implicitly, all tests of the CAPM are joint tests of the CAPM and the model used to estimate ex ante returns and betas. This section examines the simple case in which arithmetic-mean returns are used to proxy for expected returns while sample covariances and standard deviations are used to construct ex ante betas. This exercise, while fraught with problems, still helps to reveal which measure of risk is better reflected in developing-country equity returns: the beta constructed using yearly data or the beta constructed using monthly data.[9]

The data indicate that developing-country equity returns are more closely related to yearly measures of covariance risk than to monthly measures of risk. The right-hand panel of the chart plots ratios of mean country excess returns to mean world excess returns against betas calculated with annual data from 1976-91. As predicted by the CAPM, the data indicate that country excess returns bear a positive and statistically significant relationship to country betas based on annual data (see table). Whereas the CAPM, however, predicts that the slope will equal one (meaning that there will be a one-to-one relationship between betas and excess return ratios), the regression analysis indicates that the estimated slope coefficient is almost three standard deviations greater than one.

[9] A number of issues must be addressed when applying the CAPM to the international setting. A sufficient assumption is perfect correlation between the world market portfolio and world consumption. Alternatively, one can view the model as testing the mean-variance efficiency of the world market portfolio.

Equations for Capital Asset Pricing Model

Variable	Monthly Equation		Yearly Equation	
Constant term	6.3	(13.5)	-2.3	(2.1)
Beta	-7.0	(4.2)	5.2	(1.5)
Statistics				
n	32		7	
R^2	.09		.71	

Note: Standard errors are given in parentheses.

Capital Asset Pricing Model: Tests Using Monthly and Yearly Data

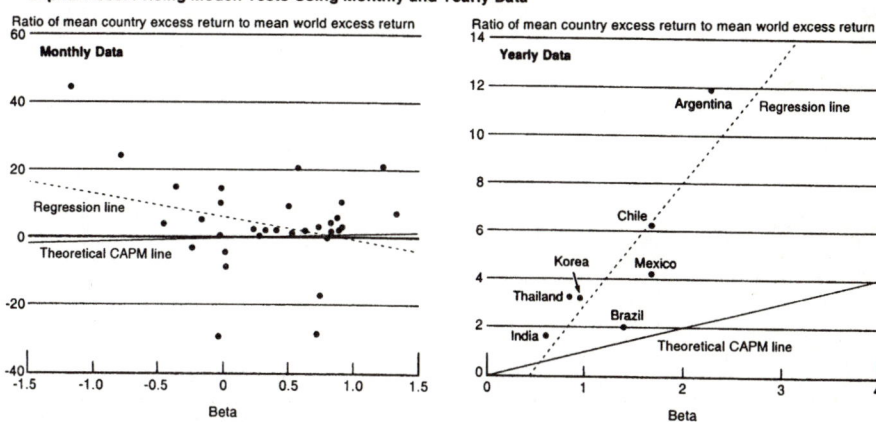

Sources: International Finance Corporation; Morgan Stanley Capital International.

Box 2: Monthly and Yearly Correlations and Covariances *(Continued)*

In contrast, betas calculated on a monthly basis are not positively correlated with relative equity returns. A test of the monthly CAPM was made using monthly excess-return data from a panel data set that was formed by breaking the experience of each country into four-year periods. The left-hand panel of the chart plots ratios of mean country excess returns to mean world excess returns against betas calculated using monthly data from the various four-year periods during 1976-91. The scatter plot reveals that we can reject with certainty the joint hypothesis that the monthly CAPM holds and that population moments (mean returns, standard deviations, and correlations) are reasonable proxies for ex ante moments.

Table 7
Total Market Capitalization: 1981-91

	1981 Billions of U.S. Dollars	1981 Percent of GDP	1986 Billions of U.S. Dollars	1986 Percent of GDP	1991 Billions of U.S. Dollars	1991 Percent of GDP
Canada	106	36	166	46	267	45
France	38	7	150	20	374	31
Germany	63	9	258	29	394	25
Italy	24	6	140	23	154	13
Japan	431	37	1,842	93	3,131	93
United Kingdom	181	35	440	78	1,003	99
United States	1,333	44	2,637	62	4,180	74
Group of Seven markets	2,176	33	5,632	60	9,503	65
All developed markets	2,502	—	6,367	—	10,760	—
Argentina	2	2	2	2	19	17
Brazil[1]	13	5	42	16	43	9
Chile	7	22	4	24	28	93
Mexico	10	4	6	5	98	40
India	7	4	14	6	48	16
Korea	4	6	14	13	96	37
Thailand	1	3	3	7	36	41
Malaysia	15	61	15	54	59	127
Taiwan	5	11	15	19	125	74
Nine emerging markets	64	6	115	12	551	32
All emerging markets tracked by International Finance Corporation	83	—	145	—	643	—

Sources: International Finance Corporation, *Emerging Stock Markets Factbook*, various issues; and International Monetary Fund, *International Financial Statistics*.
Note: Capitalization data refer to the market value of shares listed on domestic exchanges, including shares associated with international placements and those used to back American depository receipts.
[1] Sao Paulo only.

percent. This observation makes the 1991 capitalization ratios of Korea and Mexico appear all the more impressive. By 1991, capitalization ratios in these two bank-dominated economies had increased to levels surpassing the historical capitalization ratios of the more developed bank-dominated economy of Germany. Of course, the 1991 capitalization ratios of Malaysia, Chile, and Taiwan appear even more impressive when compared with the historical capitalization ratios of Germany, Italy, France, and Japan.

Another striking feature of Goldsmith's data—the large upward and downward swings of individual countries' capitalization ratios over time—suggests the possibility that some of these high capitalization ratios may be transitory. The United States' capitalization ratio increased quickly from 95 percent in 1913 to 193 percent in 1929, declined dramatically to 58 percent in 1950, and increased again to 124 percent in 1965, only to decline again to 57 percent in 1978. This sort of long-term volatility, which is common to almost all of the countries for which Goldsmith collected national balance-sheet data, implies that capitalization ratios do not tend to rise steadily or monotonically as economies develop over time. Capitalization ratios increase as stock markets boom and decline as they bust. Consequently, there does not appear to be a simple relationship between stages of economic development and capitalization ratios.

Even when viewed from a longer term perspective, however, the rapid growth of capitalization ratios among the emerging markets during the 1980s is quite impressive. For example, it may have taken as many as eighty-five years (1810-95) for the United States' capitalization ratio to rise from 7 percent to 71 percent (we cannot be absolutely sure, however, given the instability of the series). In contrast, the Taiwanese capitalization ratio rose from 11 percent to 74 percent in the ten years between 1981 and 1991. The data, therefore, suggest that the emerging stock markets of the present era have probably grown more rapidly than the stock markets of the G-7 countries during the nineteenth century.

Market capitalization remains highly concentrated
Market capitalization has been more highly concentrated in the emerging markets under study than in the highly developed markets of the United States and Japan. In Mexico, for example, shares of Telemex alone accounted for 17 percent of domestic capitalization at the end of 1991.[26] In Argentina, Telefonica de Argentina accounted for a similarly high 18.5 percent of total market capitalization. In contrast, Exxon—the most highly capitalized stock in the United States—accounted for only 2.6 percent of total market capitalization at the end of 1991.

An alternative measure of concentration reinforces the impression that emerging equity markets are often dominated by a relatively small group of highly capitalized shares. In 1991, the ten most highly capitalized stocks in Argentina together accounted for 68 percent of market capitalization, while the ten most highly capitalized stocks in Chile accounted for 50 percent of market capitalization. In contrast, the comparable figures for the United States and Japan were 15.7 percent and 16.7 percent, respectively.

In many emerging markets, however, capitalization has been less concentrated than in Germany's equity market, which is not as developed as those in the United States and Japan. The share of market capitalization attributable to the ten most highly capitalized German firms was 37.9 percent at the end of 1991, a figure that surpassed comparable concentration measures for India (23.4 percent), Brazil (27.0 percent), Korea (31.2 percent), Thailand (31.7 percent), Taiwan (35.9 percent), Malaysia (36.1 percent), and Mexico (36.5 percent).

According to one measure of equity market maturity—the ratio of capitalization to GDP—several developing-country markets appear to have converged with the world's mature markets. Nevertheless, an alternative measure, namely market concentration, indicates that these markets are less than fully developed.

Equity issuance and investment finance
With the maturation of emerging equity markets has come a greater reliance on those markets as a source of funds. Equity issuance has recently surged in the more mature developing countries, that is, those developing countries farthest along the path of industrializa-

[26] The data sources for this section are *Euromoney Guide to World Equity Markets* and International Finance Corporation, *Emerging Stock Markets Factbook.*

Table 8
Ratio of Market Capitalization to GDP: 1810-1978
Percent

	1810	1850	1875	1895	1913	1929	1939	1950	1965	1973	1978
Canada	—	—	—	—	—	—	—	**59**	46	36	41
France	0	12	38	—	**65**	23	—	25	**111**	**63**	39
Germany	—	6	17	26	37	29	17	13	31	27	24
Italy	—	11	7	11	6	3	2	19	**57**	28	10
Japan	—	—	4	32	41	**75**	**118**	24	46	29	39
United Kingdom	13	**72**	**74**	**156**	**121**	**154**	**182**	**110**	**83**	**65**	**76**
United States	7	23	**54**	**71**	**95**	**193**	**105**	**58**	**124**	**83**	**57**
India	—	1	2	3	5	9	14	12	14	15	12
Mexico	—	—	—	—	—	25	47	44	30	25	**53**

Source: Raymond Goldsmith, *Comparative National Balance Sheets* (University of Chicago Press, 1985).
Note: Capitalization ratios exceeding 50 percent appear in boldface.

tion. Equity issuance in several of the rapidly growing economies of East Asia has exceeded the post-World War II norm for G-7 economies and has been roughly in line with the high rates of equity issuance experienced by the United States during an earlier stage in its development process. These observations are consistent with the hypothesis that equity issuance as a source of finance tends to become increasingly important in the latter part of an economy's rapid-growth stage of economic development and subsequently becomes more modest.

Equity issuance in the United States earlier in the century largely reflected the transition from closely held private ownership to ownership through publicly traded equity shares. In recent years, this transition has found a developing-country parallel in a shift from government ownership of enterprises to private-sector ownership of joint-stock companies. Privatization has accelerated equity issuance in several developing countries and thereby primed the pump for additional equity issuance by private corporations seeking nondebt sources of finance.

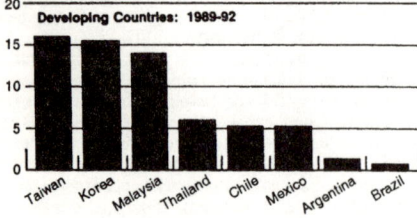

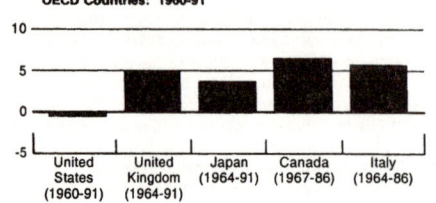

Since 1989, ratios of equity issuance to gross domestic fixed investment have been highest among those developing countries farthest along the path of industrialization. Equity issuance has been a particularly important form of investment finance in Taiwan and South Korea, developing countries that have moved beyond the manufacture of purely labor-intensive products, such as textiles, to higher value-added production. In these two countries, ratios of equity issuance to investment have recently exceeded 15 percent (Chart 6). In Malaysia and Thailand, countries that embarked on paths of rapid industrialization after Taiwan and Korea but have been growing rapidly for two decades now, issuance-to-investment ratios averaged 14 and 6 percent, respectively.

The ratio of equity issuance to investment has been smaller in the Latin American countries under consideration than in the Asian countries. Within Latin America, however, equity issuance has been highest in those countries where economic reform is most advanced. Issuance has been a steady, if not predominant, source of investment finance in Chile. Mexico's average issuance-investment ratio for the period masks the underlying fact that equity issuance in Mexico was very weak before 1990 but thereafter accelerated. Issuance of equity shares for cash, however, was relatively limited in Argentina and Brazil during 1989-1992.

The G-7 record of equity issuance during the past three decades also supports the hypothesis that equity issuance becomes increasingly important during rapid industrialization but then tapers off somewhat. In contrast to the recent experiences of the fast-growing economies of South Korea, Taiwan, and Malaysia, net equity issuance among the more mature G-7 economies has not been a quantitatively important source of investment finance. This conclusion is borne out by Chart 6, which presents ratios of net equity issuance to gross

Chart 6
Equity Issuance and Domestic Investment

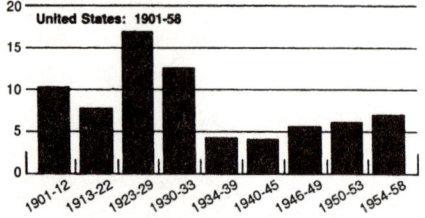

Sources: International Finance Corporation; Organization for Economic Cooperation and Development, *Financial Statistics*; Board of Governors of the Federal Reserve System, Flow of Funds Accounts; Raymond Goldsmith and Robert Lipsey, *Studies in the National Balance Sheet of the United States*, vol. 1 (Princeton University Press, 1963); U.S. Department of Commerce, *Historical Statistics of the U.S. Colonial Times to 1970* (1975).

Note: Grey-shaded bars represent developing countries.

domestic fixed investment for the United States, the United Kingdom, Japan, Canada, and Italy. Of these five developed economies, Canada has had the highest ratio of net equity issuance to gross domestic fixed investment over the past three decades. Aside from the United States, where net equity issuance has been very low relative to investment (and often negative), the ratio does not vary too widely over countries or across time: the ratio ranges from a United Kingdom low of 2.8 percent in the 1960s to a Canadian high of 7.2 percent in the 1980s.

The long-run U.S. record also fits well with the stage-of-development hypothesis. Although net equity issuance has been a relatively unimportant source of corporate finance in the United States during the past three decades, it played a much more important role in an earlier stage of the country's development, before World War II. Between 1901 and 1939, the proportion of gross domestic fixed investment financed by net equity issuance varied from 7 to 17 percent.

The stage-of-development hypothesis is also supported by a more detailed accounting of the recent experiences of several developing economies (Table 9). Although the four Asian economies under examination have grown rapidly over at least the past two decades, equity issuance has only recently begun to accelerate. During 1981-86, Malaysia had the highest issuance-investment ratio of the group at 3.9, a figure that is not unlike the G-7 norm of the past three decades. Equity issuance in these economies did not take off until the latter 1980s, at least two decades after these four economies had embarked on their rapid growth paths.

Stock market booms have frequently been the proximate cause of surges in equity issuance in both developed and developing countries. Increases in share prices lower the cost of equity financing for corporations and thereby provide strong incentives for firms to issue shares. In the United States, for example, equity issuance peaked at 17 percent of gross domestic fixed investment during 1923-29 as the NYSE rallied. In Korea and Taiwan, equity issuance peaked during 1989-90 as equity markets boomed and price-to-earnings multiples rose as high as 40 in Korea and 50 in Taiwan. Stock price movements have also played a role in Mexico's recent surge in equity issuance. Mexico's stock market opening in 1989, combined with policies to promote sustainable private sector growth, stimulated the demand for Mexican equity shares and thereby encouraged an increase in price-to-earnings multiples from 5 to 15 between 1988 and 1991.

Privatization has been a key factor underlying the recent surge in developing-country equity issuance. Malaysia's equity issuance peak of 1990, for example, coincided with the privatization of Syarikat Telekom Malaysia. In what constituted the largest flotation ever on the Kuala Lumpur Stock Exchange, more than $850 million in equity shares of Telekom were sold publicly in 1990. In Mexico also, the recent acceleration in equity issuance has been fed by privatization. Sales of Telemex shares by the Mexican government amounted to more than $3 billion between 1990 and 1992. More than two-thirds of these issues were made through international ADR sales.

Once initiated by surges in equity issuance, the process of capitalization growth in developing-country equity markets has the potential to become self-sustaining. Initial surges in equity issuance may well prime the pump for subsequent increases in equity issuance by increasing the potential investor base for domestic equity shares and thereby increasing market depth beyond a critical level. In the past, developing-country equity markets have tended to be thin markets, characterized by small numbers of traders; consequently, prices have been generally very sensitive to the impact

Table 9
Ratio of Equity Issuance to Gross Domestic Investment

	Taiwan	Korea	Malaysia	Thailand	Chile	Mexico	Argentina	Brazil
1966-75	—	—	2.5	—	—	—	—	—
1976-80	—	—	1.2	1.4	—	—	—	—
1981-86	1.9	2.0	3.9	1.3	—	—	—	—
1987	—	5.8	7.6	4.9	—	—	—	—
1988	—	20.9	4.2	2.7	—	—	—	—
1989	5.8	32.0	8.3	4.5	5.7	1.4	0.4	0.6
1990	51.7	4.8	23.1	6.1	4.6	0.6	1.9	0.6
1991	4.3	3.4	10.8	8.4	3.3	10.8	2.0	0.7
1992	2.4	1.9	13.9	4.9	7.6	8.6	—	1.0

Sources: International Finance Corporation staff estimates; International Monetary Fund, International Financial Statistics; country sources.

of individual traders' demand shifts. In deep markets, in contrast, transactors are so numerous that the uncorrelated demand shifts experienced by individual traders tend to offset each other and leave market prices unaffected. To the extent that shareholders are reluctant to participate in thin markets, thinness can lower the demand for shares and thereby inhibit equity issuance. In this way, thin equity markets can get caught in a cycle of low demand, low issuance, and lackluster capitalization growth.[27]

Government liberalization measures can potentially stimulate share demand and move an equity market from an equilibrium of thin trading and low issuance into an equilibrium of substantially higher trading and issuance. The recent experiences of several of the emerging equity markets under examination have conformed to this pattern. In particular, market openings and international equity offerings have increased the depth of trading in the shares of developing-country companies such as Telemex and appear to have thereby stimulated additional investor demand. But the international offering of Telemex ADRs had other important spillover effects. As international investors purchased Telemex ADRs, they accumulated information about the workings of the Mexican economy. Once these investors had made substantial investments in acquiring knowledge about the Mexican economy, they became more likely to invest in the equity shares of other Mexican firms. The dismantling of barriers to foreign investment and international offerings of blue-chip companies can thus pave the way for substantial increases in a market's investor base.

Turnover values and market breadth
Trading activity has increased substantially in developing-country equity markets over the past decade. The most prominent developing-country equity issues are now quite liquid and change hands as frequently as many developed-country issues listed on the NYSE or the London Stock Exchange. In an important sense, however, developing-country equity markets still lack the breadth of their more developed counterparts. High aggregate turnover values often reflect the high turnover values of a relatively small handful of issues. Outside this set of highly active issues, trading values decline greatly.

The value of turnover increased substantially in each of the nine emerging equity markets between 1981 and 1991 (Table 10). Trading exploded on Taiwan's exchange, increasing from $5.6 billion in 1981 to $365.2 billion in 1991. Trading values also increased by over 500 percent in Thailand, Korea, Mexico, and Argentina.

By 1991, the most active stocks in several of these markets appeared to be as liquid as the issues of a typical firm listed on the NYSE. The value of trading in Telebras, the Brazilian telephone company, was $3.4 billion during 1991 (Table 11). During the same year, on the Bombay Stock Exchange, turnover of the Associated Cement Company amounted to more than $3.2 billion. As a standard of comparison, the trading value of the average stock on the NYSE during the period was $334 million, or roughly 10 percent of the trading values of each of these two developing-country companies.

Listings on the NYSE have imparted increased liquidity to several developing-country stocks. Trading in Telemex shares, for example, amounted to $4.3 billion on the Mexican Bolsa in 1991. Meanwhile, the estimated value of trading in Telemex ADRs on the NYSE, where Telemex was the fourteenth most active issue during 1991, amounted to $8.4 billion. The ability of arbitragers to create and/or redeem Telemex ADRs in order to enforce price parity between Telemex ADRs on the NYSE and Telemex shares on the Bolsa implies that liquidity in one market translates into liquidity in the other. Consequently, a reasonable measure of Telemex's liquidity is the combined trading value in Telemex shares on the NYSE and the Bolsa. The combined trading value of $12.7 billion means that Telemex was one of the most liquid stocks in the world during 1991.

In an important respect, however, many of the devel-

[27]For an in-depth analysis of this argument, see Marco Pagano, "Endogenous Market Thinness and Stock Price Volatility," *Review of Economic Studies*, vol. 56 (1989), pp. 269-88.

Table 10
Value of Shares Traded
Millions of U.S. Dollars

	1981	1991	Percent Change
Argentina	454	4,824	963
Brazil	6,185	13,373	116
Chile	375	1,883	402
Mexico	4,181	31,723	659
India	6,693	24,295	263
Korea	3,721	85,464	2,197
Taiwan	5,677	365,232	6,334
Malaysia	3,498	10,657	205
Thailand	108	30,089	27,760
United States	415,760	2,254,983	442
Japan	223,835	995,939	345
Germany	13,670	818,603	5,888
Italy	10,850	43,307	299
United Kingdom	32,542	317,866	877
France	8,403	118,218	1,307

Notes: Value traded data refer to share turnover on domestic exchanges. Exchanges of American depository receipts on foreign markets are not included in the totals
Sources: International Finance Corporation, *Emerging Stock Markets Factbook*, various issues; *Euromoney Guide to World Equity Markets*, 1992

oping-economy stock markets lack breadth. In most emerging markets, trading values decrease substantially outside the small set of stocks with high trading values. A good measure of the breadth of a market's liquidity is obtained by taking the average trading value of stocks outside the ten most active. In Brazil, for example, the average value traded of stocks outside the top ten was $4 million, a very small fraction of the $3.4 billion figure for Telebras. India's markets also appear to have very little breadth by this measure: the average trading value of stocks less active than the top ten was only $2 million.

Of the Latin American markets under consideration, the Mexican Bolsa appears to have the greatest breadth. In Mexico, average turnover in 1991 for stocks outside the ten most active was $86 million, a figure that amounts to roughly 15 to 20 percent of the corresponding numbers for Japan ($427 million) and Germany ($593 million). By this measure, the Mexican stock market has much more breadth than the markets of Argentina, Brazil, and Chile, where average turnover values for stocks outside the ten most active did not exceed $7 million in 1991.

According to an alternative measure, however, the Mexican market has also lacked substantial breadth. Following the world stock market crash of October 1987, trading appears to have broken down for several of the market's most highly capitalized issues. Seven of the twenty-six stocks tracked by the IFC at the time did not trade at all on five or more trading days in November 1987, the month after the crash. In the months before the crash, most of these stocks had traded virtually every day. Apparently, the markets for these stocks were not deep enough to withstand the October 1987 shock, and liquidity consequently deteriorated.

But even during more placid times, many Mexican stocks do not trade for several days a month. During February-May 1992, for example, more than two hundred issues were listed on the Mexican Bolsa. Sixty-six of these issues were included in the IFC index for Mexico, largely on the basis of their liquidity and market capitalization. Of the sixty-six issues, thirty-three traded on fewer than 75 percent of the trading days during the period, while twenty-two traded on fewer than 50 percent of the trading days. That such a large proportion of issues trade infrequently on the Mexican Bolsa implies

Table 11
Average Value Traded: 1991
Millions of U.S. Dollars per Issue

	Among All Issues	Most Active Issue	Among Ten Most Active Issues	Among Other Issues
Argentina	28	729	373	7
Brazil	11	3,419	825	4
Chile	9	323	115	3
Mexico	152	4,309	1,462	86
India	4	3,210	1,160	2
Korea	125	—	—	—
Taiwan	1,653	—	—	—
Malaysia	33	—	—	—
Thailand	109	1,775	929	78
United States	334	38,790	16,925	310
Japan	473	20,655	10,058	427
Germany	1,227	92,449	42,922	593
Italy	124	—	—	—
United Kingdom	166	—	—	—
France	141	—	—	—

Average Share Turnover: 1991
Millions of Shares per Issue

	Among All Issues	Most Active Issue	Among Ten Most Active Issues	Among Other Issues
Korea	6	144	99	5
Taiwan	801	8,454	3,614	668
Malaysia	38	505	293	30
United States	15	553	429	14

Sources: International Finance Corporation, *Emerging Stock Markets Factbook*, 1992; *Euromoney Guide to World Equity Markets*, 1992; New York Stock Exchange; and Federal Reserve Bank of New York staff estimates.

that the market lacks breadth.[28]

In theory, market thinness is associated with increased volatility.[29] Return volatility, however, also depends importantly on the nature of information flows into a market. The historically volatile economic environments of many of the world's developing countries tend to produce the type of information flows that generate volatile asset returns.

The economics of return volatility

An important difference that remains between emerging markets and their more developed counterparts is that, in general, return volatility remains much higher among emerging markets. This section documents cross-country differences in return standard deviations and identifies factors that explain these cross-country differences. These factors include the volatility of macroeconomic fundamentals, the currency denomination of returns, and the degree to which trading within a market is concentrated among a small handful of issues.

Volatility: the stylized facts

Some, but not all, of the developing-country indexes under consideration have exhibited high levels of excess-return variance relative to the NYSE index and the MSCI world, Europe, and Japan indexes (Chart 7).[30] During 1976-91, the four Latin American countries and Taiwan registered the highest standard deviations among the markets examined, with Argentina heading the list as the most volatile market in the sample. Malaysia, India, and Thailand, in contrast, have exhibited low excess-return volatility relative to the other developing countries in the sample. Return standard deviations in these equity markets, in fact, were not much higher than the standard deviation of Japanese returns during the sixteen-year period.

Even in its earlier stages of development, the NYSE did not exhibit the degree of volatility that has been seen in the four Latin American markets and Taiwan over the past sixteen years. Chart 7 shows that the standard deviation of monthly returns on the NYSE has been remarkably steady over the past two hundred years. Between 1802 and 1831, the standard deviation

---

[28] The IFC has three main criteria for including stocks in its indexes: market capitalization, liquidity, and industry classification. In the case of Mexico, however, the IFC includes more than one class of stock for several companies. The fact that these classes are not chosen for inclusion on the basis of liquidity does not significantly modify the interpretation that only a relatively small group of shares trade continuously on the Mexican Bolsa.

[29] George Tauchen and Mark Pitts, "The Price Variability-Volume Relationship on Speculative Markets," *Econometrica*, vol. 51, no. 2 (March 1983), pp. 485-505.

[30] Unless otherwise noted, return standard deviations are dollar-denominated return standard deviations.

Chart 7
Standard Deviations of Monthly Returns

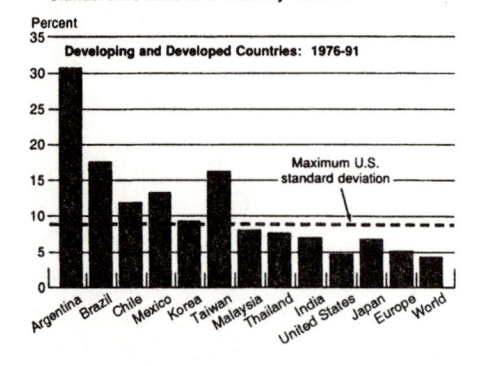

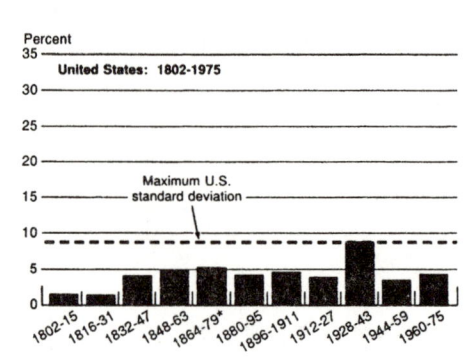

Sources: International Finance Corporation, Emerging Markets Data Base; Center for Research in Securities Prices; Morgan Stanley Capital International; William Schwert, "Indexes of United States Stock Prices, 1802-1987," *Journal of Business*, July 1990.

Note: Grey-shaded bars represent developing countries.

*During this period, standard deviation refers to rate of return calculated in British pounds.

was relatively low, hovering at roughly 1.5 percent. Volatility peaked during the 1928-43 period when the standard deviation of returns rose to 8.8 percent. Apart from these periods, however, standard deviations for the various periods under consideration remained within the narrow range of 3.5 percent to 5.3 percent.

Return volatility and macroeconomic fundamentals
That NYSE volatility exhibited no significant trend over the past two hundred years indicates that the high volatility exhibited between 1976 and 1991 by many of the emerging markets under examination cannot simply be attributed to their "stage of development." Consequently, the question arises, What causes some markets to display greater return volatility than others? Are returns more variable in countries in which economic fundamentals are more variable?

It appears that returns are more likely to be volatile in countries that pursue unstable monetary and exchange rate policies. The cross-country data, covering the period 1976-91, indicate that a statistically significant relationship exists between return volatility and the volatilities of inflation rates and real exchange rate changes (Chart 8). Equity returns were particularly volatile in the four Latin American countries under study: Argentina, Brazil, Chile, and Mexico. Rapid monetary expansion in these economies led to high and volatile rates of inflation. Furthermore, the region's governments—particularly those in Argentina and Mexico—often attempted to restore real exchange rate competitiveness by implementing large nominal exchange rate devaluations. This policy pattern, of course, bred substantial real exchange rate volatility. Frequent policy shifts generated considerable uncertainty regarding the future paths of domestic firms' input prices, output prices, sales, and therefore profitability. Since equity shares are claims on future corporate cash flows, volatile stock returns went hand-in-hand with volatile profit streams.

Additional evidence supports the notion that volatile stock returns are associated with volatile corporate profit streams. First, return volatility is closely tied to a direct measure of the volatility of corporate cash flows. Chart 8 plots the tight relationship between the standard deviation of equity returns and the standard deviation of dividend-per-share growth in U.S. dollars. Second, return volatility is correlated with the volatility of export growth, which in turn is linked to the volatility of corporate sales and therefore profits.

Return volatility: currency considerations
Another question is whether the high standard deviations of dollar-denominated returns among developing countries simply reflect the effects of converting local-currency returns into dollar returns through volatile nominal exchange rates. The answer appears to be negative. Of the seven developing economies listed in Table 12, only Mexico shows a standard deviation of dollar-denominated returns exceeding the standard deviation of local-currency returns by more than 3 percent. In Argentina and Brazil, in fact, dollar-denominated returns have had lower standard deviations than returns denominated in local currencies. In contrast, among countries belonging to the Organization for Economic Cooperation and Development, standard deviations of dollar-denominated returns have ranged between zero and 30 percent higher than standard deviations of local-currency denominated returns.

The difference between the variance of dollar-denominated and local-currency returns can be expressed as the difference between two covariances:

VAR (dollar rate of return) −

VAR (local-currency rate of return) =

COV (rate of exchange rate appreciation, dollar rate of return) −

COV (rate of exchange rate depreciation, local-currency rate of return).

The first covariance term on the right-hand side tends to exceed the second term when real shocks, as opposed to monetary shocks, are the predominant form of disturbance to an economy. Unanticipated government expenditure increases, tax cuts, and private investment booms typically cause the exchange rate to appreciate and increase dollar-denominated returns. In theory, these types of aggregate demand shock put upward pressure on interest rates, thereby inducing exchange rate appreciations. Simultaneously, these stimuli tend to increase corporate earnings, thereby increasing stock prices in both local-currency and dollar terms.[31]

By contrast, unanticipated monetary shocks tend to increase the covariance between the rate of exchange rate depreciation and local-currency returns. In theory, unanticipated monetary shocks would decrease interest rates and increase the local-currency prices of all assets, including equity shares and foreign exchange.

An implication of this analysis is that the variance of dollar returns will tend to exceed the variance of local-currency returns when real shocks predominate. Conversely, local-currency returns will be more volatile than dollar returns when monetary shocks predominate. The cross-country evidence given in the table accords well

---

[31] Local-currency returns will increase provided that the positive effect of the increase in local-currency earnings is not totally offset by the negative effect of the unanticipated increase in interest rates. Of course, dollar returns may still rise even if this condition is not met.

with this interpretation. In the cases of Argentina and Brazil, high-inflation countries where monetary shocks have presumably predominated, the second covariance term has exceeded the first, and the variance of dollar-denominated returns has been lower than the variance of returns denominated in local currency. In Italy—a high-inflation country by European standards—the two variances have been roughly equal, whereas in Ger-

Chart 8
Macroeconomic Determinants of Return Volatility

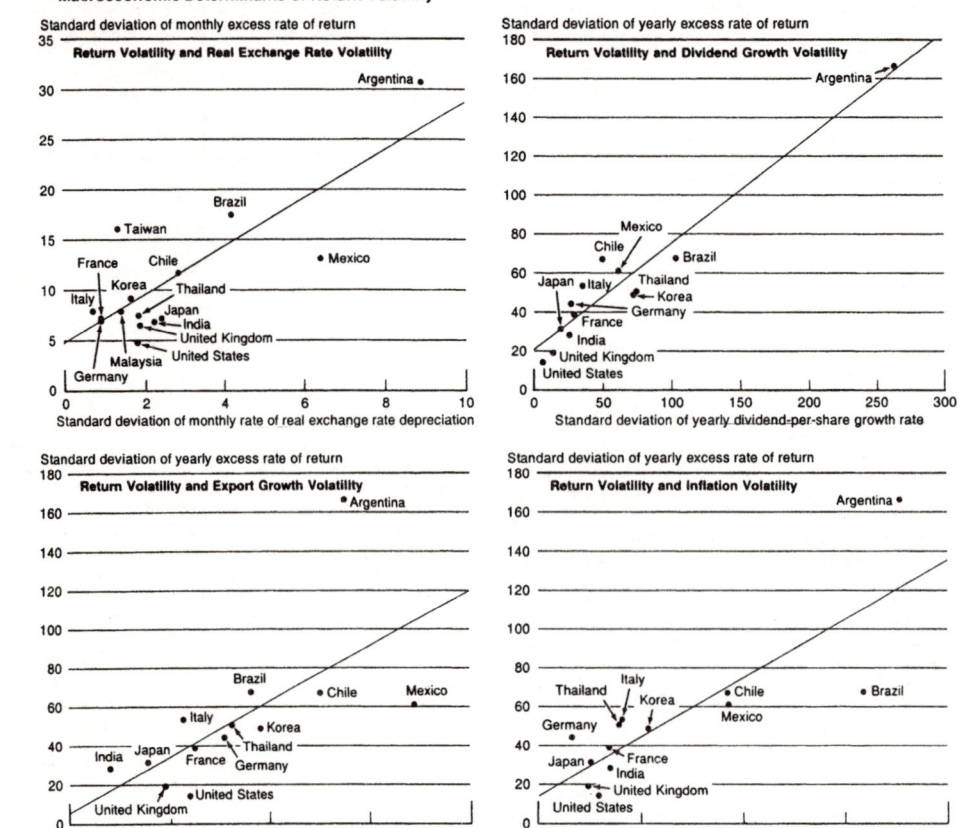

Sources: International Finance Corporation, Emerging Markets Data Base; Morgan Stanley Capital International; International Monetary Fund, International Financial Statistics; Morgan Guaranty; Bank for International Settlements.

Note: Solid line represents ordinary least squares equation.

many and Japan—two low-inflation countries—the variance of dollar-denominated returns has exceeded the variance of local-currency returns.

Additional evidence in favor of this interpretation is found in the U.S. record under the greenback standard during 1862-78. The British pound of this period should be regarded as a "hard" currency, somewhat like the modern-day dollar, and the greenback should be considered a "soft" currency, akin to many developing countries' local currencies. The Civil War period between 1862 and 1865 is of particular interest. During this period, the standard deviation of U.S. equity returns in terms of the British pound was 8.4 percent, much higher than the 5.5 percent standard deviation of returns in local currency terms.[32] Thus, during this period, the first of the two covariance terms (the term associated with real shocks) was greater than the second (the term associated with monetary shocks).[33] This finding makes sense when one considers that real shocks must have been predominant during the period. News of Union successes (failures) during the Civil War would have increased confidence (pessimism) in both business prospects and prospects of a return to the gold standard at the pre–Civil War parity. Consequently, war news would have strengthened the correlation between equity returns in British pounds and the rate of appreciation of the greenback.

This section's interpretation of the relationship between return volatility and macroeconomic volatility does not turn on the choice of unit of account or numeraire. Observe that the ordering of equity markets in terms of return volatility does not appear to depend greatly on the currency denomination of returns. One lesson to be drawn from this finding is that the positive relationship between real exchange rate volatility and dollar-denominated return volatility does not simply reflect the pass-through of nominal exchange rate movements. Instead, real exchange rate volatility implies risk for firms whose relative input and product prices, and thus rates of profit, ride the roller coaster of the real exchange rate.

Return volatility and concentration
In seeking an explanation for differences in emerging markets' return volatility, one should also consider the relationship between market concentration and volatility. It seems logical that returns would be more volatile in markets in which market capitalization and turnover are concentrated among a small subset of stocks. In a highly concentrated market, the market index is not very well diversified because it largely represents only a small handful of firms. Because less diversified portfolios tend to be more volatile, one would expect more concentrated markets to be more volatile. Evidence in favor of this hypothesis is presented in a scatter-diagram of return volatility and trading concentration, where trading concentration is defined as the share of turnover attributable to the ten most active stocks in a given market (Chart 9). The relationship is positive and statistically significant. To be sure, returns in Argentina and Brazil are more volatile than the estimated relationship between return volatility and trading concentration would predict. These discrepancies make sense, however, because Argentina and Brazil have experienced such great macroeconomic volatility. Return standard deviations in Taiwan and Japan are also greater than the fitted relationship between return volatility and concentration would predict These discrepancies can be explained by the speculative boom/crash cycles experienced by these countries during the period of analysis, 1985-91. Finally, it makes sense that low-inflation Germany has lower return volatility than market concentration alone would predict.

Table 12
Volatility of Dollar Returns Compared with Volatility of Local-Currency Returns

Country	Ratio of Standard Deviation of Returns in U.S. Dollars to Standard Deviation of Returns in Local Currency
Argentina	0.71
Brazil	0.76
Chile	1.03
Mexico	1.07
India	0.99
Korea	1.02
Thailand	1.02
Canada	1.12
France	1.17
Germany	1.16
Italy	1.00
Japan	1.30
United Kingdom	1.15

Sources: For the developing countries, data cover 1976-91 and are taken from the International Finance Corporation, Emerging Markets Data Base; for the developed countries, statistics cover 1980-88 and are taken from Sumner Levine, ed., *Global Investing* (Harper Business, 1992), p. 30.

---

[32] Data on greenback-gold exchange rates comes from Wesley C. Mitchell, *Gold, Prices, and Wages under the Greenback Standard* (University Press, 1908), pp. 288-338.

[33] Recall that the first covariance term should be interpreted as the covariance between (a) the rate of appreciation of the greenback relative to the British pound and (b) stock returns in terms of the British pound; and the second covariance term should be interpreted as the covariance between (a) the rate of depreciation of greenbacks relative to the British pound and (b) stock returns in terms of greenbacks.

Implications for international investors

The vast changes that have taken place in emerging markets over the past decade have important implications for international investors. Developing-country stocks, though volatile, are commonly thought to offer striking diversification benefits because of their impressive historical returns and the low monthly correlations between their returns and developed-country equity returns.[34] The diversification argument, however, is subject to two qualifications. The first concerns the use of historical monthly return correlations as indicators of correlation risk, a practice that tends to understate this risk. The second concerns the use of average historical returns as indicators of ex ante returns. This procedure is particularly suspect when applied to emerging markets because many of these markets have undergone important structural changes in recent years.

The diversification benefits of emerging market shares are likely to diminish as developing countries become more closely integrated with the global economy and correlations between the equity returns of developing and developed countries increase. While the strategy of portfolio diversification through the purchase of emerging market stocks may continue to offer substantial ex ante benefits, these benefits will tend to be more modest than indicated by analyses that employ historical monthly return correlations, which—as we have seen—are likely to underpredict future monthly return correlations.

Monthly return correlations also tend to understate the substantial interconnectedness of emerging and developed markets at the longer intervals that are relevant to many investors. As documented in an earlier section, correlations between emerging and developed markets tend to increase at intervals longer than one month.

Inferences based on average historical returns can also be problematic. While historical return correlations are likely to underpredict future return correlations, historical return averages are likely to overpredict future return averages. The returns of several of the developing countries under study have been quite extraordinary in recent years. Earlier sections of this article showed that these returns have exceeded levels that can be explained by covariance risk and ex post macroeconomic performance; instead, the returns appear to reflect profound changes in economic structure that will probably not be repeated.

Historical returns are typically a poor guide for predicting future developing-country equity returns. The IFC total return index for Argentina, for instance, increased at an annualized rate of 100 percent during 1976-79, declined by more than 25 percent per year during 1980-83, and increased by more than 90 percent per year during 1988-91. Returns were unstable during the period because the country underwent several significant regime changes. In fact, most of the countries under consideration experienced significant upheavals during the period. Latin American economies generally boomed in the late 1970s, contracted with the onset of the debt crisis during the early 1980s, and prospered again in the early 1990s with the implementation of economic reforms. Taiwan and South Korea each experienced speculative stock market booms during 1986-89 only to see the bottom fall out.

In general, it is difficult to form estimates of expected returns based on historical data, and the common practice of using average historical returns to construct expectations of future returns has serious pitfalls. The following example illustrates one of these potential pit-

Chart 9
Trading Concentration and Volatility

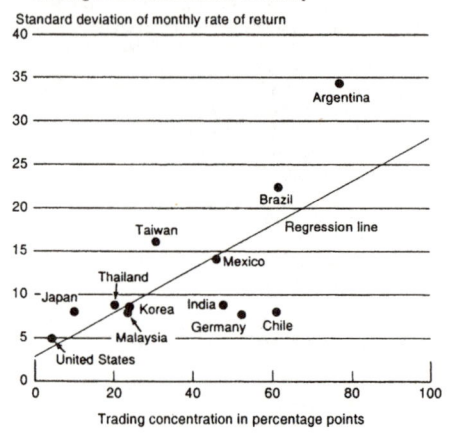

Standard deviation of monthly rate of return

[Scatter plot showing countries plotted by trading concentration (x-axis, 0-100 percentage points) versus standard deviation of monthly rate of return (y-axis, 0-40). Points include: United States, Japan, Germany, Malaysia, Thailand, Korea, India, Chile, Taiwan, Mexico, Brazil, Argentina, with a regression line.]

Trading concentration in percentage points

Sources: International Finance Corporation, Emerging Markets Data Base; *Euromoney 1992 Guide to Equity Markets*.

Notes: Concentration ratio is the share of turnover attributable to the ten most active stocks in 1991. Standard deviations are calculated over 1985-91.

---

[34] A number of studies have been published in recent years that purport to demonstrate the potential investor gains from diversification into emerging equity markets. Three of the more recent examples include: Arjun Divecha, Jaime Drach, and Dan Stefek, "Emerging Markets: A Quantitative Perspective;" Jarrod Wilcox, "Taming Frontier Markets;" and Lawrence Speidell and Ross Sappenfield, "Global Diversification in a Shrinking World." All three articles appeared in the *Journal of Portfolio Management*, Fall 1992.

falls. Divecha and his coauthors make the sensible argument that investing in emerging markets can reduce risk.[35] Using data spanning the five-year period from April 1986 to March 1991, they calculate the sample means and variances of portfolios composed partly of a mix of stocks representing the MSCI world index and partly of a mix of stocks representing the IFC composite emerging market index. Chart 10 shows their results. The portfolio composed entirely of the MSCI stocks had an average monthly return of 0.5 percent and a standard deviation of 5 percent. A portfolio that was 80 percent invested in the MSCI stocks and 20 percent invested in the IFC stocks had an average return of 0.6 percent and a somewhat lower standard deviation.

When the time frame of analysis is expanded to the seven-and-a-half year period from January 1985 to July 1992, the return-variance locus moves dramatically. Suppose that an investor is prepared to use sample means, standard deviations, and correlations as proxies for ex ante values. The investor's calculation of the increased expected return of taking on an additional unit of risk would be greatly affected by the choice of sample period. The trade-off becomes much more favorable when data from the shorter period are used. Consequently, the investor's ultimate portfolio allocation may depend significantly on the time frame of analysis.

At first glance, the investor's decision to allocate at least 20 percent of wealth to emerging-market stocks does not appear to be very sensitive to the choice of time period. When data from either time span are used, emerging market stocks account for roughly 20 percent of the derived minimum-variance portfolio. This 20 percent share, however, is not consistent with a capital market equilibrium in which investors hold emerging-market equities in proportion to their current 5 to 6 percent weight in world capitalization. The most likely path to such an equilibrium involves increases in share prices and consequent declines in future expected returns as international demand for emerging market stocks increases. The problem for investors, of course, is to determine the extent to which recent equity portfolio inflows into emerging markets have already increased share prices and lowered expected future returns.

Conclusion: Emerging equity markets and economic development

Economic reforms in developing countries—including equity market openings, international equity offerings, and policies to stabilize prices and exchange rates—have encouraged large increases in foreign purchases of emerging-market equity shares in recent years. Privatization programs have played a particularly important role in this process, a fact that was underscored by the Argentine government's recent international offering of shares in the Argentine oil company YPF, which raised roughly $3 billion. Together, economic reforms and equity portfolio inflows have helped integrate developing-country equity markets with the global financial system. Price linkages between emerging and developed markets have tightened, and as emerging markets have matured, they have come to resemble more closely their developed-country counterparts.

These findings raise the question of the possible contribution of equity markets to economic development. In recent years, a number of economists have argued that equity-based financial systems have put the Anglo-Saxon countries at a competitive disadvantage relative to the bank-dominated systems of Japan and Germany.[36] In particular, they have argued that equity-

[35]Divecha, Drach, and Stefek, "Emerging Markets: A Quantitative Perspective."

[36]See, for example, Ajit Singh, "The Stock-Market and Economic Development: Should Developing Countries Encourage Stock-Markets?" United Nations Conference on Trade and Development, Discussion Paper no. 49, October 1992.

Chart 10
Gains from Diversification

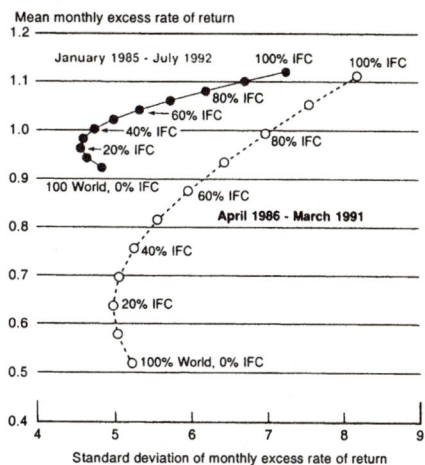

Mean monthly excess rate of return

Sources: International Finance Corporation, Emerging Markets Data Base; Morgan Stanley Capital International.

based systems tend to discourage long-term investment by producing short-term relationships between firms and their debt and equity holders. Some support for this view may be found in Japan, where investment decisions by firms with close ties to large banks are less sensitive to liquidity constraints than investment decisions by firms with weaker ties to large banks and a presumably greater reliance on credit markets.[37]

This line of argument, however, does not necessarily support the conclusion that developing countries should refrain from promoting equity market development. First, recourse to equity financing does not necessarily preclude equity stakeholders, including financial groups, from taking active and long-term roles in corporate management. Second, if promoting equity markets tends to loosen ties between commercial enterprises and banks, then some advantages may result. Although close relationships between commercial firms and banks may lessen the effects of liquidity constraints on firms' investment decisions, close ties can also increase the degree to which control over industrial activity is concentrated among a relatively small group of agents. And while close ties to a financial group may lessen an individual industrial concern's chances of going bankrupt, this advantage may come at the cost of reducing the economy-wide mobility of productive resources.

Equity markets may emerge as an important alternative to debt-based external finance for developing countries. To be sure, reliance on external financing through either equity portfolio inflows or debt inflows can expose countries to the risk of capital flight or speculative capital outflows. Nevertheless, the substitution of equity portfolio finance for debt finance reduces firms' vulnerability to earnings declines and interest rate increases. Unlike debt-service streams, which are contractually tied to interest rates, common stock dividends can be adjusted with some discretion. At the macroeconomic level, equity finance can help developing countries avoid the excessive reliance on debt accumulation that rendered many of them vulnerable to the interest rate increases of the early 1980s.

This article has shown that equity markets offer developing countries a potentially important source of investment finance. One lesson that the emerging economies of eastern Europe can draw from this experience is that even relative newcomers to the game can raise large amounts of cash through equity issuance, as China did during 1992 when it placed $654 million in shares with international investors.[38] A valuable source of funding awaits those countries that choose to develop their equity markets and encourage equity portfolio investment.

---

[37]See Takeo Hoshi, Anil Kashyap, and David Scharfstein, "Corporate Structure, Liquidity, and Investment: Evidence from Japanese Industrial Groups," *Quarterly Journal of Economics*, vol. 106, no. 1 (February 1991), pp. 33-60.

[38]Zhi Dong Kan, "Issues of B Shares in Shanghai and the Function of Domestic Securities Companies," *Shanghai Securities Market*, Swiss Bank Corporation, February 1993.

Journal of International Financial Markets,
Institutions and Money 7 (1997) 221–234

Do emerging and developed stock markets behave alike? Evidence from six pacific basin stock markets

Gregory Koutmos

School of Business, Fairfield University, Fairfield, CT 06430-7524, USA

Abstract

This paper investigates the short-term dynamics of stock returns in six emerging capital markets in the Pacific Basin area. The evidence shows that despite institutional differences, regulations and restrictions, short-term stock returns in these markets behave remarkably similar to those of major stock markets. More specifically, all stock price indices have a unit root in their univariate representation, the conditional and unconditional distributions of the returns are leptokurtic volatility, clustering is an all pervasive phenomenon, market declines are followed by greater volatility than market advances of an equal magnitude, and finally, first- and second-order autocorrelations are inversely related to volatility. © 1997 Elsevier Science B.V.

Keywords: Emerging markets; assymetric volatility; autocorrelation

JEL classification: C15

---

1. Introduction

Emerging capital markets have experienced a dramatic growth in recent years. International investors have increased their total investment from 500 million US dollars in 1984 to 25 billion in 1991 (see Park and Agtmael, 1993). Pension fund sponsors and mutual fund managers find it increasingly difficult to ignore the investment potential in these markets. In 1990, there were 22 emerging country funds listed in the New York Stock Exchange, whereas the Directory of Emerging Market Funds listed some 400 funds in 1991. According to Harvey (1955), the total capitalization of the emerging stock markets is US$13.6bn. This represents approximately 8% of the Morgan Stanley Capital International (MSCI) world capitalization.

A parallel development has been the substantial growth in American Depository Receipt programs (ADRs). Country funds and ADRs have made it easier for investors to take advantage of investment opportunities in emerging capital markets. These investment opportunities have generally been attributed to diversification benefits and growth potential. Emerging markets are less correlated with major equity markets thus offering the potential for significant risk reduction.[1] In addition, it is believed that emerging economies will experience rates of growth greater that the industrialized economies which, in turn, will be reflected in the value of their equities.

A substantial and growing body of literature is investigating the benefits of investing in emerging equity markets in terms of improving risk-return tradeoffs, e.g. Wilcox (1992), Divecha et al. (1992), Hauser et al. (1994), Errunza (1994) and Mullin (1993).[2] The diversification benefits from investing in the stock markets of the Pacific Basin are examined by Solnic (1991), Bailey and Stulz (1990) and Defusco et al. (1996). The evidence supports the case for diversifying in the Pacific Basin markets due to their low correlation with the developed markets as well as their growth potential. Bailey and Stulz caution, however, that the use of daily data may understate the true correlations.

These studies provide valuable information regarding the risk diversification potential from investing in emerging markets. However, there are very few studies dealing with the dynamics of stock returns in emerging markets and the extent to which these dynamics are similar to those of major stock markets. For example, Bailey et al. (1990) find that returns in the stock markets of the Pacific Basin depart substantially from the random walk hypothesis since the estimated first-order autocorrelations are much higher than those observed in developed markets. They also report that autocorrelations are very unstable over time and in some instances they turn negative. Ng et al. (1991) and Lee and Ohk (1991) use ARCH-type models to capture the time-varying volatility of stock returns in Pacific Basin capital markets.

This paper contributes to the ongoing investigation into the dynamic behavior of stock returns in emerging markets. Specifically, it examines the possibility that stock returns in Pacific Basin capital markets exhibit certain common characteristics that are usually found in developed stock markets. Such a possibility is very real given the substantial portfolio flows into these markets.[3] A large body of literature has established several stylized facts for stock prices in major markets. First, stock prices are not stationary, i.e. they have a unit root in their univariate representation, see, for example, Kasa (1992) and Koutmos et al. (1994) among others. Second, the empirical distributions appear to be excessively leptokurtic when compared with the normal distribution [e.g. Mandelbrot, 1963; Fama, 1965; Nelson, 1991; Booth et al., 1992 (among others)]. Third, short-term stock returns exhibit volatility clustering. Mandelbrot (1963) noted that "large changes tend to be followed by large changes, of either sign, and small changes tend to be followed by small changes". This type of behavior has been modeled very successfully with ARCH-type models (e.g. Engle, 1982; Bollerslev et al., 1994). Fourth, changes in stock prices tend to be negatively

---

[1] In the period 1985–1990, the correlation of MSCI EAFE index (a composite index for 20 established equity markets) with the IFC index (a composite index for 21 emerging equity markets) was 0.27 (see Park and Agtmael, 1993).

[2] Solnic (1988) provides a comprehensive summary on the literature on international diversification in general.

[3] Mullin (1993) finds that as emerging equity markets have opened to foreign investors, their returns have become more closely correlated with the returns of developed markets.

related to changes in volatility (e.g. Black, 1976; Christie, 1982) or, equivalently, negative returns are followed by greater volatility than positive returns of an equal magnitude. Finally, the first-order autocorrelation of index stock returns is negatively related to the level of volatility (e.g. LeBaron, 1992; Campbell et al., 1993; Sentana and Wadhwani, 1992).

The objective of this paper is to investigate whether the aforementioned stylized facts for the developed markets are also present in the Pacific Basin stock markets. Consequently, this paper can be viewed as an extension of the work of Bailey et al. (1990), Ng et al. (1991) and Lee and Ohk (1991). It differs, however, in several important ways. First, it uses more recent daily data from the post-crash period of 1987. Second, it models and tests for asymmetries in the time-varying volatility process. Third, it investigates potential linkages between volatility and autocorrelation. Fourth, it uses a more general probability density function to deal with the leptokurtic nature of the data. Finally, it assesses the robustness of the empirical findings using the set of diagnostics proposed by Engle and Ng (1993).

Daily returns are modeled as conditionally heteroscedastic processes with time-varying autocorrelations. The conditional means are assumed to follow an exponential autoregressive process of order k, EAR(k), whereas the conditional standard deviations are assumed to follow a threshold GARCH model of orders p and q, TGARCH(p, q). To allow for thicker tails, the generalized error distribution (GED) density function is used, which nests the normal as well as several other density functions. An array of diagnostics show that the EAR(k)-TGARCH(p, q) model captures the short-term dynamics of stock returns in the emerging markets under investigation remarkably well.

The remainder of this paper is organized as follows: Section 2 presents the data and some preliminary statistics. Section 3 introduces the EAR-TGARCH model which extends the studies of LeBaron (1992) and Zakoian (1994). Section 4 presents and discusses the major empirical findings, and Section 5 concludes this paper.

2. Data and preliminary statistics

The data set consists of daily figures for the stock price indexes of six Pacific Basin equity markets, namely those of Korea, Malaysia, the Philippines, Singapore, Taiwan and Thailand.[4] As of December 1991, these six markets comprised 44% of total emerging market capitalization and 3.3% of total world capitalization.[5] The time period under investigation extends from 12/17/87 to 9/13/91 for a total of 977 observations. The names of the particular indexes used along with information related to currency denomination, market capitalization, number of listings, trading value, turnover ratio, etc. are given in Table 1. The stock market of Taiwan has the highest capitalization and the highest trading value. The Korean market has the

---

[4] An excellent reference on the institutional characteristics (i.e. taxation, regulations, market mechanisms, etc.) of these markets is Park and Agtmael (1993).
[5] See IFC, Emerging Markets Fact Book (IFC, 1991).

Table 1
Emerging market indices

	Korea	Malaysia	Philippines	Singapore	Taiwan	Thailand
Index	SLINDX	KLINDX	MNINDX0	SISTRIX	TPINDX	BKINDX
Currency	Won	Ringgit	Peso	Dollar	Dollar	Baht
Market capitalization[a]	96.4	58.6	10.2	49.6	124.9	35.8
(% of GDP)	37.7	121.4	22.7	123.5	82.6	38.9
Number of listings	686	321	161	172	221	276
Trading value[b]	312.1	27.1	3.4	52.9	701.1	102.5
Turnover ratio	82.3	20.2	18.8	NA	330.1	102.2
P:E ratio	21.3	21.3	11.3	NA	22.3	12
% Dividend yield	1.6	2.4	0.8	NA	0.9	1.9
Correlation with S&P 500 (12/89–12/94)	0.20	0.39	0.36	NA	0.14	0.38

[a] Billions of US dollars.
[b] Average daily trading values in millions of US dollars. All figures are from IFC Emerging Stock Markets Factbook, and IMF International Financial Statistics, as of 1991 unless otherwise indicated.

largest number of companies listed, whereas, the market capitalization:GDP ratio is over 120% for Malaysia and Singapore. The average capitalization:GDP ratio for the six emerging markets is approximately 71%. For the same year, this ratio stood at 74% for the US stock market and at 65% for the group of seven developed markets.[6] The turnover ratio can be used to assess the liquidity of a market. By this measure, Taiwan is the most liquid and the Philippines is the least liquid. The earnings multiples are approximately in line with those of most developed markets. For example, the P:E ratio for the US has been on average 15 × over the period 1954 to 1993. Dividend yields, on the other hand, are substantially lower than those prevailing in the US. The case for diversification depends crucially on the correlations across markets. For the more recent period (12/1989–12/1994), the estimated coefficients are rather small in size, ranging from 0.38 (Thailand) to 0.39 (Malaysia).

Table 2 reports unit root test statistics calculated for the logarithm of the stock prices and several preliminary statistics calculated for the first logarithmic difference. The unit root tests are based on the Phillips–Perron procedure (Phillips and Perron, 1988).[7] The calculated Phillips–Perron (PP) statistics fail to reject the hypothesis that the logarithms of the stock price index of all six markets have a unit root in their univariate representation.[8] Consequently, further investigation of the short-term dynamics of these markets requires first differencing. Preliminary statistics

---

[6] The group of seven (G7) includes Canada, France, Germany, Italy, Japan, the United Kingdom and the United States.

[7] The Phillips–Perron procedure requires estimation of the regression $y_t = \mu + \beta(t - T/2) + \alpha y_{t-1} + u_t$, where y_t is the log of the stock price index, t is the time trend and T is the number of observations. The error term u_t could be a stationary ARMA process with time-dependent variance. The null hypothesis to be tested is that $\alpha = 1$ against the stationary alternative.

[8] The Phillips–Perron statistic was calculated using truncation lags of size 5, 10 and 20. Since there was no difference in the results only those based on the truncation lag of size 5 are reported.

Table 2
Emerging market indices and broad statistics

Statistic	Korea	Malaysia	Philippines	Singapore	Taiwan	Thailand
PP	−2.6564	−1.9349	−1.8712	−2.2179	−1.9264	−1.6285
μ	0.0337	0.0795	0.0259	0.0574	0.0610	0.0971
σ	1.6235	1.3856	1.8745	1.1471	3.0022	1.7162
S	0.5704*	0.1042*	−0.1490*	−1.1263*	−0.0845*	−0.3550*
K	8.7812*	21.2132*	2.9790*	13.0148*	1.1877*	6.1384*
D	0.0446*	0.0837*	0.1569*	0.1076*	0.0867*	0.1039*
$LB^a(10)$	22.2898*	40.2577*	61.1896*	33.7845*	28.9180*	32.6864*
$LB^b(10)$	67.8710*	226.4219*	87.8771*	72.7072*	280.0194*	340.0774*
$LB^c(10)$	135.4466*	239.3039*	149.4774*	231.0512*	331.4771*	455.3520*

*Denotes significance at the 5% level. PP is the Phillips–Perron statistic for unit root. The critical value at the 5% level is −3.41. μ and σ are the sample mean and standard deviation. S and K are measures for skewness and excess kurtosis. D is the Kolmogorov–Smirnov statistic, testing for normality; the 5% critical value is $1.36/\sqrt{T}$, where T is the number of observations. LB^a, LB^b and LB^c are the Ljung–Box statistics testing for autocorrelations in the returns, the squared returns and the absolute returns up to the 10th lag. The time period extends from 12/17/87 to 9/13/91 for a total of 977 observations.

on the logarithmic first differences, or percentage returns calculated as $R_t = 100(\log P_t - \log P_{t-1})$ are also reported in Table 2. These statistics include the mean and the standard deviation, measures for skewness and kurtosis, the Kolmogorov–Smirnov D-statistic and the Ljung–Box statistic for ten lags.[9] The daily means are statistically insignificant and the standard deviations range from 1.1471 for Singapore to 3.0022 for Taiwan. There is evidence of significant negative skewness for the markets of the Philippines, Singapore, Taiwan and Thailand, and evidence of significant positive skewness for the markets of Korea and Malaysia.[10] The positive skewness is due to some extreme positive returns that these two markets realized. Korea for example, had a 73% rate of return in 1988. Similarly, Malaysia had returns of 37% in 1988 and 58% in 1989. Excess kurtosis is statistically significant across all markets. Normality is also rejected on the basis of the Kolmogorov–Smirnov D-statistic. The rejection of normality provides the rationale for using a more general density function in the subsequent analysis.

The presence of intertemporal dependencies in the returns and some nonlinear transformations (i.e. squared and absolute returns) are tested by means of the Ljung and Box portmanteau test (LB) (e.g. Bollerslev et al., 1994). The LB statistic tests the hypothesis that autocorrelations up to the nth lag are jointly statistically insignificant. The calculated LB statistics for ten lags are significant for all return series, providing evidence of intertemporal dependencies in the first moment of the distribution of returns. This may be due to problems usually associated with the use of

---

[9] The Kolmogorov–Smirnov statistic is calculated as $D_n = \max|F_n(R) - F_0(R)|$ where F_n is the empirical cumulative distribution of R_t and $F_0(R)$ is the postulated theoretical distribution. The Ljung–Box statistic for N lags is calculated as $LB(N) = T(T+2)\Sigma_{j=1}^{N}(\rho_j^2/T-j)$ where ρ_j is the sample autocorrelation for j lags and T is the sample size.
[10] For uniformity, the 5% level of significance is used in all instances.

index returns (i.e. nonsynchronous trading of the stocks that make up the index) or it may be the manifestation of some form of market inefficiency. Evidence on higher-order intertemporal dependencies is provided by the *LB* statistic calculated for the squared and the absolute returns. As can be seen, the *LB* for the squared and the absolute returns is several times higher than that of the returns themselves. The implication is that higher-moment dependencies are much more pronounced. It should be noted that these dependencies are compatible with the volatility clustering phenomenon that has been documented for several developed stock markets. What is not clear from these statistics is: (1) whether there is asymmetry in the volatility process; and (2) whether volatility and autocorrelation are inversely related. The next section outlines the EAR–TGARCH model used to answer these questions.

3. The EAR(k)–TGARCH(p, q) model

Let R_t be the stock return at time t, I_{t-1} the information set at time $t-1$, $\mu_t = E(R_t|I_{t-1})$ the conditional mean, ϵ_t the innovation at time t [i.e. ($\epsilon_t = R_t - \mu_t$), $\sigma_t^2 = E(\epsilon_t^2|I_{t-1})$] the conditional variance, v a scale parameter or degrees of freedom, and $f(.)$ the conditional density function of R_t. The EAR(k)–TGARCH(p, q) model can then be represented by the following set of equations:

$$R_t|I_{t-1} \sim f(\mu_t, \sigma_t^2, v), \tag{1}$$

$$\mu_t = \beta_0 + \Sigma_l \phi_{l,t} R_{t-l} \text{ for } l=1, 2\cdots k, \tag{2}$$

$$\phi_{l,t} = \phi_{l,0} + \phi_{l,1} \exp(-\sigma_{t-l+1}^2/\sigma^2) \text{ for } l=1, 2\cdots k, \tag{3}$$

$$\sigma_t = \alpha_0 + \Sigma_i (\alpha_i^+ \epsilon_{t-i}^+ - \alpha_i^- \epsilon_{t-i}^-) + \Sigma_j \gamma_j \sigma_{t-j} \text{ for } i=1, 2\cdots p \text{ and } j=1, 2\cdots q. \tag{4}$$

The conditional density is given in Eq. (1) with time-varying mean μ_t and variance σ_t^2. The conditional mean in Eq. (2) follows an exponential autoregressive process of order k and is a generalized version of the equation of LeBaron (1992).[11] The autoregressive parameters $\phi_{l,t}$ in Eq. (3) consist of a constant and a time-varying term. The latter is an exponential function of past conditional variances scaled by the unconditional variance.[12] Inspection of Eq. (3) reveals that during high-volatility periods, the time-varying autocorrelation parameters approach $\phi_{l,0}$, whereas during low-volatility periods, they approach $\phi_{l,0} + \phi_{l,1}$ for $l=1, 2\cdots k$.

Eq. (4) models the conditional standard deviation rather than the conditional variance which is mostly the case with ARCH-type models. This specification allows the conditional standard deviation to respond asymmetrically to past positive and

---

[11] LeBaron (1992) allows only one lag for the exponential autoregressive parameter. However, for several Pacific Basin stock returns, Bailey et al. (1990) find persistence beyond the first lag. Consequently, a higher lag specification in the time-varying autocorrelation parameter is necessary.

[12] Estimation of the unconditional variance independent of the parameters describing the conditional variance is not possible. Consequently, in the estimation of the model, σ^2 is set equal to the sample variance.

negative innovations defined as $\epsilon_{t-1}^+ = \text{Max}(0, \epsilon_{t-1})$ and $\epsilon_{t-1}^- = \text{Min}(\epsilon_{t-1}, 0)$. This is the threshold GARCH model (TGARCH) introduced by Zakoian (1994). The advantage of the TGARCH is that the conditional variance is assured to be positive. However, the probabilistic properties of σ_t are rather complicated. As such, it is desirable to impose non-negativity constraints on Eq. (4), i.e. $\alpha_0 > 0$, $\alpha_i^+ \geq 0$, $\alpha_i^- \geq 0$ and $\gamma_j \geq 0$ for $i = 1, 2 \cdots p$ and $j = 1, 2 \cdots q$. The exponential GARCH (EGARCH), proposed by Nelson (1991) and the TGARCH process share an important feature, namely they allow the conditional variance to respond asymmetrically to positive and negative innovations. There are, however, some important differences. In the former, the conditional variance is a function of standardized innovations. As such, it does not provide any linear representation of some function of ϵ_t. In the latter, the vector $(\epsilon_t^+, \epsilon_t^-)$ can be shown to follow an ARMA process just as in the GARCH model the $\{\epsilon\}$ sequence follows an ARMA process (see Zakoian, 1994). If $\alpha_1^+ = \alpha_1^- = \alpha_1$ then Eq. (4) reduces to

$$\sigma_t = a_0 + a_1 |\epsilon_{t-1}| + \beta \sigma_{t-1}, \tag{5}$$

which is the model used by Taylor (1986) and Schwert (1989). The TGARCH specification is ideally suited to test for asymmetries in the conditional variance of the distribution of stock returns. For the US, the Japanese and the British stock markets, there has been evidence of asymmetries in the conditional variance [e.g. Nelson, 1991; Koutmos and Booth, 1995; Poon and Taylor, 1992 (among others)].

Most studies dealing with index stock returns use the normal density function. Almost invariably, however, the standardized residuals obtained from ARCH-type models that assume normality appear to be leptokurtic so that parameter estimates are not asymptotically efficient. To deal with this problem, many authors use density functions with thicker tails, such as Student's t-test (e.g. Bollerslev, 1987; Baillie and Bollerslev, 1989; Akgiray and Booth, 1991) and the generalized error distribution (GED) (e.g. Nelson, 1991; Booth et al., 1992). The advantage of using more general density functions is that parameter estimates are not excessively influenced by extreme observations occurring with low probability (e.g. market crashes). In this paper, we employ the generalized error distribution. Its density function is given by:

$$f(\mu_t, \sigma_t, v) = v/2[\Gamma(3/v)]^{1/2}[\Gamma(1/v)]^{-3/2}(1/\sigma_t) \exp\{-[\Gamma(3/v)/\Gamma(1/v)]^{v/2}|\epsilon_t/\sigma_t|^v\}, \tag{6}$$

where $\Gamma(.)$ is the gamma function and v is a scale parameter or degrees of freedom to be estimated endogenously. For $v = 2$, the GED yields the normal distribution, while for $v = 1$, it yields the Laplace or double exponential distribution.

Given initial values for ϵ_t, and σ_t^2, the parameter vector can be estimated by maximizing the log-likelihood over the sample period, which can be expressed as:

$$L(\Theta|k, p, q) = \Sigma_{t=1}^T \log f(\mu_t, \sigma_t^2, v), \tag{7}$$

where Θ, μ_t, σ_t^2 and v are the conditional mean, the conditional variance and the scale parameter, or degrees of freedom, respectively. Since the log-likelihood function is highly nonlinear in the parameters, numerical maximization techniques are used to obtain estimates of the parameter vector. The method of estimation used in this paper is based on the algorithm of Berndt et al. (1974).

4. Major empirical findings

The maximum likelihood estimates of the EAR(k)–TGARCH(p, q) are reported in Table 3. The dimensions of k, p and q are decided on the basis of likelihood ratio tests. Such tests are appropriate because lower-order EAR(k)–TGARCH(p, q) models are nested within higher-order models. In all instances, the dimension of q is unity. This is consistent with the literature on conditional heteroscedasticity of stock returns, e.g. Bollerslev et al. (1992). The dimension of k is unity for the markets of Malaysia, Singapore and Thailand and two for the markets of Korea, the Philippines and Taiwan. The dimension of p is unity with the exception of Korea and Taiwan, where the optimal order of p is two.

The constant component of the first-order autocorrelation, $\phi_{1,0}$, is insignificant across all six markets, whereas the time-varying component, measured by $\phi_{1,1}$, is statistically significant for the markets of Malaysia Singapore and Thailand. In these three markets it can be said that high volatility is associated with low first-order autocorrelation and vice versa. The constant and the time-varying components of the second-order autocorrelations, measured by $\phi_{2,0}$ and $\phi_{2,1}$, respectively, are statistically significant for the remaining three markets of Korea, the Philippines and Taiwan. For these three markets, it is the second-order autocorrelation that is inversely related to volatility. It is not clear why these three markets differ in their first-moment dynamics. The difference may be related to the trading process itself. A longer time period may be required before definite conclusions can be drawn for these markets. Overall, the findings are in general agreement with those of LeBaron (1992) and Sentana and Wadhwani (1992) for the US stock market and Booth and Koutmos (1996, submitted for publication) for the stock markets of Canada, France, Germany, Italy, Japan and the United Kingdom. None of these studies, however, have found evidence of higher-order time-varying autocorrelations. Table 3 reports the extreme values (i.e. minima and maxima) as well as the averages of the first- and second-order autocorrelations based on the estimated time-varying autocorrelation functions given in Eq. (3). Minimum values for first-order autocorrelations range from -0.05 (for Malaysia) to 0.07 (for the Philippines), whereas maximum values range from 0.10 (for Korea) to 0.39 (for Singapore). Similarly, second-order autocorrelations exhibit wide variability. Consequently, autocorrelations are quite unstable over time. They are low during volatile periods and high during calm periods.

In all markets, with no exception, volatility depends on their past history as well as past innovations (errors). High past innovations of either sign are associated with high volatility, the well-documented phenomenon of volatility clustering. An examination of the coefficients describing the volatility process reveals that in all markets the latter is an asymmetric function of past innovations. The nature of the asymmetry is such that negative innovations increase volatility more than positive ones. As

Table 3
Maximum likelihood estimates of the EAR(k)–TGARCH(p, q) model

Coefficient	Korea	Malaysia	Philippines	Singapore	Taiwan	Thailand
β_0	−0.0181	0.0604	−0.0256	0.0338	0.0259	0.0864
	(0.021)	(0.017)	(0.038)	(0.0121)	(0.074)	(0.028)
$\phi_{1,0}$	−0.0146	−0.0242	0.0761	−0.0114	0.0834	−0.0542
	(0.018)	(0.045)	(0.051)	(0.048)	(0.067)	(0.050)
$\phi_{1,1}$	0.1172	0.2559	0.2113	0.4392	0.0561	0.3792
	(0.075)	(0.106)*	(0.133)	(0.080)*	(0.129)	(0.107)*
$\phi_{2,0}$	−0.1357	–	−0.1997	–	−0.1437	–
	(0.038)*	–	(0.056)*	–	(0.056)*	–
$\phi_{2,1}$	0.4003	–	0.4487	–	0.4995	–
	(0.098)*	–	(0.158)*	–	(0.074)*	–
α_0	0.4297	0.2910	0.3936	0.1788	0.1789	0.1426
	(0.102)*	(0.054)*	(0.110)*	(0.051)*	(0.043)*	(0.026)*
α_1^+	0.1488	0.1967	0.1667	0.1419	0.0559	0.1726
	(0.057)*	(0.057)*	(0.061)*	(0.048)*	(0.041)*	(0.044)*
α_1^-	0.1669	0.3333	0.2084	0.2880	0.1224	0.3019
	(0.059)*	(0.070)*	(0.072)*	(0.058)*	(0.058)*	(0.052)*
α_2^+	0.0612	–	–	–	0.1295	–
	(0.065)	–	–	–	(0.048)*	–
α_2^-	0.1921	–	–	–	0.0558	–
	(0.093)*	–	–	–	(0.067)	–
γ_1	0.5396	0.5807	0.6184	0.6733	0.8411	0.7407
	(0.087)*	(0.066)*	(0.094)*	(0.071)*	(0.031)*	(0.035)*
v	0.7827	0.8100	0.9928	0.9921	1.4704	0.9597
	(0.035)*	(0.037)*	(0.056)*	(0.035)*	(0.085)*	(0.046)*

Range of Autocorrelations

Market	$\phi_{1,t}$			$\phi_{2,t}$		
	Minimum	Maximum	Average	Minimum	Maximum	Average
Korea	−0.0145	0.1018	0.0353	−0.1354	0.2586	0.0347
Malaysia	−0.0242	0.2095	0.1043	–	–	–
Philippines	0.0770	0.2851	0.1635	−0.1981	0.2439	0.0138
Singapore	−0.0113	0.3952	0.2018	–	–	–
Taiwan	0.0849	0.1398	0.1082	−0.1355	0.3537	0.0723
Thailand	−0.0542	0.3136	0.1370	–	–	–

*Denotes significance at the 5% level. Numbers in parentheses are the standard errors for the estimates. See also Table 2 footnotes.

mentioned earlier, this asymmetric behavior of the conditional second moment has been attributed to the leverage effect, whereby stock price declines (negative innovations) automatically increase the debt:equity ratio and therefore the risk.[13] An intuitive measure of the degree of asymmetry can be constructed by taking the ratio

---
[13] Black (1976) notes that operating leverage could have the same effect on volatility.

$\alpha_i^- : \alpha_i^+$. Focusing on the first lag, this ratio ranges from 1.12 (for Korea) to 2.19 (for Taiwan). The average degree of asymmetry across the six emerging markets is 1.67, meaning that, on average, a negative innovation will increase volatility 1.67 times more than a positive one of the same magnitude. Most studies dealing with developed markets, especially the three major markets, find that both positive and negative innovations increase volatility even though negative innovations exert a greater impact, e.g. Nelson (1991), Engle and Ng (1993) and Koutmos and Booth (1995).[14] Conventional t-tests reject the hypothesis that the conditional standard deviation is symmetric (i.e. $\alpha_1^- = \alpha_1^+$) with the exception of the Korean market. Even in this market, however, asymmetry is present in the second lag of past innovations. The other market where the second lag is significant is the Taiwanese market.

Overall, the evidence supports that notion that the daily distributions of stock returns in these six emerging markets exhibit similar behavior with those of the developed stock markets with regard to first-moment (mean) and second-moment (variance) dependencies. Some explanation for these similarities can be found in the increased amount of shares from emerging markets held by international investors. As argued by Mullin (1993), greater foreign investment has probably increased the price linkages between emerging and developed markets. A similar argument can be based on Bekaert and Harvey (1997) who find that stock returns in emerging markets are increasingly influenced by world factors rather than local factors.

The estimated degrees of freedom parameter v is well below two, the value required for normality, and very close to unity. This suggests that the empirical distributions of the returns are, in all cases, close to the double exponential or Laplace distribution. In fact, conventional t-tests reject the hypothesis that $v = 2$ for all six markets at the conventional level. This confirms the earlier assertion that departures from normality observed in the raw return series cannot be entirely attributed to temporal first- and second-moment dependencies.

In any empirical investigation, the validity of the results depends on the correct specification of the model. For ARCH-type models correct specification requires that the standardized residuals: (1) follow the assumed distribution with the estimated scale parameter, or degrees of freedom; (2) have zero mean and unit variance; and (3) they are linearly and nonlinearly independent. The appropriateness of the density function used is tested on the basis of the Kolmogorov–Smirnov D-statistic, where the null hypothesis now is that the estimated standardized residuals from each market follow the generalized error distribution (GED) with the estimated degrees of freedom v. As can be seen from Table 4, the estimated D-statistics are below their critical value in all instances such that the assumed density function is not rejected. The means and variances of the standardized residuals fulfill the requirement of zero mean and unit variance. Linear and nonlinear independence is tested again by means of the Ljung–Box statistic. The calculated LB values show that the standardized residuals, $\epsilon_t/\sigma t$, are uncorrelated up to 10 lags.

The squared standardized residuals and the absolute standardized residuals follow

---

[14] Glosten et al. (1993) find strict asymmetry in monthly US stock returns in the sense that negative (positive) innovations increase (decrease) volatility.

Table 4
Residual based diagnostics

Market	$E(\epsilon_t/\sigma_t)$	$E[(\epsilon_t/\sigma_t)_2]$	$LB^a(10)$	$LB^b(10)$	$LB^c(10)$	D
Korea	0.0325	1.0863	16.6193	14.0130	13.8523	0.0352
Malaysia	0.0068	1.0713	18.2309	6.6848	11.3179	0.0349
Philippines	0.0201	1.0056	12.3531	1.7890	5.5135	0.0334
Singapore	−0.0072	1.0585	13.9212	0.1601	7.5417	0.0298
Taiwan	0.0166	0.9973	14.9214	9.3273	8.2684	0.0322
Thailand	−0.0046	0.9864	17.6510	4.2810	6.3212	0.0376

$E(\epsilon_t/\sigma_t)$ and $E[(\epsilon_t/\sigma_t)^2]$ are the mean and the variance of the estimated standardized residuals. D is the Kolmogorov–Smirnov statistic testing the hypothesis that the standardized residuals follow the GED with the estimated degrees of freedom (5% critical value is $1.36/\sqrt{T}$, where T is sample size). $LB^a(10)$, $LB^b(10)$ and $LB^c(10)$ are the Ljung–Box statistics for $E(\epsilon_t/\sigma_t)$, $E[(\epsilon_t/\sigma_t)^2]$ and $E|\epsilon_t/\sigma_t|$. LB is distributed as χ^2 with degrees of freedom equal to the number of lags.

i.i.d. processes in all markets, as can be seen from the insignificant values of the LB statistics. This provides evidence that the volatility process is correctly specified. The LB statistic, however, does not provide any indication as to how well the model captures the impact of positive and negative innovations on volatility. For this purpose, some diagnostics proposed recently by Engle and Ng (1993) are used. These tests are based on the news impact curve implied by the particular ARCH-type model used. The premise is that if the volatility process is correctly specified then the squared standardized residuals should not be predictable on the basis of observed variables. These tests are: (1) the sign bias test; (2) the negative size bias test; and (3) the positive size bias test. The first test examines the impact of positive and negative innovations on volatility not predicted by the model. The squared residuals are regressed against a constant and a dummy S_t^- that takes the value of unity if ϵ_{t-1} is negative and zero otherwise. The test is based on the t-statistic for S_t^-. The negative size bias test examines how well the model captures the impact of large and small negative innovations. It is based on the regression of the standardized residuals against a constant and $S_t^- \epsilon_{t-1}$. The calculated t-statistic for $S_t^- \epsilon_{t-1}$ is used in this test. The positive size bias test examine possible biases associated with large and small positive innovations. Here, the standardized residuals are regressed against a constant and $(1-S_t^-)\epsilon_{t-1}$. Again, the t-statistic for $(1-S_t^-)\epsilon_{t-1}$ is used to test for possible biases. Table 5 reports the calculated t-statistics based on these regressions. The results for all six markets show no evidence of misspecification. On the basis of the various diagnostics performed, it can be said that the EAR–TGARCH model describes first- and second-moment dynamics quite well.

5. Summary and concluding remarks

This paper has investigated the dynamic behavior of the stock index returns of six emerging capital markets in the Pacific Basin area. The empirical findings suggest that the behavior of the daily returns of these markets is remarkably similar to the

Table 5
Volatility specification tests based on the news impact curve

Sign bias test: $(\epsilon_t/\sigma_t)^2 = a + bS_t^- + e_t$ (i)
Negative size bias test: $(\epsilon_t/\sigma_t)^2 = a + bS_t^- \epsilon_{t-1} + e_t$ (ii)
Positive size bias test: $(\epsilon_t/\sigma_t)^2 = a + b(1 - S_t^-)\epsilon_{t-1} + e_t$ (iii)

Market	Sign bias (t-test)	Negative size bias (t-test)	Positive sign bias (t-test)
Korea	−1.5337	0.3502	−0.4515
Malaysia	−0.3480	0.1996	0.1665
Philippines	−2.0369*	0.7435	0.4573
Singapore	1.1228	−0.2382	−0.4421
Taiwan	−0.2886	1.2740	0.1765
Thailand	−0.0181	0.1154	−0.2784

*Denotes significance at the 5% level. All t-statistics refer to coefficient b in regressions (i), (ii) and (iii).

behavior of developed capital markets despite differences in development, liquidity, institutional features and regulations. More specifically, the logarithms of stock prices have a unit root in their univariate representations. First- and, in some cases, second-order return autocorrelations are inversely related to volatility, i.e. autocorrelations are high during calm periods and low during volatile periods. The returns in all markets can be modeled as conditionally heteroscedastic processes in the sense that today's volatility depends on its immediate past as well as past innovations. The relationship of volatility to past innovations is asymmetric, meaning that negative innovations increase volatility more than positive ones. Accounting for first- and second-moment dependencies removes most of the kurtosis in the empirical distribution of the returns. However, the standardized residuals are still far from being normal. The remaining non-normality is captured quite well by the generalized error distribution which allows more peakedness and thicker tails than the normal distribution. A series of diagnostics performed on the estimated standardized residuals shows no evidence of misspecification.

References

Akgiray, V., Booth, G.C., 1991. Modeling the stochastic behavior of Canadian foreign exchange rates. J. Multinational Financial Management 1, 43–71.
Baillie, R.T., Bollerslev, T., 1989. The message in daily exchange rates: a conditional variance tale. J. Bus. Econ. Statist. 7, 297–305.
Bailey, W., Stulz, R.M., Yen, S., 1990. Properties of daily stock returns from the Pacific Basin stock markets. In: Rhee, S.G., Chang, R.P. (Eds.), Pacific Basin Capital Markets Research. Elsevier, Amsterdam, pp. 155–171.
Bailey, W., Stulz, R., 1990. Benefits of international diversification: the case of Pacific Basin stock markets. J. Portfolio Management 16, 57–61.
Bekaert, G., Harvey, C.R., 1997. Emerging equity market volatility. J. Financial Econ. 43, 29–77.

Berndt, E.K., Hall, H.B., Hall, R.E., Hausman, J.A., 1974. Estimation and inference in nonlinear structural models. Ann. Econ. Social Measmt 4, 653–666.

Black, F., 1976. Studies in stock price volatility changes. In: Proceedings of the 1976 Business Meeting of the Business and Economic Statistics Section. American Statistical Association, pp. 177–181.

Bollerslev, T., 1987. A conditional heteroskedastic time series model for speculative prices and rates of return. Rev. Econ. Statist. 69, 542–547.

Bollerslev, T., Chou, R.Y., Kroner, K.F., 1992. ARCH modeling in finance: a review of the theory and empirical evidence. J. Econ. 52, 5–59.

Bollerslev, T., Engle, R.F., Nelson, D.B., 1994. ARCH models. In: Engle, R.F., McFadden, D.L. (Eds.), Handbook of Econometrics, vol. 4. Elsevier, Amsterdam, pp. 2959–3038.

Booth, G.G., Hatem, J.J., Virtanen, I., Yli-Olli, P., 1992. Stochastic modeling of security returns: evidence from the Helsinki stock exchange. Eur. J. Opl Res. 56, 98–106.

Booth, G.G., Koutmous, G. 1996. Interaction of volatility and autocorrelation in foreign stock returns (submitted for publication).

Campbell, J.Y., Grossman, S.J., Wang, J., 1993. Trading volume and serial correlation in stock returns. Q. J. Econ. 108 (4), 905–939.

Christie, A.A., 1982. The stochastic behavior of common stock variance: value leverage and interest rate effects. J. Financial Econ. 10, 407–432.

Defusco, R.A., Geppert, J.M., Tsetsekos, G.P., 1996. Long-run diversification potential in emerging stock markets. Financial Rev. 31, 343–363.

Divecha, A., Drach, J., Stefek, D., 1992. Emerging markets: a quantitative perspective. J. Portfolio Management Summer 19 (1), 41–50.

Engle, R.F., 1982. Autoregressive conditional heteroskedasticity with estimates of the variance of UK inflation. Econometrica 50, 987–1008.

Engle, R.F., Ng, V.K., 1993. Measuring and testing the impact of news on volatility. J. Finance 48, 1749–1778.

Errunza, V.R., 1994. Emerging Markets: Some New Concepts. J. Portfolio Management Spring, 82–87.

Fama, E.F., 1965. The behavior of stock market prices. J. Bus. 38, 34–105.

Glosten, L.R., Jagannathan, R., Runkle, D.E., 1993. On the relation between the expected value and the volatility of the nominal excess return on stocks. J. Finance 48, 1779–1801.

Harvey, C.R., 1955. Predictable risk and returns in emerging stock markets. Rev. Financial Stud. 8 (3), 773–816.

Hauser, S., Marcus, M., Yaari, U., 1994. Investing in emerging stock markets: is it worthwhile hedging foreign exchange risk? J. Portfolio Management Spring, 76–81.

Kasa, K., 1992. Common stochastic trends in international stock markets. J. Monetary Econ. 29 (1), 95–124.

Koutmos, G., Booth, G.G., 1995. Asymmetric volatility transmission in international stock markets. J. Int. Money Finance 14, 747–762.

Koutmos, G., Lee, U., Theodossiou, P., 1994. Time varying betas and volatility persistence in international stock markets. J. Econ. Bus. 46, 101–112.

LeBaron, B., 1992. Some relations between volatility and serial correlations in stock market returns. J. Bus. 65, 199–219.

Lee, S.B., Ohk, K.Y., 1991. time-varying volatilities and stock market returns: international evidence. In: Rhee, S.G., Chang, R.P. (Eds.), Pacific Basin Capital Markets Research, vol. II. Elsevier, Amsterdam, pp. 261–281.

Mandelbrot, B., 1963. The variance of certain speculative price. J. Bus. 36, 394–419.

Mullin, J., 1993. Emerging equity markets in the global economy. FRBNY Q. Rev. Summer, 54–83.

Nelson, D., 1991. Conditional heteroskedasticity in asset returns: a new approach. Econometrica 59, 347–370.

Ng, V.K., Chang, R.P., Chou, R.Y., 1991. An Examination of the behavior of Pacific-Basin stock market volatility. In: Rhee, S.G., Chang, R.P. (Eds.), Pacific Basin Capital Markets Research, vol. II. Elsevier, Amsterdam, pp. 245–260.

Park, K.H., Agtmael, A.W., 1993. The World's Emerging Stock Markets: Structure, Developments, Regulations and Opportunities. Probus, Chicago.

Phillips, P.C.B., Perron, P., 1988. Testing for a unit root in time series regression. Biometrika 75, 335–346.
Poon, S-H., Taylor, S.J., 1992. Stock returns and volatility: an empirical study of the UK stock market. J. Banking Finance 16, 37–59.
Schwert, G.W., 1989. Why does market volatility change over time? J. Finance 44, 1115–1153.
Sentana, E., Wadhwani, S., 1992. Feedback traders and stock return autocorrelations: evidence from a century of daily data. Econ. J. 102, 415–425.
Solnic, B., 1988. International Investments. Addison-Wesley, Reading, MA.
Solnic, B., 1991. Pacific Basin stock markets and international diversification. In: Rhee, S.G., Chang, R.P. (Eds.), Pacific Basin Capital Markets Research, vol. II. Elsevier, Amsterdam, pp. 309–321.
Taylor, S., 1986. Modelling Financial Time Series. Wiley, New York.
Wilcox, J., 1992. Global investing in emerging markets. Financial Anal. J. JanuaryFebruary, 15–19.
Zakoian, J.M., 1994. Threshold heteroskedastic models. J. Econ. Dynamics Control 18, 931–995.

Asymmetric Price and Volatility Adjustments in Emerging Asian Stock Markets

GREGORY KOUTMOS*

1. INTRODUCTION

Emerging capital markets are becoming increasingly important for both institutional and individual investors. In the period 1984 to 1991 investment in these markets has increased from 500 million US dollars to 25 billion. Harvey (1995) reports that the market capitalization of emerging stock markets comprises approximately eight percent of the Morgan Stanley Capital International (MSCI) world capitalization.

Considerable research has been devoted to the potential benefits from investing in emerging equity markets, e.g., Wilcox (1992), Divecha, Drach and Stefek (1992), Hauser, Marcus and Yaari (1994), Errunza (1994), Mullin (1993), Solnic (1991), Bailey and Stulz (1990) and Defusco, Geppert and Tsetsekos (1996), to mention but a few. These studies provide valuable information regarding the risk diversification potential from investing in emerging markets. However, there are very few studies dealing with the dynamics of stock returns in emerging markets. For example, Bailey, Stulz and Yen (1990) find that returns in the stock markets of the Pacific Basin depart substantially from the random walk model because the estimated first-order autocorrelations are much higher than those observed in developed markets. They also report that autocorrelations are

---

*The author is from the School of Business, Fairfield University. (Paper received March 1997, revised and accepted June 1998)

Address for correspondence: Gregory Koutmos, School of Business, Fairfield University, Fairfield, CT 06430-7524, USA.
e-mail:gkoutmos.fair1.fairfield.edu

very unstable over time and in some instances they turn negative. Ng, Chang and Chou (1991), Lee and Ohk (1991) and Choudhry (1996) use ARCH-type models to capture the time varying volatility of stock returns in emerging capital markets. Harvey and Bekaert (1997) study the volatility of twenty emerging markets and they find that liberalization has led to increased correlation with the developed markets and to lower local market volatility. Studies for the developed stock markets have linked the observed autocorrelation in index stock returns to either nonsynchronous trading effects (e.g., Fisher 1966; Scholes and Williams, 1977; and Lo and MacKinlay, 1990), or to possible time variation in expected returns or, risk premia (e.g., Fama and French, 1988; and Conrad and Kaul, 1988). Regarding nonsynchronous trading, Lo and MacKinlay (1990) observe that:

> ... if nonsynchronicity is purposeful and informationally motivated, then the subsequent serial dependence in asset returns may well be considered genuine, since it is the result of economic forces rather than mismeasurement.

The implication is that market frictions may force investors to follow some sort of optimal nontrading strategies. Consequently, observed prices are likely to reflect new information with some delay which manifests itself as autocorrelation in the returns. The presence of transactions costs, for example, can delay exploitation of deviations from intrinsic value until the expected gains outweigh costs by an acceptable margin. Other important sources of market friction are (i) the cost of acquiring and processing information, (ii) the attempts of market specialists (when present) to create orderly markets and assure price continuity, and (iii) the particular institutional market mechanism by which securities are traded.[1] The role of different market mechanisms in inducing stock return autocorrelation is examined by Amihud and Mendelson (1987) by means of a partial adjustment price model. They find that returns are more persistent, i.e., they exhibit higher autocorrelation when securities are traded in a call market as opposed to a continuous auction market. Damodaran (1993) also uses the partial adjustment model and finds that stocks in NASDAQ adjust slower to new information than stocks in NYSE/AMEX. The partial adjustment model implies that stock returns follow autoregressive or, moving average processes. The underlying assumption is that costs related to market frictions are symmetric, or, equivalently, the persistence of past positive returns (good news) is equal to the persistence of past negative returns (bad news). If, for some reason, the costs of adjusting stock prices upwards are different from the costs of adjusting them downwards, then the autoregressive, or moving average models that have been used extensively in the literature are misspecified.

This paper tests the hypothesis that index stock returns in emerging stock markets adjust asymmetrically to past information. As such, it extends the work of Amihud and Mendelson (1987) and Damodaran (1993) and it offers some new insights into the dynamics of short term emerging stock index returns. For this purpose an Asymmetric Autoregressive Exponential GARCH model (asAR-EGARCH) is introduced and estimated for six emerging stock markets. The empirical evidence suggests that both prices and volatilities respond asymmetrically to past information. In agreement with studies dealing with developed markets, the conditional variance is an asymmetric function of past innovations, rising proportionately more during market declines. More importantly, the conditional mean is also an asymmetric function of past returns. Specifically, positive past returns are more persistent than negative past returns of an equal magnitude. This behavior is consistent with an asymmetric partial adjustment price model where news suggesting overpricing (negative returns) are incorporated faster into current market prices than news suggesting underpricing (positive returns). Furthermore, the asymmetric adjustment of prices to past information could be partially responsible for the asymmetries in the conditional variance if the degree of adjustment and the level of volatility are positively related, as Brorsen (1991) suggests.

The remainder of this paper is organized as follows: Section 2 outlines the model used; Section 3 discusses the data and presents some preliminary findings; Section 4 presents and discusses the main empirical findings; and the final section concludes this paper.

2. THE PARTIAL ASYMMETRIC PRICE ADJUSTMENT MODEL

The partial adjustment model used by Amihud and Mendelson (1987) and Damodaran (1993) can be described as follows:

© Blackwell Publishers Ltd 1999

$$P_t - P_{t-1} = (1 - \theta)(V_t - P_{t-1}) + u_t, \qquad (1)$$

where, P_t and V_t are the observed price and the unobserved intrinsic value respectively, both expressed in natural logarithms. u_t is a zero mean, possibly conditionally heteroskedastic error term. The adjustment costs discussed earlier give rise to the friction parameter θ. The greater the value of θ the slower the adjustment. For $\theta = 0$ the adjustment is instantaneous whereas for $\theta = 1$ there is no tendency for prices to move toward their intrinsic value. Thus, $(1 - \theta)$ measures the speed of adjustment. To assure that the price process has finite variance the friction parameter and the speed of adjustment have to satisfy $0 < \theta < 1$ and $0 < (1 - \theta) < 1$ respectively.

The intrinsic value V_t is assumed to follow a martingale process given by:

$$V_t = a + V_{t-1} + e_t, \qquad (2)$$

where a is the drift parameter and e_t is the error term. Equations (1) and (2) imply that returns follow an autoregressive process of order one, i.e.,

$$R_t = \beta + \theta R_{t-1} + \epsilon_t, \qquad (3)$$

where, $\beta = a(1 - \theta)$ and $\epsilon_t = u_t - u_{t-1} + (1 - \theta)e_t$. Estimates of the friction parameter θ can be obtained by simply estimating the AR(1) process given in equation (3). If, however, adjustment costs are asymmetric in up and down markets then the partial adjustment model with constant friction coefficient is misspecified. This study proposes extending the basic model to accommodate potential asymmetries in the adjustment process. This can be done easily by reformulating equation (1) as follows:

$$P_t - P_{t-1} = (1 - \theta^+)(V_t - P_{t-1})^+ + (1 - \theta^-)(V_t - P_{t-1})^- + u_t, \qquad (4)$$

where $(V_t - P_{t-1})^+ = \text{Max}\{(V_t - P_{t-1}, 0\}$ and $(V_t - P_{t-1})^- = \text{Min}\{(V_t - P_{t-1}, 0\}$. For $\theta^+ = \theta^- = \theta$ equation (4) reverts to the basic model. Solving (4) for V_t and substituting into (2) yields the following asymmetric autoregressive model of order one:

$$R_t = \beta + \theta^+ R_{t-1}^+ + \theta^- R_{t-1}^- \epsilon_t, \qquad (5)$$

where, $R_{t-1}^+ = \text{Max}(0, R_{t-1})$ and $R_{t-1}^- = \text{Min}(R_{t-1}, 0)$. The intercept β and the error term ϵ_t in (5) are functions of the original parameters and the original error terms respectively. Specifically, $\beta = a[(1-\theta^+) + (\theta^+ - \theta^-)D]$ and $\epsilon_t = u_t - u_{t-1} + [(1-\theta^+) + (\theta^+ - \theta^-)]e_t$ respectively where, $D=1$ if $R_t > 0$ and zero otherwise. The parameters of interest, however, θ^+ and θ^- correspond directly to those in (4). Consequently, their estimated values can be interpreted as friction parameters or, alternatively, as the degree of persistence of past positive and negative returns.

The asymmetric autoregressive process described by (4) utilizes two different filters, one for positive and one for negative past returns. When $\theta^+ = \theta^- = \theta$ the process is symmetric and the $\{R_t\}$ sequence will follow the usual autoregressive process. In this case the optimal one-step ahead forecast will be $E_{t-1}(R_t) = \beta + \theta R_{t-1}$, where E_{t-1} is the conditional expectations operator. However, when $\theta^+ \neq \theta^-$ the optimal one-step ahead forecast will depend on the sign of R_{t-1}, i.e., $E_{t-1}(R_t) = \beta + \theta^+ R_{t-1}^+$ for $R_{t-1} \geq 0$, and $E_{t-1}(R_t) = \beta + \theta^- R_{t-1}^-$ for $R_{t-1} \leq 0$.

Numerous studies report that stock prices exhibit conditional heteroskedasticity (e.g., Bollerslev, Chou and Kroner 1992). Based on these findings the error process $\{\epsilon_t\}$ is assumed to be conditionally heteroskedastic with time varying variance given by:

$$\ln(\sigma_t^2) = \alpha_0 + \alpha_1(|z_{t-1}| - E|z_{t-1}| + \delta z_{t-1}) + \phi \ln(\sigma_{t-1}^2), \quad (6)$$

where, z_t is the standardized residual, i.e., $z_t \equiv \epsilon_t/\sigma_t$, with zero mean and unit variance. This is the EGARCH suggested by Nelson (1991). It has several advantages over Engle's (1982) and Bollerslev's (1986) linear GARCH model. First, modeling the natural log of the conditional variance guarantees that σ_t^2 will be positive for all t so that parameter restrictions are unnecessary. Second, volatility at time t depends on both the size and the sign of past standardized residuals. Specifically, the term $(|z_{t-1}| - E|z_{t-1}|)$ measures the size effect whereas the term δz_{t-1} measures the sign effect. For $\delta < 0$, the sign effect is reinforcing the size effect and for $\delta > 0$, the sign effect is partially offsetting the size effect. A negative δ is consistent with the so-called 'leverage hypothesis' whereby negative returns increase the debt/equity ratio. As a result, negative returns are followed by higher volatility than positive returns of an equal size (see also Black, 1978; Nelson, 1991; Koutmos and Booth, 1995; and Koutmos and Saidi, 1995). Existence of the unconditional variance requires that $\phi < 1$. Then the logarithm of the unconditional variance will be equal to $\alpha_0/(1 - \phi)$.

Estimation of the fixed parameters describing the conditional mean and the conditional variance requires specification of the conditional density function $f(\mu_t, \sigma_t^2, \nu)$ where, μ_t, σ_t^2 and ν are the conditional mean, the conditional variance and the degrees of freedom characterizing the conditional density $f(\cdot)$ respectively. In most applications the normal density function is used. However, the standardized residuals obtained from ARCH-type models that assume normality are in most cases leptokurtic. Parameter estimates under those circumstances will still be unbiased but the standard errors are understated. Thus, hypothesis testing becomes problematic. To deal with this problem distributions with flatter tails such as the student's t or, the Generalized Error Distribution (GED) have been suggested. This paper employs the GED distribution whose density function is given by:

$$f(u_t, \sigma_t, \nu) = \nu/2[\Gamma(3/\nu)]^{1/2}[\Gamma(1/\nu)]^{-3/2}(1/\sigma_t)\exp$$
$$\{-(\Gamma(3/\nu)/\Gamma(1/\nu))^{\nu/2}|\epsilon_t/\sigma_t|^\nu\} \quad (7)$$

where, $\Gamma(\cdot)$ is the gamma function and ν is a scale parameter, or degrees of freedom to be estimated endogenously. This parameter controls the shape of the distribution allowing the GED to nest several other densities. For example, if $\nu = 2$, (7) yields the normal distribution, while for $\nu = 1$ it yields the Laplace or, double exponential distribution.

Given initial values for ϵ_t, and σ_t^2 the parameter vector $\Theta \equiv (\beta, \theta^+, \theta^-, \alpha_0, \alpha_1, \delta, \phi, \nu)$ can be estimated by maximizing the log-likelihood over the sample period. [2]

The latter can be expressed as:

$$L(\Theta) = \sum_{t=1}^{T} \log f(u_t, \sigma_t^2, \nu). \quad (8)$$

3. DATA AND DESCRIPTIVE STATISTICS

The data used are daily prices for the stock price indices of six emerging stock markets namely, those of Korea, Malaysia, the Philippines, Singapore, Taiwan and Thailand.[3] The time period

Table 1
Emerging Market Indices

	Korea	Malaysia	Philippines	Singapore	Taiwan	Thailand
Market Capitalization[a]	96.4	58.6	10.2	49.6	124.9	35.8
Market Capitalization (% of GDP)	37.7	121.4	22.7	123.5	82.6	38.9
Number of Listings	686	321	161	172	221	276
Trading Value[b]	312.1	27.1	3.4	52.9	701.1	102.5
Turnover Ratio	82.3	20.2	18.8	n.a.	330.1	102.2
P/E Ratio	21.3	21.3	11.3	n.a.	22.3	12
% Dividend Yield	1.6	2.4	0.8	n.a.	0.9	1.9
Correlation[c] with S&P 500 (12/89-12/94)	0.20	0.39	0.36	n.a.	0.14	0.38

Notes
[a] Billions of US Dollars.
[b] Average daily trading values in millions of US Dollars. All figures are from IFC *Emerging Stock Markets Factbook*, and IMF *International Financial Statistics*, as of 1991 unless otherwise indicated.
[c] Correlations are based on monthly returns.

under investigation extends from January 2, 1986 to December 1, 1995 for a total of 2,584 observations. As of December 1991, these six markets comprised 44% of total emerging market capitalization and 3.3% of total world capitalization. Table 1 provides some statistics pertaining to market capitalization, number of listings, trading value, turnover ratio, P/E ratio, dividend yield and correlation with the S&P 500 of the six stock markets under investigation. The stock market of Taiwan has the highest capitalization and the highest trading value. The Korean market has the largest number of companies listed, whereas, the market capitalization/GDP ratio is over 120% for Malaysia and Singapore. The average capitalization/GDP ratio for the six emerging markets is approximately 71%. For the same year, this ratio stood at 74% for the US stock market and at 65% for the group of seven developed markets.[4] The turnover ratio can be used to assess the liquidity of a market. By this measure, Taiwan is the most liquid and the Philippines is the least liquid. The earnings multiples are approximately in line with those of most developed markets. For example, the P/E ratio for the US has been on average 15x over the period 1954 to 1993. Dividend yields, on the other hand are substantially lower than those prevailing in the US. The case for diversification depends crucially on the correlations across markets. For the more recent period (December 1989 to December 1994) the estimated correlation coefficients with the US market based on monthly returns are rather small in size ranging from 0.39 (Malaysia) to 0.14 (Taiwan).

Table 2 reports several descriptive statistics calculated for the daily returns.[5] These statistics include the mean and the standard deviation, measures for skewness and kurtosis, the Kolmogorov-Smirnov D-statistic and the Ljung-Box statistic for 10 lags. The standard deviations range from 1.0109 (Singapore), to 2.2167 (Taiwan). The statistics of skewness and excess kurtosis suggest significant departures from normality.[6] Normality is also rejected on the basis of the Kolmogorov-Smirnov D-statistic.

The presence of intertemporal dependencies in the returns and the squared returns are tested by means of the Ljung and Box portmanteau test (LB), e.g., Bollerslev et al. (1994). The LB statistic tests the hypothesis that autocorrelations up to the nth lag are jointly statistically insignificant. With the exception of Korea, the calculated LB statistics for 10 lags are significant for the return series, providing evidence of intertemporal dependencies in the first moment of the distribution of returns.[7] Thus far, such dependencies have been attributed mostly to problems associated with the use of index returns (i.e., nonsynchronous trading of the stocks that make up the index). Evidence on second moment intertemporal dependencies is provided by the LB statistic calculated for the squared returns. As can be seen, the LB for the squared returns are several times higher than for the returns themselves. The implication is that second moment dependencies are much more pronounced. It should be noted that these dependencies are compatible with the volatility clustering phenomenon that has been documented for most developed stock markets, e.g., Bollerslev, Chou and Kroner (1992). These statistics however are not designed to detect

Table 2

Preliminary Statistical Analysis

Statistic	Korea	Malaysia	Philippines	Singapore	Taiwan	Thailand
Panel A: Descriptive Statistics						
μ	0.0673*	0.0561*	0.1129*	0.0310	0.0675	0.0847*
σ	1.3779	1.4220	1.9578	1.0109	2.2167	1.5486
S	0.2044*	−1.5397*	0.0735	−0.1899*	−0.0659	−0.5761*
K	2.5043*	21.6122*	10.1149*	28.7654*	2.4344*	7.3852*
D	0.0331*	0.1180*	0.1139*	0.1128*	0.0924*	0.1116*
$LB^a(10)$	12.9003	86.0421*	87.4062*	98.5111*	67.8986*	97.4080*
$LB^b(10)$	489.7478*	1577.6060*	743.9730*	137.8603*	1724.3967*	967.1539*
Panel B: Volatility Specification Tests						
Sign-Bias (*t*-test)	−0.5493	2.1011*	1.7909	2.6771*	2.1669*	2.9663*
Negative Size Bias (*t*-test)	−4.5664*	−16.9874*	−12.6216*	−9.7425*	−8.6049*	−14.1334*
Positive Size Bias (*t*-test)	5.0656*	3.1203*	2.3569*	0.2639	4.3018*	4.3741*
Joint Test ($F_{3,2579}$ test)	24.6822*	119.9808*	67.2014*	34.1642*	44.7449*	93.3526*

Notes:
* Denotes significance at the 5% level.
μ, σ are the sample mean and standard deviation; S and K are measures for skewness and excess kurtosis; D is the Kolmogorov-Smirnov statistic, testing for normality; the 5% critical value is $1.36/\sqrt{T}$, where T is the number of observations; LB^a, and LB^b are the Ljung-Box statistics testing for autocorrelations in the returns and the squared returns up to the 10th lag.
The sample period extends from January 2, 1986 to November 30, 1995 for a total of 2,584 observations.
The regressions for the volatility specification tests are as follows:
Sign Bias Test: $z_t^2 = a + bS_t^- + u_t$ (i)
Negative Size Bias Test: $z_t^2 = a + bS_t^- \epsilon_{t-1} + u_t$ (ii)
Positive Size Bias Test: $z_t^2 = a + b(1 - S_t^-)\epsilon_{t-1} + u_t$ (iii)
Joint Test: $z_t^2 = a + b_1 S_t + b_2 S_t \epsilon_{t-1} + b_3(1 - S_t^-)\epsilon_{t-1} + u_t$ (iv)
where, z_t^2 is the standardized return squared, ϵ_t is the de-meaned return and S_t^- is a dummy that takes the value of unity if $\epsilon_t < 0$ and zero otherwise. Individual tests are *t*-tests for coefficient *b* in (i), (ii) and (iii). The joint test is an *F*-test for regression (iv).

asymmetries in the conditional variance. For this purpose the diagnostics proposed by Engle and Ng (1993) are used. These tests are based on the premise that if returns follow an *i.i.d.* process then the squared standardized returns should not be predictable on the basis of observed variables. These tests are (i) the Sign Bias Test, (ii) the Negative Size Bias Test (iii) the Positive Size Bias Test and (iv) the Joint Test. The first test examines the asymmetric impact of positive and negative innovations on volatility not predicted by the model. The squared standardized returns are regressed against a constant and a dummy S_t^- that takes the value of unity if ϵ_{t-1} is negative and zero otherwise. The test is based on the t-statistic for S_t^-. The Negative Size Bias Test examines how well the model captures the impact of large and small negative innovations. It is based on the regression of the squared standardized returns against a constant and $S_t^- \epsilon_{t-1}$. The calculated t-statistic for $S_t^- \epsilon_{t-1}$ is used in this test. The Positive Size Bias Test examine possible biases associated with large and small positive innovations. Here, the squared standardized returns are regressed against a constant and $(1 - S_t^-)\epsilon_{t-1}$. Again, the t-statistic for $(1 - S_t^-)\epsilon_{t-1}$ is used to test for possible biases. Finally a joint test can be based on the F-statistic of a regression involving all three explanatory variables, i.e., S_t^-, $S_t^- \epsilon_{t-1}$ and $(1 - S_t^-)\epsilon_{t-1}$. The results from these tests are reported in Panel B of Table 2. Each market fails at least two of the individual tests. All markets fail the joint test. The conclusion that can be drawn is that the conditional variance in these markets is likely to be asymmetric.

4. EVIDENCE ON FIRST AND SECOND MOMENT ASYMMETRIES

Table 3 reports the maximum likelihood estimates of the asAR-EGARCH model. The autoregressive process is clearly asymmetric across all six emerging markets. Specifically, the coefficient θ^+, linking current returns to positive past returns, is larger than the coefficient θ^-, linking current returns to past negative returns. The null hypothesis $H_0: \theta^+ \leq \theta^-$ is tested on the basis of one-tail t-test. The results show that in all instances the null is rejected. Thus, θ^+ is statistically greater than θ^-.

As mentioned in Section 2, θ^+ and θ^- are friction (persistence) parameters, and their size determines the number of periods it takes to close a certain proportion of the gap between intrinsic value and past price. If the asset is underpriced (i.e., $V_t - P_{t-1} > 0$) then 50% of the gap will be closed in a number of periods m such that $(\theta^+)^m = 0.50$, or, $m = \log(0.50)/\log(\theta^+)$.

© Blackwell Publishers Ltd 1999

Table 3

Maximum Likelihood Estimates of the asAR-EGARCH Model

$$R_t = \beta + \theta^+ R_{t-1}^+ + \theta^- R_{t-1}^- + \epsilon_t$$
$$\ln(\sigma_t^2) = \alpha_0 + \alpha_1(|z_{t-1}| - E|z_{t-1}| + \delta z_{t-1}) + \phi \ln(\sigma_{t-1}^2)$$

Coefficient	Korea	Malaysia	Philippines	Singapore	Taiwan	Thailand
β	−0.0159	0.0134	0.0000	−0.0000	−0.0000	0.0309
	(0.030)	(0.019)	(0.023)	(0.011)	(0.033)	(0.020)
θ^+	0.0582	0.1575	0.1608	0.1382	0.0811	0.1583
	(0.028)*	(0.025)*	(0.022)*	(0.022)*	(0.026)*	(0.027)*
θ^-	0.0103	0.0579	0.1134	0.0735	−0.0000	0.0851
	(0.036)	(0.030)*	(0.026)*	(0.029)*	(0.029)	(0.031)*
α_0	0.0475	0.0229	0.0371	−0.0410	0.0289	0.0149
	(0.012)*	(0.008)*	(0.009)*	(0.014)*	(0.007)*	(0.007)*
α_1	0.2569	0.2943	0.2105	0.3342	0.1909	0.3214
	(0.032)*	(0.022)*	(0.024)*	(0.035)*	(0.021)*	(0.028)*
δ	−0.1681	−0.1720	−0.1143	−0.3495	−0.1784	−0.1235
	(0.071)*	(0.070)*	(0.072)	(0.085)*	(0.069)*	(0.051)*
ϕ	0.9143	0.9211	0.9665	0.8512	0.9800	0.9678
	(0.019)*	(0.013)*	(0.007)*	(0.024)*	(0.005)*	(0.007)*
ν	1.2617	0.9953	0.9309	0.9198	1.0435	1.1116
	(0.048)*	(0.022)*	(0.026)*	(0.021)*	(0.039)*	(0.038)*
t-stat	1.7107*	3.9840*	2.1545*	2.9410*	3.1192*	2.7111*
m^+	0.2437	0.3750	0.3793	0.3502	0.2759	0.3760
m^-	0.1515	0.2433	0.3184	0.2655	—	0.2813
m^+/m^-	1.6086	1.5413	1.1912	1.3190	—	1.3366
$(1+\delta)/(1-\delta)$	1.3944	1.5625	1.1278	2.0970	1.4742	1.2800

Notes:
* Denotes significance at the 5% level.
Numbers in parentheses are the standard errors for the estimates.
m^+ and m^- measure the persistence, or, half-life, of positive and negative lagged returns respectively.
m^+/m^- and $(1+\delta)/(1-\delta)$ measure the degree of asymmetry in the conditional mean and the conditional standard deviation respectively.
t-stat tests H_0: $\theta^+ \leq \theta^-$ against H_1: $\theta^+ > \theta^-$.
For a one-tail test the critical value is 1.645.

Similar reasoning holds if the asset is overpriced. The degree of persistence of positive (m^+) and negative (m^-) returns, as well as the extent of the asymmetry in the conditional mean (m^+/m^-) are reported in Table 3. For the Korean stock market, for example, it takes 0.2437 days for the price to adjust by 50% to its intrinsic value assuming underpricing and 0.1515 days assuming overpricing. Thus, positive returns are 1.6086 times more persistent than negative returns. Equivalently, bad news is incorporated much faster than good news.[8] On average the degree of asymmetry in the conditional mean is approximately 1.40. The speed of adjustment to new information has been one of the most important measures of market efficiency. By this measure, all six emerging markets appear to be at least weak-form efficient. In all instances prices adjust fully in less than one day.

The question that arises, naturally, is what could be a plausible explanation for these findings. If the persistence in returns is due to costs of adjusting prices, as the partial adjustment model suggests, why are these costs asymmetric? Asymmetry cannot be due to the usual transactions costs because these are the same for both buy and sell orders. One possibility is that investors have a higher aversion to downside risk so they react faster to bad news. The use of stop-loss orders is an example of such aversion. Also, portfolio managers, at least in such developed markets as the US, feel they are penalized more if they underperform in a falling market than in a rising market (see Sortino and Van Der Meer, 1991). As such, they are quicker to react to bad news. Similarly, in markets dominated by market makers, i.e., dealers and floor specialists, the cost of not adjusting prices downward is higher than the cost of not adjusting prices upward. Market specialists, who are required to maintain price continuity, will find it easier and less costly to do so in a rising market than in a falling market, since the latter involves building up inventory with overpriced securities. For example, during the crash of October 1987, specialists in the US market found it impossible to maintain price continuity and they became net sellers themselves. All of these possibilities suggest that bad news will be reflected into prices much faster than good news.

The parameters describing the conditional variance are statistically significant across all markets. In all instances, δ is negative and statistically significant (save for the Philippines). The implication is that negative innovations increase volatility more than positive innovations. It can be seen from (6) that the contribution of a positive unitary standardized innovation is equal to $\alpha_1(1 - \delta)$ whereas, the contribution of a negative unitary standardized innovation is $\alpha_1(1 + \delta)$. Consequently, the degree of asymmetry in the conditional variance can be measured by

$(1 + \delta)/(1 - \delta)$. On the basis of this metric the highest asymmetry is observed in Singapore and the lowest in the Philippines. Averaging across the six markets it can be said that a negative innovation increases volatility 1.5 times more than a positive innovation of an equal sign. Interestingly, the degree of asymmetry in the conditional mean is of a similar magnitude namely, 1.40. Koutmos and Booth (1995) report asymmetries in the conditional variance of the magnitude of 4.34 for the Japanese stock market, 3.27 for the UK stock market and 2.14 for the US stock market. Koutmos (1996) reports slightly smaller asymmetries in the stock returns of four major European stock markets.

This asymmetric behavior of the conditional variance has been attributed to the leverage effect, e.g., Black (1976), Christie (1982) and Koutmos and Saidi (1995). Duffee (1995) finds that, at the firm level, the leverage effect cannot explain the observed relationship between returns and volatility changes.[9] He offers, however, no alternative explanation. The evidence in this paper offers an alternative explanation that is linked to the asymmetric costs of price adjustments. The partial adjustment model implies that the speed of adjustment and the volatility of the returns are inversely related (see also Brorsen, 1991). Since prices adjust faster to past price declines it is natural to expect volatility to be higher following market declines. Consequently, the so-called 'leverage effect' is, at least partially, due to the faster adjustment of prices to past negative returns. This explanation appears to be reasonable for the six emerging markets under examination.

The estimated degrees of freedom parameter ν is well below two, the value required for normality, and very close to unity suggesting that the empirical distributions of the returns are in all cases close to the double exponential or, Laplace distribution. In fact conventional *t*-tests reject the hypothesis that $\nu = 2$ for all six markets at the conventional level. This confirms the assertion made earlier that departures from normality observed in the raw return series cannot be attributed entirely to temporal first and second moment dependencies.

To check the robustness of the results, especially the significance of asymmetries, to the international market crash in October 1987 the models are re-estimated with a crash dummy in the conditional mean and the conditional variance equations.

The crash dummy takes the value of unity for the entire month of October 1987 and zero elsewhere. Treating the entire month of October as the crash period rather than the crash date itself is a better approach since it captures any lagged influence of the crash on asymmetry. The results are reported in Table 4. The crash dummy is significant for Taiwan (conditional mean) and for Malaysia, Singapore and Thailand (conditional variance). There are minor changes in the parameters of the model but not of a qualitative nature. Most importantly, the conditional mean asymmetries remain significant. The t-test confirms that indeed $\theta^+ > \theta^-$. Interestingly, the degree of asymmetry is on average approximately the same, i.e., 1.40. Similarly, δ remains significant (Philippines is still the exception). The average asymmetry in the conditional variance drops slightly from 1.48 to 1.44. Overall, the data from the crash of October 1987 do not seem to be driving the results. Correct specification of the conditional variance is tested using the Engle and Ng (1993) diagnostics described in Section 3. Table 5 reports the results from these tests. Panel A reports the results without the crash dummy and Panel B reports the results with the crash dummy. The individual t-tests as well as the joint F-tests are insignificant suggesting that the squared standardized residuals cannot be predicted using past information. The only exception is the stock market of Taiwan which fails the Sign-Bias, the Positive Size Bias and the Joint Tests. It may be that a longer lag EGARCH structure is required for this market. Overall, the asAR-EGARCH model describes successfully the short term dynamics of these markets. More importantly, the model is able to capture asymmetries that are present in the conditional moments of the distribution of returns.

5. SUMMARY AND CONCLUDING REMARKS

This paper has tested the hypothesis that index stock returns in emerging markets adjust asymmetrically to past information. The empirical evidence supports the hypothesis that both the conditional mean and the conditional variance respond asymmetrically to past information. In agreement with studies for developed stock markets, the conditional variance is an asymmetric function of past innovations, rising proportionately

© Blackwell Publishers Ltd 1999

Table 4

Maximum Likelihood Estimates of the asAR-EGARCH Model with Crash Dummy

$$R_t = \beta + \beta_c C_t + \theta^+ R_{t-1}^+ + \theta^- R_{t-1}^- + \epsilon_t$$
$$\ln(\sigma_t^2) = \alpha_0 + \alpha_{0,c} C_t + \alpha_1(|z_{t-1}| - E|z_{t-1}| + \delta z_{t-1}) + \phi \ln(\sigma_{t-1}^2)$$

Coefficient	Korea	Malaysia	Philippines	Singapore	Taiwan	Thailand
β	−0.0182 (0.030)	0.0160 (0.020)	−0.0000 (0.023)	−0.0000 (0.011)	0.0000 (0.033)	0.0313 (0.020)
β_c	0.2048 (0.269)	0.2414 (0.458)	0.7330 (0.912)	0.0357 (0.204)	−2.5961 (0.544)*	−0.0241 (0.447)
θ^+	0.0590 (0.028)*	0.1593 (0.026)*	0.1651 (0.022)*	0.1663 (0.023)*	0.0831 (0.026)*	0.1586 (0.027)*
θ^-	0.0098 (0.036)	0.0634 (0.031)*	0.1130 (0.027)*	0.0819 (0.030)*	−0.0002 (0.028)	0.0845 (0.032)*
α_0	0.0474 (0.013)*	0.0195 (0.008)*	0.0440 (0.010)*	−0.0485 (0.015)*	0.0084 (0.006)*	0.0136 (0.007)*
$\alpha_{0,c}$	−0.0035 (0.072)	0.3296 (0.070)*	0.0122 (0.072)	0.2326 (0.098)*	0.0096 (0.045)	0.1804 (0.068)*
α_1	0.2562 (0.032)*	0.2816 (0.034)*	0.2211 (0.025)*	0.3316 (0.036)*	0.1675 (0.018)*	0.3119 (0.028)*
δ	−0.1683 (0.071)*	−0.1540 (0.075)*	−0.1120 (0.073)	−0.3320 (0.085)*	−0.1530 (0.071)*	−0.1210 (0.052)*
ϕ	0.9144 (0.019)*	0.9181 (0.014)*	0.9590 (0.008)*	0.8447 (0.025)*	0.9857 (0.004)*	0.9666 (0.070)*
ν	1.2594 (0.048)*	1.0163 (0.025)*	0.9324 (0.027)*	0.9288 (0.021)*	1.0492 (0.040)*	1.1173 (0.039)*
t-stat	1.7571*	3.6880*	2.3682*	3.6695*	3.1961*	2.7444*
m^+	0.2449	0.3773	0.3848	0.3864	0.2786	0.3764
m^-	0.1498	0.2513	0.3179	0.2770	—	0.2805
m^+/m^-	1.6343	1.5015	1.2105	1.3948	—	1.3419
$(1+\delta)/(1-\delta)$	1.4047	1.3640	1.2522	1.9940	1.3612	1.2753

Notes:
* Denotes significance at the 5% level.
Numbers in parentheses are the standard errors for the estimates.
m^+ and m^- measure the persistence, or, half-life, of positive and negative lagged returns respectively.
m^+/m^- and $(1+\delta)/(1-\delta)$ measure the degree of asymmetry in the conditional mean and the conditional standard deviation respectively.
t-stat tests $H_0: \theta^+ \leq \theta^-$ against $H_1: \theta^+ > \theta^-$.
For a one-tail test the critical value is 1.645.
C_t is a crash dummy taking the value of unity for October 1987 and zero otherwise.

© Blackwell Publishers Ltd 1999

Table 5

Volatility Specification Tests for Fitted Residuals

Test	Korea	Malaysia	Philippines	Singapore	Taiwan	Thailand
Panel A: Model without Crash Dummy						
Sign-Bias (t-test)	−0.8367	0.0109	1.5017	1.3001	0.6453	1.2139
Negative Size Bias (t-test)	0.5635	−0.0809	0.1269	−0.5613	0.5695	−0.8371
Positive Size Bias (t-test)	−0.1885	−0.2418	−0.6925	−0.6398	−2.8957*	−1.6177
Joint Test ($F_{3,2579}$ test)	0.4666	0.0288	1.0864	0.5646	3.6236*	1.7306
Panel B. Model with Crash Dummy						
Sign-Bias (t-test)	−0.7387	−0.2667	−1.8811	1.2682	2.5190*	1.1049
Negative Size Bias (t-test)	0.5614	0.2362	0.1287	−0.4047	0.2516	−0.5256
Positive Size Bias (t-test)	−0.1885	−0.1653	−0.8592	−0.6041	−3.0500*	−1.4871
Joint Test ($F_{3,2579}$ test)	0.3821	0.0753	1.9857	0.5534	4.4180*	1.6277

Notes:
* Denotes significance at the 5% level.
The regressions for the volatility specification tests are as follows:

Sign Bias Test: $z_t^2 = a + bS_t^- + u_t$ (i)
Negative Size Bias Test: $z_t^2 = a + bS_t^- \epsilon_{t-1} + u_t$ (ii)
Positive Size Bias Test: $z_t^2 = a + b(1 - S_t^-)\epsilon_{t-1} + u_t$ (iii)
Joint Test: $z_t^2 = a + b_1 S_t^- \epsilon_{t-1} + b_2(1 - S_t^-)\epsilon_{t-1} + u_t$ (iv)

where, z_t^2 is the standardized return squared, ϵ_t is the de-meaned return and S_t^- is a dummy that takes the value of unity if $\epsilon_t < 0$ and zero otherwise. Individual tests are t-tests for coefficient b in (i), (ii) and (iii). The joint test is an F-test for regression (iv).

more during market declines. On average volatility rises 1.5 times more during market declines. More importantly, the conditional mean is also an asymmetric function of past returns. Specifically, **positive past returns are on average 1.4 times more persistent** than negative past returns of an equal magnitude. This behavior is consistent with a partial adjustment price model where bad news (negative returns) are incorporated faster into current market prices than good news (positive returns). The implication is that the cost of failing to adjust prices downward is higher than the cost of failing to adjust prices upward. The faster adjustment of prices to bad news provides an alternative interpretation for the leverage effect, provided that the level of volatility rises with the speed of adjustment of prices.

NOTES

1. See Amihud and Mendelson (1987) for more details for sources of market friction.
2. Estimation of the model is done by numerical maximization techniques. The particular algorithm used is based on Berndt et al. (1974).
3. An excellent reference on the institutional characteristics (i.e., taxation, regulations, market mechanisms etc.) of these markets is Park and Agtmael (1993).
4. The group of seven (G7) includes Canada, France, Germany, Italy, Japan, the United Kingdom and the United States.
5. Daily returns are calculated as $R_t = 100(\log P_t - \log P_{t-1})$, where R_t is return and P_t is price.
6. All hypotheses testing is done at the 5% level of significance.
7. Note that the LB statistic makes no distinction between positive and negative autocorrelations.
8. The term 'bad news' is used to denote negative past returns, or, overpricing and the term 'good news' is used to denote positive past returns, or, underpricing.
9. Duffee (1995) suggests that survivorship bias may have influenced earlier findings on the significance of the leverage effect.

REFERENCES

Amihud, Y. and H. Mendelson (1987), 'Trading Mechanisms and Stock Returns: An Empirical Investigation', *Journal of Finance*, Vol. 42, pp. 533–53.
Bailey, W. and R. Stulz (1990), 'Benefits of International Diversification: The Case of Pacific Basin Stock Markets', *Journal of Portfolio Management*, Vol. 16, pp. 57–61.
────── R.M. Stulz and S. Yen (1990), 'Properties of Daily Stock Returns from the Pacific Basin Stock Markets', in S.G. Rhee and R.P. Chang (eds.), Pacific Basin Capital Markets Research, *Elsevier Science Publishers B.V.* (North Holland), pp. 155–71.
Bekaert, G. and C.R. Harvey (1997), 'Emerging Equity Market Volatility', *Journal of Financial Economics*, Vol. 43, pp. 29–77.
Berndt, E.K., H.B. Hall, R.E. Hall and J.A. Hausman (1974), 'Estimation and Inference in Nonlinear Structural Models', *Annals of Economic and Social Measurement*, Vol. 4, pp. 653–66.
Black, F. (1976), 'Studies in Stock Price Volatility Changes', *Proceedings of the 1976 Business Meeting of the Business and Economic Statistics Section. American Statistical Association*, pp. 177–81.
Bollerslev, T. (1986), 'Generalized Autoregressive Conditional Heteroskedasticity', *Journal of Econometrics*, Vol. 31, pp. 307–27.

Bollerslev, T., R.Y. Chou and K.F. Kroner (1992), 'ARCH Modeling in Finance: A Review of the Theory and Empirical Evidence', *Journal of Econometrics*, Vol. 52, pp. 5–59.

—— R.F. Engle and D.B. Nelson (1994), 'ARCH Models', in R.F. Engle and D.L. McFadden (eds.), *Handbook of Econometrics*, Vol. 4 (Elsevier Science B.V.) pp. 2959–3038.

Brorsen, W.B. (1991), 'Futures Trading, Transactions Costs and Stock Market Volatility', *Journal of Futures Markets*, Vol. 11, pp. 153–63.

Choudhry, T. (1996), 'Stock Market Volatility and the Crash of 1987: Evidence from Six Emerging Markets', *Journal of International Money and Finance*, Vol. 15, pp. 969–81.

Christie, A.A. (1982), 'The Stochastic Behavior of Common Stock Variance: Value Leverage and Interest Rate Effects', *Journal of Financial Economics*, Vol. 10, pp. 407–32.

Conrad, J. and G. Kaul (1988), 'Time-Variation in Expected Returns', *Journal of Business*, Vol. 61, pp. 409–25.

Damodaran, A. (1993), 'A Simple Measure of Price Adjustment Coefficients', *Journal of Finance*, Vol. 48, pp. 387–400.

Defusco, R.A., J.M. Geppert and G.P. Tsetsekos (1996), 'Long-Run Diversification Potential in Emerging Stock Markets', *Financial Review*, Vol. 31, pp. 343–63.

Divecha, A., J. Drach and D. Stefek (1992), 'Emerging Markets: A Quantitative Perspective', *Journal of Portfolio Management*, Vol. 19, No. 1, pp. 41-50.

Duffee, G.R. (1995), 'Stock Returns and Volatility: A Firm Level Analysis', *Journal of Financial Economics*, Vol. 37, pp. 399–420.

Engle, R.F. (1982), 'Autoregressive Conditional Heteroskedasticity with Estimates of the Variance of U.K. Inflation', *Econometrica*, Vol. 50, pp. 987–1008.

—— and V.K. Ng (1993), 'Measuring and Testing the Impact of News on Volatility', *Journal of Finance*, Vol. 48, pp. 1749–78.

Errunza, V.R. (1994), 'Emerging Markets: Some New Concepts', *Journal of Portfolio Management*, Vol. 20 (Spring), pp. 82–7.

Fama, E.F. and K.R. French (1988), 'Permanent and Transitory Components of Stock Prices', *Journal of Political Economy*, Vol. 96, pp. 246–73.

Fisher, L. (1966), 'Some New Stock Market Indexes', *Journal of Business*, Vol. 39, pp. 191–225.

Harvey, C.R. (1995), 'Predictable Risk and Returns in Emerging Stock Markets', *The Review of Financial Studies*, Vol. 8, pp. 773–816.

Hauser, S., M. Marcus and U. Yaari (1994), 'Investing in Emerging Stock Markets: Is It Worthwhile Hedging Foreign Exchange Risk?', *Journal of Portfolio Management*, Vol. 20 (Spring), pp. 76–81.

Koutmos, G. (1996), 'Modeling the Dynamic Interdependence of Major European Stock Markets', *Journal of Business Finance & Accounting*, Vol. 23, No. 7 (September) pp. 975–88.

—— and G.G. Booth (1995), 'Asymmetric Volatility Transmission in International Stock Markets', *Journal of International Money and Finance*, Vol. 14, pp. 747–62.

—— and R. Saidi (1995), 'The Leverage Effect in Individual Stocks and the Debt to Equity Ratio', *Journal of Business Finance & Accounting*, Vol. 22, No. 7 (October) pp. 1063–75.

Lee, S.B. and K.Y. Ohk (1991), 'Time-Varying Volatilities and Stock Market Returns: International Evidence', in S.G. Rhee and R.P. Chang (eds.),

© Blackwell Publishers Ltd 1999

Pacific Basin Capital Markets Research, Vol. II (Elsevier Publishers B.V., North Holland), pp. 261–81.

Lo, A.W. and C.A. MacKinlay (1990), 'An Econometric Analysis of Non-synchronous Trading', *Journal of Econometrics*, Vol. 45, pp. 181–211.

Mullin, J. (1993), 'Emerging Equity Markets in the Global Economy', *FRBNY Quarterly Review* (Summer), pp. 54–83.

Nelson, D. (1991), 'Conditional Heteroskedasticity in Asset Returns: A New Approach', *Econometrica*, Vol. 59, pp. 347–70.

Ng, V.K., R.P. Chang and R.Y. Chou (1991), 'An Examination of the Behavior of Pacific- Basin Stock Market Volatility', in S.G. Rhee and R.P. Chang (eds.), *Pacific Basin Capital Markets Research*, Vol. II (Elsevier Publishers B.V., North Holland), pp. 245–60.

Park, K.H. and A.W. Agtmael (1993), 'The World's Emerging Stock Markets: Structure, Developments, Regulations and Opportunities', *Probus Publishing Company* (Chicago Illinois).

Scholes M. and J. Williams (1977), 'Estimating Betas from Nonsynchronous Data,' *Journal of Financial Economics*, Vol. 5, pp. 309–27.

Solnic, B. (1991), 'Pacific Basin Stock Markets and International Diversification', in S.G. Rhee and R.P. Chang (eds.), *Pacific Basin Capital Markets Research*, Vol. II (Elsevier Publishers B.V., North Holland), pp. 309–21.

Sortino F.A. and R. Van Der Meer (1991), 'Downside Risk', *The Journal of Portfolio Management*, Vol. 17 (Summer), pp. 27–31.

Wilcox, J. (1992), 'Global Investing in Emerging Markets', *Financial Analysts Journal* (January–February), pp. 15–19.

Long-Run Diversification Potential in Emerging Stock Markets

Richard A. DeFusco*, John M. Geppert*, and George P. Tsetsekos**

Abstract

In this paper we use cointegration tests to examine the long-run diversification potential of 13 emerging capital markets. The Johansen [18] and Johansen and Juselius [19] cointegration procedures are applied to the U.S. and 13 emerging capital markets in three geographical regions of the world. None of the three regions examined possesses cointegrated markets. The lack of cointegration indicates that the correlation between returns from each market is independent of the investment horizon. Return correlations using weekly data correspond to the long-run investment horizon correlation. Correlations among the returns from these countries are low on average and occasionally negative. The apparent independence of markets within these three emerging regions suggests that diversification across these countries is effective.

Introduction

The stock markets of Asia and Latin America, and a handful of others, have been classified as emerging by the International Finance Corporation (IFC), the private-sector arm of the World Bank. These markets have

---

*University of Nebraska-Lincoln, Lincoln, NE 68588-0490

**Drexel University, Philadelphia, PA 19104

A version of this paper was presented at the 1993 Annual Meeting of the Financial Management Association. We would like to thank Elroy Dimson, Kathy Farrell, Gordy Karels, Stanley Martin, Mary McGarvey, Tom Zorn, participants at the Rutgers University Finance Workshop, and two anonymous referees for helpful comments. We also thank Madhumita Dutta-Sen and William V. Todd from the International Finance Corporation.

collectively grown fourfold since 1985 and together represent 5 percent of world stock market capitalization. During the last decade, academics have documented the efficiency and benefits of diversifying into emerging capital markets (e.g., Errunza [12], Errunza and Padmanabhan [13], and Bailey and Stulz [2]), and have examined the interrelationships among developed-country stock markets (e.g., Joy, Panton, Reilly, and Martin [20], Eun and Resnik [14], Philippatos, Cristofi and Cristofi [27], and Wheatly [34]). Meric and Meric [24] also document gains from international diversification among major stock markets and find that the longer the time period, the greater the degree of stability among international stock market relationships.

Recently Chan, Gup and Pan [5] tested for individual and joint efficiency of U.S. and the major Asian markets with unit root and cointegration tests. Arshanapalli and Doukas [1] use cointegration tests to examine the pre- and post-October 87 linkages and dynamic interactions among major international stock market indices. Both Chan, Gup and Pan and Arshanapalli and Doukas interpret lack of cointegration as evidence in favor of weak form market efficiency. In a recent paper, Dwyer and Wallace [9] show that the lack of cointegration is neither necessary nor sufficient for market efficiency.[1] The mounting evidence on time-varying and predictable volatility in financial markets has also been found in emerging markets (see Sewell, Stansell, Lee and Pan [31]).

The rationale for diversification benefits stems from the low value of the simple cross-country correlations estimated with weekly, monthly or quarterly data. Kasa [22] points out that the difficulty in interpreting the evidence on diversification potential is that equity prices in all national markets tend to follow an upward trend over long horizons. If all national markets share common stochastic trends, then the gains from diversification may be overstated for investors with long holding periods. With one common trend, all equity markets will be perfectly correlated in the long run. Besides common trend(s), there also could be slowly decaying transitory stochastic shocks around the trend that are of relevance to investors with long and finite holding periods.

Recent work in cointegration provides some insight on the nature of long- versus short-run correlations. Stock and Watson [32] prove that if two variables are cointegrated, then a single stochastic trend drives the pair. In the long run, the behavior of the common trend will dominate the behavior of the two series. The common stochastic trend will tie the variables together and unique shocks will die out as each variable adjusts back toward the common trend. The common stochastic trend causes the correlation between the two cointegrated series to approach 1.0 over long horizons.

The increase in the correlation in returns over long investment horizons limits the long-run diversification potential of cointegrated national markets. When more than two series are involved, the interpretation becomes less clear. With N series, if the number of stochastic trends is less than N, then the correlation between any pair of countries depends on investors' investment horizon. If the number of trends equals the number of series, N, then the correlations are independent of investors' investment horizon. Only in the special case where the number of trends equals 1, will the correlation between all pairs of countries approach 1.0 in the long run.

When markets are cointegrated, the correlation between the returns is a function of the length of the investment horizon. Previous studies that have used weekly or monthly return data to estimate the correlations among national equity markets may have overestimated the long-run diversification potential of international investing. If the national markets are cointegrated, then using monthly return data will only yield the correlation for a monthly investment horizon, because each investment horizon has its own correlation. For any other investment horizon, the monthly estimates will be inappropriate. The long-run correlations among national markets may be much higher than previously estimated if markets are cointegrated.

Our study is similar to Kasa in that tests for cointegrating relationships are conducted among national markets. Unlike Kasa, the relationship between the correlation coefficient and the length of the investment horizon in the presence of more than one common trend is explicitly modelled. The Johansen [18] and Johansen and Juselieus [19] cointegration tests are used to examine the long-run diversification potential of 13 emerging markets categorized by three geographical regions of the world. None of the three regions combined with the U.S. are cointegrated. This finding shows that independent stochastic trends generate the returns in these markets and that the correlation between the returns in these markets is independent of the investment horizon. Using weekly data, the correlation between these markets if found to be low. It would appear that international diversification across these capital markets is justified and desirable.

Cointegration and Diversification

The gains from international investing depend on the correlations among the national equity markets used to form diversified portfolios. To illustrate the behavior of the s-period return correlation in a multivariable setting, the canonical correlation analysis is used, as presented in Tsay and Tiao [33] and recently outlined in Chou and Ng [6]. This approach decomposes international stock prices into permanent (i.e., stochastic trends) and temporary (i.e., transitory) components. Let p_t be an N-dimensional time series of the natural log of international stock market prices with t indexed from 1 to T. The decomposition of Tsay and Tiao is as follows: Compute the matrix A as defined below.

$$A = \left(\sum_{t=2}^{T} p_t p_t'\right)^{-1} \left(\sum_{t=2}^{T} p_t p'_{t-1}\right) \left(\sum_{t=2}^{T} p_{t-1} p'_{t-1}\right)^{-1} \left(\sum_{t=2}^{T} p_{t-1} p_t'\right)$$

(1)

The first half of A is the coefficient matrix obtained from a matrix regression of p_{t-1} on p_t. The second half is the coefficient matrix from a matrix regression of p_t on p_{t-1}. The next step is to obtain the eigenvalues and eigenvectors of A from equation (1) such that the eigenvectors are orthogonal to each other. Let $\lambda_1 \geq \lambda_2 \geq \ldots \geq \lambda_N$ be the eigenvalues in descending order of magnitude and let $w_1, w_2, \ldots, w_N$ be the corresponding eigenvectors. The transformed series, $y_{it} \equiv w_i' p_t$ can be interpreted as the ith most persistent transformation of the original series. The y_{it}'s are called the canonical variates and are by construction uncorrelated with each other. The canonical variate approach allows a natural way to decompose the series p_t into permanent and temporary components. The decomposition outlined in Chou and Ng proceeds this way.

Let $W \equiv [w_1, \ldots, w_N]'$ and $y_t \equiv [y_{1t}, \ldots, y_{Nt}]'$ which implies that $y_t = W \cdot p_t$. Define β_{ij} as the (i,j)th element of $B \equiv W^{-1}$. Then p_{it} can be written as follows:

$$p_{it} = \sum_{j=1}^{N} \beta_{ij} y_{jt} \qquad (2)$$

As seen in equation (2) with k unit roots in p_t, $y_{1t}, \ldots, y_{kt}$ are random walks and $y_{k+1}, \ldots, y_N$ are stationary. Now define,

$$q_{it} \equiv \sum_{j=1}^{k} \beta_{ij} y_{jt}$$
$$u_{it} \equiv \sum_{j=k+1}^{N} \beta_{ij} y_{jt} \qquad (3)$$

then

$$p_{it} = q_{it} + u_{it}. \qquad (4)$$

From equation (3), the component q_{it} is the permanent part of p_{it} because $y_{1t}, \ldots, y_{kt}$ are random walks, and the component u_{it} is the temporary part due to the stationarity of $y_{k+1}, \ldots, y_{Nt}$. The one-period return for national stock index i is:

$$R_{it}^1 \equiv p_{it} - p_{it-1} \qquad (5)$$

The one-period return in equation (5) can be decomposed into its permanent and temporary components similarly used for p_{it}.

$$R_{it}^1 = \Delta q_{it} + \Delta u_{it} \qquad (6)$$

where $\Delta q_{it} \equiv q_{it} - q_{it-1}$ is the return from the permanent component and $\Delta u_{it} \equiv u_{it} - u_{it-1}$ is the return from the temporary component. This decomposition in equation (6) offers a simple way to compute the correlation of returns for varying investment horizons.

Based on the decomposition in equation (6), each log price, p_{it}, can be written as:

$$p_{it} = \sum_{g=1}^{k} \beta_{ig} y_{gt} + \sum_{g=k+1}^{N} \beta_{ig} y_{gt}, \qquad (7)$$

where the first k terms are random walks and the last $N - k$ are stationary. From (7), the s-period return can be written as:

$$R_{it}^{(s)} = \sum_{g=1}^{k} \beta_{ig}(y_{gt} - y_{gt-s}) + \sum_{g=k+1}^{N} \beta_{ig}(y_{gt} - y_{gt-s}). \qquad (8)$$

Let $\sigma_g(s)$ be the unconditional standard deviation of the s-period difference of the gth canonical variate. Because the canonical variates are uncorrelated with each other by construction, the unconditional variance of the s-period return of stock index i from equation (8) is:

$$\text{Var}(R_{it}^{(s)}) = \sum_{g=1}^{k} \beta_{ig}^2 \sigma_g^2(1) s + \sum_{g=k+1}^{N} \beta_{ig}^2 \sigma_g^2(s). \qquad (9)$$

Since the first k canonical variates are random walks, the unconditional variance of the s-period difference is simply s times the unconditional variance of the first difference. The unconditional covariance between the s-period returns of national index i and j is:

$$\text{Cov}(R_{it}^{(s)}) = \sum_{g=1}^{k} \beta_{ig}\beta_{jg}\sigma_g^2(1)s + \sum_{g=k+1}^{N} \beta_{ig}\beta_{jg}\sigma_g^2(s) \quad (10)$$

The Tsay and Tiao procedure essentially decomposes the original N series into N new orthogonal series. The first k of these new series are random walks. The remaining $(N-k)$ series are stationary variates. The number of new series which are stationary corresponds to the number of cointegrating constraints governing the system. The k non-stationary variates correspond to the stochastic trends driving the N-dimensional system.[2]

If the N national stock market indices are not cointegrated, then N independent stochastic trends drive the N series. The decomposition of Tsay and Tiao will then generate N canonical variates that are all random walks. This implies that the second sum in equations (9) and (10) will not appear, and the investment horizon, s, can be entirely factored out of the expression for the variance term and the covariance between markets i and j. Assuming that national stock market indices are not cointegrated, the s-period return correlation between indices i and j is:

$$\rho(R_{it}^{(s)}, R_{jt}^{(s)}) = \frac{\sum_{g=1}^{N} \beta_{ig}\beta_{jg}\sigma_g^2(1)}{\left[\sum_{g=1}^{N} \beta_{ig}^2\sigma_g^2(1)\right]^{1/2} \left[\sum_{g=1}^{N} \beta_{jg}^2\sigma_g^2(1)\right]^{1/2}}. \quad (11)$$

From equation (11), lack of cointegration implies that the correlation between indices i and j does not depend on the length of the investment horizon, s. Therefore, the correlations between weekly returns will be equal to the correlations of longer investment horizons. If, however, there are fewer than N independent stochastic trends (cointegrating vectors), then the s-period correlation will depend on s.

Methodology

Testing for Cointegration

The first condition for a set of series to be cointegrated is that each series must be integrated of the same order. Four regression models with their accompanying null hypothesis are used in this paper to test for the presence of a unit root. A summary of the models is presented below.

Model 1: $\quad \Delta y_t = \alpha_0 + \rho y_{t-1} + u_t \qquad H_0: \rho = 0$

Model 2: $\quad y_t = \alpha_0 + \rho y_{t-1} + u_t \qquad H_0: \rho = 1$

Model 3: $\quad \Delta y_t = \alpha_0 + \alpha_1 t + \rho y_{t-1} + u_t \qquad H_0: \rho = 0$

Model 4: $\quad y_t = \alpha_0 + \alpha_1(t - T/2) + \rho y_{t-1} + u_t \qquad H_0: \rho = 1$

In models 1 and 3, the disturbance terms are assumed to be serially uncorrelated. Models 2 and 4 allow for serial correlation in the disturbance term. Dickey and Fuller [8] show that the common test statistic, the usual "t-ratio" for the null hypothesis $\rho = 0$ does not have a t-distribution even in the limit as the sample size becomes infinite. The distribution of the t-ratio, denoted as t_μ for Model 1, or t_τ for Model 3 to distinguish it from the conventional t-statistic, has selected percentiles given in Fuller [17, p. 373].

When a variable is generated by a mixed autoregressive integrated moving average process (ARIMA) process, the critical values implied by the Dickey-Fuller simulations could be misleading. Some alternative tests for the presence of unit roots that attempt to account for mixed ARIMA processes as well as pure AR processes have been proposed by Said and Dickey [30], Phillips [28], Phillips and Perron [29], and Perron [26]. The papers by Phillips and Perron show that regardless of the order p and q of the ARIMA process, a unit root test can still be conducted. The Phillips and Perron tests, with and without trend, are presented as Models 2 and 4 above with associated test statistics denoted as $Z(t_\alpha^*)$ and

$Z(t_{\hat{a}})$. In the Phillips and Perron models the null hypothesis is $\rho = 1$, with the stationary alternative $\rho < 1$. Asymptotic critical values for $Z(t_{\alpha}^{*})$ and $Z(t_{\hat{a}})$ are found in the subtables of Table 8.5.2 of Fuller [17, p.373]. Once the series has been found to be integrated of the same order, cointegration tests can be applied.

Several different tests of cointegration have been developed.[3] The approach used in this paper is based on Johansen [18] and Johansen and Juselius [19]. To illustrate these approaches let X_t be a vector of N time series variables, each of which is integrated of order 1. Assume that X_t can be modeled by the vector autoregression,

$$X_t = \Pi_1 X_{t-1} + \ldots + \Pi_k X_{t-m} + \mu + e_t,$$

where $\Pi_1, \ldots, \Pi_m$ are $N \times N$ matrices of coefficients and μ is the constant or drift term. This equation can be written as:

$$\Delta X_t = \Gamma_1 \Delta X_{t-1} + \ldots + \Gamma_{k-1} \Delta X_{t-m+1} + \Pi X_{t-m} + \mu + e_t,$$

where

$$\Gamma_i = -(I - \Pi_1 - \ldots - \Pi_i), \quad i = 1, \ldots, m-1,$$

and

$$\Pi = -(I - \Pi_1 - \ldots - \Pi_m).$$

The last model is expressed as a traditional VAR in first differences except for the term ΠX_{t-m}. The matrix Π is called the long-run impact matrix. The appropriate lag length can be determined with the log likelihood test statistic (see Judge, et al. [21, p. 761]).

There are three possible cases for the rank of Π. If rank(Π) = 0 then $\Pi = 0$, and all of the processes in X_t are nonstationary. If rank(Π) = N, then all of the variables in X_t are stationary in levels. If $0 \leq$ rank (Π) $\leq N$, the components of X_t are cointegrated. If rank (Π) = r, where $0 \leq r \leq N$, then there are r cointegrating vectors or stationary long-run relationships among the N variables in X_t and $N - r$ common stochastic trends. In this case, there exists matrices α and β of dimension $N \times r$ such that $\Pi = \alpha\beta'$. The r cointegrating vectors β have the property that $\beta'X_t$ is stationary even though X_t is nonstationary, and the last model above can be considered an error-correction model. The α coefficients can be interpreted as measuring the average speed of adjustment toward the cointegrating relationships.

A natural way to test for the number of cointegrating relations is to examine the rank of Π, which is equal to the number of non-zero eigenvalues. Johansen and Juselius [19] develop two tests of whether the eigenvalues of the estimated Π matrix are significantly different from zero: the trace test and the maximum eigenvalue test. The maximum likelihood tests of Johansen and Juselius ensures that coefficient estimates are symmetrically distributed, median unbiased, asymptotically efficient and allows for tests of hypotheses to be conducted with standard asymptotic chi-square tests. Johansen and Juselius [19, p. 208-209] give critical values for, at most, six variables and Osterwald-Lenum [25] gives critical values for, at most, 11 variables for multivariate tests of cointegration. In the empirical tests which follow, the multivariate analysis is limited to three geographical regions of the world.

Data

Weekly price index levels published by the International Finance Corporation (IFC) for 13 emerging capital markets were collected for 228 weeks from January 1989 to May 1993. IFC reports index levels in U.S. dollars using the Friday closing stock prices. If that Friday was a holiday, the last transaction price is used in the calculation of the price index. Stocks selected for inclusion in the country indexes were based on market capitalization, liquidity, and industry classification. The indices include actively traded stocks broadly diversified by industry, whose combined market values are approximately 60 percent of total market capitalization at the end of each year. Stocks were not selected on the basis of their availability to foreign investors. In a few instances, the IFC may include in the index more than one class of stock for the same company. All IFC price indexes are weighted by market capitalization. Weekly data on the Standard & Poors 500 index were collected from the daily indices file maintained by the University of Chicago's Center for Research in Security Prices for the time period January 1989 to December 1992. S&P500 data from January 1993 to May 1993 was collected from the *Wall Street Journal*. Because of limitations on dividend data, all tests are performed on price levels only. In the Appendix, conditions on dividend behavior are derived which would leave our results unaffected.

Results

Descriptive Statistics and Unit Root Tests

Table 1 presents summary statistics for the 13 emerging capital markets and the United States. During

TABLE 1

Summary Statistics of Weekly Returns for 13 Emerging Capital Markets and the United States

Data on the 13 emerging markets and the U.S. covers the time period January 1989 to May 1993.

Country	Mean	Variance	Skewness	Kurtosis	Interquartile range
Brazil	0.0495	0.00864	−0.683	4.058	0.112
Chile	0.0060**	0.00101	0.455	0.319	0.043
Colombia	0.0059**	0.00164	1.484	7.445	0.029
Mexico	0.0067**	0.00087	−0.364	0.530	0.036
Venezuela	0.0047	0.00136	0.402	1.638	0.062
Korea	−0.0017	0.00136	0.812	1.352	0.047
Philippines	0.0018	0.00179	−1.160	6.147	0.042
Taiwan	−0.0002	0.00389	−0.199	2.777	0.067
Malaysia	0.0028	0.00080	−0.818	4.730	0.028
Thailand	0.0037	0.00189	−0.889	9.654	0.043
Greece	0.0025	0.00276	0.589	2.017	0.060
Portugal	−0.0012	0.00085	0.514	2.695	0.030
Turkey	0.0035	0.00571	0.278	0.312	0.090
United States	0.0020*	0.00032	−0.322	1.035	0.022

**Statistically different from zero at the 5 percent level of significance.

*Statistically different from zero at the 10 percent level of significance.

the period from January 1989 to May 1993, Brazil had the largest weekly return of 4.95 percent while Korea experienced the biggest loss at –0.17 percent. Only the mean weekly returns of the United States, Chile, Colombia and Mexico are found to be significantly different from zero. Of the 13 markets, Brazil has the largest amount of volatility as seen in its variance of 0.0080 and its interquartile range of 11.20 percent. For comparison purposes, the United States has the lowest variance of 0.00032.

As discussed earlier, for two series to be cointegrated, the series must be integrated of the same order. Tests of the order of integration can be conducted for individual countries with unit root tests (adjusted Dickey-Fuller (ADF) t_μ no trend; t_τ with trend, and Phillips-Peron $Z(t_\alpha^*)$ no trend; $Z(t_{\tilde{\alpha}})$ with trend) test statistics. Unit root tests are corrected for possible serial correlation and autoregressive heteroscedasticity. Table 2 presents the results of the four unit root tests. For all countries, the null hypothesis of the presence of a unit root cannot be rejected. Further testing on the first differences of each stock price index series does not indicate the presence of a second unit root. Hence, for those countries, individual stock markets appear to be $I(1)$. Because all country stock index levels are $I(1)$, all are potential candidates for cointegrated markets.

Cointegration Tests

The Johansen and Juselius cointegration test is applied to three mutually exclusive groupings of national stock markets based on their geographical region. Each of the groupings below also includes the U.S. The groups are as follows:

Latin America: U.S. and Brazil, Chile, Colombia, Mexico, and Venezuela
Pacific Basin: U.S. and Korea, Philippines, Taiwan, Malaysia, and Thailand
Mediterranean: U.S. and Greece, Portugal, and Turkey

Diversification Potential in Emerging Stock Markets

TABLE 2

Unit Root Tests on Emerging Stock Indices and the United States

Adjusted Dickey-Fuller (ADF) t_μ no trend; t_τ with trend, and Phillips-Peron $Z(t_\alpha^*)$ no trend; $Z(t_{\hat\alpha})$ with trend.

Country	t_μ	$Z(t_\alpha^*)$	t_τ	$Z(t_{\hat\alpha})$
Brazil	−0.14	−0.09	−2.68	−2.03
Chile	−1.24	−1.29	−0.99	−0.37
Colombia	−0.28	−0.15	−1.61	−1.46
Mexico	−1.80	−1.83	−1.23	−0.91
Venezuela	−0.87	−0.94	−0.42	0.10
Korea	−1.37	−1.40	−1.98	−1.92
Philippines	−1.36	−1.25	−1.36	−1.26
Taiwan	−1.17	−1.23	−2.00	−2.39
Malaysia	−1.17	−2.12	−2.19	−2.58
Thailand	−1.99	−1.40	−2.41	−2.35
Greece	−1.79	−1.69	−1.15	−1.00
Portugal	−0.66	−0.77	−2.62	−1.70
Turkey	−1.55	−1.49	−2.23	−2.18
United States	−1.53	−1.66	−2.64	−2.99

None of the above statistics are significant at conventional levels.

Statistic	Model	Null Hypothesis	1%	5%	10%
t_μ:	$\Delta y_t = \alpha_0 + \rho y_{t-1} + u_t$	$H_0: \rho = 0$	−3.46	−2.88	−2.57
$Z(t_\alpha^*)$:	$y_t = \alpha_0 + \rho y_{t-1} + u_t$	$H_0: \rho = 1$	−3.43	−2.86	−2.57
t_τ:	$\Delta y_t = \alpha_0 + \alpha_1 t + \rho y_{t-1} + u_t$	$H_0: \rho = 0$	−3.99	−3.43	−3.13
$Z(t_{\hat\alpha})$:	$y_t = \alpha_0 + \alpha_1(t - T/2) + \rho y_{t-1} + u_t$	$H_0: \rho = 1$	−3.96	−3.41	−3.12

The first step in the Johansen and Juselius cointegration test is determining the lag length for the vector autoregression (VAR). A log likelihood test statistic compares the adequacy of m versus $m + 1$ lags. Results of this test indicate that the null hypothesis of more than one lag in the vector autoregression for Latin America and the Pacific Basin, and two lags for the Mediterranean cannot be rejected. The results of the Johansen and

TABLE 3

Trace and Maximum Eigenvalue Test Statistics for Cointegration

The trace test examines the suitability of at most the number of cointegrating vectors indicated below. The maximum eigenvalue test examines the suitability of the number of cointegrating vectors indicated below versus that number plus one.

Number of Cointegrating Vectors	Group I Trace Test	Group I Maximum Eigenvalue	Group II Trace Test	Group II Maximum Eigenvalue	Group III Trace Test	Group III Maximum Eigenvalue
0	87.17	32.51	75.20	23.74	41.34	18.32
1	52.65	19.11	51.46	19.84	23.02	13.10
2	33.54	15.65	31.61	14.61	9.91	9.26
3	17.88	11.79	17.00	9.20	0.65	0.65
4	6.08	5.61	7.79	5.80	na	na
5	0.46	0.46	1.99	1.99	na	na

Group I   Latin America: U.S. and Argentina, Brazil, Chile, Colombia, Mexico, and Venezuela
Group II Pacific Basin: U.S. and Korea, Philippines, Taiwan, Malaysia, and Thailand
Group III Mediterranean: U.S. and Greece, Portugal, and Turkey

na = Test not applicable for four countries

None of the above statistics are significant at the 5 percent level

Juselius trace and maximum eigenvalue tests are presented in Table 3. In no case is a cointegrating relationship found among the counties within each grouping. In the long run, these countries stock price indices do not exhibit any tendency to move together. Because there are no cointegrating relationships, the estimated coefficients for α and β (speed of adjustment and cointegrating vectors) are not reported. The lack of cointegration implies that the second sum in equation (10) is not present and that the correlation between pairs of market does not depend on the investment horizon, s. Consequently, weekly return data can be used to measure the long investment horizon correlation. Gains from diversification are possible as long as the correlations between the national indices are low.

Table 4 presents the correlation coefficients of the weekly returns. The correlations reported in Table 4 are

TABLE 4

Correlation Coefficients of Weekly Returns for 13 Emerging Capital Markets and the United States for the Period January 1989 to May 1993

Countries are as follows: Brazil, Chile, Colombia, Mexico, Venezuela, Korea, Philippines, Taiwan, Malaysia, Thailand, Greece, Portugal, Turkey, and United States

	Bra	Chi	Col	Mex	Ven	Kor	Phil	Tai	Mal	Thai	Gre	Por	Tur	US
Bra	1.00	0.12	0.10	0.09	-0.1	0.04	0.03	0.13	0.16	0.10	0.10	0.14	0.13	0.10
Chi		1.00	-0.03	0.04	-0.10	0.09	0.06	0.04	0.04	0.002	0.06	0.06	-0.04	0.03
Col			1.00	-0.01	0.004	-0.13	0.06	0.06	-0.02	0.03	0.03	0.03	0.16	0.02
Mex				1.00	-0.02	0.09	0.20	0.21	0.38	0.23	0.12	0.18	0.02	0.37
Ven					1.00	-0.01	-0.04	-0.16	-0.03	-0.07	-0.09	-0.06	-0.03	-0.13
Kor						1.00	-0.06	0.06	0.18	0.17	-0.05	0.09	0.02	0.16
Phil							1.00	0.24	0.31	0.23	0.14	0.23	0.14	0.17
Tai								1.00	0.28	0.23	0.09	0.16	0.14	0.18
Mal									1.00	0.52	0.23	0.30	0.26	0.25
Thai										1.00	0.15	0.31	0.23	0.24
Gre											1.00	0.40	0.30	0.05
Por												1.00	0.28	0.24
Tur													1.00	0.05
US														1.00

consistent with those reported in Errunza [12], Errunza and Padmanabhan [13], and Bailey and Stulz [2]. Correlations on average are quite low and even negative for many combinations. The average correlation is 0.11, the maximum is 0.52 (Malaysia and Thailand), and the minimum is −0.16 (Taiwan and Venezuela). The distances that separate these countries does not appear to influence the degree of correlation. Even countries that are located within the same region of the world have low and/or negative correlations. It would appear that substantial gains from diversification exist among the 13 emerging markets. Correlations between the 13 emerging markets and the S&P500 index range from a maximum of 0.37 with Mexico to a minimum of −0.13 with Venezuela. The summary statistical evidence and lack of cointegration would indicate that gains exist from diversifying among emerging markets.

Conclusions

In this paper cointegration tests are used to examine the long-run diversification potential of 13 emerging capital markets. Cointegration tests are conducted based on geographical regions of the world using the Johansen [18] and Johansen and Juselius [19] procedure. None of the three regions examined possess cointegrated markets. The correlations between countries is, on average, quite low (average correlation is 0.11). The apparent independence of markets within these three emerging regions suggests that diversification across countries should be quite effective. Further analysis might include the relationships between established and emerging markets.

Appendix

The analysis in this paper was performed on international stock indices exclusive of dividend data. Because investors are concerned with total returns, ideally one would like to have an index which tracks total portfolio value, inclusive of the effect of dividend reinvestment. The value at time t of a portfolio with dividend reinvestment can be expressed as:

Diversification Potential in Emerging Stock Markets

$$V_{1t} = P_{1t}\left[\prod_{j=1}^{t}\left(1+\frac{D_{1j}}{P_{1j}}\right)\right] \quad (A1)$$

where V_{1t} is the portfolio value, P_{1t} is the level of country index 1 and D_{1j} is the dividend associated with country index 1 occurring in period j. The total return (dividend plus capital gain) can be measured as the difference of the natural log of V_{1t}. Taking the natural log of equation (A1) and rearranging terms yields

$$\ln(P_{1t}) = \ln(V_{1t}) - \sum_{j=1}^{t}\ln\left(1+\frac{D_{1j}}{P_{1j}}\right). \quad (A2)$$

Tests for cointegration between two international indices using only the index level of countries 1 and 2 involves determining whether some linear combination $\{\ln(P_{1t}) - \beta \ln(P_{2t})\}$ is stationary. Using (A2), this cointegration test is equivalent to testing whether the following is stationary:

$$\left[\ln(V_{1t}) - \sum_{j=1}^{t}\ln\left(1+\frac{D_{1j}}{P_{1j}}\right)\right] - \beta\left[\ln(V_{2t}) - \sum_{j=1}^{t}\ln\left(1+\frac{D_{2j}}{P_{2j}}\right)\right] \quad (A3)$$

Rearranging equation (A3) yields

$$\ln(V_{1t}) - \beta\ln(V_{2t}) - \left[\sum_{j=1}^{t}\ln\left(1+\frac{D_{1j}}{P_{1j}}\right) - \beta\sum_{j=1}^{t}\ln\left(1+\frac{D_{2j}}{P_{2j}}\right)\right] \quad (A4)$$

Tests for cointegration between two country indices will produce the same results whether using price levels only or prices adjusted for dividends whenever the last two terms in equation (A4) are stationary.

$$\sum_{j=1}^{t}\ln\left(1+\frac{D_{1j}}{P_{1j}}\right) \quad \text{and} \quad \sum_{j=1}^{t}\ln\left(1+\frac{D_{2j}}{P_{2j}}\right) \quad (A5)$$

These two terms in (A5) will be stationary if the discounted cash flow model of asset prices is valid and if expected discount rates and dividend growth rates are stationary processes (see Campbell and Shiller [4] for a detailed derivation).

Notes

1. It is well understood that any test of market efficiency is actually a joint test of a particular model and the efficiency of the market. Predictability of asset returns is often interpreted as evidence of weak form market inefficiency. However, just as with statements about market efficiency, market inefficiency cannot be discussed separately from a specific modelling framework. Asset return predictability and market efficiency are inconsistent in an environment with time invariant risk premiums. However, there is mounting evidence that such an environment is not rich enough to describe many asset returns. Eckbo and Liu [10] discuss that univariate predictability is consistent with market efficiency in an environment with time varying risk premia. Time variation in the risk premium could be driven by predictable variation in economic aggregates (e.g., Fama and French [15],[16] Keim and Stambaugh [23], Daniel and Torous [7] and Engle and Rothschild [11]). Bossaerts [3] shows that a Lucas type representative consumer model can lead to asset prices which are cointegrated. In such an environment, asset returns are predictable, yet each agent is behaving optimally. While it is true that cointegration among asset prices does imply an error-correction representation and necessarily a predictable component in asset returns, markets can still be efficient (in the sense that agents are behaving optimally) if risk premiums are allowed to be time varying.

2. Conceptually, cointegrating vectors can be thought of as representing constraints that an economic system imposes on the movement of the variables in the system in the long-run. Consequently, the more cointegrating vectors there are, the more stable the system. Consider a system with N variables and no common trends (or no unit roots), so the system is stationary (i.e., all changes in the level of the variables are temporary). The variables never deviate too far from their steady-state equilibrium value. If there is one common trend ($N - 1$ cointegrating vectors) there are only $N - 1$ directions where the variance is finite and one direction in which it is infinite. And, if there is only one cointegrating vector, the system can deviate in $N - 1$ independent directions and is stable in only one direction. Geometrically, if there are three variables that span R^3 and if these variables are stationary, the system converges to a steady state equilibrium. In this case it is a point in R^3 and variation around that point is finite. If there is one common trend (two cointegrating vectors) the system converges to a long-run equilibrium represented by a line, determined by the intersection of the planes of the two cointegrating vectors in R^3. This is a stationary equilibrium in the sense that the variance about this line is finite. With two common trends (one cointegrating vector), the long-run equilibrium is represented by a plane defined by the single cointegrating vector. The variables are unbounded in the plane, but cannot move too far from it. The variance in the plane is infinite, but

the variance about the plane is finite. With no cointegrating vectors the variables are free to wander in R^3.

3. Several researchers have developed tests for cointegration and methods for estimating cointegrating vectors. All of these tests involve locating the "most stationary" linear combinations (among all the possible ones) of the time series in question. Estimation methods of cointegration have been proposed with ordinary least squares, nonlinear least squares, and principal components. Johansen and Johansen and Juselius use maximum likelihood estimation in a fully specified error-correction model.

References

[1] Arshanapalli, Bala, and John Doukas. "International Stock Market Linkages: Evidence From the Pre- and Post-October 1987 Period." *Journal of Banking and Finance* 17(1993): 193-208.

[2] Bailey, Warren, and Rene M. Stulz. "Benefits of International Diversification: The Case of Pacific Basin Stock Markets." *Journal of Portfolio Management* 16(1990): 57-61.

[3] Bossaerts, Peter. "Common Nonstationary Components of Asset Prices." *Journal of Economic Dynamics and Control* 12(1988): 347-364.

[4] Campbell, John Y., and Robert J. Shiller. "The Dividend-Price Ratio and Expectations of Future Dividends and Discount Factors." *Review of Financial Studies* 1(1989): 195-228.

[5] Chan, Kam C., Benton E. Gup, and Ming-Shiun Pan. "An Empirical Analysis of Stock Prices in Major Asian Markets and the United States." *Financial Review* 27(1992): 89-307.

[6] Chou, Raymond Y., and Victor K. Ng. "Correlation Structure of the Permanent and Temporary Components of International Stock Market Prices." Paper presented at the 1993 meeting of the Financial Management Association.

[7] Daniel, Kenneth, and Walter Torous. "Common Stock Returns and the Business Cycle." Working paper, University of British Columbia (1991).

[8] Dickey, David A., and Wayne A. Fuller. "Distributions of the Estimates for Autoregressive Time Series with a Unit Root." *Journal of the American Statistical Association* 74(1979): 427-432.

[9] Dwyer, Gerald P. Jr, and Myles S. Wallace. "Cointegration and Market Efficiency." *Journal of International Money and Finance* 11(1992): 318-327.

[10] Eckbo, B. Espen and Jian Liu. "Temporary Components of Stock Prices: New Univariate Results." *Journal of Financial and Quantitative Analysis* 28(1993): 161-176.

[11] Engle, Robert F., and Michael Rothschild. "A Multi-Dynamic Factor Model for Stock Returns." *Journal of Econometrics* 52(1992): 245-266.

[12] Errunza, Vihang R. "Emerging Markets: A New Opportunity for Improving Global Portfolio Performance." *Financial Analysts Journal* (Sept-Oct 1983): 51-58.

[13] Errunza, Vihang R., and Prasad Padmanabhan. "Further Evidence on the Benefits of Portfolio Investments in Emerging Markets." *Financial Analysts Journal* (July-Aug 1988): 76-78.

[14] Eun, Cheol S., and Bruce Resnik. "Estimating the Correlation Structure of International Share Prices." *Journal of Finance* (1984): 1311-1324.

[15] Fama, Eugene F., and Kenneth French. "Dividend Yields and Expected Stock Returns." *Journal of Financial Economics* 22(1988): 3-25.

[16] Fama, Eugene F., and Kenneth French. "Business Conditions and Expected Returns on Stocks and Bonds." *Journal of Financial Economics* 25(1989): 23-49.

[17] Fuller, Wayne A. "Introduction to Statistical Time Series." New York, Wiley & Sons, 1976.

[18] Johansen, Soren. "Statistical Analysis of Cointegrating Vectors." *Journal of Economic Dynamics and Control* 12(1988): 231-254.

[19] Johansen, Soren, and Katarina Juselius. "Maximum Likelihood Estimation and Inference on Cointegration—With Applications to the Demand for Money." *Oxford Bulletin of Economics and Statistics* 52(1990): 169-210.

[20] Joy, O. Maurice, Don B. Panton, Frank K. Reilly, and Stanley A. Martin. "Comovements of Major International Equity Markets." *Financial Review* 11(1976): 1-20.

[21] Judge, George G., R.C. Carter, William E. Griffiths, Helmut Lutkepohl, and Tsoung-Chao Lee. "Introduction to the Theory and Practice of Econometrics." New York: Wiley & Sons 1988.

[22] Kasa, Kenneth. "Common Stochastic Trends in International Stock Markets." *Journal of Monetary Economics* 29(1992): 95-124.

[23] Keim, Donald B., and Robert F. Stambaugh. "Predicting Returns in the Stock and Bond Markets." *Journal of Financial Economics* 17(1986): 357-390.

[24] Meric, Ilhan and Gusler Meric. "Potential Gains from International Portfolio Diversification and Inter-temporal Stability and Seasonality in International Stock Market Relationships." *Journal of Banking and Finance* 13(1989): 627-640.

Diversification Potential in Emerging Stock Markets

[25] Osterwald-Lenum, Michael. "A Note with Quantiles of the Asymptotic Distribution of the Maximum Likelihood Cointegration Rank Test Statistics." *Oxford Bulletin of Economics and Statistics* 54(1992): 461-472.

[26] Perron, Pierre. "Trends and Random Walks in Macroeconomic Time Series: Further Evidence from a New Approach." *Journal of Economic Dynamics and Control* 12(1988): 297-332.

[27] Philippatos, Geroge C., Andreas Cristofi, and Petros Cristofi. "The Intertemporal Stability of Stock Market Relationships: Another View." *Financial Management* (Winter 1983): 63-69.

[28] Phillips, Peter C.B. "Time Series Regression with a Unit Root." *Econometrica* 55(1987): 277-301.

[29] Phillips, Peter C.B., and Pierre Perron. "Testing for a Unit Root in Time Series Regression." *Biometrika* 75(1988): 335-346.

[30] Said, Said E., and David A. Dickey. "Testing for Unit Roots in Autoregressive Moving Average Models of Unknown Order." *Biometrika* 71(1984): 599-607.

[31] Sewell, Susan, Stanley Stansell, Insup Lee, and Ming-Shiun Pan. "Nonlinearities in Emerging Foreign Capital Markets." *Journal of Business Finance & Accounting* 20(1993): 237-248.

[32] Stock, James H., and Mark W. Waston. Testing for common trends, Discussion paper no. 1222, Harvard University, Institute for Economic Research, Cambridge, MA 1987.

[33] Tsay, Ruey S., and George C. Tiao. "Asymptotic Properties of Multivariate Nonstationary Processes with Applications to Autoregressions." *The Annals of Statistics* 18(1990): 220-250.

[34] Wheatly, Simon. "Some Tests of Equity Integration." *Journal of Financial Economics* 20(1988): 177-212.

[18]
New Perspectives on Emerging Market Bonds

Looking beyond the current crisis.

Claude B. Erb, Campbell R. Harvey, and Tadas E. Viskanta

CLAUDE B. ERB is a managing director at First Chicago NBD Investment Management Company in Chicago (IL 60670).

CAMPBELL R. HARVEY is a professor at the Fuqua School of Business at Duke University in Durham (NC 27708), and a fellow at the National Bureau of Economic Research in Cambridge, Massachusetts.

TADAS E. VISKANTA is a vice president at First Chicago NBD Investment Management Company in Chicago (IL 60670).

Emerging market bonds have attracted considerable interest for their very high average returns. Indeed, from 1991 through early summer 1997, the average returns on emerging market bonds exceeded return on the Standard & Poor's 500 index. Since August 1997, however, the value of these bonds has plummeted along with equity market values. We argued in the summer of 1997 that any judgment on the viability of emerging market bonds as an asset class is difficult, given 1) the short history of data, and 2) that characteristics were being measured over a long bull market (Erb, Harvey, and Viskanta [1997b]).

Nemerever [1996], Dahiya [1997], and Froland [1998] all argue the case for investment in emerging market bonds, but there is very little research on emerging market debt. Emerging market equities, on the other hand, have garnered far more attention. Harvey [1995] finds that standard asset pricing models fail when applied to these markets. He attributes the failure of these models to a lack of integration of emerging capital markets with global capital markets. Bekaert and Harvey [1995, 1997] propose and test models of expected returns in emerging markets that explicitly take the degree of market integration into account. Erb, Harvey, and Viskanta [1996a] propose a model of expected returns based on risk ratings in emerging market countries.

With more data from both up and down cycles, it is now more appropriate to examine the characteristics of EM bonds. We have several objectives. First, we explore the yields of these bonds over U.S. Treasury bonds in the context of a country risk model. Second, we consider the risk and expected return characteristics of these bonds, broadening the view of risk to include conditional skewness risk. Third, we explore the shifting cross-asset class correlations of emerging market bonds. Finally, we conduct an analysis of style to determine to what degree these bonds figure in other asset classes.

HISTORICAL PERSPECTIVE

Although many of the discussions about emerging market bonds apply only to the last decade, global bond investing has a long history. Through at least the first World War, London was the center of global finance. Latin American lending had already become quite widespread in the nineteenth century. The sale of foreign bonds to individual investors, and the subsequent losses, played a role in enactment of the Glass-Steagall Act in 1933 (see Chernow [1990]).

Volatility has been a hallmark of emerging market bonds throughout time. Exhibit 1A shows yields on Argentine and Brazilian bonds from 1859 through 1959.[1] One can clearly see periodic bouts of distress and volatility. This long-term historical perspective allows us to put recent experience into context.

Exhibit 1B shows the stripped yields over U.S. Treasuries for Argentina and Brazil from 1991

EXHIBIT 1A
EMERGING MARKET BONDS —
LONG-TERM HISTORICAL YIELDS

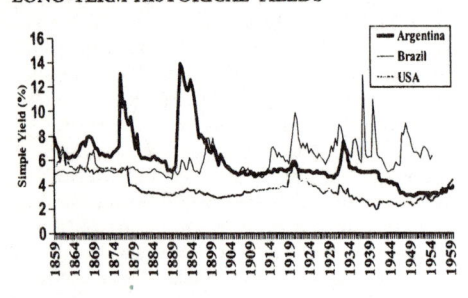

Semiannual observations.

Source: Global Financial Database.

EXHIBIT 1B
EMERGING MARKET BONDS —
RECENT HISTORICAL YIELDS

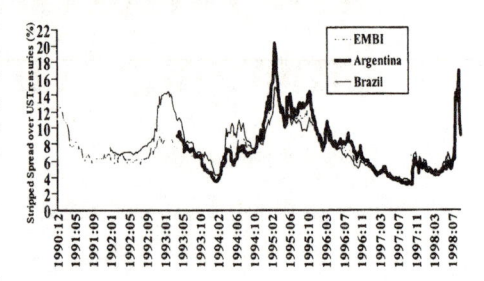

Weekly observations.

Source: J.P. Morgan Securities.

through mid-1998. Again we see both high yields and ample volatility.

DATA

Data on emerging market bonds are limited in large part by the short history of many of these instruments. J.P. Morgan Securities, however, provides an impressive source of data on emerging market bonds, and we use its data throughout.

The two major indexes are EMBI (Emerging Market Bond Index) and EMBI+. EMBI consists of U.S. dollar-denominated Brady bonds.[2] EMBI+ expands on EMBI by including other non-local currency-denominated bonds and has more restrictive liquidity requirements. As of September 30, 1998, the EMBI included bonds from thirteen countries.

A problem in regard to emerging market equities is market survivorship. Goetzmann and Jorion [1996] demonstrate that emerging equity markets that rebound after a period of dormancy have higher returns for some initial period than their long-term expected return. Such an upward bias should be evident in emerging market bond markets as well. The effects of debt renegotiation and market liberalization drove returns over this period above their sustainable long-term average. Therefore, these data likely need to be interpreted with great care.

J.P. Morgan also produces the ELMI+ (Emerging Local Market Index), a local currency-denominated money market index that covers twenty-four countries. It differs from the earlier indexes in a number of respects. First, it comprises securities denominated in each country's local currency. Second, the index has a short duration (forty-day average life as of September 30, 1998). Third, the country composition differs materially from the hard currency indexes. To date most foreign emerging market investment has been in the longer-duration hard currency bonds. It is likely, however, that local currency bonds will become increasingly important.

EMERGING MARKET BOND CAPITALIZATION

Emerging market bonds remain a relatively small part of the world capital markets. In September 1998, the market capitalization of J.P. Morgan's EMBI was U.S. $71 billion. This compares to $252 billion for the CS First Boston high-yield index. The Lehman long-term U.S. government index has $748 billion in capitalization, while the Lehman U.S. intermediate and aggregate indexes have $1.828 trillion and $5.408 trillion, respectively. The Salomon Smith Barney non-U.S. bond index has $4.336 billion in capitalization. Clearly, emerging market bonds are a very small fraction of the fixed-income market.

The emerging market bonds are also small compared to equity capitalization. The International Finance Corporation Global index has $668 billion in market capitalization while the IFC Investables index has $482 billion. The Morgan Stanley Capital International EAFE has $6.063 trillion in capitalization and the Standard & Poor's 500 has $8.153 trillion.

Through 1997, local currency bonds seemed to be expanding their market presence. Hinchberger [1997] cites estimates that the market capitalization of local currency emerging market fixed-income instruments is two times the hard currency market. Even at this size, there remain some concerns for foreign investors. The market is dominated by short-term (shorter than one year) instruments, as represented in J.P. Morgan's ELMI+. Other issues related to an expanding local currency debt market include potential illiquidity and complex regulatory issues in certain countries.

Emerging market bonds were initially viewed by many market participants as high-yield substitutes. Indeed, for a time in 1997, emerging market bonds appeared to be approaching U.S. high-yield bonds in terms of market capitalization. If local currency-denominated securities are taken into account, then emerging market debt might surpass the size of the U.S. high-yield market.

The Asian financial crisis has pointed out the danger for countries and companies of relying on debt issues denominated in hard currencies (see Harvey and Roper [1998]).

RISK AND EXPECTED RETURNS OF EMERGING MARKET BONDS

We need to exercise some caution in any historical analysis of emerging market bond performance. The J.P. Morgan EMBI dates back only to January 1991. There are great dangers in drawing inferences on the basis of such short samples. For example, in the summer of 1997, the average performance of the EMBI was better than that of the S&P 500 and considerably better than the U.S. high-yield index. Such return differentials are often used to promote investment in emerging market bonds.

One year makes a huge difference. Both emerging market equities and bonds were subject to massive selloffs beginning in August 1997. Average returns decreased, and volatility increased.

Exhibits 2A and 2B show that emerging market bonds (JPM EMBI) stand out in terms of both return and volatility. Over the January 1991 to September 1998 period, emerging market bonds have higher returns than emerging market equities (IFCG and IFCI) and U.S. high-yield corporate debt (CSFB High Yield). The return advantage, however, comes at the cost of higher volatility, which we will see for emerging market bonds is largely idiosyncratic.

DISTRIBUTIONAL CHARACTERISTICS OF EMERGING MARKET BONDS

Research into the distributional characteristics of emerging market equities has shown significant deviations from normality. Bekaert and Harvey [1997] and Bekaert et al. [1997] demonstrate that emerging market equities exhibit skewness and excess kurtosis. They show that, given a typical investor's preferences, optimal investment weights should reflect the asset's contribution to portfolio skewness.

The intuition for this is straightforward. People like assets that deliver high positive skewness and are

EXHIBIT 2A
WORLD CAPITAL MARKETS:
RISK, RETURN, AND RELATIVE
CAPITALIZATION IN SEPTEMBER 1998

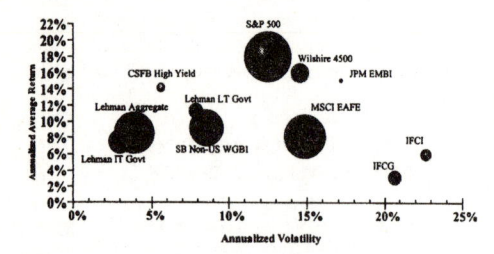

Data: Monthly U.S.$ total returns (1991:01-1998:09).

EXHIBIT 2B
WORLD CAPITAL MARKETS:
RISK, RETURN, AND RELATIVE
CAPITALIZATION IN SEPTEMBER 1998

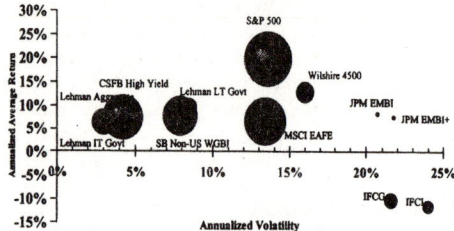

Data: Monthly U.S.$ total returns (1994:01-1998:09).

willing to accept low (or even negative) expected returns for these assets (viz. lottery tickets, option payoffs). Investors do not like negative skewness. To take on negative skewness, investors demand a higher expected return.[3]

One difficulty with measuring skewness is that it likely changes through time. That is, past data may give no indication of future expected skewness. This is the so-called peso problem in economic theory. Looking at past currency movements, you may see little variation in rates during a managed float regime. Yet there is a probability of a devaluation that you cannot detect from looking at past data. This is the definition of negative skewness.

The inability to detect negative skewness using past data does not appear to be relevant for emerging market bonds. For example, in the January 1991 through May 1997 period, the EMBI has a negative skewness of –0.7. In the January 1994 to May 1997 period, the negative skewness is –0.5. During the same period, the EMBI+ has a negative skewness of –0.06. There was considerable evidence — before the emerging market meltdown — that emerging market bonds possessed negative skewness. This negative skewness is consistent with the high expected returns.

The events beginning in the summer of 1997 caused an even greater measured negative skewness. Exhibit 3 shows that the skewness of the EMBI portfolio in the January 1991 through September 1998 period is –2.1.

Bonds and Equities

Are emerging market equities and bonds sub-

Abbreviation	Index
CSFB High Yield	Credit Suisse First Boston High Yield Bond Index
IFCI	International Finance Corporation Investable Composite
IFCG	International Finance Corporation Global Composite
JPM EMBI	J.P. Morgan Emerging Market Bond Index
JPM EMBI+	J.P. Morgan Emerging Market Bond Index Plus
Lehman Aggregate	Lehman Brothers Aggregate Bond Index
Lehman LT Government	Lehman Brothers Long-Term Government Bond Index
Lehman IT Government	Lehman Brothers Intermediate-Term Government Bond Index
MSCI EAFE	Morgan Stanley Capital International Europe, Australasia, and Far East Index
S&P 500	Standard & Poor's 500 Index
SB Non-U.S. WGBI	Salomon Brothers Non-United States World Government Bond Index (Unhedged)
Wilshire 4500	Wilshire Associates 4500 Stock Index

stitutes? Intuition suggests that high-yield bonds should behave much like equities — especially in times of distress. Our intuition is that emerging market stocks and bonds should have higher intramarket correlations than those in the developed markets because of their country-specific risk. This would

EXHIBIT 3
WORLD CAPITAL MARKETS: SKEWNESS

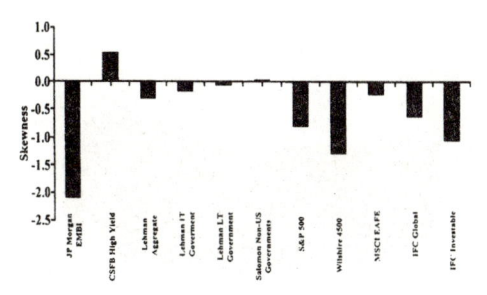

Data: Monthly U.S.$ total returns (1991:01-1998:09).

allow an investor the chance to more readily substitute bonds and stocks within an emerging country. This could be very helpful in markets where liquidity or investability are issues.

Exhibit 4 details the equity-bond correlations for eleven countries. We report three subperiods: January 1991-September 1998, January 1991-July 1997, and August 1997-September 1998. The third period isolates the emerging market selloff. The correlations are generally very high, which is consistent with intuition.

The most striking pattern in Exhibit 4 is the dramatic increase in the intramarket correlations during the most recent year. Argentina, Brazil, Mexico, Russia, and Venezuela all have intramarket correlations around 0.8. For the index as a whole, the correlation increases from 0.55 in the period up to July 1997 to 0.82 over the last fourteen months of the period.[4]

Asset Class Correlations

Exhibit 5 presents the correlation of J.P. Morgan's EMBI with other asset classes. The time periods correspond to the start of the EMBI and the EMBI+. The correlation between EMBI and EMBI+ is very high at 0.98.

Examining the data through July 1997, one notices that the highest correlations are with the two IFC emerging market indexes. Correlations against other U.S. dollar bond indexes are in the 0.35 to 0.50 range up to July 1997. A first glance at the data suggests that emerging market bonds are unique in their return patterns, but there is a extraordinary shift in the patterns when the most recent data are examined.

In the fourteen months after July 1997, the correlation with the CSFB high-yield index doubles. The correlation with the S&P 500 is higher than 0.8 and surprisingly higher than the correlation with the IFC indexes. The correlation with the government bond indexes shifts from positive in the earlier period to negative in the most recent period.

Another way of approaching this question is to examine emerging market bond returns in a multivariate setting. We use a Sharpe-style attribution methodology to examine both the overall and time series

EXHIBIT 4
EMERGING MARKET BONDS: INTRACOUNTRY BOND VERSUS EQUITY INDEX CORRELATION

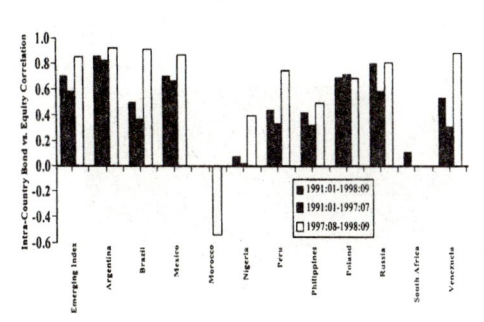

Data: Monthly U.S.$ total returns.
Equities: IFC Investable; Bonds: J.P. Morgan EMBI+.

EXHIBIT 5
EMERGING MARKET BONDS: ASSET CLASS CORRELATIONS

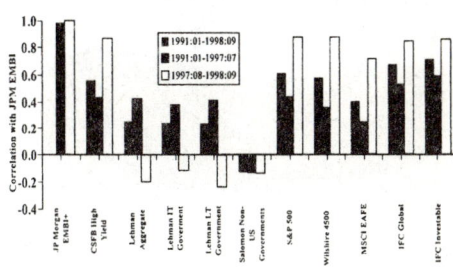

Data: Monthly U.S.$ total returns.

properties of the asset class.[5] If we can determine which asset classes emerging market bonds correlate with, we gain a better understanding of how they might fit into a portfolio.

Exhibits 6A-6C show the results for an analysis from January 1991 through September 1998 and subsamples of the last two years and the last year. Over the full sample, the greatest contributor to variation in emerging market debt returns is the IFC index. The S&P 500 is the second-most important, followed by the high-yield index and long-term U.S. government bonds.

Examining more recent data reveals a different story. Over the past two years, the contribution of the IFC investables shrinks from 41% to 30% while the contribution of the S&P increases from 26% to 37%. Over the past year, the emerging market bond returns are explained by two factors: the S&P 500 and the IFC index. The S&P accounts for 64% of the variation. One can also see this pattern in the rolling style analysis presented in Exhibit 7.

Another pattern is the degree of explanatory power. In the overall period, the style analysis can account for 60% of the variation in the emerging market debt with four asset classes. In the most recent period, 87% of the returns can be accounted for using only two asset classes. The message here is that the effect of emerging market debt can be gained through other asset classes more recently.

EXHIBIT 6A
EMERGING MARKET BONDS: OVERALL STYLE ANALYSIS

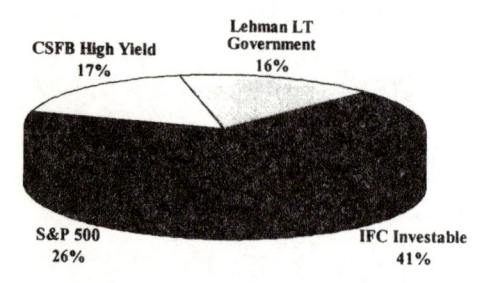

CSFB High Yield 17%
Lehman LT Government 16%
S&P 500 26%
IFC Investable 41%

Emerging market bonds: J.P. Morgan EMBI.
Data: 1991:01-1998:09.
R-squared: 60%.

EXHIBIT 6B
EMERGING MARKET BONDS: TRAILING TWENTY-FOUR-MONTH STYLE ANALYSIS

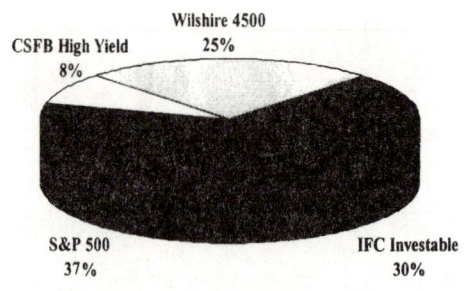

CSFB High Yield 8%
Wilshire 4500 25%
S&P 500 37%
IFC Investable 30%

Emerging market bonds: J.P. Morgan EMBI.
Data: 1996:10-1998:09.
R-squared: 83%.

COUNTRY RISK RATINGS AND CREDIT SPREADS

Investors in the emerging markets face three primary sources of risk. The first is interest rate risk. This is a non-trivial issue in regard to some emerging market bonds. Some bonds issued through loan restructurings have complex structures that must be properly modeled to capture the interest rate sensitivities. This is particularly important because many emerging market bonds have relatively long durations.

EXHIBIT 6C
EMERGING MARKET BONDS: TRAILING TWELVE-MONTH STYLE ANALYSIS

S&P 500 64
IFC Investable 36%

Emerging market bonds: J.P. Morgan EMBI.
Data: 1997:10-1998:09.
R-squared: 87%.

EXHIBIT 7
EMERGING MARKET BONDS —
ROLLING STYLE ANALYSIS: J.P. MORGAN EMBI

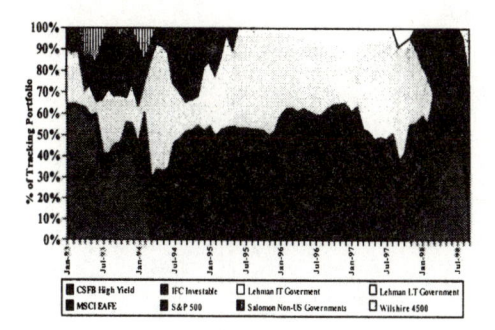

Source: Ibbotson Associates EnCorr Attribution, twenty-four-month rolling window.
Data: 1997:10–1998:09.
Overall R-squared: 60%.

The second risk is currency risk. We have not focused on currency risk because most of our analysis focuses on U.S. dollar-based debt. As local currency bond issuance increases, the management of currency risk will undoubtedly become more important over time.

The third type of risk is sovereign or country risk. Emerging markets represent not only a wide geographic area, but also cover a wide range of situations. Most observers, for example, would recognize that the issues facing Brazil are quite different from those facing Russia or the Philippines. Accordingly, researchers must focus more on explaining the pricing of sovereign risk and how various services rate and rank sovereign risk.

Eichengreen and Mody [1999] study the fundamental determinants of yield spread on emerging market debt. They determine that sentiment has played a key role in determining emerging market bond spreads in 1991-1996. Cantor and Packer [1996] examine the factors that go into determining sovereign ratings. They find that macroeconomic factors are able to explain a large amount of the variation in commonly used sovereign ratings. They also examine the impact of changes in ratings on sovereign credit spreads. Dym [1997] also uses a model to derive credit sensitivities for a number of emerging markets and uses them to create a credit model investment strategy.

Purcell [1996] examines the sources of sovereign risk and their role in emerging market bond investing. Erb, Harvey, and Viskanta [1997a] model various commercial rating services' country risk ratings using macroeconomic variables, and examine their use in the portfolio management process.

Given this research, we should not be surprised to see that perceptions of country risk are reflected in sovereign yields and country bond returns. Erb, Harvey, and Viskanta [1996b] show that commonly used country risk ratings do an impressive job in explaining the cross-section of real yields in a sample of developed market bonds. In the emerging markets we study bonds denominated in U.S. dollars. This allows us to directly examine cross-country yield spreads over the appropriate (maturity-adjusted) Treasury yields.

Exhibit 8 shows the relation between Political Risk Services' *International Country Risk Guide* (ICRG) composite rating and the spread over U.S. Treasuries for the EMBI+ universe of countries. To simplify the analysis, and to keep it in two dimensions, we estimate for each country the spread over Treasuries for a five-year spread duration.[6]

Exhibit 9 presents regression analysis of the spread over Treasuries on the difference between the country rating and the U.S. ICRG composite rating. The regression analysis, which uses 618 monthly observations, confirms the graph in Exhibit 8. There is a

EXHIBIT 8
EMERGING MARKET BONDS
SPREADS VERSUS COUNTRY RISK

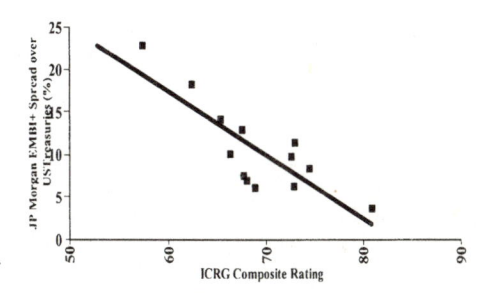

Estimated five-year spread durations for EMBI universe (x-Russia).
Data (9/98): J.P. Morgan Securities, International Country Risk Guide.

EXHIBIT 9
EMERGING MARKET BOND SPREADS AND COUNTRY CREDIT RISK

PANEL A. DEPENDENT VARIABLE: JPM EMBI COUNTRY SPREAD OVER U.S. TREASURIES (IN %)

Independent Variable	Coefficient	Standard Error	t-Statistic
Constant	4.19	0.48	8.81
ICRGC(EM)$_t$ − ICRGC(US)$_t$	−0.24	0.03	−8.52
Observations	618		
R-Squared	0.12		
Adjusted R-Squared	0.12		
Standard Error of Regression	4.87		
F-Statistic	84.15		
Prob (F-Statistic)	0.00		

PANEL B. DEPENDENT VARIABLE: MONTHLY DIFFERENCE IN JPM EMBI COUNTRY SPREAD OVER U.S. TREASURIES (IN %)

Independent Variable	Coefficient	Standard Error	t-Statistic
Constant	0.02	0.08	0.27
(ICRGC(EM)$_t$ − ICRGC(US)$_t$) × (ICRGC(EM)$_{t-1}$ − ICRGC(US)$_{t-1}$)	−2.35	5.31	−0.44
Observations	607		
R-Squared	0.00		
Adjusted R-Squared	0.00		
Standard Error of Regression	1.98		
F-Statistic	0.17		
Prob (F-Statistic)	0.68		

ICRGC: International Country Risk Guide Composite Rating.
EM: Emerging market.
Data period: January 1991–September 1998.
Standard errors use a heteroscedasticity-consistent (White) covariance matrix.

EXHIBIT 10
COUNTRY RISK MODEL-DERIVED BOND SPREADS (OVER U.S. TREASURIES IN %)

Country	Country Weight in: EMBI+	IFCI	ICRG Composite	Fitted Bond Spread
Argentina	28.4	4.9	74.3	6.7
Brazil	24.5	10.2	67.5	11.6
Bulgaria	2.3		72.8	7.7
Chile		5.8	78.3	3.9
China		0.6	78.3	3.9
Colombia		0.9	60.0	17.7
Czech Republic		0.3	77.3	4.6
Ecuador	2.1		62.3	15.8
Egypt		1.2	71.0	9.0
Greece		5.2	77.5	4.4
Hungary		1.5	78.5	3.8
India		2.4	64.5	14.0
Indonesia		0.9	43.0	35.0
Israel		3.4	69.0	10.5
Jordan		0.3	74.3	6.7
Malaysia		5.8	67.3	11.8
Mexico	19.7	11.9	67.8	11.4
Morocco	1.6	1.9	72.5	7.9
Nigeria	1.1		57.3	20.2
Pakistan		0.5	53.3	23.9
Panama	2.4		72.8	7.7
Peru	1.5	1.2	66.3	12.6
Philippines		1.3	69.0	10.5
Poland	4.0	1.1	80.8	2.3
Portugal		5.2	84.3	0.1
Russia	2.7	0.7	55.8	21.5
Slovakia		0.1	76.8	4.9
South Africa		12.6	68.8	10.7
South Korea	3.2	5.1	68.0	11.2
Sri Lanka		0.1	62.3	15.8
Taiwan		10.0	81.0	2.1
Thailand		1.1	66.8	12.2
Turkey		3.2	53.0	24.2
Venezuela	6.6	0.7	65.3	13.4
Zimbabwe		0.0	54.8	24.5

Data: J.P. Morgan EMBI+ (9/98), IFC Investables (9/98), ICRGC (9/98).
Spreads fitted on EMBI+ universe (five-year constant spread duration).

highly significant negative relation between country risk and spread to Treasuries.

Exhibit 10 provides fitted bond spreads for a number of countries based on the September 1998 ICRG composite rating. The model predicts, for example, that the Brazilian debt should be trading at 1,160 basis points above the Treasury. There are fitted values for a number of countries that do not have U.S. dollar debt actively traded in the market. We can apply this model to any country that has a risk rating.

CONCLUSIONS

The pricing of emerging market bonds is an important issue not only for its own sake, but also for our understanding of other emerging market assets. All financial valuation models require some estimate of the discount function. Understanding the dynamics of emerging market interest rates will help in accurately discounting cash flows in the emerging markets.

One unanswered question is the nature of the term structure of emerging market interest rates. There is evidence for an upward-sloping term structure of credit spreads (interest rates over comparable U.S. Treasuries) in many of the emerging markets. The market is demanding higher compensation for out-year risk, and cash flow models need to take this observation into account.

There is much left to learn about emerging market bonds. We believe that it is premature to debate whether emerging market bonds are a new asset class. Indeed, our analysis suggests that the characteristics of these bonds change through time.

In relatively good times, the emerging market bonds seem unique in return characteristics. They have very high tracking error with known asset classes. In times of crisis, they are highly correlated with equity markets. The bonds have negative skewness that needs to be compensated for in terms of higher expected returns.

It is also important to look beyond the current crisis in emerging markets. Most observers believe that the capital needs of these countries will continue to grow. This implies growth in both sovereign and corporate debt in these markets. Our work provides some insights on the role of emerging market debt in global portfolios. Currently, the price of emerging market debt is low, and expected returns are high. This is a logical consequence of the perceived negative skewness risk.

ENDNOTES

Some of this material was presented at the Association for Investment Management and Research 1997 Financial Analysts Seminar. The authors would like to thank Brian Mitchell at J.P. Morgan Securities for his helpful comments.

[1] One can argue that Argentina was at the time a relatively well-developed country. Its equity market capitalization in the early 1920s exceeded England's.

[2] Brady bonds are bonds issued under a Brady Plan debt restructuring. Named after former U.S. Treasury Secretary Nicholas Brady, a Brady Plan generally exchanges debt for freely traded bonds, reduces the overall level of debt and interest payments, and often offers new bonds with a pledge of U.S. Treasury zero-coupon bonds.

[3] In the context of a portfolio, we measure the contribution to the skewness of a portfolio, or coskewness. This measure is analogous to the beta for contribution to variance. See Harvey and Siddique [1998].

[4] We tested to see if non-synchronous trading affects the results for the emerging markets. We find some limited evidence for data lags lowering correlations, but it is concentrated in two observations: Nigeria and South Africa.

[5] The asset class factor model seeks to explain the target returns using a predefined set of asset class returns. This can give us some insight into the strength of the relationship between asset classes. See Sharpe [1992] for an introduction to the style measurement process.

[6] For each country we use the spread over Treasuries and spread duration for a number of sovereign bonds in each country. We then fit a linear regression for each country and calculate the spread over Treasuries for a five-year duration. We choose five years because that approximates the overall spread duration on the J.P. Morgan EMBI+.

REFERENCES

Bekaert, Geert, and Campbell R. Harvey. "Emerging Equity Market Volatility." *Journal of Financial Economics*, Vol. 43, No. 1 (1997), pp. 29-77.

——. "Time-Varying World Market Integration." *Journal of Finance*, Vol. 50, No. 2 (1995), pp. 403-444.

Bekaert, Geert, Claude B. Erb, Campbell R. Harvey, and Tadas E. Viskanta. "Distributional Characteristics of Emerging Market Equities and Asset Allocation." *Journal of Portfolio Management*, Winter 1998, pp. 102-116.

Cantor, Richard, and Frank Packer. "Determinants and Impact of Sovereign Credit Ratings." *Journal of Fixed Income*, December 1996, pp. 76-91.

Chernow, Ron. *The House of Morgan*. New York: Simon & Schuster, 1990.

Dahiya, Sandeep. "The Risks and Returns of Brady Bonds in a Portfolio Context." *Financial Markets, Institutions & Instruments*, Vol. 6, No. 5 (December 1997), pp. 45-60.

Dym, Steven. "Country Risk Analysis for Developing Country Bond Portfolios." *Journal of Portfolio Management*, Winter 1997, pp. 99-103.

Eichengreen, Barry, and Ashoka Mody. "What Explains Changing Spreads on Emerging Market Debt: Fundamentals or Market Sentiment?" In Sebastian Edwards, ed., Capital Inflows to Emerging Markets. Chicago: University of Chicago Press, 1999.

"EMBI Index Summary" and "EMBI+ Index Summary." J.P. Morgan Securities, September 30, 1998.

"Emerging Market Bond Index Monitor." J.P. Morgan Securities, December 31, 1997.

Erb, Claude B., Campbell R. Harvey, and Tadas E. Viskanta. *Country Risk in Global Financial Management*. Charlottesville, VA:

Research Foundation of the Institute for Chartered Financial Analysts, 1997a.

———. "Emerging Market Bonds: A Global Perspective." Proceedings of the Association for Investment Management and Research Financial Analysts Seminar, Northwestern University, July 24, 1997b.

———. "Expected Returns in 135 Countries." *Journal of Portfolio Management*, Spring 1996a, pp. 46-58.

———. "The Influence of Political, Economic, and Financial Risk on Expected Fixed-Income Returns." *Journal of Fixed Income*, September 1996b, pp. 7-31.

Froland, Charles. "Opportunities for Institutional Investors in Emerging Market Debt." *Journal of Pension Plan Investing*, Vol. 2, No. 3 (Winter 1998), pp. 84-99.

Goetzmann, William, and Philippe Jorion. "Re-Emerging Markets." Working paper, Yale University, 1996.

Harvey, Campbell R. "Predictable Risk and Returns in Emerging Markets." *Review of Financial Studies*, Fall 1995, pp. 773-816.

Harvey, Campbell R., and Andrew Roper. "The Asian Bet." Working paper, Duke University, 1998.

Harvey, Campbell R., and Akhtar Siddique. "Conditional Skewness in Asset Pricing Tests." Working paper, Duke University, 1998.

Hinchberger, Bill. "Local Heroes." *Institutional Investor*, July 1997, pp. 137-145.

Nemerever, William L. "Opportunities in Emerging Market Debt." In *Investing Worldwide VII: Focus on Emerging Markets*. Charlottesville, VA: Association for Investment Management and Research, 1996.

Purcell, John F.H. "Sovereign Risk in Emerging Markets," in *Investing Worldwide VII: Focus on Emerging Markets*. Charlottesville, VA: Association for Investment Management and Research, 1996.

Sharpe, William F. "Asset Allocation: Management Style and Performance Measurement." *Journal of Portfolio Management*, Winter 1992, pp. 7-19.

[19]
Is There a Free Lunch in Emerging Market Equities?

In some markets, but investors need to be more selective going forward.

Geert Bekaert and Michael S. Urias

GEERT BEKAERT is an associate professor at the Graduate School of Business at Stanford University in Stanford (CA 94305).

MICHAEL S. URIAS is a vice president at Morgan Stanley Dean Witter & Co., Inc., in New York (NY 10036).

In the early 1990s, people began to refer to investments in emerging markets as a "free lunch." It was argued that emerging equity markets reduce risk and increase expected returns, rendering significant diversification benefits for globally minded investors. Speidell and Sappenfield [1992] even advocated portfolio allocations of 10% to 15% for quantitative asset managers who maximize expected return for a given risk tolerance. In 1993, as foreign capital flows to emerging markets reached an all-time high, most markets gave an unprecedented performance as measured by the International Finance Corporation's (IFC) global indexes, providing some measure of support for the "free lunch" doctrine (see Exhibit 1).

Since 1994, two severe financial and economic shocks have afflicted emerging markets, one following the collapse of the Mexican peso, and the other the collapse of the Thai baht. The result has been slower economic growth, lower average equity market returns, and greater market volatility in emerging markets as a whole. Yet emerging markets still seem to have found a place in many institutional portfolios as a strategic asset class, not just an asset to be exploited tactically.

Several characteristics of emerging markets support the argument of a free lunch. Emerging markets exhibit higher average returns than developed markets (when measured over the medium to long term), but also higher volatility as represented by standard market indexes. More important, they tend to have low correlations with most developed markets, as well as low cor-

EXHIBIT 1

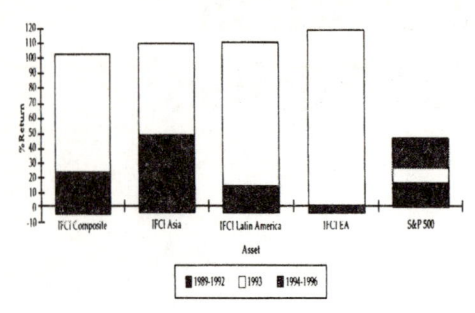

Annualized Returns 1989-1996

Annualized Volatility 1989-1996

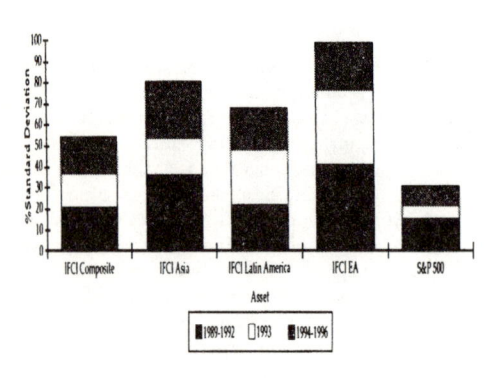

Correlation with S&P 500 1989-1996

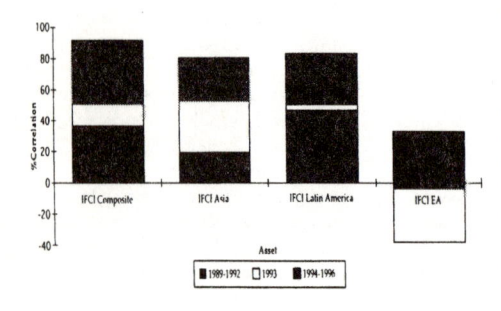

relations among themselves.[1] Low correlation means that adding emerging markets to a portfolio can actually reduce risk and still provide the benefits of higher average returns.

These conclusions depend critically on the investor's ability to achieve the performance of the market indexes used in the calculation of means and correlations.[2] Most recent studies of emerging markets are based on the IFC global indexes, which may not always accurately reflect the costs of emerging market investments relative to developed markets, or the restrictions that affect such investments.

For example, according to Bekaert et al. [1997], the bid-ask spreads in Argentina imply an average cost of approximately 155 basis points for foreign investors, considerably higher than the cost of trading stocks in most developed markets. Markets such as South Korea and Taiwan have foreign ownership restrictions that are often binding. Index providers attempt to correct for ownership restrictions in the weights applied to stocks or countries in certain indexes, but the prices often do not represent those faced by most global investors. In some cases, such as the Alien Board in Thailand, a different set of prices apply to foreigners dealing in restricted stock from those applying to local investors (see Bailey and Jagtiani [1994]).

Once investments are made, moreover, the free flow of capital can also be restricted, such as in Chile, where foreign investors cannot repatriate invested capital for one year. Furthermore, factors such as poor liquidity and currency and macroeconomic instability can impact emerging market performance in ways not reflected by benchmark indexes.[3]

An important implication is that, although indexes provided by the IFC, Morgan Stanley Capital International, and others have enabled researchers to gain valuable insights into emerging equity markets, the performance of direct investment in emerging markets as represented by such benchmarks may not always be achievable. Hence the "free lunch" doctrine should be qualified, particularly for retail investors. A more realistic picture of the true diversification benefits from emerging equity markets is available from three investment vehicles that provide access to emerging market returns, while circumventing many of the restrictions and costs described above.

We focus on the benefits from holding closed-end mutual funds, ADRs, and open-end mutual funds in a global equity portfolio. Closed-end country funds

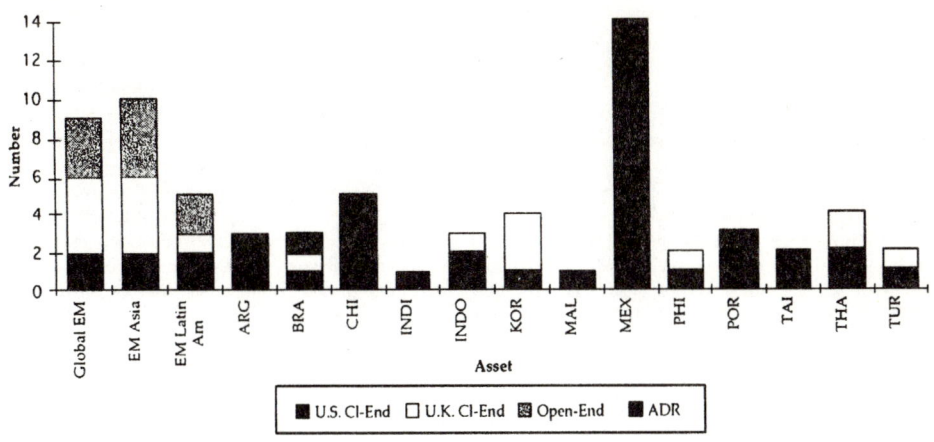

EXHIBIT 2
SAMPLE OF ADRS, OPEN-END FUNDS, AND CLOSED-END FUNDS

were among the earliest investment vehicles providing access to emerging markets, beginning with the New York-traded Mexico Fund in 1981. They often trade at prices different from their portfolio value (known as net asset value or NAV), since they generally do not redeem or issue new shares. Often, country funds that invest in closed or restricted markets will trade at a premium. There are a sizable number of emerging market closed-end funds trading in the U.S. and the U.K.

Since the early 1990s, U.S.- or U.K.-traded receipts representing emerging market shares have been available. ADRs trade close to parity with the underlying foreign shares they represent, because they can be redeemed or created from the foreign shares by paying a fee to the depository bank. Nevertheless, it still may be difficult to build a portfolio of ADRs that adequately tracks the local market.[4]

Like ADRs, open-end funds representing the emerging markets are a relatively new phenomenon. Open-end mutual funds (ignoring transaction costs) trade at prices that are the same as their portfolio values because they redeem or issue new shares periodically. Because of this, managers may tend to invest in more-liquid emerging market issues than they otherwise would. Moreover, because they are actively managed, open-end funds may offer protection in down markets that other investment vehicles do not.[5]

The goal of this article is a better understanding of the rewards and risks from holding emerging markets in a global equity portfolio. While closed-end funds, open-end funds, and ADRs provide emerging market returns that are actually attainable, they may sacrifice some of the benefits of direct access to the local markets they represent.[6]

Any assessment of the rewards and the trade-off between investable performance and benchmark index performance is inherently ex post and constrained by the data at hand. Our analysis attempts to shed light on these matters from several angles. We begin with a discussion of expected returns, correlation, and tracking error using the different investment vehicles. Finally, we attempt to use robust statistical tests to evaluate the diversification benefits of emerging markets in a mean-variance framework.

THE DATA

Exhibit 2 shows the geographic coverage of emerging market closed-end funds, open-end funds, and ADRs in our sample. The sample also includes the IFC investable country and regional indexes, and FT-Actuaries indexes to represent the developed equity markets.

The sample of closed-end funds consists of twenty-three U.S. funds and nineteen U.K. funds that invest in emerging markets as defined by the IFC. The sample attempts to include all publicly traded U.S. and U.K. emerging market funds with initial offerings prior to 1992.[7]

The sample of open-end emerging market funds is limited to U.S. funds that target a particular region: Asia, Latin America, or the world. In the test period there were no available open-end emerging market funds targeting individual countries.

Finally, the ADR sample represents equities trading in five emerging markets as early as September 1993. It is restricted to ADRs that trade on a U.S. exchange as opposed to over-the-counter or in the institutional market, in order to avoid stale pricing.[8]

The empirical analysis focuses on two sample periods, September 1990 through August 1993 for the closed-end funds, and September 1993 through August 1996 for the closed-end funds, open-end funds, and ADRs. All the analysis uses weekly dollar total returns.

EXPECTED RETURNS ON CLOSED-END FUNDS, OPEN-END FUNDS, ADRS, AND EMERGING MARKET INDEXES

The traditional practice of portfolio optimization requires estimates of expected returns and the covariance and volatility of returns for a set of candidate investments. Much of the portfolio management business is driven by decisions based in some way on expected return estimates, usually relative to a benchmark. Unfortunately, it is well known that estimating expected returns from the mean of historical returns is problematic. The noise and short time series of equity returns in typical applications result in very poor estimates of expected returns from historical means. Estimates of the covariance of asset returns from historical data tend to be somewhat more precise.

Exhibit 1 illustrates the relative stability of the historical volatility and correlations of emerging equity market returns with the S&P 500 index.

If we are willing to use historical estimates of the covariance of equity market returns, we can infer expected returns in the mean-variance paradigm. Specifically, it is possible to construct expected excess returns that correspond to hypothetical "efficient" portfolios using these covariance estimates. Given the limitations inherent in our data, this may be a good place to start understanding the potential benefits of emerging equity markets under different scenarios, and the trade-offs between different investment vehicles that access these markets.

Let Σ_R denote the covariance matrix of the developed world equity market index return and a portfolio of emerging market investment returns, and let δ represent the market price of risk. The market price of risk can be interpreted as the ratio of the required return in excess of the riskless return by the marginal investor in risky assets, and the variance of that return.[9]

Then, for an optimal portfolio (one that lies on the efficient frontier of asset returns) of developed and emerging market equities, ω, the expected excess returns are given by

$$ER - r_f = \delta \Sigma_R \omega \qquad (1)$$

where ER is the vector of expected returns, and r_f is the riskless rate of return. This relation assumes no borrowing or lending by the marginal or representative investor.

The expected excess returns can be viewed as those implied by an efficient portfolio, ω, held in a world where Σ_R describes the riskiness of the assets. A long investor who thinks that 20% is the efficient amount to put to work in emerging markets can think of $ER - r_f$ as the expected excess returns consistent with such a portfolio.

Exhibit 3 shows required excess returns of candidate emerging market portfolios when the optimal allocation to emerging markets ranges between 5% and 20%. The excess return of the emerging market portfolio over the FT-Actuaries developed world market return is given in parentheses. The table assumes that the market price of risk is 3.5.[10] The covariance matrix is estimated using weekly returns data from the 1993-1996 sample period.

The results indicate higher expected returns for the U.S. and the U.K. closed-end funds than for the open-end funds, ADRs, and IFC investable composite index, at all allocation levels. In most cases, the expected excess return for the emerging market assets exceeds that of the developed world equity market index for optimal portfolios with at least 10% invested in emerging markets.

From Equation (1), higher expected excess returns for the closed-end funds than for the open-end funds, ADRs, and IFC investable index can be explained by their higher covariance with the devel-

EXHIBIT 3
COMPARING CLOSED-END FUNDS, ADRS, AND OPEN-END FUNDS (REQUIRED EXCESS RETURNS FROM OPTIMAL ALLOCATION TO EMERGING MARKET)

		Allocation	
Asset	5%	10%	20%
U.K. Closed-End Fund Index	2.07	3.41	4.30
	(0.35)	(0.80)	(1.70)
U.S. Closed-End Fund Index	3.76	4.48	5.93
	(1.12)	(1.82)	(3.22)
ADR Index	1.20	2.11	3.95
	(-1.21)	(-0.27)	(1.80)
Open-End Fund Index	2.58	2.86	3.44
	(-0.03)	(0.27)	(0.88)
IFC Composite	2.39	2.73	3.40
	(-0.20)	(0.16)	(0.90)

Annualized expected return of the candidate emerging market portfolio in excess of the riskless rate, in U.S. dollars. Numbers in parentheses are the expected return of the emerging market portfolio in excess of the expected excess return of the developed world market. Calculations are based on returns from 1993-1996.

oped world market portfolio. Investors therefore demand higher returns for closed-end funds when holding them in optimal portfolios in the 1993-1996 period. This result is consistent with the costliness of arbitrage between closed-end funds and their underlying assets, resulting in a high correlation of closed-end funds with the markets where they trade in the U.S. and the U.K. (and thus the developed world market).

By contrast, there are cases where investors are willing to hold open-end funds, ADRs, and the IFC investable index in their portfolios even though expected returns are lower than for the developed world market. Exhibit 3 shows this to be the case for optimal allocations to emerging markets of 5% and 10%. An interpretation of this result is that open-end funds, ADRs, and the IFC investable index are desirable in optimal portfolios, even with inferior returns, for risk reduction purposes alone.

Under the assumptions of the experiment in Exhibit 3, on an expected return basis, investment vehicles like closed-end funds, open-end funds, and ADRs appear more attractive than the IFC investable index. Of course, the risk reduction benefits from emerging markets in a global equity portfolio must be balanced with the potential for higher returns, and on that basis the IFC investable indexes may be superior, although full attainability of the index performance is difficult.

HISTORICAL TRACKING ERROR OF CLOSED-END FUNDS, OPEN-END FUNDS, AND ADRS

Exhibit 4 reports the tracking error from several portfolios of closed-end funds, open-end funds, and ADRs with respect to the IFC investable composite, Asia, and Latin America indexes. Tracking error is defined as the annualized standard deviation of the difference between the portfolio return of the funds or ADRs and the return on the IFC index.

The table reports results for equally weighted portfolios of funds and ADRs using returns for the 1993-1996 sample period. While analytically determined weights that vary with time may provide better tracking, equally

EXHIBIT 4
TRACKING THE IFC INDEXES — WEEKLY RETURNS 1993-1996

	Asia	Latin America	Composite
U.K. Closed-End Funds	19.47%	18.66%	23.26%
U.S. Closed-End Funds	14.61	29.41	13.60
ADRs	NA	35.40	NA
Open-End Funds	9.35	7.02	5.92

Annualized tracking error for the best-tracking portfolio of funds or ADRs in each category. Tracking error is defined as the standard deviation of the difference in the returns on the portfolio and the target index. NA indicates not available.

weighted portfolios give us a sense of the opportunity for smaller or unsophisticated investors.

Strikingly, by far the lowest tracking error is achieved by the open-end funds. The U.K. closed-end funds track the IFC indexes better than the U.S. funds, with the exception of the Latin America index, where there is only one U.K. fund in the sample. ADRs do not seem to cover enough of the local market to provide close tracking of the IFC indexes. The ADR tracking errors are somewhat greater than those reported by Jorion and Miller [1997], who use optimization techniques to improve tracking.

To sum it up, during the 1993-1996 sample period, equally weighted portfolios of open-end funds were the superior investment vehicle for matching the performance of the IFC indexes.

TESTING FOR DIVERSIFICATION BENEFITS

Mean-Variance Spanning Tests

We measure diversification benefits in the standard mean-variance framework. The mean-standard deviation frontier depicts the highest expected return that is attainable from a portfolio of assets for a given level of risk, where risk is measured as standard deviation of return (the square root of the variance). It has the familiar hyperbolic shape in expected return-standard deviation space.

We begin with a set of developed market returns a global investor might hold, which we call the benchmark assets. We can construct the frontier from the means and covariances of the historical returns. Suppose we add emerging market assets to our benchmark, and recompute the mean-standard deviation frontier. It will always be true that the frontier either stays the same or shifts to the left; that is, for each level of expected return, the expanded set of assets means you will be able to do at least as well as before in terms of risk.

The inputs to the calculation are very important here. Even with a reasonably long time series of historical data, there may be little confidence in a statistical sense that the risk-return trade-off is truly better when emerging markets are added. This is the essence of what we formally test: Is there a statistically significant leftward shift in the mean-standard deviation frontier?

The test examines whether the frontiers intersect at two prespecified points along the benchmark frontier. We identify one of the points using a "riskless" asset, which defines a tangency portfolio.[11]

The test, formally called a mean-variance spanning test, was first described by Huberman and Kandel [1987]. We use a modern, more robust version of the test that builds on recent results in dynamic asset pricing theory developed by Hansen and Jagannathan [1991].

The main intuition for the test can be seen using the following notation. Let $R_e(t)$ represent an emerging market asset return or "test" asset return, and let $R_b(t, j)$ represent the return on the j-th benchmark asset, where j is indexed from 1 to K. Then $R_e(t)$ is spanned by the K benchmark returns if it can be written as a portfolio of the benchmark returns with the weights summing to one, plus an uncorrelated, mean-zero error term, $\upsilon(t)$:

$$R_e(t) = a + w_1 R_b(t, 1) + ... + w_K R_b(t, K) + \upsilon(t) \quad (2)$$

with

$$a = 0$$
$$w_1 + ... + w_K = 1$$

In effect, Equation (2) says that the emerging market return is spanned by the benchmark if we can use the benchmark returns to mimic the return on the emerging market fund. The emerging market return does not offer real diversification benefits if that is the case, and hence we cannot reject that the frontier of the benchmark plus emerging market returns is the same as the frontier generated by only the benchmark returns. The mean-variance spanning test we employ is equivalent to a test of the econometric restrictions given by Equation (2).

Our test is robust to the non-standard features of equity market data such as fat tails and the fact that we are using a relatively short time series to infer market relationships. Nevertheless, the turbulent period in emerging markets from 1990 to 1996 significantly complicates our tests by increasing the difficulty of estimating expected returns and covariance from the historical data. In the end, we hope to be able to say something about the diversification benefits of emerging equity markets going forward, despite the limitations of the data.

The appendix describes the method we employ in more detail.

EXHIBIT 5

PANEL A. CONFIDENCE LEVELS 1990-1993: CLOSED-END FUNDS AND IFC INDEXES

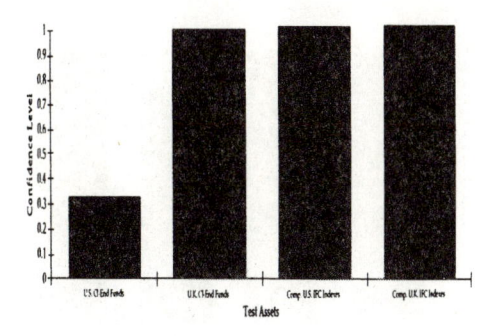

PANEL B. CONFIDENCE LEVELS 1993-1996: CLOSED-END FUNDS AND IFC INDEXES

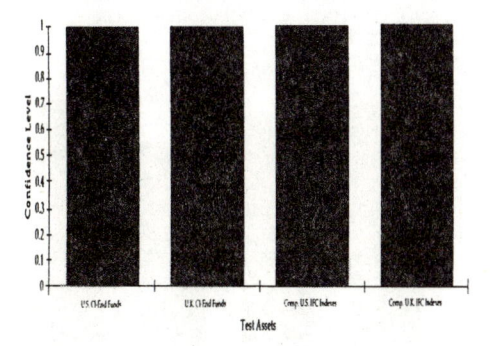

Summary of Evidence from Closed-End Funds, Open-End Funds, and ADRs: 1990-1996

We report the results of mean-variance spanning tests using a set of benchmark returns that consists of the FT-Actuaries U.S. index, U.K. index, Europe less U.K. index, and Pacific index, a possible benchmark for a well-diversified global investor in the developed markets. The test assets are sets of emerging market closed-end funds in the U.S. and the U.K., U.S. open-end funds, and U.S.-traded ADRs. For comparison, we examine the diversification benefits of investing in the corresponding IFC investable indexes — e.g., if the test assets include a Chilean closed-end fund, we include the IFC's Chile index in our set of investable indexes.

Test results are shown for two periods: September 1990 through August 1993 for the closed-end funds, and September 1993 through August 1996 for the closed-end funds, open-end funds, and ADRs. The first period includes the top of the performance cycle for emerging markets this decade, and the second period includes the global selloff in 1995 but avoids the more recent Asian crisis beginning in 1997.

The bars in Exhibits 5 through 8 show confidence levels from the mean-variance spanning tests. The confidence level is a number between zero and one. A confidence level of 95% means that, given the data inputs to the test, we are 95% sure that spanning is rejected, and consequently that emerging markets offer diversification benefits.

Closed-End Funds. The full sample of closed-end fund test assets consists of twelve individual U.S. emerging market funds and six individual U.K. funds. The sample includes funds that target specific countries as well as regional funds.[12]

For the 1990-1993 test period, we find strong evidence of diversification benefits for the U.K. funds. The confidence level for the U.S. funds is about 33%, but over 99% for the U.K. funds (see Exhibit 5). The confidence level for the IFC investables is greater than 99% in the 1990-1993 period.

For the 1993-1996 test period, the confidence level for both the U.S. and the U.K. closed-end funds is greater than 99% (Exhibit 6). The confidence level is greater than 99% for the corresponding IFC investable indexes in 1993-1996. It therefore appears that both the U.S. and the U.K. closed-end funds provided significant diversification benefits in 1993-1996, but the benefits are less pronounced in the earlier 1990-1993 test period, with a confidence level greater than 95% only for the U.K. funds. The IFC investable indexes provided significant benefits in both periods.

We carry out a number of robustness checks to ensure the validity of the closed-end fund results. In several cases, more than one fund targets the same emerging market country or region. We find that the pattern of results is robust to whichever fund is chosen in these cases. Furthermore, since there is broader country coverage in the U.S. sample, and this full available coverage is used for the U.S. test assets, we exam-

EXHIBIT 6

**PANEL A. CONFIDENCE LEVELS 1990-1993:
CLOSED-END FUNDS AND IFC INDEXES,
RESTRICTED SAMPLE**

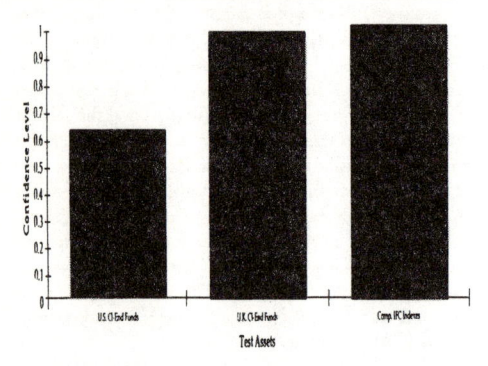

**PANEL B. CONFIDENCE LEVELS 1993-1996:
CLOSED-END FUNDS AND IFC INDEXES,
RESTRICTED SAMPLE**

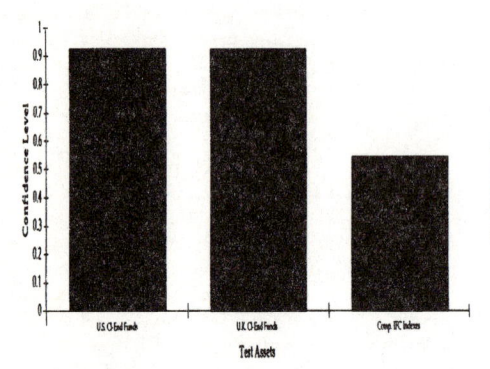

EXHIBIT 7

**PANEL A. CONFIDENCE LEVELS 1993-1996 (ASIA):
OPEN-END FUND, CLOSED-END FUNDS, AND
IFC INCEXES**

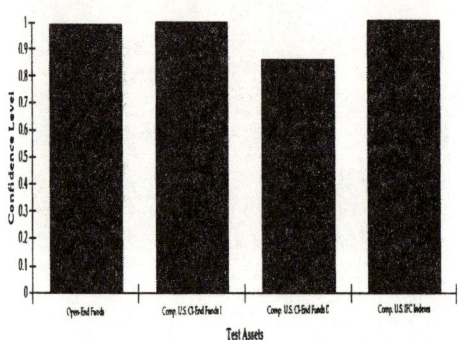

**PANEL B. CONFIDENCE LEVELS 1993-1996 (ASIA):
OPEN-END FUND, CLOSED-END FUNDS, AND
IFC INDEXES**

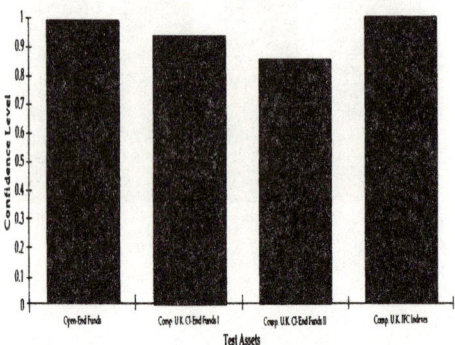

ine whether requiring common coverage by U.S. and U.K. funds alters the results.

Overall, both U.S. and U.K. emerging market closed-end funds provided significant diversification gains in the 1993-1996 period, and the U.K. funds provided benefits in some combinations in the earlier 1990-1993 period.

Open-End Funds. Exhibit 7 presents results from mean-variance spanning tests using global and Asian open-end funds and the FT-Actuaries benchmark of four indexes (Latin American open-end funds are examined with the ADR results). The open-end funds provide clear diversification benefits, with a confidence level near 99%. Robustness checks confirm that the particular choice of funds does not affect the results when there is duplicate coverage.

The results for closed-end funds from the U.S. or the U.K. covering the same regional markets are

EXHIBIT 8

PANEL A. CONFIDENCE LEVELS 1993-1996 (LATIN AMERICA): ADRS AND CLOSED-END FUNDS

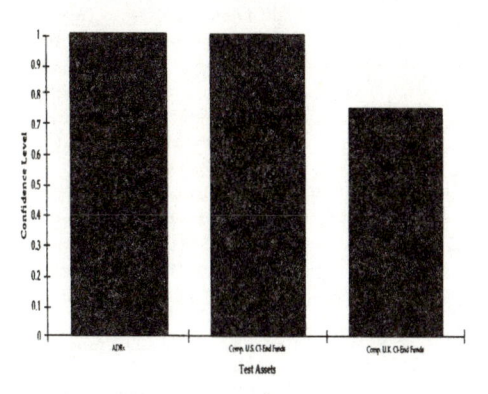

PANEL B. CONFIDENCE LEVELS 1993-1996 (LATIN AMERICA): ADRS, OPEN-END FUNDS, AND IFC INDEXES

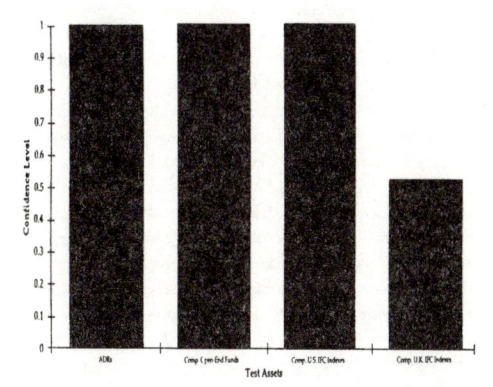

ambiguous, and depend on the particular funds chosen when there is duplicate coverage. (Exhibit 7 shows the worst case for the U.S. and U.K. funds.) The corresponding IFC investable indexes provide strong evidence of diversification benefits from Asian markets during the test period, with a confidence level greater than 99% for the indexes.

ADRs. For the ADRs, equally weighted indexes of eligible ADRs in each of the five markets constitute the test assets, and the benchmark is the same FT-Actuaries benchmark of four indexes. In Exhibit 8, the confidence level for the ADR indexes is close to 100%.

The ADR results are compared with tests using open-end and closed-end funds from the U.S. or the U.K. covering the same markets. The confidence level for the comparable U.S. closed-end funds is 99%, but only 75% for the comparable U.K. closed-end funds. These levels are robust to the choice of funds when there is duplicate coverage. The U.S. closed-end funds therefore appear to offer diversification benefits in line with comparable ADRs during the test period (only one Latin American U.K. closed-end fund was available).

Comparing a set of four global and Latin American open-end funds to the ADR sample, there are significant diversification benefits for the open-end funds, at a confidence level greater than 99%. Here again the results are robust to the particular open-end fund chosen when there is duplicate coverage. The IFC investable indexes corresponding to the ADR coverage provide significant diversification benefits, at a confidence level of more than 99%.

How Practical Are Our Tests?

Recall that a mean-variance spanning test is equivalent to examining whether the frontier of benchmark assets intersects the frontier of benchmark and test assets at two points. The two-fund separation principle then guarantees that if the frontiers intersect at two points, they intersect at all points (i.e., the frontiers are the same). Of course, the asset frontiers in the test depend on the historical time series we use to estimate them.

When we reject the null hypothesis that the benchmark assets span the test assets, it is relevant to ask whether the portfolios at which we test for intersection are realistic. In fact, in some cases the portfolio implied by the frontier of benchmark and test assets and the riskless rate has negative weights, since our mean-variance spanning tests do not constrain the weights of assets in the tangency portfolio to be positive. Results based on these portfolios may suggest diversification benefits that are not available when shorting is disallowed or prohibitively costly.

To assess the importance of shorting in our results, in Exhibit 9 we report the change in the Sharpe ratio implied by the addition of the test assets when shorting more than 10% of an asset is allowed and when it is not, for groups of test assets where short positions

EXHIBIT 9
THE IMPACT OF SHORTING ON MEAN-VARIANCE SPANNING TESTS (1993-1996)

Test Assets	Sharpe Ratio Change Shorting	No Shorts < -10%
U.K. Closed-End Fund Index	0.0061	0.0015
U.S. Closed-End Fund Index	0.0398	0.0111
ADRs	0.0971	0.0601
Open-End Funds	0.0978	0.0386

are a problem.[13]

Shorting was most in evidence for the closed-end funds during the 1993-1996 period, and for tests using the open-end Asian and Latin American funds. Exhibit 9 suggests that excluding funds that are shorted in the original tests reduces the incremental Sharpe ratio obtained from the emerging market assets, but for some investors this loss may be reasonable compared to the costs of undertaking short positions.

CONCLUSION

On an expected return basis, it is possible to compare the advantages of emerging market investments in the context of a mean-variance efficient portfolio. Our experiment shows that, if we are willing to accept the integrity of estimates of the covariance between emerging and developed equity market returns from historical data, we can distinguish among closed-end funds, open-end funds, ADRs, and the IFC investable indexes. The higher correlations between closed-end fund returns and developed market equity returns imply that higher expected returns are required to justify emerging market closed-end funds in optimal portfolios compared to the other emerging market investment vehicles. With optimal allocation levels greater than 10%, emerging market open-end funds, ADRs, and the IFC index may actually have lower expected returns than developed equity markets owing to low correlations with the developed markets. Open-end funds offer the best tracking of the IFC investable index from 1993-1996 using equally weighted portfolios.

As for evidence of diversification benefits from emerging equity markets, using mean-variance spanning tests, we find that benefits are sensitive to the time period of the tests and, in some cases, to the particular investment vehicle. Direct exposure to emerging market indexes almost always gives benefits at least as strong as those from managed funds (both publicly traded and not) or ADR portfolios. Closed-end funds, open-end funds, and ADRs provided statistically significant diversification benefits in the 1993-1996 test period.

When accessing emerging markets through closed-end funds, performance may depend on who manages the portfolio. In the earlier 1990-1993 test period, it appears that U.K. fund managers as a whole provided benefits superior to the U.S. managers. These test results rely on estimates of both expected returns and covariance from the historical data.

Are the benefits we document likely to persist? Clearly, as the equity markets in emerging economies mature, the restrictions and costs associated with investing will be reduced. The diversification potential reflected in market indexes will gradually become a more attainable benchmark for all types of investors.

Global capital market integration is likely to continue, however, and in the process the correlations between emerging and developed markets are likely to strengthen. Bekaert and Harvey [1997a] show how correlations between the world market and emerging markets increase over time as the degree of integration increases. Furthermore, the returns investors can expect to earn in emerging markets are likely to fall as integration proceeds. Specifically, the integration process may lead to one-time, discrete price hikes that bring about lower expected returns going forward (see Bekaert and Harvey [1997b] for a formal discussion).

This does not mean that emerging markets are not attractive from a return perspective. Many still are, but investors will need to be more selective going forward, and entertain the prospects of unfamiliar new markets as well. Before the large influx of capital in the early 1990s, most emerging equity markets were small relative to the size of their economies and had ample room to grow. Their market capitalization as a proportion of GDP is approximately 17% today, according to MSCI in December 1997.

As these markets mature, more sophisticated asset management approaches may have value. For example, some Latin American markets offer liquid local stocks that are affiliated with ADR programs as well as illiquid local shares with less international visibility. Urias [1996] shows that these two categories of stocks should exhibit different expected return and correlation characteristics, although the presence of ADRs should lead to some international influence on the pricing of the less-liquid local shares.

Finally, as the Mexican peso and Asian currency crises demonstrate, even with increasing integration of world and emerging capital markets, certain risks specific to emerging markets remain. Occasional calamities suggest that asset allocation models need to be improved to accommodate the asymmetric return distributions that characterize equity markets, especially emerging markets. Risk management systems must incorporate expectations of low-probability negative events. Forecasting such calamities is an important topic for future research.

APPENDIX
Mean-Variance Spanning Tests

Our test for mean-variance spanning relies on the asset pricing framework of Hansen and Jagannathan [1991] and is equivalent to the restrictions on the regression coefficients in Equation (1) in the text. The primary advantage of our test is its robustness to non-standard characteristics of asset return data like conditional heteroscedasticity and autocorrelation. Here we provide some intuition for the test by establishing the connection between mean-variance spanning and changes in the Sharpe ratio (see Sharpe [1994]). Bekaert and Urias [1996] provide a more formal development of the test and its equivalence with the Huberman and Kandel [1987] test described in Equation (1).

We begin with the fundamental asset pricing equation that, under very general conditions, relates the price of any asset today to its payoff next period. The equation says that the asset's price today is equal to the mathematical expectation of its price plus payoff next period times a stochastic discount factor. This can be written as

$$E\{[R(t+1) + \iota]m(t+1)\} = \iota \qquad (A\text{-}1)$$

where $R(t+1)$ represents a vector of net security returns at time $t+1$, $m(t+1)$ is the stochastic discount factor, and ι is a vector of ones.

The distinguishing feature of an asset pricing model is its specification for the discount factor, $m(t+1)$. Equation (A-1) assumes frictionless markets and that the law of one price holds. It turns out that any asset pricing model, including the CAPM, multifactor models, or Black-Scholes, can be written according to Equation (A-1).

Hansen and Jagannathan [1991] show that the linear projection of $m(t+1)$ onto the set of asset returns being priced has minimum variance in the class of all discount factors that satisfy Equation (A-1). For example, the discount factor:

$$m^\alpha(t+1) \equiv \alpha + [R(t+1) - ER(t+1)]'\beta^{(\alpha)} \qquad (A\text{-}2)$$

formed from the projection of $m(t+1)$ onto one-period returns also satisfies Equation (A-1). The discount factor depends on a pre-specified value for α, which equals $Em(t+1)$.

Now partition $R(t+1) \equiv [R_b(t+1)', R_e(t+1)']'$ and $\beta^{(\alpha)} \equiv [\beta_b^{(\alpha)'}, \beta_e^{(\alpha)'}]$. Hence $R_b(t+1)$ can be thought of as the benchmark asset returns in Equation (1), and $R_e(t+1)$ can be thought of as the emerging market test asset returns.

We use this framework to test whether the benchmark vector of returns, $R_b(t+1)$, spans the vector of benchmark and test returns, $R(t+1)$. The mean-variance spanning restriction in this framework amounts to:

$$\beta_e^{(\alpha)} = 0 \qquad \forall \qquad (A\text{-}3)$$

in Equation (A-2), and is equivalent to the restriction described in Equation (2). The test asks whether the test assets $R_e(t+1)$ are needed to "price" the benchmark and test assets in $R(t+1)$.

Suppressing time subscripts and assuming $m^{(\alpha)}$ is the fitted value from Equation (A-2), we can calculate $\beta^{(\alpha)}$ using standard regression theory as:

$$\beta^{(\alpha)} = \Sigma_R^{-1}[\iota - (Em)(ER)] \qquad (A\text{-}4)$$

where Σ_R^{-1} is the inverse of the variance-covariance matrix of the returns, and $Em = Em^{(\alpha)}$. Substituting $\beta^{(\alpha)}$ into Equation (A-2), it follows that the volatility of the true discount factor, σ_m^2, is bounded below by the volatility of the discount factor $m^{(\alpha)}$:

$$\sigma_m^2 \geq \sigma_{m^{(\alpha)}}^2 = [\iota - (Em)(ER)]'\Sigma_R^{-1}[\iota - (Em)(ER)] \qquad (A\text{-}5)$$

Finally, using the fact that Em equals one divided by the riskless rate, $1/r_f$ [substitute a riskless return into Equation (A-5)], we see that the discount factor volatility, scaled by its mean, is bounded below by the Sharpe ratio:

$$\frac{\sigma_m}{Em} \geq \{[ER - r_f]'\Sigma_R^{-1}[ER - r_f]\}^{1/2} \qquad (A\text{-}6)$$

Note that the right-hand side of Equation (A-6) is the Sharpe ratio for the mean-standard deviation frontier formed by the benchmark and test asset returns $R(t+1)$. It is the slope of the line emanating from the point $(0, r_f)$ that intersects the frontier. Thus

Equation (A-6) says that changes in the volatility of the discount factor correspond to changes in the Sharpe ratio. For example, when the discount factor in Equation (A-6) is restricted to be a function of a smaller set of returns [e.g., $R_b(t + 1)$ instead of $R(t + 1)$], the change in its volatility corresponds to a change in the Sharpe ratio.

Testing the restriction in Equation (A-3) when $\alpha = 1/r_f$ can then be viewed as a test that the mean-standard deviation frontiers formed by $R_b(t + 1)$ and $R(t + 1)$ intersect at one point. Equation (A-3) requires that the frontiers intersect at every point (for any α), including that corresponding to $\alpha = 1/r_f$. Mean-variance spanning therefore implies that the change in the Sharpe ratio resulting from adding the test assets to the benchmark assets is zero at all points.

ENDNOTES

The authors would like to thank Albert Perez for excellent research assistance. The article has benefitted also from the comments of Campbell Harvey, Eugene Fama, Peter Wall, and Ingrid Werner; and participants in sessions at the NYSE Conference on Global Equity Issuance and Trading; Berkeley Program in Finance, April 1997; Swedish School of Economics; Financial Research Initiative Colloquium, Stanford University, February 1997; Tilburg University; Institutional Investor Symposium on Emerging Markets; and the Security Analysts of San Francisco (SASF) Quantitative Program.

[1] There is some evidence, however, that the correlations are higher in down markets. See Harvey [1995] for a summary of emerging equity market characteristics.

[2] Another important consideration, although not developed in this article, is the stability of correlations over time as the relationship between emerging and developed markets changes. Bekaert and Harvey [1997a] study this issue.

[3] Bekaert [1995] provides a classification of the various costs associated with emerging market investments.

[4] More recently, publicly traded shares representing the performance of a basket of equities built to track a market index have been introduced. One such product, known as WEBS, has been trading since 1996.

[5] A more recent open-end alternative is Vanguard Group's International Equity Index Fund Emerging Markets Portfolio, which tracks the MSCI Select Emerging Markets Free index.

[6] Comparing the costs of different emerging market investments is a complex subject that we do not fully address here. Our interest is the direct or indirect impact of these costs on the realized and expected performance of alternative investments.

[7] U.K. closed-end funds are known as investment trusts, and while they are technically equivalent to their U.S. counterparts, there are a number of institutional differences. The most important are that U.K. funds are held mainly by institutions, and fund expenses are deductible from taxable income for U.K. trusts (see Bekaert and Urias [1996] and Ammer [1990] for details). In the U.S., closed-end funds are largely the province of retail investors, and fund expenses are not tax-deductible. The capitalization of U.K. trusts also tends to be more complex than for U.S. funds, with multiple classes of shares and warrants common in the U.K.

[8] Urias [1996] describes the differences in regulatory and other costs associated with the different categories of ADRs.

[9] It also corresponds to the coefficient of relative risk aversion for an investor with constant relative risk aversion preferences who invests in assets with normally distributed returns.

[10] This number is obtained by computing the price of risk using the historical excess return and volatility of the world market return.

[11] The return on this asset is the average of the U.S. dollar LIBOR for the period of the test.

[12] The two sets of funds include only funds that are available in both test periods and have corresponding IFC investable indexes.

[13] Variants of our mean-variance spanning test that correct for shorting exist, but discussion of them is beyond the scope of our investigation. See deRoon, Nijman, and Werker [1996] for an analysis.

REFERENCES

Ammer, J. "Expenses, Yields, and Excess Returns: New Evidence on Closed End Funds Discounts from the UK." LSE Financial Markets Discussion Paper No. 108, 1990.

Bailey, W. and J. Jagtiani. "Foreign Ownership Restrictions and Stock Prices in the Thai Capital Market." *Journal of Financial Economics*, 36 (1994), pp. 57-87.

Bekaert, G. "Market Integration and Investment Barriers in Emerging Equity Markets." *The World Bank Economic Review*, 1995, pp. 75-107.

Bekaert, G., C.B. Erb, C.R. Harvey, and T.E. Viskanta. "The Cross-Sectional Determinants of Emerging Equity Market Returns," in Peter Carman, ed., *Quantitative Investing for the Global Market*. Chicago: Glenlake Publishing, 1997, pp. 221-272.

Bekaert, G., and C. Harvey. "Emerging Equity Market Volatility." *Journal of Financial Economics*, 43 (1997), pp. 23-77.

——. "Foreign Speculators and Emerging Equity Markets." NBER, Working Paper No. W6312, 1997b.

——. "Time-Varying World Market Integration." *Journal of Finance*, 50 (1995), pp. 403-444.

Bekaert, G., and M.S. Urias. "Diversification, Integration, and Emerging Market Closed-End Funds." *Journal of Finance*, 51 (1996), pp. 835-869.

deRoon, F.A., T.E. Nijman, and B.J.M. Werker. "Testing for Mean Variance Spanning in Case of Short Sales Constraints and Transaction Costs." Tilburg University, 1996.

Hansen, L.P., and R. Jagannathan. "Implications of Security

Market Data for Models of Dynamic Economies." *Journal of Political Economy*, 99 (1991), pp. 225-262.

Harvey, C. "Predictable Risk and Returns in Emerging Markets." *Review of Financial Studies*, 8 (1995), pp. 773-816.

Huberman, G., and S.A. Kandel. "Mean-Variance Spanning." *Journal of Finance*, 42 (1987), pp. 383-388.

Jorion, P., and D. Miller. "Investing in Emerging Markets Using Depository Receipts." *Emerging Markets Quarterly*, 1 (1997), pp. 7-13.

Sharpe, W.F. "The Sharpe Ratio." *Journal of Portfolio Management*, 20 (1994), pp. 47-58.

Speidell, L.S., and R. Sappenfield. "Global Diversification in a Shrinking World." *Journal of Portfolio Management*, 19 (1992), pp. 57-67.

Urias, M. "The Impact of ADR Programs on Emerging Stock Market Risk." Working paper, Stanford University, 1996.

THE PRICING OF COUNTRY FUNDS FROM EMERGING MARKETS: THEORY AND EVIDENCE

VIHANG ERRUNZA

McGill University, Faculty of Management, Montreal, Quebec H3A 1G5, Canada

LEMMA W. SENBET

University of Maryland, The Maryland Business School, College Park, MD 20742, USA
E-mail: lsenbet@mbs.umd.edu

and

KED HOGAN

McGill University, Faculty of Management, Montreal, Quebec H3A 1G5, Canada

Received 22 August 1997

This paper provides a theoretical and empirical analysis of country funds focusing on emerging economies whose capital markets are not readily accessible to outside investors. We study country fund pricing and the associated policy implications under alternative variations of international market structure segmentation. We show that country funds traded in the developed capital markets can be beneficial in promoting the efficiency of pricing in the emerging capital markets and in enhancing capital mobilization by local firms. These efficiency gains vary depending upon the degree to which the emerging market securities are spanned by the core or advanced market securities, and cross-border arbitrage restrictions. A country fund premium or discount arises in our framework owing to access and substitution effects characterizing the relationship between the host and emerging markets. We present some empirical evidence supporting our principal predictions. In particular, we investigate the issues of country fund pricing, relative influences of the home market, the international market, the global closed-end fund factor, and the behavior of fund premia/discounts.

1. Introduction

Closed-end country funds primarily invest in the stocks of the originating countries, such as Spain, Germany, Japan, India, Korea, Brazil, and are typically traded on the organized exchanges of the US and the UK. Country funds (CFs) have expanded phenomenally over the recent past, but they beg important issues which are not sufficiently explored. For example, what drives the return on CFs or what are the determinants of fund premia? Are there efficiency gains, particularly to emerging markets, from the introduction of country funds?

Explanations for the behavior of closed-end domestic (US) funds, particularly for the persistence of discounts include, informational inefficiency, illiquidity, tax liability, transaction costs, or noise trading and they offer valuable insights regarding behavior of CFs.[a,b] However, in contrast to domestic closed-end funds, some CFs have consistently sold at a premium (e.g. Korea Fund), some have fluctuated between premium and discount over time (e.g. Malaysia and Germany Funds), and some have consistently sold at a discount (e.g. UK Fund). Thus, although factors that are important in pricing domestic (US) closed-end funds may also influence CF valuation, the structure of global capital market, in particular, the impact of barriers to international capital flows must be considered, since CF shares and their underlying portfolios are priced in different market segments.[c]

Our purpose here is to provide a theoretical and empirical analysis of country funds focusing on emerging economies whose capital markets are not readily accessible to outside investors. By utilizing a segmented markets framework, we link the pricing of country funds in the reference or core markets (say the US) with the pricing of the component underlying assets (or net asset valuation) in the originating securities markets. We study various scenarios of international capital market structure and draw important implications for valuation and premia on country funds, and their impact in enhancing pricing efficiency in the local securities markets. We allow for imperfect substitution between the country fund and the underlying assets based on the notion of excess price volatility that has received ample attention in finance. This is because the component assets traded in the originating countries are fundamental to country funds traded in the core market, and excess volatility is measured by price volatility relative to fundamental volatility. This notion of imperfect substitution is reinforced by the time series pattern of country funds prices and the corresponding net asset values (see Table 1). We show that the country fund will deliver premium or discount, depending on the access and substitution effects characterizing the core and the restricted markets.

If we allow country funds to serve as a perfect substitute for the component securities, the results depend on cross-border arbitrage restrictions. Specifically, under capital inflow controls and prohibitive restrictions on international arbitrage, resulting from such factors as absence of short sales opportunities, taxes, borrowing constraints, and other legal investment barriers, there will be a premium on the country fund, and the pricing of the country fund conforms to the core market rather than the originating country.[d] On the other hand, if local investors can engage in free cross-border arbitrage, there will be no premium or discount on the country fund.

---

[a] See [22] and [10] for literature on US closed-end funds.
[b] A noise trading approach argues that systematic variations in investor sentiment would render closed-end funds riskier and underpriced relative to fundamentals. See for example, [12, 7].
[c] In our framework, if price and underlying net asset value are determined in the same market segment (i.e. in a fully integrated market), no premium/discount would be observed, a result similar to that delivered by well-known asset pricing models.
[d] Since the legal restrictions are prohibitive and binding, we do not consider the impact of market frictions on the arbitrageur's behavior in the spirit of Tuckman and Vila [32].

Table 1. Country fund descriptive statistics.

	\multicolumn{3}{c}{Premia/Discount}			
	mean	max	min	var(r_p)	var(r_{nav})	$\dfrac{\text{var}(r_p)}{\text{var}(r_{nav})}$
Emerging Markets						
Argentina Fund	−.0918	1.3838	−.0727	.0525	.0337	1.5578
Brazil Fund	−.0765	.5514	−.5625	.0698	.0734	.9509
Brazilian Equity Fund	.0343	.3079	−.1489	.0737	.0705	1.0454
Chile Fund	−.0586	.1827	−.4772	.0591	.0408	1.4485
India Growth Fund	.0406	.5424	−.3124	.0537	.0385	1.3948
Indonesia Fund	.1428	.4789	−.2104	.0558	.0261	2.1379
Korea Fund	.4390	1.5658	−.0515	.0629	.0412	1.5266
Korea Investment Fund	.0724	.4418	−.1649	.0423	.0524	.8072
Malaysia Fund	−.0198	.7454	−.4143	.0636	.0325	1.9569
Mexico Equity and Income Fund	−.0599	1.6639	−.5137	.0722	.0614	−.1759
Mexico Fund	−.02622	.4311	−.2698	.0560	.0376	1.4893
Emerging Mexico Fund	−.0148	.3805	−.2035	.0617	.0478	1.2907
First Philippine Fund	−.1690	.6319	−.3359	.0497	.0241	2.0622
Portugal Fund	−.0491	.3980	−.2753	.0497	.0221	2.2488
Taiwan Fund	.2389	2.2955	−.2527	.0795	.0510	1.5588
ROC Taiwan Fund	−.0073	.3412	−.3155	.0575	.0382	1.5052
Thai Capital Fund	.0735	.8829	−.2177	.0544	.0362	1.5027
Thai Fund	−.0819	.1435	−.2401	.0499	.0378	1.3201
Turkey Fund	.0859	1.0025	−.3610	.0615	.0739	.8322
Developed Stock Markets						
Australia Fund	−.1117	.1968	−.2753	.0394	.0227	1.7356
France Growth Fund	−.1235	.1743	−.3324	.0422	.0214	1.9761
Germany Fund	.0231	1.00	−.2388	.0606	.0323	1.8761
Future Germany Fund	−.1319	.0782	−.2647	.0384	.0255	1.5058
New Germany Fund	−.1377	.0131	.2523	.0403	.0237	1.7004
Emerging Germany Fund	−.1066	.7293	−.2174	.0454	.0243	1.8683
Irish Investment Fund	−.1500	.0407	−.3341	.0353	.0224	1.5758
Italy Fund	−.0639	.3795	−.3368	.0501	.0283	1.7703
Japan Equity Fund	.0637	.4751	−.2619	.0532	.0363	1.4655
Japan OTC Equity Fund	.0116	.3169	−.1373	.0428	.0332	1.2891
Singapore Fund	−.0192	.3165	−.2753	.0436	.0251	1.7370
Spain Fund	−.1421	.0903	−.2805	.0343	.0272	1.2610
United Kingdom Fund	−.1219	.0457	−.2420	.0359	.02210	1.6244

Finally, we present empirical evidence supporting our principal findings. In particular, we investigate the issues of country fund pricing, relative influences of the home market, the international market, the global closed-end fund factor, and the behavior of fund premia/discounts.

The paper is organized as follows. In Sec. 2, we provide foundation for the pricing of country funds on the basis of recent theoretical advances on the pricing of assets in segmented markets. In Sec. 3, we present the model, draw implications for pricing and premia on country funds under alternate market structures and derive testable implications. In Sec. 4, data and empirical results are reported. Concluding remarks follow.

2. Foundations for Country Fund Pricing

We begin with the pricing of the underlying component assets traded in the originating countries. We characterize the price of a representative portfolio of assets in a restricted environment as a starting point and draw implications for CF pricing and premia under various international market segmentation and arbitrage conditions.

2.1. *Market setting for trading of country funds and their underlying securities*

The market setting follows the tradition of market segmentation as posited by Lintner [21], Rubinstein [26], Glenn [18] in the domestic context, and by Black [6], Stulz [29], Errunza and Senbet [16], Errunza and Losq [15] in an international context. More recently the structure has been used fruitfully by Merton [24] and Mauer and Senbet [23] to study the effects of limited followership (imperfect information) and the underpricing anomaly of initial public offerings, respectively.[e] In particular, we find it convenient to follow the approaches of EL [15] and MS [23], although their respective motivations are different from ours. This would then serve as a starting point in deriving relevant implications for country funds as we study them for alternative variations of market structure and arbitrage conditions.

In our setting, there are N country funds from N markets that trade in the advanced capital market. The advanced reference market is denoted as "core" which is costlessly accessed by all investors (T) in the universe. The originating markets are accessible only to local investors, and hence they are completely segmented from each other. However, there is partial segmentation between the core and each of the N markets in the sense that investors from the originating countries have access to the core.

For an analytical convenience we deal with only one restricted asset for the most part of our initial analysis, accessible only to $M(M < T)$ local investors in the restricted market. This representation of the market structure is simple and it captures the focal issues in a reasonable way. In fact, as we shall see later, it is rich enough to generate important implications regarding country funds. The implications for the country funds arise from the recognition that the model for an

---

[e]See also Errunza [14] for a similar application, A variation of this structure is used by Alexander, et al. [1] to price a dually listed security in an otherwise fully segmented two-country setting, whereby investors have access only to their respective markets.

individual restricted asset is applicable to a collection or a portfolio of restricted assets which can be viewed as component assets to the fund.

2.2. Technology

We treat the risky securities of the core market (say the US) as an aggregate index with the end-of-period cash flow specified in terms of multiple factors as follows:

$$Y_c = \overline{Y_c} + \sum_k \beta_{ck} F_k + \varepsilon_c, \qquad (1)$$

where

Y_c = the core market's end-of-period cash flow,

$\overline{Y_c}$ = the expected value of Y_c,

F_k = the kth economic factor,

β_{ck} = the core market asset sensitivity to the kth economic factor,

ε_c = the residual core market cash flow.

We also invoke standard orthogonality conditions such that $E(F_k) = E(\varepsilon_c) = E(\varepsilon_c F_k) = E(F_k F_j)$ This is a two-date or single period framework in which the final date cash flows specified above include the liquidation proceeds. As a reference point we consider an asset in a restricted market which is accessed only by M local investors, but its cash flow has a stochastic technological relationship with the assets in the core market. In general, the relationship is such that the asset is not perfectly spanned by the core assets; that is, it does not have a perfect substitute in the core market. We posit the spanning relationship following MS [23], whereby the restricted asset's terminal cash flow can be stated as:

$$Y_F = \overline{Y_F} + \beta_F [Y_C - \overline{Y_C}] + \varepsilon_F, \qquad (2)$$

or alternatively,

$$Y_F = \overline{Y_F} + \beta_F \sum_k \beta_{CK} F_K + \beta_F \varepsilon_C + \varepsilon_F, \qquad (3)$$

where

$\beta_F \beta_{CK}$ = the sensitivity of the restricted market asset to the kth economic factor,

ε_F = the component of the restricted asset cash flow unspanned by the core market

$E(\varepsilon_F) = E(\varepsilon_C \varepsilon_F) = E(\varepsilon_F F_K) = 0.$

A similar spanning relationship follows for the remaining restricted assets from the other $N-1$ countries; we can again think of them in an aggregate for the purpose of cash flow specification. Thus, the aggregate cash flows for the remaining group of restricted assets can be specified as:

$$Y_W = \overline{Y_W} + \beta_W \sum_K \beta_{CK} F_K + \beta_W \varepsilon_C + \varepsilon_W, \qquad (4)$$

where

$\beta_W \beta_{CK}$ = the sensitivity of the aggregate cash flows for the assets of the rest of the restricted markets to the kth economic factor,

ε_W = the component of the restricted asset cash flows unspanned by the core market.

$E(\varepsilon_W) = E(\varepsilon_C \varepsilon_W) = E(\varepsilon_F F_K) = 0$.

For completeness, we also recognize a spanning relationship existing between the reference restricted security (F) and the aggregate (W) of the remaining restricted assets from $N-1$ countries; recognizing this particular spanning relationship, we can restate the cash flows for the restricted asset:

$$Y_F = \left[\overline{Y_F^C} + \beta_F \left(\sum_k \beta_{CK} F_K + \varepsilon_C\right)\right] + \left[\overline{Y_F^*} + b_F \varepsilon_W + \varepsilon_F^*\right]. \qquad (5)$$

The cash flows are split into those spanned by the core market (first square parenthesis) and those "core unspanned" or specific to the asset (second square parenthesis). The latter parenthesis recognizes that there is a spanning relationship between the "core-unspanned" and the remaining aggregate of restricted assets, with a factor of proportionality b_F and the unique residual ε_F^*.

2.3. Portfolio and market equilibria

While our motivation is specific to pricing of country funds, the technological specifications are adaptations of the frameworks utilized by MS [23] in the context of underpricing anomaly of initial public offerings and by EL [15] in the context of international asset pricing. Consequently, the initial valuation that we wish to use as a starter follows from these works, and we will state it without proof.[f] The approach is fairly standard in that individual investors are allowed to optimize their portfolio choices by picking fractional holdings in various categories of assets, depending upon accessibility of these assets. The efficient portfolio optimization is in a mean-variance paradigm, whereby individuals maximize their utility over current consumption, the expected value of portfolio wealth (or equivalently expected consumption) at a final date, and portfolio risk as reflected in the volatility of future consumption at a final date. Portfolio demands are then aggregated and equated

[f]The detailed proof is in Appendix I.

to aggregate existing supply of securities to derive a market equilibrium valuation. Note that the aggregation process takes explicit account of limited access, or alternatively as in Merton [24], the Lagrange multipliers are used to measure a shadow price of imperfect access. However, the model delivers the same structure under either treatment of access restrictions. Thus, the value of a restricted asset can be specified as:

$$V_F = (1+r_f)^{-1}\left[\overline{Y_F} - \theta^{-1}(\beta_F Z) - (\theta^M)^{-1}(b_F^2 \sigma^2(\varepsilon_W) + \sigma^2(\varepsilon_F^*))\right], \qquad (6)$$

where

$$Z = (1+\beta_F+\beta_W)\left[\Sigma\beta_{CK}^2\sigma^2(F_K) + \sigma^2(\varepsilon_C)\right].$$

The valuation in (6) recognizes that there is also risk-free lending and borrowing available to all participants at a rate equal to r_f.[g] The risk premium is of two forms:- (a) "complete pricing" risk premium which is a function of Z, and (b) the risk premium associated with limited risk sharing or "nationalistic risk" factor which is shared only by local investors. The complete pricing risk factor is subject to the universal price of risk, θ^{-1}, and the nationalistic risk factor is subject to $(\theta^M)^{-1}$.

The nationalistic risk factor is separately priced only due to limited risk sharing resulting from limited access. If access were complete, the model converges to the familiar capital asset pricing model, where the reference benchmark portfolio is the international portfolio. Also, if the restricted asset had a perfect substitute in the core market, it would be priced as an unrestricted asset with identical characteristics. The two important dimensions — access and substitution effects — can be dramatized if we make additional restrictions without much loss of generality. Following Merton [24] and MS [23], if we assume individuals everywhere have identical preferences and initial wealth, we can express the degree of access and substitution effects more explicitly as follows:

$$V_F = (1+r_f)^{-1}\left\{\left[\overline{Y_F} - \left(\frac{\gamma}{T}\right)(\beta_F Z + b_F^2\sigma^2(\varepsilon_W) + \sigma^2(\varepsilon_F^*))\right]\right.$$
$$\left. - \left(\frac{\gamma}{T}\right)(b_F^2\sigma^2(\varepsilon_W) + \sigma^2(\varepsilon_F^*))\frac{1-\alpha}{\alpha}\right\}. \qquad (7)$$

The interaction between the degree of access and substitution effects are reflected in the last term of the model. The degree of access is now measured by (α) = the number of investors accessing the security (M)/ the number of all investors in the universe (T). The universal risk aversion measure or "price of risk" is given by $\left(\frac{\gamma}{T}\right)$,

---

[g]This assumption may turn out to be important, because, as we remark later, the interest rate differential (in real terms) across national boundaries may alone generate premia/discounts on the country funds. This is particularly so if the interest rate markets are segmented, along with the stock markets which is the focus of this paper.

while the nationalistic price of risk is given by $(\frac{\gamma}{\alpha T})$. The latter is greater than the former to the extent that $\alpha < 1$, reflecting the extra risk premium demanded by local investors due to incomplete risk sharing. Note that if the "core-unspanned" risk (or the volatility of the unspanned cash flows in (5)) were zero, which is the case under the existence of perfect substitutes in the core, the last term would collapse to zero. In that case the effect of limited access is undone, because investors can achieve complete hedging by taking long and short positions in the core and restricted markets.

In the following section we shall link the pricing of the restricted assets in the originating countries with the pricing of country funds in the core market. Under alternative structures of market segmentation and arbitrage conditions, we derive various implications by using the model in (7) as a starting point.

3. Country Fund Pricing and Net Asset Valuation

The model in (7) can also be used to price a portfolio of restricted foreign assets. In the parlance of country funds, the price of such a portfolio is the net asset value of the fund. Hereinafter we reinterpret asset F as a portfolio of the component assets underlying the country fund. We can restate the net asset value in an implicit functional form:

$$V_F = f[\overline{Y}_F, Z, \alpha, \sigma^2(\varepsilon_F)], \qquad (8)$$

where

$\overline{Y}_F$ = expected portfolio cash flow at the final date,

Z = the complete pricing or spanning risk subject to the aggregate international price of risk $\left(\theta^{-1} = \frac{\gamma}{T}\right)$,

α = the degree of access, wherein $\alpha = 1$ denotes complete access,

$\sigma^2(\varepsilon_F)$ = the unspanned risk factor subject to the nationalistic price of risk $\left[(\theta^M)^{-1} = \frac{\gamma}{\alpha T}\right]$; also the degree of substitution, wherein $\sigma^2(\varepsilon_F) = 0$ denotes perfect substitution,

T = number of investors in the entire universe, including both the core and restricted local markets.

Now we are ready to value a country fund in the core (say the US) market in relation to its net asset value. Throughout we maintain a mildly segmented market structure in the sense that investors in the local, emerging economies are unrestricted, but investors from the advanced, core markets are restricted from holding securities in the emerging economies directly. Thus, restrictions are imposed on capital inflows, but not on outflows, into the emerging economies.

3.1. The model

Recognizing that a country fund is an unrestricted asset which was previously restricted, its risk is now subject to the universal price of risk ($\frac{\gamma}{T}$). In other words, it will be priced with complete access ($\alpha = 1$) so that

$$V_p = (1+r_f)^{-1}\left[\overline{Y_F} - \frac{\gamma}{T}(\beta_F Z + b_F^2 \sigma^2(\varepsilon_W) + \sigma^2(\varepsilon_F^*))\right], \qquad (9)$$

where V_p is the price of a country fund. The pricing of a country fund in the core market, relative to its component assets traded in the local market, depends on the degree of its substitutability with the underlying assets and cross-border arbitrage between the two markets. In the usual models where the country fund serves as a perfect substitute for its underlying component assets (in a portfolio sense), there will be no differential between country fund pricing and net asset valuation, assuming unimpeded cross-border arbitrage.

Imperfect substitution between the country fund and the underlying assets traded in the emerging countries may arise from a number of factors, including but not limited to, (a) sovereign risk exposure for holders of country funds, such as the possibility of exchange control, (b) exchange risk arising from market conditions and the use of differential numeraire,[h] (c) noise trading and excess volatility.[i] As mentioned earlier, there is evidence that time series behavior of fund prices (and the associated volatility) differs from that of the net asset values (see Table 1). The volatility is higher for fund prices and this divergence appears larger for less developed economies. This gives credence to the notion of imperfect substitution.

Consider a new spanning (albeit imperfect substitution) relationship between the component assets and the country fund now in the core market:

$$\varepsilon_F = b_F^* \varepsilon_P + \varepsilon_F^{**}, \qquad (10)$$

where

$\varepsilon_P =$ the component of the country fund cash flow unspanned by the core market,

$\varepsilon_F^{**} =$ the component of the underlying asset cash flow unspanned by the country fund.

Rewriting (9) to recognize the possibility of divergence in the volatilities of the country fund and the underlying assets:

$$V_p = (1+r_f)^{-1}\left[\overline{Y} - \frac{\gamma}{T}(\beta_F Z + \sigma^2(\varepsilon_P))\right], \qquad (11)$$

---

[h]Under a different numeraire for translating cash flows holders of the country fund and the component assets may face divergent or heterogeneous expectations, resulting in differential valuations for the two classes of investments and hence premia or discount on the fund.

[i]The notion of excess volatility fits in well with such studies as Summers [31] and Shiller [28] who claim that observed price volatility is excessively high relative to its fundamental counterpart. Under our framework the component securities are *fundamental* to the country fund securities.

where it is assumed that complete pricing risk factor (Z) is unchanged, but there is divergence in the unspanned risks (i.e. there is differential in the component risks of the fund and its underlying assets unspanned by the core market).

It also follows that the net asset value of the component securities is:

$$V_F^* = (1+r_f)^{-1}\left[\overline{Y_F} - \frac{\gamma}{T}\left(\beta_F Z + b_F^{*2}\sigma^2(\varepsilon_P)\right) - \frac{\gamma}{\alpha T}\sigma^2(\varepsilon_F^{**})\right]. \quad (12)$$

Comparing (12) with (7) or (8), we see that $V_F^* > V_F$, because only a component of the previously unspanned risk, $\sigma^2(\varepsilon_F^{**})$, is subject to the nationalistic price of risk upon the introduction of the country fund in the core market. Consequently, the net asset value increases in spite of imperfect substitution or imperfect spanning relationship between the country fund and its underlying assets traded in the emerging market. Comparing (12) with (11), though, $V_P - V_F^*$ can be positive or negative, or it is possible for the country fund to sell at either a discount or premium.

3.2. Model implications and comparative statics

We shall pursue the implications of the model by performing some simple comparative statics. These implications are all potentially testable, although due to limited data we are able to conduct tests on only part of them.

The first set of implications are related to the determinants of pricing efficiency gains to emerging markets from the introduction of a country fund into the core market. In general, the local security prices get bid up to reflect the fact that a larger component of the asset risks are subject to the universal price of risk.[j] The efficiency effect can be stated more explicitly as

$$Q = \frac{\gamma}{T}\left(\frac{1}{\alpha} - 1\right)\lambda\sigma^2(\varepsilon_F)$$

where

$$\lambda = b_F^{*2}\frac{\sigma^2(\varepsilon_P)}{\sigma^2(\varepsilon_F)}$$

= the degree of substitution between the unspanned risks.

Thus, among the determinants of the efficiency gains are:

the degree of substitution:

$$\frac{\delta Q}{\delta \lambda} = \frac{\gamma}{T}\left(\frac{1}{\alpha} - 1\right)\sigma^2(\varepsilon_F) > 0$$

the degree of initial access:

$$\frac{\delta Q}{\delta \alpha} = -\frac{\gamma}{T}\sigma^2(\varepsilon_F)\frac{1}{\alpha^2} < 0$$

---
[j]This result is similar to Stulz and Wasserfallen [30].

the risk unspannable by the core:

$$\frac{\delta Q}{\delta \sigma^2(\varepsilon_F)} = \frac{\gamma}{T}\left(\frac{1}{\alpha} - 1\right)\lambda > 0$$

Discussion: Other things being equal, emerging countries with larger unspannable risk benefit more from the introduction of the country fund in the core (advanced) market. Such countries typically have idiosyncratic investment opportunities or unique natural resources. At the limit, of course, the effect is nil if either (a) $\lambda = 0$, or (b) $\alpha = 1$. Also, other things being equal, the gain is larger if the local price of risk is higher relative to the world or universal price of risk, which may be the case for small emerging markets with limited risk-sharing opportunities. This effect is reflected in α. Finally, a greater substitutability of the country fund and its underlying assets increases the efficiency gain. This effect increases with λ.

An additional testable implication can be drawn from imperfect substitution stemming from additional factors affecting country fund prices, in the sense that there is now an additional pricing factor common to certain segments of the country funds. In the language of the arbitrage pricing theory (APT), this factor conforms *neither* to the originating countries *nor* to the reference countries. The additional factor is analogous to the risk factors in (3), exclusive of the complete pricing risk, $\beta_P Z$. It is also possible to generate this additional factor through the spanning relationship that exists between restricted assets as suggested in Eq. (5) to the extent that these assets have become components of country funds traded in the core market. We pursue the existence of a "global fund index" in our empirical analysis.

Another set of implications relates to the country fund premium or discount. Among the determinants of the premium/discount are the degree of accessibility to the restricted market and the volatility ratio of the country fund to its net assets. From Eqs. (11) and (12), the premium/discount can be stated as

$$\Pi = (1+r_f)^{-1}\left[\beta\sigma^2(\varepsilon_F)\{b_F^{*2} - 1\} + \frac{\sigma^2(\varepsilon_F^{**})}{\alpha}\right]\left(\frac{\gamma}{T}\right),$$

where β is defined from

$$\sigma^2(\varepsilon_P) = \beta\sigma^2(\varepsilon_F),$$

such that

Access:

$$\frac{\delta\Pi}{\delta\alpha} = -\frac{\sigma^2(\varepsilon_F^{**})}{\alpha^2}\frac{\gamma}{T}(1+r_f)^{-1} < 0$$

Excess volatility:

$$\frac{\delta\Pi}{\delta\beta} = (1+r_f)^{-1}\frac{\gamma}{T}\sigma^2(\varepsilon_F)\{b_F^{*2} - 1\} < 0 \text{ since } b_F^* < 1$$

Other things constant, the premium is smaller for emerging markets which have greater access. The premium is also smaller if the country fund becomes more volatile, relative to the underlying assets.

3.3. Specialized cases

3.3.1. Perfect substitution and ban on cross-border arbitrage

Consider a simple case of market segmentation, where investors in the emerging markets face a ban on cross-border arbitrage between the country fund and its component assets, although the country fund is presumed to be a perfect substitute in terms of cash flow (technological uncertainty) for the cash flows of the portfolio of the component securities. The sense in which there is restriction on arbitrage may arise from explicit legal restrictions, the absence of short-sales or differential tax penalties (e.g. Germany; see the appendix on taxes), or that there is limited supply of funds due to control considerations. In this case, investors in the emerging countries would be unable to undo the price differential between the country fund and its net asset value through arbitrage operations. The introduction of a country fund has no impact on the pricing of the component assets in the local market, but the country fund sells at a premium relative to its net asset value.

In the absence of cross-border arbitrage, the restricted asset will have its entire risk, including the spanning risk, subject to the nationalistic price of risk; the country fund and the portfolio of restricted component assets will have differential value, with the net asset value expressed as:

$$V_F^* = (1+r_f)^{-1}\left[\overline{Y_F} - \frac{\gamma}{\alpha T}(\beta_F Z + b_F^2 \sigma^2(\varepsilon_W) + \sigma^2(\varepsilon_F^*))\right]. \tag{13}$$

Comparing (9) with (13), the country fund price $= V_P > V_F^* =$ the net asset value, since $\frac{\gamma}{T} < \frac{\gamma}{\alpha T}$. The risk premium would be larger for the restricted security, as the cash flow uncertainty is identical for both the country fund and the component securities (by assumption of perfect substitution). Consequently, the country fund sells at a premium over the net asset value.

Under this market structure the introduction of the country fund in the core market is of no consequence to the pricing of the component assets in the restricted emerging market from which the fund originates, although there may be diversification gain to the core (international) investors through their holdings of the fund. Indeed, the country fund and its component assets will be priced as though they are completely segmented, where the price of risk for the country fund conforms to the price of risk in the core (host) market, whereas the price of risk for the underlying assets conforms to the market in the originating country. They plot on two different security market lines, so to speak. This is a subject of our empirical analysis, since this case establishes the possibility that prices of certain funds behave so as to "resemble" their hosts (e.g. the US) rather than their origins.

3.3.2. Perfect substitution and unimpeded cross-border arbitrage

As above, if we allow the country fund to be a perfect substitute for the underlying assets traded in the originating market and unrestricted cross-border arbitrage, the capital inflow restriction is inconsequential, because the pricing differential will be eliminated by virtue of unimpeded arbitrage by local investors from the originating countries.

The introduction of a country fund will enhance the value of the component assets (at a decreasing rate) in the originating country, but the fund trades at zero premium. Since the country fund is trading now in the core with complete access ($\alpha = 1$), the net asset value of the component underlying assets will be bid up to $V_F^* = V_P$, because of perfect substitution between the fund and the component assets and perfect cross-border arbitrage by local investors. Consequently, there will be no premium or discount on the fund.

There is pricing efficiency in the sense that the prices of the component securities in the originating countries (i.e. emerging economies) rise, on average, upon the introduction of the country fund. Thus, the country fund serves as a mechanism to complete the market. The efficiency gains come about as local investors are able to reduce, and as the core investors increase, their holdings of domestic risks. This is achieved in two ways: first, investors in the core market can now hold local risk by buying into the country fund. Second, local investors can short sell the fund and acquire core assets with the proceeds. The important point is that unrestricted trade in local risk becomes possible with the establishment of a country fund of any size when domestic investors are able to short sell the fund in the core market.

3.4. Some possible extensions

The preceding analysis has focused primarily on the risk dimension and incomplete risk sharing in an international environment characterized with investor restrictions. However, there are significant cases where country funds trade at a discount even when they do not originate from countries with limited capital and inflow restrictions. As a starter, this observation is consistent with long-standing anomaly that closed-end funds trade typically at a discount even when they trade in the domestic market (e.g. closed-end funds traded in the US). In this section, we wish to catalogue additional factors that have a bearing on the pricing of country funds relative to their net asset values.

3.4.1. Interest rate differential

The preceding analysis assumed that investors faced the same real rate of interest across national boundaries. This may not hold between pairs of countries with differential creditworthiness such that the induced interest rate differential between the core market and the originating emerging country may deliver discount or premium on the country fund originating from the latter country. Suppose that the core country is the US and the emerging country is Brazil with lower creditworthiness and higher real rate of interest. This may alone deliver a premium on the Brazilian fund, since the underlying securities traded in Brazil are presumably discounted by Brazilians at a higher rate than the rate applicable to the country fund by US investors.

The preceding argument is incomplete, though, because Brazilian investors may fully access the US risk-free government securities and hence face the same benchmark rate of interest as investors in the US for lending purposes. In addition, they may use the US asset investments as a collateral for borrowing purposes in the event that credit enforcement is an issue. Thus, in the absence of investor restrictions leading to segmentation in the international money markets, the interest rate differential alone may not deliver a price differential on the country fund relative to its net asset value. Moreover, the interest rate differential may reflect country risk differential, affecting the core market discount rate applicable to the country fund. While the interest rate differential between Brazil and the US may alone lead to a premium, the country risk factor leads to a discount that reflects the risk of expropriation of the foreign portfolio investors. When the probability of expropriation is low, which is likely when country funds are small, a premium may emerge. At any rate, it is difficult to determine the net effect of the interest rate differential on the price of the fund relative to its net asset value.

3.4.2. *Tax and regulatory factors*

Our analysis thus far has not explicitly considered the impact of the tax treatment of country funds, although implicit in our model is the possibility of differential tax treatment rendering imperfect substitution between the country fund and the component securities traded in the originating countries. A stylized description of the US tax treatment of country funds is provided in Appendix II. The impact of tax treatment can be appreciated just on the basis of the most straightforward case defined as follows:

(1) The fund qualifies as a Regulated Investment Co. (IRC) and hence subject to no *corporate taxation*.
(2) *All* distributions of net investment income (dividends, interest, net short-term capital gains, etc.) are taxable at an *ordinary personal tax rate*. [Note: Taxes are imposed even when income is reinvested.]
(3) Foreign withholding taxes and foreign income taxes paid by the fund are treated as *paid by shareholders* who then claim these as credits/deductions for US tax purposes (US is the host country here).

Under the above scenario the controlling tax rate on the fund income is the US income tax rate. If the controlling tax rate is identical to the foreign (originating country) tax rate, there will be no tax-induced differential between the fund price and its net asset value. Note that the net asset value is impacted only by the foreign taxes imposed on component assets in the originating country. Thus, the premium/discount = f(US/foreign income tax rate differential).[k]

4. Empirical Perspectives

This section provides an empirical investigation of country funds based on the principal theoretical predictions of our model. Specifically, we investigate the relative significance of the home market, host market and the global closed-end fund factors in CF pricing and their associated premia/discounts. The testable implications of our model regarding efficiency gains are left for future investigation pending availability of reliable local market data sets on component securities of the funds in our sample.

4.1. The data and sample

The study covers all closed-end single country funds publicly traded in New York by the end of 1993. Nineteen funds are from emerging markets (EMs) and thirteen are from developed markets (DMs). The data base contains weekly observations for each fund since its inception comprising Friday closing prices as reported in the NYSE records; net asset value (NAV) as obtained from fund managers and Wall Street Journal; dividends and distributions of capital gains. MSCI and IFCG total return indices are used to proxy local market returns for DMs and EMs respectively. Table 1 reports summary statistics on the sample funds. Unlike their domestic closed-end fund counterparts, in many instances closed-end country funds exhibit average premiums. Specifically, in 9 of 18 EMs and 3 of 13 DMs we find price exceeding NAV on average. Furthermore, we note extreme swings in country fund premia, with premiums at times in excess of 50% in 10 cases (9 EMs and 1 DM). We also find country fund discounts at times in excess of −50% in only 2 cases (both of which are EMs). Further, we report the unconditional variance of price and NAV returns. In all but three cases we find the variance of price returns to exceed that of NAV returns.

4.2. Pricing of country funds

The empirical evidence to date suggests that, although country funds provide substantial diversification benefits to US investors, the gains are smaller than if they had access to the originating market portfolios or if the funds had been designed to mimic the local index (i.e. a true national index fund).[l] On the other hand, Bekaert and Urias [5] find that country funds traded in the UK improve

---

[k]In some cases the tax treatment is complex (e.g. *Germany*), affecting the extent to which investors engage in arbitrage. Rather than treating regulatory and tax factors as separate predictors of pricing, one could view them as engendering imperfect substitution. That way the model can accommodate them in its current structural form. For instance, sovereign risk may impact the substitution effect negatively.

[l]See, for example, Bailey and Lim [3] and Diwan, Errunza and Senbet [13].

diversification gains while those which trade in the US do not. Furthermore, they find that diversification gains from passive IFC investible index position to be superior to that of country funds. This raises an important question as to the pricing of these funds. Specifically, do these funds behave like domestic US securities or follow the originating country returns? Bailey and Lim [3] conclude that country fund returns are often more like domestic US stock returns than returns from foreign stock portfolios. They consider intraday correlations and volatilities during trading and non-trading hours. Their tests follow the existing empirical literature on cross-border stock market relationships. Although they attempt to explain these results, we must study this issue further based on the insights of our theoretical model. Note that their conclusion is consistent with the prediction of the specialized case of our model which rests on perfect substitution and restricted arbitrage.

4.2.1. Imperfect substitution

As noted earlier, the return behavior of country funds in our sample does not qualify them as perfect substitutes for the underlying assets traded in the home market. As further evidence, consider the ratio of standard deviations of price returns and NAV returns for the sample funds as reported in Table 1. In all cases the price returns display substantially higher volatility compared to the NAV returns. The only exceptions are Turkey, Korea Investment and Brazil funds whose portfolios had substantial holdings of the US T-bills during the period studied. This leads us to consider the empirical implications of our model which admits imperfect substitution.

4.2.2. Methodology

To assess the relative importance of the domestic, US factor and global country fund factors in explaining country fund price returns we first compute the R-square from the regression of the country fund price return (r_c) on each of the factors in isolation, i.e. the return on the domestic market (r_d), the US factor (r_{us}), and the return on global country fund index (r_g). The global fund index is obtained by equally weighting the return on the oldest country fund from each of the markets in our total sample. Note that the tests using global fund factor, that conforms neither to the originating countries nor to the host countries, are based on the prediction of our model. As we argued, there are other factors unrelated to either the originating countries or the reference countries that affect country fund prices. With such "imperfect substitution", we postulate that there should be a factor (e.g. noise trading activity) common to all funds. We attempt to capture this factor through the construction of the global fund index.

Next, we compute first order partial correlation coefficients, i.e.

$$\rho(r_c, r_i | r_j) = \frac{\rho(r_c, r_i) - \rho(r_c, r_i)\rho(r_c, r_j)}{\sqrt{1 - \rho(r_c, r_i)^2}\sqrt{1 - \rho(r_c, r_j)^2}} \quad \text{for } i \neq j. \tag{14}$$

The square of the partial correlation represents the portion of country fund price return explained by factor i after controlling for factor j. These figures are reported in columns 2 and 3 of Tables 2, 3 and 4. Finally, we calculate the second order multiple correlation coefficients which provide a measure of how much of the variance of the country fund return that is explained by one factor that cannot be jointly accounted for by the other two factors. Essentially, the analysis nets out the effects of the other factors to isolate the extent to which each factor explains country fund pricing.

4.2.3. Results

The R-squares for the regressions of fund returns (r_c) on each of the three factors $(r_d, r_{us}$ and $r_g)$ are reported in the first column of Tables 2-4, respectively. The partial correlations are reported in columns 2 and 3, and the multiple correlations are reported in column 4 of the Tables 2-4. Several general conclusions are in order. First, with few exceptions (Brazilian Equity, Malaysia and Taiwan) the domestic factor alone, accounts for a larger fraction of the country fund return variance. Netting out the effects of the US factor has little or no effect on the degree to which the domestic factor explains the EM country fund pricing. This is consistent with the well-documented low degree of correlation between the US and emerging market indices. Somewhat surprising is the fact that this result also holds for the DM country funds. Netting out the effects of the global country fund factor has a far greater impact on the explanatory power of the domestic factor. For example, the explained variance of the Malaysia fund attributable to the domestic factor declines from 0.1605 to 0.039 once the global factor is accounted for. Other dramatic examples include Portugal, Mexico Equity and Income Fund, Thai Fund, Thai Capital Fund, Australia Fund, France Growth Fund and Germany Fund. Again, there appears to be no discernible difference in this dimension between DMs and EMs.

Second, for the majority of EM country funds (13 out of 19 cases), the global fund factor alone explains more of the country fund return than the domestic factor. A similar result is found for 10 of 13 DM country funds. This conclusion is not much affected once the domestic factor is netted out. Finally, comparing the last column across Tables 2, 3 and 4, we note that in 19 cases the global factor accounts for the largest portion of country fund price behavior after netting out the other two factors. The corresponding numbers for the domestic and the US factor are 12 and 1, respectively.

To summarize, the results of this subsection provide strong support for the theoretical predictions of our model which admits imperfect substitution. The presence of the additional factor common to all country funds is borne out by the importance of the global index factor in explaining returns of country funds from emerging and developed markets as reported in this subsection. This finding has important implications for the design of country funds and policies to reduce imperfect substitutability of the funds and their component assets traded in the home markets, as we remark later in the concluding section.

Table 2. The relative importance of the domestic factor.

The portion of the variance of the country fund price return explained by the domestic market factor alone is inferred from the squared correlation coefficient $\rho^2(r_c, r_d)$, where r_c is the country fund price return and r_d is the domestic market return. The squared first-order partial correlation coefficients $\rho^2(r_c, r_d | r_{us})$ reveal the fraction of country fund price attributable to the domestic factor net of the affects of the US factor. Similarly $\rho^2(r_c, r_d | r_{gl})$ reveals the fraction of the country fund price attributable to the domestic factor net of the global factor. The squared second-order partial correlation coefficients $\rho^2(r_c, r_d | r_{gl}, r_{us})$ reveal the fraction of country fund price return attributable to the domestic factor net of both the US factor and the global factor.

	Domestic Factor			
	$\rho^2(r_c, r_d)$	$\rho^2(r_c, r_d | r_{us})$	$\rho^2(r_c, r_d | r_{gl})$	$\rho^2(r_c, r_d | r_{gl}, r_{us})$
Emerging Markets				
Argentina Fund	.2351	.2031	.1336	.1310
Brazil Fund	.2076	.1925	.1554	.1552
Brazilian Equity Fund	.0000	.0004	.0004	.0002
Chile Fund	.1533	.1495	.1140	.1158
India Growth Fund	.0916	.0954	.0976	.0938
Indonesia Fund	.1037	.1099	.0701	.0606
Korea Fund	.2411	.2309	.2045	.2049
Korea Investment Fund	.0877	.0874	.0710	.0664
Malaysia Fund	.1605	.1267	.0390	.0382
Mexico Fund	.0668	.0529	.0206	.0222
Mexico Equity and Income Fund	.1205	.1093	.0942	.0935
Emerging Mexico Fund	.3413	.3306	.2652	.2689
First Philippine Fund	.1972	.1841	.1059	.1056
Portugal Fund	.1032	.0827	.0254	.0253
Taiwan Fund	.0000	.0000	.0017	.0015
ROC Taiwan Fund	.2968	.2754	.2178	.2173
Thai Fund	.1861	.1527	.0629	.0621
Thai capital Fund	.2571	.2065	.0806	.0814
Turkey Fund	.1584	.1515	.1277	.1280
Developed Stock Markets				
Australia Fund	.1334	.1089	.0444	.0468
France Growth Fund	.2140	.1579	.0632	.0656
Germany Fund	.1425	.1111	.0245	.0245
New Germany Fund	.3062	.2555	.1498	.1486
Future Germany Fund	.2959	.2519	.1341	.1348
Emerging Germany Fund	.0003	.0003	.0018	.0016
Irish Investment Fund	.0061	.0038	.0000	.0001
Italy Fund	.1532	.1433	.0852	.0885
Japan OTC Fund	.2211	.1670	.1308	.1239
Japan Equity Fund	.2200	.2216	.2100	.2129
Singapore Fund	.0407	.0331	.0000	.0000
Spain Fund	.3332	.2402	.1483	.1375
United Kingdom Fund	.2279	.1495	.1231	.0988

Table 3. The relative importance of the US factor.

The portion of the variance of the country fund price return explained by the US market factor alone is inferred from the squared correlation coefficient $\rho^2(r_c, r_{us})$, where r_c is the country fund price return and r_{us} is the US market return. The squared first-order partial correlation coefficients $\rho^2(r_c, r_{us}|r_d)$ reveal the fraction of country fund price attributable to the US factor net of the affects of the domestic factor. Similarly $\rho^2(r_c, r_{us}|r_{gl})$ reveals the fraction of the country fund price attributable to the US factor net of the global factor. The squared second-order partial correlation coefficients $\rho^2(r_c, r_{us}|r_d, r_{gl})$ reveal the fraction of country fund price return attributable to the US factor net of both the domestic factor and the global factor.

	US Factor			
	$\rho^2(r_c, r_{us})$	$\rho^2(r_c, r_{us}|r_d)$	$\rho^2(r_c, r_{us}|r_{gl})$	$\rho^2(r_c, r_{us}|r_d, r_{gl})$
Emerging Markets				
Argentina Fund	.0398	.0063	.0030	.0003
Brazil Fund	.0595	.0446	.0062	.0058
Brazilian Equity Fund	.0188	.0193	.0329	.0326
Chile Fund	.0711	.0671	.0038	.0061
India Growth Fund	.0058	.0086	.0092	.0051
Indonesia Fund	.0338	.0213	.0197	.0109
Korea Fund	.0662	.0219	.0004	.0010
Korea Investment Fund	.0025	.0030	.0240	.0195
Malaysia Fund	.1625	.0954	.0109	.0101
Mexico Fund	.0179	.0101	.001	.003
Mexico Equity and Investment Fund	.0144	.0019	.0014	.0007
Emerging Mexico Fund	.01646	.0004	.0046	.0103
First Philippine Fund	.03975	.0241	.0009	.0005
Portugal Fund	.0626	.0411	.0001	.0000
Taiwan Fund	.0009	.0027	.0130	.0128
ROC Taiwan Fund	.0688	.0405	.0020	.0014
Thai Fund	.077	.0618	.0034	.0026
Thai Capital Fund	.1350	.077	.0051	.0060
Turkey Fund	.0282	.0205	.0014	.0020
Developed Stock Markets				
Australia Fund	.0456	.01946	.0025	.0051
France Growth Fund	.0903	.0269	.0003	.0028
Germany Fund	.0686	.0341	.0000	.1378
New Germany Fund	.1378	.0704	.0039	.0025
Future Germany Fund	.0936	.0375	.0005	.0012
Emerging Germany Fund	.0001	.0000	.0020	.0017
Irish Investment Fund	.0036	.0013	.0017	.0018
Italy Fund	.0156	.0043	.0128	.0163
Japan OTC Fund	.1693	.1106	.0464	.0387
Japan Equity Fund	.0506	.0491	.0188	.0235
Singapore Fund	.0088	.0009	.0114	.0114
Spain Fund	.1780	.0719	.0284	.0154
United Kingdom Fund	.1739	.0897	.0621	.0361

Table 4. The relative importance of the global factor.

The portion of the variance of the country fund price return explained by the country fund global factor alone is inferred from the squared correlation coefficient $\rho^2(r_c, r_{gl})$, where r_c is the country fund price return and r_{gl} is the global factor. The squared first-order partial correlation coefficients $\rho^2(r_c, r_{gl}|r_d)$ reveal the fraction of country fund price attributable to the global factor net of the affects of the domestic factor. Similarly $\rho^2(r_c, r_{gl}|r_{us})$ reveals the fraction of the country fund price attributable to the global factor net of the US factor. The squared second-order partial correlation coefficients $\rho^2(r_c, r_{gl}|r_d, r_{us})$ reveal the fraction of country fund price return attributable to the global factor net of both the US factor and the domestic.

	Global Fund Factor			
	$\rho^2(r_c, r_{gl})$	$\rho^2(r_c, r_{gl}\|r_d)$	$\rho^2(r_c, r_{gl}\|r_{us})$	$\rho^2(r_c, r_{gl}\|r_d, r_{us})$
Emerging Markets				
Argentina Fund	.1325	.02936	.0989	.0251
Brazil Fund	.1672	.1124	.1172	.0763
Brazilian Equity Fund	.0045	.0050	.0188	.0186
Chile Fund	.2063	.1694	.1487	.1150
India Growth Fund	.1060	.119	.1103	.1087
Indonesia Fund	.2913	.2213	.2795	.2130
Korea Fund	.1934	.1544	.1651	.1363
Korea Investment Fund	.1773	.1594	.1951	.1752
Malaysia Fund	.4065	.3206	.3248	.2565
Mexico Fund	.1719	.1309	.1521	.1248
Mexico Equity and Income Fund	.0292	.0017	.0163	.0005
Emerging Mexico Fund	.1615	.0680	.1512	.0766
First Philippine Fund	.2562	.1718	.2261	.1517
Portugal Fund	.2986	.2376	.2519	.2049
Taiwan Fund	.01151	.0131	.0217	.0231
ROC Taiwan Fund	.2328	.146	.1776	.1117
Thai Fund	.3579	.2607	.2895	.2140
Thai Capital Fund	.3556	.2048	.2572	.1431
Turkey Fund	.20155	.1723	.1794	.1567
Developed Stock Markets				
Australia Fund	.3065	.2353	.2753	.2241
France Growth Fund	.3439	.2185	.2772	.1979
Germany Fund	.3265	.2338	.2769	.2064
New Germany Fund	.3891	.2509	.2926	.1905
Future Germany Fund	.3647	.2190	.2978	.1881
Emerging Germany Fund	.0033	.0047	.0052	.0063
Irish Investment Fund	.2226	.1602	.2204	.1703
Italy Fund	.0321	.02625	.0302	.0265
Japan OTC Fund	.2184	.1285	.1026	.0560
Japan Equity Fund	.0631	.0576	.0317	.0282
Singapore Fund	.1113	.0730	.1128	.0827
Spain Fund	.3428	.1635	.2225	.1122
United Kingdom Fund	.2430	.1403	.1406	.0893

4.3. Determinants of country fund premia

In this section we test theoretical predictions of the model with respect to fund premia. Our model highlights the impact of international market segmentation on country fund premia. Segmentation stems from two sources in our model: (1) market access, and (2) incomplete international risk sharing or spanning. The model suggests that neither source of segmentation is meaningful in the absence of the other. That is, limited access to a foreign market will have no impact on the country fund premia if foreign securities are perfectly spanned in the host market. Likewise, incomplete spanning is irrelevant if foreigners have full access to foreign markets. It is the interaction of both imperfect spanning and limited access which drives a wedge between a country fund price and net asset value. Although Bekaert and Harvey [4] have investigated their combined effect, an explicit decomposition of spanning and access has yet to be addressed in the empirical literature.

In addition to market segmentation, country fund premia are influenced by a multitude of other factors. Our model accounts for a generic lack of substitutability between price and its fundamental value as well as a common factor that may be attributed to noise trading. What follows is an attempt to proxy spanning, access, imperfect substitution, and the global factor, towards investigating the extent to which these factors affect country fund premia.

Spanning

A set of eligible securities $(R_1^e, \ldots, R_m^e)$ (returns on freely accessible securities in host market) is said to span restricted security R^i (e.g. country fund NAV return) if a vector δ can be found such that $R^i = \Sigma_1^m \delta_j R_j^e$. Partitioning R^i into a spanned and unspanned component can be accomplished by estimating the following regression:

$$R_t^i = \delta_1 R_{1,t}^e + \cdots + \delta_m R_{m,t}^e + \epsilon_{i,t}, \qquad (15)$$

where the degree of spanning is inversely related to the variance of the unspanned component $\sigma^2(\epsilon_i)$. Theoretically, the spanning measure in our model $\sigma^2(\epsilon_F^{**})$ should be derived from the set of all eligible securities, including the country fund itself. Empirically, some operational assumptions must be made. We follow along the lines of Breedon, Gibbons and Litzenberger [9] and proxy the investible universe by constructing 12 US 2-digit SIC industry portfolios. In this spirit we construct a measure of spanning based on the following regression:

$$R_t^F = \beta_1 R_{1,t}^{II} + \cdots + \beta_{12} R_{12,t}^{II} + \beta_{13} R_t^P + \epsilon_{F,t}^{**}, \qquad (16)$$

where $R_{j,t}^{II}$ is the return on jth industrial index, R_t^F is the net asset value return on country fund and R_t^P is the country fund price return. We account for time variation in $\sigma^2(\epsilon_F^{**})$ by estimating simple GARCH(1,1) models with mean equations as stated in (16). Our model suggests that an increase in the variance of the unspanned component of the NAV will lead to an increase in the country fund premium.

Access

Another testable implication of our model is that the premium is inversely related to the degree of access. Unfortunately, it is very difficult to systematically classify our sample by the degree of access. No study exists (to our knowledge) that would provide us with indicators or benchmarks to proxy access over time. However, the International Finance Corporation emerging markets database provides market information for a global set and an investible set. The investible set is defined over the population of securities for which foreigners have free access. The global set is defined over both accessible and inaccessible securities. Hence a reasonable proxy for market access can be constructed as the differential between market capitalizations of the global and investible sets. Thus,

$$\text{Access}_t = IFCG_t - IFCI_t, \qquad (17)$$

where $IFCG_t$ and $IFCI_t$ are the global and investible market capitalizations, respectively.[m]

Imperfect substitution

As suggested in the theoretical model, we use the ratio of conditional volatilities of price and NAV returns as a reasonable proxy to capture the degree of imperfect substitution. Based on the model implications, we would expect a higher ratio to result in a lower premium. We estimate conditional volatilities based on simple GARCH(1,1) models with mean equations specified as follows:

$$R_t^F = \beta_1^F R_{1,t}^{II} + \cdots + \beta_{12}^F R_{12,t}^{II} + \epsilon_t^F, \qquad (18)$$

$$R_t^P = \beta_1^P R_{1,t}^{II} + \cdots + \beta_{12}^P R_{12,t}^{II} + \epsilon_t^P. \qquad (19)$$

Global country fund premia

Given the theoretical prediction of a common country fund factor and the results of the previous subsection that suggest the significance of the global factor, we incorporate the global premium/discount as an independent variable. We would expect a positive relationship between the individual fund premium/discount and the global premium/discount.

Country fund premia

The country fund premium/discount is defined as follows:

$$\text{PREM}_t^i = \frac{P_t^i - NAV_t^i}{NAV_t^i}. \qquad (20)$$

Note that the premium is defined in terms of price levels and not returns. Hence stationarity issues are of great importance when undertaking empirical tests of

---

[m] In a similar vein, Bekaert and Urias [5] investigate the exposure of NAV and the country fund premia to the residuals from the regression of the global return index on the investible index.

country fund premia. Given that both the country fund price and its corresponding NAV are driven by fundamentals, it is plausible that these series are cointegrated and hence the premium a stationary variable. Chang, Eun, and Kolodny [11] find cointegration for 6 of 12 countries in their study. Alternatively, Hardoveleous, La Porta, and Wizman [19] conclude that for "most of the country funds" in their study, a unit root in country fund premia can be rejected. Our model offers key insights into the nature of the source of nonstationarity in country fund premia. Specifically, of the above-mentioned determinants of country fund premia, the most plausible source of nonstationarity is market access — all other determinants being a function of the second moments of the joint distribution of price returns and NAV returns.

4.3.1. Model specification

We estimate a linear approximation of the theoretical model as follows:

$$d(\text{PREM}_t) = \beta_0 + \beta_1 \text{Sub}_t + \beta_2 d(\text{Access}_t) + \beta_3 \text{Span}_t + \beta_4 \text{Global}_t + e_t, \quad (21)$$

where $d(\text{PREM}_t)$ denotes the first difference in the premium as a means of inducing stationarity, (Sub_t) refers to imperfect substitution which is proxied by the ratio of conditional volatilities of price return over NAV return. The model suggests that an *increase* in (Sub_t) will lead to a *decrease* in the premium, i.e. $\beta_1 < 0$. $d(\text{Access}_t)$ refers to the change in market access. The model predicts that as access increases (as proxied by a decline in the difference between the global and investible market caps) the country fund premia should decrease, hence we anticipate $\beta_2 > 0$. The access variable is differenced in order to induce stationarity, i.e.

$$d(\text{Access}_t) = \frac{IFCG_t}{IFCG_{t-1}} - \frac{IFCI_t}{IFCI_{t-1}}. \quad (22)$$

Since this data is only available for EM countries, the analysis for DMs will not include this variable. (Span_t) denotes the conditional variance of the NAV return series unspanned by eligibles and the country fund price return. The model predicts that an increase in the unspanned variance will lead to an increase in the premium, i.e. $\beta_3 > 0$. Finally, (Global_t) refers to the model prediction of a common country fund factor with $\beta_4 > 0$.

4.3.2. Results

Table 5 reports the time series results for EMs. Parameter estimates are based on simple ordinary least squares. The substitution parameter is significant/marginally significant in 6 of 19 cases. The sign is negative as anticipated in all cases except for one. The access variable is significant/marginally significant in 10 of 19 cases with the anticipated positive sign in all but 2 instances. The spanning factor is statistically significant in only 3 of the 19 cases with the anticipated positive sign.

Table 5. Time series regression results for EM country fund premia.

The change in EM country fund premia are regressed on proxies for substitution, spanning and the global factor. The proxy for substitution is the ratio of the conditional variance of price to NAV unspanned by the US market and estimated as GARCH(1,1) with mean specification as follows:

$$R_t^i = \beta_1^i R_{1,t}^{II} + \cdots + \beta_{12}^i R_{12,t}^{II} + \varepsilon_t^i \quad i = F, P.$$

R_t^i is the return of the country fund or NAV and $R_{1,t}^{II}$ refers to 1 of 12 US industrial portfolios. The proxy for access is the percentage change in the IFC Global market capitalization minus the percentage change in the IFC investible market capitalization. Spanning is proxied by the conditional variance of the NAV unspanned by the US market and the country fund and estimated as GARCH(1,1) with mean specification as follows:

$$R_t^F = \beta_1 R_{1,t}^{II} + \cdots + \beta_{12} R_{12,t}^{II} + \beta_{13} R_t^P + \varepsilon_t.$$

The global factor proxy is computed as the percentage change of the equally weighted country fund premia across both emerging and developed markets.

	Substitution		Access		Spanning		Global Factor		adj. R^2
	Coeff.	t-stat	Coeff.	t-stat	Coeff.	t-stat	Coeff.	t-stat	
Argentina	.1025	1.2892	.0102	**2.0528	.1128	*1.6474	12.0644	.3417	.0376
Brazil	−.0215	−*1.6722	.1839	**6.1958	−.7029	−.8956	.0367	**3.2805	.1593
Brazil (Equity)	.0014	.7393	.3643	**2.9285	−3.875	−1.0432	.0566	**2.1519	.1070
Chile	−.1707	−1.1920	.0673	1.0228	.0626	.0047	.0521	**7.1204	.1961
Indonesia	.0300	.4320	−.0096	−.1218	8.8113	.2294	.0562	**5.1154	.1065
India	−24.32	−*1.8927	.1804	1.0988	87.83	*1.6872	.0585	**2.3264	.1325
Jakarta	−.0002	−.2795	.1576	*1.6869	5.3639	.2555	.0380	**3.6780	.0610
Korea	−.2296	−.7046	−.1417	−1.1740	13.9725	.1721	.0854	**5.0652	.1837
Korea (Investment)	1.8808	.9841	.2973	*1.8248	9.6546	**2.1187	.0056	.2292	.0586
Mexico	.0442	.4802	.0072	.7179	.2845	.2337	.0390	**5.8160	.1042
Mexico (Equity)	.0389	.6918	−.0024	-.0323	61.6828	1.2481	.0203	**2.0223	.0130
Mexico (Emerging)	−.0991	−.2237	−.1351	−*1.9358	−10.4906	−1.0945	.0369	**3.9975	.1096
Philippine	.0001	**2.8553	−.0701	−1.1121	−33.6962	−1.4324	.0302	**3.8351	.0901
Portugal	−.0846	−1.2058	.0911	1.2188	−5.9467	−0.4765	.0532	**7.4498	.2004
Taiwan	−.3146	−**1.9875	−.05472	−1.1245	−7.0588	−1.2983	.0225	1.4989	.0171
Taiwan (ROC)	.0216	1.1986	−.0586	−*1.7352	5.7791	.8668	.0260	**2.4811	.0415
Thai	−.1672	−*1.7254	.2483	**3.5930	−.1897	−.0509	.0723	**7.5032	.1978
Thai (Capital)	−.0009	−.0290	.1854	**4.0677	−7.2231	−.9578	.0426	**5.5243	.1734
Turkey	−1.6630	−**2.0610	.07939	**3.4973	9.3549	.1842	.0674	**6.6565	.2078

*Denotes 90% significance and ** denotes 95% significance.

Table 6. Time series regression results for DM country fund.

The change in DM country fund premia are regressed on proxies for substitution, access, spanning and the global factor. The proxy for substitution is the ratio of the conditional variance of price to NAV unspanned by the US market and estimated as GARCH(1,1) with mean specification as follows:

$$R_t^i = \beta_1^i R_{1,t}^{II} + \cdots + \beta_{12}^i R_{12,t}^{II} + \varepsilon_t^i \quad i = F, P.$$

R_t^i is the return of the country fund or NAV and $R_{1,t}^{II}$ refers to 1 of 12 US industrial portfolios. The proxy for access is the percentage change in the IFC Global market capitalization minus the percentage change in the IFC investible market capitalization. Spanning is proxied by the conditional variance of the NAV unspanned by the US market and the country fund and estimated as GARCH(1,1) with mean specification as follows:

$$R_t^F = \beta_1 R_{1,t}^{II} + \cdots + \beta_{12} R_{12,t}^{II} + \beta_{13} R_t^P + \varepsilon_t.$$

The global factor proxy is computed as the percentage change of the equally weighted country fund premia across both emerging and developed markets.

Country	Substitution Coeff.	t-stat	Spanning Coeff.	t-stat	Global Factor Coeff.	t-stat	adj. R^2
Ausralia	−.0024	.0405	11.0813	.7287	.0141	*1.7221	.0103
France	−.0030	−*1.7604	−26.2496	−1.0903	.04976	**4.8363	.1932
Germany	−.0045	−1.0605	−17.4057	−1.2611	.05844	**4.4147	.1838
Germany (New)	−.0145	−1.0434	124.695	*1.6487	.03645	**4.7267	.1887
Germany (Future)	.0010	.1372	17.5054	.8933	.0396	**4.0764	.1396
Germany (Emergin)	.00278	.4658	23.1003	.3826	−.0228	**−2.0222	.0151
Irish Investment	−.0178	−.4260	−133.2228	−.0708	.0107	1.0441	−.008
Italy	−.0040	−1.2967	−15.6389	−.6898	.0212	1.4510	.0169
Japan (OTC)	−.0053	−.7604	−17.8545	−**2.2364	.0499	− −3.5588	.1393
Japan (Equity)	−.0002	−.7087	−3.4315	−1.5445	.01526	1.2533	.0158
Singapore	.00572	1.4955	213.9122	*1.8171	.0630	**4.9141	.2343
Spain	.0011	.0921	−2.0755	−.2953	.01639	1.5572	−.003
United Kingdom	−.0075	−*1.8583	9.7833	.1552	.0304	**2.8366	.0057

*Denotes 90% significance and ** denotes 95% significance.

The global fund factor is significant and with the anticipated positive sign in 16 of 19 cases. Thus, we find significant evidence in support of the theoretical model in terms of the impact of global fund factor and market access on country fund premia.

Table 6 reports the evidence for DMs. In general the results are not as supportive for DMs. In only 2 of 13 cases is the substitution factor significant and of the right sign. Similarly, in only 1 case of 13 do we find the spanning variable to be significant and of the right sign. However, we do find evidence of a significant global factor in 7 out of 13 cases. The lower ability to predict country fund premia for DMs relative to EMs is not entirely inconsistent with our model since the primary focus of our analysis is on market segmentation factors which are more relevant for EMs than for DMs.[n]

Finally, we estimated the cross-sectional model for EM funds in our sample over the period January 89–December 93. The averages of weekly OLS coefficient estimates for the substitution, spanning and access variables are consistent with our theoretical expectations and the time-series results reported above. Specifically, the substitution factor is negative and marginally significant ($t = -1.60$), the spanning variable is positive but insignificant ($t = 0.16$) and the access variable is positive and highly significant ($t = 4.14$).

5. Conclusion and Policy Implications

We have provided a theoretical and empirical analysis of country funds focussing on emerging economics whose capital markets are not readily accessible to outside investors. We use a model structure that is based on imperfect substitution between the country fund returns (as generated in the advanced core market) and the underlying asset returns (as generated in the originating emerging market). This may stem from the notion of excess price volatility (or noise trading) relative to fundamental volatility. We emphasize that the component assets traded in the originating countries are fundamental to country funds traded in the core advanced market.

Under imperfect substitution between the country fund and its underlying assets, the fund sells at a discount or premium depending upon the degree of international investor access to the originating market, the degree to which the core market securities span the securities in the emerging markets, and the degree of comovement of the country fund universe.

Our analysis shows that country funds traded in the developed capital markets can be beneficial in promoting the efficiency of pricing in the emerging capital markets and in enhancing capital mobilization by local firms of the originating countries. The specific determinants of the pricing efficiency gains to emerging capital markets and resource mobilization by local firms are: (a) the risks of the local assets constituting the fund unspanned by the core developed financial market in which the fund is traded, (b) the differential between local price of risk and universal price of risk, and (c) the degree of substitution between the fund and the underlying assets traded in the originating (emerging) markets. Other things being equal, emerging countries with larger unspannable risk benefit more from the introduction of the country fund in the core (advanced) market. Such countries typically have idiosyncratic investment opportunities or unique natural resources.

---

[n]Based on suggestions of Geert Bekaert, we conducted two additional sets of time series tests of our model (Eq. (21)). In the first set, the local market (corresponding to the CF being tested) was purged from the construction of the global factor. In the second set, the global factor was completely excluded from the test specification. The results for both sets were similar to those reported in this paper and do not affect our conclusions. Results are available from the authors upon request.

Moreover, the gain is larger if the local price of risk is higher relative to the world or universal price of risk, which may be the case for thinly capitalized emerging markets with limited risk-sharing opportunities.

The empirical evidence supports the principal predictions of our theoretical model. The prediction of a common pricing factor is borne out by the importance of the global country fund factor in explaining the returns of CFs from emerging and developed markets. Further, the variables that proxy the degree of access (for EMs), spanning and substitution effects as well as the global country fund factor, show up as significant determinants of country fund premia.

The analysis leads to some policy implications relating to the composition of country funds, the desirability of price stabilization, and possible subsidization of creation of certain country funds. On the first issue, country funds should be targeted at those local assets with imperfect or no substitutes in the advanced core markets.[o] On the second issue, since imperfect substitution between the country fund and the component assets traded in the local markets mitigates the efficiency gains, policies for country fund price stabilization may deserve consideration by international agencies. Finally, when new issues of country funds are expected to trade at a discount, it would become unprofitable for underwriters to introduce the funds through public offerings, since the initial investors would stand to lose relative to waiting and buying when the funds are seasoned. When efficiency gains exist from new issues of country funds, even when they trade at a discount, the issue arises as to whether some institutions, particularly domestic public authorities or development agencies, take the initial loss so as to promote the fund into existence.

Appendix I. Portfolio Equilibrium

While our motivation is country fund pricing in the international context, the derivation of the portfolio equilibrium is a straightforward application of the Mauer-Senbet [23] framework for the pricing of initial public issues in the domestic market. The MS approach itself is a variation of earlier frameworks by Errunza and Senbet [16], EL [15], and Merton [24]. Although all of these models possess similar structure, they are set apart by their respective motivations and the implications that are drawn for the particular economic phenomena under study. The implications regarding country funds are studied for alternative variations of market structures in the text of the paper.

The investor's choice problem is to maximize his Von Neumann–Morgenstern utility, $U^i(\cdot)$, of current and expected future consumption by picking fractional holdings in the core market assets (α_C^i), in the restricted assets from emerging markets (α_F^i), in the aggregate restricted market assets (α_W^i), and riskless borrowing

---

[o]There is, however, some evidence suggesting that the actual choice of the underlying securities is too conservative with excessive usage of "blue chips". We reach this conclusion by comparing the residual volatilities of the component assets in the country funds and those of the assets in the local market.

or lending in the amount B^i at one-plus the riskless rate of interest, R.[p] If the investor lacks access to the restricted securities, $\alpha_F^i = \alpha_W^i = 0$. We shall explicitly include investor access restrictions at the demand aggregation stage.[q] In a mean-variance world, the investor faces the following objective function:

$$\text{Maximize } U^i\left(C_0^i, \overline{C_1^i}, \sigma^2\left(C_1^i\right)\right) \tag{A1}$$

with respect to α_C^i, α_F^i, α_W^i and B^i. Subject to

$$C_0^i = W_0^i = [B^i + \alpha_C^i V_C + \alpha_F^i (V_F^C + V_F^F) + \alpha_W^i (V_W^C + V_W^W)], \tag{A2}$$

$$\overline{C_1^i} = RB^i + \alpha_C^i \overline{Y_C} + \alpha_F^i \left(\overline{Y_F^C} + \overline{Y_F^F}\right) + \alpha_W^i \left(\overline{Y_W^C} + \overline{Y_W^W}\right), \tag{A3}$$

$$\sigma^2(C_1^i) = (\alpha_C^i)^2 \sigma^2(Y_C) + (\alpha_F^i)^2 [\sigma^2(Y_C^F) + \sigma^2(Y_F^F)]$$
$$+ (\alpha_W^i)^2 [\sigma^2(Y_W^C) + \sigma^2(Y_W^W)] + 2\alpha_C^i \alpha_F^i COV(Y_C, Y_F^C)$$
$$+ 2\alpha_C^i \alpha_W^i COV(Y_C, Y_W^C) + 2\alpha_W^i \alpha_F^i COV(Y_W, Y_F), \tag{A4}$$

where

W_0^i = the initial wealth of investor i,

C_0^i = the current consumption of investor i,

$\overline{C_1^i}$ = the expected future consumption of investor i,

$\sigma^2(C_1^i)$ = the variance of future consumption,

V_C = the current value of all securities in the core market,

$V_F = V_F^C + V_F^F$ = the current value of assets in the emerging market; decomposable into the core market spanned component, V_F^C, and the unspanned value, V_F^F;

$V_W = V_W^C + V_W^W$ = the current value of restricted assets in the aggregate of the rest of emerging markets; decomposable into spanned, V_W^C, and unspanned, V_W^W, components.

The constraints in (A2)–(A4) can be substituted into (A1), yielding the unconstrained objective function to be maximized with respect to the decision variables. The resulting first-order conditions are:

$$\frac{\delta U^i}{\delta B^i} = -U_0^i + \overline{U_1^i} R = 0, \tag{A5}$$

[p]The risk-free asset is assumed internal with zero net supply.
[q]Like Mauer and Senbet, we do not distinguish between those investors with access and those without access to emerging market securities when deriving first-order necessary conditions. Access restrictions are taken into account in the demand aggregation process. This differs, for example, from Merton [24] wherein Lagrange multipliers are utilized to measure the shadow price of imperfect accessibility.

$$\frac{\delta U^i}{\delta \alpha_C^i} = U_0^i(-V_C) + \overline{U_1^i} Y_C$$

$$+ 2U_\sigma^i[\alpha_C^i \sigma^2(Y_C) + \alpha_F^i COV(Y_C, Y_F^C) + \alpha_W^i COV(Y_C, Y_W^C)]$$

$$= 0, \qquad (A6)$$

$$\frac{\delta U^i}{\delta \alpha_F^i} = U_0^i(-V_F) + \overline{U_1^i} Y_F$$

$$+ 2U_\sigma^i[\alpha_F^i \sigma^2(Y_F) + \alpha_C^i COV(Y_C, Y_F^C) + \alpha_W^i COV(Y_F, Y_W)]$$

$$= 0, \qquad (A7)$$

$$\frac{\delta U^i}{\delta \alpha_W^i} = U_0^i(-V_W) + \overline{U_1^i} Y_W$$

$$+ 2U_\sigma^i[\alpha_W^i \sigma^2(Y_W) + \alpha_C^i COV(Y_C, Y_W^C) + \alpha_F^i COV(Y_F, Y_W)]$$

$$= 0, \qquad (A8)$$

where

$$U_0^i = \frac{\delta U^i}{\delta C_0^i} > 0; \quad \overline{U_0^i} = \frac{\delta U^i}{\delta \overline{C_0^i}} > 0; \quad \overline{U_\sigma^i} = \frac{\delta U^i}{\delta \sigma(C_0^i)} < 0.$$

The foregoing inequalities follow the standard conditions of non-satiation and risk aversion.

We now explicitly recognize emerging market accessibility restrictions to derive asset demands. Let M and H denote the number of investors with exclusive access to the emerging market and the rest of the aggregate emerging markets, respectively. The two sets of investors, M and H, are disjoint. The remaining L investors are completely excluded from the primary markets, and invest only in the core market securities. We obtain the following implicit asset demand functions by rearranging the first-order conditions:

risk-free asset;

$$\frac{U_0^i}{\overline{U_1^i}} = R \quad i = 1, \ldots, L + M + H$$

core market asset;

$$COV(Y_C, \alpha_C^i Y_C + \alpha_F^i Y_F^C + \alpha_W^i Y_W^C) = \theta^i [\overline{Y_C} - RV_C] \quad i = L + M + H \qquad (A9)$$

restricted emerging market asset;

$$COV(Y_F, \alpha_F^i Y_F + \alpha_C^i Y_C) = \theta^i [\overline{Y_F} - RV_F] \quad i = 1, \ldots M, \qquad (A10)$$

the aggregate of the rest of emerging markets;

$$COV(Y_W, \alpha_W^i Y_W + \alpha_C^i Y_C) = \theta^i [\overline{Y_W} - RV_w] \quad i = 1, \ldots H, \qquad (A11)$$

where θ^i is the marginal rate of substitution between expected future consumption and volatility (risk), or the inverse of the Pratt–Arrow absolute risk aversion coefficient.

Note that (A9)–(A11) explicitly recognize that emerging market investors can access the core market and only their *own* securities markets. As a consequence, in (A10) $\alpha_W^i = 0$ for $i = 1, \ldots, M$, and in (A11) $\alpha_F^i = 0$ for $i = 1, \ldots, H$.

In equilibrium, universal aggregate demand for all assets must equal universal aggregate supply. Consider first the demand for core market assets. Equation (A9), which is the demand function for the core market asset, must hold for all $L + M + H$ investors. Hence, summing (A9) over all investors yields:

$$\sum_{i=1}^{L+M+H} COV(Y_C, \alpha_C^i Y_C + \alpha_F^i Y_F^C + \alpha_W^i Y_W^C) = [\overline{Y_C} - RV_C] \sum_{i=1}^{L+M+H} \theta^i.$$

Market Clearing conditions require that

$$\sum_{i=1}^{L+M+H} \alpha_C^i = \sum_{i=1}^{M} \alpha_F^i = \sum_{i=1}^{H} \alpha_i^W = 1.$$

Therefore, letting

$$\sum_{i=1}^{L+M+H} \theta^i = \theta,$$

we have

$$COV(Y_C, Y_C + Y_F^C + Y_W^C) = [\overline{Y_C} - RV_C] \theta. \qquad (A12)$$

Or equivalently, upon rearrangement

$$V_C = R^{-1} [\overline{Y_C} - \theta^{-1} COV(Y_C, Y_A^C)], \qquad (A13)$$

where

$$Y_A^C = Y_C + (Y_F^C + Y_W^C).$$

Equation (A13) is the certainty equivalent valuation of Y_C, where Y_A^C is the aggregate of the core market cash flow and spannable emerging market cash flow components, and θ^{-1} is the aggregate "price" of risk.

Similarly, aggregation of the demand function (A10) and market clearing conditions, along with the factor structure for cash flows in (1)–(5) in the text, delivers the valuation for the restricted emerging market asset in (6) [see text], where

$$\theta^M = \sum_{i=1}^{M} \theta_i.$$

Appendix II. US Tax Treatment of the Investment Entity (Fund)

The fund may be able to obtain preferred tax treatment relative to other corporate forms by qualifying as a Regulated Investment Company (RIC). To qualify the following three conditions must be met:

(1) derive 90% of gross income from investment activities;
(2) derive less than 30% of gross income from short term investments of less than three months;
(3) meet certain diversification criteria.

Foreign tax credit: The fund can file an election with the IRS to pass-through to the fund's shareholders the amount of foreign taxes paid by the fund if more than 50% of the funds total assets are foreign. Subject to certain technicalities (see below) the foreign taxes paid can be used by shareholders as a credit or deduction of foreign taxes.

US tax rates:
(1) Income tax and all distributions: 0%
This is provided that the fund distributes at least 90% of net investment income (dividends and distributions received less operating expenses) and 90% of its net short-term capital gains (excess of net short-term capital gains over long-term capital losses, if any). If these requirements are not met, a non-deductible excise tax of 4% is incurred.
(2) Undistributed net long-term capital gains: 34%
Net long-term capital gains are net long-term capital gains less net short-term capital losses. If these are distributed, no tax is paid. If undistributed, a tax rate of 34% is imposed.
(3) Carrybacks and carryovers:
No carrybacks are permitted for an RIC but capital losses can be carried over for 8 years.

US tax treatment of individual investors
This is just an outline of tax treatment of US residents or citizens. Note also that foreigners with trade/business connections are treated as residents for tax purposes.

(1) Distributions of net investment income and net short-term capital gains are taxed at ordinary tax rates.
(2) Distributions of net long-term gains are taxed at ordinary tax rates. This includes a return of capital.
(3) Undistributed net long-term gains: These are included in a shareholder's income as long-term capital gains, and the tax paid by the company (34%) is credited to the shareholders US income tax payable. Therefore, the effect seems to have no effect on individual taxes paid. The tax basis of the shareholder's shares in the fund is increased by the net amount which is 66% of the undistributed capital gain.

(4) Foreign tax credit: The fund needs to qualify every year to pass through foreign taxes to its shareholders.

Foreign income is composed of distributions from foreign entities. Foreign capital gains and foreign exchange gains or losses are part of US operations.

US individuals typically receive credit for foreign taxes paid. Hence, the objective is to treat shareholders of the fund the same as individuals who receive foreign income.

Shareholders have two options: (a) to deduct their share of foreign income taxes paid by the fund, or (b) use them as a tax credit, but not a mixture. Deductions are available only to those shareholders who itemize deductions and have to exceed 2% of the individual's adjusted gross income. Deductions reduce the taxable income, and hence do not provide a one-for-one saving, unlike credit. On the other hand, the foreign tax credit cannot be used to diminish the tax liability from US sources.

Acknowledgments

We acknowledge helpful comments from Geert Bekaert, Cheol Eun, Vikram Nehru, Larry Summers, Thierry Wizman and Morty Yalovsky. We are especially grateful to Ishac Diwan for his involvement with the initial stages of this research. Earlier versions were presented at the World Bank Workshop, American Finance Association 1997 annual meetings, the Pacific-Basin Conference in Hong Kong, and the World Bank Conference "Portfolio Investment in Developing Countries". Financial support was received from the World Bank, Faculty of Management at McGill, SSHRC of Canada and the William E. Mayer Chair at Maryland. Santiago Galindez and Philip O'Connor have provided valuable research assistance.

References

[1] G. Alexander, C. Eun and S. Janakiramanan, *Asset pricing and dual listing on foreign capital markets: A note*, J. Finance **42** (1987) 151–158.

[2] S. Anderson, *Closed-end funds and market efficincy*, J. Portfolio Management (Fall 1986) 63–67.

[3] W. Bailey and J. Lim, *Evaluating the diversification benefits of the new country funds*, J. Porfolio Management **18** (1992) 74–80.

[4] G. Bekaert and C. Harvey, *Time-varying world market integration*, J. Finance **50** (1995) 403–444.

[5] G. Bekaert and M. Urias *Diversification, integration and emerging market closed-end funds*, J. Finance **51** (1996) 835–869.

[6] F. Black, *International capital market equilibrium with investment barriers*, J. Financial Economics **1** (1974) 337–352.

[7] J. Bodurtha, D. Kim and C. Lee, *Closed-end country funds and US Market sentiment*, Rev. Financial Studies **8** (1995) 879–918.

[8] C. Bonser-Neal, G. Brauer, R. Neal and S. Wheatley, *International investment restrictions and closed-end country fund prices*, J. Finance **45** (June 1990) 523–547.

[9] D. Breedon, M. Gibbons and R. Litzenberger, *Empirical tests of the consumption oriented CAPM*, J. Finance **2** (1989) 231–262.

[10] G. A. Brauer, *Closed-end fund shares' abnormal returns and the information content of discounts and premiums*, J. Finance **43** (1988) 113–128.

[11] E. Chang, C. Eun and R. Kolodny, *International diversification through closed-end country funds*, Working Paper, Univ. of Maryland (1993).

[12] J. B. De Long, A. Shleifer, L. Summers and R. J. Waldman, *Noise trader risk in financial markets*, J. Political Economy **98** (1990) 703–738.

[13] I. Diwan, V. Errunza and L. Senbet, *Diversification benefits of country funds*, in *Investing in Emerging Markets*, ed. M. Howell, Euromoney/World Bank (1995) 199–218.

[14] V. R. Errunza, *Pricing of national index funds: Theory and evidence*, Rev. Quantitative Finance and Accounting **1** (January 1991) 91–100.

[15] V. R. Errunza and E. Losq, *International asset pricing under mild segmentation: Theory and test*, J. Finance **40** (March 1985) 105–124.

[16] V. R. Errunza and L. Senbet, *The effect of international operations on the market value of the firm: Theory and evidence*, J. Finance **36** (1981) 401–417.

[17] C. Eun, S. Janakiramanan and L. Senbet, *The design and pricing of country funds under market segmentation*, Working Paper, Univ. of Maryland (March 1993).

[18] D. Glenn, *Super premium security prices and optimal corporate financing*, J. Finance **32** (May 1976) 479–492.

[19] G. Hardouvelis, R. Laporta and T. Wizman, *What moves the discount on country equity funds?*, Mimeo (1993).

[20] C. Lee, A. Shleifer and R. Thaler, *Investor sentiment and the closed-end fund puzzle*, J. Finance **46** (March 1991) 75–109.

[21] J. Lintner, *Expectations, mergers and equilibrium in purely competitive securities markets*, Amer. Econ. Rev. **61** (May 1971) 101–111.

[22] B. Malkeil, *The valuation of closed-end investment company shares*, J. Finance **32** (1997) 847–859.

[23] D. C. Mauer and L. Senbet, *The effect of the secondary market on the pricing of initial public offerings: Theory and evidence*, J. Financial and Quantitative Analysis **27** (March 1992) 55–79.

[24] R. C. Merton, *A simple model of capital market equilibrium with incomplete information*, J. Finance **42** (July 1987) 483–510.

[25] S. A. Ross, *A simple approach to the valuation of risky streams*, J. Business **51** (July 1981) 453–475.

[26] M. E. Rubinstein, *Corporate financial policy in segmented security markets*, J. Financial and Quantitative Analysis **8** (Dec. 1973) 749–761.

[27] A. Shleifer and L. Summers, *The noise trader approach to finance*, J. Econ. Perspectives **4** (Spring 1990) 19–33.

[28] R. J. Shiller, *Do stock prices move too much to be justified by subsequent changes in dividends?*, Amer. Econ. Rev. **71** (June 1981) 421–436.

[29] R. Stulz, *On the effects of barriers to international investment*, J. Finance **36** (September 1981) 923–934.

[30] R. Stulz and W. Wasserfallen, *Foreign equity investment restrictions and shareholder wealth maximization: Theory and evidence*, Working Paper (1992).

[31] L. Summers, *Does the stock market rationally reflect fundamental values?*, J. Finance **41** (July 1986) 591–601.

[32] B. Tuckman and J.-L. Vila, *Arbitrage with holding costs: A utility-based approach*, J. Finance **47** (September 1992) 1283–1302; K. Weiss, *The post-offering price performance of closed-end funds*, Financial Management (1989) 57–67.

Part IV
International Derivative Securities

[21]
EQUILIBRIUM PRICING FUNCTIONS OF FOREIGN EXCHANGE FORWARD, FUTURES, AND OPTION CONTRACTS

Tribhuvan N. Puri* and George C. Philippatos[†]

INTRODUCTION

This paper seeks to develop equilibrium pricing formulas for forward and futures currency contracts and European options on spot exchange rate and to provide an intuitive economic meaning of the underlying relationships.

The differences between forward and futures commodity contracts and commodity options were first pointed out by Black (1976). Jarrow and Oldfield (1981) further clarified the differences between the two contracts using an arbitrage argument to price forward contracts and to relate forward prices to spot prices and futures prices. They argue that forward prices need not equal futures prices unless

---

*Department of Finance, School of Business and Management, Temple University.
[†]Department of Finance, The University of Tennessee, Knoxville.

risk-free interest rate is constant. Richard and Sundaresan (1981) set up a general equilibrium model in continuous time to study the equilibrium pricing relationships for the commodity contracts. They show that the value of a contract which promises a stochastic commodity flow in the future can be determined by using the intertemporal marginal rate of substitution across commodities as the discount factor and then taking the expected value of the discounted stochastic commodity flows. Cox, Ingersoll, and Ross (1981) consolidate some known results in the literature and develop a number of propositions characterizing the forward and futures prices. They also discuss the effects of taxes and other institutional factors on prices of these contracts. Cornell and Reinganum (1981) measured the differences in forward and futures exchange rates and concluded that the results were consistent with the Cox–Ingersoll–Ross model.

The studies cited in the extant literature pertain to the valuation of commodity contracts in closed economies. Equilibrium pricing functions of foreign exchange contracts have not been derived. This paper seeks to fill this gap. The valuation functions of currency contracts in the open economy developed here are structurally similar to those for closed economy as in Richard and Sundaresan (1981) and Cox, Ingersoll, and Ross (1985). In addition, more formulas are derived and intuitively appealing interpretations are provided for an international setting. The model constructed here is characterized by a simple two-country general equilibrium continuous-time framework to obtain equilibrium pricing functions of currency contracts. The world economy consists of utility-maximizing homogeneous consumer-investors across countries producing different consumption-investment goods through the use of stochastic constant-returns-to-scale technologies. The exchange rates are flexible and are assumed to be perfectly correlated with the terms of trade. Money is not explicitly introduced so that changes in the exchange rates are real. Principles of stochastic control theory (see Arnold [1974], Fleming and Rishel [1975]) are used to obtain equilibrium pricing functions reflecting relationship with fundamental macroeconomic variables.

FOREIGN EXCHANGE FORWARDS, FUTURES, AND OPTIONS

In a flexible exchange rate regime, foreign exchange contracts are risky financial assets promising stochastic payoff and providing opportunities to diversify portfolios. Before developing the model, it will be useful to define the forward and futures exchange rates and various types of foreign exchange contracts.

A. Forward Exchange Rate and Forward Contracts

The forward price of a foreign currency, $e_F(t,T)$, is the price at which parties to the contract agree to buy or sell the foreign currency at a given expiration date T in

Equilibrium Functions of Foreign Exchange Contracts 219

the future. The forward exchange rate $e_F(t,T)$ does not change during the life of the contract. No money transactions take place either at the time of writing of the contract or during the lifetime of the contract. Only at the expiration date, the holder of a long position in forward contract receives the specified amount of foreign currency in exchange for the home currency at the forward exchange rate as stipulated in the contract.

The value of the forward contract, F_1, fluctuates over the course of the contract as the spot exchange rate $e(t)$ changes. The initial value of the forward contract is zero at the time of writing of the contract since no initial investment is required. At maturity, the value of the forward contract is the difference between the spot exchange rate at maturity, $e(T)$, and the contracted forward exchange rate. These initial and boundary conditions can be expressed as $F_1[t,e_F(t,T)] = 0$, and $F_1[(T,e_F(t,T)] = [e(T) - e_F(t,T)]$, respectively.

B. Futures Exchange Rate and Futures Currency Contracts

The futures exchange rate $F_2(t,T)$ is the price of the foreign currency in terms of the home currency at time t for a future delivery at T. A futures contract is rewritten every day with a new futures exchange rate. Thus a futures contract is like a series of forward contracts. The value of the futures contract is reset to zero every day. The stochastic payoff to the holder of the contract is established from marking to the market and is equal to the difference in the futures exchange rates on two consecutive days. At the equilibrium futures exchange rate, the value of the futures contract is zero. In the continuous-time model developed in this paper, the futures contract is assumed to be rewritten every instant. The stochastic payoff to the holder of the contract is $dF_2(t,T)$ over the next differential time interval dt. Unlike forward contracts, currency futures are homogeneous contracts to be traded in standardized amounts specified by the clearing house. This institutional arrangement is ignored in the model developed here.

C. Currency Options

Like a forward currency contract, currency options are also maturity contracts, but they contrast with the forward contracts, which obligate the holder of the contract to complete the transaction at the expiration date. The holder of a currency option has a choice whether or not he would like to buy foreign currency at the contracted forward exchange rate, which is usually termed the exercise price. Options to buy are calls and options to sell are puts. Options exercised on expiration date are known as European. In the present work only options on spot exchange rate are considered. The value of an option contract, F_3, at maturity is given by

$$F_3(e_F(T,T),T) = \begin{cases} e(T) - e^*, & \text{if } e(T) \geq e^* \\ 0 & \text{if } e(T) < e^*, \end{cases} \quad (1)$$

where e^* is the exercise price.

THE MODEL

Without loss of generality, it is assumed that the world economy consists of two countries, home and foreign, populated by homogeneous investors whose endowments, tastes, and preferences are identical in continuous time.[1] Each country produces a distinct consumption good by employing a distinct stochastic-constant-returns-to-scale technology. Each good produced is used as an input in its respective production process. It is assumed that the price of each good is always one unit of its home currency. Thus the exchange rate is perfectly correlated with the terms of trade. The output of the two countries randomly fluctuates in continuous time in response to exogenous technological shocks imparted by state variables whose dynamics are

$$dX(t) = \mu[X(t),t]dt + \sigma[X(t),t]dz, \quad (2)$$

where μ is the drift vector of order $(k \times 1)$, σ is the diffusion matrix of order $k \times (k + n)$, dz is the increment of Wiener process of order $(k + n) \times 1$, k is equal to the number of contingent claims, and n is the number of risky production technologies[2].

It is assumed that there are no barriers against perfect capital mobility. The law of one price holds continuously. The dynamics of spot exchange rate are

$$\frac{de}{e} = \mu_e dt + \sigma_e dz, \quad (3)$$

where μ_e is the drift coefficient and σ_e is the diffusion matrix of order $1 \times (k + n)$.

A. Investment Opportunity Set

All homogeneous investors of a country are represented by a composite investor who faces an investment opportunity set comprised of one risky production function[3] in each country, one forward contract requiring purchase of foreign currency, one futures currency contract, one European currency option, one foreign bond, and one domestic bond promising risk-free return in terms of the domestic currency. With these assumptions, $k = 3$ and $n = 2$.

The rates of return from investment, I_i [i = 1(home), 2(foreign)], in risky production processes follow stochastic differential equations:

Equilibrium Functions of Foreign Exchange Contracts

$$\frac{dI_i}{I_i} = \alpha_i(X,t)dt + \sum_{j=1}^{k+n} g_{ij}dz_j; \quad i = 1, 2, \tag{4}$$

where α_i is the average productivity of process i, and g_{ij} are elements of the diffusion matrix G of order $2 \times (k + n)$. In matrix notation

$$\frac{dI}{I} = \alpha dt + G dz. \tag{5}$$

The rate of return from the foreign industry in terms of the home currency is given by

$$\frac{d(eI_2)}{eI_2} = \frac{dI_2}{I_2} + \frac{de}{e} + \frac{de}{e} \cdot \frac{dI_2}{I_2}. \tag{6}$$

The dynamics of stochastic rates of returns on various currency contracts[4] are given by

$$\frac{dF_i}{F_i} = \beta_i(X,t)dt + \sum_{j=1}^{5} h_{ij}dz_j; \quad i = 1, 2, 3. \tag{7}$$

In matrix notation,

$$\frac{dF}{F} = \beta dt + H dz, \tag{8}$$

where β is the drift vector of order 3×1 of the expected rates of return and h_{ij} are the elements of diffusion matrix H of order 3×5.

The endogenous values of these parameters are obtained by applying Itô's lemma and are given as follows:

$$\beta F = A^v(t)F + \frac{\partial F}{\partial t}, \tag{9}$$

$$H = F_X \sigma + F_W G, \tag{10}$$

where F_X and F_W are the partial derivatives of F with respect to X and W, and the differential operator $A^v(t)$ is given by

$$A^v(t) = W\mu_W \frac{\partial}{\partial W} + \sum_{i=1}^{k} \mu_i \frac{\partial}{\partial X_i} + \frac{1}{2} W^2 \sigma_W \sigma'_W \frac{\partial^2}{\partial W^2}$$

$$+ W \sum_{i=1}^{k} (\sigma_W \sigma')_i \frac{\partial^2}{\partial W \partial X_i} + \sum_{i=1}^{k} \sum_{j=1}^{k} (\sigma \sigma')_{ij} \frac{\partial^2}{\partial X_i \partial X_j}, \tag{11}$$

where W is the wealth or capital stock denominated in the investor's home currency, and it grows according to the following stochastic process:

$$\frac{dW}{W} = \mu_W dt + \sigma_W dz. \tag{12}$$

The drift μ_W and diffusion σ_W of the above stochastic process are endogenously determined in terms of the exogenously specified rates of return on production processes.

Rates of return on home and foreign bonds are

$$\frac{dB_i}{B_i} = r_i dt; \quad i = 1, 2, \tag{13}$$

where $r(t) = [r_1(t), r_2(t)]$ is the vector of home and foreign instantaneously risk-free interest rates.

The rate of return from the foreign bond in the home currency is given by

$$\frac{d(eB_2)}{eB_2} = \frac{dB_2}{B_2} + \frac{de}{e} + \frac{de}{e} \cdot \frac{dB_2}{B_2}. \tag{14}$$

B. Consumption Opportunity Set

The domestic investor at each instant includes the domestic and the foreign good in his or her consumption bundle. Since the relative price of the two goods is the exchange rate, its current value and future distribution constitute the consumption opportunity set.

C. Optimization Problem

Each investor maximizes an expected lifetime von Neumann Morgenstern time additive function:

$$\max E_t \left[\int_t^\infty \exp(-\rho t) U[c_1(t), c_2(t)] dt \right], \tag{15}$$

where $U(\cdot)$ is the utility function assumed to be strictly concave, increasing and twice differentiable continuously with respect to its arguments $c(t) = [c_1(t), c_2(t)]$ which are consumption rates at any time t, of home and foreign goods, respectively; and ρ is a discount factor. The optimization is subject to an instantaneous budget constraint as follows:

Equilibrium Functions of Foreign Exchange Contracts

$$\sum_{i=1}^{2} a_i + \sum_{i=1}^{3} b_i + \sum_{i=1}^{2} b_{oi} = 1, \tag{16}$$

where vectors $a = (a_i, i = 1, 2)$, $b = (b_i, i = 1, 2, 3)$ and $b_o = (b_{oi}, i = 1, 2)$ represent investment shares in home and foreign productions, foreign exchange contracts, and bonds, respectively. The flow budget constraint for the home investor is the process given in Equation (12), in which the drift μ_W is the instantaneous expected average productivity of the capital stock and is given by

$$\mu_W = [a_1(\alpha_1 - r_1) + a_2(\alpha_2 - r_2 + \sum_{j=1}^{5} \sigma_{ej}g_{2j})$$

$$+ \sum_{i=1}^{3} b_i(\beta_i - r_1) + b^*(r_2 - r_1 + \mu_e) - \frac{1}{W}(C_1 + ec_2)], \tag{17}$$

where $b^* = a_2 + b_{o2}$.

The diffusion terms are given as

$$\sigma_{Wj} = \sum_{i=1}^{2} a_i g_{ij} + \sum_{i=1}^{3} b_i h_{ij} + b^* \sigma_{ej}. \tag{18}$$

The Bellman equation of dynamic programming is

$$\max_{a,b,b_o,c} [A^\nu(t)J + U(a,b,b_o,c,t) - \rho J] = -J_t, \tag{19}$$

where $J(W, X, t)$ is the state-dependent indirect utility of wealth W denominated in home currency when state is described by vector X at time t. It is shown in Cox, Ingersoll, and Ross (1985) that J is a strictly concave and increasing function of W and twice continuously differentiable. A consumer-investor will derive optimal expected lifetime utility by making optimal choices at each instant. It is further assumed that there exist internal solutions for value function J and controls (a,b,b_o,c) which satisfy the Bellman equation.[5]

The necessary and sufficient first-order conditions are

$$\frac{\partial U}{\partial c_i} + \frac{\partial (A^\nu J)}{\partial c_i} = 0, \quad i = 1, 2,$$

$$\frac{\partial (A^\nu J)}{\partial a_i} = 0, \quad i = 1, 2,$$

$$\frac{\partial (A^\nu J)}{\partial b_i} = 0, \quad i = 1, 2, 3, \text{ and}$$

$$\frac{\partial(A^v J)}{\partial b^*} = 0. \qquad (20)$$

The first-order conditions in Equation (20) with Bellman Equation (19) are solved for optimal allocations, optimal consumption rates, and indirect utility function J for equilibrium prices (F,r,e). In the next section, market clearing conditions and equilibrium conditions are specified. These specifications will be used for simultaneous determination of equilibrium prices and exchange rates for optimal rules (a,b,b_0,c).

MARKET EQUILIBRIUM AND EQUILIBRIUM PRICES

In equilibrium all the output is held by the consumer-investors. The market clearing conditions require that net demand for contingent claims and risk-free borrowing and lending be zero and that all the capital stock be invested in real production processes. The market clearing conditions are

$$b = 0,$$
$$b_0 = 0, \text{ and} \qquad (21)$$
$$a_1 + a_2 = 1.$$

The assumption of rational expectations closes the model and requires that optimal intertemporal pricing functions obtained from the above market clearing conditions and, as implied by Itô's lemma, be precisely those which are anticipated by continuously optimizing consumer-investors. The rational expectation equilibrium is defined as a set of stochastic processes $(F,r,e,J; a,c)$ satisfying optimality conditions in Equations (19) and (20) and market clearing conditions in Equations (21).

Theorem 1. *Valuation of the forward currency contract using random rate of return*[6]

The value of the forward contract at any time τ where $t < \tau \le T$ is given as follows:

$$F_1[W(\tau),X(\tau),\tau,T] = \underset{W,X,\tau}{E}\left[\xi_1(W,X,T)\exp\left(\int_\tau^T -\beta_1(W(\lambda),x(\lambda),\lambda)d\lambda\right)\right], \qquad (22)$$

where the expectation operator E is conditional upon the dynamics of state variables given in Equation (2) and the growth of capital stock given in Equation (12), such that μ_W and σ_W are obtained under market clearing conditions given in Equation (21). The boundary value of the forward contract at maturity is $\xi_1(T)$ and is equal to $[e(T) - e_F(T)]$.

Equilibrium Functions of Foreign Exchange Contracts

The formula in Equation (22) suggests an intuitive explanation that the present value of a forward currency contract is obtained by discounting the terminal value at a randomly fluctuating rate of return and then taking its expected value. The expectation is conditional upon the information on state (W, X) including the endogenously determined parameters μ_W and σ_W when market clearing conditions in Equation (21) are satisfied. In particular

$$\sigma_W^2 = \sigma_I^2 + 2a_2\mathrm{cov}(I,e) + a_2^2\sigma_e^2, \qquad (23)$$

where $\sigma_I^2 = a'GG'a$.

The growth of capital stock involves a productivity risk σ_W^2 due to the volatility in the average productivity, μ_W, of the world production processes. The first component of this risk is the variance of the optimal rates of returns from the domestic and foreign production processes and depends upon the optimal investment shares in these processes. The other two components arise due to the volatility of the exchange rate and its covariance with the vector of optimal rates of return. The contribution of the second and the third components toward the entire productivity risk depends upon the optimal foreign investment a_2. Thus, the investor's expectations crucially depend upon the information on the distribution of the exchange rate and the level of foreign investment.

Investors would also consider technology risk arising due to random technological shocks imparted by changes in state variables. This risk is given by

$$\sigma_W\sigma' = \mathrm{cov}(I,X) + a_2\mathrm{cov}(e,X). \qquad (24)$$

The components of this fundamental risk depend upon the covariance of optimal rates of return on production processes and the rate of change of the exchange rate with the changes in state variables and the level of optimal foreign investment.

Theorem 2. *Valuation of forward currency contracts using risk-free interest rate*

The value of the forward currency contract is also given by

$$F_1[W(\tau),X(\tau),\tau,T] = \overline{E}_{W,X,\tau}\left\{\xi_1(W,X,T)\exp\left(\int_\tau^T -r_1[W(\lambda),X(\lambda),\lambda]d\lambda\right)\right\}, \qquad (25)$$

where the expectation operator $\overline{E}$ is conditional upon the growth process given as follows:

$$\frac{dW}{W} = (\mu_W - \theta_W)dt + \sigma_W\,dz, \text{ and}$$

$$dX = [\mu - (\theta_{X_1}\ldots\theta_{X_K})'dt + \sigma dz, \qquad (26)$$

where θ_W and θ_X are the risk premium factors and are given as

$$\theta_W = A^r[\sigma_I^2 + 2a_2\text{cov}(I,e) + a_2^2\sigma_e^2] + \sum_{i=1}^{k} A^{X_i}[\text{cov}(I,X_i) + a_2\text{cov}(e,X_i)],$$

$$\theta_{X_i} = A^r[\text{cov}(I,X_i) + a_2\text{cov}(e,X_i)] + \sum_{i=1}^{k} A^{X_i}\text{cov}(X_i,X_j), \qquad (27)$$

where $A^r = -(WJ_{WW})/J_W$ is the coefficient of relative risk aversion, and $A^X = -J_{WX}/J_W$ is the vector of coefficients of risk aversion with respect to changes in state variables.

According to Equation (25), the present value of the forward currency contract held by the home investor before expiration may be obtained by discounting the terminal value using the instantaneously risk-free interest rate in the investor's home country when the expectation is conditional upon a risk-adjusted growth process in which the expected average productivity of the capital stock and expected changes in state variables are reduced by their respective factor risk premia, θ_W and θ_X.[7] These factor risk premia depend upon the investor's degree of relative risk aversion and the fundamental sources of risk, namely, the productivity risk and the technology risk.

The formula in Equation (25) is more convenient from the practical point of view because interest rates are observable variables. On the contrary, the formula in Equation (22) requires calculation of the equilibrium rate of return, β_1, on the forward currency contracts.

Corollary 1. *Valuation of the forward contract in terms of intertemporal marginal rate of substitution*

The value of the forward currency contract at any time τ before maturity T is also given by

$$F_1[W(\tau),X(\tau),\tau,T] = \underset{W,X,\tau}{E}\left[\frac{J_W(T)\cdot\exp(-\rho T)}{J_W(\tau)\cdot\exp(-\rho\tau)} \cdot \xi_1[W(T),X(T)]\right] \qquad (28)$$

It may be inferred that the present value before expiration, at τ, of a random payoff on a forward currency contract at maturity T is obtained by multiplying the payoff by the intertemporal stochastic marginal rate of substitution, $J_W(T)\exp(-\rho T)/J_W(t)\exp(-\rho t)$, of one unit of home currency at maturity T for one unit of home currency at time τ and taking its expected value.[8] A risk-averse investor will invest in the forward foreign exchange asset if it improves upon his or her future consumption.

Corollary 2. *Equilibrium forward exchange rate*

Equilibrium Functions of Foreign Exchange Contracts

The equilibrium forward exchange rate at which the forward contract is written at time t is given by

$$e_F(t,T) = \frac{E_t[(J_W(T)e(T)]}{E_t[J_W(T)]}. \tag{29}$$

The formula in Equation (29) suggests that the forward exchange rate is the ratio of the expected marginal utility of one unit of foreign currency at maturity [or $e(T)$ units of home currency] and the expected marginal utility of one unit of home currency at maturity.

If the distribution of the marginal utility of wealth denominated in home currency at maturity T is correlated with the distribution of the spot exchange rate, it can be inferred that $e_F(t,T)$ is not equal to $E_t[e(T)]$, implying that the forward exchange rate is not an unbiased predictor of the future spot exchange rate. If the marginal utility of wealth is either nonstochastic or distributed independently of the future spot exchange rate, then the forward exchange rate is an unbiased predictor of the future spot exchange rate. Also under risk neutrality, marginal utility of wealth being constant, the forward rate will be an unbiased predictor of future spot rate.

For risk-averse investors, the hedging forward risk premium, Φ, can readily be obtained from Equation (29).[9] With the initial condition that the value of the forward contract at inception is zero, Φ is given by

$$\phi = e_F(t,T) - E_t[e(T)] = \frac{\text{cov}[e(T), J_W(T)]}{E_t[J_W(T)]}. \tag{30}$$

Note that the risk premium in the formula in Equation (30) does not depend upon the tastes and preferences of consumer-investors. Given the expected marginal utility of wealth denominated in home currency, the sign and size of the premium will depend upon the marginal utility of the home investor's wealth at maturity and its covariability with the future spot exchange rate at maturity. When the marginal utility of domestic wealth is positively correlated with the future spot exchange rate, the forward rate will overpredict the future spot rate, a case of contango. A negative correlation will result in normal backwardation with a downward bias in forward exchange rates.

Suppose that the covariance between the marginal utility of one unit of home currency at maturity and the spot exchange rate at maturity is negative; then an above average depreciation of home currency will be accompanied by a below average marginal utility of future consumption. Assuming that the risk-averse home investor (foreign investor) holds a net long (short) position in the forward contract, any payoff at maturity, $[e(T) - e_F(t,T)]$, due to unanticipated depreciation of home currency will provide relatively lower utility from future consumption and hence a relatively lower demand by the long position holder for forward contracts. The foreign investor will derive relatively higher utility from one unit of home currency in the future in the event of an unanticipated appreciation of the home currency (given the negative covariance). The foreign investor, going short in forward contract, must pay a compensating premium to the home investor to induce him or her into holding long forward foreign currency. The forward exchange rate, therefore, will be less than the expected future spot exchange rate by the amount of risk premium. The equilibrium value of the premium, $[e(T) - e_F(t,T)]$, will be commensurate with the systematic risk assumed by the holders of either of the positions as the forward contract reduces the risk of the home investor against the unanticipated depreciation of the home currency inasmuch as it reduces the risk of the foreign investor against the unanticipated appreciation of the home currency. Similarly, when the marginal utility of one unit of home currency is positively correlated with the future spot rate, an above average depreciation of home currency against the foreign currency will be accompanied by an above average marginal utility of future consumption. This outcome brings a relatively stronger demand for forward contracts by the home investor, who will issue a premium to the foreign investor to induce the latter into holding an offsetting short position, resulting in a forward exchange rate in excess of the expected future spot rate by the amount of risk premium. In equilibrium, the cost of hedging $[e_F(t,T) - e(T)]$ to the long investor will be the premium earned by the short investor.

Theorem 3. *Futures exchange rate*

The equilibrium futures exchange rate quoted at time t on a futures currency contract of maturity T is given by

$$F_2(t,T) = \mathop{E}_{w,x,t} \left[\frac{J_W(T)\exp(-\rho T)}{J_W(t)\exp(-\rho t)} \cdot \exp\left(\int_t^T r_1(\lambda)d\lambda\right) \right]. \tag{31}$$

Recognize that $\{J_W(T)\exp[-\rho(T - t)]/J_W(t)\}e(T)$ is the marginal rate of substitution of one unit of foreign currency at maturity [or equivalently, $e(T)$ units of home currency] for one unit of home currency at time t. Then, the futures exchange rate is the expected present value of $\exp\int_t^T r_1(\lambda)d\lambda$, which is a random number of foreign currency units to be delivered at maturity. This random number is independent of any currency and depends solely on the instantaneously risk-free rate in the investor's home country. Equation (31) also suggests that the futures exchange rate, like the forward exchange rate, is a biased predictor of the future spot exchange rate. This is due to the fact that the marginal utility of wealth and the instantaneous interest rate in the investor's home country are stochastic. If the interest rates were deterministic, Equation (31) would give the forward exchange rate for the same maturity. The next corollary demonstrates the premia which separate the futures exchange rate from the expected future spot exchange rate.

Corollary 3. *Premia in futures exchange rate*

Equilibrium Functions of Foreign Exchange Contracts

The futures exchange rate is also given by

$$F_2(t,T) = E_t[e(T)] + E_t[e(T)] \left(\frac{E_t[J_W(T)]\exp(-\rho T)}{J_W(t)\exp(-\rho t)}\right) \left(E_t\left\{\exp[\int_t^T r_1(s)ds]\right\} - 1\right)$$

$$+ \frac{E_t[J_W(T)]\exp(-\rho T)}{J_W(t)\exp(-\rho t)} \left(\text{cov}[e(T), \exp[\int_t^T r_1(s)ds]]\right)$$

$$+ \text{cov}\left(\frac{J_W(T)\exp(-\rho T)}{J_W(t)\exp(-\rho t)}, \left\{e(T)\exp[\int_t^T r_1(s)ds]\right\}\right). \qquad (32)$$

Equation (32) states that, like the forward exchange rate, the futures exchange rate is also different from the future spot exchange rate. The difference, however, is not only due to hedging premium, as in the forward exchange rate, but also due to a term premium and a reinvestment rate premium. For risk-averse investors, the term premium represented by the second term in Equation (32) arises from the presence of liquidity premium in the term structure. The distribution of cash flows until maturity due to the marking-to-market feature of futures contract has the effect of reducing the duration of the contract. Therefore, a long investor in futures pays a premium for this additional liquidity, unlike as in a forward contract, where cash flows are realized only at maturity. If the instantaneous interest rates were deterministic, the random number of foreign currency units equal to $\exp\int_t^T r_1(\lambda)d\lambda$ would converge to a known number of foreign currency units equal to $\exp\int_t^T R_1(t,\lambda)d\lambda$, and the term premium would be zero.

Cash flows distributed over the life of a futures contract due to marking to market and stochastic interest rates give rise to reinvestment rate premium also given by the third term in Equation (32). Suppose this covariance term is negative, implying that a below-average decline in the domestic instantaneous interest rate is associated with an above-average depreciation of the domestic currency against the foreign currency. Further, suppose the domestic investor holds a long position and the foreign investor a matching short position. Then, the gain from the domestic investor's long position tends to be offset by reinvestment of the instantaneous margins at a lower domestic interest rate. In equilibrium, to ensure against the loss due to the lower reinvestment rate, the foreign investor holding the short position must pay a premium to the home investor holding the long position, resulting in a downward bias in the futures exchange rates. If the covariance between r_1 and $e(T)$ is positive so that an above-average increase in the instantaneous domestic interest rate is associated with an above-average depreciation of the domestic currency, then the gain from the long position is reinforced by reinvestment of margins at a higher domestic interest rate. In this case the long home investor must issue an insurance to the short foreign investor, resulting in an upward bias in the futures exchange rate.

The hedging premium for the forward and futures exchange rate has the same explanation. It is not possible to infer the sign and size of the net bias due to the three premia. If the domestic interest rate is constant or deterministic, the term premium as well as the reinvestment rate premium will vanish and there will be no difference between the forward and futures exchange rates of identical maturity.

Theorem 4. *Valuation of currency options contract on spot exchange rate*[10]

The equilibrium price of the foreign currency option written on the spot exchange rate with an exercise price e^* units of home currency per unit of foreign currency is given by

$$F_3(t,T,e^*) = \underset{w,x,t}{E} \left\{ \frac{Jw(T)}{Jw(t)} \exp[-\rho(T-t)] \cdot \max[0,(e(T) - e^*)] \right\}. \qquad (33)$$

If the option is exercised, the value of the European option is the present value of a random payoff $[e(T) - e^*]$ at the expiration date T found by discounting by the intertemporal marginal rate of substitution. The value of the option is zero if unexercised.

CONCLUSIONS

A theoretical framework in a general equilibrium continuous-time setting has been presented in this paper to study the equilibrium prices of foreign exchange contracts. With stochastic constant-returns-to-scale technologies, frictionless foreign exchange markets, and continuous trading, pricing theorems on forward, futures, and currency option contracts have been established. In particular, the following conclusions merit attention.

One of the contributions of this paper is to develop several alternative expressions for the valuation of foreign exchange forward and futures contracts and to provide intuitive economic meaning of the relationships. In general, it is shown that under a flexible exchange rate regime, the value of a forward contract at any time during the course of the contract can be found by discounting the terminal value of the contract at a randomly fluctuating rate of return and then taking its expected value. In this valuation, productivity risk, technology risk, exchange rate variability, and market risk are reflected in the stochastic rate of return on the forward contract. Alternatively, discounting can be done at the instantaneously risk-free interest rate in the investor's home country. In this case, the expected value of a forward contract is based on a process in which the capital stock and the economy's exogenously specified state variables providing technology shocks drift at a slower rate by an amount determined by factor risk premia. These factor risk premia depend upon the investor's degree of relative risk aversion and fundamental sources of risk arising due to stochastic productivity, technological shocks, and exchange rate variability.

Another alternative form of valuation of foreign exchange contracts emphasizes a fundamental way in which the intertemporal marginal rate of substitution on the rate of time preference across currencies enters in the present value formulations.

In general, it is shown that forward and futures exchange rates are not unbiased predictors of the future spot exchange rate. This is due to the uncertainty of the marginal utility of future consumption, which depends on the interest rates, and to random changes in the exchange rates. If the co-movement of the spot exchange rate and the marginal utility of wealth or the future consumption are in the same (opposite) direction, there is a positive (negative) hedging risk premium for risk-averse investors in forward foreign currency. Accordingly, the forward exchange rate is greater (less) than the expected future spot exchange rate by the amount of the equilibrium risk premium. In addition to the hedging premium, a term premium and a reinvestment rate premium set apart the futures exchange rate from the expected future spot exchange rate. This is due to the marking-to-market feature and stochastic domestic interest rates. The valuation of a currency option of the European type is essentially similar to a forward contract, with the only difference that the terminal payoff of the option may be different from that of a forward contract depending upon whether the option is exercised or not.

APPENDIX: PROOFS OF THEOREMS AND COROLLARIES

Theorem 1. *Valuation of forward contracts using random rate of return*

By Itô's lemma, the price of the forward contract satisfies the stochastic partial differential equation:

$$A^v(t)F + \frac{\partial F}{\partial t} = \beta F, \tag{A1}$$

where the differential operator $A^v(t)$ is given by Equation (11) of the text. Substituting equilibrium values of μ_W and σ_W in Equation (11) and the boundary condition for the forward contract and applying theorem 5.2 of the Friedman (1975, p. 147) solution to Equation (A1) give the value of the forward contract in terms of the stochastic rate of return on the forward contract.

Theorem 2. *Valuation of forward currency contract using risk-free interest rate*

Excess return on a contingent claim is given by

$$\beta F - rF = F_W\theta_W + \sum_{i=1}^{k} F_{X_i}\theta_{X_i} \qquad (A2)$$

$$\frac{1}{2}W^2 F_{WW} \sum_{j=1}^{k+2} \sigma_{W_j}^2 + \sum_{i=1}^{k} F_{WX_i} \sum_{j=1}^{k+2} \sigma_{W_j}\sigma_{ij} + \frac{1}{2}\sum_{i=1}^{k}\sum_{j=1}^{k} F_{X_i}F_{X_j} \sum_{m=1}^{k+2} \sigma_{im}\sigma_{jm}$$

$$+ F_W(W\mu_W - \theta_W) + \sum_{i=1}^{k} F_{X_i}(\mu_i - \theta_{X_i}) = r_1 F. \qquad (A3)$$

Equation (A3) is similar to Equation (A1) except that drift terms W_{μ_W} and μ_i are reduced by factor risk premium θ_W and θ_{X_i}, respectively, given in Equation (27).

Corollary 1. *Valuation of forward contracts in terms of intertemporal marginal rate of substitution*

Differentiating the Bellman Equation (19) of the text with respect to W and recalling that J is an implicit function of t, we have $J_t = 0$, and

$$\frac{\partial(A^v J)}{\partial W} - \rho J_W = 0, \qquad (A4)$$

or,

$$A^v \frac{\partial J}{\partial W} + J \frac{\partial A^v}{\partial W} - \rho J_W = 0. \qquad (A5)$$

But,

$$\frac{\partial A^v}{\partial W} = r_1 \frac{\partial}{\partial W}. \qquad (A6)$$

Therefore,

$$r_1 J_W + A^v J_W - \rho J_W = 0. \qquad (A7)$$

From the first-order condition in Equation (20) of the text we obtain

$$A^v(F_1 J_W) + \frac{\partial(F_1 J_W)}{\partial t} - r_1(F_1 J_W) - F_1(A^v J_W) = 0,$$

$$\frac{\partial F_1}{\partial W} = 0,$$

Equilibrium Functions of Foreign Exchange Contracts 233

$$\frac{\partial J_W}{\partial t} = 0. \tag{A8}$$

Using (A7) we get

$$A^v(J_W F_1) + \frac{\partial(J_W F_1)}{\partial t} = \rho(J_W F_1). \tag{A9}$$

Equation (A9) is similar to Equation (A1) except that F_1 is replaced by $J_W F_1$ and β_1 replaced by ρ. Using theorem 5.2 of Friedman (1975, p. 147) the solution of the corollary can be obtained.

Corollary 2. *Equilibrium forward exchange rate*

At initial time when contract is written the value of the contract is zero. Substituting $F_1[W(t),X(t),t,T] = 0$ in Equation (28) of the text, we get the result.

Theorem 3. *Equilibrium futures exchange rate*

From first-order condition for futures contract we have

$$A^v(J_W F_2) + \frac{\partial(J_W F_2)}{\partial t} = F_2(A^v J_W). \tag{A10}$$

Proof is exactly the same as for corollary 1. The boundary condition for futures contract is $F_2[W(T),X(T),T,T] = e(T)$. Using Equation (A7) and theorem 5.2 of Friedman (1975, p. 147), we get the result.

Corollary 3. *Premia in the futures exchange rate*

The result in Equation (32) of the text can be directly obtained by applying the expectation operator to the product of the three random terms in Equation (32) and rearranging terms.

Theorem 4. *Valuation of currency options*

The boundary condition for a European currency option is

$$\xi_3[W(T),X(T)] = \max[0,e(T) - e^*)]. \tag{A11}$$

Proceed as in corollary 1 to get the result.

NOTES

1. The assumption of homogeneous consumer-investors is restrictive for the open economies modeled here. Nevertheless, country-specific technologies producing different goods for domestic and foreign consumption and investment provide sufficient international dimension to the model.

2. In a heterogeneous society the capital markets are complete in the Arrow–Debreu sense if the number of firms and contingent claims is equal to the number of state variables. Then, there exists, for a risk-averse investor, a perfect hedge against unanticipated changes in each state variable. In case of a homogeneous society, markets for all or some financial claims may be closed without affecting Pareto optimality because homogeneous investors need not trade with each other. Clearly in the present model, the number of state variables need not be equal to $(n + k)$. Here state variables are assumed to be equal to k.

3. Each good may be produced by using several competing risky production functions in each country. Since risk-averse investors can always diversify across risky assets, therefore, one technology per good is not a restrictive assumption.

4. The reader is reminded that F_1 is the value of the forward contract whereas F_2 is the futures exchange rate. This is done merely for notational convenience.

5. In addition, some regularity conditions are also specified to guarantee a well-behaved solution. The controls belong to a set of admissible control functions having the Markov property which are narrowed down by boundedness. Further, the controls are Borel measurable, satisfying growth and Lipshitz conditions. See Arnold (1974), Fleming and Rishel (1975, chap. 6), and Cox, Ingersoll, and Ross (1985).

6. Proofs of all the theorems and corollaries are provided in the Appendix.

7. The factor risk premia are different from those in the closed economy model of Cox, Ingersoll, and Ross (1985). The differences arise due to the variability of the exchange rate and the foreign investment facilitated through an expanded investment opportunity set.

8. Intuitively, the expected value of the intertemporal marginal rate of substitution of one unit of home currency is equal to $\exp[-\int_t^T R_1(t,\lambda)d\lambda]$ where R_1 is the known domestic interest rate at t for a maturity at λ.

9. Hodrick (1981) concludes that the bias is introduced by the time-varying risk premia. This conclusion, however, is obtained via interest rate parity without explicitly introducing the forward market. See also Huang (1989). He uses an intertemporal latent variable asset pricing model with unobservable time-varying risk premia to price forward foreign exchange contracts and to determine the term structure of forward foreign exchange contracts.

10. The Black–Scholes (1973) model is not a general equilibrium model. Their approach is to price options with respect to an asset whose price is exogenously specified.

REFERENCES

Arnold, L. *Stochastic Differential Equations: Theory and Applications.* John Wiley, New York, 1974.

Black, F. "The Pricing of Commodity Contracts." *Journal of Financial Economics* 3 (1976), pp. 167–179.

Black, F. and M. Scholes. "The Pricing of Options and Corporate Liabilities." *Journal of Political Economy* 81 (May–June 1973), pp.637–654.

Cornell, B. and M. R. Reinganum. "Forward and Futures Prices: Evidence from the Foreign Exchange Markets." *Journal of Finance* 36, No. 12 (December 1981), pp. 1035–1045.

Cox, J. C., J. E. Ingersoll, Jr., and S. A. Ross. "The Relation Between Forward Prices and Future Prices." *Journal of Financial Economics* 9 (1981), pp. 321–346.

———. "An Intertemporal General Equilibrium Model of Asset Prices." *Econometrica* 53, No. 2 (March 1985), pp. 363–384.

Fleming, W. H. and R. W. Rishel. *Deterministic and Stochastic Optimal Control.* New York: Springer-Verlag, 1975.

Friedman, A. *Stochastic Differential Equations and Applications*, Vol. 1. New York: Academic Press, 1975.

Hodrick, R. J. "International Asset Pricing With Time-varying Risk Premia." *Journal of International Economics* 11 (1981), pp. 573–587.

Huang, R. D. "An Analysis of Intertemporal Pricing for Forward Foreign Exchange Contracts" *Journal of Finance*, 44, No. 1 (March 1989), pp. 183–194.

Jarrow, R. A. and G. S. Oldfield. "Forward Contracts and Futures Contracts." *Journal of Financial Economics* 9 (1981), pp. 373–382.

Richard, S. F. and M. Sundaresan. "A Continuous Time Equilibrium Model of Forward Prices and Futures Prices in a Multigood Economy." *Journal of Financial Economics* 9 (1981), pp. 347–371.

Credit Swap Valuation

Darrell Duffie

This review of the pricing of credit swaps, a form of derivative security that can be viewed as default insurance on loans or bonds, begins with a description of the credit swap contract, turns to pricing by reference to spreads over the risk-free rate of par floating-rate bonds of the same quality, and then considers model-based pricing. The role of asset swap spreads as a reference for pricing credit swaps is also considered.

Credit swaps pay the buyer of protection a given contingent amount at the time of a given credit event, such as a default. The contingent amount is often the difference between the face value of a bond and its market value and is paid at the time the underlying bond defaults. The buyer of protection pays an annuity premium until the time of the credit event or the maturity date of the credit swap, whichever is first. The credit event must be documented with a notice, supported with evidence of public announcement of the event in, for example, the international press. The amount to be paid at the time of the credit event is determined by one or more third parties and based on physical or cash settlement, as indicated in the confirmation form of the OTC credit swap transaction, a standard contract form with indicated alternatives.

The term "swap" applies to credit swaps because they can be viewed, under certain ideal conditions to be explained in this article, as a swap of a default-free floating-rate note for a defaultable floating-rate note.

Credit swaps are currently perhaps the most popular of credit derivatives.[1] Unlike many other derivative forms, in a credit swap, payment to the buyer of protection is triggered by a contractually defined event that must be documented.

The Basics

The basic credit swap contract is as follows. Parties A and B enter into a contract terminating at the time of a given credit event or at a stated maturity, whichever is first. A commonly stipulated credit event is default by a named issuer—say, Entity C, which could be a corporation or a sovereign issuer.

Credit events may be defined in terms of downgrades, events that could instigate the default of one or more counterparties, or other credit-related occurrences.[2] Swaps involve some risk of disagreement about whether the event has, in fact, occurred, but in this discussion of valuing the credit swap, such risk of documentation or enforceability will be ignored.

In the event of termination at the designated credit event, Party A pays Party B a stipulated termination amount. For example, in the most common form of credit swap, called a "default swap," if the termination is triggered by the default of Entity C, A pays B an amount that is, in effect, the difference between the face value and the market value of the designated note issued by C.

In compensation for what it may receive in the event of termination by a credit event, until the maturity of the credit swap or termination by the designated credit event, Party B pays Party A an annuity at a rate called the "credit swap spread" or, sometimes, the "credit swap premium."

The cash flows of a credit swap are illustrated in **Figure 1**, where U is the swap's annuity coupon rate, τ is the time of the default event, $Y(\tau)$ is the market value of the designated underlying note at time τ, and T is the maturity date. The payment at credit time τ, if before maturity T, is the difference, D, between the underlying note's face value—100 units, for example—and $Y(\tau)$, or in this case, $D = 100 - Y(\tau)$.

For instance, in some cases, the compensating annuity may be paid as a spread over the usual plain-vanilla (noncredit) swap rate.[3] For example, if the five-year fixed-for-floating interest rate swap rate is 6 percent versus LIBOR and B is the fixed-rate payer in the default swap, then B pays a fixed rate higher than the usual 6 percent. If, for example, B pays 7.5 percent fixed versus LIBOR and if the C-issued note underlying the default swap is of the same notional amount as the interest rate swap, then

---

Darrell Duffie is a professor of finance at the Stanford University Graduate School of Business.

January/February 1999

Financial Analysts Journal

Figure 1. Credit Swap Cash Flows

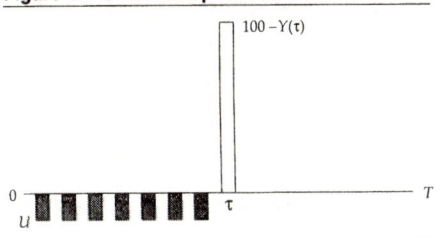

Note: Receive par less market value $Y(\tau)$ of underlying note at τ if $\tau \le T$.

in this case, the default swap spread is 150 basis points (bps). If B is the floating-rate payer on the interest rate swap, then B pays floating plus a spread in return for the usual market fixed rate on swaps or, in effect, receives fixed less a spread. The theoretical default swap spread is not necessarily the same in the case of B paying fixed as in B paying floating.

In general, combining the credit swap with an interest rate swap affects the quoted credit swap spread because an interest rate swap whose fixed rate is the at-market swap rate for maturity T but has a random early termination does not have a market value of zero. For example, if the term structure of forward rates is steeply upward sloping, then an at-market interest rate swap to maturity T or the credit event time, whichever is first, has a lower fixed rate than a plain-vanilla at-market interest rate swap to maturity T. A credit spread of 150 bps over the at-market plain-vanilla swap rate to maturity T, therefore, represents a larger credit spread than does a credit swap without an interest rate swap that pays a premium of 150 bps.

Apparently, when corporate bonds are the underlying securities, default swaps in which the payment at default is reduced by the accrued portion of the credit swap premium are not unusual. This variation is briefly considered later.

In short, the classic credit swap can be thought of as an insurance contract in which the insured party pays an insurance premium in return for coverage against a loss that may occur because of a credit event.

The credit swap involves two pricing problems:
- At origination, the standard credit swap involves no exchange of cash flows and, therefore (ignoring dealer margins and transaction costs), has a market value of zero. One must, however, determine the at-market annuity premium rate, U, for which the market value of the credit swap is indeed zero. This at-market rate is the credit swap premium, sometimes called the "market credit swap spread."

- After origination, changes in market interest rates and in the credit quality of the issuing entity, as well as the passage of time, typically change the market value of the credit swap. For a given credit swap with stated annuity rate U, one must then determine the current market value, which is not generally zero.

When making markets, the first pricing problem is the more critical. When hedging or marking to market, the second problem is relevant. Methods for solving the two problems are similar. The second problem is generally the more challenging because off-market default swaps have less liquidity and because pricing references, such as bond spreads, are of relatively less use.

This article considers simple credit swaps and their extensions.[4] In all the following discussions, the credit swap counterparties A and B are assumed to be default free in order to avoid dealing here with the pricing impact of default by counterparties A and B, which can be treated by the first-to-default results in Duffie (1998b).

Simple Credit Swap Spreads

For this section, the contingent-payment amount specified in the credit swap (the amount to be paid if the credit event occurs) is the difference between the face value of a note issued by Entity C and the note's market value $Y(\tau)$ at the credit event time, τ—that is, the contingent-payment amount is $D = 100 - Y(\tau)$.

Starter Case. The assumptions for this starter case are as follows:
- The swap involves no embedded interest rate swap. That is, the default swap is an exchange of a constant coupon rate, U, paid by Party B until termination at maturity or at the stated credit event (which may or may not be default of the underlying C-issued note.) This constraint eliminates the need to consider the value of an interest rate swap with early termination at a credit event.
- There is no payment of the accrued credit swap premium at default.
- The underlying note issued by C is a par floating-rate note (FRN) with the maturity of the credit swap. This important restriction will be relaxed later.
- For this starter case, the assumption is that an investor can create a short position by selling today the underlying C-issued note for its current market value and can buy back the note on the date of the credit event, or on the credit swap maturity date, at its then-current market value, with no other cash flows.

Credit Swap Valuation

- A default-free FRN exists with floating rate R_t at date t. The coupon payments on the FRN issued by C (the C-FRN) are contractually specified to be $R_t + S$, the floating rate plus a fixed spread, S. In practice, FRN spreads are usually relative to LIBOR or some other benchmark floating rate that need not be a pure default-free rate. Having the pure default-free floating rate and reference rate (which might be LIBOR) differ by a constant poses no difficulties for this analysis. (Bear in mind that the short-term U.S. Treasury rate is not a pure default-free interest rate because of repo [repurchase agreement] "specials" [discussed later] and the "moneyness" or tax advantages of Treasuries.[5] A better benchmark for risk-free borrowing is the term general collateral rate, which is close to a default-free rate and has typically been close to LIBOR, with a slowly varying spread to LIBOR in U.S. markets.) For example, suppose the C-FRN is at a spread of 100 bps to LIBOR, which is at a spread to the general collateral rate that, although varying over time, is approximately 5 bps. Then, for purposes of this analysis, an approximation of the spread of the C-FRN to the default-free floating rate would be 105 bps.
- In cash markets for the default-free note and C-FRN, there are no transaction costs, such as bid–ask spreads. In particular, at the initiation of the credit swap, an investor can sell the underlying C-FRN at its market value. At termination, the assumption is that an investor can buy the C-FRN at market value.
- The termination payment if a credit event occurs is made at the immediately following coupon date on the underlying C-issued note. (If not, the question of accrued interest arises and can be accommodated by standard time value of money calculations, shown later.)
- If the credit swap is terminated by the stated credit event, the swap is settled by the physical delivery of the C-FRN in exchange for cash in the amount of its face value. (Many credit swaps are settled in cash and, so far, neither physical nor cash settlement seems to have gained predominance as the standard method.)
- Tax effects can be ignored. (If not, the calculations to be made are applied after tax and using the tax rate of investors that are indifferent to purchasing the default swap at its market price.)

With these assumptions, one can "price" the credit swap; that is, one can compute the at-market credit swap spread, on the basis of a synthesis of Party B's cash flows on the credit swap, by the following arbitrage argument:

An investor can short the par C-FRN for an initial cash receivable of, say, 100 units of account and invest the 100 units in a par default-free FRN. The investor holds this portfolio through maturity or the stated credit event. In the meantime, the investor pays the floating rate plus spread on the C-FRN and receives the floating rate on the default-free FRN. The net paid is the spread.

If the credit event does not occur before maturity, both notes mature at par value and no net cash flow occurs at termination.

If the credit event does occur before maturity, the investor liquidates the portfolio at the coupon date immediately following the event and collects the difference between the market value of the default-free FRN (which is par on a coupon date) and the market value of the C-FRN—in this example, the difference is $D = 100 - Y(\tau)$. (Liquidation calls for termination of the short position in the C-FRN, which involves buying the C-FRN in the market for delivery against the short sale through, for example, the completion of a repo contract.)

Because this contingent amount, the difference D, is the same as the amount specified in the credit swap contract, the absence of arbitrage implies that the unique arbitrage-free at-market credit swap spread, denoted U, is S, the spread over the risk-free rate on the underlying floating-rate notes issued by C. (That is, combining this strategy with Party A's cash flows as the seller of the credit swap results in a net constant annuity cash flow of $U - S$ until maturity or termination. Therefore, in the absence of other costs, for no arbitrage to exist, U must equal S.)

This arbitrage under its ideal assumptions, is illustrated in **Figure 2**.

Extension: The Reference Par Spread for Default Swaps. Provided the credit swap is, in fact, a default swap, the restrictive assumption that the underlying note has the same maturity as the credit swap can be relaxed. In this case, the relevant par spread for fixing the credit swap spread is that of a (possibly different) C-issued FRN that is of the same maturity as the credit swap and of the same priority as the underlying note. This note is the "reference C-FRN." As long as absolute priority applies at default (so that the underlying note and the reference note have the same recovery value at default), the previous arbitrage pricing argument applies. This argument works, under the stated assumptions, even if the underlying note is a fixed-rate note of the same seniority as the reference C-FRN.

Some cautions are in order here. First, often no reference C-FRN exists. Second, absolute priority need not apply in practice. For example, a senior short-maturity FRN and a senior long-maturity

Figure 2. Synthetic Credit Swap Cash Flows

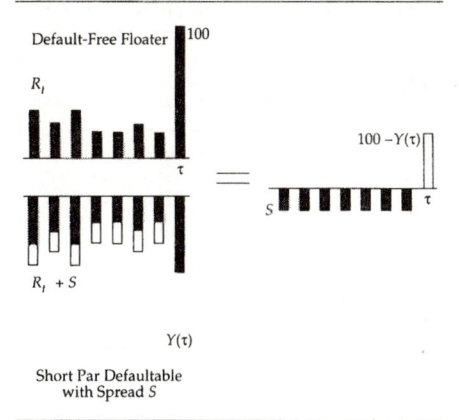

Default-Free Floater

R_l

$R_l + S$

$Y(\tau)$

Short Par Defaultable with Spread S

Figure 3. Reverse Repo Combined with Cash Sale

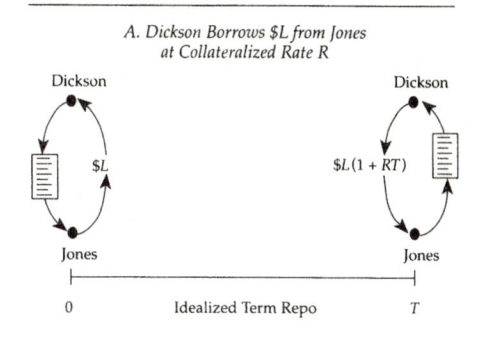

A. Dickson Borrows $L from Jones at Collateralized Rate R

0 — Idealized Term Repo — T

B. Jones Shorts Collateral through Reverse Repo and Sale to Thomas

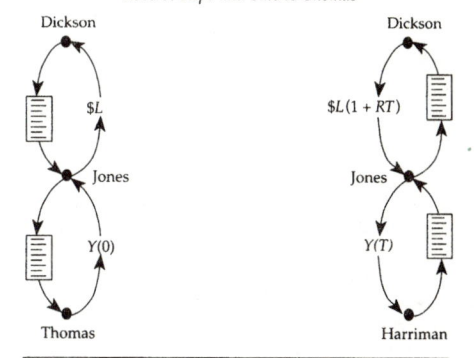

fixed-rate note may represent significantly different bargaining power, especially in a reorganization scenario precipitated by default.

Extension: Adding Repo Specials and Transaction Costs. Another important and common relaxation of the assumptions in the starter case involves the ability to freely short the reference C-FRN. A typical method of shorting securities is via a reverse repo combined with a cash sale. That is, through a reverse repo, an investor can arrange to receive the reference note as collateral on a loan to a given term. Rather than holding the note as collateral, the investor can immediately sell the note. In effect, the investor has then created a short position in the reference note through the term of the repo. As shown in the top part of **Figure 3** (with Dickson as the investor), each repo involves a collateralized interest rate, or repo rate, R. A loan of L dollars at repo rate R for a term of T years results in a loan repayment of $L(1 + RT)$ at term. As shown in the bottom part of Figure 3, the repo counterparty—in this case, Jones—who is offering the loan and receiving the collateral may, at the initiation of the repo, sell the collateral at its market value, $Y(0)$. Then, at the maturity date of the repo contract, Jones may buy the note back at its market value, $Y(T)$, so as to return it to the original repo counterparty, in this case, Dickson. If the general prevailing interest rate, r, for such loans, called the "general collateral rate," is larger than the specific collateral rate R for the loan collateralized by the C-issued note in question, Jones will have suffered costs in creating the short position in the underlying C-issued note.[6]

In many cases, one cannot arrange a reverse repo at the general collateral rate (GCR). If the reference note is "scarce," an investor may be forced to offer a repo rate that is below the GCR in order to reverse in the C-FRN as collateral. This situation is termed a repo special (see, e.g., Duffie 1996). In addition, particularly with risky FRNs, a substantial bid–ask spread may be present in the market for the reference FRN at initiation of the repo (when one sells) and at termination (when one buys).

Suppose that a term reverse repo collateralized by the C-FRN can be arranged, with maturity equal to the maturity date of the credit swap. Also suppose that default of the collateral triggers early termination of the repo at the originally agreed repo rate (which is the case in many jurisdictions). The term repo special, Z, is the difference between the term GCR and the term specific collateral rate for the C-FRN. Shorting the C-FRN, therefore, requires an extra annuity payment of Z. The arbitrage-based default swap spread would then be approximately $S + Z$. If the term repo does not necessarily terminate at the credit event, this spread is not an exact arbitrage-based spread. Because the probability of a credit event occurring well before maturity is typically small, however, and because term repo specials are often small, the difference may not be large in practice.[7]

Now consider the other side of the swap: For the synthesis of a short position in the credit swap, an investor purchases the C-FRN and places it into a term repo to capture the term repo special.

If transaction costs in the cash market are a factor, the credit swap broker/dealer may incur risk from uncovered credit swap positions, transaction costs, or some of each, and may, in principle, charge an additional premium. With two-sided market making and diversification, how quickly these costs and risks build up over a portfolio of positions is not clear.[8]

The difference between a transaction cost and a repo special is important. A transaction cost simply widens the bid–ask spread on a default swap, increasing the default swap spread quoted by the broker/dealer who sells the default swap and reducing the quoted default swap spread when the broker/dealer is asked by a customer to buy a default swap from the customer. A repo special, however, is not itself a transaction cost; it can be thought of as an extra source of interest income on the underlying C-FRN, a source that effectively changes the spread relative to the default-free rate. Substantial specials, which raise the cost of providing the credit swap, do not necessarily increase the bid–ask spread. For example, in synthesizing a short position in a default swap, an investor can place the associated long position in the C-FRN into a repo position and profit from the repo special.

In summary, under the assumptions stated up to this point, a dealer can broker a default swap (that is, take the position of Party A) at a spread of approximately $S + Z$ with a bid–ask spread of K, where

- S is the par spread on a reference floating-rate note issued by a named entity, called here Entity C, of the same maturity as the default swap and of the same seniority as the underlying note;
- Z is the term repo special on par floating-rate notes issued by C or else an estimate of the annuity rate paid, throughout the term of the default swap, for maintaining a short position in the reference note to the termination of the credit swap; and
- K contains any annuitized transaction costs (such as cash market bid–ask spreads) for hedging, any risk premium for unhedged portions of the risk (which would apply in imperfect capital markets), overhead, and a profit margin.

In practice, estimating the effective term repo special is usually difficult because default swaps are normally of much longer term than repo positions. In some cases, liquidity in the credit swap market has apparently been sufficient to allow some traders to quote term repo rates for the underlying collateral by reference to the credit swap spread.

Extension: Payment of Accrued Credit Swap Premium. Some credit swaps, more frequently on underlying corporate rather than sovereign bonds, specify that, at default, the buyer of protection must pay the credit swap premium that has accrued since the last coupon date. For example, with a credit swap spread of 300 bps and default one-third of the way through a current semiannual coupon period, the buyer of protection would receive face value less recovery value of the underlying asset less one-third of the semiannual annuity payment, which would be 0.5 percent of the underlying face value.

For reasonably small default probabilities and intercoupon periods, the expected difference in time between the credit event and the previous coupon date is approximately half the length of an intercoupon period. Thus, for pricing purposes in all but extreme cases, one can think of the credit swap as equivalent to payment at default of face value less recovery value less one-half of the regular default swap premium payment.

For example, suppose there is some risk-neutral probability $h > 0$ per year for the credit event.[9] Then, one estimates a reduction in the at-market credit swap spread for the accrued premium that is below the spread that is appropriate without the accrued-premium feature—approximately $hS/2n$, where n is the number of coupons a year of the underlying bond. For a pure default swap, spread S is smaller than h because of partial recovery, so this correction is smaller than $h^2/2n$, which is negligible for small h. For example, at semiannual credit swap coupon intervals and for a risk-neutral mean arrival rate of the credit event of 2 percent a year, the correction for the accrued-premium effect is less than 1 bp.

Extension: Accrued Interest on the Underlying Notes. For calculating the synthetic arbitrage described previously, the question of accrued interest payment on the default-free floating rate note arises. The typical credit swap specifies payment of the difference between face value *without* *accrued interest* and market value of the underlying note. However, the arbitrage portfolio described here (long a default-free floater, short a defaultable floater) is worth face value *plus accrued interest on the default-free note* less recovery on the underlying defaultable note. If the credit event involves default of the underlying note, the previous arbitrage argument is not quite right.

Consider, for example, a one-year default swap with semiannual coupons. Suppose the LIBOR rate is 8 percent. Then, the expected value of the accrued interest on the default-free note at default is approximately 2 percent of face value for small default probabilities. Suppose the risk-neutral probability of occurrence of the credit event is 4 percent a year. Then, the market value of the credit swap to the buyer of protection is reduced roughly 8 bps of face value and, therefore, the at-market credit swap spread is reduced roughly 8 bps.

Generally, for credit swaps of any maturity with relatively small and constant risk-neutral default probabilities and relatively flat term structures of default-free rates, the reduction in the at-market credit swap spread for the accrued-interest effect, below the par floating rate-spread plus effective repo special, is approximately $hr/2n$, where h is the annual risk-neutral probability of occurrence of the credit, r is the average of the default-free forward rates through credit swap maturity, and n is the number of coupons per year of the underlying bond. Of course, one could work out the effect more precisely with a term-structure model, as described later.

Extension: Approximating the Reference Floating-Rate Spread. If no par floating-rate note of the same credit quality is available whose maturity is that of the default swap, then one can attempt to "back out" the reference par spread, S, from other spreads. For example, suppose C issues an FRN of the swap maturity and of the same seniority as the underlying note and it is trading at a price, p, that is not necessarily par and paying a spread of $\hat{S}$ over the default-free floating rate.

Let AP denote the associated annuity price—that is, the present value of an annuity paid at a rate of 1 unit until the credit swap termination (default of the underlying note or maturity).

For reasonably small credit risks and interest rates, AP is close to the default-free annuity price because most of the market value of the credit risk of an FRN is associated in this case with potential loss of principal. A more precise computation of AP is considered later.

The difference between a par and a nonpar FRN with the same maturity is the coupon spread (assuming the same recovery at default); therefore,

$$p - 1 = AP(\hat{S} - S),$$

where S is the implied reference par spread. Solving for the implied reference par spread produces

$$S = \hat{S} + \frac{1-p}{AP}.$$

With this formula, one can estimate the reference par spread, S.

If the relevant price information is for a fixed-rate note issued by C of the reference maturity and seniority, one can again resort to the assumption that its recovery of face value at default is the same as that of a par floater of the same seniority (which is again reasonable on legal grounds in a liquidation scenario). And one can again attempt to "back out" the reference par floating-rate spread.

Spreads over default-free rates on par fixed-rate notes and par floating-rate notes are approximately equal.[10] Thus, if the only reference spread is a par fixed-rate spread, F, using F in place of S in estimating the default swap spread is reasonably safe.

An example in **Figure 4** shows the close relationship between the term structures of default swap spreads and par fixed-coupon yield spreads for the same credit quality.[11] Some of the difference between the spreads shown in Figure 4 is, in fact, the accrued-interest effect discussed in the previous subsection.

If the reference pricing information is for a nonpar fixed-rate note, then one can proceed as before. Let p denote the price of the available fixed-rate note, with spread $\hat{F}$ over the default-free rate. Then,

$$p - 1 = AP(\hat{F} - F),$$

where AP is again the annuity price to maturity or default. So, with an estimate of AP, one can obtain an estimate of the par fixed spread, F, which is a close approximation of the par floating-rate spread, S, the quantity needed to compute the default swap spread.[12]

Estimating Hazard Rates and Defaultable Annuity Prices

The hazard rate for the credit event is the arrival rate of the credit event (in the sense of Poisson processes). For example, a constant hazard rate of 400 bps represents a mean arrival rate of 4 times per 100 years. The mean time to arrival, conditional on no event arrival date by T, remains 25 years after T for any T. Begin by assuming a constant risk-neutral

Figure 4. Term Structures of Bond and Default Swap Spreads

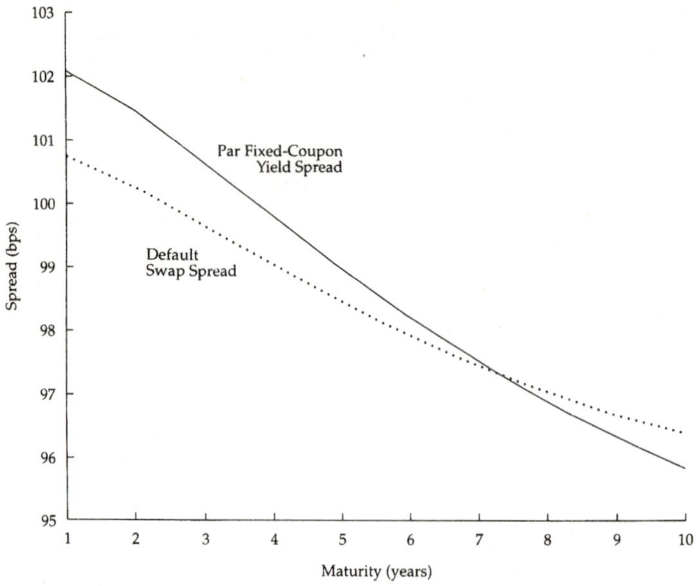

hazard rate, h, for the event. In this simple model (to be generalized shortly), at any time, given that the credit event has not yet occurred, the amount of time until it does occur is risk-neutrally exponentially distributed with parameter h. For small h, the probability of defaulting during a time period of small length, Δ, conditional on survival to the beginning of the period, is then approximately $h\Delta$. This section contains some intermediate calculations that can be used to estimate implied hazard rates and the annuity price.

The Case of Constant Default Hazard Rate.

Suppose default by Entity C occurs at a risk-neutral constant hazard rate of h. In that case, default occurs at a time that, under "risk-neutral probabilities," is the first jump time of a Poisson process with intensity h. Let

- $a_i(h)$ be the value at time zero of receiving 1 unit of account at the ith coupon date in the event that default is after that date and
- $b_i(h)$ be the value at time zero of receiving 1 unit of account at the ith coupon date in the event default is between the $(i-1)$th and the ith coupon date.

Then,

$$a_i(h) = \exp\{-[h + y(i)]T(i)\},$$

where $T(i)$ is time to maturity of the ith coupon date and $y(i)$ is the continuously compounding default-free zero-coupon yield to the ith coupon date. Similarly, under these assumptions,

$$b_i(h) = \exp[-y(i)T(i)]\{\exp[-hT(i-1)] - \exp[-hT(i)]\}.$$

The price of an annuity of 1 unit of account paid at each coupon date until default by C or maturity $T(n)$ is

$$A(h, T) = a_1(h) + \ldots + a_n(h).$$

The market value of a payment of 1 unit of account at the first coupon date after default by C, provided the default date is before maturity date $T(n)$, is

$$B(h, T) = b_1(h) + \ldots + b_n(h).$$

Now, consider a classic default swap:

- Party B pays Party A a constant annuity U until maturity T or the default time τ of the underlying note issued by C.
- If $\tau \leq T$, then at τ, Party A pays Party B 1 unit of account minus the value at τ of the underlying note issued by C.

Suppose now that the loss of face value at default carries no risk premium and has an expected value of f.[13] Then, given the parameters (T, U) of the default swap contract and given the default-risk-free term structure, one can compute the market value of the classic default swap as a function of any assumed default parameters h and f:

$$V(h, f, T, U) = B(h, T)f - A(h, T)U.$$

The at-market default swap spread, $U(h,T,f)$, is obtained by solving $V(h, f, T, U) = 0$ for U, leaving

$$U(h, T, f) = \frac{B(h, T)}{A(h, T)}.$$

For more accuracy, one can easily account for the difference in time between the credit event and the subsequent coupon date. At small hazard rates, this difference is slightly more than half the intercoupon period of the credit swap and can be treated analytically in a direct manner. Alternatively, one can make a simple approximating adjustment by noting that the effect is equivalent to the accrued-interest effect in adjusting the par floating-rate spread to the credit swap spread. As mentioned previously, this adjustment causes an increase in the implied default swap spread that is on the order of $hr/2n$, where r is the average of the intercoupon default-free forward rates through maturity. (One can obtain a better approximation for a steeply sloped forward-rate curve.)

Estimates of the expected loss, f, at default and the risk-neutral hazard rate, h, can be obtained from the prices of bonds or notes issued by Entity C, from risk-free rates, and from data on recovery values for bonds or notes of the same seniority.[14] For example, suppose a C-issued FRN, which is possibly different from the note underlying the default swap, sells at price p, has maturity $\hat{T}$, and has spread $\hat{S}$. And suppose the expected default loss of this note, relative to face value, is $\hat{f}$. Under the assumptions stated here, a portfolio containing a risk-free floater and a short position in this C-issued FRN (with no repo specials) has a market value of

$$1 - p = A(h, \hat{T})\hat{S} + B(h, \hat{T})\hat{f}.$$

This equation can be solved for the implied risk-neutral hazard rate, h.

Provided the reference prices of notes used for this purpose are near par, a certain robustness is associated with uncertainty about recovery. For example, an upward bias in f results in a downward bias in h and these errors (for small h) approximately cancel each other out when the mark-to-market value of the default swap, $V(h, f, T, U)$, is being estimated. To obtain this robustness, it is best to use a reference note of approximately the same maturity as that of the default swap.

If the C-issued note that is chosen for price reference is a fixed-rate note with price p, coupon rate c, expected loss $\hat{f}$ at default relative to face value, and maturity $\hat{T}$, then h can be estimated from the pricing formula

$$p = A(h, T)c + B(h, \hat{T})(1 - \hat{f}).$$

To check the sensitivity of the model to choice of risk-neutral default arrival rate and expected recovery, one can use the intuition that the coupon yield spread of a fixed-rate bond is roughly the product of the mean default intensity and the fractional loss of value at default. This intuition can be given a formal justification in certain settings, as explained in Duffie and Singleton (1997). For example, **Figure 5** contains plots of the risk-neutral mean (set equal to initial default) intensity $\bar{h}$ implied by the term-structure model and that mean intensity implied by the approximation $S = f\bar{h}$, for various par 10-year coupon spreads S at each assumed level of expected recovery of face value at default, $w = (1 - f)$.

Figure 5 shows that, up to a high level of fractional recovery, the effects of varying h and f are more or less offsetting in the fashion previously suggested. (That is, if one overestimates f by a factor of 2, even a crude term-structure model will underestimate h by a factor of roughly 2 and the implied par-coupon spread will be relatively unaffected, which means that the default swap spread is also relatively unaffected.) This approximation is more accurate for shorter maturities. The fact that the approximation works poorly at high spreads is mainly because par spreads are measured on the basis of bond-equivalent yield (compounded semi-annually) whereas the mean intensity is measured on a continuously compounded basis.

If multiple reference notes with maturities similar to that of the underlying default swap are available, an investor might average their implied hazard rates, after discarding outliers, and then average the rates. An alternative is to use nonlinear least-squares fitting or some similar pragmatic estimation procedure. The reference notes may, however, have important institutional differences that will affect relative recovery. For example, in negotiated workouts, one investor group may be favored over another for bargaining reasons.

Default swaps seem to serve, at least currently, as a benchmark for credit pricing. For example, if the at-market default swap quote, U^*, is available and an investor wishes to estimate the implied risk-neutral hazard rate, the process is to solve $U(h, T, f) = U^*$ for h. As suggested previously, the model result depends more or less linearly on the modeling

Figure 5. Hazard Rate Implied by Spread and Expected Recovery

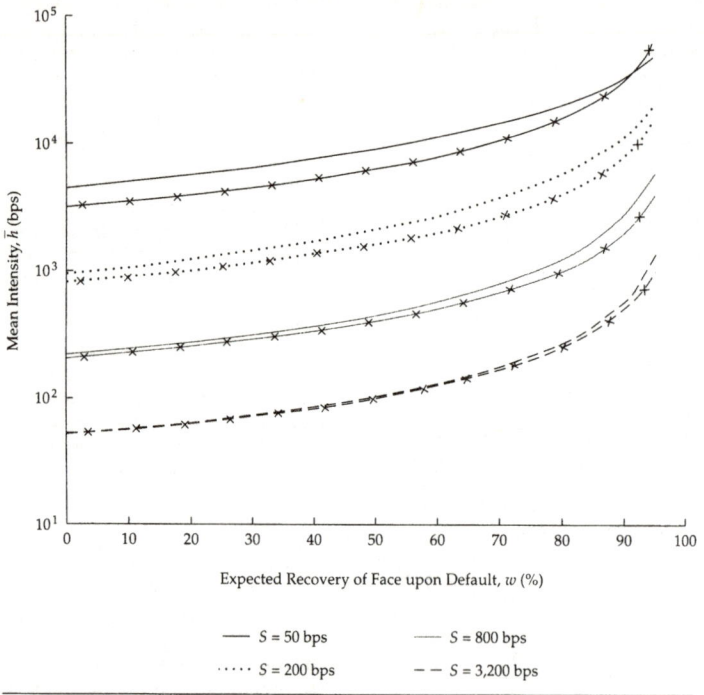

Note: Lines with cross marks are the approximations.

assumption for the expected fractional loss at default. Sensitivity analysis is warranted if the objective is to apply the hazard-rate estimate to price an issue that has substantially different cash flow features from those of the reference default swap.

The Term Structure of Hazard Rates. If the reference credit's pricing information is for maturities different from the maturity of the credit swap, an investor is advised to estimate the term structure of hazard rates. For example, one could assume that the hazard rate between coupon dates $T(i-1)$ and $T(i)$ is $h(i)$. In this case, given the vector $h = [h(1), \ldots, h(n)]$, and assuming equal intercoupon time intervals, we have the more general calculations:

$$a_i(h) = \exp\{-[H(i) + y(i)]T(i)\},$$

where

$$H(i) = \frac{h_1 + \ldots + h_i}{i},$$

and

$$b_i(h) = \exp[-y(i)T(i)]\{\exp[-H(i-1)T(i-1)] - \exp[-H(i)T(i)]\}.$$

Following these changes, the previous results apply.

Because of the well-established dependence of credit spreads on maturity, the wise analyst will consider the term structure when valuing credit swaps or inferring default probabilities from credit swap spreads.

When information regarding the shape of the term structure of hazard rates for the reference entity C is critical but not available, a pragmatic approach is to assume that the shape is that of comparable issues. For example, one might use the shape implied by Bloomberg par yield spreads for issues of the same credit rating and sector and then scale the implied hazard rates to match the pricing available for the reference entity. This *ad hoc* approach is subject to the modeler's judgment.

A more sophisticated approach to estimating hazard rates is to build a term-structure model for a stochastically varying risk-neutral intensity process, as in Duffie (1998a), Duffie and Singleton (1997), Jarrow and Turnbull (1995), or Lando (1998). Default swap pricing is reasonably robust, however, to the model of intensities, calibrated to given spread correlations and volatilities. For example, **Figure 6** shows that default swap spreads do not depend significantly on how much the default arrival intensity is assumed to change with each 100 bp change in the short-term rates. The effect of default-risk volatility on default swap spreads becomes pronounced only at relatively high levels of volatility of h, as indicated in **Figure 7**. For this figure, volatility was measured as percentage standard deviation, at initial conditions, for an intensity model in the style of Cox–Ingersoll–Ross. The effect of volatility arises essentially from Jensen's inequality.[15]

Even the general structure of the defaultable term-structure model may not be critical for determining default swap spreads. For example, **Figure 8** shows par coupon yield spreads for two term-structure models. One, the RMV model, is based on Duffie and Singleton (1997) and assumes recovery of 50 percent of *market value* at default. The other, the RFV model, assumes recovery of 50 percent of *face value* at default. Despite the difference in recovery assumptions, with no attempt to calibrate the two models to given prices, the implied term structures are similar. With calibration to a reference bond of maturity similar to that of the underlying bond, the match of credit swap spreads implied by the two models would be even closer. (This discussion does not, however, address the relative pricing of callable or convertible bonds with these two classes of models.)

Some cautions or extensions are as follows:

- The risk-neutral hazard-rate need not be the same as the hazard rate under an objective probability measure. The "objective" (actual) hazard rate is never used here.
- Even if hazard rates are stochastic, the previous calculations apply as long as they are independent (risk-neutrally) of interest rates. In such a case, one simply interprets $h(i)$ to be the rate of arrival of default during the ith interval, conditional only on survival to the beginning of that interval. This "forward default rate" is by definition deterministic.[16]

Figure 6. Two-Year Default Swap Spread by Expected Response of Default Intensity to Change in Short-Term Default-Free Rate

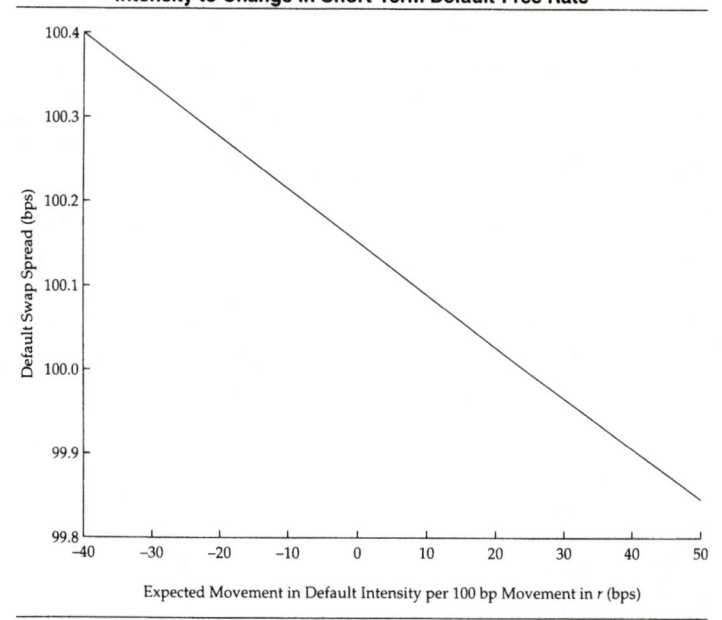

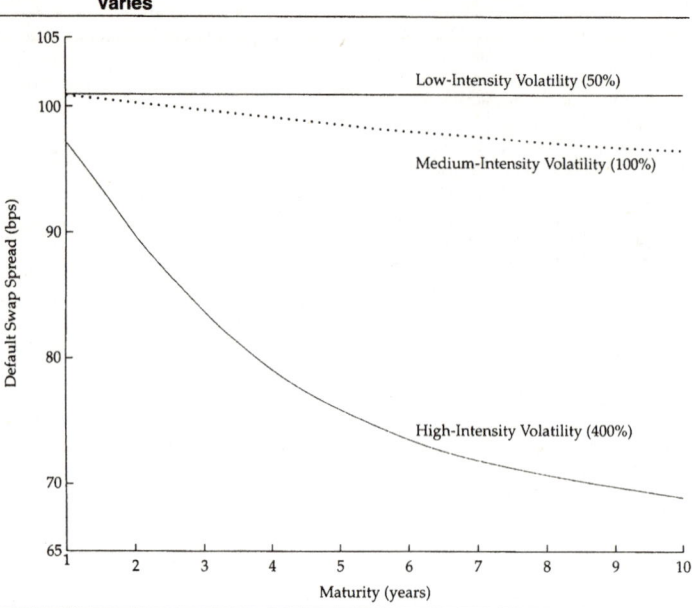

Figure 7. Term Structure of Default Swap Spreads as Intensity Volatility Varies

[Graph showing Default Swap Spread (bps) on y-axis from 65 to 105, vs Maturity (years) on x-axis from 1 to 10, with three curves: Low-Intensity Volatility (50%), Medium-Intensity Volatility (100%), and High-Intensity Volatility (400%).]

- If the notes used for pricing reference are on special in the repo market, an estimate of the "hidden" specialness, Y, should be included in the preceding calculations as an add-on to the floating-rate spread, $\tilde{S}$, or the fixed-rate coupon, c, when estimating the implied risk-neutral hazard rate, h.
- If necessary, one can use actuarial data on default incidence for comparable companies and adjust the estimated actual default arrival rate by a multiplicative corrective risk-premium factor, estimated cross-sectionally perhaps, to incorporate a risk premium.[17]
- If one assumes "instant" payment at default, rather than payment at the subsequent coupon date, the factor $b_i(h)$ is replaced by

$$b_i^*(h) = \exp\{-[y(i-1) + H(i-1)]T(i-1)\,k_i[h(i)]\},$$

where

$$k_i[h(i)] = \frac{h(i)}{h(i)+\varphi(i)}$$
$$\langle 1 - \exp\{-[h(i)+\varphi(i)][T(i)-T(i-1)]\}\rangle,$$

is the price at time $T(i-1)$, conditional on survival to that date, of a claim that pays 1 unit of account at the default time provided the default time is before $T(i)$ and where φ_i is the instantaneous default-free forward interest rate, assumed constant between $T(i-1)$ and $T(i)$. This equation can be checked by noting that the conditional density of the time to default, given survival to $T(i-1)$, is over the interval $[T(i-1), T(i)]$. For reasonably small intercoupon periods, default probabilities, and interest rates, the impact of assuming instant recovery rather than recovery at the subsequent coupon date is relatively small.

The Role of Asset Swaps

An asset swap is a derivative security that can be viewed in its simplest version as a portfolio consisting of a fixed-rate note and an interest rate swap that pays the fixed rate and receives the floating rate to the stated maturity of the underlying fixed-rate note. The fixed rate on the interest rate swap is conventionally chosen so that the asset swap is valued at par when traded. An important aspect is that the net coupons of the interest-rate swap are exchanged through maturity even if the underlying note defaults and its coupon payments are thereby discontinued.

Recently, the markets for many fixed-rate notes have sometimes been less liquid than the markets for associated asset swaps, whose spreads are thus often used as benchmarks for pricing default swaps. In fact, because of the mismatch in

Figure 8. Par Coupon Yield Spreads for RMV and RFV Term-Structure Models

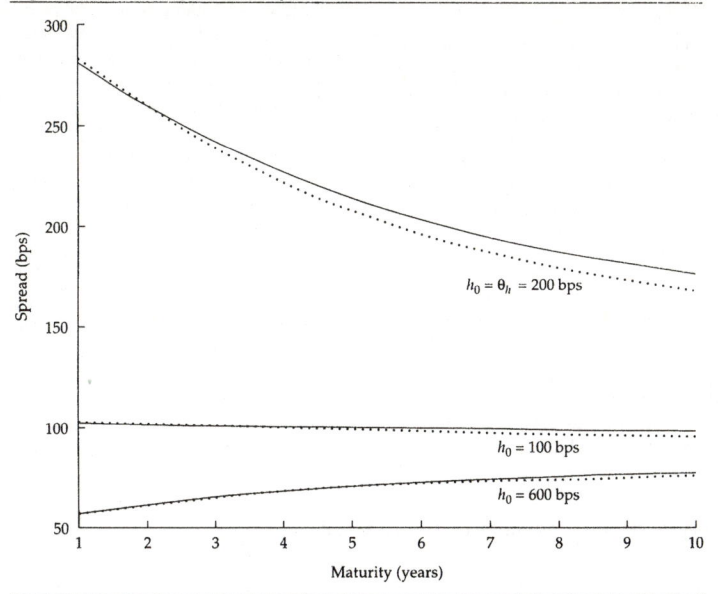

Notes: The solid line in each pair is the RMV model, and the dotted line in each pair is the RFV model, with 50 percent recovery upon default; long-run mean intensity, θ_h, of 200 bps; mean reversion rate, κ, of 0.25; and initial intensity volatility of 100 percent. All coefficients are risk neutral.

termination with default between the interest rate swap embedded in the asset swap and the underlying fixed-rate note, the asset swap spread does not on its own provide precise information for default swap pricing. For example, as illustrated in **Figure 9**, a synthetic credit swap *cannot* be created from a portfolio consisting of a default-free floater and a short asset swap.

The asset swap spread and the term structure of default-free rates together, however, can be used to obtain an implied par floating-rate spread from which the default swap spread can be estimated. For example, suppose an asset swap is at quoted spread $\hat{S}$ to the default-free floating rate. (In the following, repo specials and transaction costs are ignored, but they can be easily added.) Suppose the stated underlying fixed rate on the note is c and the at-market default-free interest-rate swap rate is c^*. Then, the interest rate swap underlying the asset swap is an exchange of the floating rate for $c - \hat{S}$. An analyst can compute the desired par fixed-rate spread, F, over the default-free coupon rate of the same credit quality from the relationship implied by the price of a portfolio consisting of the asset swap and a short position in a portfolio consisting of a par fixed-rate note of the same credit quality as the underlying C-issued fixed-rate note combined with an at-market interest rate swap. This portfolio is worth

$$1 - 1 = 0 = AP(c - F) + AP^*(c^* - c + \hat{S}),$$

where AP is the defaultable annuity price described previously and AP^* is the default-free annuity price to the same maturity. All the variables c, c^*, $\hat{S}$, and AP^* are available from market quotes. Given the defaultable annuity price AP, which can be estimated as discussed previously, an analyst can thus solve this equation for the implied par fixed-rate spread:

Figure 9. Failed Attempt to Synthesize a Credit Swap from an Asset Swap

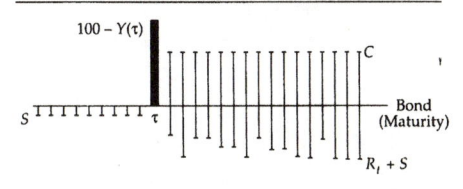

Note: Par default-free floater with short asset swap.

Credit Swap Valuation

$$F = c - \frac{AP^*}{AP}(c - \hat{S} - c^*).$$

The implied par rate F is approximately the same as the par floating-rate spread, S, which is then the basis for setting the default swap spread. For small default probabilities, under the other assumptions given here, the default swap spread S and the par asset swap spread are approximately the same.

To assume that the asset swap spread is a reasonable proxy for the default swap spread is dangerous, however, for premium or discount bonds. **Figure 10** shows the divergence between the term structures of asset swap spreads for premium bonds (coupon rate 400 bps above the par rate), par bonds, and discount bonds (coupon rate 400 bps under the par rate).

Concluding Remarks

This article has explained how the superficially simple arbitrage pricing (and synthesis) of a credit swap through a portfolio of default-free and defaultable floating-rate notes may, in fact, be difficult. Key concerns are (1) the ability to short the underlying note without incurring the cost of repo specials and (2) the valuation and recovery of reference notes used for pricing purposes in relation to the actual note underlying the swap. Model-based pricing may be useful because it adds discipline to the measurement and use of default probabilities and recoveries. For additional modeling of default swaps, see Davis and Mavroidis (1997).

Research assistance by Jun Pan is gratefully acknowledged. Discussions with Angelo Aravantis, David Lando, Jean-Paul Laurent, Wolfgang Schmidt, Ken Singleton, and Lucie Tepla are much appreciated. This work was supported in part by the Gifford Fong Associates Fund at the Graduate School of Business, Stanford University. A previous version of this document can be found at http://www.stanford.edu/~duffie/working.htm.

Figure 10. Term Structure of Asset Swap Spreads

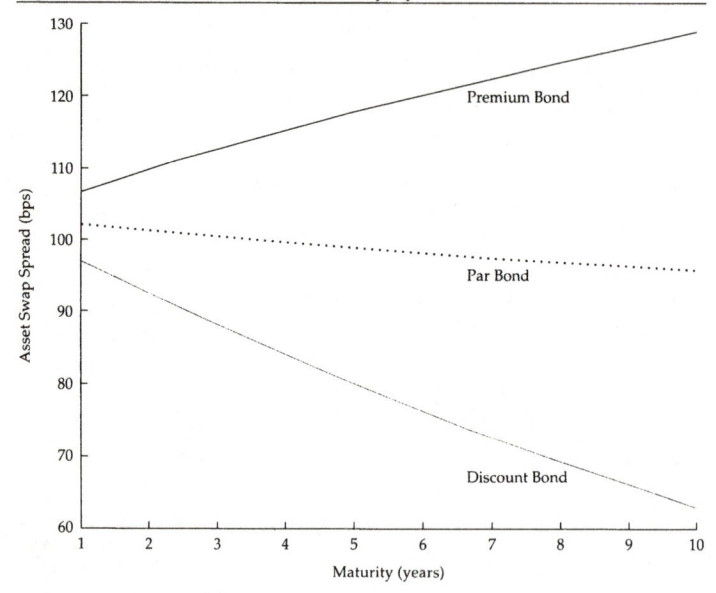

Financial Analysts Journal

Notes

1. Key credit derivatives in addition to credit swaps include *total-return swaps*, which pay the net return of one asset class over another (if the two asset classes differ mainly in terms of credit risk, such as a U.S. Treasury bond versus a corporate bond of similar duration, then the total-return swap is a credit derivative); *collateralized debt obligations*, which are typically tranches of a structure collateralized by a pool of debt whose cash flows are allocated according to a specified priority schedule to the individual tranches of the structure; and *spread options*, which typically convey the right to trade bonds at given spreads over a reference yield, such as a Treasury yield.
2. At a presentation at the March 1998 International Swap Dealers Association conference in Rome, Daniel Cunningham of Cravath, Swaine, and Moore reviewed the documentation of credit swaps, including the specification of such credit event types as "bankruptcy, credit event upon merger, cross-acceleration, cross-default, downgrade, failure to pay, repudiation, or restructuring."
3. My discussions with a global bank indicate that of more than 200 default swaps, approximately 10 percent of the total were combined with an interest rate swap.
4. I do not consider here "exotic" forms of credit swaps, such as "first-to-default" swaps, for which credit event time τ is the first of the default times of a given list of underlying notes or bonds, with a payment at the credit event time that depends on the identity of the first of the underlying bonds to default. For example, the payment could be the loss relative to face value of the first bond to default.
5. The moneyness of Treasuries refers to their usefulness as a medium of exchange in, for example, securities transactions that are conducted by federal funds wire or for margin services. This usefulness conveys extra value to Treasury securities.
6. As to the costs, a haircut would normally apply. For example, at a haircut of 20 percent, a note trading at a market value of $100 would serve as collateral on a loan of $80. At a general collateral rate of 5 percent, a specific collateral rate of 1 percent, and a term of 0.5 year, Jones incurs an extra shorting cost of which the present value is $80 × (5 percent − 1 percent) × [0.5/(1 + 5 percent × 0.5)] = $1.56.
7. If the term repo rate applies to the credit swap maturity, then $S + Y$ is a lower bound on the theoretical credit swap premium.
8. This article does not consider these effects directly, but traders have noted that, in practice, the credit swap spread for illiquid entities can vary substantially from the reference par FRN spread.
9. This rate may be interpreted as a Poisson arrival rate, in the sense of hazard rates explained later in the article.
10. The floating-rate spread is known theoretically to be slightly higher than the fixed-rate spread in the case of the typical upward-sloping term structure, but the difference is typically on the order of 1 bp or less on a five-year note per 100 bps of yield spread to the default-free rate. See Duffie and Liu (1997) for details.
11. Figures 4–10 are based on an illustrative correlated multifactor Cox–Ingersoll–Ross model of default-free short rates and default arrival intensities. The short-rate model is a three-factor Cox–Ingersoll–Ross model calibrated to recent behavior in the term structure of LIBOR swap rates. The model of risk-neutral default-arrival intensity is set for an initial arrival intensity of 200 bps, with 100 percent initial volatility in intensity, mean reverting in risk-neutral expectation at 25 percent a year to 200 bps until default. Recovery at default is assumed to be 50 percent of face value. For details, see Duffie (1998b). The results depend on the degree of correlation, mean reversion, and volatility among short-term rates and default-arrival intensities.
12. Sometimes the statement is made that if the underlying asset is a fixed-rate bond, the reference par floating-rate spread may be taken to be the asset swap spread. The usefulness of this assumption is considered in the last section of this article.
13. Recovery risk is sometimes viewed as reasonably diversifiable and relatively unrelated to the business cycle. No rigorous test of these hypotheses is available.
14. Sources of recovery data include annual reports by Moody's Investors Service and Standard & Poor's Corporation, Altman (1993) for bonds, and Carey (1998) and sources cited in it for loans. The averages reported are typically by seniority.
15. The risk-neutral survival probability to term T for a risk-neutral intensity process h under standard regularity assumptions is given by $E^*\left\{\exp\left[-\int_0^T h(t)dt\right]\right\}$, where E^* denotes risk-neutral expectation. See Lando for a survey. Because $\exp(\cdot)$ is convex, more volatility of risk-neutral intensity causes, other things being equal, a higher risk-neutral survival probability and thus narrower credit spreads.
16. This idea is based on the "forward default probability" introduced by Litterman and Iben (1991).
17. Multiplicative factors are preferred to additive factors in light of general economic considerations and the form of Girsanov's Theorem for point processes, as in Protter (1990). Fons (1994) provides information on the pricing of notes at actuarially implied default rates, but Fons does not provide an estimate of default arrival intensity.

References

Altman, E. 1993. "Defaulted Bonds: Demand, Supply and Performance 1987–1992." *Financial Analysts Journal*, vol. 49, no. 3 (May/June):55–60.

Carey, M. 1998. "Credit Risk in Private Debt Portfolios." *Journal of Finance*, vol. 53, no. 4 (August):1363–88.

Davis, M., and T. Mavroidis. 1997. "Valuation and Potential Exposure of Default Swaps." Technical Note RPD-18. Tokyo: Mitsubishi International.

Duffie, D. 1998a. "Defaultable Term Structure Models with Fractional Recovery of Par." Working paper. Graduate School of Business, Stanford University.

———. 1998b. "First-to-Default Valuation." Working paper. Graduate School of Business, Stanford University.

———. 1996. "Special Repo Rates." *Journal of Finance*, vol. 51, no. 2 (June):493–526.

Duffie, D., and J. Liu. 1997. "Floating–Fixed Credit Spreads." Working paper. Graduate School of Business, Stanford University.

Duffie, D., and K. Singleton. 1997. "Modeling Term Structures of Defaultable Bonds." Working paper. Graduate School of Business, Stanford University (forthcoming in *Review of Financial Studies*).

Fons, J. 1994. "Using Default Rates to Model the Term Structure of Credit Risk." *Financial Analysts Journal*, vol. 50, no. 5 (September/October):25–32.

Jarrow, R., and S. Turnbull. 1995. "Pricing Derivatives on Financial Securities Subject to Default Risk." *Journal of Finance*, vol. 50, no. 1 (March):53–86.

Lando, D. 1998. "On Cox Processes and Credit Risky Securities." Working paper. Department of Operations Research, University of Copenhagen (forthcoming in *Review of Derivatives Research*).

Litterman, R., and T. Iben. 1991. "Corporate Bond Valuation and the Term Structure of Credit Spreads." *Journal of Portfolio Management*, vol. 17, no. 3 (Spring):52–64.

Protter, P. 1990. *Stochastic Integration and Differential Equations*. New York: Springer-Verlag.

ASIAN OPTIONS WITH THE AMERICAN EARLY EXERCISE FEATURE

LIXIN WU and YUE KUEN KWOK

Department of Mathematics, Hong Kong University of Science and Technology, Clear Water Bay, Kowloon, Hong Kong

HONG YU

Department of Information Systems, School of Computing, National University of Singapore, 10 Kent Ridge Crescent, Singapore 119260

Received 19 May 1998

By appropriate scaling of the variables, the reduction in the dimensionality of the partial differential equation formulation of an American-style Asian option model is achieved. The integral representation of the early exercise premium can be obtained in a succinct manner. The exercise policy of Asian options with the early exercise provision can then be examined.

JEL classification code: G130

1. Introduction

Asian options are averaging options where the terminal payoffs depend on some form of averaging prices of the underlying asset over a part or the whole life of the option. Averaging options are particularly useful for business involved in trading on thinly traded commodities. These types of options are used by traders who are interested to hedge against the average price of a commodity over a period rather than, say, the price at the end of period.

A wide variety of averaging options have been proposed, and summaries of some of these options can be found in the papers by Boyle [1] and Zhang [11]. The most commonly used sampled average is the discrete *arithmetic average*. However, the pricing of this class of Asian options is almost analytically intractable since the sum of lognormal densities has no explicit representation. On the other hand, if the *Geometric Brownian* motion is assumed for the underlying asset price, the analytic derivation of the price formula for Asian options with geometric averaging is feasible since the product of lognormal prices remains to be lognormal.

The analytic procedures for deriving pricing formula of geometrically averaged Asian options can be broadly classified into two types, one uses the probabilistic approach and the other uses the partial differential equation approach. In the probabilistic approach, one evaluates the price of an Asian option following the risk neutralized discounted expectation approach. The density function of the joint distribution of the asset price and its geometric averaging is derived. This probability approach has been well explored in numerous papers for a wide variety of European-style Asian option models, for examples, in the papers by Kemna and Vorst [8], Conze and Viswanathan [2], Vorst [10], etc. However, the extension of the probabilistic approach to derive pricing formula for American-style Asian options appears to be less straightforward [5]. For the other approach, Dewynne and Wilmott [3, 4] derived the most general partial differential equation formulation of Asian option models. They have also attempted to analyze the properties of the early exercise provision of American-style Asian options. However, they have not come up with the analytical representation of the early exercise premium.

This paper presents the valuation of the floating strike Asian options with American early exercise feature whose payoff functions depend on the continuous geometrical averaging of the asset price. The value of the American Asian option is expressed as the sum of the value of its European counterpart and the early exercise premium, where the premium term is in the form of an integral. The complexity of the derivation is reduced by an appropriate choice of similarity variables, which reduces the dimensionality of the governing equation of the Asian option model. The availability of the integral representation of the early exercise premium leads to an integral equation for the early exercise boundary. The solution of the exercise boundary can be obtained effectively by the recursive integration method [6].

In the next section, we present the partial differential equation formulation of a floating strike American Asian option with continuous geometrical averaging of the asset price.

2. Partial Differential Equation Formulation

Let t denote the current time and T denote the expiration date of the contract of a floating strike Asian call option with continuous geometrical averaging of the asset price. The terminal payoff function of this Asian call option is given by

$$C(S_T, G_T, T) = \max(S_T - G_T, 0), \qquad (1)$$

where S_T is the asset price at time T and G_T is the continuous geometrical averaging of the asset price with averaging period starting at the time zero. Accordingly, G_t is defined by

$$G_t = \exp\left(\frac{1}{t}\int_0^t \ln S_u du\right), \quad 0 < t \leq T. \qquad (2)$$

The current asset price S_t is assumed to follow the risk neutral lognormal process:

$$dS_t = (r-q)S_t\, dt + \sigma S_t\, dZ(t). \qquad (3)$$

Here, r, q and σ denote the constant riskless interest rate, constant dividend yield and constant volatility, respectively, and $Z(t)$ is the standard Wiener process. By solving the stochastic differential Eq. (3) and using Eq. (2), we obtain

$$\ln S_T = \ln S_t + \left(r - q - \frac{\sigma^2}{2}\right)(T - t) + \sigma[Z(T) - Z(t)], \tag{4}$$

and

$$\ln G_T = \frac{t}{T} \ln G_t + \frac{1}{T}\left[(T-t)\ln S_t + \left(r - q - \frac{\sigma^2}{2}\right)\frac{(T-t)^2}{2}\right]$$

$$+ \frac{\sigma}{T}\int_t^T [Z(u) - Z(t)]du, \tag{5}$$

where it is known that [2]

$$Z(T) - Z(t) = \phi(0, \sqrt{T-t}), \tag{6a}$$

$$\int_t^T [Z(u) - Z(t)]du = \phi\left(0, \frac{1}{\sqrt{3}}(T-t)^{\frac{3}{2}}\right). \tag{6b}$$

Here, $\phi(\mu, \sigma)$ denotes the normal distribution with mean μ and standard deviation σ. The above relations reveal that G_T is also lognormally distributed.

Following the riskless hedging approach and applying the no arbitrage argument, the governing equation of the value of the European counterpart of the above Asian call is given by

$$\frac{\partial c}{\partial t} + \left(\frac{G}{t}\ln\frac{S}{G}\right)\frac{\partial c}{\partial G} + \frac{\sigma^2}{2}S^2\frac{\partial^2 c}{\partial S^2} + (r-q)S\frac{\partial c}{\partial S} - rc = 0, \quad 0 < t < T, \tag{7a}$$

with terminal condition:

$$c(S, G, T) = \max(S - G, 0). \tag{7b}$$

Let $S^*(G, t)$ denote the optimal exercise asset price above which it is optimal to exercise the American Asian option. Using the argument of delay exercise compensation as advocated by Jamshidian [7], the governing equation of the above American Asian option is obtained by modifying Eq. (7a) as follows:

$$\frac{\partial C}{\partial t} + \left(\frac{G}{t}\ln\frac{S}{G}\right)\frac{\partial C}{\partial G} + \frac{\sigma^2}{2}S^2\frac{\partial^2 C}{\partial S^2} + (r-q)S\frac{\partial C}{\partial S} - rC$$

$$= \begin{cases} 0 & \text{if } S \leq S^*(G, t) \\ -qS - \dfrac{dG}{dt} + rG & \text{if } S > S^*(G, t) \end{cases} \tag{8}$$

The above partial differential equation formulation involves two spatial variables: S and G, and also the optimal exercise asset price S^* depends on G and t. The non-homogeneous term in Eq. (8) contains the extra term, $\frac{dG}{dt}$, which corresponds to the change of the strike price due to the temporal rate of change of the averaging asset value.

Various attempts have been made to reduce the dimensionality of the governing equation by seeking appropriate scaling of the variables [4, 9]. We propose the following choice for the set of similarity variables:

$$y = t \ln \frac{G}{S},$$

$$V(y,t) = \frac{C(S,G,t)}{S}, \tag{9}$$

where the asset price S is used as the numeraire. In terms of the new similarity variables, the partial differential equation formulation of the American Asian option model is reduced to

$$\frac{\partial V}{\partial t} + \frac{\sigma^2 t^2}{2} \frac{\partial^2 V}{\partial y^2} - \left(r - q + \frac{\sigma^2}{2}\right) t \frac{\partial V}{\partial y} - qV$$

$$= \begin{cases} 0 & \text{if } y \geq y^*(t) \\ -q + re^{y/t} + \frac{y}{t^2} e^{y/t} & \text{if } y < y^*(t) \end{cases}, \tag{10a}$$

and

$$V(y,T) = \max(1 - e^{y/T}, 0). \tag{10b}$$

In the stopping region, the American Asian option value is given by

$$V(y,t) = 1 - e^{y/t}, \quad y \leq y^*(t). \tag{10c}$$

The above new formulation paves the path for the effective derivation of the pricing formula of the American Asian option.

3. Integral Representation of the Early Exercise Premium

The solution for the American call option value obtained from the above pricing model can be formally represented as integrals involving the Green function of the governing equation. Let $G(y,t;Y,T)$ be the Green function which satisfies the following reduced equation:

$$\frac{\partial V}{\partial t} + \frac{\sigma^2 t^2}{2} \frac{\partial^2 V}{\partial y^2} - \left(r - q + \frac{\sigma^2}{2}\right) t \frac{\partial V}{\partial y} = 0. \tag{11}$$

The Green function is found to be

$$G(y,t;Y,T) = n\left(\frac{Y - y + \mu \int_t^T u\, du}{\sigma \sqrt{\int_t^T u^2\, du}}\right), \tag{12}$$

where $\mu = r - q + \frac{\sigma^2}{2}$ and $n(x)$ is the standard normal density function. The solution to the governing Eqs. (10a) and (10b) can be formally represented by

$$V(y,t) = e^{-q(T-t)} \int_{-\infty}^{\infty} \max(1 - e^{Y/T}, 0) G(y,t;Y,T) \, dY$$

$$+ \int_t^T e^{-q(u-t)} \int_{-\infty}^{y^*(u)} \left(q - re^{Y/u} - \frac{Y}{u^2} e^{Y/u} \right) G(y,t;Y,u) \, dY \, du, \quad (13)$$

where $y^*(u)$ is the critical value of y at time u, such that when $y \leq y^*(u)$, the American option value assumes its intrinsic value. The first term in Eq. (13), when multiplied by S, gives the option value of the European counterpart of the present American Asian call option. By brute force integration of the first integral, the value of the European counterpart is found to be

$$c(S,G,t) = S e^{-q(T-t)} N(d_1) - G^{t/T} S^{(T-t)/T} e^{-q(T-t)} e^{-Q} N(d_2), \quad (14)$$

where

$$d_1 = \frac{t \ln \frac{S}{G} + \frac{\mu}{2}(T^2 - t^2)}{\sigma \sqrt{\frac{T^3 - t^3}{3}}}, \quad d_2 = d_1 - \frac{\sigma}{T} \sqrt{\frac{T^3 - t^3}{3}}, \quad Q = \frac{\mu}{2} \frac{T^2 - t^2}{T} - \frac{\sigma^2}{6} \frac{T^3 - t^3}{T^2}.$$

We let $e(S, G, t)$ denote the early exercise premium, that is,

$$e(S, G, t) = C(S, G, t) - c(S, G, t). \quad (15)$$

Here, $c(S, G, t)$ is given in Eq. (14) and $C(S, G, t)$ is the solution to Eq. (8). Let the second integral in Eq. (13) be $V_e(y, t)$ so that $e(S, G, t) = S V_e(y, t)$. Again, by performing the integration accordingly, we obtain the integral representation of the early exercise premium as follows:

$$e(S, G, t) = S \int_t^T \left\{ q e^{-q(u-t)} N(\hat{d}_1) \right.$$

$$\left. - \left(\frac{G}{S} \right)^{t/u} e^{-q(u-t)} e^{\hat{Q}} \left[\left(r + \hat{d}_3 \right) N(\hat{d}_2) - \frac{\hat{\sigma}}{u^2} n(\hat{d}_2) \right] \right\} du, \quad (16)$$

where

$$\hat{d}_1 = \frac{u \ln \frac{G}{S^*(G,u)} - t \ln \frac{G}{S} + \frac{\mu}{2}(u^2 - t^2)}{\hat{\sigma}}, \quad \hat{d}_2 = \hat{d}_1 - \frac{\hat{\sigma}}{u},$$

$$\hat{d}_3 = \frac{t \ln \frac{G}{S} - \frac{\mu}{2}(u^2 - t^2) + \frac{\hat{\sigma}^2}{u}}{u^2},$$

$$\hat{Q} = \frac{\hat{\sigma}^2}{2u^2} - \frac{\mu(u^2 - t^2)}{2u}, \quad \hat{\sigma}^2 = \frac{\sigma^2}{3}(u^3 - t^3).$$

The above early exercise premium integral resembles that of an American vanilla option. The availability of the early exercise premium term in analytic form proves to be valuable in subsequent analysis of the early exercise policy.

4. Early Exercise Boundary

From the integral representation of the early exercise premium, we can deduce the following two properties of the optimal exercise asset value, $S^*(G,t)$.

(1) The optimal exercise asset value is homogeneous in G. In fact,

$$\frac{S^*(G,t)}{G} = e^{-y^*(t)/t}, \tag{17}$$

and $e^{-y^*(t)/t}$ is a function of time. This agrees with the homogeneity property of the present floating strike Asian option model.

(2) The asymptotic limit of $y^*(t)$ as $t \to T^-$, at instant right before the expiration time, is given by

$$y^*(T^-) = \min(y^*, 0), \tag{18a}$$

where y^* is the solution to the non-linear algebraic equation

$$q - \left[\frac{y^*}{T^2} + r\right] e^{y^*/T} = 0. \tag{18b}$$

The results given by Eqs. (18a) and (18b) are obtained based on the following arguments. Since the payoff of the American Asian call option when exercised prematurely is $S - G$, which must be non-negative; and so correspondingly, $y^*(T^-)$ must be non-positive. In order that the American Asian call option remains alive at time right before the expiration time, the condition $\frac{\partial V}{\partial t}|_{t=T^-} < 0$ must be observed. At the critical value $y = y^*(T^-)$, we should have $\frac{\partial V}{\partial t}|_{t=T^-} = 0$. The critical value $y^*(T^-)$ is then obtained by setting the non-homogeneous term in Eq. (10a) to be zero, thus giving Eq. (18b).

In particular, when $q = 0$, Eq. (18b) can be solved analytically to give

$$y^*(T^-) = -rT^2. \tag{19}$$

Hence, it is still optimal to exercise the present American Asian call option at sufficiently high asset price even when the underlying asset is non-dividend paying, a property not shared by the American vanilla call option.

In order to solve for the critical exercise boundary, we derive the following integral equation for the critical value $y^*(t)$ above which the option value assumes the intrinsic value. Setting $V(y^*,t) = 1 - e^{y^*/t}$ along the critical boundary $(y^*(t),t), t \leq T$, we obtain

$$1 - e^{y^*/t} = V_E(y^*(t),t) + \int_t^T f(y^*(t),t;y^*(u),u)du, \tag{20}$$

where $f(y^*(t), t; y^*(u), u)$ denotes the integrand in the integral representing $V_e(y^*(t), t)$. The solution of $y^*(t), t \leq T$, can be effected by applying the following numerical procedure, which has been coined as the recursive integration method [6].

In the recursive integration method, one attempts to find the numerical approximation of $y^*(t)$ at discrete instants $t_k, k = 0, 1, \ldots, n$, where $t_0 = t$, $t_n = T$ and $\Delta t = \frac{T-t}{n}$. Let y_k^* denote the numerical approximation of $y^*(t_k), k = 0, 1, \ldots, n$. By approximating the integral in Eq. (20) using the trapezoidal rule in numerical integration, we obtain the following non-linear algebraic equation for y_k^*:

$$1 - e^{y_k^*/t_k} = V_E(y_k^*, t_k)$$
$$+ \frac{\Delta t}{2} \left[f(y_k^*, t_k; y_k^*, t_k) + f(y_k^*, t_k; y_n^*, t_n) + 2 \sum_{i=k+1}^{n-1} f(y_k^*, t_k; y_i^*, t_i) \right]. \quad (21)$$

Provided that $y_i^*, i = k+1, \ldots, n$ are known, one can solve for y_k^* from the above equation by any iterative method.

The following procedure is adopted to solve for y_n^*, y_{n-1}^*, y_{n-2}^*, $\ldots$, y_0^* in sequential manner. First, y_n^* is obtained by solving Eqs. (18a) and (18b). Next, we solve for y_{n-1}^* from the equation obtained by taking $k = n-1$ in Eq. (21). Once y_{n-1}^* is known, we take $k = n-2$ in Eq. (21) and again solve for y_{n-2}^* from the corresponding equation. The same procedure is repeated until we have found y_n^*, $y_{n-1}^*, \ldots, y_0^*$ sequentially.

5. Numerical Examples

We apply the above recursive integration method to determine the early exercise boundary of a floating strike American-style Asian call option whose payoff function is given by Eq. (1). The other parameter values of the Asian model are (i) annualized riskless interest rate $r = 4\%$, (ii) annualized dividend yield q is set to be 0, 4%, and 8% successively, (iii) annualized volatility $\sigma = 20\%$, (iv) averaging period from $t = 0$ till the expiration time, $t = 1.5$. In Fig. 1, we plot $S^*(G,t)/G = e^{-y^*(t)/t}$ against time t for varying values of dividend yield q. At any moment when the asset price S is above $S^*(G,t)$, the American Asian option should be optimally exercised. It is observed that the function $S^*(G,t)/G$ is not a monotonic function in t. The higher fluctuation level of G to changes in asset price S at the earlier time of the averaging period compared to that at the later time may explain the concavity property of the plot of $S^*(G,t)/G$ shown in Fig. 1. Premature exercise becomes more attractive when the dividend yield becomes higher, as evidenced by decreasing value of $S^*(G,t)/G$ with increasing dividend yield (see Fig. 1). Even when the underlying asset is non-dividend paying, that is, $q = 0$, the American floating strike Asian call option will be exercised prematurely when it is sufficiently deep-in-the-money, a property not shared by the American vanilla call option. This

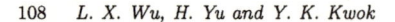

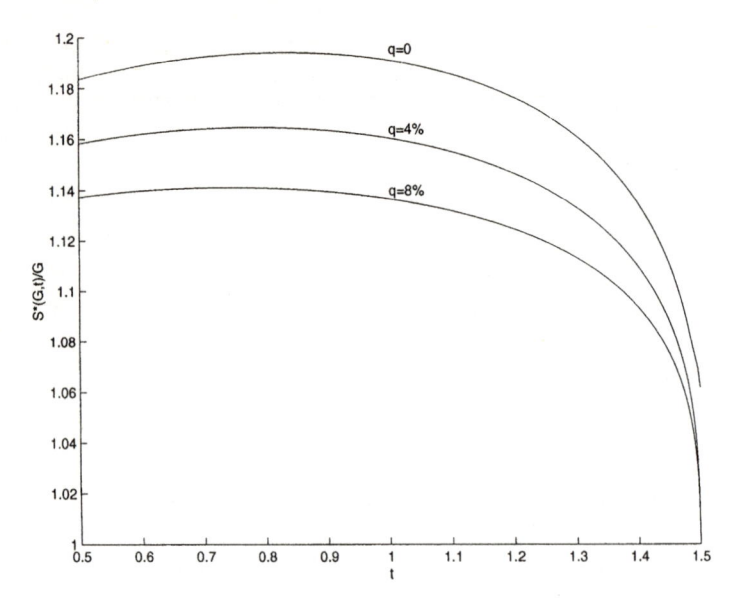

Fig. 1. Plot of $S^*(G,t)/G$ against time t.

is because the strike price, which equals the averaging price G, is changing at all times in the present floating strike option.

We would also like to explore the effects of interest rate and dividend yield on the early exercise policy of the American Asian options and examine how these may differ from those of the American vanilla options. The American value, $C(S,t)$, consists of two parts: the early exercise premium, $e(S,t)$, and the value of the European counterpart, $c(S,t)$. The ratio $R(S,t) = e(S,t)/c(S,t)$ somewhat reveals the value of the early exercise privilege, where higher value of the ratio would indicate that the potential of taking advantage of premature exercise is higher. We consider an American vanilla call option and an American floating strike Asian call option with continuous geometrically averaging, and compute the corresponding $R(S,t)$ in both models. In the numerical calculations, the asset price and the time to expiry are chosen to be $S = 100$ and $\tau = 1.0$, respectively, in both options. The strike price for the vanilla option is $X = 100$ and the geometrical average value is $G = 100$. The annualized volatility σ is chosen to be 20% in all calculations. We take the dividend yield q to be $r/2$, r and $2r$ successively. Figures 2 and 3 show the plots of the ratio $R(S,t)$ against the interest rate r for the American vanilla call option and the American Asian call option, respectively.

We observe that the ratio $R(S,t)$ normally has a higher value for the American Asian option comparing with that of the American vanilla option in similar situation. This is attributed to the positive correlation between S and G, so that the intrinsic value $S - G$ of the American Asian option fluctuates at a lower level

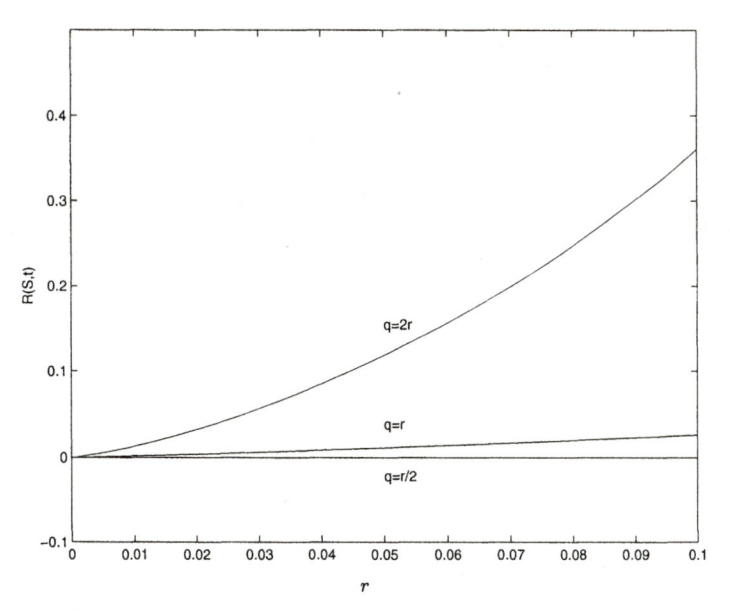

Fig. 2. Plot of $R(S,t)$ against r for the American vanilla call option model.

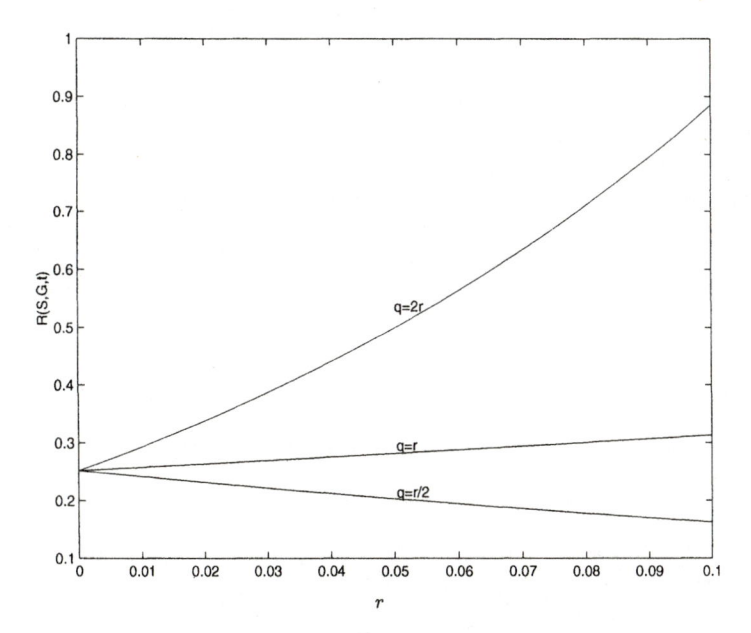

Fig. 3. Plot of $R(S,G,t)$ against r for the American Asian call option model.

compared to $S - X$ of the American vanilla option. The lower level of fluctuation leads to higher potential of taking the early exercise advantage and so higher value of $R(S,t)$. It is interesting to observe that when $q > r$, the ratio $R(S,t)$ increases steeply with increasing r in both the Asian and vanilla options. In the risk neutral world, the drift rate becomes negative when $q > r$ so that the asset value has higher tendency to drop then to rise. Correspondingly, the early exercise privilege becomes more valuable when the drift rate becomes more negative and so the ratio $R(S,t)$ increases with increasing value of r.

6. Conclusion

The apparent difficulties of analyzing the pricing models of American Asian options stem from the dependence of the option value on the stochastic movements of both the asset price and its averaging value. In this paper, we illustrate that the option value, when normalized by the asset price, depends only on a single stochastic variable. This stochastic variable is the ratio of the averaging price to the asset price. The early exercise policy of the American Asian options can be analyzed by solving an integral equation for the exercise boundary, the complexity of which resembles that of an American vanilla option. Some interesting properties of the early exercise policy unique to averaging options have been obtained in the present analysis. Compared to the American vanilla options, it is shown that the ratio of the early exercise premium to the value of the European counterpart is higher for the American Asian options.

One may query that this paper only deals with the pricing of a floating strike American Asian option with continuous geometrical averaging, which is considered to be one of the simplest option model among the whole class of American Asian options. However, the methodology discussed here can be applied to price other types of American-style Asian options, including models whose averaging is sampled discretely, and with other terminal payoff structures. In addition, more efficient numerical algorithms may also be constructed from the more succinct partial differential equation formulation derived using the scaling technique proposed in this paper.

References

[1] P. P. Boyle, *New life forms on the option landscape*, J. Financial Engineering **2** (1993) 217–252.

[2] A. Conze and Viswanathan, *European path dependent options: the case of geometric averages*, Finance **12** (1991) 7–22.

[3] J. N. Dewynne and P. Wilmott, *A note on average rate options with discrete sampling*, SIAM J. Appl. Math. **55** (1995) 267–276.

[4] J. N. Dewynne and P. Wilmott, *Asian options as linear complimentarity problems: analysis and finite difference solutions*, Advances in Futures and Options Research **8** (1995b) 145–173.

[5] A. T. Hansen and P. L. Jorgensen, *Analytical valuation of American-style Asian options*, Working paper of Univ. of Aarhus (1997).
[6] J. Z. Huang, M. G. Subrahmanyam and G. G. Yu, *Pricing and hedging American options: a recursive integration method*, Rev. Financial Studies **9** (1996) 277–300.
[7] F. Jamshidian, *An analysis of American options*, Rev. Futures Markets **11** (1992) 72–82.
[8] A. G. Z. Kemna and A. C. F. Vorst, *A pricing method for options based on average asset values*, J. Banking and Finance **14** (1990) 113–129.
[9] L. C. G. Rogers and Z. Shi, *The value of an Asian option*, J. Appl. Probability **32** (1995) 1077–1088.
[10] T. Vorst, *Prices and hedge ratios of average exchange rate options*, Int. Rev. Financial Analysis **1** (1992) 179–193.
[11] P. G. Zhang, *Flexible Asian options*, J. Financial Eng. **3** (1994) 65–83.

The pricing of dollar-denominated yen/DM warrants*

AJAY DRAVID

Salomon Brothers Inc, New York, NY 10048, USA

MATTHEW RICHARDSON

The Wharton School, University of Pennsylvania, Philadelphia, PA 19104, USA

AND

TONG-SHENG SUN

Graduate School of Business, Columbia University, New York, NY 10025, USA

> This paper investigates the pricing of dollar-denominated cross-currency warrants (options) traded in US markets. In a Black–Scholes setting, we obtain closed-form option pricing formulas for European warrants. We describe the intuition behind the differences in the properties of these securities versus standard foreign currency options, concentrating on parameter sensitivity as well as hedging aspects. We show that US cross-currency warrants can be hedged using three underlying assets although the fundamental PDE involves only one asset. This analytical framework is applied to observed prices for AT&T's NYSE-traded US yen/DM cross-currency warrant. We examine and attempt to explain the deviations between model and observed prices uncovered by the empirical work. We find evidence of misspecification in standard currency option-pricing models. (JEL F31).

In October, 1990 the first US public market offering of a cross-currency warrant was made by AT&T Capital Corporation. The security was essentially an option on the cross exchange rate between two foreign currencies, the yen and the Deutsche mark (DM).[1] The interesting aspect of this warrant is that the strike price, although nominally stated in units of the cross-rate (yen/DM), is actually denominated in US dollars, as is the payoff to the option when exercised. Hence, it offers US investors an opportunity to speculate on movements in the yen relative to the DM without resorting to the currency markets. In addition, this warrant allows individual and institutional investors to hedge currency risk

*Support from the Weiss Center for International Financial Research is gratefully acknowledged. We would like to thank two anonymous referees for their helpful comments and suggestions.

between German- and Japanese-based assets using US dollar-denominated securities. As capital markets (and, for that matter, investors' holdings) become more global, one can expect these types of securities to increase in importance and volume worldwide.[2]

The pricing of these warrants, however, introduces an interesting issue relative to standard currency options. The pricing of such options—for example, an option on the yen/DM exchange rate—is relatively simple when the strike price and payoff are denominated in either of these currencies.[3] It is less obvious when their payoffs are specified in terms of a third currency. In this paper, we view these warrants as dollar-denominated options with payoffs written on two risky assets: the yen/dollar and DM/dollar exchange rates. The price of the underlying asset, therefore, is simply the ratio of these two asset prices, which implies that the options can be priced using the Margrabe (1978) approach.[4]

The purpose of this paper is threefold. First, we provide closed-form European option pricing formulas (in a Black–Scholes setting) for cross-rate call and put warrants. Next, we describe the intuition behind the differences in the properties of these options and those of standard currency options. We uncover an interesting difference between the pricing and hedging of US cross-currency warrants. Finally, we apply our analysis to the prices of the NYSE traded US yen/DM cross-currency warrant issued by AT&T Capital Corporation.

I. Pricing cross-currency warrants: theory

In this section, we first discuss briefly the pricing of options with payoffs based on the ratio of two traded financial assets. This framework lays the foundation for the yen/DM warrants, which are essentially options on the ratio of the yen/dollar and DM/dollar exchange rates. Finally, we derive closed-form pricing formulas for European yen/DM options, and study their comparative statics in comparison to standard currency options.

I.A. Options on the ratio of two securities

Let M_t and Y_t denote the prices at time t of two dollar-denominated financial assets traded in the USA. The two prices are assumed to follow correlated diffusion processes. Define the ratio of the two prices by $S_t \equiv M_t/Y_t$. Let r denote the instantaneous riskless rate in the USA, and δ_m and δ_y the instantaneous proportional dividend payout rates of the two assets.

As shown by Harrison and Kreps (1979), among others, under the risk-neutral probability (or the martingale measure) for US dollar investors, M and Y must satisfy the following stochastic differential equations:

$$\langle 1 \rangle \qquad dM = (r - \delta_m)M\,dt + \sigma_m M\,dZ_1,$$

$$\langle 2 \rangle \qquad dY = (r - \delta_y)Y\,dt + \sigma_y Y\,dZ_2,$$

where σ_m and σ_y are the instantaneous volatilities of the two assets, and Z_1 and Z_2 are two standard Brownian motions with correlation coefficient ρ. From Itô's

Lemma, the dynamics of S_t are described by

$$\langle 3 \rangle \qquad dS = (\delta_y - \delta_m + \sigma_y^2 - \rho\sigma_m\sigma_y)S\, dt + \sigma_m S\, dZ_1 - \sigma_y S\, dZ_2.$$

Note that the expected rate of return on S under the risk-neutral probability is not the US riskless interest rate, because S is not a traded (dollar-denominated) financial asset.[5]

A yen/DM cross-rate warrant can be viewed as an option based on the ratio of the prices of two dollar-denominated underlying assets. Specifically, let M_t and Y_t denote the spot German and Japanese exchange rates at time t, specified in units of dollars per DM and dollars per yen respectively. Then S_t is the yen/DM cross-rate, and the dividend payout rates in $\langle 1 \rangle$ and $\langle 2 \rangle$ are simply the constant instantaneous riskless rates in Germany and Japan, r_m and r_y. Dollars converted into DM and yen are held in the corresponding foreign riskless bonds and pay implicit dividends at the rate of r_m and r_y respectively.[6]

Let $F(S_t, \tau)$ be the price at time t of a contingent claim expiring at time $t + \tau$ with payoff based on the cross-exchange rate between t and $t + \tau$. By the standard technique of constructing a riskless hedge portfolio, it can be shown that F must satisfy the fundamental partial differential equation (PDE):[7]

$$\langle 4 \rangle \qquad -\frac{\partial F}{\partial \tau} + \frac{1}{2}(\sigma_m^2 - 2\rho\sigma_m\sigma_y + \sigma_y^2)S^2 \frac{\partial^2 F}{\partial S^2} + (r_y - r_m + \sigma_y^2 - \rho\sigma_m\sigma_y)S \frac{\partial F}{\partial S} - rF = 0.$$

The boundary conditions of the PDE are specified according to the contractual provisions of the contingent claim to be priced. In general, the price for a contingent claim is derived by numerically solving the PDE.

The cross-rate warrant has a unique feature: although its PDE involves only the underlying asset (S), investors who wish to replicate its payoffs must use *three* assets: US, Japanese and German riskless bonds. Recall that hedging a general contingent claim written on the price of only one asset will generally involve only two assets: the underlying asset and a riskless bond. For example, to hedge a standard yen currency option, US investors need to use Japanese and US riskless bonds. It is therefore interesting that an additional third asset is needed in order to hedge the cross-currency warrant.

The explanation for this paradox is as follows: the warrant can be *priced* by solving a PDE that involves the 'price' of only one asset—the cross-rate—since only the ratio of the two exchange rates appears in the PDE. However, this asset is not traded in the USA. Hence, the cross-currency warrant is in fact a contingent claim based on two traded assets, so that investors must use three assets to replicate its payoffs. In our case, these are the riskless bonds in each of the three countries involved.[8]

Next, we derive exact pricing formulas for European yen/DM options. It is obviously simpler to study the comparative statics of these prices, which in turn provide intuition about the properties of American cross-currency options, the subject of our empirical work.

I.B. *European yen/DM options*

Consider a European yen/DM call option expiring at $t + \tau$. Let the payoff be specified as a fixed dollar multiple, A, of the percent difference between the strike yen/DM rate, K, and the future spot yen/DM rate, $S_{t+\tau}$. Specifically, the payoff is given by

$$\max\left[0, A \cdot \frac{(S_{t+\tau} - K)}{K}\right].$$

Under the risk-neutral probability, the price of a yen/DM European option equals its expected payoff at expiration discounted at the US risk-free rate. That is,

$$c(S_t, K, \tau) = e^{-r\tau} E_t\left\{\max\left[\frac{A}{K}(S_{t+\tau} - K), 0\right]\right\},$$

where $E_t\{\cdot\}$ is the conditional expectation at time t with respect to the risk-neutral probability.

Since the solution to equation ⟨3⟩ is (see, e.g., Arnold, 1974, theorem 8.4.2):

⟨5⟩ $\quad S_{t+\tau} = S_t \exp\{(r_y - r_m + \sigma_y^2 - \rho\sigma_m\sigma_y)\tau - \tfrac{1}{2}(\sigma_m^2 - 2\rho\sigma_m\sigma_y + \sigma_y^2)\tau$
$\qquad + \sigma_m(Z_{t+\tau}^{(m)} - Z_t^{(m)}) - \sigma_y(Z_{t+\tau}^{(y)} - Z_t^{(y)})\},$

it is straightforward to evaluate this conditional expectation. The call price at time t is given by:

⟨6⟩ $\quad c(S_t, K, \tau) = \dfrac{A}{K}[S_t e^{-(r-r_y+r_m-\sigma_y^2+\rho\sigma_m\sigma_y)\tau} N(d_1) - K e^{-r\tau} N(d_1 - \sigma\sqrt{\tau})],$

where

⟨7⟩
$$d_1 \equiv \frac{\ln(S_t/K) + (r_y - r_m + \sigma_y^2 - \rho\sigma_m\sigma_y)\tau}{\sigma\sqrt{\tau}} + \frac{1}{2}\sigma\sqrt{\tau},$$

$$\sigma^2 \equiv \sigma_m^2 + \sigma_y^2 - 2\rho\sigma_m\sigma_y,$$

and $N(\cdot)$ is the standard normal distribution function. Similarly, the price at time t of a corresponding European put option is:

⟨8⟩ $\quad p(S_t, K, \tau) = e^{-r\tau} E_t\left\{\max\left[\dfrac{A}{K}(K - S_{t+\tau}), 0\right]\right\}$

$\qquad = \dfrac{A}{K}[K e^{-r\tau} N(-d_1 + \sigma\sqrt{\tau}) - S_t e^{-(r-r_y+r_m-\sigma_y^2+\rho\sigma_m\sigma_y)\tau} N(-d_1)].$

As expected, the pricing equations resemble the Black–Scholes formula, with σ^2 being the volatility of S, the quotient of M and Y.

The prices of dollar-denominated European yen/DM options possess a number of interesting features, which are different from more standard currency options. In particular, comparative statics results for the parameters are summarized in Table 1, and some key results are discussed here.

Time to expiration: In the standard formula for currency options such as Garman and Kohlhagen (1983), the effect of time to expiration is ambiguous. For example, consider DM foreign currency options traded in Japan. When the foreign interest rate rises far above the domestic rate (corresponding to $r_m \gg r_y$ in this example)

TABLE 1. Comparative statics for European call and put options with strike prices and payoffs denominated in dollars.

	Partial derivatives of call price	Partial derivatives of put price
Time to maturity (τ)	>0 if $r_y - r_m + \sigma_y^2 - \rho\sigma_m\sigma_y \geq r$ ≥ 0 otherwise	≥ 0
US risk-free rate (r)	<0	<0
Japanese risk-free rate (r_y)	>0	<0
German risk-free rate (r_m)	<0	>0
Correlation (ρ)	<0	≥ 0
Exchange rate volatilities (σ_y & σ_m)	>0 if $\rho \leq 0$ ≥ 0 otherwise	≥ 0

The underlying asset is the cross-currency yen/DM rate, defined by $S_t = M_t/Y_t$, where M and Y are dollar/DM and dollar/yen exchange rates.

or similarly when the call option is deep-in-the-money, an increase in the time to maturity can result in a decrease in the call price. The cross-rate warrants have some additional interesting features. While the relative magnitudes of r_m and r_y are still important, the US risk-free rate r and the volatility parameters σ_y and σ_m also play an important role.

In particular, the price of a yen/DM call increases with time to expiration only if $r_y - r_m + \sigma_y^2 - \rho\sigma_m\sigma_y \geq r$. Otherwise, the effect of an increase in time to expiration is indeterminable. This can be understood in terms of the replicating portfolio, which consists of a long position in the cross-exchange rate—in fact, a long position in DM and a short position in yen—coupled with a short position in US riskless bonds. The cross-exchange rate is expected to appreciate at the rate $r_y - r_m + \sigma_y^2 - \rho\sigma_m\sigma_y$, while the US riskless bond appreciates at the rate r. If $r_y - r_m + \sigma_y^2 - \rho\sigma_m\sigma_y \geq r$, the long position will appreciate more than the short position. For this case, the price of the call warrant therefore increases with time to expiration. For cross-currency put options, the standard Black–Scholes result holds: the sign of the partial derivative of the put price with respect to time to maturity cannot be determined unambiguously.

Interest rates: In the usual Black–Scholes framework, under the risk-neutral probability, an increase in r does not affect today's present value of the price of the asset received at expiration. However, the call-holder benefits from the decrease in the present value of the strike price paid. Hence, an increase in r leads to a net increase in the call value. For the yen/DM call warrant, as in Black–Scholes, an increase in r will result in a lower present value of the exercise price. However, the present value of the underlying asset is now lower since its rate of appreciation is no longer r. This decrease dominates the lower present value of the exercise price because at maturity only in-the-money options are exercised. Hence, the net effect is that the price of the yen/DM call decreases as

Pricing dollar-denominated yen/DM warrants: A Dravid, M Richardson and T Sun

r increases. Analogous reasoning explains why the price of the put also decreases as r increases.

The comparative statics with respect to the other interest rates are similar to those for standard currency options. Specifically, when the Japanese risk-free rate r_y increases, the yen/DM call price increases. As r_y increases, the cross-exchange rate appreciates at a faster rate, while there is no change in the present value of the exercise price. Thus, the holder of the call benefits. Similar arguments show that the yen/DM call price decreases as the German risk-free rate r_m increases. Further, the converse results can be shown to hold for put options.

Covariance and volatilities: Consider the covariance (ρ) between the two exchange rates. A decrease in ρ results in a higher call price. The intuition behind this result is as follows: a low correlation implies that high draws of M and low draws of Y are more likely to occur simultaneously at expiration, which benefits the holder of the yen/DM call warrant. Though simultaneous low draws of M and high draws of Y are also more probable at expiration, they do not affect the call price since it will not be exercised in these states. The converse argument holds for put options.

As for the volatilities of the exchange rates, an increase in σ_m or σ_y has two effects on the options. First, we have the usual result that an increase in volatility leads to higher option prices. The second effect is felt through the covariance of the exchange rates. If the correlation between the exchange rates is negative (*i.e.* $\rho < 0$), the second effect is positive and hence reinforces the volatility effect and increases the call price. On the other hand, when $\rho \geqslant 0$, the covariance effect is negative. The net effect on the call price therefore cannot be determined unambiguously, as it depends on the relative magnitudes of the volatilities. For example, consider the volatility of the yen exchange rate, σ_y. If σ_y exceeds $\rho\sigma_m$, then it is possible to show that the effect on the call price tends to be positive. For puts, unfortunately, the effect of changes in volatilities cannot be identified unambiguously.

II. Estimation method and data description

II.A. Estimation method

Since the yen/DM warrants traded on the NYSE are of the American type, model prices of the options must be calculated by substituting values for the parameters and numerically solving the PDE described in $\langle 4 \rangle$. The difficulty with this approach is that some of the model parameters are not observable and must therefore be estimated. This introduces sampling error into the model prices; however, these prices can be compared statistically to actual option prices using the methodology described by Lo (1986).

To see this, note that the pricing equations for the warrants involve three unobservable parameters—the volatilities of and correlation between the yen and DM exchange rates. Let us denote this vector of parameters by $\Theta' \equiv (\sigma_m, \sigma_y, \rho)$. Given the assumed geometric Brownian motion processes for the exchange rates, these moments can be estimated via discretely sampled data using maximum likelihood (ML) techniques. The ML estimate $\hat{\Theta}$ has the asymptotic distribution

$$\sqrt{T}(\hat{\Theta} - \Theta) \stackrel{asy}{\sim} N(0, V_\Theta),$$

where T is the number of observations used in estimation, and V_Θ is its asymptotic variance–covariance matrix (see, *e.g.*, Kendall and Stuart, 1979):

$$V_\Theta = \begin{pmatrix} \sigma_{s^*}^2/2 & \rho^2 \sigma_{s^*} \sigma_y/2 & -\rho(\rho^2-1)\sigma_{s^*}/2 \\ \rho^2 \sigma_{s^*} \sigma_y/2 & \sigma_y^2/2 & -\rho(\rho^2-1)\sigma_y/2 \\ -\rho(\rho^2-1)\sigma_{s^*}/2 & -\rho(\rho^2-1)\sigma_y/2 & (1-\rho^2)^2 \end{pmatrix}.$$

Since functions of ML estimators are also ML estimators, option values as functions of the parameter estimators possess easily characterized asymptotic normal distributions centered around the true value of the option. Specifically,

$$\sqrt{T}(F(\hat{\Theta}) - F(\Theta)) \stackrel{asy}{\sim} N\left(0, \frac{\partial F(\Theta)}{\partial \Theta'} V_\Theta \frac{\partial F(\Theta)}{\partial \Theta}\right),$$

where $F(\hat{\Theta})$ and $F(\Theta)$ are the model and true price of the option respectively (as a function of the volatility parameters). Standardized normal tests are then available for testing the pricing model on any particular date.

Within the framework of this procedure, it should be pointed out, however, that the errors across the time-series are singular since there are only three sources of uncertainty.[9] One possibility is to treat each time-series observation as separate, adopting the view that each is unique in terms of measurement error resulting from factors such as bid–ask spreads, non-synchronous trading, etc. Here, we simply treat the confidence bands as a useful intuitive metric rather than a formal statistical test per se. In evaluating statistical significance across the time-series of the options, therefore, the results need to be interpreted cautiously.

II.B. *Features of AT&T's yen/DM warrants*

On October 31, 1990 five million yen/DM cross-rate put warrants were issued by AT&T Capital Corporation. The managing underwriters (Goldman Sachs, Dean Witter and Oppenheimer) offered these warrants to the public at a price of $3.50, and they were approved for listing on the NYSE.

These warrants could have been exercised on or before October 30, 1992, approximately two years from the date of issue. The strike rate for these puts was 85.20 yen/DM. On exercise, the cash settlement value in US dollars was specified to be

$$\max\left[0, \$50 \times \frac{85.20 - S}{85.20}\right].$$

For example, if the yen/DM rate on the exercise date were $S = 76.68$, the payoff per warrant would be $5.

While the underlying motivation for this issue is not completely obvious, it appears that the warrants were designed to be of special interest to US investors (whether corporations, institutions or individuals) who have assets and cash flows denominated in both yen and DM.[10] For example, consider a US multinational which plans to use the cash flows from its German operation, say one million in DM, to finance a project in Japan which will cost 85.2 million in yen. In the face of possible appreciation of yen relative to DM, the company can purchase the yen/DM put to hedge unfavorable changes in the two currencies. While it is theoretically possible to hedge these currency risks by taking positions in either standard foreign currency options or futures, using a cross-currency option can be justified if it is a lower transaction cost means of achieving the same objective. Based on the analysis of Rogalski and Seward (1991), there are two possible explanations for AT&T's issuing the warrants. First, the firm may have been trying to hedge its own yen/DM exposure. Secondly, it may have viewed the issue as potentially creating wealth for its shareholders based on the anticipation that investors would pay a premium for the warrants relative to their fair value.

II.C. Data sources

We investigate the pricing of the yen/DM warrant over the period January 1991 to July 1992. We collect daily closing prices for the yen/DM warrant from the Bloomberg Financial Markets quote system.[11] Closing spot exchange rate data (yen/$ and DM/$) were also collected from the same source. Since the warrants have long expirations (2 years) relative to the nine months or less for standard equity options, it is not easy to identify the appropriate risk-free interest rates to use. We use the yield on US Treasury Strips maturing in October 1992 as our estimate of the US risk-free rate r. Despite the obvious problems, we use the yield on the benchmark Japanese and German long-term government bonds as proxies for r_y and r_m. Data for these three series are also obtained from the Bloomberg quote system.

Figure 1 plots the three exchange rates during the sample period. The yen exchange rate fluctuates between about 125 yen/$ and 140 yen/$, while the DM rate exhibits a fair amount of variation, between about 1.45 DM/$ and 1.85 DM/$.[12] Note that the yen/DM cross-rate is relatively more stable, ranging from 75 yen/DM to 90 yen/DM. Similarly, Figure 2 plots the three riskless interest rates during the overall period. German and Japanese interest rates change very little: the former fluctuates narrowly between 7 percent and 8 percent, and the latter between about 5.5 percent to 7.5 percent. The US riskless rate exhibits considerably more variation. After holding almost constant around 7 percent during the first half of 1991, it falls to around 4 percent by the end of the year and stays at about that level thereafter.

III. Empirical application

In this section, the option pricing analysis of Section I is applied to AT&T's dollar-denominated yen/DM warrants that traded on the NYSE.[13] In particular, model prices are compared to observed prices via the estimation methodology described in Section II.A. Systematic mispricing by the model in one subperiod is documented. We propose and investigate a number of explanations for the observed deviations. Finally, volatility estimation and its implications are discussed.

Pricing dollar-denominated yen/DM warrants: A Dravid, M Richardson and T Sun

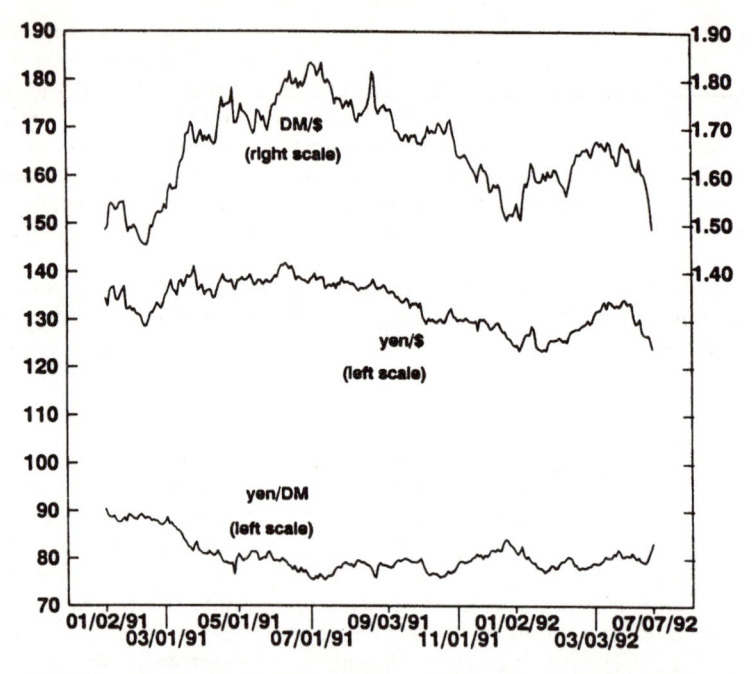

FIGURE 1. Exchange rates over the period January 1991 to July 1992. Specifically, Figure 1 plots yen/dollar, yen/Deutsche mark and Deutsche mark/dollar exchange rates. (Note that the DM/$ scale is on the right-hand side of the figure.)

III.A. Summary of results

Figures 3 and 4 graph the observed and the model prices of the warrants with corresponding '95 percent confidence bands' over the sample subperiods January 1991–September 1991 and October 1991–July 1992.[14] Note that the band in each graph represents the model price plus or minus 1.96 standard errors.[15] In order to assess the performance of the model at various levels of the spot yen/DM rate relative to the exercise price, we denote the observed prices of the warrants by a circle (○) when the warrant is out-of-the-money and a cross (×) when it is in-the-money.

Figures 3 and 4 tell two quite different stories. In the first subperiod, the results are very encouraging. For the most part, observed prices lie within the confidence bands, and there is no obvious systematic bias. The second subperiod, however, is quite different. Ignoring the issue of autocorrelated daily pricing errors, there appears to be a systematic downward bias: the model consistently underprices the warrant relative to the market. In fact, several of the deviations are between 50 and 75 cents, which represents errors as high as 15–20 percent of the observed price. The width of the confidence band, however, tends to be quite small (generally less than 25 cents) during this sample subperiod.

Pricing dollar-denominated yen/DM warrants: A Dravid, M Richardson and T Sun

FIGURE 2. Interest rates over the period January 1991 to July 1992. Figure 2 plots the US interest rate (r), the Japanese interest rate (r_y), and the German interest rate (r_m) covering the relevant maturity of the yen/DM warrants.

III.B. Pricing error explanations

We discuss four factors that appear capable of explaining our results. Although we are unable to explain completely the difference in the pricing deviations across the two subperiods, we find that all the factors discussed below provide an explanation for a piece of the puzzle.

III.B.1. Moneyness

It is of some interest to note that the pricing deviations appear to be related to the moneyness of the options.[16] As seen from Figure 3, the warrants were generally out-of-the-money during the first subperiod. By way of contrast, Figure 4 shows that they were almost consistently in-the-money—and in fact quite deeply so—during the second subperiod. Thus, similar to the well-known Black–Scholes 'moneyness' bias, our model appears to underprice the warrants during the second subperiod, when they are deep in-the-money relative to the first subperiod when they are at-the-money or out-of-the-money.

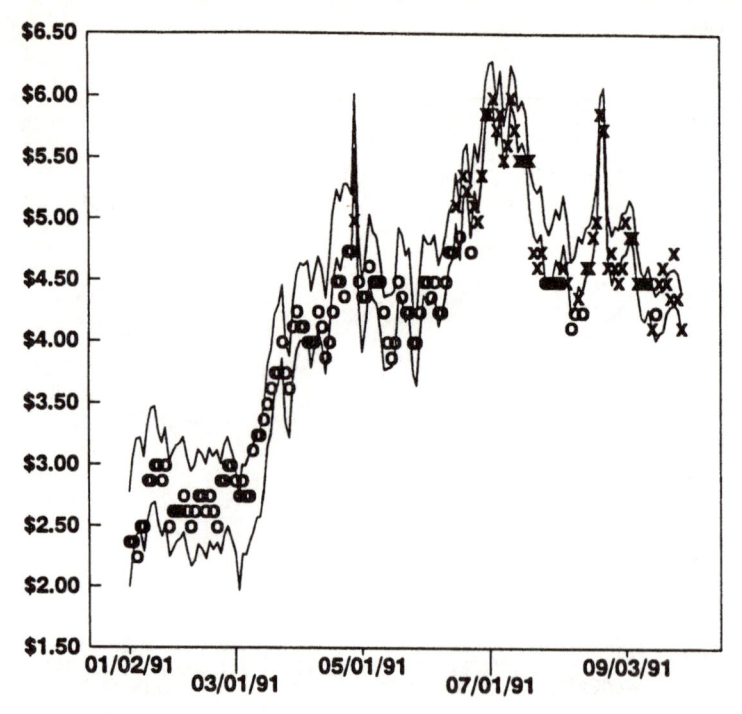

FIGURE 3. The market and model prices of the warrants with corresponding '95% confidence bands' over the sample period January 1991 to September 1991. The market prices of the warrants are represented by either a circle (○) when the warrant is out-of-the-money or a cross (×) when the warrant is in-the-money.

III.B.2. Time to maturity

It has been observed empirically that option-pricing models are more consistent for options that are farther away from the expiration date relative to short-maturity options. Specifically, the implied volatilities derived from in- and out-of-the-money options are most different for options near to maturity (see, *e.g.*, Rubinstein, 1985; Canina and Figlewski, 1993; and Fleming, 1993). To the extent these papers imply deviations from Black–Scholes pricing are more frequent with short-maturity options, our results are somewhat consistent with the time to maturity biases. It has been found that errors in pricing short-maturity options are generally larger than for longer-maturity options. However, it is unlikely that such biases could explain the sharp change in the error pattern from the first subperiod to the second: instead, we might expect the magnitude of the errors to increase gradually as we approach maturity.

II.B.3. Trading volume

We find a major difference in the volume of contracts traded during the two

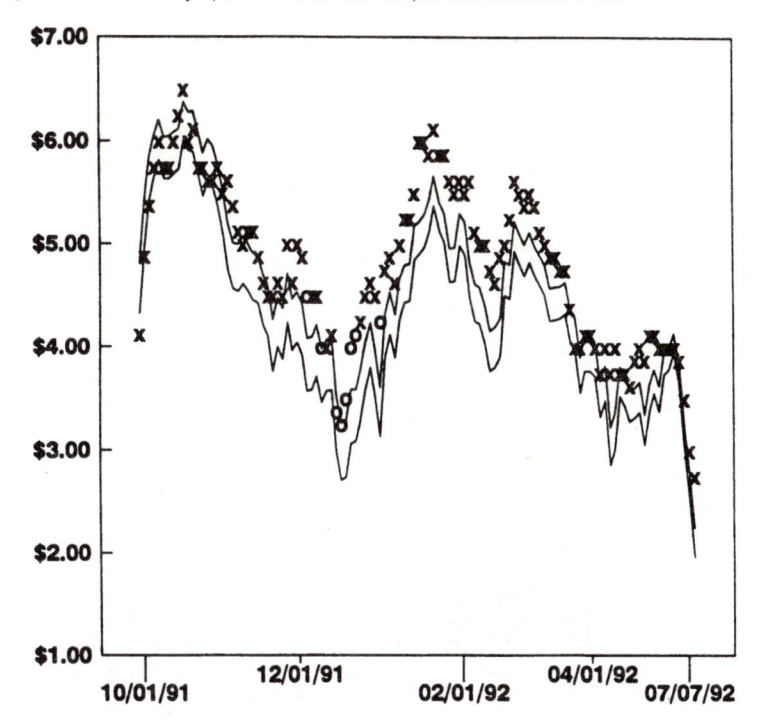

Pricing dollar-denominated yen/DM warrants: A Dravid, M Richardson and T Sun

FIGURE 4. The market and model prices of the warrants with corresponding '95% confidence bands' over the sample period October 1991 to July 1992. The market prices of the warrants are represented by either a circle (○) when the warrant is out-of-the-money or a cross (×) when the warrant is in-the-money.

sample subperiods. Figure 5 provides a graph of the daily trading volume during the two subperiods. In the first subperiod, an average of approximately 40,000 contracts were traded daily relative to only about 15,000 in the second subperiod. In fact, there are several instances during the latter when the warrant does not trade at all for intervals between one and five days. This decrease in volume in the latter period has two adverse effects.

First, note that the observed warrant prices are not identified as bid or ask prices. Since the size of the bid–ask spread is inversely related to liquidity, for which trading volume serves as a proxy, pricing deviations may be partially attributable to an increase in the bid–ask bias. Secondly, the warrant data are more likely to be non-synchronous with respect to exchange rate data when there is low volume.

However, even if we account for the correlation from one observation to the next, it seems unlikely that bid–ask spreads could consistently lead to a systematic upward bias in the traded price, unless every closing transaction were initiated by a buy order. Similarly, the likelihood that non-synchronous data would cause a systematic bias seems remote. Both these factors certainly serve to reduce the

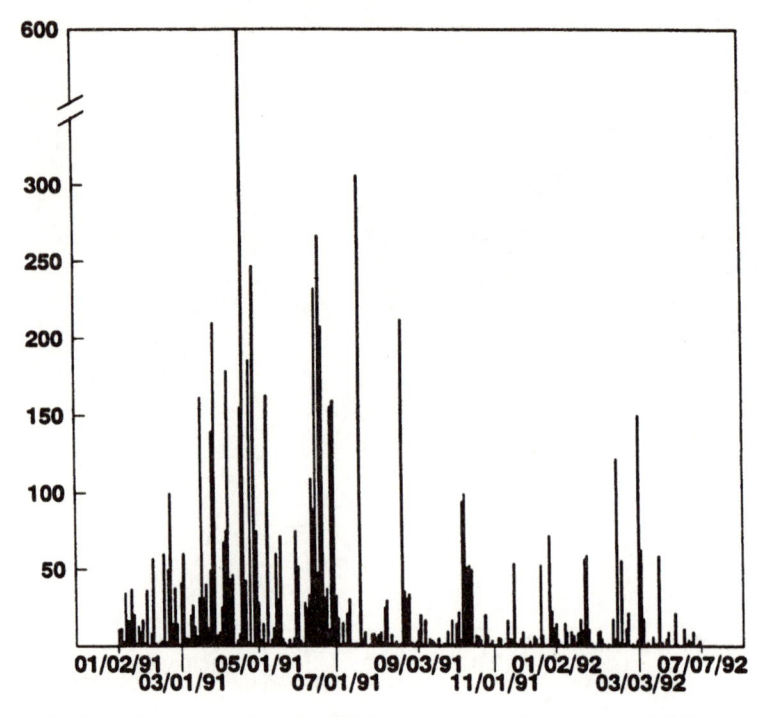

Pricing dollar-denominated yen/DM warrants: A Dravid, M Richardson and T Sun

FIGURE 5. The daily volume of the yen/DM warrants over the sample period January 1991 to July 1992.

reliability of the observed data, but the effects of this type of measurement error should not generally result in a systematic bias.

III.B.4. Credit risk

As discussed earlier, the warrants under investigation are unsecured liabilities issued by AT&T Capital Corporation. They are not backed by the Options Clearing Corporation or any other guarantor. Hence, investors may justifiably demand a default risk premium for holding them. A possible explanation for the differences between the results in the two subperiods could lie in a change in the perceived credit risk associated with the warrants. Using the LEXIS/NEXIS database, we conducted an electronic search for news stories relating to AT&T during the entire period between September 15 and October 15. Recall that the change in the performance of the model begins around October 1. We found that the long-term debt of AT&T and its subsidiaries was upgraded on September 25, 1991 by Duff and Phelps from AA-Minus to AA-Plus. It was also removed from their rating watch-unfavorable list.

As anecdotal evidence, it is worth mentioning that the market price of the warrants registered a large increase—from $4.375 to $4.75—while the model

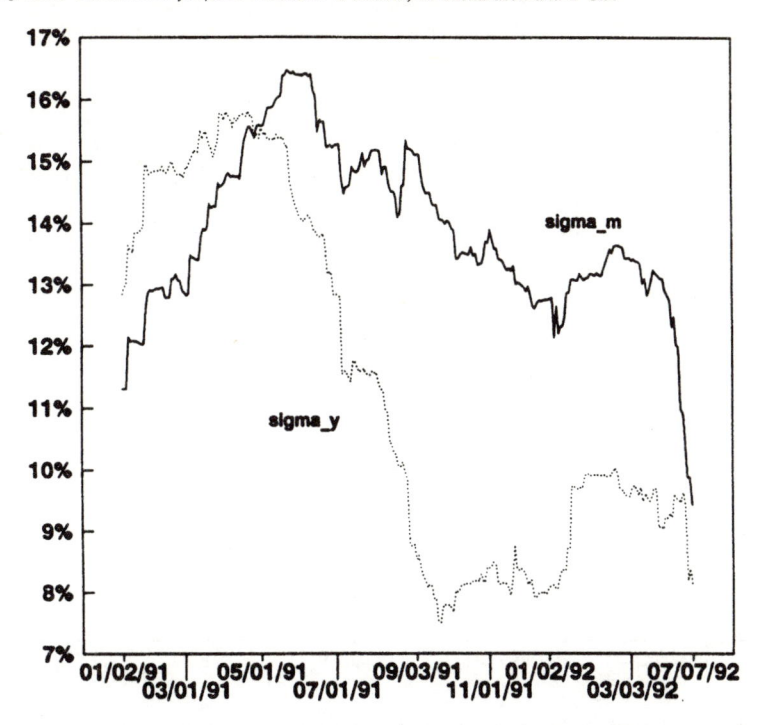

Pricing dollar-denominated yen/DM warrants: A Dravid, M Richardson and T Sun

FIGURE 6. Historical rolling estimates of the volatility of the yen/$ and DM/$ exchange rates over the period January 1991 to July 1992. The estimates are calculated using the past 100 observations on the exchange rates via maximum likelihood.

price hardly moved at all—from $4.44 to $4.46—on September 25. Thus, as a result of this change in credit rating, it appears as though investors viewed the warrants as being less risky in the second subperiod, and consequently bid up their prices relative to the first subperiod. The fact that the warrants are deep-in-the-money during the second subperiod complements this explanation: if the warrants were deep-out-of-the-money and the probability of exercising them were very small, the ability of the issuer to pay off the warrantholders upon exercise would not be an issue. Credit risk is obviously of much greater significance when the warrants are likely to be exercised.[17]

III.C. Model misspecification: evidence from implied volatilities

In our pricing model, we assume that yen and DM exchange rates follow geometric Brownian motions. There is evidence that exchange rate processes may be characterized by stochastic volatility.[18] As discussed earlier, there are also instances of large changes in daily exchange rates, which may be construed as evidence in favor of modeling them as jump-diffusions.[19] Any explanation along these lines, however, would need to account for both the satisfactory performance

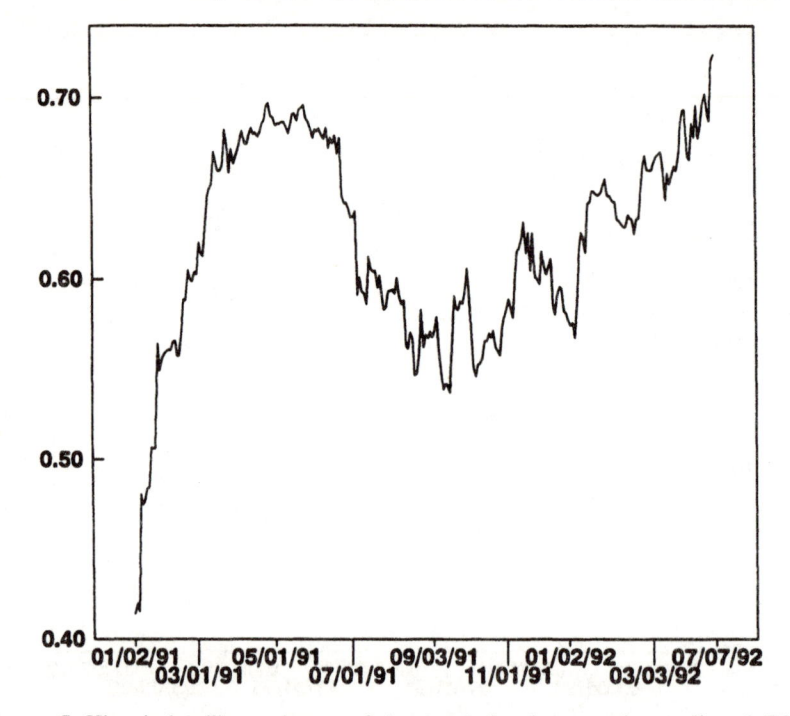

FIGURE 7. Historical rolling estimates of the correlation between the yen/$ and DM/$ exchange rates over the period January 1991 to July 1992. The estimates are calculated using the past 100 observations on the exchange rates via maximum likelihood.

of the model in the first subperiod, as well as its systematic underpricing during the second subperiod.

In the context of the pricing model, to further understand the effect of volatility, Figure 6 plots rolling estimates of the sample volatilities for the yen and DM, while Figure 7 plots their correlation coefficient.[20] Correlation across observations aside, the three parameter estimates seem to exhibit fluctuations during the sample period. Of particular importance, there is a general decline in the level of volatilities between the two subperiods in question. In order to assess the impact of these changing parameters on the warrant, Figure 8 plots σ as defined in $\langle 7 \rangle$, which plays the role of the 'effective volatility' for the options in question. After fluctuating narrowly between about 12 percent and 13 percent until September 1991, the volatility exhibits a downward trend throughout 1992. Although the rolling estimates are difficult to compare statistically from observation to observation, a formal test using non-overlapping data confirms that there was a statistically reliable decline in volatilities between the subperiods.

There is, however, another diagnostic test we can perform on the yen/DM cross-rate warrants. Since standard yen and DM currency options are traded in the USA, we can obtain independently estimates of yen and DM implied

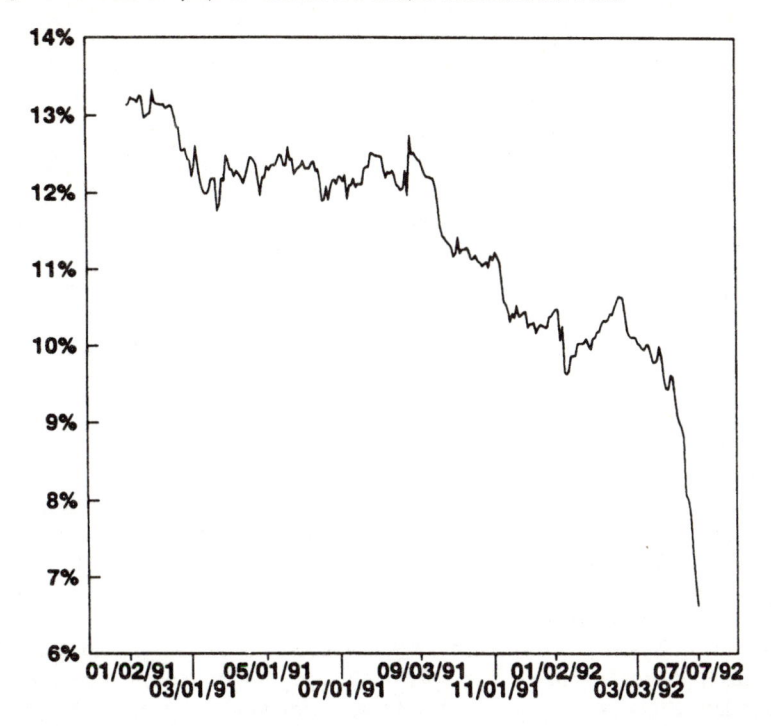

FIGURE 8. The volatility of the yen/DM cross-rate as implied by the yen/$ volatility (σ_y), DM/$ volatility (σ_m), and their cross-correlation over the period January 1991 to July 1992.

volatilities. For the last trading day of each quarter in our sample period, we obtain data on standard exchange-traded dollar/yen and dollar/DM currency call options. We calculate the implied yen and DM volatility using standard currency option pricing models. We use the longest term available, and average the implied volatilities for options with three different strike prices, all near-the-money. This is designed to minimize bid–ask and other biases that might result from the use of a single option.[21]

The implied volatilities and corresponding historical volatilities obtained are shown in Table 2. On most dates, the historical and implied volatility estimates are within 2–3 percent of each other. The largest exceptions occur during the second half of 1991. For example, on September 30, 1991 the estimates of σ_y are 7.8 percent versus 12.8 percent, while those of σ_m are 14.1 percent versus 11.4 percent. Let us assume that the historical correlation estimate between the exchange rates is representative of that used by the market. The implied volatility estimates in late 1991 then imply that model prices (using historical estimates) should be higher than observed prices. To see this, note that the difference in historical and implied values of σ_y is much greater than that between historical and implied σ_m. The increase in σ_y dominates the decrease in σ_m, as can be seen

TABLE 2. Implied and historical volatilities.

	σ_y		σ_m	
	Historical	Implied	Historical	Implied
March 28, 1991	0.1507	0.1293	0.1428	0.1279
June 28, 1991	0.1284	0.1000	0.1522	0.1182
September 30, 1991	0.0779	0.1282	0.1405	0.1136
December 27, 1991	0.0800	0.1157	0.1273	0.1170
March 27, 1992	0.0949	0.0948	0.1291	0.1112
June 26, 1992	0.0838	0.0845	0.0990	0.1084

by examining $\langle 8 \rangle$. Hence, relatively lower model prices will result when using the implied volatility estimates in place of their historical counterparts.

Unfortunately, the use of implied volatility estimates from currency options does not explain the mispricing error in the second subperiod: it exacerbates the problem. This is because the model prices are already too low relative to observed prices when historical volatilities are used. The use of implied volatilities lowers them even further. As additional evidence, note that the historical and implied estimates are very similar in March through July of 1992. The mispricing errors, however, still persist in this period.[22] The existence of exchange-traded currency options and cross-currency warrants (with similar maturities) is an example of redundant contingent claims. If our option pricing models are correctly specified, implied volatilities from the individual currency options must be consistent with the cross-currency option implied volatility. The fact that this is not the case can be viewed as further evidence of misspecification in standard option pricing models.

IV. Conclusion

This paper provides an investigation of cross-currency warrants and, in particular, the AT&T yen/DM warrant traded on the NYSE. The first part of the paper concentrates on pricing the warrant (in a Black–Scholes setting). Special attention is devoted to intuition regarding the sensitivity of the warrant price to the underlying parameters, and differences in these results relative to standard currency options. An interesting result is that three underlying assets are needed to hedge cross-currency warrants, although their price appears to be a function of only one asset.

The second part of the paper applies the analysis to observed data on the NYSE-traded American yen/DM warrant. The results are mixed, depending on the sample period—the model performs well during the first subperiod, while it results in consistent underpricing relative to observed prices during the second subperiod. The later mispricing can be partially explained by the option's being in-the-money, being closer to maturity, and having lower perceived credit risk during the second subperiod. Finally, we address the issue of volatility estimation. By exploiting the redundancy provided by the cross-currency option in conjunction with two standard currency options, we uncover further evidence of

Pricing dollar-denominated yen/DM warrants: A Dravid, M Richardson and T Sun

model misspecification in standard (Black–Scholes) currency option pricing models.

Notes

1. Although these warrants are unsecured liabilities of the issuing firm and not backed by the Options Clearing Corporation, they are for practical purposes very close to options. We use the two terms interchangeably in this paper.
2. Rogalski and Seward (1991) have studied similar foreign currency exchange warrants (FCEWs) issued by other corporations. In their view, such securities are demanded by investors for hedging or speculative purposes. They claim further that corporations help complete markets by issuing these 'innovative securities', whilst simultaneously creating shareholder wealth because the securities appear to be overpriced in the market. At the same time, they recognize that issuing corporations may be hedging their own foreign currency exposure by issuing such warrants.
3. Traditional currency options were first studied, among others, by Garman and Kohlhagen (1983) and Grabbe (1983). For more recent work, see, *e.g.*, Hull and White (1987) and Shastri and Tandon (1987). Melino and Turnbull (1990) and Amin and Jarrow (1991) extend pricing models to allow for stochastic volatility and interest rates respectively.
4. This approach to pricing two risky assets has been recently applied to foreign index warrants. See, *e.g.*, Gruca and Ritchken (1991), Rumsey (1991), Dravid *et al.* (1993), Reiner (1992) and Wei (1992a, 1992b, 1992c). For cross-currency warrants, Rumsey (1991) discusses volatility estimation in this framework. Independently Gruca and Ritchken (1991) and Ritchken and Sankarasubramanian (1991) have derived theoretical results similar to those in this paper.
5. The above discussion is generally valid as long as the stochastic volatilities and the interest rate satisfy regularity conditions, as shown by Huang (1985). However, in order to provide intuition and to perform simple empirical tests of our model, we assume standard Black–Scholes assumptions throughout the rest of the paper, namely that the instantaneous volatilities and the interest rates are all constant. Equivalently, M and Y are assumed to follow correlated geometric Brownian motions.
6. Alternatively, let $B_t \equiv e^{\int_0^t r_t dt}$, $B_{m,t} \equiv e^{\int_0^t r_{m,t} dt}$, and $B_{y,t} \equiv e^{\int_0^t r_{y,t} dt}$. Then for US investors MB_m/B and YB_y/B are martingales under the risk-neutral probability, which implies $\langle 1 \rangle$ and $\langle 2 \rangle$.
7. Heuristically, the portfolio consisting of one unit of F, $\left(\frac{\partial F}{\partial S}\frac{M}{Y^2}\right)$ units of Y, and $\left(-\frac{\partial F}{\partial S}\frac{1}{Y}\right)$ units of M is locally riskless because the diffusion term of $\left(dF + \frac{\partial F}{\partial S}\frac{M}{Y^2}dY - \frac{\partial F}{\partial S}\frac{1}{Y}dM\right)$ is zero. Therefore, the portfolio should yield a rate of return r, which implies equation $\langle 4 \rangle$.
8. The hedge ratios for the Japanese bond $\left(\frac{\partial F}{\partial S}\frac{M}{Y^2}\right)$ and the German bond $\left(\frac{\partial F}{\partial S}\frac{1}{Y}\right)$ are related to each other through the cross-rate M/Y, which eliminates one variable from the PDE. Thus, a reduction in the dimensionality of the PDE is obtained, which does not carry through to the hedge portfolio.
9. In the empirical work, we actually employ rolling estimates of the parameters, so some additional uncertainty in the estimation is introduced. Nevertheless, these rolling estimates will be highly correlated.
10. An NYSE official stated that the warrants would 'for the first time provide retail investors in the U.S. with the opportunity to invest in a security based on the relative movements of two foreign currencies. This is an important addition to the choices available to investors and another step forward in the global reach and diversity of investments available at the NYSE.'
11. In order to verify the accuracy of the data, prices and trading volumes of the warrants on several randomly selected days were checked against data published in the *Wall Street Journal*. No errors were found.

12. In fact, there were a few days during the sample period on which the DM rate changed dramatically. For example, on April 30, the rate rose to 1.708 DM/$ relative to 1.783 on April 29. Again, on January 9, 1992, the rate fell to 1.5617 DM/$ from 1.508 on January 8. These large changes were ignored in computing the 100-day rolling historical volatilties discussed later.
13. The empirical results for US cross-rate warrants are obtained by employing the implicit finite difference method to solve the fundamental PDE $\langle 4 \rangle$ numerically.
14. The sample period is subdivided based on differences in the results.
15. The ML estimates of the parameters Θ are computed using the 100 most recent observations on the exchange rates, providing 'heuristic' confidence intervals around each estimated model price. As mentioned in Section II.A, over the sample period, warrant prices and pricing errors will be highly correlated from one observation to the next. One needs to be cautious, therefore, in evaluating the pricing errors jointly in a formal statistical setting.
16. 'Moneyness' is defined with respect to the present value of the exercise price.
17. In addition to the search for news pertaining to AT&T, we also look for major macroeconomic news related to Japan, Germany and the USA during the same period. For example, announcements of changes in interest rates, currency revaluations, devaluations, or crises, news about budget or trade deficits, etc., if significant enough, could have resulted in a 'regime change'. We were unable to uncover any such events, except for the fact that during the period between October 1 and October 8, the yen appreciated against the dollar while the DM simultaneously depreciated, resulting in the cross-rate moving from 79.976 yen/DM to 76.503 yen/DM, a gain of almost 4 percent. During this period, the price of the warrants increased from $4.125 to $6.000 or 45 percent, as the puts moved deeper into the money.
18. See McFarland *et al.* (1982), Hsieh (1986), Boothe and Glassman (1987), Melino and Turnbull (1990) and others for volatility's effect on exchange rate movements and foreign currency options.
19. On two occasions the DM rate underwent large changes (see note 12). The rolling estimates of historical volatility showed large jumps on those days, and corresponding jumps in the opposite direction 100 days later. This sudden change in the historical volatility is not relevant for pricing the option, since we are trying to forecast future volatility. Hence, we elect to drop the outliers when we compute historical volatility. We also repeated the tests with the outliers included, and found that the results were qualitatively unchanged.
20. These are, of course, the same values that are used to compute model prices for the warrants.
21. The three implied estimates of σ_y and σ_m at each date are all within 1 percent of each other. Of course, the implied volatilities are calculated from shorter-term options than the yen/DM warrants. The market's volatility expectations over longer horizons may well be different, possibly higher. Any explanation along these lines, however, would need to reconcile Figures 3 and 4.
22. An additional assumption, which is not satisfied by the data, is the assumption of constant interest rates (see Figure 2). A detailed examination of how stochastic interest rates affects the pricing of these options is beyond the scope of the paper. Nevertheless, related work by Wei (1992b) in examining theoretical implications of stochastic interest rates in pricing Nikkei index options (which are also denominated in dollars) suggests that this assumption is not important. We surmise that similar results may follow here.

References

AMIN, K. AND R. JARROW, 'Pricing foreign currency options under stochastic interest rates,' *Journal of International Money and Finance*, September 1991, **10**: 310–329.

ARNOLD, L., *Stochastic Differential Equations: Theory and Applications*, Wiley-Interscience, New York, NY, 1974.

BLACK, F. AND M. SCHOLES, 'The pricing of options and corporate liabilities,' *Journal of Political Economy*, June 1973, **81**: 637–654.

BOOTHE, P. AND D. GLASSMAN, 'The statistical distribution of exchange rates,' *Journal of International Economics*, May 1987, **22**: 297–319.

CANINA, L. AND S. FIGLEWSKI, 'The informational content of implied volatility,' *Review of Financial Studies*, 1993, **6**: 659–681.

DRAVID, A., M. RICHARDSON AND T. SUN, 'Pricing foreign index contingent claims: an application to Nikkei index warrants,' *Journal of Derivatives*, 1993, **1**: 33–51.

FLEMING, J., 'The rationality of market volatility forecasts implied by S&P 100 Index option prices,' working paper, Fuqua School of Business, Duke University, 1993.

GARMAN, M. AND S. KOHLHAGEN, 'Foreign currency option values,' *Journal of International Money and Finance*, December 1983, **2**: 231–237.

GRABBE, J. O., 'The pricing of call and put options on foreign exchange,' *Journal of International Money and Finance*, December 1983, **2**: 239–253.

GRUCA, E. AND P. RITCHKEN, 'Exchange-traded foreign warrants,' working paper, Case Western Reserve University, 1991.

HSIEH, D., 'The statistical properties of daily exchange rates,' *Journal of International Economics*, 1986, **5**: 234–250.

HARRISON, J. M. AND D. KREPS, 'Martingales and arbitrage in multiperiod securities markets,' *Journal of Economic Theory*, June 1979, **20**: 381–408.

HUANG, C. F., 'Information structures and viable price systems,' *Journal of Mathematical Economics*, 1985, **14**: 215–240.

HULL, J. AND A. WHITE, 'Hedging the risks from writing foreign currency options,' *Journal of International Money and Finance*, June 1987, **6**: 131–152.

KENDALL, M. AND A. STUART, *Advanced Theory of Statistics*, Vol. 2, Macmillan, New York, 1979.

LO, A., 'Statistical tests of contingent-claims asset-pricing models,' *Journal of Financial Economics*, September 1986, **17**: 143–173.

MARGRABE, W., 'The value of an option to exchange one asset for another,' *Journal of Finance*, March 1978, **33**: 177–186.

MCFARLAND, J. R., R. PETTIT AND S. SUNG, 'The distribution of foreign exchange price changes: trading day effects and risk measurement,' *Journal of Finance*, June 1982, **37**: 693–715.

MELINO, A. AND S. TURNBULL, 'Pricing foreign currency options with stochastic volatility,' *Journal of Econometrics*, July/August 1990, **45**: 239–265.

REINER, E., 'Quanto mechanics,' *Risk*, 1992, **5**: 59–63.

RITCHKEN, P. AND L. SANKARASUBRAMANIAN, 'On contingent claim valuation in a stochastic interest rate economy,' working paper, Univerisity of Southern California, 1991.

ROGALSKI, R. AND J. SEWARD, 'Corporate issues of foreign currency exchange warrants,' *Journal of Financial Economics*, December 1991, **30**: 347–366.

RUBINSTEIN, M., 'Nonparametric tests of alternative option pricing models using all reported trades and quotes on the 30 most active CBOE option classes from August 23, 1976 through August 3, 1978,' *Journal of Finance*, June 1985, **4**: 455–480.

RUMSEY, J., 'Pricing cross-currency options,' *Journal of Futures Markets*, February 1991, **11**, 89–93.

SHASTRI, K. AND K. TANDON, 'Valuation of American option on foreign currency,' *Journal of Banking and Finance*, June 1987, **11**: 245–270.

SHAW, J., E. THORP AND W. ZIEMBA, 'Convergence to efficiency of the Nikkei put warrant market of 1989–91,' working paper, University of British Columbia, 1992.

WEI, J., 'Pricing Nikkei put warrants,' *Journal of Multinational Financial Management*, **2**, 1992 (1992a).

WEI, J., 'Pricing forward contracts and options on foreign assets,' working paper, University of Toronto, 1992 (1992b).

WEI, J., 'Pricing options on foreign assets when interest rates are stochastic,' working paper, University of Toronto, 1992 (1992c).

WIGGINS, J., 'Option values under stochastic volatility: theory and empirical estimates,' *Journal of Financial Economics*, December 1987, **19**, 351–372.

Do we really need more regulation of financial derivatives?

Merton H. Miller

Graduate School of Business, University of Chicago, 1101 E. 58th St., Chicago, IL 60637, USA

Keywords: Regulation; Financial derivatives

JEL classification: G28

1. What are financial derivatives and why do we have them?

Financial derivatives, for those who may have been too preoccupied with their own concerns to notice, come these days in basically 3 different flavors, like the quarks in nuclear physics. First, historically were exchange-traded futures and options which burst on the scene in their modern form in the early 1970's, in Chicago, naturally (though their ancestry traces back to Holland in the 17th century and, surprisingly, to Japan at about the same time). Next in time came so-called swaps - contracts, in which, as the name suggests, two counterparties exchange payment streams, typically a floating interest rate stream for a fixed interest rate stream; or a stream in dollars for a stream in marks or yen. And, finally, and most recently, has come an explosive revival in so-called "structured notes" which might, to take one wild example, let a Brazilian firm, say, borrow at 5 percent in U.S. dollars plus the amount by which the returns on the Brazilian stock market exceed that on the Mexican market. These customized structured deals, admittedly, may sometimes strike outsiders as a bit bizarre, but the fact remains that the use of derivatives of all three flavors has grown rapidly over the last twenty years. And why is that? Their use has grown, I insist, because they have satisfied an important business need; they have allowed firms and banks, at

---

[*] A keynote address at the Sixth Annual PACAP Finance Conference, Jakarta, Indonesia, July 6-8, 1995.

long last, to manage effectively and at low cost, business and financial risks that have plagued them for decades, if not for centuries.

But despite what I and most other economists, at least of the Chicago variety, see as the social benefits of these financial derivatives, they have, let us face it, also been getting a very bad press recently. Everyone by now surely has read about Procter and Gamble, that sweet little old Ivory Soap company that dropped $150 million or so on derivatives; and about the big German conglomerate, Metallgesellschaft that supposedly dropped 10 times that amount, or close to a billion and a half, on oil futures. These and other horror stories have created the impression that derivatives have brought us close to a financial Chernobyl that threatens to bring the whole economy down around our ears unless derivatives are brought under strict government control and supervision.

2. The real threat: derivatives or central banks?

So, before going any further, let me emphasize that no serious danger of a derivatives-induced financial collapse really exists. Note, however, how I have carefully phrased that: no *derivatives-induced* financial collapse. Firms will continue to lose money on bad judgment and bad derivatives deals, just as they always have in deals on ordinary assets like stocks and real estate. And a major crack in one of the world's financial markets is always possible. But crashes in financial markets are not exogenous calamities like earthquakes. They are *policy* disasters, tracing not to transactions between *private-sector* parties, but to the deliberately deflationary actions of a central bank somewhere, usually overreacting to its previous policy errors in the other direction.

A classic example, of course, has been the turmoil in the U.S. bond market since the Spring of 1994 after our Federal Reserve System suddenly nudged up short-term interest rates. And why did the Fed feel it had to nudge them up? Because the Fed had previously driven short rates far too low, hoping that lower short rates would lead to lower long rates which in turn, the Fed hoped, would pull the U.S. economy more rapidly out of its recession. That announced policy of driving interest rates down gave the banks, the hedge funds and the big institutional investors generally, what seemed a sure-fire, money-coining strategy: borrow short and lend long. The low short rates kept their cost of borrowing small; and the Fed's fears of throttling the then still-weak economic expansion would keep them low. Prices of long-term bonds, then, could go only one way: up. For more than a year, those leveraged bets on falling long-term interest rates paid off handsomely.

But the Fed eventually discovered, or should I say rediscovered, that the short-term rate could be held below its warranted level only by rapidly expanding the money supply and risking a resurgence of price inflation. The Fed thereupon suddenly stepped on the monetary brakes by raising short-term interest rates, hoping that its anti-inflation rhetoric would keep the more inflation-sensitive long-term rates from rising. But the Fed guessed wrong. Long-term rates rose right along with short-term rates and blood began to flow on Wall Street (and in Orange County). So far, the fall-out on the U.S. real economy from the Fed's monetary tightening has been small. But more tightening is on the way and we must not become complacent. We need only look to the mismanagement by the Federal Reserve System in the early 1930's to see how much permanent damage a central bank can inflict on an economy.

3. The current state of derivatives regulation

For what further comfort it may offer to those worried about the dangers from unregulated derivatives, let me also assure them that derivatives already are very extensively regulated. The futures exchanges, for example, are regulated, and very heavy-handedly so by the Commodity Futures Trading Commission (the CFTC), one of the largest producers of bureaucratic red tape this side of Japan. The securities broker/dealer firms like Goldman, Sachs or Salomon Bros. are regulated by the SEC, an agency with a world-recognized reputation as a tough cop.

On that score, however, some critics, including our U.S. General Accounting Office, have complained recently that while the SEC may regulate the dealer firms and their capital requirements, the agency has no special or specific requirements for their derivatives operations. But if you know how the derivatives business is structured in Wall Street these days, that line of argument by our GAO makes no real sense. The name of the game in the derivatives business is *credit quality*. Nobody will deal swaps with you if you can't convince them that you have adequate capital; or unless you post substantial collateral if you don't. For further reassurance to the particularly credit-sensitive sector of the market, moreover, some of the big brokerage firms have even split parts of their derivatives business off into separate subsidiaries, with dedicated capital of their own. The subs have received triple A credit ratings from the private credit-rating agencies like Moody's and Standard and Poors - agencies who do a more stringent capital and credit analysis, incidentally, than the SEC ever has or ever could. And far from suggesting any looming capital inadequacy, the ratings of the subs, in fact, are actually higher than that of the banks that do most of the derivatives business.

Those banks, moreover, which currently account for about 70 percent of the derivatives business, are themselves heavily regulated indeed, to say the least. The derivatives activities of every bank dealer are regulated by at least one, and sometimes by as many as three separate regulators - the bank officers often finding themselves saying good-bye to one group of examiners going out the back door, just as another group is being ushered in at the front door.

4. The Savings and Loan crisis and the supposed dangers of inadequate regulation

But if derivatives, as I insist, are already adequately (or more than adequately regulated), how do I answer people who say we've heard that same talk about overregulation back in the early 1980's when the Savings and Loan industry was insisting that *its* regulation was adequate. And look what happened!

But are the two cases really parallel? Very definitely not! The so-called deregulation of the S&L's in the early 1980's was less a matter of allowing free market magic to do its work, than an attempt by Congress to prolong the life of an industry that a truly free market would have ended years before. The industry was not allowed to die a natural death because residential housing and everything connected with it had become a sacred cow of American politics. Congress in the 1930's and even more so in the years after World War II was encouraging American citizens to buy homes and finance them with 30-year, fixed-rate mortgages from deposit-funded local Savings and Loan associations. By the mid-60's however, as inflation and hence interest rates began to rise in the U.S., the S&L's found themselves having to pay 6 percent or more to keep from losing their deposits, while the fixed-rate 30-year mortgages on their books had been made years before at 4 to 5 percent. By the late 1970's, in fact, as inflation accelerated, most of the industry had become technically insolvent on a mark-to-market basis.

At that point, rather than face up to closing down the politically potent local S&L industry and bailing out their Federally insured depositors with tax money, Congress gave the S&L's one last chance to stay alive, by allowing them to invest in more than just the mortgages on single family homes, which had been their traditional market niche. They could now invest in commercial real estate, luxury condos and resort properties, a form of diversification which, by itself, might not have been so troublesome. But the S&L's were allowed to support commercial property developments of that kind, without having to face the normal market tests for funding such risky ventures. Congress, in the dark of night, literally, i.e., without holding hearings or any public debate, had raised the limit on government guaranteed deposit accounts of S&L's from $10,000 to $100,000 per *account* - not per individual or per family. That would be equivalent, in today's prices, to close to $200,000 per account - a non-trivial sum. S&L's could thus raise virtually unlimited funds for speculative property development merely by offering to pay 50 or 75 basis points above the going deposit rate. Deposit brokers would then funnel them money from all over the country. The depositors didn't ask any questions about how the S&L's hoped to earn those extra 50 or 75 basis points. Why should they care? The U.S. government was guaranteeing their deposits.

To cite the S&L bailouts as grounds for regulating derivatives is thus not only to miss the point of that government-spawned disaster, but is doubly ironic. Financial derivatives, if they had only been more readily available in the early

1980's could have kept the S&L industry viable as a residential housing lender without massive life-support from subsidized deposits. If maturity mismatch between floating-rate deposits and fixed-rate mortgages is your problem, then interest-rate swaps, futures and options can be your solution. Indeed, that is precisely the direction in which what's left of the S&L industry is going at the moment. The industry has also been helped, of course, by the development of variable-rate mortgages and even more by its ability to securitize its locally raised mortgages by bundling them into mortgage pools. Those pools in turn, serve as inputs to still another class of derivatives securities - the so-called CMO's or collateralized mortgage obligations - which support many new strategies for controlling interest-rate risks, though alas, also some new ways for the unskilled or the unlucky to lose big chunks of money.

5. Derivatives and the safety of the banking system

Not only are the S&L's much safer institutions today, thanks to derivatives, than they were in the past, but so too are the commercial banks. Despite all the hullabaloo in the press, and all the bad publicity surrounding derivatives, banks are safer today, not riskier. And for several reasons.

For one thing, the customers in the banks' derivatives book are now much better credit risks, on the whole, than those in their regular loan portfolio. Top-rated, blue-chip clients had been leaving the banks steadily for many years in favor of public-market funding, especially commercial paper. Swaps and options have brought them back. And even for some of the banks' so-so, intermediate customers, swaps strengthen a bank's hand on long-term fixed-rate credits. They let a bank pull the plug on a firm when its condition is just beginning to deteriorate, without having to wait for an actual default.

The swaps and options book, moreover, is typically highly diversified whereas banks' commercial portfolios are often heavily concentrated by region, or by industry (like Continental Bank and its oil credits) or by foreign country (like Citibank and its Latin American credits). And, of course, as noted earlier for the S&L's, a bank's swaps and derivatives book can be managed to control interest rate risk. If more of a bank's customers want to take the floating-rate side than want the fixed rate side of interest-rate swaps, the bank simply lays off the excess directly with other dealers who happen to have the reverse position. Or, I am happy to say, the bank can make an offsetting transaction using exchange-traded financial futures, like the Eurodollar futures of the CME.

But if swaps and derivatives have really made the financial system safer, not riskier, as I have claimed, why are we hearing so many calls these days for more regulation? Part of the answer, I suspect, comes from misunderstanding by the public and the financial press about how serious the risks really are. A tell-tale sign of how deep those misunderstandings go is the almost universal practice of citing the nominal size of swaps outstanding and treating that number as if it were the amount at risk. Last year the conventional number was $8 trillion; this year it's $12 trillion. But 8 or 12, it's a huge amount; and if that really did measure the risk exposure, it would be hard to blame people for being worried.

Those multi-trillion dollar numbers, however, are just bookkeeping entries, or better, score-keeping entries, not transaction amounts. Whenever I hear those trillions being tossed around, I am always reminded of the two bored floor traders on a quiet day at the exchange, keeping their trading skills honed by offering to trade two million-dollar cats for one 2 million-dollar dog. And similarly for interest-rate swaps. What gets swapped is *not* the trillions of principal amount, but only the *interest* on the principal which is an order of magnitude smaller. And even that is an overstatement, because only the *difference* between the fixed and the floating rates is exchanged, which cuts it in half again. So we're talking not about $12 trillion at risk, but something like 1 or 2 percent of that amount, which is certainly not trivial, but it's not terribly frightening either, given the elaborate risk-control programs installed by all the major banks and dealers.

6. Derivatives regulation from a University of Chicago perspective

While these and related misunderstandings about derivatives have certainly contributed to the public's sense of uneasiness about derivatives, automatically blaming the public's ignorance for any demand for new government regulation can be a mistake. When it comes to appraising regulation and other government interventions in economic life, the Chicago School of free-market economics has two quite different streams. One stream, associated with Milton Friedman, attributes the interventions to mistakes in reasoning by the public. Some people sincerely believe that the country could be made better off, say, by imposing tariffs or quotas on Japanese automobiles and it is the task of a country's economists to expose the fallacies in that line of thought. The other Chicago stream, typified by the late George Stigler, is much more cynical. The regulations we see, says Stigler, are put there not by ignorance, but by design. Whatever may be the rhetorical arguments invoked in their favor, their real purpose is usually to benefit their sponsors at the expense of their competitors, domestic as well as foreign.

The field of financial regulation has a multitude of examples supporting the cynical Stigler position, as I have been showing in a variety of papers and speeches over the last few years (e.g., Miller, 1994a,b). My favorite, of course, is the campaign waged after the Crash of 1987 by the New York Stock Exchange, the SEC and parts of the New York brokerage industry for tighter regulation of the Chicago futures exchanges (Miller, 1993). The New York attackers were claiming that index arbitrage was causing market crashes and raising market volatility, which was false. What they *really* meant, of course, was that the new Chicago index futures products were taking commission and fee income away from the New York firms, which was certainly true. Such are the conventions of America politics, however, that the brokerage industry and the SEC couldn't come right out and say that. They had to frame their case in higher, public-interest terms by demanding tighter regulation of the interlopers. As it turned out, the threat of crippling regulation of stock index futures was eventually beaten back in that case, not, I am sorry to say, because we economists acting in the Friedman tradition had successfully disabused the New York firms of the errors in their reasoning; but because the New York firms became index futures players in a big way themselves. Or, as I like to say, the competitive problem between the two groups was solved by intermarriage.

With the stock index futures case and so many similar ones in mind, the natural place to look for where the calls for regulating derivatives must be coming from is to the competitive structure of the derivatives industry. Surprisingly, however, this time the calls for more regulation are *not* coming from the more highly regulated sectors demanding a levelling of the regulatory playing field. Alan Greenspan, in fact, the Chairman of the Federal Reserve Board and the main regulator of the banks, has on numerous occasions recently, pointedly refused to endorse calls for further regulation of the banks' broker/dealer competitors. Nor are we seeing attempts by regulatory commissions to expand their jurisdiction - turf wars, as we call them.

The failure of the regulators and their Congressional overseers to call for more restrictions on their industry's competitors cannot be traced to Congressional indifference to the business success of the industry they supervise. If nothing else, campaign contributions can be counted on to keep the interests of the Congressional overseers aligned with their industries. And while Congressmen don't usually participate directly in the industry profits - that would be considered "corruption" in the U.S. - they do so indirectly when they retire or are defeated and then capitalize on their contacts and influence.

In Japan, this post-retirement link between the regulators and their industry has been institutionalized in a form known, sarcastically, as *amakudari*, literally "the descent from heaven". Every hardworking Japanese bureaucrat in the Ministry of Finance who has served his regulatory clients well can look forward on retirement to a well-paying sinecure on the board or on the top management of some Japanese bank, or insurance company or brokerage firm. And while the Japanese, admittedly, have raised this and similar forms of industry "capture" to an art form, comparable, if perhaps less blatant, industry/regulator links exist in the U.S., and most western countries. The major difference is the two-way nature of the flow of top regulators and top executives in most countries other than Japan. The current chairman of our SEC, for example, is the former chairman of the American Stock Exchange. In Japan, by contrast, all senior regulatory posts are filled by long-term bureaucrats who entered the Ministry of Finance in a junior capacity many years earlier, usually fresh from the University of Tokyo Law School.

7. Prospects for Congressional action on derivatives

But while Congressmen in the U.S. have deep and enduring ties to the industries they oversee, they have other constituencies as well and it is perhaps these constituencies that are fueling the calls for regulation. Congressmen know they will be blamed by those constituents if a disaster occurs on their watch. And often even if it's not really a disaster.

The reaction of Congress to news sometimes reminds me of my undergraduate college whose rules for governing our behavior was: There *are* no rules governing off-campus behavior, as long as you don't get the university's name in the papers. But if newspaper stories did appear, they'd have to do something. And our Congress too has been wondering whether to do something in response to what seem like horror stories about derivatives in the newspapers recently. Barring a catastrophe, however, and it's hard to imagine one, I don't see them doing anything of great consequence. We may well see more calls for disclosure which has long been a magic word in Washington. It's not clear, of course, as a matter of purely scientific evidence, whether the SEC's disclosure rules really ever *have* saved anybody from a bad investment or even that an SEC prospectus is readable by anyone other than a plaintiff's lawyer looking to levy some extortion on a luckless corporation willing to settle rather than fight. But it's hard for anyone, except perhaps a cynical academic, to argue against the proposed therapeutic value of disclosure.

As for who will be asked to disclose the details of their derivatives holdings, one group will surely be the mutual funds and especially the money market funds. Some of those supposedly no-risk funds were trying to steal a march on their competitors by using exotic options of one kind or another to raise their advertised yields. The stakes in playing the yield-enhancement game can be enormous not in terms of the investment returns themselves, but thanks to the presence of firms that specialize in ranking fund performance. An edge of even a few basis points can sometimes move a money market fund well up in the rankings, leading to a big surge to the fund in deposits (and fees to the managers). But when interest rates rose in early 1994, some of the more aggressive no-risk funds that had been enhancing their reported yields with derivatives took big hits and had to be bailed out by their parent brokerage firms; or in one case, actually liquidated.

Although money market funds will almost surely be reined in by the disclosure route (or possibly by outright prohibitions on derivatives), I don't see detailed disclosures on derivative usage being applied either to the corporate customer end-users of derivatives or to the dealers who peddle them. Nobody has yet figured out what it makes sense to disclose! A derivative is not like a piece of real estate you put on your books and appraise from time to time. The dealer's book and risk-exposure changes from minute to minute. And estimates of "value at risk" often can be quite sensitive to the particular risk model being used. Model errors are *always* a problem, of course, but for these errors of mandated disclosure you could wind up as a defendent in a class-action lawsuit.

Even if Congress is tempted to win publicity points by imposing disclosure requirements on dealers, the threat of foreign competition will quickly cool the Congressional ardor. The European banks may have been somewhat slow at getting into the derivatives game, but they are in it now in a big way. These late-comer European banks are much larger than the American banks that pioneered the derivatives business; and they have much better credit ratings, always the key in this field. Tough disclosure requirements for U.S. dealers make it harder and riskier for them to do business. I don't see any American Congress cheerfully conceding this industry to Europe.

If Congress feels it must do *something* to allay the public's concerns over derivatives, it may try imposing so-called suitability requirements; that is, giving dealers the affirmative obligation of assuring that the risks in the derivatives peddled to their customers are both carefully explained and appropriate to the customers' circumstances. If not, and the derivatives later go bad, the dealer can be sued. This is a uniquely American approach to regulation, replacing the doctrine of *caveat emptor* with *caveat venditor*. And pushed to an extreme (for example by applying securities law rather than common law to swaps) that approach could effectively kill the U.S. swaps industry (or, at least move it to subsidiaries abroad). Remember that one party loses on *every* derivatives deal.

8. A closer look at some recent derivatives horror stories

The public's concerns over derivatives may also be allayed, we can hope, by further academic research into the reality behind some of the recent conspicuous horror stories about derivatives disasters. Just as a child's fears that something is lurking under the bed can be made to vanish by shining a light down there, so perhaps will the public's fears diminish when the true facts of the seeming horror stories become known.

To understand what really happened, the key first question must always be *how* the derivatives were being used. Were the derivatives used to take a position on which way particular market prices, interest rates or exchange rates were likely to move; or were they used to *avoid* having to take a position on market movements? Comparing Procter and Gamble, Orange County and Metallgesellschaft, currently the three leading horror tales on that score, the differences are striking.

The treasurers of Procter and Gamble and of Orange County were making bets-and highly leveraged bets at that-that the general level of interest rates would fall (or, at least, not rise). Let there be no misunderstanding, however, about the term "betting" in this context. Corporate treasurers, and corporate officials generally are paid, after all, to "take intelligent risks". A disclaimer might perhaps have to be entered on that score for the Orange County treasurer who might be construed as having had "fiduciary" obligations to the local communities whose funds he was investing and who therefore shouldn't have been gambling at all. But the fault to be laid on the treasurer of P&G - a large profit-making corporation, after all, whose stockholders can be presumed adequately diversified - is not that of gambling, but of gambling on matters where he had no special expertise. Loathe as they may be to admit it, the belief by many corporate treasurers that they can forecast interest rates rests on nothing but *hubris*.

In the P&G case, the *hubris* was even worse than usual. The treasurer was not only betting that interest rates would not rise, but making that bet in the riskiest possible way, that is by *selling* what amounted to naked put options on long-term bond prices. *Buying* put options can be a conservative, loss-limited strategy; but *selling* naked put options exposes the seller to virtually limitless losses if the price of the underlying asset falls (as long-term bond prices did in early 1994). That is not to suggest, of course, that selling put options is never defensible. Selling an option, like selling any commodity, *could* make perfect sense if the seller had reason to believe the option was substantially overpriced. But why should corporate treasurers, with their limited expertise in option pricing, imagine they could sell an overpriced lemon of an option to the seasoned professionals who make their living dealing in options? That's *really hubris*.

9. The MG case

The Metallgesellschaft case, by contrast, did not involve the use of derivatives as part of a *treasury* function. MG Refining and Marketing (MGRM for short) was a U.S. subsidiary of the giant German conglomerate corporation Metallgesellschaft AG and was concerned, as its name suggests, with the marketing, refining and delivery of heating oil gasoline and other petroleum products on a long-term, fixed-price basis to a variety of large and small customers in Eastern and South Central U.S. MGRM as a business operation, was betting, as it were, primarily on its ability to manage efficiently the seasonal and longer-term variations in the cost of storing oil products for future delivery. The company used derivatives in its storage management program precisely so that it could concentrate on its marketing and storage activities *without* having to place big bets on which way oil prices were likely to move in the months and years ahead. Unlike the treasurers described earlier, the MGRM team did not suffer from *hubris*. Recognizing that they had no comparative advantage in forecasting oil prices, they chose to hedge their long-term fixed-price delivery commitments with futures and futures equivalents.

They hedged by rolling over successively a "stack" of highly liquid, short-maturity (one to 3 months) futures contracts. Hedging long-term deliveries with short-term futures seems to suggest the kind of borrowing short/lending long mismatch that did in the S&L's in the 1980's. But the cases are not really parallel. Christopher Culp and I (Culp and Miller, 1994,1995), after taking a close look at

MGRM's hedging strategy - or at least as close a look as available to any outsiders forced to rely only on the limited information actually published - have concluded that maturity mismatch was not the real culprit. We show that hedged storage/delivery programs, like MGRM's, are not fatally flawed, provided - and a very critical proviso it is indeed-that top management understands the program and the long-term funding commitments needed to make the program successful. Neither of those key conditions, alas, appear to have obtained in the MG case.

We believe that the top management of the parent corporation was surprised by the large temporary cash drains needed to meet variation margin calls on the stacked futures hedge when oil prices fell for several months running in the Fall of 1993. Rather than continuing to supply the financing on which the marketing staff had been relying, the supervisory board sold off the futures hedge in mid-December 1993, a decision that proved unfortunate on several counts. The decision turned paper losses on the futures hedge into realized losses; sent a distress signal to MGRM's swap counterparties; and left the company's profit margins on its fixed-price delivery contracts subject to erosion when oil prices later rebounded in the Spring of 1994.

10. The real lesson of the horror stories

Although the MG case was a painful episode indeed for all concerned, it may serve at least to bring a better sense of perspective to the current agitation over derivatives. The real problems at MG, and at Orange County and P&G as well, trace not to the derivatives as such, but ultimately to top management's failure to ask their technicians the right questions *before* the programs were set under way. Top managers do that routinely with most other big-money commitments, but derivatives are just too new and unfamiliar to set managements' standard control reflexes into motion. And understandably so.

The derivatives revolution, after all, is barely twenty years old; and some parts of it are much more recent than that. The top managers of most U.S. or German corporations and banks are too old to have studied derivatives during their college or MBA days. Derivatives hadn't been invented yet! And the tools themselves, though far less complicated, when properly taught, than the "rocket science" image they have acquired, do require some diligent study and homework - something for which busy CEO's cannot always and perhaps should not be expected to find the time. So we will just have to live with travails like the MG case or the P&G case for another decade or so until a whole new generation of corporate leaders, who have grown up with derivatives and computers finally takes over.

Many present-day executives, wrestling with the problems, and the opportunities posed by the derivatives revolution may envy their younger soon-to-be successors with all their glib talk of megabytes and modems and knock-out options. But the current group of business leaders shouldn't really be envious. Today's young Turks, they should eventually remember, will eventually become old fogies themselves. The next generation of business leaders will have to face technical revolutions of their own - revolutions whose outlines today can still only dimly be perceived. That's the way it has always been in vibrant and progressive societies. And who really would want it any different?

References

Culp, Christopher L. and Merton H. Miller, 1994, Hedging a flow of commodity deliveries with futures: Lessons from Metallgesellschaft. Derivatives Quarterly 1(1).
Culp, Christopher L. and Merton H. Miller, 1995, Metallgesellschaft and the economics of synthetic storage, Journal of Applied Corporate Finance 7(4).
Miller, Merton H., 1993, The economics and politics of index arbitrage in the U.S. and Japan, Pacific Basin Finance Journal 1(1), 3-11.
Miller, Merton H., 1994a, Functional regulation. Pacific Basin Finance Journal 2(2/3), 91-106.
Miller, Merton H., 1994b, Inside financial derivatives. Taxes 72(12).

Part V
European Monetary Union and Implications for Financial Markets

Investment Implications of a Single European Capital Market

Stronger correlations, fewer decision variables, diminished manager opportunities.

Stan Beckers

STAN BECKERS is president of BARRA International in London.

European economic, fiscal, and monetary harmonization will cause fundamental changes in the relative behavior of European capital markets. For example, over the last decade we have witnessed a gradual movement toward a more integrated equity market. This evolution implies higher correlations, possibly leading to a reduction in diversification potential and therefore to higher portfolio risk.

In the first part of this article we quantify the structural changes that have had an impact on the risk profile of European equity portfolios. In particular, we concentrate on whether and to what extent these portfolios have become riskier as a result of the gradual shift toward tighter integration.[1]

We also discuss the effect of the European Monetary Union on the currency risk embedded in European equity and fixed-income portfolios. Obviously this currency risk will disappear completely for an EMU-based investor, but it is interesting to quantify how great the risk reduction could be. Conversely, it is not clear how the EMU will affect non-EMU based investors; multiple sources of risk will now be replaced with one source.

Whether this reduction in risk dimensionality also leads to lower portfolio risk depends crucially on the correlation structure between the disappearing currencies. Looking at the historic behavior of the EMU currencies (and the ECU), we conjecture whether non-EMU-based investors will end up with higher or

EXHIBIT 1
EMU "INS" AND "OUTS"

First-Round Participants

Austria	Ireland
Belgium	Italy
Finland	Netherlands
France	Spain
Germany	

First-Round "Outs"

Denmark	Sweden
Norway	U.K.
Switzerland	

Portugal and Luxembourg are also part of the first round, but are not covered in this study due to lack of data.

EXHIBIT 2
FTI SECTOR DEFINITIONS

Basic Industries
Capital Goods
Consumer Goods
Transport
Utilities
Energy
Finance

lower currency risk in their European portfolios.

Finally, the emergence of a "United States of Europe" would also have a fundamental impact on active managers' potential to add value. We assume that Europe will evolve toward a United States of Europe consisting of a fully amalgamated set of twelve core European countries. A top-down asset allocator will then have eleven fewer country and eleven fewer currency decision variables. As the playing field shrinks, the potential to add value is reduced as well.

DATA

All our equity data originate from Financial Times International, which calculates daily indexes for regions, countries, and sectors. The daily exchange rate data are also provided by FTI. The J.P. Morgan fixed-income indexes are used as reflective of the European government bond markets.

In all cases we use roughly ten years of data (i.e., starting January 1, 1988). To eliminate currency effects, we translate nominal local currency returns into local excess returns by subtracting the local risk-free rate. (This local excess return is the return that would have been achieved by an investor hedging the currency exposure.)

Exhibit 1 lists the European countries used in this study, grouped into the EMU first-round participants and the "outs." Exhibit 2 summarizes the equity market sector definitions used by FTI. We use the broad sector classification, rather than the more detailed industry one, since the latter is extremely sparsely populated in some countries.

ARE EUROPEAN EQUITY MARKETS BECOMING MORE HOMOGENEOUS?

If the harmonization in economic, monetary, and fiscal policies across the European Economic Community has any impact on the behavior of European equity markets, we would expect this to be reflected in the correlations between and among the different indexes. To get an idea of the trend in correlations at the market and sector level, we fit a trend line through the average three-month correlations (based on daily data) over the last ten years. In other words, for a three-month period we calculate the correlations between the different markets (sectors), using daily local excess returns. We then calculate the average correlation across these markets (sectors).

Repeating the exercise for the next (non-overlapping) three-month period yields a total of forty average correlations through which a simple trend line is fitted.[2] The objective is to establish whether there has been a significant increase in the average correlation over the last ten years. Exhibit 3 summarizes these results for the core nine EMU countries.

At the market level, we can see a statistically significant upward trend in the correlations, with the average correlation increasing by 0.024 per year. At the sector level, it is mainly the energy, finance, and (somewhat) utility sectors that are behaving increasingly alike. Conversely, the European transport, capital goods, and basic industries do not seem to be significantly affected by the economic integration.

Although the breakdown is not represented, it is noteworthy that the results in Exhibit 3 do not differ significantly when we combine the "ins" and "outs." The European economic integration seems to affect all coun-

EXHIBIT 3
AVERAGE AND TREND OF CORRELATIONS ACROSS MARKETS FOR EUROPE JANUARY 1988–DECEMBER 1997

	Average	Trend (Annualized)	T-Statistic
Market Indexes	0.40	0.024	2.91
Basic Industries	0.26	0.003	0.05
Capital Goods	0.21	–0.002	–0.08
Consumer Goods	0.29	0.010	1.45
Transport	0.22	–0.010	–1.32
Utilities	0.22	0.012	1.78
Energy	0.29	0.021	4.55
Finance	0.33	0.023	2.94

Correlations calculated on daily local excess returns over non-overlapping three-month periods.

---

tries alike, whether they are enthusiasts or skeptics within the European Economic Community.

The relevant insights of Exhibit 3 are that European stocks are starting to behave more and more similarly, especially in the finance and energy sectors. Given that these two sectors also dominate most market indexes, it is not surprising that the increase in correlation is also noticeable and significant at the market index level. The data in Exhibit 3 indicate that transnational effects increasingly drive European stocks, thereby confirming the insights of earlier studies (see, for instance, Heston and Rouwenhorst [1994] and Beckers, Connor, and Curds [1996]).

The corollary of the insights in Exhibit 3 is that the behavior of stocks within a given country is increasingly driven by transnational stock events. In fact, Roll [1992] suggests that the correlation (or lack thereof) between market indexes is mainly driven by the industrial structure of the relative markets. He argues that stocks within the same industry behave alike, irrespective of their nationality. This means that sectors within a given country will lead increasingly independent lives as the "nationality" common factor weakens.

This view is addressed in Exhibit 4, which summarizes the trend in quarterly average cross-sector correlations within a given country (again based on daily data). In nine out of the fourteen European countries, the average cross-sector correlations have indeed shown a decreasing trend over the last ten years (six of them statistically significant); the divergence between the different sectors within a given country typically increases. Belgium, Finland, and Spain prove to be the exception, with statistically significantly growing cross-sector correlations.

It is interesting to observe that the weakening interdependence of the sectors applies not only at the individual country level, but also across the European sectors. Europe in this respect conforms to the behavior of the U.S. stock market, where sectors also have led increasingly independent lives over the last ten years. Japan, on the other hand, has experienced a strengthening of cross-sector ties over the last decade; sectors in Japan are behaving more alike now than they did ten years ago.

The analysis in Exhibit 4 also introduces a dummy variable for rising markets; i.e., it differentiates correlations in quarters when on average the market was up from those when the market was down. Since Erb, Harvey, and Viskanta [1995] have shown that correlations are typically higher in down markets than in up markets, the dummy helps ensure that the result we obtain is not a corollary of the decade-long bull market.

The results in Exhibit 4 confirm that on average the cross-sector correlations are indeed lower in up markets. The lower cross-sector correlations cannot be exclusively attributed to the bull-market, however, since the trend in most markets remains firmly negative, even after correcting for the up market quarters.

IS THE EUROPEAN EQUITY MARKET BECOMING RISKIER?

It is impossible to evaluate the impact of stronger ties of stocks within the same sector (across national boundaries) and of a weakening of the correlations between the sectors without discussing the other component of portfolio risk: volatilities. Exhibit 5 summarizes the average annualized quarterly volatility (based on daily data) for each European equity market (and for the U.S. and Japan). We also calculate the trend in the annualized quarterly standard deviations (based on daily data) over the last decade.

Almost every single market (with the exception of Finland, Italy, and Spain) has experienced a downward trend in volatility. In fact, in most markets, the annualized volatilities are now at an all-time low. The numbers for the U.S. (and to some degree for Japan) confirm that this phenomenon is not restricted to Europe. With the exception of the U.K. and Ireland,

EXHIBIT 4
AVERAGE AND TREND OF CORRELATIONS ACROSS SECTORS WITHIN A GIVEN MARKET
JANUARY 1988–DECEMBER 1997

Country	Average	Trend Coefficient	T-Statistic	Up Market Coefficient	T-Statistic
Austria	0.40	0.005	0.43	−0.492	−2.13
Belgium	0.45	0.027	2.97	−0.422	−2.11
Denmark	0.32	−0.011	−1.44	−0.049	−0.30
Finland	0.28	0.016	2.27	0.275	1.83
France	0.60	−0.010	−1.63	−0.215	−1.51
Germany	0.69	−0.009	−1.32	−0.112	−0.74
Ireland	0.25	−0.011	−2.40	0.042	0.38
Italy	0.74	−0.013	−2.08	−0.297	−2.19
Netherlands	0.49	−0.041	−6.22	−0.314	−1.83
Norway	0.41	−0.002	−0.23	−0.140	−0.79
Spain	0.53	0.028	3.38	−0.299	−1.71
Sweden	0.52	−0.028	−3.75	−0.404	−2.31
Switzerland	0.46	−0.017	−2.23	−0.434	−2.36
U.K.	0.63	−0.022	−2.80	−0.047	−0.24
Average	0.48	−0.006		−0.208	−1.14
Europe	0.80	−0.011	−2.61	−0.101	−1.10
U.S.	0.62	−0.040	−6.18	−0.764	−2.08
Japan	0.72	0.029	3.61	−0.032	−0.25

Correlations calculated on daily local excess returns over non-overlapping three-month periods.

---

the reduction in volatility is also more pronounced in up markets than in down markets (although rarely significantly so).

The question can be asked whether this reduction in volatility is a temporary aberration or a structural change. It is hard to believe that the typical stock market volatility in the next decade would continue to decrease the way it has over the last ten years. A reversion toward the long-term mean therefore seems more likely than a continued decline.

In summary: Stocks within the same European sector are starting to behave more and more alike, but the sectors themselves are leading increasingly independent lives. In addition, volatilities are decreasing.

What does this all add up to? Is Europe becoming riskier or less risky? How do the changes in correlations and volatilities interact?

Exhibit 6 summarizes the combined impact of these effects by subdividing the last ten years into five-year subperiods. We notice that Europe, the U.S., and Japan all have experienced lower risk in the last five years (whether we are equal-weighting or capitalization-weighting the fourteen European countries). The proportional risk decrease in Europe, though, is much lower than in the rest of the world. This is probably because the increases in correlations (across markets and across stocks within the same sectors) somewhat offset the secular downward trend in volatilities.

This gradual structural change — on balance — results in an increase in correlations, leading to a much less pronounced risk reduction for the European equity market (as compared to the U.S. or Japan).

WHAT ABOUT CURRENCY RISK?

The moment a number of core European countries sign up for the common currency (the Euro), a source of investment risk for Euro-based investors will disappear overnight. These investors will no longer carry currency risk, and their diversified European equity or bond portfolios will suddenly become less risky. It is interesting to quantify how large this risk reduction could be for a typical European investor.

For a non-Euro-based investor, it is not clear

EXHIBIT 5
AVERAGE AND TREND OF STANDARD DEVIATIONS — JANUARY 1988-DECEMBER 1997

Country	Average	Trend Coefficient	Trend T-Statistic	Up Market Coefficient	Up Market T-Statistic
Austria	14.89	−0.60	−1.22	−6.61	−0.64
Belgium	10.10	−0.39	−1.49	−7.05	−1.23
Denmark	11.82	−0.22	−1.06	−3.55	−0.77
Finland	18.65	1.33	4.01	−4.74	−0.67
France	14.73	−0.28	−1.16	−5.80	−1.05
Germany	15.27	−0.91	−2.54	−5.52	−0.66
Ireland	15.25	−1.05	−3.23	8.08	1.08
Italy	19.32	0.66	1.86	−9.85	−1.29
Netherlands	11.83	−0.52	−2.82	−7.11	−1.46
Norway	18.56	−1.16	−2.75	−6.14	−0.64
Spain	14.65	0.24	0.72	−3.72	−0.50
Sweden	16.85	−0.26	−0.72	−2.16	−2.59
Switzerland	13.76	−0.68	−2.53	−2.68	−3.20
U.K.	11.83	−0.47	−2.65	1.45	0.35
Average	14.82	−0.31		−6.60	−0.95
Europe	12.41	−0.56	−2.55	−3.68	−0.54
Japan	17.35	−0.16	−0.34	−4.85	−0.46
U.S.	11.67	−0.79	−4.11	−3.45	−0.60

Standard deviations calculated on daily local excess returns over non-overlapping three-month periods (all numbers annualized).

what the impact of the Euro will be; sources of risk (the different currencies) disappear. At the same time, the associated risk diversification opportunities vanish. It is not a priori clear which of these effects will dominate.

In Exhibit 7 we summarize the historic currency risk associated with investing in European equity or bond markets from different currency perspectives. The increase in risk is expressed in standard deviation terms, and takes into account the pure currency risk as well as the covariance between currency movement and local market movement.

A U.S. dollar- or yen-based investor would have incurred between 8% and 12% currency related risk when investing in the European equity market over the last decade. The corresponding currency risk when investing in the European bond markets is about 9%. Note that the currency risk associated with the ECU bond market is virtually indistinguishable from that associated with an investment in a diversified portfolio of European government bond markets. In other words, switching from a multicurrency European bond portfolio to an ECU bond portfolio would historically have had no impact on the currency risk incurred by a U.S. dollar- or yen-based investor.

For European ("domestic") investors, the currency risk associated with a European equity portfolio is about the same order of magnitude as for a U.S. dollar- or yen-based investor. For these investors, however, the European diversified fixed-income portfolios historically had a small (absolute) amount of currency risk. (Although, relatively speaking, the majority of the risk in a fixed-income portfolio is still currency-related.)

EXHIBIT 6
TOTAL LOCAL MARKET RISK: THE BOTTOM LINE

	1988-1992	1993-1997	Change
Europe Cap-Weighted	15.19	13.31	−12.4%
Europe Equal-Weighted	14.80	13.14	−11.1%
U.S.	13.30	9.42	−29.2%
Japan	24.04	19.40	−19.3%

Annual standard deviation based on monthly data, equal-weighted.

EXHIBIT 7
ANNUAL STANDARD DEVIATION ATTRIBUTABLE TO CURRENCY EXPOSURE (INCLUDING COVARIANCE TERM) — JANUARY 1988-DECEMBER 1997

Market	$ Base Equity	$ Base Bond	Yen Base Equity	Yen Base Bond	£ Base Equity	£ Base Bond	DM Base Equity	DM Base Bond	ECU Base Equity	ECU Base Bond
Europe	8.22	9.27	11.52	9.04	9.10	5.33	11.26	3.54	8.64	3.84
ECU		9.90		9.32		6.21		3.15		
Proportion of Total Risk	20%	80%	37%	82%	30%	85%	40%	80%	26%	67%

Data based on monthly observations, equally weighted.

If we take history as a guide, we would infer that, for Euro-based investors, the emergence of the Euro could eliminate up to 4% risk in standard deviation units from a European bond portfolio, and up to 11% risk in standard deviation terms from a European equity portfolio. Relatively speaking, a European bond portfolio would become about 70% less risky than before, while a European equity portfolio would become about 30% less risky.

This extrapolation assumes that currency risk is completely separable from local market risk. An alternative hypothesis argues that there is an amount of "real" risk in the world that is currently partially absorbed by the equity and bond markets and partially by the currency market. The disappearance of the currency markets in Europe would lead to evaporation of the currency market sponge. Under this scenario, currency risk would not dissolve into thin air but would be at least partially reallocated across the equity and bond markets.

Although it is difficult to predict what the effect of the European Monetary Union will be on the risk of European equity or bond markets, our numbers should act as an upper bound on the risk reduction that can be expected.

THE FUTURE RISK OF EUROPEAN PORTFOLIOS: A CONJECTURE

Let us conjecture what the risk of a diversified European equity or bond portfolio would look like under the Euro regime. Exhibit 8 summarizes the historic risk of the ECU from U.S. dollar, yen, and sterling perspectives, and the historic risk of a fully hedged European equity portfolio, a European bond portfolio, and an ECU bond portfolio. It then combines these historical numbers with some assumed correlations between Euro movement and local market movement, to estimate the total volatility of European equity or bond portfolios.[3]

Almost all the risk in the equity portfolio will be local market risk, with the currency risk and the correlation between currency and local market playing a relatively minor role in the makeup of the total risk number. Conversely, for the European bond portfolio, almost all the risk will be currency risk. Most impor-

EXHIBIT 8
WHAT HAPPENS WITH EMU: SOME CONJECTURE

Historic Risk of ECU		Historic Risk of Fully Hedged European Market	
$ Base	10.39%	Equity	15.37%
Sterling Base	7.36%	Bond	3.83%
Yen Base	10.12%	ECU Bond	4.31%

Risk of Unhedged European Portfolio from Dollar or Yen Base

Currency Risk	10%
Local Market Equity Risk	15%
ECU Bond Risk	4%

Correlation of Currency Return with Local Market Return	Equity Risk	Bond Risk
−0.2	16.28	10.00
−0.1	17.17	10.39
0.0	18.03	10.77
0.1	18.84	11.14
0.2	19.62	11.49

All standard deviations calculated using equal-weighted monthly return over the last ten years.

tant, though, the resulting numbers are not dramatically different from those incurred historically over the last decade by non-Euro-based investors.

From a risk perspective, the emergence of the Euro appears to be a non-event for a U.S. dollar- or yen- (and possibly sterling-) based investor.

IMPLICATIONS FOR ACTIVE MANAGEMENT

Even if the emergence of the Euro may be something of a non-event from a risk point of view, the implications for a top-down active manager could be dramatic. Suppose you are an active portfolio manager who heretofore has managed an international equity portfolio with the twenty-three-market MSCI or FT World index as a benchmark. If suddenly you find yourself in a fully integrated United States of Europe, twenty-two decision variables would disappear overnight. There would be eleven fewer markets to allocate money to, and there would be eleven fewer currencies to time. A skillful manager would obviously be hurt by this significant constriction of the playing field.

We will try to quantify the magnitude of this effect using a Monte Carlo simulation. We simulate the behavior of an asset allocator or currency manager who originally operates in a twenty-three-market/currency environment and subsequently — with the same skill set as before — in a constricted environment.

The managers in the Monte Carlo simulation are assigned a skill level. On average, they have an information coefficient (correlation between their forecast and realization) of 0.1; i.e., on average the correlation between their monthly market (or currency) forecast and the subsequent return realization is 0.1. The information coefficients vary (randomly) from a high of 0.21 for some markets (currencies) to a low of 0.001 for others.

The managers are assumed to create optimized portfolios, using the historic covariance matrix — without data snooping — of the markets or currencies using quadratic optimization to solve a mean-variance objective function. They operate either as hedge fund managers (long-short managers with cash as the benchmark) or as traditional long-only managers with the capitalization-weighted portfolio as benchmark. In the case of the currency manager, the benchmark is the currency basket with the same weights as the corresponding capitalization-weighted equity portfolio.

The Monte Carlo simulations are repeated fifty times (or, conversely, we are studying the behavior of fifty equally skillful managers). The managers are assumed to make forecasts (and to rebalance their portfolios) on a monthly basis. The simulation extends over a 240-month period. We present the results of the average manager at regular intervals over the twenty-year period, concentrating on the managers' ability to add value as expressed by their information ratios (active return over the benchmark, divided by the standard deviation of this active return).

Exhibit 9 summarizes the results for the asset allocators or currency managers operating in either a twenty-three- or twelve-market/currency environment. Note that the reported information ratios are higher than those typically observed in the real world (a good upper-quartile manager would — at best — have an information ratio of 0.5). Column 1 in each set of results summarizes the results for the twenty-three-market/currency environment; column 2 reports the results for the twelve-market/currency case.

Among the asset allocators, the conservative long-only manager is hit most badly by the reduction in the opportunity set; this manager loses up to two-thirds of the potential to add value. The more aggressive manager, on the other hand, is less affected, mainly because this manager starts off with a much lower information ratio.[4]

Comparing the asset allocator to the currency manager, it is striking that the latter — given the same level of skill — can add more value per unit risk in the twenty-three-currency environment. The information ratios in column 1 are invariably higher for the currency manager. This implies that the broad currency market environment (i.e., its covariance structure) is more supportive of active management than the corresponding equity markets.

The reduction of the information ratios due to the shrinking of the opportunity set is, however, also much more dramatic for the currency managers. In fact, the currency manager whose attention is restricted to twelve currencies invariably ends up worse off than the corresponding asset allocator. The long conservative currency manager ends up losing most (about 85%) of the potential to add value due to the shrinking of the playing field. The long-short manager loses about 75%; the more aggressive long-only managers lose about 40% of their information ratios.

EXHIBIT 9
AVERAGE INFORMATION RATIOS FOR ASSET ALLOCATOR

	After 36 Months		% Decrease	After 60 Months		% Decrease	After 120 Months		% Decrease	After 180 Months		% Decrease	After 240 Months		% Decrease
	(1)	(2)		(1)	(2)		(1)	(2)		(1)	(2)		(1)	(2)	
Long – Short Active Risk 1.50%	1.07	0.73	32	1.39	0.73	48	1.73	0.76	56	1.84	0.76	59	1.91	0.76	60
Long – Active Risk 0.50%	1.32	0.69	47	1.49	0.59	60	1.42	0.48	66	1.42	0.48	66	1.42	0.45	68
Long – Active Risk 2.00%	0.52	0.52	0	0.69	0.48	30	0.55	0.31	44	0.48	0.31	35	0.45	0.28	37

AVERAGE INFORMATION RATIOS FOR CURRENCY MANAGER

	After 36 Months		% Decrease	After 60 Months		% Decrease	After 120 Months		% Decrease	After 180 Months		% Decrease	After 240 Months		% Decrease
	(1)	(2)		(1)	(2)		(1)	(2)		(1)	(2)		(1)	(2)	
Long – Short Active Risk 2.0%	1.77	0.62	65	2.04	0.55	73	2.49	0.69	73	2.70	0.66	75	2.84	0.66	77
Long – Active Risk 0.5%	1.77	0.38	79	1.94	0.38	80	2.08	0.42	80	2.15	0.35	84	2.15	0.35	84
Long – Active Risk 1.5%	0.42	0.31	26	0.35	0.28	20	0.48	0.28	41	0.45	0.28	37	0.42	0.24	43

Column (1): Twenty-three markets or currencies.
Column (2): Eleven non-European markets/currencies and Europe/ECU.

SUMMARY

On balance, the structural change arising from the European monetary, fiscal, and economic integration has led to a relative increase in the risk of the European equity market (as a result of the increases in correlations between markets and between the same sectors in different markets). The EMU is probably a non-event from a currency risk perspective for a non-EMU-based investor. European equity and bond portfolios will most likely have the same currency risk after as before the EMU. A Euro-based investor, to the contrary, will see a risk reduction of up to 70% in a European bond portfolio and 40% in a European equity portfolio.

As Europe becomes more integrated, active management will become harder, as the number of decision variables drops. Currency managers will suffer more than asset allocators, although both classes of investors will lose somewhere between 40% and 85% of their potential to add value, due to the reduction in their opportunity set. None of these changes will make the life of an active manager any easier. Basically, the increase in correlations represents a diminution of opportunities.

ENDNOTES

The author thanks Gregory Conner for his usual helpful advice and Ross Curds for invaluable computational assistance.

[1] For a good summary of the macroeconomic implications of the European Monetary Union, see, for instance, DeGrauwe [1997].

[2] That is, we regress the time series of correlations on an intercept and time index using ordinary least squares. Under the hypothesis that the true correlation is constant over time, the estimated trend coefficient is consistent, and the t-statistics are approximately normal.

[3] For those who believe that the Euro will behave more like the DM than like the ECU, the historical risk numbers of the

DM versus U.S. dollar, sterling, and yen are 11.17%, 7.83%, and 10.41%, respectively (i.e., they are virtually identical to the historical ECU numbers).

[4]Given the constraints associated with long-only management, the potential of a moderately aggressive active manager to add value in a twenty-three-market environment may be only a third of that of more conservative colleagues.

REFERENCES

Beckers, Stan, Gregory Connor, and Ross Curds. "National Versus Global Influences on Equity Returns." *Financial Analysts Journal*, 52, No. 2 (1996), pp. 31-39.

DeGrauwe, Paul. *The Economics of Monetary Union*, 3rd ed. Oxford: Oxford University Press, 1997.

Erb, C.B., C. Harvey, and T.E. Viskanta. "Forecasting International Equity Correlations." *Financial Analysts Journal*, 51 (6) (1995), pp. 32-45.

Heston, Steven L., and K Geert Rouwenhorst. "Does Industrial Structure Explain the Benefits of International Diversification?" *Journal of Financial Economics*, 36 (1994), pp. 3-27.

Roll, Richard. "Industrial Structure and the Comparative Behavior of International Stock Market Indices." *Journal of Finance*, 47 (1992), pp. 3-42.

The role of banks in monetary policy: A survey with implications for the European monetary union

Anil K Kashyap and Jeremy C. Stein

Much of the debate about European monetary union (EMU) has focused on the likely macroeconomic effects. On the benefits side, there is clearly the reduction in transactions costs that comes from eliminating all the competing currencies. For some countries there is also the possibility that the shift to the new European central bank will bring enhanced inflation-fighting credibility. If so, these countries will enjoy lower nominal interest rates and perhaps even lower real interest rates if they can eliminate an inflation risk premium. On the cost side, some countries may see their inflation-fighting credibility decline. In addition, all countries will presumably have less freedom to use monetary policy to stimulate their own economy.

While these issues are important, we believe another crucial factor is being overlooked: the banking system aspects of monetary policy under the EMU. This article reviews some recent work, which suggests that monetary policy has significant distributional effects that operate through the banking system. We briefly discuss how this bank transmission channel may operate in the EMU.

First, we describe the conceptual differences between the bank-centric view of monetary transmission and the conventional view, in which banks do not play a key role. The bank-centric theory hinges on two key propositions: that monetary interventions do something special to banks; and that once banks are affected, so are firms and/or consumers. Then we review the empirical evidence, which tends to support the bank-centric view. Finally, we look at how a common monetary policy will affect banks throughout Europe and how this, in turn, might influence real economic activity in different countries.

A byproduct of our work is that we have developed a large amount of documentation and experience working with U.S. bank-level data, which we describe in the appendix at the end of this article. The appendix also provides details of how researchers can access these data via the Federal Reserve Bank of Chicago's Web site.

Contrasting views of monetary transmission

Conventional monetary economics

The classic textbook treatment of monetary policy focuses on how the central bank's actions affect households' portfolios. In simple terms, household portfolios are allocated between

---

Anil K Kashyap is a professor of economics at the University of Chicago Graduate School of Business, a consultant to the Federal Bank of Chicago, and a research associate at the National Bureau of Economic Research (NBER). Jeremy C. Stein is the J.C. Penney Professor of Management at the MIT Sloan School of Management and a research associate at the NBER. The authors thank Magda Bianco, Giovanni Ferri, Dario Focarelli, and Luigi Guizo for providing data and suggestions, as well as Christopher Tang of Thomson BankWatch and Sharon Standish of the OECD for supplying unpublished data. The Web site for the Call Report data could not have been built without the help of many Bank staff members; however, Nancy Andrews, Larry Chen, and Peter Schneider deserve special recognition for their efforts. This research was supported by a National Science Foundation grant made to the NBER.

"bonds," shorthand for all types of financial assets that are not used for transactions purposes, and money (which is the asset used in transactions). Importantly, money can be more than just currency, with checking accounts being the obvious substitute to include in narrow measures of money.

It is assumed that central banks can control the quantity of money. If the central bank can control one of the two asset types in household portfolios, it follows that by adjusting the relative supply of the two asset types, the central bank can control their relative prices. For simplicity, we often assume that transaction-facilitating assets do not pay interest. In this case, the relative price of money and bonds is the nominal interest rate. If we alter the characterization to allow transactions accounts to pay interest, the central bank will be able to influence the gap between this rate and the rate on assets with no transactions services.

Regardless of whether transactions accounts pay interest, the conventional view rests on two assumptions. First, there must be some well-defined asset called money, which is essential for transactions. Second, the monetary authority must be able to control (with some precision over intermediate horizons) the supply of money.

Historically, when demand deposits and currency were about the only assets used in transactions, it was easy to see how this control might work. Because the central bank is the only entity that can create currency, it can determine how much currency comes into circulation. Furthermore, the ability of banks (and other financial institutions) to create checking accounts has typically been limited by the requirement that banks hold reserves (which can be thought of as vault cash) against these accounts. By managing the rules regarding reserves, the monetary authority indirectly controls the noncurrency component of transaction balances.

Typically, the central bank decides both the level of reserves to be held against a given level of transactions balances and the types of assets that can be used as reserves. When the central bank wants more money in the economy, it provides the banks with more currency that can be used as reserves (say by trading reserves for other bank securities). Banks then lever up the reserves through lending and crediting the checking accounts of the borrowers who receive the funds. In this framework, the willingness of banks to lend matters only to the extent to which it influences the creation of transaction-facilitating assets, that is, deposits.

Once the supply of transactions accounts has been adjusted following the central bank's reserve injection, interest rates respond in a predictable manner. When more transactions balances become available to households, the valuation of these balances falls and money becomes cheaper to hold than before—that is, nominal interest rates fall. For this change in nominal rates to matter, one must assume that prices do not adjust instantly to the change in the money supply. Then with more money, people will have more *real* purchasing power, and the nominal interest decline will correspond to a lower real interest rate.

The major problem with the conventional theory of monetary policy is the sharp two-asset dichotomy that underlies the model. There is an increasing proliferation of assets, which, from the household perspective, mimic checking accounts but are not controllable by the central bank (for example, mutual funds with check writing privileges). As these non-reservable transactions-type accounts become more prevalent, the central bank's power over currency and transaction deposits becomes less relevant in the determination of interest rates. This does not mean the central bank will no longer be able to influence rates; however, we believe that the basic logic underlying the textbook model is becoming much less compelling.

The bank-centric view

In view of the above limitation of the conventional theory, a large literature has developed based on the assumption that there are three important asset types: money, bonds, and bank loans. In this context, the special response of banks to changes in monetary policy is their *lending* response (not just their role as deposit creators). Thus, the ambiguity over what constitutes money is much less important. For this mechanism to operate, it is essential that some spending that is financed with bank loans will not occur if the banks cut the loans (that is, there is no perfect substitute available for a bank loan). The assumed sensitivity of bank loan supply to monetary policy together with the assumed dependence of some spending on bank lending generate a number of predictions about how monetary policy will work.[1]

One basic prediction is that the firms and individuals whose creditworthiness is most difficult to gauge (that is, those borrowers about whom information is imperfect) will be most dependent on banks for financing. Because these borrowers face the extra cost of raising funds from third parties, they are not indifferent about the composition of their liabilities. Banks have a particular advantage in lending to such borrowers because they can specialize in information gathering to determine creditworthiness. Moreover, by developing repeat business, banks can stay informed about their customers. They are therefore better able to make prudent lending decisions than lenders that don't have access to this information.[2]

The question of who will fund the banks remains. Banks that lend to relatively small, little known borrowers will have collections of assets that are difficult to value. This implies that individual investors are not as well informed as bank management about the value of the bank's existing assets. Depending on the type of liability the bank issues to finance itself, this may create an adverse selection problem. Banks with high levels of opaque assets need to pay a relatively high interest rate to offset the risk associated with these assets. Some banks may prefer to make fewer loans than to pay the rates required to attract funds.

One way to overcome this problem is through deposit insurance. If banks can issue insured deposits, account holders need not worry about the lending decisions made by their bank. To fund themselves with insured deposits, banks typically have to allow the entity that is providing the deposit guarantee to oversee their lending decisions. In addition, they are usually required to put aside reserves (generally currency) against the insured deposits. This link between deposit insurance and reserve requirements gives the monetary authorities a powerful lever. In effect, the reserves allow banks to raise funds without having to generate comprehensive information about the quality of their own assets. (See Stein, 1995, for the formal model.)

In this context, a reduction in the supply of reserves has an impact beyond those emphasized in the conventional textbook description: It pushes the banks toward a more costly form of financing. Because of the extra premium that banks will have to pay to bring in noninsured deposits, the banks will make fewer loans after the reserve outflow. If the borrowers that lose their loans cannot obtain new funds quickly, their spending levels may fall. Because these consequences can be partially anticipated, banks and firms will hedge this risk. Banks will not fully loan out their deposits, holding some securities as a buffer stock against a reserve outflow. Similarly, firms will hold some liquid assets on their books in case a loan is withdrawn.

Nevertheless, there are good reasons to believe that such buffer stocks will not fully offset the effects of contractionary monetary policy. For one thing, buffer stocks are costly for the banks. Banks make money by making loans, not by sitting on securities that offer returns close to the rates the banks pay on deposits. Moreover, the tax code makes it inefficient for the banks to hold securities. As with any equity financed corporation, holding these types of assets imposes double taxation on the bank's shareholders.

In summary, unlike the traditional theory that emphasizes households' preferences between money and other less liquid assets, the new theory of monetary policy asserts that the role of the banking sector is central to the transmission of monetary policy. Specifically, two key factors shape the way in which monetary policy works: 1) the extent to which banks rely on reservable deposit financing and adjust their loan supply schedules following changes in bank reserves; and 2) the extent to which certain borrowers are bank-dependent and cannot easily offset these shifts in bank loan supply.

Empirical evidence on the role of banks in monetary policy

A growing literature tests the bank-centric theory described above. Although relatively little of this research has been done using European data, we will explain in a later section why the existing results suggest there may be powerful effects in Europe.[3]

The work (which mostly focuses on the U.S.) can be summarized by the following picture of monetary policy transmission. When the Federal Reserve tightens policy, aggregate lending by banks gradually slows down and there is a surge in nonbank financing, such as commercial paper. When this substitution of financing is taking place, aggregate investment is reduced by more than would be predicted solely on the basis of rising interest rates.

Small firms that do not have significant buffer cash holdings are most likely to trim investment (particularly inventory investment) around the periods of tight money. Similarly, small banks seem more prone than large banks to reduce their lending, with the effect greatest for small banks with relatively low buffer stocks of securities at the time of the tightening. Overall, the results suggest that monetary policy may have important real consequences beyond those generated by standard interest rate effects. Below, we review this evidence in detail.

Do banks change their supply of loans when monetary policy changes?

Perhaps the simplest aggregate empirical implication of the bank-centric view of monetary transmission is that bank loans should be closely correlated with measures of economic activity. Following changes in monetary policy, there is a strong correlation between bank loans and unemployment, GNP, and other key macroeconomic indicators (see Bernanke and Blinder, 1992). However, such correlations could arise even if the "bank lending channel" is not operative. The correlations may be driven by changes in the demand for bank loans rather than the supply of bank loans. For example, bank loans and inventories might move together because banks always stand willing to lend and firms finance desired changes in inventory levels with bank loans.

Kashyap, Stein, and Wilcox (KSW, 1993) use macroeconomic data to overcome the difficulty of separating the role of loan demand from loan supply. According to KSW, movements in substitutes for bank financing should contain information about the demand for bank financing. For example, if bank loans are falling while commercial paper issuance is rising, one can infer that bank loan supply has contracted.[4] KSW examine movements in the mix between bank loans and loan substitutes following changes in monetary policy. They find that when the Fed tightens, commercial paper issuance surges while bank loans (slowly) decline.

Hoshi, Scharfstein, and Singleton (1993) conduct an analogous set of tests using aggregate Japanese data. Specifically, they compare the behavior of bank loans subject to informal control by the Bank of Japan with loans from insurance companies that are the main alternative to bank financing. As predicted by the lending channel theory, they find that when the Bank of Japan tightens, the fraction of industrial loans coming from banks drops noticeably. Arguably, the Japanese evidence is less surprising because the Bank of Japan appears to exert some direct control over loan volume in addition to any indirect control that might come from changing reserves.

Evidence relying on changes in the aggregate financing mix has been questioned because alternative explanations exist that do not rely on bank loan supply shifts. For instance, one could argue that *large* firms that typically use commercial paper financing might tend to increase *all* forms of borrowing, while smaller firms that are mostly bank-dependent receive less of all types of financing. In this case, heterogeneity in loan demand rather than differences in loan supply would explain the results above. In response to this criticism, however, Kashyap, Stein, and Wilcox (1996) show that even among a composite of large U.S. firms, there is considerable substitution away from bank loans toward commercial paper.

Calomiris, Himmelberg, and Wachtel (1995) use data on individual firms to make a similar point. Using a sample of firms that are issuing commercial paper, Calomiris et al. show that when monetary policy tightens, commercial paper issuance rises and so does the trade credit extended by these firms. This finding suggests that these larger firms are taking up some of the slack created as their smaller customers lose their bank loans. While this mechanism partially offsets the impact of the loan supply shock, it does not eliminate the shock.

Recently, Ludvigson (1996) developed a test for loan supply effects that is immune to the loan demand explanation. Comparing the extension of auto credit by banks and finance companies, the author finds that bank lending to consumers declines relative to finance company lending when monetary policy tightens, as predicted by the lending channel. The vast majority of the borrowers in this case are individuals, so it is not possible to appeal to differences in large and small buyers to explain the pattern. Furthermore, Ludvigson finds that finance company borrowers default more than bank borrowers, so finance companies are not lending more after a monetary contraction simply because they have higher-quality customers. Thus, Ludvigson's findings strongly indicate a loan supply effect of monetary policy.

The search for loan supply responses to monetary policy has also been carried out using disaggregated bank data. The theory outlined above suggests that banks that have trouble raising external finance respond differently to a monetary policy tightening from banks that can easily raise uninsured external funds. One natural proxy for the ability to raise such financing is bank size. Particularly in the U.S. where there are thousands of banks, small banks tend not to be rated by credit agencies and, therefore, have trouble attracting uninsured nondeposit financing.

In Kashyap and Stein (1995), we created a composite of small and large banks to study this question. As predicted by the theory, we find that banks of different sizes use different forms of financing. Only the larger banks have much success in securing nondeposit financing. More importantly, we find that small banks' lending is more sensitive to Fed-induced deposit shocks than that of large banks.

While these results are consistent with the idea that policy shifts induce changes in loan supply, there is also a loan demand interpretation. In this case one would have to argue that the customers of small banks differ from the customers of large banks and that loan demand drops more for customers of small banks. To take account of this possibility, we conducted further tests at the individual bank level, comparing the behavior of different small banks (Kashyap and Stein, 1997). Because most U.S. bank-level data are collected for regulatory purposes rather than for use in research, bank-level analysis requires a considerable amount of effort to get the data into usable form. As mentioned earlier, one of the byproducts of this effort is that we have developed a large amount of documentation and experience working with these data. The appendix provides a description of the data, available on the Bank's Web site; table 1 also summarizes some of the data.

At the individual bank level, the theory predicts that banks that have difficulty making up for deposit outflows should typically hold a buffer stock of securities, so that they can reduce securities holdings rather than having to cut back loans. Consistent with this prediction, table 1 shows strong evidence that small banks hold a higher fraction of assets in cash and securities than large banks. The data in table 1 also bear out other predictions of the imperfect information theory, such as small banks not being able to borrow in the federal funds market (where collateral is not used).

In terms of the search for loan supply effects, the buffer stocks will make it more difficult to find lending responses to shifts in monetary policy. Nevertheless, our research suggests that securities holdings do not seem to completely insulate bank lending from monetary policy. Even among small banks where the tendency to hold buffer stocks is most pronounced, banks with more cash and securities at the onset of a monetary contraction respond differently from less liquid banks (Kashyap and Stein, 1997). Specifically, the liquid banks are much less prone to reduce their lending following a tightening of monetary policy. Gibson (1996) shows that this pattern holds over time: When the aggregate bank holdings of securities are low, lending is more responsive to monetary policy.

The accumulated evidence shows that the bank loan supply shifts when monetary policy changes. However, there are various ways in which this loan supply shock could be neutralized. For instance, borrowers could find other nonbank lenders to fully offset the shortfall in bank lending. As a result, we must go beyond data on the volume of lending alone to see if the lending channel has any real effects on economic activity.

Does spending respond to changes in bank loan supply?

KSW check whether the financing mix has any additional explanatory power for investment once other fundamental factors, such as the cost of capital, are taken into account. The authors find that the mix does seem to have independent predictive power for investment, particularly inventory investment. Similarly, Hoshi, Scharfstein, and Singleton (1993) find that in a four-variable vector autoregression (which includes interest rates), the credit mix variable is a significant determinant of both fixed investment and finished goods inventories. Thus, the Japanese and U.S. data give the same basic message.

Working at a lower level of aggregation, Ludvigson looks at whether the financing mix (which in this case separates bank loans and finance company lending) is an important predictor of automobile sales. The author finds that the mix is a significant predictor even controlling for income, auto prices, and interest rates. This evidence strikes us as particularly

TABLE 1
Composition of bank balance sheets

As of 1976:Q1	Below 75th percentile	75th to 90th percentile	90th to 95th percentile	95th to 98th percentile	98th to 99th percentile	Above 99th percentile
Number of banks	10,784	2,157	719	431	144	144
Mean assets *(1993 $ millions)*	32.8	119.1	247.7	556.6	1,341.5	10,763.4
Median assets *(1993 $ millions)*	28.4	112.6	239.0	508.1	1,228.7	3,964.6
Fraction of total system assets	0.128	0.093	0.064	0.087	0.070	0.559
Fraction of total assets in size category						
Cash and securities	0.426	0.418	0.418	0.408	0.396	0.371
Fed funds lent	0.049	0.040	0.038	0.045	0.045	0.025
Total domestic loans	0.518	0.531	0.531	0.531	0.539	0.413
Real estate loans	0.172	0.191	0.106	0.179	0.174	0.087
C&I loans	0.102	0.131	0.153	0.160	0.168	0.171
Loans to individuals	0.147	0.162	0.148	0.147	0.138	0.059
Total deposits	0.902	0.897	0.890	0.969	0.841	0.810
Demand deposits	0.312	0.301	0.301	0.313	0.327	0.248
Time and savings deposits	0.590	0.596	0.589	0.554	0.508	0.326
Time deposits > $100 K	0.067	0.095	0.119	0.139	0.143	0.156
Fed funds borrowed	0.004	0.010	0.019	0.039	0.067	0.076
Subordinated debt	0.002	0.003	0.004	0.005	0.006	0.005
Other liabilities	0.008	0.012	0.013	0.014	0.017	0.057
As of 1993:Q2						
Number of banks	8,404	1,681	560	336	112	113
Mean assets *(1993 $ millions)*	44.4	165.8	370.1	1,072.6	3,366.0	17,413.4
Median assets *(1993 $ millions)*	38.6	155.7	362.7	920.8	3,246.3	9,297.7
Fraction of total system assets	0.105	0.078	0.060	0.101	0.106	0.551
Fraction of total assets in size category						
Cash and securities	0.399	0.371	0.343	0.333	0.325	0.311
Fed funds lent	0.045	0.040	0.035	0.041	0.041	0.040
Total loans	0.531	0.562	0.596	0.594	0.599	0.587
Real estate loans	0.296	0.331	0.337	0.302	0.252	0.209
C&I loans	0.087	0.101	0.111	0.117	0.132	0.183
Loans to individuals	0.086	0.098	0.120	0.144	0.166	0.097
Total deposits	0.879	0.868	0.850	0.794	0.760	0.690
Transaction deposits	0.258	0.257	0.254	0.240	0.258	0.193
Large deposits	0.174	0.207	0.225	0.248	0.244	0.212
Brokered deposits	0.022	0.004	0.008	0.017	0.016	0.013
Fed funds borrowed	0.010	0.021	0.039	0.063	0.097	0.093
Subordinated debt	0.000	0.000	0.001	0.002	0.004	0.017
Other liabilities	0.013	0.021	0.026	0.054	0.059	0.129
Equity	0.098	0.090	0.084	0.086	0.080	0.072

Source: Kashyap and Stein (1997).

strong, because the mix variable is added to a structural equation that is already supposed to account for monetary policy.

Among other work using disaggregated data, perhaps the most intriguing studies focus on inventory investment. Inventory reductions are large during recessions and monetary policy is typically tight prior to recessions. However, the simple story that tight money and high carrying costs lead to inventory runoffs is undermined by the difficulty in documenting interest rate effects on inventories. The previously discussed aggregate findings provide some support for the view that monetary policy and financial factors may be important for inventory movements, even though standard security market interest rates do not have much predictive power for inventories.

Gertler and Gilchrist (1994) compare the aggregate investment of a sample of large firms with that of a sample of small firms, which are presumably more bank-dependent.

They find that the small firms' inventory investment is much more sensitive to changes in monetary policy than that of the large firms. The differences are large enough that as much as half of the aggregate movement in inventory investment two years after a major monetary tightening may be attributable to the small firms. The authors find similar effects in terms of sales.

Using individual firm data, Kashyap, Stein, and Lamont (1994) look at the differences in inventory investment between publicly traded companies with bond ratings and those without bond ratings. The non-rated companies are typically much smaller than the rated companies and are more likely to be bank-dependent. The authors find that during the 1982 recession, prior to which Federal Reserve policy was restrictive, the inventory movements of the non-rated companies were much more sensitive to their own cash holdings than were the inventory movements of the rated companies. (In fact, there was no significant liquidity effect for the rated companies.) They find a similar pattern for the 1974–75 recession, which also followed a significant tightening of monetary policy by the Fed.

In contrast, in other "easy money" periods there is little relation between cash holdings and inventory movements for the non-rated companies. For instance, during 1985 and 1986, when many argue that U.S. monetary policy was particularly loose, the correlation between inventory investment and cash holdings is completely insignificant. The difference in the cash sensitivity of inventory investment for the bank-dependent firms is precisely to be expected if loan supply is varying with monetary policy.

Subsequent work by Carpenter, Fazzari, and Petersen (1994) confirms these patterns using a sample that includes information on quarterly (rather than annual) adjustments in inventories. Similarly, Milne (1991) finds similar credit availability effects on inventory investment for British firms. Thus, several independent pieces of evidence now point toward the importance of loan supply effects.

Other work with disaggregated data shows cross-sectional differences among firms involving margins other than inventory investment. As mentioned above, Gertler and Gilchrist find differences in the sales response of large and small firms following a monetary policy shock. Gertler and Hubbard (1988) find differences in the correlation between fixed investment and cash flow for firms that pay dividends and those that do not pay dividends in recessions and normal periods. If we accept a low dividend payout ratio as a proxy for bank dependence and assume that monetary policy shifted prior to the recessions, we can read these results as supporting a bank lending channel.

Focusing on Japanese firms that are not part of bank-centered industrial groups and, therefore, are susceptible to being cut off from bank credit, Hoshi, Scharfstein, and Singleton (1993) find that when monetary policy is tight, liquidity is more important for independent firms' investment than in normal times.

Finally, Sharpe (1994) contrasts the employment adjustment of different sized firms to changes in the real federal funds rate. He finds that small firms' employment is more responsive than that of large firms. Furthermore, firms that are more highly leveraged tend to show greater sensitivity to funds rate shocks. If we assume that more highly leveraged firms are more bank-dependent, this finding is also consistent with the lending channel.

Taken together, these findings strongly support the view that banks play an important role in the transmission of monetary policy. The evidence from different countries, different time periods, and for different agents suggests that 1) restrictive monetary policy reduces loan supply by banks and 2) this reduction in loan supply depresses spending.

Implications for monetary transmission under the EMU

We believe the work reviewed above answers a number of questions about the ways consumers, firms, and banks respond to monetary policy. Furthermore, it implies that the degree of bank dependence in the economy and the extent to which central bank actions move loan supply are the key factors determining the importance of the lending channel. In light of the vast differences in institutions across Europe, this story could have important implications for how monetary policy operates under the EMU.

Consider a uniform tightening of monetary policy. Suppose one country has a set of mostly creditworthy banks and relatively few bank-dependent firms. In this case, the banks may be able to offset the contraction in reserves by picking up uninsured nondeposit financing in the capital markets. Accordingly, bank lending will not fall by much. Moreover, if most firms can continue producing even if some bank loans are cut, the aggregate lending channel effect will be fairly weak.

In a country with many bank-dependent firms and a weak banking system, the impact might be quite different. Banks with poor credit ratings may not be able to attract uninsured funds to offset their deposit outflow. As the banks are driven to cut their lending, their customers will need to find other funding. If this funding is not available in the short run, a sizable spending drop may occur. Thus, a uniform contraction in monetary policy across the two countries may lead to a very asymmetric response, raising potentially problematic distributional issues.

This hypothetical comparison focuses on the differences in the aggregate conditions in the two countries. A key lesson from the work on the U.S. is that the banking-related effects of monetary policy are subtle and that microlevel studies are often required. Nevertheless, in light of the difficulty of getting reliable micro data for a large number of countries, we make an illustrative first pass at the problem with some, admittedly crude, aggregate-level calculations. We infer the degree of bank dependence in different countries by looking at the size distribution of firms and the availability of nonbank finance. To gauge loan supply effects, we study the size distribution of the banking industry and the health of the banks. These are no doubt highly imperfect proxies. We hope this exercise, which we view as a somewhat speculative first step, will spur researchers who have access to better data to build on our results.

Cross-country responsiveness of loan supply to policy changes

Since it is still too early to be certain which countries initially join the monetary union, we work with data for the following countries in the European Union: Belgium, Denmark, France, Germany, Greece, Ireland, Italy, Luxembourg, Netherlands, Portugal, Spain, and the UK. We report similar statistics for the U.S. and Japan, wherever possible.

As mentioned above, Kashyap and Stein (1995) show that small banks are more responsive to monetary tightening than large banks. If bank size is an appropriate proxy for the ability to access noninsured sources of funds,

this contrast makes sense (in the context of the lending channel). In some European countries, even large banks may find it difficult to obtain nondeposit financing. We have not been able to find any good data on differences in bank financing options across countries, however, and must therefore rely on size proxies to infer the sensitivity of loan supply to monetary policy.

Our first size distribution indicator (shown in column 4 of table 2) is the three-firm concentration ratio for commercial banks (that is, the share of total commercial bank assets controlled by the three largest commercial banks) as reported by Barth, Nolle, and Rice (BNR, 1997). Although the statistics are a bit dated (from 1993), they cover all of the countries. However, the ratio covers only commercial banks and for some countries, such as Germany, commercial banks are of limited overall importance. The data shown in column 5 of table 2 have been rescaled to correct for this coverage effect; where BNR report the share of commercial bank assets relative to total bank assets, we restate the three-firm concentration ratio in terms of all bank assets.

Even after making this adjustment, looking at only the top three firms may be misleading. For example, consider a country with ten roughly equally sized banks versus a country that has three dominant banks and hundreds of small banks. Depending on the size of the large banks in the second country, small banks might appear to be more or less important than in the first country, even though there may be no small banks in the first country. This problem can occur where there is a sharp discontinuity in the size distribution of banks. To partially address it, we show five- and ten-firm concentration ratios, based on data for 1995 from the Bank for International Settlements (BIS). The BIS data are broader (relative to all banks not just commercial banks) and more current than the BNR measure but, regrettably, they are not available for all countries.

For the most part, the different size distribution statistics paint a similar picture. In Belgium, Netherlands, and the UK, the large banks appear to hold a dominant position. Conversely, Italy, Germany, and Luxembourg stand out as countries in which the smaller banks control a significant fraction of the assets. The limitations of the data preclude drawing any sharp distinctions among the remaining countries.

TABLE 2
Size distribution of banks in selected countries

Country	Range of banks covered by OECD	Banks covered by OECD in 1995	Total assets of 1995 OECD reporting banks (billions U.S. $)[a]	1993 commercial bank assets in the 3 largest commercial banks[b]	1993 assets of all credit institutions in 3 largest commercial banks[c]	1995 assets in 5 largest institutions[c]	1995 assets in 10 largest institutions[c]
				(----------percent----------)			
Belgium	All banks	143	843.3	44	44	59[e]	73[e]
Denmark	Commercial and savings banks	114	166.7	64	NA	NA	NA
France	All banks	1,453	3797	64	33	47	63
Germany	All banks	3,500	4,151.4	89	24	17	28
Greece	Commercial banks	18	69.7	98	73	NA	NA
Ireland	Commercial banks[d]	434[d]	71.24[d]	94	76	NA	NA
Italy	All banks	269	1,519.7	36	28	29	45
Luxembourg	Commercial banks	220	612.9	17	17	NA	NA
Netherlands	All banks	173	916.5	59	59	81	89
Portugal	All banks	37	201.1	38	NA	NA	NA
Spain	All banks	318	951	50	34	49	62
UK	Commercial banks	40	1,184.1	29	NA	57[e]	78[e]
U.S.	Commercial banks	9,986	4,149.3	13	10	13	21
Japan	Commercial banks	138	6,733.9	28	NA	17[e]	28[e]

[a]Exchange rates are taken from 1996 IMF *Financial Statistics Yearbook*, p. 15. All domestic figures are converted into special drawing rights and then into dollars.
[b]Source is Barth, Nolle, and Rice (1997), table 3.
[c]Source is Bank for International Settlements, *Annual Report* (1996).
[d]These data are for 1993 and are taken from Barth, Nolle, and Rice (1997), table 3.
[e]These data are for 1994.

In addition to the data on bank size, we use a number of measures of bank profitability and capital. In principle, the uninsured liabilities of banks with high levels of capital should have lower credit risk. Thus, well-capitalized (or highly rated) banks should have a much easier time going to securities markets to raise funds in the face of a deposit shock. This implies that monetary policy would have less of an impact when banks are well capitalized.[5] However, for most countries, data on capitalization and credit-worthiness are available only for the major institutions; smaller banks tend not to be monitored by the rating agencies that collect most of these statistics. Our benchmark measure of creditworthiness comes from Thomson BankWatch, one of the leading global bank rating agencies. According to its Web page, Thomson constructs ratings which:

"Incorporate a combination of pure credit risk with performance risk looking over an intermediate horizon. These ratings indicate the likelihood of receiving timely payment of principal and interest, and an opinion on the company's vulnerability to negative events that might alter the market's perception of the company and affect the marketability of its securities."[6]

Because these ratings (shown in column 1 of table 3) do not cover all the banks in each country, we supplemented the Thomson data with another measure of bank health. The OECD publishes a stylized income statement for banks in its member countries. The processing lags required to generate comparable data are such that 1995 data are just becoming available. To calibrate the Thomson sample to the broader OECD sample, we calculated the return on average assets (ROA) for both samples. To control for year-to-year volatility, we averaged the numbers over three years and the results are shown in table 3. The ROA estimates from the two sources are very similar. Table 3 also shows loan losses relative to loans from the Thomson data.

Looking across table 3, the countries seem to fall into three fairly distinct groups. The evidence for the first group, Netherlands, Luxembourg, and the UK, suggests that the banks are in good shape. (The U.S. is also in this group.) In the case of the second group, France and Italy, the numbers consistently show that the banking sectors are relatively weak, with high levels of bad loans and low profit rates. (Japan also belongs in this group.) The third group, comprising all remaining countries, falls somewhere in between.

Options for substituting toward nonbank financing

Our first measure of bank dependence is culled from employment data. Using information from the European Commission, we compare the importance of small firms in different countries. The data exclude the self-employed, but include very small firms employing between one and nine people. We believe monitoring costs for these micro firms are likely to be so high that they will have trouble attracting nonbank financing.[7] Because of the processing lags, the data we analyze are from 1990, but a comparison with similar statistics from 1988 suggests that these employment patterns are fairly stable over time.

Table 4 shows that the smallest firms generally account for a larger fraction of employment in Europe than they do in the U.S., although they vary significantly in importance from one European country to another. In Spain and Italy, more than 40 percent of the work force is attached to these firms, while in Belgium, Germany, and Luxembourg, they are of much more limited significance.[8] Similar heterogeneity exists for mid-sized and large firms.

The last column in table 4 reports the ratio of each country's share of total European employment to its share of the total number of enterprises. A ratio of one would be the typical size distribution for European countries. Ratios below one indicate a preponderance of smaller firms, while ratios above one indicate more larger firms.

Again, these data can be used to sort the countries into three categories. In Greece, Italy, Netherlands, Portugal, and Spain, smaller firms are most important. Germany, Luxembourg, and the UK are dominated by larger firms, with employment distributions that look much more like those of the U.S. The remaining cases are not clear cut.

The second indicator of bank dependence is based on the structure of capital markets across Europe. Ideally, we would like to have a measure of the switching costs firms would incur if they lost their bank financing. We would not expect these firms to be able to issue publicly traded securities directly. However, through trade credit, they may have access to funds raised in the securities markets (see Calomiris, Himmelberg, and Wachtel, 1995). Similarly, although equity financing is rarely an important source of funding for most firms, deep equity markets are often correlated with the existence of other public markets that might be tapped when bank credit contracts.[9]

Accordingly, table 5 provides information from the World Bank on stock market capitalization across different countries. The table also shows OECD data on the public bond markets for each country. However, these data are only for firms listed on the specific exchanges shown in the table and, in some cases, this significantly understates the size of the bond market (for example, in the U.S. where only bonds of the NYSE firms are counted). The bottom line is in the last two columns of the table, which show the ratio of stock market capitalization to gross domestic product (GDP) and the ratio of public bonds to GDP. Subjectively weighting these two measures, we conclude that the availability of nonbank finance is greatest in Belgium, Denmark, and the UK. Conversely, Greece, Italy, and Portugal appear to be the least developed by this metric.

TABLE 3
Bank health in selected countries

Country	Fiscal 1995 Thomson average rating of tracked banks (no. of banks)[a]	Thomson estimated ROA for major banks, 1993–95 (average no. of major banks)	OECD profit before tax relative to assets, 1993–95 (average no. of rated banks)	1995 Thomson estimated loan losses relative to loans for major banks (no. of major banks)
Belgium	B (8)	0.28 (54)	0.23 (147)	NA (NA)
Denmark	B/C (3)	0.55 (74)	0.52 (113)	0.91 (86)
France	B/C (22)	0.15 (298)	0 (1,569)	2.56 (269)
Germany	B/C (24)	.22 (205)	0.26 (3,627)	0.17 (204)
Greece	B (9)	0.39 (22)	0.84 (19)	0.57 (23)
Ireland	B (3)	1.03 (29)	NA (NA)	0.78 (28)
Italy	C (30)	−0.01 (57)	0.11 (296)	7.47 (57)
Luxembourg	B (3)	0.6 (128)	0.36 (220)	0.14 (127)
Netherlands	A/B (3)	0.57 (52)	0.5 (174)	NA (NA)
Portugal	B/C (4)	0.46 (48)	0.62 (36)	3.61 (46)
Spain	B/C (14)	0.20 (101)	0.45 (317)	4.09 (105)
United Kingdom	B (25)	1.84[b] (6)	0.67 (38)	1.21[b] (6)
United States	B (29)	1.23 (29)	1.18 (10493)	0.74 (29)
Japan	C (10)	−0.06[c] (10)	−0.07 (139)	3.96[c] (10)

[a]Thomson normally requires banks to pay to be evaluated. In some cases struggling banks decide not pay for the rating but Thomson assigns a rating anyway (although it may not store all of the financial information for these banks). The country averages pertain to all banks for which a rating was assigned.

The Thomson rating scale is as follows:

A—Company possesses an exceptionally strong balance sheet and earnings record, translating into an excellent reputation and very good access to its natural money markets. If weakness or vulnerability exists in any aspect of the company's business, it is entirely mitigated by the strengths of the organization.
A/B—Company is financially very solid with a favorable track record and no readily apparent weakness. Its overall risk profile, while low, is not quite as favorable as for companies in the highest rating category.
B—Company is strong with a solid financial record and is well received by its natural money markets. Some minor weaknesses may exist, but any deviation from the company's historical performance levels should be limited and short-lived. The likelihood of significant problems is small, yet slightly greater than for a higher rated company.
B/C—Company is clearly viewed as a good credit. While some shortcomings are apparent, they are not serious and/or are quite manageable in the short term.
C—Company is inherently a sound credit with no serious deficiencies, but financial statements reveal at least one fundamental area of concern that prevents a higher rating. Company may recently have experienced a period of difficulty, but those pressures should not be long term in nature. The company's ability to absorb a surprise, however, is less than that for organizations with better operating records.
C/D—While still considered an acceptable credit, the company has some meaningful deficiencies. Its ability to deal with further deterioration is less than that of better rated companies.
D—Company financials suggest obvious weaknesses, most likely created by asset quality considerations and/or a poorly structured balance sheet. A meaningful level of uncertainty and vulnerability exists going forward. The ability to address further unexpected problems must be questioned.
D/E—Company has areas of major weakness that may include funding and/or liquidity difficulties. A high degree of uncertainty exists about the company's ability to absorb incremental problems.
E—Very serious problems exist for the company, creating doubt about its continued viability without some form of outside assistance, regulatory or otherwise.

[b]United Kingdom data are averaged for two years only.
[c]Japanese data cover fiscal years 1995 through 1997.

Predicted potency of the lending channel under the EMU

Given the noisy nature of our data, it is not possible to make strong claims about how important the lending channel might be in different countries. However, we believe the proxies reviewed above provide some interesting information, particularly at the extremes of their respective distributions. To summarize these results, we assigned each country a letter grade (from A to C) for each of our four factors. A grade of "A" indicates the *least* sensitivity to monetary policy.

Table 6 shows these grades and an overall grade (shown in the last column) based on a subjective weighting of the factors. The UK emerges as the country for which the evidence most clearly suggests a relatively weak lending channel. UK banks are in relatively good

TABLE 4
1990 size distribution of employment in selected countries

	% of total Euro 12 employment	% in firms with fewer than 10 people	% in firms with 10–499 people	% in firms with 500+ people	% of total enterprises in Euro 12	Ratio of share of employment to share of enterprises
EURO 12	100	30.3	39.4	30.3	100	1.00
Belgium	3.0	17.0	47.7	35.3	3.5	0.86
Denmark	1.8	31.6	49.1	19.3	1.8	1.00
France	15.5	28.0	41.0	31.0	13.9	1.12
Germany	23.2	18.3	45.6	36.1	14.8	1.57
Greece	NA	NA	82.7	17.3	NA	NA
Ireland	0.25	NA	NA	NA	.072	3.46
Italy	15.7	42.5	37.8	19.7	21.5	0.73
Luxembourg	0.2	15.1	40.6	25.5	0.1	2.00
Netherlands	NA	30.1	45.4	24.5	NA	NA
Portugal	3.0	24.3	54.7	21.0	4.2	0.71
Spain	10.5	45.8	38.9	15.3	17.0	0.62
United Kingdom	20.9	27.1	39.1	33.8	17.2	1.22
United States	107	12.0	41.4	46.6	NA	NA

Notes: Greek data only cover NACE 1–4 and 67; employment figures only cover establishments with an average of 10 or more employees. Irish data only cover enterprises in NACE 1–4 averaging 3 employees or more and NACE establishments averaging 20 employees or more. Data are reported for 3–19 employees or 20 plus employees. NA indicates not available.

Source: Commission of the European Communities, *Enterprises in Europe, Third Report*, Brussels, Belgium (1994).

shape, there are not a lot of small firms, and firms have many other financing options. Belgium and Netherlands also appear to be on the relatively insensitive end of the spectrum. Netherlands has large, creditworthy banks, and Belgium appears to be in moderately good shape in terms of both loan supply sensitivity and bank dependence.

At the opposite end of the spectrum, Italy is clearly the country in which we would expect strong effects of monetary policy, based on each of the factors we have studied. Portugal also fits into this part of the distribution.

In the remaining countries, the picture is less clear. For example, in Germany and Luxembourg there are many small banks, but bank health appears at least adequate and large firms are relatively important. Our data are not sufficiently precise to identify more than the extreme cases.

Conclusions

Research strongly suggests that banks play a role in the transmission of monetary policy. The factors that determine the significance of this role are the degree of bank dependence on the part of firms and consumers and the ability of banks to offset monetary-policy-induced deposit outflows. Based on the best available data, we find considerable differences in these dimensions across member countries of the European Union.

When it goes into effect, the EMU may provide answers to key questions regarding the potency of the bank lending channel. Given the wide heterogeneity in bank health, a sudden shift in monetary conditions (such as an increase in interest rates by the European central bank) would provide a live test of this mechanism. In the meantime, our research suggests that it would be desirable to consider integration in banking and securities markets in tandem with the move to a single currency European

TABLE 5
Nonbank financing options

Country	Stock exchange tracked by World Bank	1995 listed firms on exchange tracked by World Bank	1995 market capitalization (world rank)	1995 GDP	Exchange for bond market data (year)	Public bonds of traded firms	Equity value as a % of GDP	Public bonds as a % of GDP
			(---- U.S. $ billions ----)			(U.S. $ billions)		
Belgium	Brussels	143	104.96 (22)	269.2	Brussels (1995)	235.0	0.39	0.87
Denmark	Copenhagen	213	56.22 (27)	175.2	Copenhagen (1995)	301.1	0.32	1.72
France	Paris	450	522.05 (5)	1,549.2	Paris (1993)	662.9	0.34	0.43
Germany	German Stock Exchange Inc.	678	577.37 (4)	2,420.5	Frankfurt (1995)	1,223.8	0.24	0.51
Greece	Athens	99	10.16 (NA)	111.8	Athens (1989)	17.5	0.09	0.16
Ireland	Irish Stock Exchange	80	25.82 (37)	60.1	Not shown separately	NA	0.43	NA
Italy	Italian Stock Exchange Council	250	209.52 (13)	1,091.1	Milan (1994)	760.5	0.19	0.70
Luxembourg	Luxembourg	61	30.44 (36)	16.8	Luxembourg (1989)	1.5	1.81	0.09
Netherlands	Amsterdam	387	356.48 (8)	396.9	Amsterdam (1995)	0.294	0.90	0.00
Portugal	Lisbon	169	18.36 (39)	103.2	NA	NA	0.18	NA
Spain	Madrid	362	197.79 (14)	557.4	Madrid (1995)	27.7	0.35	0.05
United Kingdom	London	2,078	1,407.74 (3)	1,099.7	Ireland and UK (1993)	554.4	1.28	0.50
United States	Combined NYSE, AMEX, NASDAQ	7,671	6,857.62 (1)	6,981.7	New York (1995)	2,495.9	0.98	0.36
Japan	Combined all major exchanges[a]	2,263	3,667.29 (2)	4,960.7	Tokyo (1994)	1,789.6[b]	0.74	0.36

[a]The Japanese exchanges include Fukoka, Hiroshima, Kyoto, Nagoya, Niigata, Osaka, Sapporo, and Tokyo.
[b]Japanese bond data cover both domestic and foreign firms.
Sources: *Emerging Stock Markets Factbook*, International Finance Corporation (1996); OECD, "OECD financial statistics, part 1," *Financial Statistics Monthly*, various issues, and OECD, *Non-Financial Enterprises Financial Statements* (1995).

TABLE 6
Summary of factors affecting the lending channel

Country	Importance of small banks (Table 2)	Bank health (Table 3)	Importance of small firms (Table 4)	Availability of nonbank finance (Table 5)	Overall predicted potency
Belgium	A	B	B	A	A/B
Denmark	B	B	B	A	B
France	B	C	B	B	B/C
Germany	C	B	A	B	B
Greece	B	B	C	C	B/C
Ireland	B	B	B	B	B
Italy	B	C	C	C	C-
Luxembourg	C	A	A	B	B
Netherlands	A	A	C	B	A/B
Portugal	B	C	C	C	C
Spain	B	B	C	B	B
United Kingdom	A	A	A	A	A

Note: A grade of "A" indicates low effect of lending channel sensitivity to monetary policy; "C" indicates high sensitivity.

banking regulations have officially been harmonized for several years. However, the health of the banking system varies significantly from one country to another, and few banks have begun lending outside their own borders. Countries with weak banking systems might benefit from the entry of foreign banks into their markets. The development of deeper securities markets that would be available to all European firms could also help offset a potential credit crunch.

APPENDIX

The data shown in table 1 and used in Kashyap and Stein (1995 and 1997) are taken from the quarterly regulatory filings made by all U.S. commercial banks. These reports, commonly referred to as Call Reports, contain detailed quarterly balance sheet and income statement data for all banks. In addition to this basic information, the reports contain data on a variety of off-balance-sheet items, a special supplement on small business lending that is collected as part of the June Call Report, geographic information, and the holding company status of the banks.

The Federal Reserve Bank of Chicago is now making the most popular items from the Call Reports available through its Web site. Initially, the post-1990 data will be available; eventually data going back to 1976 will be on-line. The data for each quarter are stored in a SAS transport data set, which has been compressed in a zip format. The zipped files are typically 4.5 megabytes and expand to about 48 megabytes when they are uncompressed. It took us about 15 minutes to download the 1995 fourth quarter file in our tests. You can access the data at www.frbchi.org/rcri/rcri_database.html. (The site also shows current reporting forms filled out by the banks.)

To supplement the raw Call Report data, the Bank's research staff is making a file available that lists all the mergers between U.S. commercial banks from 1976 onward. This merger file can easily be combined with the Call Report data for a number of projects, for example, an event study analysis. We have used the file to screen out banks for which mergers make the accounting statements discontinuous.

The Bank's Web site also contains a simple data access program. This program allows a user to create consistent time series for several of the major items on the banks' balance sheets. Similarly, there is documentation describing the known breaks in all of the series.

A picture of the Web site appears on the following page.

Go To: http://www.frbchi.org/rcri/rcri_database.html

Report of Condition and Income Database

The Report of Condition and Income database contains selected data for all banks regulated by the Federal Reserve System, Federal Deposit Insurance Corporation, and Comptroller of the Currency. The financial data are on an individual bank basis and were selected from the following schedule: assets and liabilities, income, capital, off-balance-sheet transactions, risk-based capital, and other memoranda items. Files are available quarterly and only for downloading purposes.

About the Data

Documentation files:

Data Description contains a list of all the variables in this database.

Data Definitions contains the definitions of the variables and notes on forming consistent time series.

Data Access contains information on how to import the zipped SAS files into various software packages and a sample SAS program.

Sample Form shows the reporting form currently used to collect the data.

Merger Data

The merger file contains information that can be used to identify all bank acquisitions and mergers since 1976. These data can be merged into the Call Report data.

Quarterly Call Report Data

Each quarterly data file contains income and balance sheet items for all the banks. The files are zipped using PKZIP. The files are in SAS transport data file format. The files are about 4.5 megabytes in compressed form and about 48 megabytes when expanded.

Year	1st quarter	2nd quarter	3rd quarter	4th quarter
1990	1st	2nd	3rd	4th
1991	1st	2nd	3rd	4th
1992	1st	2nd	3rd	4th
1993	1st	2nd	3rd	4th
1994	1st	2nd	3rd	4th
1995	1st	2nd	3rd	4th
1996	1st	2nd	3rd	4th

Document: Done

NOTES

[1] Throughout all of what follows we are implicitly relying on the conventional assumption that there is imperfect price adjustment. See Bernanke and Gertler (1995), Cecchetti (1995), Hubbard (1995), and Kashyap and Stein (1994) for other surveys of this literature.

[2] See Diamond (1984) for a formal treatment of this problem.

[3] See Borio (1996) and Berran, Coudert, and Mojon (1996) for two exceptions.

[4] A finding that these forms of financing move in opposite directions following a monetary contraction should not be taken as an indication that those firms that are cut off from banks are the same ones that begin issuing commercial paper. A much more realistic mechanism is that smaller firms that are cut off from bank lending receive increased trade credit, and the trade credit is supplied by larger firms that can access the commercial paper market.

[5] For the U.S., Kashyap and Stein (1994) note that things may have worked differently in the credit crunch of the early 1990s. If a regulatory risk-based capital standard binds banks at the margin, then the banks' loan supply can become disconnected from changes in monetary policy. In this case, the binding capital requirement can generate a "pushing on a string" problem for the central bank, in which monetary policy becomes *less* effective.

[6] Description of Thomson issuer ratings from www.bankwatch.com, as of July 17, 1997. We thank Christopher Tang for supplying the BankWatch data and answering our questions about them.

[7] One caveat to this assumption is that if firms are part of a holding company structure that creates the appearance of many small firms in order to skirt certain regulations, then it is possible that these firms may have access to the internal capital market of the holding company.

[8] Of course, the Gertler and Gilchrist numbers shown earlier demonstrate that small firms generally may account for a much larger fraction of fluctuations than suggested by their average share of the aggregate economy.

[9] For example, Demirgüç-Kunt and Levine (1996) show that stock market capitalization tends to be fairly highly correlated with the ratio of domestic credit to GDP.

REFERENCES

Bank for International Settlements, *Annual Report*, Basel, Switzerland: BIS, 1996.

Barth, James R., Daniel E. Nolle, and Tara N. Rice, "Commercial banking structure, regulation, and performance: An international comparison," Office of the Comptroller of the Currency, economics working paper, No. 97-6, 1997.

Berger, Allen N., Anil K Kashyap, and Joseph M. Scalise, "The transformation of the U.S. banking industry: What a long, strange trip it's been," *Brookings Papers on Economic Activity*, 1995, pp. 55–218.

Bernanke, Ben S., and Alan S. Blinder, "The federal funds rate and the channels of monetary transmission," *American Economic Review*, Vol. 82, September 1992, pp. 901–921.

Bernanke, Ben S., and Mark Gertler, "Inside the black box: The credit channel of monetary policy transmission," *Journal of Economic Perspectives*, Vol. 9, Fall 1995, pp. 27–48.

Berran, Fernando, Virginie Coudert, and Benoit Mojon, "The transmission of monetary policy in European countries," Centre D'Études Prospectives et D'Informations Internationales, working paper, 1995.

Borio, Claudio, "Credit characteristics and the monetary transmission mechanism in fourteen industrial countries: Facts, conjectures, and some econometric evidence," in *Monetary Policy in a Converging Europe*, Koos Alders, Kees Koedijk, Clemens Kool, and Carlo Winder (eds.), Amsterdam: Kluwer Academic Press, 1996, pp. 77–115.

Calomiris, Charles W., Charles P. Himmelberg, and Paul Wachtel, "Commercial paper, corporate finance, and the business cycle: A microeconomic perspective," *Carnegie-Rochester Conference Series on Public Policy*, Vol. 42, 1995, pp. 203–250.

Carpenter, Robert E., Steven M. Fazzari, and Bruce C. Petersen, "Inventory investment, internal-finance fluctuations, and the business cycle," *Brookings Papers on Economic Activity*, 1994, pp. 75–138.

Cecchetti, Stephen G., "Distinguishing theories of the monetary transmission mechanism,"

Review, Federal Reserve Bank of St. Louis, Vol. 77, May/June 1995, pp. 83–97.

Demirgüç-Kunt, Asli, and Ross Levine, "Stock market development and financial intermediaries: Stylized facts," *The World Bank Economic Review*, Vol. 10, No. 2, 1996, pp. 291–321.

Diamond, Douglas W., "Financial intermediation and delegated monitoring," *Review of Economic Studies*, Vol. 51, No. 166, July 1984, pp. 393–414.

Gertler, Mark, and Simon Gilchrist, "Monetary policy, business cycles, and the behavior of small manufacturing firms," *Quarterly Journal of Economics*, Vol. 109, May 1994, pp. 309–340.

Gertler, Mark, and R. Glenn Hubbard, "Financial factors in business fluctuations," *Financial Volatility: Causes, Consequences, and Policy Recommendations*, Washington, DC: Federal Reserve Board, 1988.

Gibson, Michael, "The bank lending channel of monetary policy transmission: Evidence from a model of bank behavior that incorporates long-term customer relationships," Federal Reserve Board, working paper, 1996.

Hoshi, T., David Scharfstein, and Kenneth J. Singleton, "Japanese corporate investment and Bank of Japan guidance of commercial bank lending," in *Japanese Monetary Policy*, Kenneth J. Singleton (ed.), NBER, 1993, pp. 63–94.

Hubbard, R. Glenn, "Is there a 'credit' channel for monetary policy?," *Review*, Federal Reserve Bank of St. Louis, Vol. 77, May/June 1995, pp. 63–77.

International Finance Corporation, *Emerging Stock Markets Factbook*, Washington, DC, 1996.

Kashyap, Anil K, and Jeremy C. Stein, "Monetary policy and bank lending," in *Monetary Policy*, N. Gregory Mankiw (ed.), Chicago: University of Chicago Press, 1994, pp. 221–256.

_____, "The impact of monetary policy on bank balance sheets," *Carnegie-Rochester Conference Series on Public Policy*, Vol. 42, 1995, pp. 151–195.

_____, "What do a million banks have to say about the transmission of monetary policy," National Bureau of Economic Research, working paper, No. 6056, June 1997.

Kashyap, Anil K, Jeremy C. Stein, and Owen Lamont, "Credit conditions and the cyclical behavior of inventories," *Quarterly Journal of Economics*, Vol. 109, August 1994, pp. 565–592.

Kashyap, Anil K, Jeremy C. Stein, and David W. Wilcox, "Monetary policy and credit conditions: Evidence from the composition of external finance," *American Economic Review*, Vol. 83, March 1993, pp. 78–98.

_____, "Monetary policy and credit conditions: Evidence from the composition of external finance: Reply," *American Economic Review*, Vol. 86, March 1996, pp. 310–314.

Ludvigson, Sydney, "The channel of monetary transmission to demand: Evidence from the market for automobile credit," Federal Reserve Bank of New York, working paper, No. 9625, 1996.

Milne, Alistair, "Inventory investment in the UK: Excess volatility, financial effects, and the cost of capital," University of London, unpublished Ph.D. thesis, 1991.

Organization for Economic Cooperation and Development, *Bank Profitability: Financial Statements of Banks 1986–1995* (preliminary), Paris: OECD, 1997.

_____, *Non-Financial Enterprises Financial Statements*, Paris, 1995.

_____, "OECD financial statistics, part 1," *Financial Statistics Monthly*, Paris, various issues.

Sharpe, Steven A., "Bank capitalization, regulation, and the credit crunch: A critical review of the research findings," Federal Reserve Board, working paper, No. 95-20, 1995.

Stein, Jeremy C., "An adverse selection model of bank asset and liability management with implications for the transmission of monetary policy," National Bureau of Economic Research, working paper, No. 5217, 1995.

EMU and Capital Markets: Big Bang or Glacier?[1]

Daniel Gros
Centre for European Policy Studies, Brussels.

Abstract

EMU is a non-event from a macroeconomic point of view; financial market regulations will not change and households will barely notice that something has changed on 1 January 1999. In this sense EMU does not constitute a big bang. European financial markets will retain their national characteristics for some time because of the many national regulations (prudential and fiscal) that make assets expressed in euro imperfect substitutes across borders. Moreover, national central banks have a vested interest in preserving local idiosyncrasies, and prudential supervision will also continue to be handled differently from country to country. But these national indiosyncracies cannot forever survive competitive pressures in the euro area. The year 1999 will thus see the beginning of a process of unification of financial markets that will be irresistible in the end, but will take some time to complete.

I. Introduction

On 1 January 1999 the European Central Bank (ECB) starts conducting a common monetary policy for the (initially 11) participating member countries of the EU. But this does not necessarily constitute a 'big bang'. From a

---

[1]This contribution draws on joint work with Niels Thygesen and Karel Lannoo.

macroeconomic point of view little changes, since the core countries of the EMS have already had a *de facto* common monetary policy over the last decade. Inflation and interest rates converged several years ago for this group of countries, and even for the relative newcomers to price stability (Spain, Italy and Portugal) low inflation and interest rates do not constitute news any more. The convergence of interest rates, inflation and fiscal policy was obtained over the last years as member countries made enormous efforts to meet the Maastricht criteria. In this sense, the real news about EMU came much before 1 January 1999 as governments surprised markets by being much tougher than anticipated. But the fact that convergence was achieved before the formal start of EMU implies that the creation of the ECB is a non-event from a macroeconomic point of view.

The start of the third stage of EMU will also, *per se*, have no effect on the regulatory environment for financial markets. Most of the internal market programme for financial services has already been implemented, and the European passport for banking has in principle allowed for unfettered cross-country competition for a number of years. But until now national capital markets have retained many distinguishing features and show little sign of converging rapidly towards a single model. Households will in any case have to wait until 2002 before they can use euro banknotes, and in the meantime they are limited to seeing the euro as a memo item on their bank account statements.

So, one is tempted to ask: What will change with EMU?

There are, of course, a few minor 'bangs' happening in January 1999. The foreign exchange and the inter-bank markets immediately switch over to the euro and there will be a unified payments system that allows for real-time transfers within the euro zone. Moreover, most government debt will be redenominated. There will thus be some large and liquid segments that operate in euros. But this does not imply that national capital markets lose their characteristics because of the many national regulations (prudential and fiscal) that make assets expressed in euros imperfect substitutes across borders. The purpose of this paper is to provide a description of the major obstacles to the emergence of an integrated European capital market.

The paper starts in Section II with the institutional elements of EMU, namely the ECB. It is not widely recognized how decentralized the decision-making and implementation of monetary policy will be in the euro area. This is important, as national central banks will retain a lot of leeway (perhaps too much) in championing their local clients. Section III touches on other central banking tasks that are not assigned to the ECB, making it thus an incomplete central bank. Section IV discusses briefly whether the minor big bangs of January 1999 are sufficient to create a critical mass of euro-users during the incomplete monetary union of 1999–2002. Section V illustrates some of the fiscal regulations that separate capital markets. Section VI concludes with a reflection on the implications for capital markets.

II. The Institutional Environment

A. *The Governing Bodies of the European System of Central Banks: Centre versus National Central Banks*

The European System of Central Banks (ESCB) consists of a central institution, the European Central Bank (ECB), and the national central banks (NCBs) of EU member states that have joined EMU. The ECB (located in Frankfurt) has two governing bodies: the Executive Board and the Governing Council.[2] The Executive Board has six members, including the President (Wim Duisenberg) and a Vice-President (Christian Noyer), all nominated by the historic European Council of May 1998.[3]

The Governing Council comprises the six members constituting the Executive Board and the governors of the participating national central banks. All members of Council have one vote.[4] This last provision is very important. Acceptance of the one-man-one-vote principle must be seen as an important concession by Germany (and to a lesser extent by other large member states). It was obtained in return for the explicit mandate to preserve price stability and the high degree of independence for the ESCB. Together with assured long periods of tenure, and the role of the ECB Governing Council in future nominations for the Executive Board, the voting rule should assure that this decisive policy-making body develops a high degree of cohesiveness and collegiality. Weighted voting could have fostered the thinking that governors were primarily representing national interests and were not equal members of a collegiate body charged with formulating a common policy for Europe.

The Governing Council is vested with the main overall authority: 'The Governing Council shall formulate the monetary policy of the Community

---

[2] Central bank governors from EU countries which have not entered EMU will not take part in the joint decisions in the Governing Council of the ECB as foreseen by Article 109k of the Treaty which states that, in case of some Member states having been given a derogation in the final stage of EMU, the voting rights for the representatives of the central bank governors concerned on the ECB Council will be suspended. The excluded governors will have a seat on the ECB *General* Council, which has, however, no influence on monetary policy.

[3] For a detailed description of the institutional set-up see chapter 12 in Gros and Thygesen 1998.

[4] This principle does not apply to voting on financial matters (distribution of profits and loss), for which the capital key, based on GDP and population weights; it can be set and revised every five or ten years (Article 28).

© Blackwell Publishers Ltd. 1998

including, as appropriate, decisions relating to intermediate monetary objectives, key interest rates and the supply of reserves in the system, and shall establish the necessary guidelines for their implementation' (Article 12.1 of the Statutes of the ESCB). But, as policy could hardly be set in sufficient detail by a Council likely to meet only on a monthly basis, this paragraph continues with 'The Executive Board shall implement monetary policy ... including by giving the necessary instructions to national central banks' (Article 12.1). This formulation seems to leave no doubt as to the hierarchical nature of the system.

In reality, however, important practical issues concerning the division of responsibilities for implementing policies between the ECB and the participating national central banks have been left open since the Statutes stipulate that:

> To the extent deemed possible and appropriate and without prejudice to the provisions of this Article (i.e. the capacity to give instructions), the ECB shall have recourse to the national central banks to carry out operations which form part of the tasks of the ESCB.
> (Article 12.1)

A further element that highlights the uneasy balance between the centre and the participating NCBs is that the ECB Executive Board members will have only six votes out of a total number of votes in the Governing Council of, initially, 17. That latter number will rise further, as EU/EMU membership widens. This minority position resembles that of the Bundesbank Board (Direktorium) prior to 1992, which had, for most of the time,[5] seven members and a Council (Rat) with a total (maximum) of 18 members, given that there were 11 presidents of Landeszentralbanken. However, in Germany all significant monetary policy operations were centralized in Frankfurt, which made up for any perception of weakness at the centre. Moreover, even in Germany a need was felt to redress the balance when five new Länder joined. The 16 members representing Länder were reduced to nine so that currently the balance is eight:nine (for a total of 17).[6]

---

[5] The law on the Bundesbank of 1957 foresaw that the 'Direktorium' would consist of up to 10 members, as much as there were 'Landeszentralbanken' at the time. But the maximum possible number of members of the Direktorium was never reached.

[6] A seldom-mentioned side-effect of EMU is that it makes the internal decision-making structures of national central banks obsolete. The governors or presidents cannot be bound by instructions from their own organizations. As only the arguments and votes expressed by the President in the Governing Council of the ECB will count, the national substructures, such as the Zentralbankrat in Germany, will in effect become mere debating clubs and lose all influence. National central banks will *de facto* become hierarchical.

© Blackwell Publishers Ltd. 1998

In the United States, the Federal Open Market Committee (FOMC), which meets every five to six weeks, has functions analogous to those envisaged for the ECB Governing Council in setting monetary objectives and in formulating guidelines for the main policy instrument, open-market operations, to be undertaken through the Federal Reserve Bank of New York. The FOMC meetings are attended by the seven members of the Board of Governors, nominated by the President of the United States, subject to confirmation by the US Senate, and the 12 Presidents of the regional Federal Reserve Banks. Of the latter only five have the right to vote at any one meeting, so the majority lies with the Board – provided they agree, obviously. The central position of the Board is further underlined by the attribution to it alone of two important policy instruments: discount rate changes and variations in reserve requirements. Although these latter two instruments have recently lost their importance, the Board of Governors retains its dominant influence both on decisions and on implementation of policy. This was not always the case. As analysed in Eichengreen 1992, during its early years the Federal Reserve was even less unified than the ESCB. But the uncertain and belated response of the Federal Reserve to the depression was then also the main reason why its statutes were changed.

The experience of the Bundesbank and the Federal Reserve also shows that the strength of centrally appointed members of governing councils of NCBs is usually based on their superior back-up in terms of analysis, rather than their numbers. Even in otherwise rather federally structured NCBs, almost the entire analytical staff (mainly, but not exclusively research) who prepare the background material for major policy decisions are concentrated at headquarters, and work under the direction of the centrally appointed members of the governing councils, or whatever institution represents the highest decision-making body at the national level. This will be different in the case of the E(S)CB, as can be seen from Table 1, which shows the headquarters staff of a number of NCBs. The total staff of the ECB of some 400–500 is minuscule compared to the 60,000–70,000 employed by the component NCBs. Monetary policy is supposed to be executed ('to the extent possible', according to the Treaty) by the latter, and hence they will need more personnel. But even if one looks only at the analytical staff (i.e. the ones not directly involved in the execution of monetary policy), it is clear that the ECB will be rather weak compared to most of the NCBs in the euro area.

Table 1 thus suggests clearly that the six members of the Board of the ECB will be in a rather weak position vis-à-vis the (initially) 11 governors of the NCBs who will also sit in the Council of the ECB. A number of NCB presidents will be able to rely on a larger staff for analysis at their home base than the board members in Frankfurt. There is thus a danger that some governors will arrive at the bi-monthly meetings with analysis that has been prepared by their national staff and that is thus likely to be at least 'coloured'

© Blackwell Publishers Ltd. 1998

by a national view; possibly if only because of the fact that national data will become available before EMU-area-wide data.[7]

Something like this has actually also been taking place within the Zentralbankrat of the Bundesbank. The presidents of Landeszentralbanken in eastern Germany are more interested in low interest rates, given the depressed state of industry in their region. The president of the Landeszentralbank of Hesse (which includes Frankfurt) is at times accused by his colleagues from other Länder that he looks only after the interest of the large banks headquartered in 'his' Frankfurt, whereas they have to take into account the interest of the myriad smaller banks that dominate the banking scene in the province.

The background notes on which decisions of the ECB Governing Board will have to be based (e.g. notes on the inflation outlook to serve as a basis for a decision on interest rates) will thus not come mainly from ECB staff. Moreover, during the first few years of operation the ECB staff will be absorbed by technical tasks to ensure that the framework for the execution of monetary policy works smoothly, whereas a number of operational personnel at NCBs (e.g. in foreign exchange markets) will no longer be needed, and, as they must be occupied somehow, many might turn to research. The system might thus produce too much analytical material; but this would mostly originate in NCBs. The ECB will try to impose a uniform framework on the entire system (as is done in the Federal Reserve), but this might work only for 'ordinary administration', not during critical periods or for the many new issues that the ECB will have to face.

The excess supply of personnel at the national level[8] suggests that the ECB will be pushed initially to continue the practice adopted under the EMI regime, namely to have most important decisions prepared by committees drawn from NCBs. These committees are in many cases not even chaired by EMI personnel, and have to reach a consensus before a position can be taken. The ECB is likely to continue the staffing policy of the EMI, which recruited almost all of its staff through secondments from NCBs. As these secondments are usually for limited periods, the ECB staff will retain their loyalty to their home national central banks and will not develop the *esprit de corps* that has characterized, for example, the Bundesbank, and which becomes crucial when the institution is under pressure.

Moreover, it is difficult to see how the views of the governors, who come to Frankfurt only every two weeks or so (for at most one and a half days), can

---

[7]Dornbusch and Giavazzi 1998 speak of 'clones' that replicate national preferences.

[8]According to press reports the French Parliament was induced to include some provisions that effectively guarantee the employment of the staff of the French central bank when it had to make some final minor changes to the statute of the Banque de France to render it fully compatible with the Maastricht Treaty.

fail to be strongly influenced by their national background. The governors will spend most of their time and efforts in their home countries, dealing with national problems and addressing a national audience most of the time. This diversity in outlook creates the risk that reaching an agreement will be difficult because the starting points in the discussion will be so different.[9] The danger is that this might paralyse the ECB in the face of crisis. At the very least the ECB is thus likely to be slow in its decisions, unable to react quickly to market developments. Under these circumstances it will also take some time to develop the unity of views (or corporate culture) that would enhance credibility with markets and deliver efficient decision-making.[10]

A first comparison of the ESCB with either of the two main federal models – the Deutsche Bundesbank and the Federal Reserve System – in their present form must arrive at the conclusion that the ECB Executive Board is likely to have a relatively weaker position with respect to both decision-making and policy implementation than its German and US counterparts. The Board will be squeezed from one side by the Governing Council, the repository of all major policy-making authority, and from the other side by the participating NCBs, which will be anxious to preserve as many operational tasks as possible, partly to retain influence for themselves, and partly to defend the perceived interests of their employees. The national governors will argue, on the basis of the principle of subsidiarity, that they can implement policy at least as efficiently as a new and inexperienced operational centre at the ECB under the daily management of the Board.

The ECB will not have a significant balance sheet as all monetary policy operations will be on the books of the NCBs. The ECB will thus not be in constant contact with the markets. It will not have a significant dealing room, so that it could not act on its own account, even if it wanted to. In terms of market developments it has to rely on what is reported by the NCBs. Another consequence of the absence of a normal central bank balance sheet for the ECB is that seigniorage revenues will accrue at the national level and have to be redistributed. Agreeing on a procedure for this redistribution has been difficult because the provisions in the Statutes have proven unacceptable (see Gros 1998 for details).

---

[9]The disagreements that surfaced when the 1998 convergence report of the EMI was prepared apparently convinced at least one governor that the ECB will not be a truly European institution '*super partes*' and that he will have to defend his country in the Governing Board. (Rampari 1998)

[10]See von Hagen 1997 for a discussion of the dangers of majority voting in a heterogeneous body.

© Blackwell Publishers Ltd. 1998

B. Consequences of Excessive Decentralization

The ambition to decentralize policy implementation 'to the full extent possible' will have an impact on capital markets because it implies preservation of some of the idiosyncrasies that currently characterize local capital (and especially money) markets. Incentives to retain operations in the national financial centres, arising from a) the desire to protect the employment of specialized staff in the central banks, and b) to extend favours to the private financial institutions in a particular country, remain.

i) Regarding staff, EU15 central banks currently employ a total of over 60,000.[11] Total employment in the Federal Reserve System, which performs similar tasks to those to be assigned to the ECB and the NCBs, including supervisory and reporting functions, is less than half this number.

NCBs are difficult to compare. Differences in geography, financial structure and historically inherited tasks can explain some of the striking differences in staffing. The number of central bank staff per million inhabitants ranges from 294 for Belgium (and 292 for France) to 83 for Spain, with an EU15 average of 160; against 82 for the US and 50 for Japan. For example, some undertake extensive printing activities beyond those related to the note issue; others (of which the largest – the Banque de France, with about 17,000 employees – is the prime example) are heavily involved in the production of economic statistics, the analysis of company financial statements, etc. Some even still offer domestic private clients and banks financial services. Some of these additional activities might be only marginally affected by the move to a single currency but they still imply that different national central banks will tend to be more involved with their national financial systems.

ii) Commercial banks will be able to obtain funds from the ESCB mainly from the central bank of their own country of origin because that is where most of their capital is (access to US Federal Reserve credit is also only through the regional Reserve bank in one's own district). Moreover, NCBs can accept two types of assets in repo operations: a) 'tier one' assets that are standardized throughout the euro area, and b) 'tier two' assets that are used only in some national financial markets. Some national central banks insist on using these tier two, i.e. national, assets. This gives them an instrument to protect their local clients. For example, the Bundesbank (or rather the Landeszentralbanken) insists on using the 'Wechsel' (bill of trade dating from the 19th century) that have so far constituted the base for discount operations in Germany. As this type of IOU is not used in other countries it will be difficult to compare the conditions under which funds are provided through this

---

[11] The total wage and salary bill may be close to ECU 3–4 billion. Running Europe's monetary systems is a relatively labour-intensive industry.

© Blackwell Publishers Ltd. 1998

channel with the conditions under which the ECB provides funds against the euro-area-wide standardized (tier one) assets. In theory, the existence of two types of collateral should not lead to discrimination, as it can be used in the entire area. However, it is not likely that, for example, a French bank would deal in 'Wechsels', and would thus be in a position to use them as collateral with the Banque de France. The existence of local collateral is thus *de facto* likely to give monetary policy a national nuance. The ECB has to approve the list of securities included in the tier-two assets, and can thus limit any abuse. But as all NCBs are in a similar situation, they are unlikely to be strict with their colleagues. A permissive consensus could easily develop under these circumstances.

The two elements discussed so far might be only of folklorist interest if they did not interact with a serious issue; namely the fact that given the existing differences in financial structures, the common monetary policy is likely to have slightly different effects in different countries.[12] How strong these asymmetric effects are has been subject to some debate. Broadly speaking, one can distinguish three angles of attack, as follows.

Some studies have documented differences in financing patterns. Borio 1995 is the best example.[13] For example, a finding that in some countries enterprises rely more on long-term capital (e.g. in Germany) than in others (e.g. Italy) is usually interpreted as implying that any move of the ECB that somehow twists the yield curve would have differential national effects. An increase in short-term rates that reduces inflationary expectations and hence leads to lower long-term interest rates might then have the opposite effects in Germany and Italy.

Other studies have relied on small VAR models to estimate the short-run impact of changing short-term interest rates (the main policy instrument of the ECB) on prices and demand.[14] However, this approach is subject to the Lucas critique in its severest form. Past correlation cannot contain a lot of information in this case. For example, the central bank reaction functions must all change, if only because there can no longer be a correlation between national variables and monetary policy. Moreover, the reaction function of the ECB will surely be different from that of a follower in the EMS or that of a central bank that has spent the last ten years trying to achieve convergence towards Germany.

A third way is to use existing small-scale models whose structural relations can be assumed to be less affected by EMU. A comparative study along these

---

[12]Differences in industrial structures and trade patterns are relatively minor for the larger member countries and do not constitute another important source of asymmetric effects of a common policy.

[13]See also ECC 1997 for more recent data or Dornbusch et al. 1998 for further references.

[14]See Gerlach and Smets 1995.

© Blackwell Publishers Ltd. 1998

lines organized by the BIS[15] showed that there were differences in the timing and the strength of the transmission of monetary policy. In general, France and Germany show a slower response than other countries. Somewhat surprisingly, the differences in the impact effects reported by Dornbusch et al. 1998 are actually small and statistically not significant, whereas the effect after two years is twice as strong for Italy as for Germany, France or Spain. One reassuring element of these studies is the fact that the Franco-German couple, which accounts for about two-thirds of the GDP of the EMU11 area, shows a very similar pattern.

Differences in financial structures, which lie behind differences in the monetary policy transmission mechanism, are, of course, not exogenous to the monetary policy regime. However, there has been little convergence in financing structures, even between countries that have had essentially the same macro policies for a decade (Germany, France, Austria, Belgium, etc.). The main reason is that tax systems (see below) are more important for financing structures than inflation (as long as it remains moderate), and EMU will not lead quickly to a harmonization of taxes.

Differences in the transmission channels of monetary policy are not just of interest for macroeconomists. They have important implications for the reaction of national stock markets to monetary policy. The larger the differences in the effects of monetary policy, the lower will be the correlation of stock-market returns. Frankel 1996 finds that exchange-rate variability had in the past little impact on the covariance of national stock-market returns. Fixing exchange rates and sharing a common monetary policy will thus not lead automatically to a perfect correlation of national stock markets. This in turn gives shares a certain 'nationality' and has implications for the incentives to diversify away from the home market.[16]

III. The ECB: a Central Bank or a Monetary Policy Rule?

It has so far been argued that the European System of Central Banks (ESCB) does not, in contrast to the Federal Reserve System of the US, constitute a unified organization, but is really much more a coalition of NCBs that have to agree on one common monetary policy. This has important implications for financial markets, as there is much more to central banking than deciding every two weeks on some short-term interest rate. The essence of central banking is often described as consisting of a trilogy: i) control of inflation through

---

[15] See Bank for International Settlements 1996.

[16] See also Biais 1998.

© Blackwell Publishers Ltd. 1998

monetary policy; ii) the safeguarding of the stability of the banking and financial system through prudential policies; and iii) ensuring the efficiency and integrity of payments systems. It is difficult to disentangle a part of this trilogy without losing the global objective, namely to maintain overall economic and financial stability. For example, it is difficult to maintain price stability when the banking system needs large injections of liquidity because it is in a systemic crisis.

Within the euro area, the ECB will not manage all the elements of this trilogy. The ECB was granted exclusive competence in the areas of monetary policy, but its functions in payments systems and prudential supervision are limited, or exercised in co-operation with the participating NCBs. In this latter area the ECB's role is limited to giving advice to the EU Council of Ministers and the Commission regarding draft Community legislation relating to the prudential supervision of credit institutions and the stability of the financial system. The ECB will, however, collaborate in an extremely important technical mechanism that makes immediate cross-border payments possible within the euro area, namely the TARGET system, which will encompass national real-time gross settlement (RTGS) systems. This system will have to be used for all transactions connected with ECB monetary policy and ensures that euros held on different bank accounts within the EMU area are perfectly substitutable.[17]

This limitation to monetary policy has led some observers to characterize the E(S)CB as a monetary policy rule, rather than a full central bank. Folkerts-Landau and Garber 1992 argue that this could stifle the development of liquid and securitized financial markets because such markets need to be supported by a central bank with broad functions. The ECB will not be in constant contact with financial markets, unlike most NCBs, which not only intervene frequently but also participate in the development of new activities. By contrast, the draft ECB monetary policy instruments provide for only weekly refinancing operations, and likely supporting instruments for its monetary policy, such as reserve requirements, limit short-term funding in the banking system. This could already be observed in Germany, where the existence of reserve requirements provoked the flight of the Deutschmark repo market to the UK.

One simple reason why the ECB could not be made responsible for banking supervision in the euro area is the fact that monetary policy and banking supervisory functions are separated in one half of the Community countries, and combined in the other half (see Table 4). This is not the place to review in depth the academic and policy discussion on this issue. Generally speaking, the arguments in favour of combining both functions derive from the

---

[17] See Folkerts-Landau et al. 1996 on the importance of payments systems for the structure of financial markets.

objective of ensuring the stability of the financial system and preventing contagious systemic crises. One argument is that assigning supervisory and regulatory functions to the central bank should contribute to a better control of overall financial stability. Another argument is that as central banks cannot avoid playing a role in rescues of commercial banks they should also be involved in supervision. But this argument cuts two ways. As has often been argued, especially by the Bundesbank, a conflict of interest might arise as the injection of additional liquidity in the financial system might endanger price stability and increase moral hazard.

The fact that both regimes are equally represented in the EU suggests that there are no definitive arguments for either model. According to Goodhart and Schoenmaker 1995, the question of the appropriate design has to be seen more against the background of the particular financial or banking structure of each country rather than as an abstract generality. Moreover, there is a general trend of retreat in central banks away from supervisory functions, which was exemplified recently by the breakaway of the supervisory functions from the Bank of England and the establishment of the new Financial Services Authority. This new regulatory authority will bring all financial-sector supervision under one roof.

If one takes these arguments seriously, there is a potential 'catch-22': as long as there are large differences among the national financial systems, prudential control must remain at the national level. But as long as national authorities exercise prudential supervision, national financial systems might never converge.

Another reason why any involvement of the ECB in banking supervision would be difficult to accept is that this could force it to act as a lender of last resort, which has, at least potentially, fiscal implications. How would one share the cost of a large banking rescue operation (à la Credit Lyonnais)? Moreover, the ECB might feel that keeping the banking system afloat could at times be difficult to reconcile with the task of maintaining price stability, thus compromising its independence.

NCBs can also argue that, on practical grounds, bank supervision can be better executed at the local level because of the availability of specific expertise and the knowledge of the local market. Because the participating NCBs will be involved in open market and credit operations with banks, they will have hands-on experience with financial markets and institutions and information on market conditions.

All this implies that there is another source of potential trouble, unless excellent communication lines are established between NCBs (or supervisory authorities) and the ECB. The ECB might at times have to constrain lender-of-last-resort operations at the local level, if these threaten to undermine the common monetary policy. But if it wants to avoid acting too late, i.e. when a crisis has become systemic, it needs to develop a capacity systematically to monitor financial markets and to assess financial stability. For the time being it does not look as if it would be able to do so with the structures at hand.

Keeping prudential supervision and control in national hands has important implications for cross-border competition in a number of areas. Despite the existence of an EU passport for banking, there has so far been limited competition in this area. One of the reasons behind this lack of competition is that NCBs (or national supervisory authorities) tend to get involved in all cases where a bank comes into difficulties and might thus represent a target for a takeover from abroad. Rescues, whether open or concealed, often also involve concessions from the fiscal authorities, and this only increases the bias towards 'national' solutions. National authorities in all larger member countries have a tendency to keep control over domestic institutions in national hands. Formally, this can be justified by national supervisory authorities (whether in a central bank or not does not matter) by the 'general good' clause. This clause is contained in all key financial services directives, and stipulates that the free provision of services can be restricted if it is against the 'general good' of the host country. But this clause does not need to be invoked formally, as private-sector financial institutions realize that they cannot proceed in the face of opposition from a local central bank, whatever the motives for this opposition. For example, the Banca d'Italia is said to have blocked for a number of years any expansion of a large German bank in Italy, allegedly in retaliation for the role of the German bank in the 1995 crisis of the lira. Host-country supervision gives national authorities a lot of leeway to influence the structure of their local financial markets. EMU will at least eliminate the escape clause in the Second Banking Directive that allows national supervisory authorities to intervene whenever the 'implementation of their monetary policies' might be affected. As related in Steil 1998 this was used in the past, *inter alia*, to justify the prohibition of interest-bearing current accounts in France. But even under EMU, NCBs can still intervene to protect the ill-defined 'general good'.

IV. The Incomplete Monetary Union (1999–2002)

Another reason why there will be no big bang in 1999 is that the euro will not be available immediately in the form of banknotes. National currencies will thus remain the predominant unit of accounts for households. The legal framework for stage IIIa, as it is sometimes called, is the following. Between 1999 and 2002, only a core of operations has to be carried out in euros. The private sector will be free to change to the euro for all other operations at any time during the three-year period: the basic principle is 'no compulsion, no prohibition' in the use of the euro. The euro will not be available in physical form, but a Council regulation provides a legally enforceable equivalence between the euro and the participating national currency units for all transactions that do not involve cash by stipulating that the national currencies are only (non-decimal) denominations of the euro. Nevertheless, these national denominations of the euro remain the sole legal tender in the respective countries until 2002.

This official reference scenario for the period until 2002 had to be based on the premise that before the euro becomes the sole legal tender, the authorities cannot force the private sector to use it instead of national currency. The private sector will have to be convinced on purely economic grounds. This might be difficult because the use of a currency as a unit of account involves external economic effects similar to the network economies in telecommunications: the marginal cost of using a particular currency depends on how much it is used. A widely used currency has lower transactions costs.[18] The basic concept is that switching to a new currency is costly, and so it will not be in the interest of any single private operator to switch to the euro if everybody else is using only national currencies. If the euro is already widely used, however, the benefits from switching are much greater and it might be in the interest of many private operators to start using it too. Hence it is possible that there are two equilibria for stage IIIa:

i. The euro is used only where mandated, or
ii. The euro is used widely even where not mandated.

Under the second equilibrium, transactions costs might be lower, but the private sector would not adopt this equilibrium on its own because no individual operator would have an interest in taking the first step.

A key determinant for a fast take-off is thus the initial size of the market in euros. At present, there are only three areas where the euro will be used with some certainty: monetary policy operations, public debt and inter-bank operations. The use of the euro in a fourth area, that of non-bank deposits, is much less certain, as the greatest share is held by households. The three latter issues are discussed below.

A. Public Debt

Under the official changeover scenario, only *new tradable* debt had to be issued in euro. This changed when the French Trésor indicated in early 1996

---

[18]See Dowd and Greenaway 1993 for an analysis of network economies in the use of currencies.

© Blackwell Publishers Ltd. 1998

that all its outstanding debt would be converted to euros from the start, which would immediately create a deep euro market with products of different maturities. Other governments then announced similar plans, and under these circumstances even the German (federal) government had to follow.

Redenomination of public debt could be important for the retail sector because the largest holders of government debt in the EU are households. But this does not imply that they will come directly into contact with the euro. Their government debt is often held indirectly via unit trusts and other savings instruments. In the countries where banks are big holders in government debt (e.g. Belgium), over 50% of the asset side of their balance sheets will be in euro, whereas the liabilities side would remain predominantly in national currency (deposits) during the transition period, unless banks convince their clients to use the euro for savings deposits.

The decision to convert public debt is the logical outcome of the intense competition for the position of leading financial centre in EMU. Connected with this issue is the contest to become the benchmark issuer for the euro area. If bond markets remain separate, the contest would be between France and Germany. Although the total volume of German public debt is much higher, the French market is in some respects more attractive. One important element is that federal government debt only amounts to about half of the total German public debt and the debt of the Länder and Gemeinden (the other half) is usually in a non-tradable form. Moreover, French government paper is almost totally dematerialized, which should make it much easier to convert it at once into euros than German public debt. Furthermore, French government bonds cover the maturity spectrum more evenly than the German Bunds, and thus provide sufficient liquidity in all segments of the market. Hence French debt might be a more suitable benchmark. However, it now appears that bond markets will converge on a benchmark that is an index of, for example, government bonds that are all rated triple A.

The emergence of a common benchmark does not change the fact that French and German government debt would still represent distinct securities, trading at slightly different risk premia, but they would both be contained in the relevant benchmark yield curve. Governments with a significantly lower credit rating would of course pay higher risk premia, as markets know that they can no longer rely on their NCB to bail them out if needed. How large these premia have to be is difficult to predict. The existing premia on foreign-currency debt are not a reliable guide, as this debt typically accounted for only a small fraction of overall debt. Nielsen 1998 argues that, at least relative to the past, default premia will become more important, and that individual governments would consider themselves small players on the euro capital market and thus have an incentive to over-issue nominal euro debt, which would imply that some co-ordination of public debt management would be desirable.

© Blackwell Publishers Ltd. 1998

The markets for local government debt outside the three countries with the largest public debts (France, Germany and Italy) will be even more transformed by EMU. There is no longer any reason why governments in the smaller countries should try to cover the entire maturity spectrum, as they have been doing up to now. They will probably have to concentrate on the medium to long end, and they might have to use the instruments that are used by the benchmark issuers.

B. Inter-bank and Foreign Exchange Operations

In most EMU11 countries inter-bank operations (in domestic currency) constitute about one third of the overall balance sheet of the banking system. Most of these operations will be conducted in euros from day one because the wholesale inter-bank market is closely linked to the execution of monetary policy. Moreover, inter-bank operations have to be denominated in euro to be processed by the TARGET payment system. The total of inter-bank deposits in the initial euro zone will amount to 3,000 billion, or more than 50% of the GDP of these countries. To this sum one should add the intra-EMU11 cross-border operations in the currencies of the participating countries. This implies that from early 1999 onwards bank deposits in euros of well over 3 trillion will already exist. This is again a stock effect, but inter-bank deposits are traded frequently; hence this will be a very active and liquid market segment. Moreover, a group of large banks will provide a single EURIBOR (euro inter-bank offered rate) as the benchmark reference rate for the EMU area.

Even before the euro has physically replaced national currencies, the dollar and other third currencies will be quoted and traded only against the euro. This is an extremely active market that turns over the equivalent of hundreds of billion of dollars or euros each day. Even after eliminating inter-EMU area transactions there is still a huge market here in which the euro will be used.[19] Most of the foreign exchange transactions will, however, be between private agents, as official foreign exchange reserves are dwarfed by private holdings of foreign assets. Moreover, foreign exchange interventions will not play an important role in the common monetary policy because the mandate of the ECB is to look at domestic price stability, and because the euro area will not be very exposed to foreign trade (which will account for about 10% of GDP).

The importance of foreign exchange intervention in the common monetary policy will also be affected by the size of the foreign exchange reserves of the ECB. *A priori* one might have thought that the full and definitive transfer of

---

[19]See Hartman 1998 for detailed estimates.

© Blackwell Publishers Ltd. 1998

ownership of all international reserve assets (excluding, of course, holdings of EMU currencies and ECU) from the national level to the ECB would have been a logical step to take to mark the irrevocable nature of the final stage. But this is not foreseen. The ESCB Statute (Article 30) says only that national central banks are to endow the ECB initially with non-EU currency reserves up to ECU 50 billion. The key for contributions will be based on that for capital subscriptions, viz. weights determined equally by the national shares in EU population and GDP (Article 29.1).

Is this sum sufficient? One might take the US as an example, as it is roughly the same size as the euro area in terms of GDP and trade.[20] In this case, the ECU 50 billion limit foreseen by the Treaty appears generous, since that would be considerably more than the amount held today by the US. Even the pro rata reduction for the non-participation of the UK and some smaller countries (about 20%) would still leave the ECB with about the same amount as the two US foreign exchange authorities combined, i.e. about ECU 40 billion.[21]

With one foreign exchange market and area-wide benchmarks in the wholesale banking sector, it is likely that outside investors will perceive a unified euro area long before Europeans, especially households, who have to pay local taxes and are used to putting their investments into certain instruments whose characteristics vary from country to country.

C. Non-bank Deposits

About 75% of non-bank deposits, i.e. the money supply, originate in the household sector, which is likely to be guided by different considerations to the corporate sector in its choice of unit of account. Table 4 shows the proportion of the different monetary aggregates held by households, the corporate and the public sector in Germany and France. It is apparent that almost all long-term deposits are held by households, and that the share of the corporate sector is higher for short-term deposits. One has to keep in mind that a large fraction of the demand deposits of the corporate sector is likely to arise from their dealings with households. A significant fraction of non-bank deposits (i.e. the money supply) will thus be converted into euros only if households start to use it more. Whether this will happen is difficult to predict. But it is likely that as long as households continue using the national currency for

---

[20] The EU11 and the US each account for about 19% of world GDP and 17–18% of world trade.

[21] There are two monetary authorities in the US that hold foreign exchange reserves: the Federal Reserve and the US Treasury Exchange Stabilization Fund. As of end 1996 both held about US$20 billion worth of reserves, mainly DM, yen (and some Mexican pesos!).

© Blackwell Publishers Ltd. 1998

their daily transactions, they will use national currency as their preferred unit of account.

The transitional period will also bring some clarity regarding the root causes of the 'home bias' of investors. It has often been observed that in almost all countries investors hold a portfolio that consists of over 90% domestic assets. Portfolio theory suggests that this is not efficient since, given the low international correlation in returns, investors would gain a lot in lower variance by diversifying internationally. One reason often adduced for the home bias is that foreign exchange transaction costs make cross-border investment more costly. However, Tesar and Werner 1995 report that the turnover on international portfolios is not different from that on domestic portfolios, which would contradict this argument. Under EMU the covariance of returns should increase and the benefits from cross-border diversification should thus fall. At the same time the transactions costs and psychological barriers should also fall. It thus remains to be seen whether EMU will actually lead to a large rebalancing of portfolios and whether this happens already before 2002. Two contrasting opinions can be found in De Santis et al. 1998, who argue that the reduced benefits in terms of diversification of currency fluctuations are more important, and Smith 1998, who takes the opposite position.

A more widespread use of the euro by the private sector will encounter one important obstacle, namely local public administrations that in most cases are not prepared to deal with the euro before 2002. The fact that most tax administrations will not recognize accounts in euro for income tax purposes already implies that firms that want to switch to the euro in their internal account will have to keep an additional set of books. One might think that switching to the euro should only involve multiplying all entries by one number and should thus be easy to do and easy to undo for the local tax offices if they so desire. However, this is not the case as most enterprises carry a lot of unrealized foreign exchange losses and gains on their books, which would have to be fully recognized once they shift to the euro. Switching to the euro as a unit of account can thus have important consequences for tax purposes.

V. Regulatory Barriers to a Fully Integrated Capital Market: Differences in Taxation and Related Regulations

The delay in the appearance of the euro for households is one reason why EMU will not lead immediately to a unified market from the point of view of households, which are ultimately the owners of most investments. But there are other barriers that are much more important and that will operate even long after 2002. The main reason why EMU will not create a truly unified capital market is that investors and borrowers are subject to complicated fiscal regimes that differ greatly from country to country, and this will not change with the introduction of the euro. The importance of this is difficult to document systematically as there is no rule without exception – almost every country and every instrument is a special case. A few examples should, however, suffice to illustrate that differences in tax regimes are crucial for investors:

– in Germany, as in other EU member states, a withholding tax is levied on dividends, paid out of profits on which the company has already paid a 36% corporate income tax. German residents can, however, get a tax credit for the corporate income tax. This tax credit is not available to non-residents. Non-residents can, depending on the existence of a bilateral tax treaty, benefit only from a lower withholding tax rate. Moreover, the German Ministry of Finance accords a tax credit only to dividends from German firms;

– in the UK, a tax credit equivalent to the advance corporation tax paid by a local corporation is available for dividend income of UK residents. Some of the UK's double taxation treaties allow this tax credit also to non-resident individuals and to institutional investors, but reduced by a 15% withholding tax. This tax credit is not applicable to dividends from abroad;

– in Italy, a dividend credit of 56.25% of the amount of the dividend applies to residents and local firms. This tax credit is extended only to France and the UK under double taxation treaties. Italy, furthermore, applies different withholding tax rates on interest income depending on the instrument. Income from Italian Treasury bills is effectively taxed lower than bonds of other member states.[22]

These are only a few examples from the tax jungle. It is difficult to identify a forest from this mass of trees although the basic issues are simple, at least in theory. Personal income taxation is based in all member countries on the worldwide principle; i.e. each individual (or household) is subject to the regime of the country of residence and should pay taxes there on the aggregated income from all sources. The problem is to ensure the application of this principle in reality when there are large differences in the national tax regimes and when national tax administrations do not collaborate and exchange no information. Until now this was not a major problem for most of the population because most income comes from labour (which is not mobile internationally) and the home bias of investors ensured that – apart from corporations – only very rich individuals derived a significant fraction of their overall capital income from foreign sources. But this might change with the euro.

---

[22]Examples based upon *Corporate Taxes, A Worldwide Summary*, by Price Waterhouse 1997.

The prospect of EMU was already enough to bring discussions on an effective enforcement of capital income taxation back on the agenda. The agreement reached in the Council of Finance Ministers (Ecofin) on 1 December 1997 on taxation policy can be considered as a landmark in EU direct tax harmonization. The Council agreed on a package of measures to combat *harmful* tax competition in the EU, including a code of conduct on corporate taxation and elements which should enable the Commission to draft a new proposal for a directive on the taxation of income from savings.[23] The Council created an *ad hoc* group of special representatives of the Finance Ministers, the Taxation Policy Group, and agreed on a Code of Conduct according to which member states promise not to introduce new tax measures which are 'harmful' and to eliminate existing harmful tax measures – the 'standstill' and 'rollback' procedure. According to the Council definition, harmful tax measures are those which provide for a significantly lower effective level of taxation, including zero taxation, than that which generally applies in the member state in question and in the Community as a whole. Such an agreement cannot be expected to have any immediate effect; but the Council also created a forum for regular consultation between the member states to discuss and comment on any new tax measures which may fall within the scope of the code. This 'Review Group' will be co-ordinated by the European Commission and report regularly to Ecofin. Hence even if the agreement is not legally binding, a permanent structure is now in place to discuss tax co-ordination in the EU.

However, one immediate practical step will be taken, namely the drafting of an EU Directive on the taxation of savings. Reaching agreement even on this limited issue will not be easy because a number of member states immediately added their desiderata to the Council conclusions, such as the French request for a minimum rate of withholding tax of 25% and the UK request that it should not apply to Eurobonds and similar instruments (without specifying what the meaning of Eurobonds would be under EMU).[24] However, even if agreement on a Commission proposal is reached quickly by European standards, say during 1998, formal adoption by the Council would take until the end of 1999, with implementation unlikely before 2002.

The basic principle of the draft directive on interest income would be an important step towards the creation of an integrated financial market because

---

[23] The Commission started from the overall assessment that taxation on income from labour was rising too strongly as a result of a downward spiral of unfair tax competition between the member states to attract investments. This was considered harmful since it led to a loss of tax revenue, distorted the single market and destroyed employment.

[24] The existing definition in European law of what constitutes a 'Euro-security' would formally not be affected by EMU as, somewhat surprisingly, it has nothing to do with the currency of issue. This has to change under EMU.

it would imply that a citizen from any member state should no longer be considered a 'foreigner' for tax administrations in other member states. Until now tax administrations did not care whether non-residents declared their income or not in their home country because the loss of revenue was a problem for a foreign country.

One practical problem with the planned European withholding tax (which would be EU-wide, not just EMU-wide) is that two systems of capital income taxation systems are applied in the EU, one where withholding taxes are levied directly when interest income is received, and another where this income is reported to the tax authorities and added to the income tax declaration (a 'reporting system'). Although the reporting system is applied only by two small countries under the Council conclusions, both systems would co-exist, whereby either withholding taxes would be received or information would be provided on savings income to the tax authorities in the other member states.

An overview of general (resident) withholding taxes rates and the tax system applicable in EU member states is given in Table 5. This is an assessment of the most common situation, to which exist many exceptions. In most EU states, withholding taxes are also levied on non-residents, except in Austria, Luxembourg and Sweden, or when a reporting system applies. Since there is little exchange of information between tax administrations yet, the reporting systems *de facto* discriminate between residents and non-residents. Non-resident individuals and corporates often enjoy lower withholding tax rates, depending on the existence of double taxation treaties.

Withholding taxes are in theory only a means to ensure that income is declared so that it can be effectively taxed. However, in reality, withholding taxes are often final on cross-border investments, as national tax administrations give only partial credit for taxes withheld abroad and procedures for tax credits on taxes withheld at source often discriminate against non-residents, or do not apply to them, as illustrated above. Moreover, some national tax administrations (e.g. Italy) are known to take years to pay reimbursements of excess taxes. Even a European-wide uniform withholding tax could thus be perceived differently from country to country; in countries with slow reimbursement it effectively would represent an additional tax.

A detailed description of the tax regimes applicable in EU member states would exceed the scope of this paper. The examples are intended only to give a flavour of the mixture of differential treatment based on the 'nationality' of the instrument and the investor applicable within the EU today, which might keep markets fragmented for some time to come. The EU Taxation Policy Group faces a huge task.

One important issue that is not widely recognized is that of the 'Eurobonds' that are so far exempt from withholding tax. The official definition of a 'Eurobond' is one that is placed by a multinational syndicate simultaneously

© Blackwell Publishers Ltd. 1998

in several countries. As this type of bond was so far mainly bought by institutional investors, there was no need for a withholding tax. But in an integrated bond market most issues should be placed by a syndicate from several countries and be sold in the entire euro area. Hence in future most bonds might qualify as 'Eurobonds' (to avoid confusion the name should be 'Xenobonds'). As this is clearly unacceptable, the 'Euro' market as it existed until 1999 will shrink considerably as many of the issuers were located in the area itself.

However, differences in the taxation of capital income are not the only elements to separate capital markets. There are many further regulations concerning trading of securities, and accounting and disclosure rules, to name just a few. A few examples must again suffice to give an impression of what still remains to be done before one can speak of a single European capital market.

Regarding the organization of securities markets, Article 15.5 of the Investment Services Directive gives member states the right to 'prohibit the creation of new markets within their territories'. This provision could be used to effectively negate the freedom of the single passport provisions and would not be affected by EMU (Steil 1998). The very concept of a 'regulated' market enshrined in this directive gives member states a weapon to defend the perceived interests of their national financial centres.

The lack of comparability of the financial information published by companies across member states is a further reason for the limited integration of Europe's equity markets. Several EU directives regarding harmonization of basic accounting standards, auditing of accounts and rules on disclosure do exist, but they have failed to ensure comparability because the underlying conceptual frameworks differ so much. In some countries the accounting process is driven by the needs of financial markets, whereas in others it is primarily driven by law – the former being mainly the English-speaking countries (and to a certain extent the Netherlands), the latter including the other western European countries. In the former grouping, the accounts should convey information of an adequate quality, in accordance with the currently accepted standards and practices developed by the profession. In the latter, it is based on compliance with statutory requirements. The tax authorities have retained a strong influence on the accounting regulation process in these countries, as national laws state that the taxable profit should be very close to the profit reported in the individual financial statements. Setting an overall conceptual framework for accounting could deprive these authorities of their influence.

Disclosure requirements (e.g. listing particulars for the quotation on stock markets and public-offer prospectuses of securities) also differ from country to country and the mutual recognition foreseen under the single-market programme does not work. Several directives exist in this area, but they are not being implemented or are too vague. The same applies to issues such as the disclosure of major holdings and the prohibition of insider trading.

Progress in these areas is important also for institutional investors, some of which were constrained by prudential rules. Pension funds and insurance companies had usually to invest most of their capital in the home market, or rather in the home currency. These regulations (see Davis 1996 or Gros and Lannoo 1998 for a summary) are redundant under EMU. However, it is not a foregone conclusion that insurance companies will rush to acquire a balanced EMU-wide portfolio as long as the tax treatment is different and it is more difficult to evaluate companies abroad.

Compared to the regulatory and tax differences, the effects of national private-market conventions and of differences in the microstructures should be second order. Private-sector associations are also much more likely to agree on new area-wide conventions. These associations are dominated by the big internationally orientated institutions that have the most to gain from the larger market that is created through the euro. Whether complete harmonization in market conventions is desirable and whether competition will lead to it is a different question.

VI. Conclusions: Implications for Capital Markets

EMU constitutes a quantum step in the process of European integration. But it will not lead to a situation that can be compared to the dollar area. Within the US monetary union it does not make sense to speak of different regional capital markets. Nothing differentiates the New York from the Californian market, except that some market participants are located (and deal) in New York and some others deal primarily in California. This will not be the case in Europe. Even after the introduction of the euro, capital markets will retain a strong 'national' flavour. This does not apply to all market segments, but to most of the important ones. There are many reasons for this. They can best be organized by distinguishing between the retail and the wholesale level (Steil 1998).

At the retail level the reasons for differentiation are clear. National regulations and habits of consumers mean that in each country different instruments are used. Regulation at the retail level is concerned mainly with consumer protection and will therefore remain in national hands. Moreover, there is very little cross-border trade in financial services at the retail level because personal contact is in most cases indispensable. These factors can also explain why political efforts have concentrated on opening the wholesale markets.

National idiosyncrasies at the retail level are myriad. For example, in some countries simple savings accounts are still very popular (and protected by

© Blackwell Publishers Ltd. 1998

legislation), whereas in others they have been supplanted by money-market certificates. Another example is mortgages, which show large differences from country to country. Some of these differences can be related to differences in past monetary policy performance. In Germany, with a history of low and stable inflation, mortgages are long-term fixed-rate loans whereas in the UK, with a history of higher and more variable inflation, mortgage rates are indexed on short-term interest rates. These idiosyncrasies at the retail level will not disappear immediately, even within the euro area, as the adjustment takes time. While these differences at the retail level are not the focus of the present contribution, they are important because they can affect even the wholesale level when they influence the preferred mode of refinancing of local financial institutions. For example, in Germany banks need a stable deposit base at long-term fixed rates. UK banks, in contrast, can live with a higher proportion of short-term deposits.

It is often argued that EMU will lead to problems in the banking sector because the larger market for debt that opens up in the euro area will offer more opportunities for disintermediation. But this is not a foregone conclusion. The integration of the (wholesale part of the) banking market will actually be quicker and deeper than the integration of securities markets. EMU could thus favour the banking sector over the securities markets (whether organized or not) if some truly European banks were to emerge. This would be difficult to achieve for the retail part, which still absorbs most of the personnel and which has strong national roots. But if some of the larger European banks were to be able to merge their wholesale operations it is possible that EMU will initially favour bank finance over securities markets.

The present contribution has concentrated on four aspects of the institutional and regulatory regime under which EMU will operate and has found in all four cases that the integration of financial markets will be much less than complete.

A first basic point is that it is the European System of Central Banks (ESCB), rather than its central component, the ECB, that will set and execute policy. National central banks (NCBs) have a big advantage in terms of manpower and local knowledge over the ECB. And they are likely to give monetary policy a national twist by using local assets in the execution of the common policy. On top of this comes a second point, namely that the ESCB is not a full central bank: prudential controls remain firmly in national hands; in some cases, but not everywhere, in the hands of NCBs.

There are two additional factors beyond the structure of the E(S)CB. The first is temporary, namely the fact that euro notes and coins will be introduced only in 2002. Until then only some wholesale markets will switch to the euro. Households (and national administrations) are likely to keep national currencies as their unit of account and will thus continue to regard investments in other EMU countries as 'foreign' investment, which would imply that there will be little asset reallocation by them.

The biggest and most permanent obstacles to a full integration of capital markets, especially equity markets, are in the fiscal field. The financing structure of enterprises, that differs so strongly from country to country, and which characterizes national financial systems, is to a large extent determined by the structure of national tax systems (corporate taxation, personal taxation, etc.). The same differences in taxation also discriminate *de facto* against cross-border investments, mainly, but not exclusively in the equity market, because many tax credits are available only to residents and withholding taxes are never fully credited.

All this does not mean that there will be no change on 1 January 1999. Some wholesale markets, e.g. the foreign exchange and inter-bank markets, will immediately switch to the euro. One of the initial consequences of EMU might therefore be an increasing dichotomy between (mainly national) retail markets and a more and more unified wholesale market whose sheer size favours securitization and hence large organized exchanges.

The start of EMU in 1999 will thus not constitute a big bang for most market segments; it will not lead immediately to a unification of financial markets. Local habits, regulations and vested interests will keep markets, especially retail and equity markets, segmented for some time. Whether or not the home bias of retail investors will disappear with the introduction of a common currency is subject to some dispute. But it is also certain that competitive pressures will become irresistible in the long run. Local habits are not immutable, and only the most efficient instruments and practices will survive the competition in the euro area. The same applies to regulations. Governments are also feeling this competitive pressure in the area of taxation of income from capital. Only some timid first steps towards the required co-ordination in this field have been taken so far, but the need for further action is already widely accepted. The year 1999 will thus see the start of a process of integration of European capital markets, rather than its completion. The pace might be slow at the beginning, but progress will be as inexorable as the advance of a glacier. It would not be the first time in the history of European integration that major steps are oversold at the beginning, but develop their full potential over time and turn out in the end to have been even more important than originally assumed, but in different areas.

Does it matter whether change in the structures of national capital markets comes slowly or quickly? The pace of change, obviously, has nothing to do with the overall level of interest rates and thus the broad allocation of capital. But the pace of change in capital markets will be an important factor in a number of policy areas. Stable structures in retail banking imply that the demand for money might be more stable than anticipated. If the

© Blackwell Publishers Ltd. 1998

widely anticipated switch to disintermediation does not materialize, concerns for the stability of the European banking system might become less important for regulators. Persistence in the differences in financing structures of enterprises implies that the short-term transmission channel for monetary policy might continue to differ across countries. Policy-makers will thus have to watch closely the evolution of capital markets in the euro area. Investors will also find that the promised emergence of another market of the size of that of the US dollar might take some time.

Professor Daniel Gros
Centre for European Policy Studies
Place du Congrès 1
B-1000 Brussels
Belgium

References

Bank for International Settlements (1995), *Financial Structures and the Monetary Policy Transmission Mechanism*. Basel.

Biais, Bruno (1998), 'European Stock Markets and European Unification', Chapter 8, in Jean Dermine and Pierre Hillion, eds, *European Capital Markets With a Single Currency*. European Capital Markets Institute.

Borio, Claudio (1995), *The Structure of Credit to the Non-Government Sector and the Transmission Mechanism of Monetary Policy: A Cross Country Comparison*. Bank for International Settlements, Working Paper No. 24.

—— (1997), *Monetary Policy Operating Procedures in Industrial Countries*. Bank for International Settlements, Working Paper No. 40.

Borio, Claudio, and Wilhelm Fritz (1995), *The Response of Short-term Bank Lending Rates to Policy Rates: A Cross Country Perspective*. Bank for International Settlements, Working Paper No. 27.

Choi, Frederick, and Richard Levich (1996), 'Accounting Diversity', Chapter 8, in Benn Steil, ed., *The European Equity Markets*. The Royal Institute of International Affairs for the European Capital Markets Institute.

Davis, Phil (1996), 'Pension Funds Investments', Chapter 6, in Benn Steil, ed., *The European Equity Markets*. The Royal Institute of International Affairs for the European Capital Markets Institute.

Dermine, Jean (1998), 'European Capital Markets with a Single Currency, an Overview', Chapter 1, in Jean Dermine and Pierre Hillion, eds, *European Capital Markets With a Single Currency*. European Capital Markets Institute.

De Santis, Giorgio, Bruno Gerard and Pierre Hillion (1998), 'The Single European Currency and World Equity Markets', Chapter 7, in Jean Dermine and Pierre Hillion,

© Blackwell Publishers Ltd. 1998

eds, *European Capital Markets With a Single Currency*. European Capital Markets Institute.

Dornbusch, Carlo Favero, and Francesco Giavazzi (1998), 'A Red Letter Day?', CEPR Discussion Paper No. 1804, February.

Dowd, Kevin, and David Greenaway (1993), 'Currency Competition, Network Externalities and Switching Costs: Towards an Alternative View of Optimum Currency Areas', *Economic Journal*, 103, 1180–89.

Eichengreen, Barry (1992), 'Designing a Central Bank for Europe: A Cautionary Tale from the Early Years of the Federal Reserve System', in Mathew Canzoneri, Vittorio Grilli and Paul Masson, eds, *Establishing a Central Bank: Issues in Europe and Lessons from the US*, 13–48. Cambridge University Press.

European Commission (1997), *The Impact of the Introduction of the Euro on Capital Markets*, July.

—— (1997a), *European Economy*, Supplement A, No. 12, December, Background Paper 'Advancing Financial Integration'.

European Monetary Institute (1996), *First Progress Report on the TARGET Project*. Working Group on EU Payment Systems, August.

—— (1997), *The Single Monetary Policy in Stage III of EMU – Specification of the Operational Framework*, January.

European Mortgage Federation (1997), *Mortgage Credit in the EU in 1996*.

Folkerts-Landau, David, Peter Garber and Dirk Schoenmaker (1996), *The Reform of Wholesale Payment Systems and Its Impact on Financial Markets*. Group of Thirty, Occasional Paper, No. 51.

Folkerts-Landau, David, and Peter Garber (1992), 'The ECB: a Bank or a Monetary Policy Rule?', in M. Canzoneri et al., eds, *Establishing A Central Bank: Issues in Europe and Lessons from the US*. Cambridge: Cambridge University Press.

Frankel, Jeffery (1996), 'Exchange Rates and the Single Currency', Chapter 10, in Benn Steil, ed., *The European Equity Markets*. The Royal Institute of International Affairs for the European Capital Markets Institute.

Gerlach, Stefan, and Frank Smets (1995), *The Monetary Transmission Mechanism: Evidence from the G-7 Countries*. Bank for International Settlements, Working Paper No. 26.

Goodhart, Charles, et al. (1997), *Financial regulation: Why, How and Where Now?*, Monograph for the Central Bank Governors' Meeting, Bank of England, June.

Goodhart, Charles, and Dirk Schoenmaker (1995), 'Should the Functions of Monetary Policy and Banking Supervision be Separated?', *Oxford Economic Papers*, 47, 539–60.

Grilli, Vittorio, Donato Masciandaro and Guido Tabellini (1991), 'Political and Monetary Institutions and Public Financial Policies in the Industrial Countries', *Economic Policy*, 13, 341–92.

Gros, Daniel (1998), *Distributing Seigniorage under EMU*, manuscript. Brussels: Centre for European Policy Studies (CEPS), March.

© Blackwell Publishers Ltd. 1998

Gros, Daniel, and Niels Thygesen (1998), *European Monetary Integration, From the European Monetary System to European Monetary Union*. London: Longman (second revised edition).

Gros, Daniel, and Karel Lannoo (1996), *The Passage to the Euro*. Brussels: Centre for European Policy Studies (CEPS), Working Party Report No. 15, November.

—— (1998), *EMU and European Capital Markets*. Brussels: Centre for European Policy Studies (CEPS), Working Party Report No. 20, May.

Hartman, Philip (1996), *The Role of the Euro as an international Currency*. Brussels: Centre for European Policy Studies, Research Report No. 20, December.

—— (1998), *Currency Competition and Foreign Exchange Markets, The Dollar, the Yen and the Future International Role of the Euro*. Cambridge: Cambridge University Press.

IMF (1995), *World Economic Outlook*. Washington DC: IMF.

McCauley, Robert (1997), *The Euro and the Dollar*. Essays in International Finance, No. 205, Princeton, NJ: Princeton University, November.

Monticelli, Carlo, and Ugo Papi (1996), *European Integration, Monetary Coordination, and the Demand for Money*. Oxford: Oxford University Press.

Nielsen, Lars Tyge (1998), Chapter 4, in Jean Dermine and Pierre Hillion, eds, *European Capital Markets With a Single Currency*. European Capital Markets Institute.

OECD (1996), *Banking Profitability Statistics*.

Orr, Adrian, Malcolm Edey and Michael Kennedy (1995), *The Determinants of Real Long-term Interest Rates: 17 Country Pooled Time Series Evidence*. OECD Working Paper No. 155.

Prati, Alessandro, and Gary Shinasi (1997), *European Monetary Union and International Capital Markets: Structural Implications and Risks*, paper prepared for IMF conference on 'EMU and the International Monetary System', Washington DC, February.

Rampari, Federico (1998), 'Fazio contro Duisenberg', *La Republica*, 22 March.

Schoenmaker, Dirk (1994), *Externalities in Payment Systems: Issues for Europe*. CEPS Research Report No. 15.

—— (1995), 'Banking supervision in stage III of EMU', in *The Single Market in Banking: From 1992 to EMU*. CEPS Research Report No. 17.

Smith, Roy (1998), 'The European Securities Industry Under a Single Currency, Part IV', in Jean Dermine and Pierre Hillion, eds, *European Capital Markets With a Single Currency*. European Capital Markets Institute.

Steil, Benn (1996), 'Equity Trading IV: The ISD and the Regulation of European Market Structure', Chapter 4, in Benn Steil, ed., *The European Equity Markets*. The Royal Institute of International Affairs for the European Capital Markets Institute.

—— (1998), *Regional Financial Market Integration: learning from the European Experience*, Special Paper Series, London: The Royal Institute of International Affairs.

© Blackwell Publishers Ltd. 1998

Tesar, Linda, and Ingrid Werner (1995), 'Home Bias and High Turnover', *Journal of International Money and Finance*, Vol. 14, No. 4, August, 467–92.

von Hagen, Jürgen (1997), 'Monetary Policy and Institutions in the EMU', *Swedish Economic Policy Journal*, Vol. 4, No. 1, Spring, 51–116.

Data Appendix

Table 1: A Weak Centre: Headquarters Staff at National Central Banks

	Total staff	At headquarters	In analytical functions (research, statistics, economics, etc.)	Research
E(S)CB		400–500	100–150	20–50
For comparison NCBs:				
Germany	17,632	2,770	360	70
France	16,917		750	280
Italy	9,307	2,000	300	150
Spain	3,269		350	
Netherlands	1,721	1,500	165	60
US	23,727	1,700	350	

Sources: Morgan Stanley Central Banking Directory (1997); national central banks (1995 data).

Table 2: Size of Inter-bank Deposits in Selected EU Countries (1994)

	bn ECU	% of balance sheet
Belgium	162.6	32.9
Denmark	24.3	21.6
France	936.8	39.0
Germany	644.3	21.3
Italy	86.4	6.7
Luxembourg	267.6	60.1
Netherlands	121.6	18.3
Spain	110.1	15.8
Austria	108.7	29.0
United Kingdom	146.1	15.7
Total	2,608.5	26.0

Source: OECD (1996).

Table 3: Sectoral Distribution of Monetary Aggregates in France and Germany (1995, in national currency)

	Germany (bn DM)		France (bn FFr)	
M3	2,007.4		5,478.5	
Minus savings deposits	−750.3		−2,215.5	
M2	1,257.1		3,263.0	
Minus time deposits	−441.0		−1,446.0	
of which:		% shares		% shares
Corp. sector	110.7	25.1	3.4	0.2
Households	285.8	64.7	1,442.4	99.8
Public sector	45.1	10.2	0.2	0.0
M1	816.1		1,817.0	
Minus demand deposits	−578.6		−1,561.1	
of which:		% shares		% shares
Corp. sector	196.6	33.9	433.4	27.8
Households	352.0	60.7	948.0	60.7
Public sector	31.3	5.4	179.7	11.5
Cash	237.5		255.9	
Shares in M3:				
cash	11.8		4.7	
M1	40.7		33.2	
M2	62.6		59.6	

Sources: Banque de France; Deutsche Bundesbank (1995 data).

Table 4: Monetary and Bank Supervisory Functions in EU Countries

	Regime	Monetary agency	Supervisory agency
Austria	S	National Bank of Austria (CB)	(Federal) Ministry of Finance (MF)
Belgium	S	National Bank of Belgium (CB)	Banking and Finance Commission
Denmark	S	Danmarks Natonalbank (CB)	Finance Inspectorate (MI)[1]
Finland	S	Bank of Finland (CB)	Bank Inspectorate (MF)/ Bank of Finland (CB)
France	C	Banque de France (CB)	Banque de France (CB)/ Commission Bancaire[2]
Germany	S	Deutsche Bundesbank (CB)	Federal Banking Supervisory Office/ Deutsche Bundesbank[3]
Greece	C	Bank of Greece (CB)	Bank of Greece (CB)
Ireland	C	Central bank of Ireland (CB)	Central Bank of Ireland (CB)
Italy	C	Banca d'Italia (CB)	Banca d'Italia (CB)
Luxemb.	C	Luxembourg Monetary Institute (CB)	Luxembourg Monetary Institute (CB)
Netherl.	C	De Nederlandsche Bank (CB)	De Nederlandsche Bank (CB)
Portugal	C	Banco de Portugal (CB)	Banco de Portugal (CB)
Spain	C	Banco de Espana (CB)	Banco de Espana (CB)
Sweden	S	Sveriges Riksbank (CB)	Swedish Financial Supervisory Authority
UK	S	Bank of England (CB)[4]	Financial Services Authority
Switzerland	S	Swiss National Bank (CB)	Federal Banking Commission
US	S/C	Federal Reserve Board (CB)	Office of the Comptroller of the Currency (CB)/ Federal Reserve board (CB)/ State Governments/ Federal Deposit Insurance Corporation[5]

Notes:
C = Combined; S = Separated; CB = Central Bank; MF = Ministry of Finance; MI = Ministry of Industry; (1) The Danish National Bank is the granter of liquidity support, while the Inspectorate is responsible for the supervision of banks. The inspectorate has no formal link with the Nationalbank, although there is in practice co-operation between the two on many issues; (2) The Banking Commission (Commission Bancaire) is a composite body chaired by the governor of the Banque de France, with representatives from the treasury. The Banking Commission supervises compliance with the prudential regulations. The inspections and on-site examinations are carried out by the Banque de France on behalf of the Banking Commission; (3) The Federal Banking Supervisory Office (Bundesaufsichtsamt für das Kreditwesen) is entrusted entrusted with the supervision of banks. It is responsible for sovereign acts, such as licensing and issuing regulations, whereas the Bundesbank is involved in current supervision by collecting and processing bank prudential returns. The Banking Act provides for co-operation between the Supervisory Board and the Bundesbank (i.e. the two bodies communicate information to each other, and the Supervisory Office has to consult the Bundesbank on new regulations); (4) Under proposals of the Blair government, the banking supervisory responsibilities will be taken away from the Bank of England and put into an extended Securities and Investment Board, which will supervise the whole financial sector; (5) The Office of the Comptroller of the Currency, an agency within the US Treasury Department, supervises national banks and federally licensed branches of foreign banks. The Federal Reserve Board and the State Governments supervise state chartered banks which are members of the federal Reserve System. State chartered non-member banks are supervised by the State Governments. The Federal Reserve Board has the authority to supervise all bank holding companies and their subsidiaries. In addition, the autonomous Federal Deposit Insurance Corporation has some supervisory responsibilities.

Source: adapted from Goodhart and Schoenmaker 1995, p. 558.

© Blackwell Publishers Ltd. 1998

Table 5: Resident Withholding Taxes on Interest and Dividends in the EU (1997)

	Withholding tax		Application
	Interest income	Dividends	
B	15	25	final
DK	RS	25	declared
DE	25	25	declared
EL	15	0	final
E	25	25	declared
F	15	25	final
I	12.5	12.5	final
IRL	26	0	final
L	0	25	declared
NL	RS	25	declared
AU	25	25	final
P	20	30	final
SF	28	28	final
SW	30	30	declared
UK	20	0	declared
CH	35	35	declared
US	RS	30	declared

Source: Price Waterhouse 1997.

© Blackwell Publishers Ltd. 1998

Part VI
International Financial Crises

# Brazilian debt crisis and financial markets: an analysis of major economic events leading to the Brazilian debt moratorium

GEORGE C. PHILIPPATOS* and K. G. VISWANATHAN[†]

*432 Stokely Management Center, University of Tennessee, Knoxville, Tennessee 37996, USA and [†]110 Phillips Hall, Department of Banking and Finance, Hofstra University, Hempstead, New York 11550, USA

The effects of the February 20, 1987 Brazilian debt moratorium announcement on US bank equity prices are analysed. Standard event study methodology is applied to a large sample of loan-exposed and non-exposed banks to detect new information or contagion effects. Intervention analysis and Chow-tests are used to confirm the results. Additionally, 178 related events prior to and after the default announcement are reviewed to detect any equity price adjustments. The absence of any adverse effect of the announcement of both exposed and non-exposed banks is explained by the significant stock price adjustments following many of the related events prior to the announcement.

I. INTRODUCTION

On 19 August 1982, Mexico declared a moratorium on its foreign debt payments, and sought additional funds from US banks and the International Monetary Fund to service its huge obligations in order to remain technically solvent. Since the Mexican announcement in 1982, Peru, Bolivia, Argentina, Chile, and, more recently, Brazil and Venezuela have faced difficulties in meeting their foreign debt obligations. On 20 February 1987, Brazil became the latest large borrower to default, when it announced that it would also halt payments on its $100 billion external debt.

Given their potential to disrupt the US banking industry and perhaps the world monetary order, it is important to analyse and understand the effects of large sovereign debt defaults from the creditors' perspective. The primary objective of the creditor banks, like any other publicly held firms, is to maximize the wealth of their shareholders. Hence, creditor banks should be concerned about events that affect them adversely. The event that is considered in this study is considered critical, with the potential to cause financial distress and failure to individual banks as well as have negative externalities to the entire US banking industry.

The purpose of this research is to test for the effects of the Brazilian foreign debt moratorium within a framework that allows a better understanding of all events that led up to the 20 February suspension of debt servicing by Brazil. Toward this goal, we employ a sample of all US banks with available relevant information around the time of the Brazilian event. Specifically, we test for market value effects on a grand sample of 87 banks traded in the NYSE, the AMEX and the OTC markets. The tests are performed on the entire sample of banks and on various subsamples as follows: (1) high and low exposure to Brazilian loans; (2) type of stock exchange where bank stocks are traded; (3) bank holding company affiliates and unit banks; and (4) large, medium and small banks segmented by asset size. In addition to the above, we review 178 subevents (public announcements) regarding the Brazilian foreign debt situation between 1 April 1985 and 30 June 1987, and statistically analyse 42 of the most important subevents for price effects on US bank stocks. Also, we retest the grand sample and the various subsamples for

0960-3107 © 1991 Chapman & Hall

differential effects in response to longer estimation periods. Finally, we perform intervention analysis in order to verify the results from the conventional event-study methodology.

The results of our study can be summarized as follows: (1) The announcement of the debt moratorium did not convey a negative signal to the market and bank stock prices were not adversely affected – both Brazilian loan-exposed and non-exposed banks. (2) Breaking down the exposed banks into high and low loan-exposure groups did not produce distinguishable results. (3) Effects on NYSE/AMEX-traded bank stocks were indistinguishable from that of OTC-traded bank stocks. (4) Unit or independent bank stocks suffered heavier and longer-sustained losses than the stocks of bank-holding company affiliates. (5) Large bank stocks experienced the largest and longest-sustained market value declines vis-a-vis those of the medium-size banks whose overall loss profiles are nearly indistinguishable. (6) Analysis of important subevents along an event window of 580 days before and after the event indicates that the market adjusted stock prices downward in many of these Brazilian new announcements. (7) Increases in the length of the estimation period do not affect the above results, although tests on market anticipation prior to the event may be sensitive to the estimation interval. (8) The results from the intervention analysis corroborate the findings from the standard methodology of cumulative residuals.

II. MARKET EFFICIENCY IN THE BANKING INDUSTRY: A REVIEW OF THE LITERATURE

The empirical evidence on the efficiency of the markets for bank equities is mixed. If the market for the shares of banks (or bank-holding companies) is efficient, information about events that have adverse affects on creditor banks, such as the moratorium announcements by major third world borrowers, should immediately translate into lower market prices. But, if the relevant market has some inefficiencies due to asymmetric information between the affected institutions and the market participants, there should be no significant adjustments to the market prices of the securities.

Bank regulators tend to defend regulation by rejecting the notion of efficient markets for bank equities, although academic researchers (Pettway, 1980, among others) find the market for large bank equities to be efficient. Regulators argue that the market for bank equities lacks the necessary information to price correctly bank obligations and portfolio of assets consistent with their risk. The imperfect information on the part of some market participants results in inefficiencies in bank equity markets.[1] Several studies have attempted to determine if the default announcements by Mexico and other Latin American borrowers had any significant impact on the market prices of bank equities and shareholder wealth. They have also tried to detect any adjustments prior to and long-after the announcements by focusing on the 'announcement' effects of the default and subsequent regulatory responses. Other studies have concentrated on the rapidity with which the market reacted to the announcement and its ability to price securities proportionately with the risk of the banks issuing the securities. The latter has important implications for the policies implemented by regulating agencies. If the market is mispricing securities due to asymmetric information, the regulators are justified in mandating more disclosure by banks in order to improve the operational efficiency of capital markets.

One of the first studies to analyse the US stock market responses to the Mexican default announcement in 1982 was conducted by Cornell and Shapiro (1986). They use a cross-sectional regression approach to test for a Latin American exposure effect on annual, bi-annual, and monthly returns of exposed US banks. Implicitly, they test the extent to which the market incorporates the riskiness of foreign loans and bank-specific exposure in valuing bank stocks. Cornell and Shapiro (CS) test 43 NYSE-listed banks and find Latin American exposure to be a significant determinant of annual returns,[2] but insignificant in determining monthly returns around the announcement day (19 August 1982). Hence, they conclude that the market had factored the information about the Mexican debt crisis in pricing bank stocks prior to the announcement date.

Schoder and Vankudre (1986) (SV) test for a Mexico exposure effect on the announcement date returns. They use the standard event study methodology to a sample of 45 banks and find a negative and statistically not significant effect on the announcement day, and no specific price effects associated with loan exposure.[3] Smirlock and Kaufold (1987) (SK) use a modified version of the standard event study methodology to test for a Mexico exposure effect on

---

[1] For example, Pettway (1980) suggests that while it may be true that the market for small- and medium-sized bank equities may be lacking the necessary information to make them efficient, the market for large-bank stocks is active and, hence, efficient. He analyses stock returns of failed and non-failed large banks, and concludes that there is no support for the view of bank regulators that the market is inefficient.
[2] The empirical tests show that during 1982 each percentage point increase in the ratio of Latin American loan exposure to total assets cost a bank, on average, 4.3% in annual return. The authors contend that money centre banks, which had high Latin American exposure, experienced larger losses in annual returns compared to non-money centre banks.
[3] Smirlock and Kaufold (1987) contend that the study by SV has some shortcomings that make it difficult to draw the correct conclusions. SV use book value of loans and market value of equity to measure exposure. This makes the loan exposure figures inaccurate as they fluctuate with changes in bank stock prices. Also, the power of the tests used by SV may be lower as they do not account for the covariance of returns across bank stocks.

bank stock returns around the event date. Since the returns are cross-sectionally correlated for the exposed and the non-exposed banks, they apply a Seemingly Unrelated Regressions (SUR) technique on a sample of 60 banks. Exposure is measured by the ratio of book value of loans to the book value of equity. SK conclude that there was a significant relationship between exposure and returns during the announcement period. They also suggest that the investors were able to differentiate between banks with different exposures.

In contrast to the above studies, Bruner and Simms (1987) (BS) test for 'The rapidity of the market's response to the actual deterioration in asset quality caused by Mexican exposure.' They test two sets of hypotheses on 48 bank stocks utilizing the standard event-study methodology, and conclude that the market impounded the information quickly in the share prices of the exposed banks. They also report that initially the market penalized all banks regardless of their degree of exposure, but after four days, it recognized the varying exposure levels and priced securities accordingly.

Lamy et al. (1986) (LMT) also use the standard event study methodology to test for announcement and contagion effects. They test a sample of 57 exposed banks in 10 exposure subgroups and non-exposed banks. The authors conclude that the market possesses a high level of informational efficiency, as exhibited by significant exposure coefficients. However, they find that the equity market discounted the Mexican loans by only a small fraction of the actual loans. LMT attribute this to the 'bailout theory', which holds that the Federal Reserve System and the IMF are expected to protect the commerical banking industry through beneficent intervention.

To the best of our knowledge, there has been only one study that has looked at the announcement and contagion effects of the Brazilian debt default of February, 1987. Musumeci and Sinkey (1990) examine bank security returns surrounding Brazil's debt moratorium announcement using regression analysis and standard event-study methods. Individual bank returns and excess bank returns are regressed against exposure data for the Brazilian default announcement. However, they use a narrow prediction period of 3 days before and 3 days after the event. They acknowledge that their tests do not capture any adjustments outside their prediction window. They also use only 25 banks in their sample: 10 money-centre banks and 15 regional banks. Their study concludes that the market reacted negatively to the moratorium announcement by Brazil, but does not find any evidence of mispricing or investor contagion. The authors conclude that the market was informationally efficient.

III. METHODOLOGY, DATA, AND HYPOTHESES TESTED

Methodology

As is common in the event-type of studies, intially we employ here the market model, as follows:

$$r_{it} = \alpha_i + \beta_i r_{mt} + \varepsilon_{it} \qquad (1)$$

where, r_{it} is the return for security i on day t; r_{mt} is the return for the market on day t; α_i and β_i are firm specific parameters; ε_{it} is the white noise disturbance term; and the joint distribution of r_{it} and r_{mt} is bivariate normal.[4]

Data

The day on which a specific debtor nation announced that it will stop principal and debt-service payments on its external debt is used as the event date. The *Wall Street Journal* reported that the Brazilian announcement was made on Friday, 20 February 1987. However, not all investors became immediately aware of events as they occurred and news arrived on the wire. Some investors were informed about the events only when they read about them in the print media the following day. Hence, as is customary in such cases, the event period focuses on two trading days – the day of the announcement and the following trading day. Figure 1 shows the time period for the Brazilian event. Different estimation periods and estimation intervals are used to reduce any time-related bias in the parameter estimation process.

Our study uses all US banks listed in the Center for Research in Security Prices (CRSP) tape that are traded in the NYSE, the AMEX, and the OTC markets for which data are available. The data are screened to eliminate from the sample banks whose returns migh have been affected by other contaminating events (such as acquisitions or operational irregularities) during the parameter estimation period or during the event period. The daily returns for individual bank stocks and market returns are obtained from the CRSP tapes. Estimates of loan exposures to third world borrowers are obtained from various sources including bank SEC filing (10-K reports), FDIC Call and Income reports, bank annual reports, and the Freedom of Information Office of the Federal Reserve Board of Governors. Typically, two different measures of foreign loan exposure are employed in similar studies: (1) The ratio of external loans outstanding in a country to the sum of shareholder equity (book value) and loan-loss reserves of a bank; and (2) the ratio of external loans outstanding in a country to the

---

[4]This implies that under Ordinary Least Squares Estimation, the following conditions hold:
(a) ε_{it} is normally distributed; (b) ε_{it} has a mean value of zero, $E(\varepsilon_{it})=0$; (c) Var $(\varepsilon_{it})=\sigma^2(\varepsilon_{it})$; (d) the disturbance terms are cross-sectionally independent, $\text{Cov}(\varepsilon_{it}, \varepsilon_{jt})=0$; and (e) r_{mt} is non-stochastic, $\text{Cov}(\varepsilon_{it} r_{mt})=0$.

Estimation Period: t_{-150} to t_{-30} (15 July–2 January)
Prediction period: t_{-30} to t_{+30} (5 January–31 March)
Event period: Feb 20, Feb 23

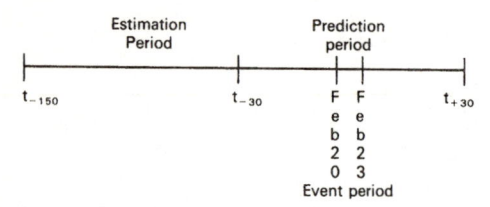

Fig. 1. *Estimation, prediction and event periods for the Brazilian default announcement*

Event date: 20 February, 1987
Estimation period: t_{-150} to t_{-30} (15 July–2 January)
Prediction period: t_{-30} to t_{+30} (5 January–31 March)

total assets of the bank. Here, we report on the former measure since both measures yield similar results.[5]

Hypotheses tested

Tests of announcement effects. The first set of two hypotheses tests whether the market recognizes the adverse information generated by the event – the public announcement of a moratorium on the debt payments by the borrower – and incorporates it into the market valuation of bank equities. It also tests the market's efficiency in anticipating the event, and attempts to determine when the market impounds the information conveyed by the announcement by adjusting the market value of the stocks of the affected banks with exposure to Latin America.

H_{01}: *New information hypothesis*. The moratorium announcement conveyed a negative signal about the quality of assets held by the creditor banks causing a downward adjustment of bank share prices.

H_{02}: *Information leakage hypothesis*. The market had information about the deterioration of the quality of banks assets even before the default announcement and had made prior adjustment.

The new information hypothesis states that as a result of the moratorium announcement by the borrower the inferior quality of the loan assets held by banks is revealed, resulting in downward price adjustments in the market. The information leakage hypothesis states that the market has anticipated the deterioration in the quality of loan assets, and has already impounded the information in the stock prices of the affected banks prior to the announcement.

Tests of industry contagion effects. The second set of hypotheses is related to the size of the stock price reaction to the moratorium announcement. It is designed to detect any industry contagion effect in the market following the Brazilian default. If there exists a contagion effect, the impact of the moratorium spills over to the other non-involved banks and affects them adversely.

H_{03}: *Rational pricing hypothesis*: The size of the share price response is related to the actual exposure of the bank to the borrower.

H_{04}: *Industry contagion hypothesis*: The size of the share price response is not related to the actual exposure of the bank.

The first hypothesis, the rational pricing hypothesis, states that the size of the share price response is related to the actual exposure of the bank to external loans. It assumes that the market is efficient and rational in impounding the information and applying it to the appropriate bank equity valuation. Banks with high exposure experience a larger drop in share prices than banks with low exposure. The industry contagion hypothesis states that the market reacts to the event by lowering the stock prices of the affected banks, but the size of the response does not reflect the exposure level of the bank. There is a contagion effect which results in the market penalizing all banks regardless of their degree of exposure.[6]

IV. RESULTS AND DISCUSSION

The results of our study are discussed in terms of the grand sample and various subsamples, as outlined earlier in the paper.

Sample attributes

The population of banks for which all the relevant data are available is used to analyse the reaction of bank stock prices to the Brazilian moratorium announcement and events leading up to and following it. The asset and equity variates for the overall sample and the various subgroups are shown in Table 1. The initial sample consists of 87 banks, 48 of which are listed in the NYSE/AMEX and 39 in the

---

[5] For the similarity of results obtained from both measures, see Cornell and Shapiro (1986).
[6] Saunders (1988) identifies two mechanisms through which contagion effects can be transmitted. (1) Institutional that may imply disintermediation and portfolio adjustments that are transmitted and affect the entire banking system. (2) Informational that result in reduced confidence in the banking system. The latter case is further classified into (a) 'pure information contagion' that implies symmetric information and 'noisy information contagion' that implies asymmetric information. It should be noted that, while Smirlock and Kaufold find the market's repricing of bank equities rational, Schoder and Vankudre detect the presence of contagion effects associated with the Mexican moratorium. Similar contagion effects are found by Bruner and Simms.

Brazilian debt crisis and financial markets

Table 1. Characteristics of the sample of banks

Subgroup	Number of banks	$million Minimum value	$million Maximum value	$million Average value
Total assets				
All banks	87	333.45	196 124.00	19 196.45
Exposed banks	48	593.45	196 124.00	31 283.16
Non-exp banks	39	333.45	20 228.90	5 635.75
NYSE banks	48	333.45	196 124.00	28 671.00
OTC banks	39	1201.97	26 820.21	7535.47
BHC banks	60	369.99	196 124.00	22 716.05
Non-BHC banks	27	333.45	21 539.41	9957.52
Small banks	25	333.45	4509.65	2760.93
Medium banks	21	5060.02	9982.51	7233.17
Large banks	41	10 697.40	196 124.00	35 345.65
Equity				
All banks	87	16.96	13 446.00	1356.80
Exposed banks	48	65.56	13 446.00	2200.11
Non-exp banks	39	16.96	1456.65	410.64
NYSE banks	48	16.96	13 446.00	2026.72
OTC banks	39	95.03	1846.93	532.27
BHC banks	60	16.96	13 446.00	1597.87
Non-BHC banks	27	22.60	1720.20	723.99
Small banks	25	16.96	426.47	200.92
Medium banks	21	349.29	712.92	514.64
Large banks	41	694.27	13 446.00	2492.95

NASDAQ. The purpose of distinguishing between NYSE/AMEX and NASDAQ banks is to identify any effects associated with the exchange in which the bank stocks are traded. NYSE/AMEX bank stocks are more actively traded and widely held, whereas NASDAQ bank stocks are less actively traded and not widely held. The banks vary in total asset size from $333.45 million to $191.12 billion. The average size of the total assets is $19.20 billion and average equity is $1.36 billion. The 48 NYSE/AMEX banks have an average size $28.67 billion in total assets and $2.03 billion in equity. The corresponding numbers for the 39 NASDAQ banks are $7.54 billion and $532.27 million. No distinction is made between NYSE and AMEX bank stocks as the number of banks in the sample that are listed in AMEX is too small to make any meaningful inferences. Forty eight of the banks in the initial sample had loans outstanding to Brazil at the time of the default, while the remaining 39 banks are mostly regional banks without any direct exposure to Brazil. Here, the purpose is to find out if the market was able to distinguish between exposed and non-exposed banks. If the market was not able to distinguish between the two groups, it implies that the market lacked sufficient information about bank loan exposure to value bank securities correctly. The exposed banks have average total assets of $31.28 billion and average equity of $2200.11 million,

while the non-exposed banks have average total assets of $5.6 billion and average equity of $410.64 million. The exposed banks have a mean exposure of 13.11 percent of capital. The 48 exposed banks are divided into two groups of (20) high exposure and (28) low exposure banks along the mean exposure level. A distinction is also made between bank-holding companies (BHCs) and non-bank-holding companies (non-BHCs). The adverse effects on bank stocks associated with a negative signal should be less for BHCs due to their greater degree of diversification relative to non-BHCs. The sample of 87 banks contains 60 BHCs and 27 non-BHCs. The BHCs have average total assets of $22.716 billion and average equity of $1597.87 million. The corresponding number for the non-BHCs are $9.957 billion and $723.99 million.

Tests on loan exposure, bank-holding status, exchange membership, and size effects

The daily average excess returns for the period surrounding the Brazilian default announcement are computed using an estimation period of 120 days starting 150 days before the event and ending 30 days before the event. The test period ranges from 30 days before the event to 30 days after the event.

The daily average excess returns for the different subgroups are presented in Table 2.[7] The first three columns show the announcement effect results for the sample of all banks, as well as exposed and non-exposed banks. On 20 February 1987 (t_0) Brazil announced the unilateral suspension of debt service payments to its creditors. The Wall Street Journal reported this on 23 February 1987 (t_{+1}). The announcement day excess returns for the different subgroups are positive, though not significant (0.53% for all banks, 0.56% for exposed banks and 0.50% for non-exposed banks). The excess returns on the press day become negative for the sample of all banks (−0.07%) and the sample of exposed banks (−0.32%), but are not significant. The 2-day excess returns are positive for all three subgroups (0.46%, 0.24% and 0.73% respectively). This implies that the announcement did not have any adverse effect on these three subgroups of banks. Unlike the case of the Musumeci and Sinkey (1990) study, there appears to be no negative effect associated with the Brazilian default announcement. This could mean that the announcement, by itself, is a non-event, or that it did not convey any new information to the market about the quality of assets held by creditor banks. It could also mean that the market anticipated the event and had already impounded it in the share prices of banks prior to the announcement. Since the Mexican debt crisis in 1982, the market has been continuously monitoring the activities of the Third World borrowers and the creditor banks. In the intra-event period, other borrowers like Peru and Argentina had defaulted on their loans to the industrialized nations. The market might have anticipated the suspension of debt service payments by Brazil in 1987. This explains the non-negative excess returns for the two-day event period. The weak negative effect for the samples of all banks and exposed banks on the press day may be minor corrections by a small group of market participants that did not previously anticipate correctly the value of bank equities.

The excess returns for high and low exposure banks during the test period are shown in columns 4 and 5. Again, the announcement period returns are positive on the event day and negative, but insignificant on the press day. The two-day event period returns are 0.31% and 0.19% respectively. The event period returns for the subsamples of NYSE/AMEX and OTC banks are shown in the next two columns. The two-day event period returns for these subgroups of banks are positive and insignificant (0.24% and 0.73%). Columns 8 and 9 show the event for both subgroups (0.65% and 0.29% respectively), the two-day event period excess returns are positive for the BHCs (0.85%) and negative for the non-BHCs (−0.36%). The negative sign on the excess returns of non-BHCs indicates the higher risk faced by investors in non-BHCs vis-à-vis investors in BHCs.

The sample of 87 banks is divided into subgroups of small, medium and large banks. The group of small banks have less than $5 billion in total assets. Medium banks have total assets ranging from $5 billion to $10 billion. Banks with over $10 billion in total assets are classified as large banks. The sample contained 25 small banks, 21 medium banks and 41 large banks. The average size of the total assets for the three groups is $2.76 billion, $7.23 billion and $35.35 billion respectively. The last two columns present the excess returns of these three subgroups for the test period. The announcement day excess returns of these three subgroups for the test period. The announcement day excess returns for the group of small banks is positive and significant (1.21%). The corresponding returns for medium and large banks are also positive, though not significant (0.72% and 0.03% respectively). The 2-day excess returns for the three groups are 2.23% (signficant), 1.07% and −0.97%. On the press day, only the excess returns of the group of large banks is negative and significant (−0.99%).

The excess returns of the different subgroups around the announcement indicate that the share prices of bank equities did not experience any decline immediately following the Brazilian announcement. The excess returns on the announcement day are not significantly negative for any of the subgroups. The excess returns on the press day are negative and significant only in the case of large banks. This implies that only the share prices of large-bank equities were affected by the Brazilian moratorium announcement. None of the other groups of banks were adversely affected by the announcement. Again, this shows that the announcement did not reveal any new information about the quality of assets held by banks. Either the market had anticipated the deterioration of the quality of bank assets and had previously adjusted for this decline in value, or the market did not feel that the announcement represented a decline in the value of bank equities.

Tests on longer estimation intervals and selected subevents

Some perspectives on the estimation period. Since the Mexican debt default of 1982, the market had been concerned about the unprecedented growth in international lending, especially to Latin American nations. Several unfavourable reports about the borrowers and their ability to meet their debt obligations were published in the financial press. Some or all of the market participants might have been monitoring these reports and might have anticipated the Brazilian default prior to 20 February 1987. To capture these effects, if any, a larger event period is used. The abnormal returns are computed using an estimation period starting 620 days before the event and ending 500 days before the event. The abnormal returns for the 500 days before the event and 500 days after the event are analysed. Due to the larger time interval, 12 of the banks used in the initial sample had to be eliminated for lack of all relevant data.

---

[7] Due to limitation of space, the excess returns are reported for only selected time periods. Results not reported are available on request.

Table 2. Daily average excess returns of subgroups of banks[a]

Time relative to event	All banks (n=87)	Exposed banks (n=48)	Non-exposure banks (n=39)	High exposure banks (n=20)	Low exposed banks (n=28)	NYSE/AMEX banks (n=48)	OTC banks (n=39)	BHC banks (n=60)	Non-BHC banks (n=27)	Small banks (n=25)	Medium banks (n=21)	Large banks (n=41)
t−30	0.3148	0.4801	0.1113	0.1596	0.7090	0.4775	0.1144	0.3553	0.2292	0.8033	−0.1330	0.2462
t−20	−0.9264**	−0.9495*	−0.8978**	−1.2376*	−0.7438	−1.4448*	−0.2883	−0.7641*	−1.2682**	−0.4736	−1.1209*	−1.1028**
t−10	0.0306	0.1053	−0.0615	0.3285	−0.0541	0.1020	−0.0573	0.0725	−0.0578	−0.2118	0.3725	0.0032
t−9	0.6073*	0.5057	0.7323*	0.7953	0.2989	0.7178	0.4712	0.6640*	0.4878	1.0127*	0.9277*	0.1960
t−8	−0.0696	−0.1001	−0.0319	−0.4972	0.1835	−0.2770	0.1858	−0.2660	0.3443	−0.8230	0.2351	0.2338
t−7	0.1611	−0.0582	0.4310	−0.2436	0.0743	−0.0232	0.3879	0.2156	0.0463	0.6483	−0.0796	−0.0127
t−6	−0.4739	−0.6557	−0.2501	−0.8447	−0.5208	−0.4063	−0.5572	−0.4126	−0.6032	−0.3013	−0.0519	−0.5560
t−5	0.0301	−0.0182	0.0894	0.0127	0.0743	0.0963	−0.0515	0.0545	−0.0214	−0.2856	0.3277	0.0701
t−4	−0.0916	0.1343	−0.3697	0.3873	−0.0465	0.1855	−0.4327	−0.1063	−0.0607	−0.0222	−0.4911	0.0707
t−3	−0.4166	−0.1137	−0.7895*	−0.1117	−0.1151	−0.3906	−0.4486	−0.3950	−0.4621	0.7899	−0.9311*	−0.8887*
t−2	0.1902	0.0668	0.3420	−0.5565	0.5121	0.4090	−0.0791	0.1621	0.2494	−0.1025	−0.0324	0.4827
t−1	0.9446**	1.1960**	0.6353*	1.8114**	0.7564	1.1294*	0.7173*	0.8732**	1.0953**	0.5973	0.4914	1.3886**
t0	0.5341	0.5635	0.4978	0.7515	0.4292	0.4604	0.6247	0.6482	0.2936	1.2112*	0.7183	0.0268
t+1	−0.0724	−0.3224	0.2353	−0.4434	−0.2360	−0.2180	0.1069	0.2016	−0.6498	1.0688*	0.3617	−0.9906**
t+2	0.0292	−0.0021	0.0677	−0.2897	0.2033	−0.1463	0.2452	0.0779	−0.0735	−0.0473	0.2062	−0.0148
t+3	−0.7103**	−0.8734*	−0.5096	−1.3070*	−0.5637	−0.8895*	−0.4898	−0.5717	−1.0024*	−1.4587**	−0.3792	−0.4236
t+4	−0.0620	0.1025	−0.2644	0.4055	−0.1140	0.1630	−0.3388	−0.2277	0.2871	0.4016	−0.4099	−0.1664
t+5	0.3243	0.4918	0.1182	0.5725	0.4341	0.4218	0.2044	0.2282	0.5268	0.1441	−0.1183	0.6609*
t+6	0.9274*	0.6815	1.2300*	1.6683**	−0.0234	1.0050*	0.8318*	0.9235*	0.9355*	1.0867*	0.6275	0.9837**
t+7	−0.1579	−0.2693	−0.0207	0.0784	−0.5176	−0.3805	0.1161	−0.1772	−0.1171	−0.7563	0.0200	0.1159
t+8	−0.1699	0.1874	−0.6097*	0.4465	0.0023	−0.2906	−0.0213	−0.0143	−0.4978	0.9863	−0.1590	−0.9805*
t+9	0.0968	0.3085	−0.1638	−0.2867	0.7336	0.2075	−0.0395	0.1870	−0.0933	0.3397	0.0343	−0.0193
t+10	0.1619	0.1105	0.2253	−0.1288	0.2814	0.3287	−0.0433	0.3339	−0.0200	0.5830	0.0043	−0.0140
t+20	−0.1487	−0.1659	−0.1276	−0.6027	0.1462	−0.1181	−0.1865	−0.1064	−0.2378	−0.5784	0.5927	−0.2664
t+30	−0.7187*	−0.8763*	−0.5247	−0.3219	−1.2723**	−0.8962*	−0.5002	−0.3869	−1.4178**	0.6817	−1.0594*	−1.3981**

[a] Estimation period ranges from 150 days before the event to 30 days before the event.
* Significant at the 0.95 level.
** Significant at the 0.99 level.

In general, analysis of the abnormal returns of banks for the 30 days before and after the event (not shown here), using a different estimation period yields results similar to those discussed above. The announcement day returns are not negative and significant for any of the subgroups. The two-day event period excess returns for the group of all banks is negative, but not significant (-0.49%). The group of 41 exposed banks account for most of this decline (-0.62%), while the group of non-exposed banks experience a smaller two-day decline (-0.33%). A major part of the decline experienced by the exposed banks is associated with the decline faced by low exposure banks (-1.05%). The high exposure banks adjust downward by 0.07%. This implies that over the two days, banks with lower exposure were penalized more than banks with higher exposure to Brazil. Although the market was able to distinguish correctly between exposed and non-exposed banks and penalize banks with exposure proportionately, it was not rational in penalizing banks with low exposure more than banks with high exposure.

The two-day excess returns for the NYSE and OTC banks do not appear to be different (-0.56% and -0.41%). This means that there were no listed exchange-related effects over these two days. At the same time, there appears to be a difference in the market's analysis of BHCs and non-BHCs. While the two-day excess returns for the BHCs is -0.02%, the corresponding two-day excess return for non-BHCs is -1.57% and significant. This is consistent with the higher risks faced by investors in non-BHC equity. Most of the two-day adverse reaction in bank stock prices is associated with the decline in stock prices of large banks. The group of large banks experienced a two-day decline of 1.42%. During the same time-period, the medium bank suffered a 0.59% decline while small banks experienced an increase of 1.55%.

Further research uncovered 178 separate *Wall Street Journal* write-ups related to the Third World debt, and specifically, the Brazilian debt, during 1985–87. One or more of these reports may have affected the valuation of bank equities prior to the Brazilian default. To identify any such anticipations, the abnormal returns of the different subgroups for a 580-day event window are computed. This event window consists of 500 days the announcement and 80 days after the announcement. Abnormal returns were computed and cross-matched to isolate those days during which both reports about the deteriorating quality of bank loans to Third World countries were published in the *Wall Street Journal* and one or more bank subgroups suffered significant declines in market value. Most of the unfavourable reports following the Brazilian default were followed by negative bank equity price adjustments, in many cases, statistically significant. Prior to the Brazilian default, unfavourable press reports were followed by both positive and negative price adjustments, indicating that there was some anticipation of the quality of loan assets held by banks.

A total of 42 subevents were identified. These included events such as new lending by creditor banks to Brazil, statements by Brazilian authorities regarding its willingness to fulfil its debt obligations, announcements related to LDC debt by the Federal Reserve, the US Treasury and the IMF, and loan–loss reserve announcements by creditor banks. Each of these events represents either an improvement in the debt servicing capacity of Brazil, or a deterioration in its economic position and hence, a deterioration in the quality of loan assets held by the lending banks. For example, one of the events included was the announcement of the 'Baker Plan' in Ocotober 1985, which was a new initiative by the US Treasury to try to solve the debt problem. Another example is the announcement by Citicorp in May 1987 that it was raising its loan–loss reserves to specifically offset non-performing foreign loans. (The 42 events are not shown here due to limitation of space. However, they are available from the authors on request.)

A multivariate regression model of the following form is used to analyse the effect of these events on the bank returns:

$$R_{it} = a_i + b_i R_{mt} + c_{ik} D_{kt}$$

where R_{it} is the return of bank i on day t, R_{mt} is the market return on day t, D_{kt} is a series of binary indicator variables, and a, b, and c are regression coefficients.

Each subevent is represented by an indicator variable with a value of 1 if the event occurred and 0 if otherwise. Separate multivariate regressions are run for each subgroup using the 30 indicator variables. The regression coefficients for some of the variables are shown in Panel A of Table 3.

Analysis of subevents

The various subevents had varying impacts on each group of banks. Most of the 42 subevents represented adverse information about the ability of Third World countries, especially Brazil, in servicing their external debts. However, not all of them are associated with negative regression coefficients. Table 3 shows that most of the statistically significant coefficients are negative. This implies that the market was aware of the problems faced by Brazil in servicing its external debt to creditor banks. The market was also aware of the deteriorating quality of assets held by US creditor banks. Events 4, 8, 15, 18, 20, 21, 26, 29, 31, 33, 37 and 39 are associated with statistically significant regression coefficients for a majority of the subgroups of banks. An analysis and explanation of these events follow.

Event 4 is report on 22 May 1985 in the *Wall Street Journal* that the various efforts to prevent a financial disaster among Third World debtor nations have failed to address the underlying economic problems faced by the debtor nations. With the exception of small, OTC and non-exposed groups of banks, all other groups were associated with statistically significant and negative regression coefficients. Since 1982, the borrowers had been resisting all efforts by the lenders to impose economic austerity programmes on

Table 3. *Regression coefficients of the indicator variables and intervention analysis coefficients for subevents before and after the Brazilian announcement*

Event	All banks (n=75)	Exposed banks (n=41)	Non-exposed banks (n=34)	NYSE banks (n=39)	OTC banks (n=36)	BHC banks (n=51)	Non-BHC banks (n=24)	Small banks (n=18)	Medium banks (n=20)	Large banks (n=37)
					PANEL A					
1	0.0046	0.0046	0.0046	0.0014	0.0081	0.0049	0.0040	-0.0013	0.0146**	0.0021
4	-0.0077**	-0.0113**	-0.0034	-0.0118**	-0.0034	-0.0075**	-0.0083*	-0.0016	-0.0060	-0.0117**
6	0.0052	0.0065	0.0037	0.0073	0.0030	0.0030	0.0098*	0.0120*	0.0058	0.0016
7	0.0053	0.0038	0.0071	0.0024	0.0085*	0.0073	0.0010	0.0078	0.0043	0.0046
8	-0.0082*	-0.0091*	-0.0071	-0.0078*	-0.0087*	-0.0094*	-0.0057	-0.0062	-0.0064	-0.0102*
10	-0.0058	-0.0041	-0.0078	-0.0028	-0.0090	-0.0075*	-0.0021	-0.0045	-0.0079	-0.0053
13	0.0068	0.0073	0.0062	0.0071	0.0065	0.0070	0.0064	0.0057	0.0015	0.0102*
14	0.0057	0.0071	0.0040	0.0076	0.0037	0.0033	0.0109*	0.0066	0.0065	0.0048
15	-0.0190**	-0.0247**	-0.0121**	-0.0285**	-0.0087*	-0.0173**	-0.0226**	-0.0160**	-0.0150**	-0.0226*
16	0.0072	0.0108*	0.0029	0.0110*	0.0031	0.0038	0.0145*	0.0118*	0.0063	0.0055
18	-0.0124**	-0.0109*	-0.0141**	-0.0112*	-0.0137**	-0.0137**	-0.0095*	-0.0048	-0.0174**	-0.0134*
20	-0.0115*	-0.0116*	-0.0113*	-0.0140**	-0.0087*	-0.0121*	-0.0101*	-0.0145*	-0.0087*	-0.0115*
21	-0.0060	-0.0086*	-0.0029	-0.0106*	-0.0010	-0.0071	-0.0037	-0.0147**	-0.0026	-0.0036
23	0.0079*	0.0067	0.0093	0.0046	0.0115*	0.0110*	0.0013	0.0069	0.0111*	0.0066
26	-0.0095*	-0.0120*	-0.0065	-0.0130*	-0.0057	-0.0115*	-0.0054	-0.0085*	-0.0095*	-0.0100*
29	0.0092**	0.0119*	0.0059	0.0124*	0.0058	0.0082	0.0112*	0.0060	0.0038	0.0137*
30	0.0033	0.0043	0.0021	0.0033	0.0032	0.0052	-0.0008	0.0126*	0.0020	-0.0006
31	-0.0121*	-0.0158**	-0.0076	-0.0157**	-0.0082	-0.0083*	-0.0201**	0.0018	-0.0092*	-0.0203*
33	-0.0044	-0.0072	-0.0009	-0.0086*	0.0002	-0.0030	-0.0073	-0.0161*	0.0003	-0.0017
34	0.0062	0.0032	0.0098*	0.0069	0.0054	0.0060	0.0067	0.0068	0.0029	0.0077
35	-0.0032	-0.0004	-0.0067	0.0025	-0.0094*	-0.0010	-0.0079	-0.0007	-0.0060	0.0030
36	0.0038	0.0027	0.0051	0.0050	0.0024	0.0063	-0.0015	0.0140*	-0.0002	0.0009
37	-0.0130**	-0.0156**	-0.0098*	-0.0138**	-0.0121*	-0.0153**	-0.0081*	-0.0196**	-0.0083*	-0.0123*
39	-0.0079*	-0.0077*	-0.0082*	-0.0090*	-0.0068	-0.0046	-0.0150*	-0.0118*	-0.0076	-0.0062
40	0.0060	0.0066	0.0054	0.0070	0.0050	0.0039	0.0107*	0.0057	0.0057	0.0115*
41	-0.0042	-0.0068	-0.0012	-0.0059	-0.0025	-0.0021	-0.0088*	-0.0101*	0.0018	-0.0046
42	-0.0052	-0.0172**	0.0093**	-0.0181**	0.0088*	-0.0081*	0.0010	-0.0331**	0.0038	0.0036
					PANEL B					
Variable										
Int1	0.0003	0.0001	0.0005	0.0001	0.0005	0.0003	0.0001	0.0005	0.0005	0.0000
Int2	0.0000	-0.0001	0.0000	0.0000	-0.0001	-0.0002	0.0003	-0.0002	-0.0002	0.0001
Beta1	0.7595*	0.8300*	0.6745*	0.8346*	0.6782	0.7610*	0.7563*	0.6315*	0.6656*	0.8726*
Beta2	0.7150*	0.7308*	0.6960*	0.7773*	0.6474*	0.7287*	0.6858*	0.5122*	0.6182*	0.8659*
Event1	0.0028	0.0029	0.0027	0.0000	0.0059	0.0030	0.0024	-0.0031	0.0127	0.0003
Event42	-0.0077	-0.0197*	0.0068	-0.0205**	0.0063	-0.0106	-0.0014	-0.0347*	0.0017	0.0004
Beta1-Beta2	0.0446	0.0993	-0.0214	0.0573	0.0308	0.0323	0.0706	0.1193	0.0474	0.0067
t-value	0.1322	0.2664	-0.0766	0.1764	0.0869	0.0993	0.1925	0.2759	0.1522	0.0222

* Significant at the level of 0.05.
** Significant at the level of 0.01.

them. Resistance by the borrowers could have been construed as a negative signal by the market. Event 8 further reinforced the reluctance on the part of borrowers, and particularly Brazil, to accept any conditions placed by the lenders for continued lending. Brazilian President Sarney stated that his government would persue a hard line in negotiating with the lenders. The regression coefficients in Table 7 associated with this event are negative and statistically significant for all groups of banks.

On 23 January 1986, the *Wall Street Journal* reported that the 'Baker Plan' to solve the Third World debt problem was not well accepted, 3 months after it was first revealed (event 15). The market did not react favourably to this news. The regression coefficients are statistically significant, negative and relatively large. Earlier on, when the 'Baker Plan' was first revealed (events 11 and 12), the market did not react favourably, either.

On 8 September 1986, Brazil and its creditors signed an agreement that would restructure its foreign debt (event 18). This further indicated that Brazil was facing serious problems in servicing its foreign debts and the market reacted negatively. The problem was becoming too large for the creditor banks to salvage their investments in Third World loans.

Events 20 and 21 showed that the Latin American borrowers had to increase the size of their debt burdens and that none of the existing proposals were helping to solve the debt problem. Event 26 indicated the further deterioration of the Brazilian economy and its increasing dependence on new loans from foreign lenders. The market reacted to these adverse events by adjusting downward the prices of bank stocks.

On 23 February 1987, it was reported that Brazil had formally suspended servicing its external debt (event 31). All subgroups of banks were adversely affected on that day. (The regression coefficients are statistically significant for all groups of banks except small banks.) Two days later, the *Wall Street Journal* reported that Brazil was not going to impose the economic austerity needed to solve its debt problem (event 33). On 9 April 1987, Brazil's Finance Minister, Funaro, reiterated his government's opposition to the austerity programme (event 37). The market reacted negatively to Brazil's unwillingness to accept the conditions placed by its creditors and other international authorities.

Recognizing the seriousness of the problem, Citicorp became the first major lender to increase its Third World loan–loss reserves and write off a part of its assets on 19 May 1987, thereby experiencing an accounting loss (event 39). The market expected other lenders to increase their loan-loss reserves and show larger than expected losses for the following quarters. It resulted in the market adjusting the prices of all banks stocks downward .

The only subevent when the market reaction is not consistent with the signal conveyed by the event happened on 19 February 1987 (event 29). Brazil took steps to conserve its foreign currency reserves, an indication of its impending suspension of debt servicing, but the market did not react negatively. In fact, most of the groups of banks experienced price appreciations on that day.

The above regression analysis results explain the lack of any announcement effect associated with the Brazilian default announcement of February 1987. Previous studies find a significant announcement effect associated with the Mexican default announcement of August 1982. This study does not detect any negative effects around the Brazilian announcement as the market had already incorporated this in its valuation of bank securities. The negative coefficients associated with the earlier subevents indicate that the market was constantly monitoring the activities of both the lending banks and the borrowers. Compared to the Mexican default, the market had more information at the time of the Brazilian default, and hence, there was no significant reaction to the latter event.

Intervention analysis

The Cumulative Average Residuals methodology estimates the parameters of the market model for a prior time period, and uses these estimates to compute the residuals during the event period. DeJong and Collins (1985) and Bar-Yosef and Brown (1977) find that the systematic risk of a firm changes during the event period. Kalay and Loewenstein (1985) find that the volatility of returns and risk characteristics of a firm increase dramatically around any event affecting the firm. They argue that the traditionally measured excess returns over an event period could be merely the higher compensation that risk averse investors demand to hold the asset over the risky event period, and do not necessarily represent economic profits. Thus, when the systematic risk of a firm changes over the event period, the cumulative average residual methodology may yield biased results. Drawing inferences about market efficiency based on these biased results may not be appropriate. Indeed, Born and Anderson (1986), employing a sample of 45 banks listed in CRSP, find that shifts in the systematic risk for the banking industry did occur in 1982, and that the shifts were centred around the Mexican default announcement. Hence, computation of abnormal returns using residual analysis may have introduced a bias.

Larker *et al.* (1980) have developed a model based on the work by Box and Tiao (1975), which separates risk changes from the information content of an event. This model, also known as Intervention Analysis or Dummy Variable Regression, improves the estimates of the parameters by removing the autocorrelation of the residuals. Intervention Analysis is appropriate when there is reason to believe that the economic event may have caused or is accompanied by a change in the stochastic process that generates the security returns. The model uses a series of dummy variables that capture shifts in both the intercept and slope coefficients.

The model can be expressed as

$$R_{it} = a_1 + b_1 R_{mt} E[t^- t^0] + b_2 R_{mt} E[t^0, t^+] + c_1 E_1 + c_2 E_2 \ldots c_n C_n + u_{it}$$

where R_{it} is the return on a security i for time period t, R_{mt} is the return on a market portfolio for time period t, a_1 is a constant, b_1 is the systematic risk of the firm prior to the event, b_2 is the systematic risk of the firm after the event, $c_1, \ldots c_n$ are coefficients specifying the information content associated with specific subevent $E_1, \ldots E_n$, u_{it} is the noise component, t^0 is the event time, $[t^-, t^0]$ is the time period before the event, $[t^0, t^+]$ is the time period following the event, $E[t^-, t^0] = \{1 \text{ if } t < t^0; 0 \text{ otherwise}\}$ and $E[t^0, t^+] = \{1 \text{ if } t^0 <= t; 0 \text{ otherwise}\}$.

In this model, the coefficients b_1 and b_2 are associated solely with the changes in the systematic risk while the coefficients $c_1 \ldots$ and c_n are associated solely with the information content of the subevents. The coefficients can be tested for statistical significance. Hence, b_1 and b_2 represent the slope of the regression model before and after the event. If the slope parameters that estimate the individual security returns experience a shift due to the event, then the term $(b_1 - b_2)$ will be statistically significantly different from zero. The advantage of using Intervention Analysis is that unlike the case of using the standard residual methodology, it separates changes in the systematic risk from the changes associated with the information content of an event. The confounding influence of shifts in the slope coefficients are detected and separated from the information content represented by $c_1 \ldots c_n$.

Panel B to Table 3 presents the results of tests using the Intervention Analysis for the Brazilian event. The reduced sample of 75 banks used in the standard event study methodology for longer estimation periods is used in the Intervention Analysis. The 75 banks are also divided into subgroups based on their exposure, size, exchange membership and bank-holding company status. The pre-event period consists of 500 trading days prior to the Brazilian default announcement of 20 February 1987. The post-event period consists of 80 trading days after the announcement. A total of 42 subevents around the Brazilian announcement are identified and tested. Each of these subevents is represented by a dummy variable in the regression model. The table shows the intervention analysis coefficients for the intercepts and the slopes before and after the default announcement.

The slope coefficients range from 0.512 to 0.873. The pre-event slope coefficient for the entire sample of banks is 0.759.

The post-event slope coefficients for the same sample is 0.715. Table 3 also shows the differences in the slope coefficients before and after the event and the corresponding t-values for each of the subgroups.[8] The t-values indicate that the slope differences for the various subgroups are not significantly different from zero. This implies that the systematic risk of the sample of banks did not experience any shifts due to the Brazilian announcement. The slope difference for the sample of all banks is 0.045.

For the various subsamples, the slope differences range from -0.021 to 0.119, but none are significantly different from zero. This implies that any abnormal return associated with the Brazilian announcement is due to the information content of the events and not due to shifts in the systematic risks associated with the banks.[9] It also implies that the results obtained using the standard residual methodology are valid and need not be adjusted for changes in systematic risk as all of the abnormal return during the prediction period reflects the information content of the announcement.

A comparison of the coefficients associated with the 42 subevents with the regression coefficients using indicator variables in Table 3, Panel A show that the signs are consistent in the two cases. Many of the events, especially those close to the Brazilian default announcement have negative regression coefficients, reflecting the adverse information conveyed by these events. However, not all of them are statistically significant.

V. SUMMARY AND CONCLUSIONS

In this study we test for announcement and contagion effect of the Brazilian debt default announcement of 20 February 1987. We test the effects for the entire sample of 87 banks, and for smaller samples, grouped by size, foreign-loan exposure, exchange membership and bank-holding status. We find that the default announcement by Brazil did not convey any new information to the market. With the exception of the group of large banks, none of the other groups experienced significant negative abnormal returns. For the group of large banks, the excess returns are negative and significant on the day following the announcement (the press day). However, they are not significant on the announcement day or the 2-day announcement period. This contradicts the results of Musumeci and Sinkey (1990). Using a smaller sample of banks, they find that the market reacted negatively following the announcement.

[8] The standard error to test the slope differences is computed as:

$$\sigma(\beta 1 - \beta 2) = \sqrt{[\sigma^2(\beta 1) + \sigma^2(\beta 2) - 2\operatorname{cov}(\beta 1, \beta 2)]}$$

[9] An alternative version of the intervention analysis model was also used to detect any shifts in the systematic risk of the bank. The results (not shown here) are similar to the results obtained with the original formulation. The slope coefficient for the announcement period is higher than the coefficients before and after the announcement. However, the differences are not statistically significant.

The results of the announcement effect tests were verified using different estimation periods and Intervention Analysis.

To test for any valuation adjustments prior to the default announcement, several subevents during the 500 days before and 80 days after the announcement are analysed. We find that the market adjusted the equity prices of banks following many of these subevents, responding to the signal conveyed by them. Consequently, the actual default by Brazil on 20 February 1987, by itself, did not have a significant effect on bank equity prices.

ACKNOWLEDGEMENTS

This paper was presented at various University Workshops and at the 1990 Annual ASSA meeting, Washington DC, 28–30 December 1990. The authors wish to thank H. Black, W. Dowling, D. Ketcham, P. Koveos, C. Garrison, R. Shrieves, G. E. Morgan, J. Simms, and R. Pettway for constructive criticism and comments on earlier versions. Special thanks are also due to the Editor and an anonymous reviewer for comments that led to the present streamlined and improved version.

REFERENCES

Bar-Yosef, S. and Brown, B. (1977) A reexamination of stock splits using moving betas, *Jounal of Finance*, **32**, 1069–80.

Born, J. A. and Anderson, S. C. (1986) A comparison of intervention and residual analysis, *Journal of Financial Research*, **9**, 261–70.

Box, G. E. P. and Tiao, G. (1975) Intervention analysis with applications to economic and environmental problems, *Journal of American Statistical Association*, March, 70–9.

Brown, S. and Warner, J. (1980) Measuring security price performance, *Journal of Financial Economics*, **8**, 205–58.

Brown, S. and Warner, J. (1985) Using daily stock returns, *Journal of Financial Economics*, **14**, 3–31.

Bruner, R. F. and Simms, J. M. (1987) The international debt crisis and bank security returns in 1982, *Journal of Money, Credit and Banking*, **19**, 46–55.

Cornell, B. and Shapiro, A. C. (1986) The reaction of bank stock prices to the international debt crisis, *Journal of Banking and Finance*, **10**, 55–73.

DeJong, D. and Collins, D. (1985) Explanation for the instability of equity beta: risk-free rate changes and leverage effects, *Journal of Financial and Quantitative Analysis*, **20**, 73–94.

Deshpande, S. and Philippatos, G. (1988) Leverage decision and the effect of corporate eurobond offerings, *Applied Economics*, **20**, 901–16.

Fama, E. (1976) *Foundations of Finance*, Basic Books, New York.

Kalay, A. and Loewenstein, U. (1985) Predictable events and excess returns, *Journal of Financial Economics*, **14**, 423–49.

Larker, D., Gordon, L. and Pinches, G. (1980) Testing for market efficiency: a comparison of the cumulative average residual methodology and intervention analysis, *Journal of Financial and Quantitative Analysis*, **15**, 267–87.

Musumeci, J. and Sinkey, J. (1990) The international debt crisis, investor contagion, and bank security returns in 1987, *Journal of Money, Credit and Banking*, **22**, 209–20.

Pettway, R. (1980) Potential insolvency, market efficiency, and bank regulation of large commercial banks, *Journal of Financial and Quantitative Analysis*, **15**, 219–36.

Pettway, R. and Sinkey, J. (1980) Establising on-site bank examination priorities: an early warning system using accounting and market information, *Journal of Finance*, **35**, 137–50.

Schoder, S. and Vankudre, P. (1986) The market for bank stocks and banks' disclosure of cross-border exposure: the 1982 Mexican debt crisis, working paper, Wharton School of Finance, University of Pennsylvania.

Smirlock, M. and Kaufold, H. (1987) Bank foreign lending, mandatory disclosure rules, and the reaction of bank stock prices to the Mexican debt crisis, *Journal of Business*, **60**, 347–64.

[30]

by Richard Roll

The International Crash of October 1987

All major world markets declined substantially in October 1987—an exceptional occurrence, given the usual modest correlations of returns across countries. Of 23 markets, 19 declined more than 20 per cent. The U. S. market had the fifth smallest decline in local-currency units, but came in only 11th out of 23 when returns are restated in a common currency.

The U.S. market was not the first to decline sharply. Non-Japanese Asian markets began a severe decline on October 19 (their time). This decline was echoed first by a number of European markets, then by North America and, finally, by Japan. Most of these same markets, however, had experienced significant but less severe declines in the latter part of the previous week. With the exception of the U.S. and Canada, markets continued downward through the end of October, and some of the declines were as large as the great crash on October 19.

Various institutional characteristics have been blamed as contributors to the crash. Univariate regressions indicate that the presence of an official specialist, computer-directed trading, price limits and margin requirements were associated with less severe stock market declines in October 1987, while continuous auctions and automated quotations were associated with larger declines. In multiple regressions, however, several of these variables, including price limits and margin requirements, were found to be insignificant.

October's crash could be ascribed to the normal response of each country's stock market to a worldwide market movement. A world market index was found to be statistically related to monthly returns in every country during the period from the beginning of 1981 up until the month before the crash. The magnitude of market response differed materially across countries. The response coefficient, or beta, was by far the most statistically significant explanatory variable in the October crash, swamping the influences of the institutional market characteristics. Only one institutional variable—continuous auctions—had even a marginally significant influence on the estimated beta.

Richard Roll is Allstate Professor of Finance at the Anderson Graduate School of Management of the University of California, Los Angeles.

The author thanks Jim Brandon for his assistance and advice and Robert Barro, Michael Brennan, Eugene Fama, Robert Kamphuis, Roger Kormendi and Alan Meltzer for their helpful comments.

This article will appear in Black Monday and the Future of Financial Markets, *by The Mid-America Institute for Public Policy Research, published by Dow Jones-Irwin. It is printed here with the permission of Dow Jones-Irwin.*

THE SHARP DROP in U.S. stock prices in October 1987 gave birth to at least one industry—the production of explanations for the crash. Among the most popular are those related to the U.S. market's institutional structure and practices—computer-assisted trading, portfolio insurance, the organized exchange specialists, concurrent trading in stock index futures, margin rules, and the absence of

---

Footnotes appear at end of article.

Table I Stock Price Index Percentage Changes in Major Markets (calendar year 1987 and October 1987)[a]

	Local Currency Units 1987	October	U.S. Dollars 1987	October
Australia[b]	−3.6	−41.8	4.7	−44.9
Austria	−17.6	−11.4	0.7	−5.8
Belgium	−15.5	−23.2	3.1	−18.9
Canada[b]	4.0	−22.5	10.4	−22.9
Denmark	−4.5	−12.5	15.5	−7.3
France	−27.8	−22.9	−13.9	−19.5
Germany	−36.8	−22.3	−22.7	−17.1
Hong Kong	−11.3	−45.8	−11.0	−45.8
Ireland	−12.3	−29.1	4.7	−25.4
Italy	−32.4	−16.3	−22.3	−12.9
Japan	8.5	−12.8	41.4	−7.7
Malaysia	6.9	−39.8	11.7	−39.3
Mexico[b,c]	158.9	−35.0	5.5	−37.6
Netherlands	−18.9	−23.3	0.3	−18.1
New Zealand[b]	−38.7	−29.3	−23.8	−36.0
Norway	−14.0	−30.5	1.7	−28.8
Singapore	−10.6	−42.2	−2.7	−41.6
South Africa[b]	−8.8	−43.9	33.5	−29.0
Spain	8.2	−27.7	32.6	−23.1
Sweden	−15.1	−21.8	−0.9	−18.6
Switzerland	−34.0	−26.1	−16.5	−20.8
United Kingdom	4.6	−26.4	32.5	−22.1
United States	0.5	−21.6	0.5	−21.6

a. Annual average dividend yields are generally in the 2 to 5 per cent range except for Japan and Mexico, which have average dividend yields less than 1 per cent.
b. The currencies of these countries depreciated against the dollar during October 1987.
c. Mexico is the only country whose currency did *not* appreciate against the dollar during 1987.

"circuit breakers" such as trading suspensions and limitations on price movements. Several commission reports about the crash focus on these institutional arrangements.

As regulatory agencies and potential regulatees debate the most appropriate means for preventing another crash, the focus again is on institutional form. The debaters seem to accept without question that the arrangements in place during October were somehow related to the event. Yet there is virtually no evidence to support such a view. If institutional structure of the U.S. market had been the sole culprit, the market would have crashed even earlier. There must have been an underlying "trigger." Some have pointed to the U.S. trade deficit, to anticipations about the 1988 elections, to fears of a recession. But no one has been able to substantiate the underlying cause of the October market decline.

The likely impact of both market structure and macroeconomic conditions can perhaps be deduced by comparing circumstances in the United States with circumstances prevailing in other markets around the world. Indeed, we are blessed with a natural laboratory experiment, for conditions varied widely across countries. To the extent that institutions and economics influence the stock market, we should be able to detect those influences by comparing behaviors in various markets during October 1987.

Table II Correlation Coefficients of Monthly Percentage Changes in Major Stock Market Indexes (local currencies, June 1981–September 1987)

	Australia	Austria	Belgium	Canada	Denmark	France	Germany	Hong Kong	Ireland	Italy
Austria	0.219									
Belgium	0.190	0.222								
Canada	0.568	0.250	0.215							
Denmark	0.217	−0.062	0.219	0.301						
France	0.180	0.263	0.355	0.351	0.241					
Germany	0.145	0.406	0.315	0.194	0.215	0.327				
Hong Kong	0.321	0.174	0.129	0.236	0.120	0.201	0.304			
Ireland	0.349	0.202	0.361	0.490	0.387	0.374	0.067	0.320		
Italy	0.209	0.224	0.307	0.321	0.150	0.459	0.257	0.216	0.275	
Japan	0.182	−0.025	0.223	0.294	0.186	0.361	0.147	0.137	0.183	0.241
Malaysia	0.329	−0.013	0.096	0.274	0.151	−0.134	−0.020	0.159	0.082	−0.119
Mexico	0.220	0.018	0.104	0.114	−0.174	−0.009	0.002	0.149	0.113	0.114
Netherlands	0.294	0.232	0.344	0.545	0.341	0.344	0.511	0.395	0.373	0.344
New Zealand	0.389	0.290	0.275	0.230	0.148	0.247	0.318	0.352	0.314	0.142
Norway	0.355	0.009	0.233	0.381	0.324	0.231	0.173	0.356	0.306	0.042
Singapore	0.374	0.030	0.133	0.320	0.133	−0.085	0.037	0.219	0.102	−0.038
South Africa	0.279	0.159	0.143	0.385	−0.113	0.267	0.007	−0.095	0.024	0.093
Spain	0.147	0.018	0.050	0.190	0.019	0.255	0.147	0.193	0.175	0.290
Sweden	0.327	0.161	0.158	0.376	0.131	0.159	0.227	0.196	0.122	0.330
Switzerland	0.334	0.401	0.276	0.551	0.283	0.307	0.675	0.379	0.290	0.287
United Kingdom	0.377	0.073	0.381	0.590	0.218	0.332	0.263	0.431	0.467	0.328
United States	0.328	0.138	0.250	0.720	0.351	0.390	0.209	0.114	0.380	0.224

The Comparative Performance of Major Stock Markets in 1987

During the entire calendar year 1987, stock market performance varied widely across major countries. Table I gives the total percentage change in the major stock price index for each of 23 countries, in both local-currency and U.S.-dollar terms.[1] The best performer in dollar terms was Japan (+41.4 per cent), the worst performer New Zealand (−23.8 per cent). The local-currency results, however, are quite different from the dollar-denominated results. For example, Mexico had a 5.5 per cent dollar-denominated return in 1987, but was up 158.9 per cent in local currency!

The wide disparity in 1987 returns is typical. Table II shows the simple correlation coefficients of monthly percentage changes in the (local currency) indexes over the pre-crash period for which simultaneous data were available for all countries (mid-1981 through September 1987). The intercountry correlations are mostly positive, but moderate in size. Correlations above 0.5 are relatively rare, and there are only two above 0.7.[2] These modest correlations are in marked contrast to the usual correlation found between any two well-diversified portfolios within the same country. Randomly selected portfolios of U.S. stocks, for example, generally have correlations above 0.9 when there are 50 or more issues included in each portfolio.

Table I also reports total percentage market movements for each country during the month of October 1987. They are all negative! This alone is a cause of wonder. During the whole period of data availability (calendar years 1981 through 1987, inclusive), October 1987 is the *only* month when all markets moved in the same direction, but in that month every stock market fell, and most fell by more than 20 per cent. When just the last three months of 1987 are added to data from the previous 76 months used in Table II, the average correlation coefficient increases from 0.222 to 0.415.[3]

In October Austria, the world's best-performing country, experienced an 11.4 per cent local-currency decline, and Japan declined 12.8 per cent, but the currencies of both countries appreciated significantly against the dollar. The worst performer, Hong Kong, had the same result in both local currency and in U.S. dollars, −45.8 per cent. The rank of the U.S. improves considerably (from 11th to fifth) when the results are expressed in local currency, because the dollar depreciated against most countries during October.

Given the generally low correlations between countries, the uniformity during October 1987, even in local-currency units, is all the more striking. There seems to have been an international trigger that swamped the usual influences of country-specific events.

Table II continued

Japan	Malaysia	Mexico	Netherlands	New Zealand	Norway	Singapore	South Africa	Spain	Sweden	Switzerland	UK
0.109											
−0.021	0.231										
0.333	0.151	0.038									
−0.111	0.136	0.231	0.230								
0.156	0.262	0.050	0.405	0.201							
0.066	0.891	0.202	0.196	0.212	0.280						
0.225	−0.013	0.260	0.058	0.038	0.156	−0.056					
0.248	−0.071	0.059	0.170	0.095	0.075	0.056	−0.088				
0.115	0.103	0.000	0.324	0.136	0.237	0.180	0.070	0.181			
0.130	0.099	0.026	0.570	0.397	0.331	0.157	0.112	0.192	0.334		
0.354	0.193	0.068	0.534	0.014	0.313	0.250	0.168	0.209	0.339	0.435	
0.326	0.347	0.063	0.473	0.083	0.356	0.377	0.218	0.214	0.279	0.500	0.513

Movements Around the Crash

During the month of October, the declines experienced in all markets were concentrated in the second half of the month. Figures A through F present the day-to-day closing index numbers for each market over the entire month of October, restated to 1.0 currency units on October 1. Figure G plots equal-weighted regional indexes over a shorter period around the crash, beginning on October 14 and ending on October 26. Figure H gives a similar portrait of the six largest individual markets. All eight graphs are plotted in actual world time; the tick marks reflect each index's value at the daily New York market close—4:00 p.m. U.S. Eastern Standard Time.[4] The graphs are on the same vertical scale and plotted for the same world time, so they can easily be compared.

The earliest significant declines occurred on October 14 (in the North American markets and in France, The Netherlands and Spain). Most world markets experienced at least some decline for the week ending October 16. In the U.S. market, by far the largest daily decline occurred on October 19. However, many European markets split their declines between their 19th (preceding the U.S. decline) and their 20th. In the cases of Belgium, France, Germany, The Netherlands, Sweden and Switzerland, the biggest down day was their 19th.

In the Asian markets, Hong Kong, Malaysia and Singapore had major declines on both their 19th and 20th, the movement on their 19th preceding the U.S. decline by more than 12 hours. (These markets close before the North American markets open.) Japan fell only slightly on its 19th, but it joined Australia and New Zealand for a major drop on the 20th (i.e., late in the day on October 19 in the U.S.), lagging the major U.S. decline by several hours.

On a given calendar day, the North American markets are the last to trade. Most of the other markets around the world displayed dramatic declines on their October 19—foreshadowing the crash in North America. With just a few exceptions, the most important being Japan, other countries experienced most of their declines either prior to the opening of the U.S. market on the 19th or approximately straddling the U.S. market's October 19 session (i.e., on October 19 and 20, local time).

This seems to be some evidence against the widely expressed view that the U.S. market pulled down all the other world markets on October 19. However, it is true that the U.S. experienced one of the largest declines in the previous week (see Figure H). So there remains the possibility that other market crashes, though generally occurring before the major U.S. crash, were in fact precipitated by the relatively modest U.S. decline from October 14 through 16.[5]

Following the crash, there was a one-day advance in most markets (including the U.S.) on the 21st. Figure G shows that this advance began first in the Asian and Pacific markets, then spread to Europe and finally to North America. Many markets resumed a substantial decline after October 21, however. From the 22nd through the end of October, every market except the U.S. fell, and every decline except that of Canada was substantial (in local-currency units).[6] Some of these cases were at least partial holdovers from market closures on the 19th (e.g., Hong Kong) or drawn out by successive encounters of exchange price limits. In Europe and Asia, however, the weekend from the 23rd to the 25th was just as bad, and in a few cases worse, than the great crash weekend of October 16 to 19. (See Figures C, D and E or Figure G.)

The overall pattern of intertemporal price movements in the various markets suggests the presence of some underlying fundamental factor, but it debunks the notion that an institutional defect in the U.S. market was the cause. It also seems inconsistent with a U.S.-specific macroeconomic event. If anything, the U.S. market lagged the initial price movements that began in earnest on October 14, and it also did not participate in further declines that occurred during the last weekend in October. This would not be the observed empirical pattern if, for instance, portfolio insurance and program trading in New York and Chicago were the basic triggers of the worldwide crash.

October 1987—Before and After

The strong market decline during October 1987 followed what for many countries had been an unprecedented market increase during the first nine months of the year. In the U.S. market, for instance, stock prices advanced 31.4 per cent over those nine months. Some commentators have suggested that the real cause of October's decline was overinflated prices generated by a speculative bubble during the earlier period. Of the 23 countries in our sample, 20 experienced

Figure A October 1987 Stock Prices—North America

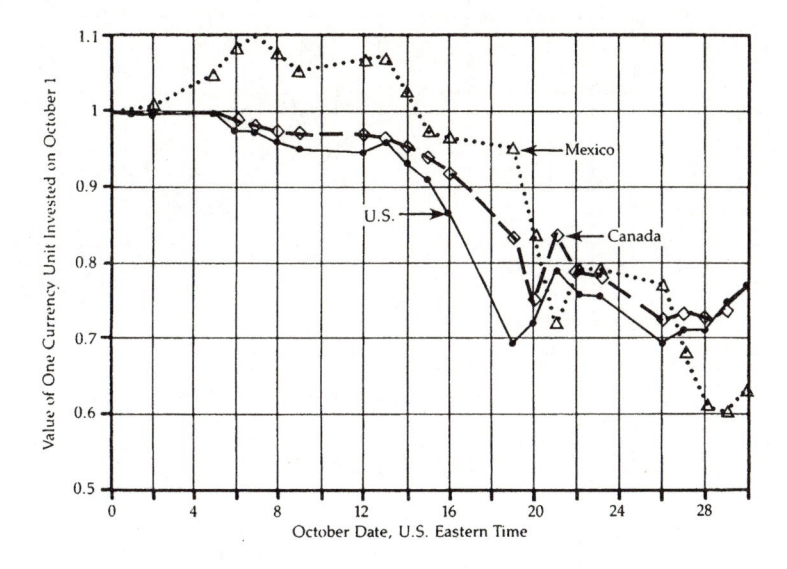

Figure B October 1987 Stock Prices—Ireland, South Africa, U.K.

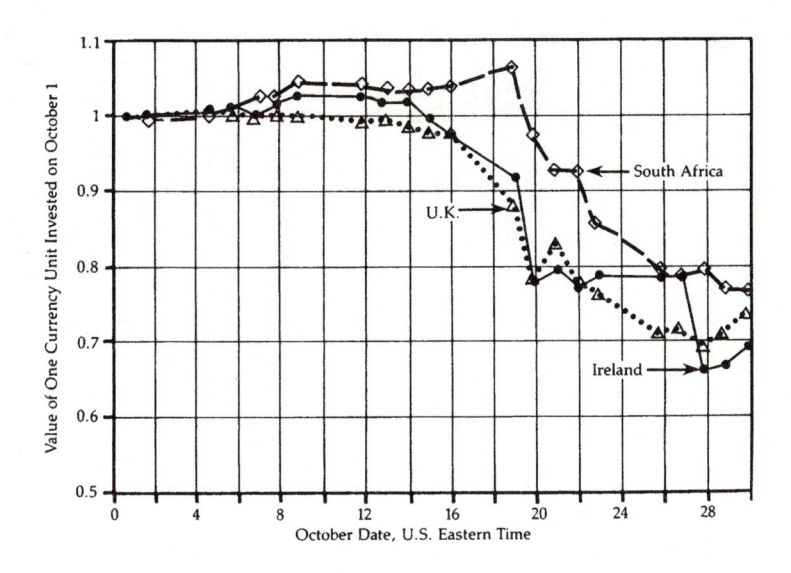

Figure C October 1987 Stock Prices—Larger European Countries

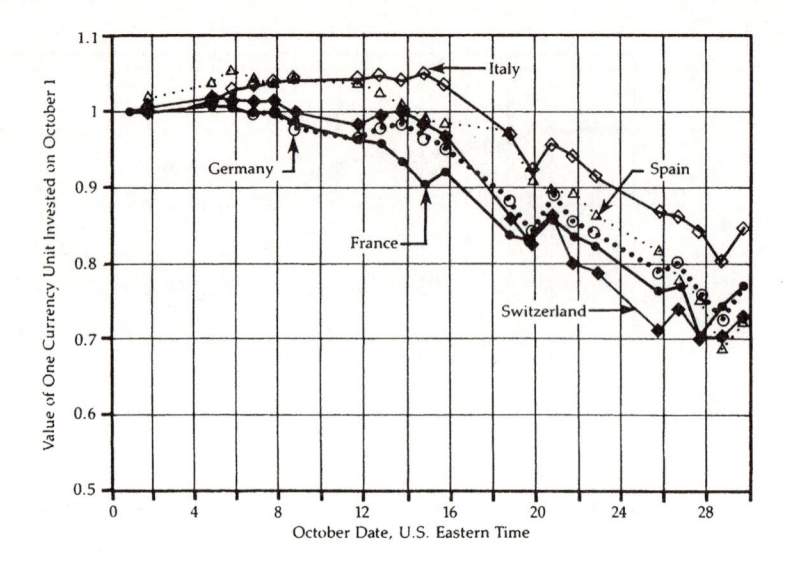

Figure D October 1987 Stock Prices—Smaller European Countries

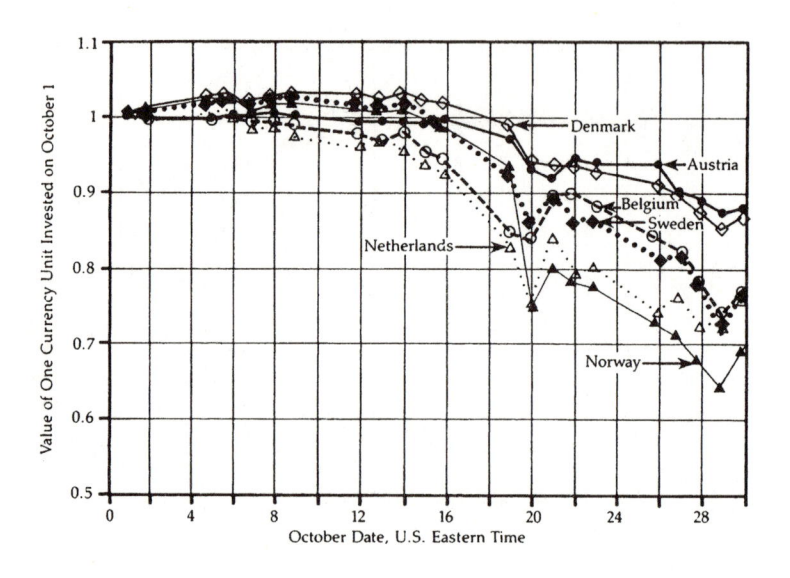

Figure E October 1987 Stock Prices—Asian Markets

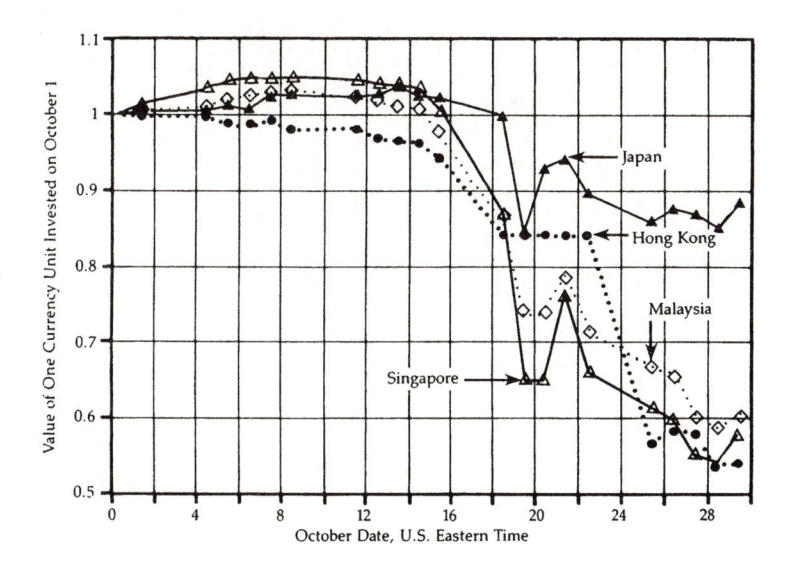

Figure F October 1987 Stock Prices—Australia and New Zealand

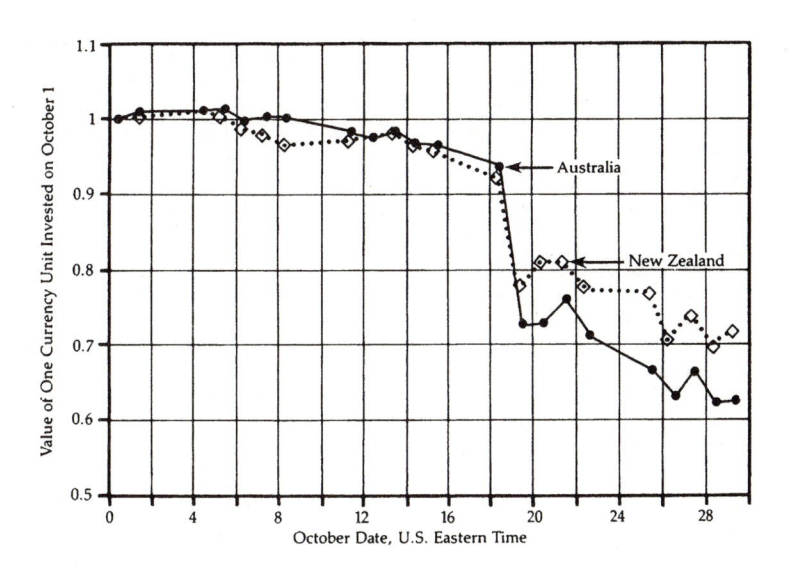

Figure G   Regional Indexes—October 14–October 26

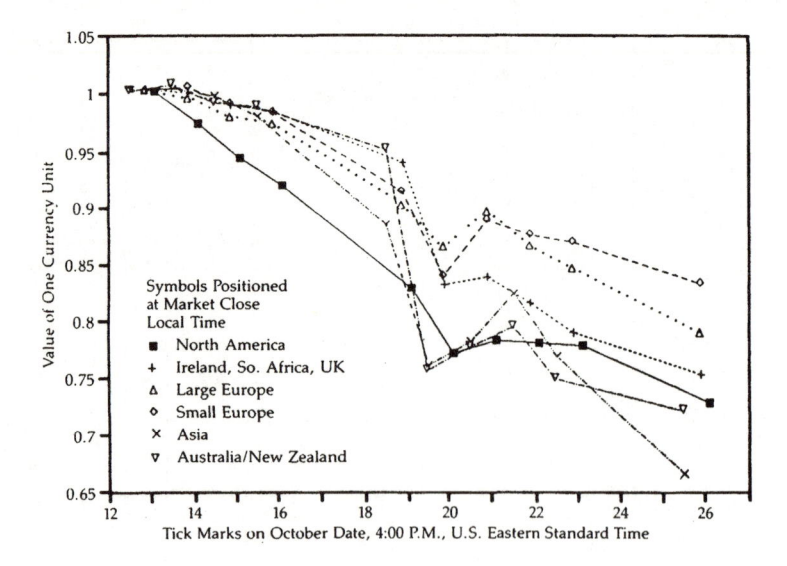

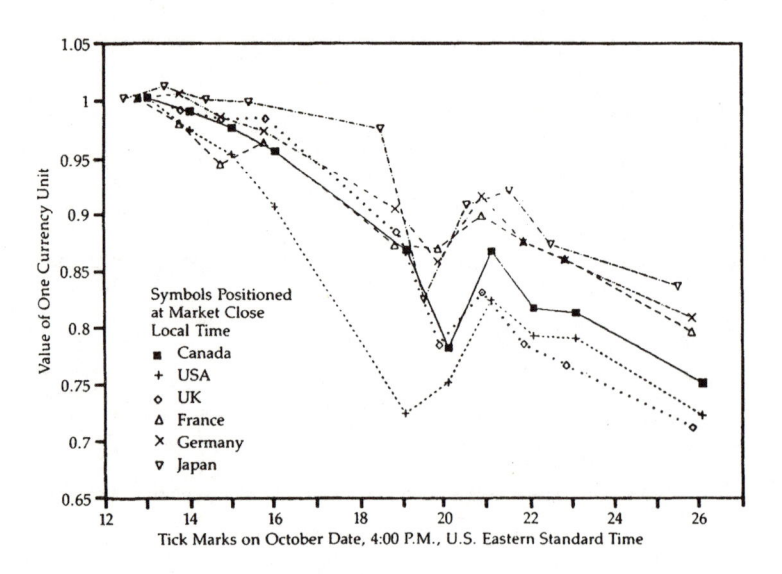

Figure H   The Six Largest Markets—October 14–October 26

stock price increases over the January to September period. There was, however, wide disparity in the extent of the advance.

One symptom of a speculative bubble might be an inverse relation between the price increase and the extent of the subsequent crash. Figure I presents a cross-country comparison of the January-September 1987 return versus the October decline.[7] There is in fact a significant negative cross-country relation. The regression line shown on the figure indicates a statistically significant association, with an R^2 of 0.543.

There is, however, a conceptual difficulty in ascribing these results to the existence of a speculative bubble: The same pattern would arise if there were underlying common factors driving stock price changes in all countries. Suppose, for instance, that there is a fundamental macroeconomic factor related to world industrial activity, that it influences the market in every country, but that each country's amplitude of response is different. If that factor happened to be positive from January through September of 1987, while other country-specific influences happened to be relatively stable, we would have observed price advances in most countries (although advances of widely-varying amounts). If the same factor happened to decline dramatically in October, those countries with the greatest amplitude of reaction would have displayed the largest stock price declines. The overall result would be a cross-country negative relation such as that indicated in Figure I. In other words, high "beta" countries do better in worldwide bull markets and worse in bear markets, thus inducing a cross-country negative relation when a bull market period is compared cross-sectionally with a bear market period.

To ascertain whether 1987 was really a speculative bubble followed by a crash, as opposed to a simple manifestation of the usual world market behavior, one would be obliged to identify and estimate a factor model over an entirely different period and use the prefitted response coefficients with fundamental macroeconomic factors measured during 1987.

Since the Crash
In the aftermath of the crash, some have alleged that it was actually an overreaction and that it will soon be reversed; i.e., that it represented just the opposite of a corrected speculative bubble (but was still irrational). If this is true, strong and sharp price increases should occur sometime. However, as Figure J shows, there has been no evidence of a rebound during the successive four calendar months.

Certain regions have performed better than others. Asia, North America and the smaller European countries have experienced moderate price increases, particularly after the first of December 1987. Conversely, other regions (Australia, New Zealand) have performed rather poorly, or have shown little movement in either direction from the level established at the end of October. The interocular test in Figure J reveals an ordinary pattern, one that could be expected over just about any four-month interval—some differences across markets, but certainly no dramatic and worldwide reversal anywhere close to the size of October's decline.

A world index constructed by equally weighting the local currency indexes and normalized to 100 on September 30, 1987 fell to 73.6 by October 30. By February 29, 1988, the index stood at 72.7. Thus the price level established in the October crash seems to have been a virtually unbiased estimate of the average price level over the subsequent four months. If a sizable correction is going to occur, it is apparently going to take a while.

Institutional Arrangements and Market Behavior
Our world laboratory experiment provides insights into the possible influence of each major element of a market's institutional structure. The stock markets around the world are amazingly diverse in their organization. Table III provides a list of some of the particular features in place during October 1987.[8]

Among the features that have figured prominently in post-crash discussions are the extent of computerized trading, the auction system itself, the presence or absence of limits on price movements, regulated margin requirements, and off-market or off-hours trading. Additional features that could be of significance include the presence or absence of floor brokers who conduct trades but are not permitted to invest on their own accounts, the extent of trading in the cash market versus the forward market, the identity of traders (i.e., institutions such as banks or specialized trading firms), and the significance of transaction taxes.

Some markets have trading for both immediate and forward settlement. When forward set-

Figure I   1987 Returns, October vs. January–September

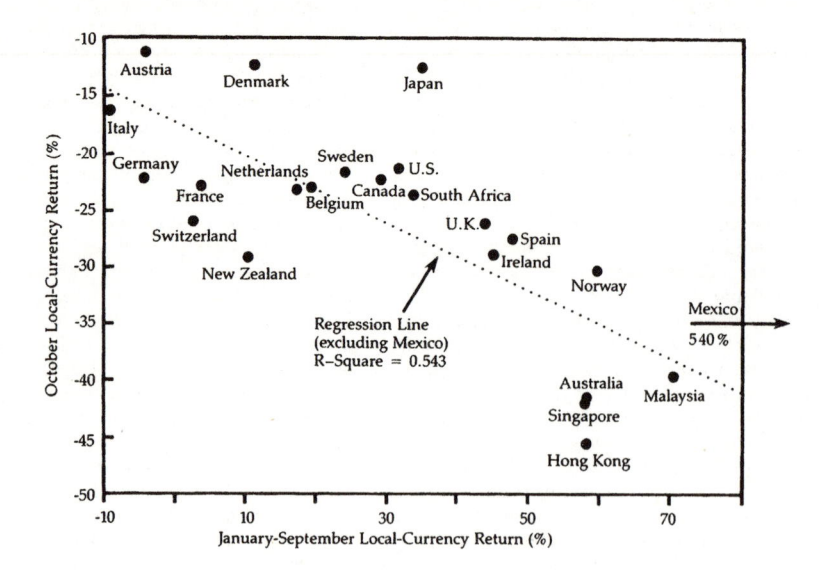

Figure J   Regional Indexes—October 14, 1987–February 29, 1988

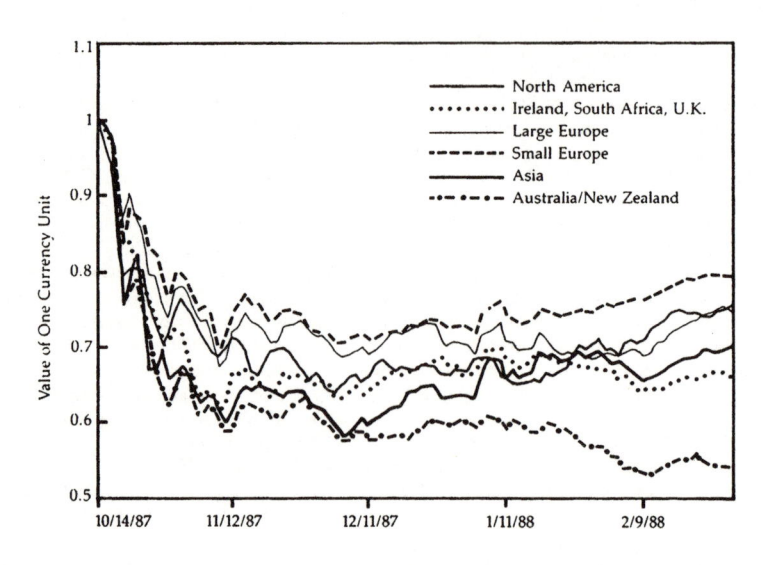

Table III Institutional Arrangements in World Markets

Country	Auction	Official Specialists	Forward Trading on Exchange	Automated Quotations	Computer-Directed Trading	Options/Futures Trading	Price Limits	Transaction Tax (Round-Trip)	Margin Requirements	Trading Off Exchange
Australia	Continuous	No	No	Yes	No	Yes	None	0.6%	None	Infrequent
Austria	Single	Yes	No	No	No	No	5%	0.3%	100%	Frequent
Belgium	Mixed	No	Yes	No	No	No[a]	10%/None[b]	0.375%/0.195%	100%/25%[b]	Occasional
Canada	Continuous	Yes	No	Yes	Yes	Yes	None[c]	0	50%[d]	Prohibited
Denmark	Mixed	No	No	No	No	No	None	1%	None	Frequent
France	Mixed	Yes	Yes	Yes	Yes	Yes	4%/7%[c]	0.3%	100%/20%[f]	Prohibited
Germany	Continuous	Yes	No	No	No	Options	None	0.5%	None	Frequent
Hong Kong	Continuous	No	No	Yes	No	Futures	None[g]	0.6%+	None	Infrequent
Ireland	Continuous	No	No	Yes	No	No	None	1%	100%	Frequent
Italy	Mixed	No	Yes	No	No	No	10–20%[h]	0.3%	100%	Frequent
Japan	Continuous	Yes	No	Yes	Yes	No[i]	–10%	0.55%	70%[j]	Prohibited
Malaysia	Continuous	No	No	Yes	No	No	None	0.03%	None	Occasional
Mexico	Continuous	No	Yes	No	No	No	10%[k]	0	None	Occasional
Netherlands	Continuous	Yes	No	No	No	Options	Variable[l]	2.4%[m]	None	Prohibited
New Zealand	Continuous	No	No	No	No	Futures	None	0	None	Occasional
Norway	Single	No	No	No	No	No	None	1%	100%	Frequent
Singapore	Continuous	No	No	Yes	No	No[n]	None	0.5%	71%	Occasional
South Africa	Continuous	No	No	Yes	No	Options	None	1.5%	100%	Prohibited
Spain	Mixed[o]	No	No	No	No	No	10%[p]	0.11%	50%[p]	Frequent
Sweden	Mixed	No	No	Yes	No	Yes	None	2%	40%	Frequent
Switzerland	Mixed	No	Yes	Yes	No	Yes	5%[q]	0.9%	None	Infrequent
United Kingdom	Continuous	No	No	Yes	Yes	Yes	None	0.5%	None	Occasional
United States	Continuous	Yes	No	Yes	Yes	Yes	None	0	Yes	Occasional

a. Calls only on just five stocks.
b. Cash/forward.
c. None on stocks; 3-5% on index futures.
d. 10% (5%) for uncovered (covered) futures.
e. Cash/forward, but not always enforced.
f. Cash/forward; 40% if forward collateral is stock rather than cash.
g. "Four Spread Rule": offers not permitted more than four ticks from current bids and asks.
h. Hitting limit suspends auction; auction then tried a second time at end of day.
i. Futures on the Nikkei Index are traded in Singapore.
j. Decreased to 50% on October 21, 1987 "to encourage buyers."
k. Trading suspended for successive periods, 15 and then 30 minutes; effective limit: 30–40%.
l. Authorities have discretion. In October, 2% limits every 15 minutes used frequently.
m. For non-dealer transactions only.
n. Only for Nikkei Index (Japan).
o. Groups of stocks are traded continuously for 10 minutes each.
p. Limits raised to 20% and margin to 50% on October 27.
q. Hitting limit causes 15-minute trading suspension. Limits raised to 10–15% in October.

tlement exists, the forward contracts often have a greater volume of trading than cash contracts. For instance, on the Paris *Bourse,* there is a once-a-day auction in the cash market conducted by designated brokerage houses, but there is continuous forward trading in the larger stocks from 9:30 to 11:00 a.m. and repeated call auctions thereafter in forward contracts for all stocks. The limit moves are different too; they are 7 per cent in the forward market and 4 per cent in the cash market.[9] However, there are no limits on the price movements of foreign securities. All trading is done by registered stock brokers, a requirement of French law. Block trading is conducted between the previous day's high and low prices, and block volume constitutes about one-half of all equity trading.

To judge the importance of any particular institutional characteristic, one could compare the market behavior in Table I or in Figures A to F with the presence or absence of the characteristic given in Table III. For example, computer-directed trading is prevalent in Canada, France, Japan, the United Kingdom and the United States. In local-currency terms, these five countries experienced an average decline of 21.25 per

Table IV Local-Currency Returns in October 1987 and Market Characteristics

	Auction	Official Special.	Forward Trading	Auto. Quot.	Comp. Trading	Options/ Futures	Price Limits	Trans. Tax	Margin Reqs.	Off-Ex. Trading
	Cont. = 1 Else = 0	Yes = 1 Else = 0	Yes = 1 Else = 0	Yes = 1 Else = 0	Yes = 1 Else = 0	Yes = 1 Else = 0	None = 0 Else = 1	Non-0 = 1 Else = 0	None = 0 Else = i	None & Infr. = 0 Else = 1
	Average October Local-Currency Return for Countries in Zero/One Variable Group (%)								
Group 1	-29.69	-19.53	-24.70	-28.99	-21.25	-27.31	-22.08	-26.31	-23.54	-25.94
Group 0	-21.39	-29.47	-26.93	-23.14	-27.89	-25.50	-29.25	-27.08	-30.22	-27.38
Diff.	-8.31	9.94	2.23	-5.85	6.63	-1.80	7.17	0.78	6.68	1.44
T-Value	-2.66	3.53	0.51	-2.05	2.31	-0.57	2.25	0.22	2.20	0.41
	Multiple Regression of October Local Currency Return on Zero/One Variables								
Coeff.	-7.324	6.528	-2.867	-6.065	7.518	1.194	1.638	1.845	2.111	1.452
T-Value	-1.304	1.068	-0.417	-0.954	1.110	0.222	0.232	0.298	0.449	0.258
TS T-Val	-1.762	1.628	-0.592	-1.287	1.631	0.267	0.335	0.343	0.594	0.406

intercept = -26.5; adjusted R-squared = 0.254

cent during October; the 18 countries without widespread computer-directed trading experienced an average decline of 27.89 per cent. Taken as a characteristic in isolation, computer-directed trading (e.g., portfolio insurance and index arbitrage), if it had any impact at all, actually helped mitigate the market decline.

The Quantitative Impact of Market Arrangements on the Extent of the Crash

To obtain a quantitative estimate of the impact of each qualitative institutional characteristic, we converted the entries in Table III into zero/one values and computed both univariate and multivariate results based on the converted numbers. Table IV defines the zero/one variables and presents the basic results.

The top panel of the table shows simple cross-country means for the countries in each univariate zero/one category. For example, if the auction in a particular country is conducted on a continuous basis, that country is assigned to group 1; if there is a single daily auction, or a mixed auction, the country is in group 0. Table IV shows that continuous-auction countries had October declines of 29.69 per cent on average, while the non-continuous-auction countries had October declines that averaged 21.39 per cent.

The t-value of the difference provides a statistical measure of significance. If the t-value is above 1.65 (in absolute terms), the odds are roughly 10 to one that the variable is significant, when judged on a univariate basis (i.e., in isolation).[10] Six of the 10 variables were related to the magnitude of the crash. Continuous auctions and automated quotation systems were associated with larger declines, while the presence of an official specialist, computer-directed trading, price limits and margin requirements were associated with smaller declines. Forward trading, options and futures trading, transaction taxes and trading off the exchanges were not significantly associated with the size of the crash.

Univariate results may be misleading, however. A characteristic that appears to be significant may merely be a proxy for some other characteristic that is the true cause of the observed difference. This is certainly possible here, not only because the different institutional characteristics are correlated across countries, but also because other relevant influences may have been omitted.

The bottom panel of Table IV presents a multivariate comparison in the form of a cross-country regression of October returns (in local-currency units) on all the zero/one variables. The explained variance (adjusted R^2) was 25.4 per cent, but none of the ordinary t-values from the cross-sectional regression indicates statistical reliability. This reveals the presence of multicollinearity in the explanatory variables, which makes it difficult to assess the relative importance of each one.

Moreover, the observations in this cross-sectional regression may not be cross-sectionally independent, in which case the ordinary t-values will be biased, although the direction of bias is impossible to determine without knowledge of the covariance structure of the residuals. In an attempt to repair both multicollinearity and cross-sectional dependence, we constructed another t-value by using the time series of cross-sectional returns for the period prior to October. The method is explained in the appendix.

With the time-series-derived TS t-values, several characteristics have at least marginal statistical reliability. The presence of an official monopolistic specialist and computer-directed trading were associated with less severe market declines in October. Continuous auctions were marginally significant and associated with greater market declines. Note that these three variables have coefficients with roughly the same magnitude in both the univariate and the multivariate computations, while variables such as price limits and margin requirements have much larger coefficients in the univariate calculations.[11]

Although the regression in Table IV indicates some statistically significant associations between certain market characteristics and the October decline, one should hesitate to conclude that even a strongly associated variable actually contributed to the decline. Markets differ in their amplitudes of response to the same underlying trigger, and certain institutional features may have been adopted because of a high amplitude. For example, it is conceivable, though perhaps improbable, that price limits are abandoned in markets with great volatility. This could have given rise to an association between the absence of price limits and the severity of price decline in October 1987, without there actually having been a mitigating influence of limits.

The Typical Market Response to World Movements and the Crash

In addition to institutional arrangements, another potential explanation for the variety of declines in different markets is that a fundamental, worldwide triggering variable caused the crash, and that the relative movement of each market was simply the usual relation between that particular market and the underlying factor. In order to assess this possibility, we used data from February 1981 through September 1987 to construct a world market index.[12] The index was equally weighted across countries using local-currency-denominated returns.[13] The following simple market model was fitted to the available time series of monthly returns for each country:

$$R_{j,t} = a_j + b_j R_{M,t} + e_{j,t},$$

where

$R_{j,t}$ = the monthly percentage change in the index of country j for month t,

$R_{M,t}$ = the world market index percentage change,

$e_{j,t}$ = an unexplained residual, and

a_j and b_j = fitted coefficients.

The slope coefficient b_j is the so-called beta, which measures the relative magnitude of response of a given country to changes in the world market index. The appendix gives details of these regressions for each country. Every country exhibited a statistically significant relation with the world market index, with the average R-square being 0.243.

The market model fitted for each country up through September 1987 was used to predict the country's return in October 1987, conditional on the world market index movement in October. The prediction errors (or out-of-sample residuals) were then related cross-sectionally to market characteristics (i.e., to the zero/one variables used previously). The top panel of Table V gives the results.

No coefficient is statistically different from zero. Thus none of the institutional market characteristics was associated with an unusually large or small October return after the worldwide market movement was taken into account. In other words, the magnitude of each market's decline was explained by that market's ordinary relation with world market events. Nothing was left to be explained by the particular institutional arrangements in place.[14]

The second panel of Table V gives some additional evidence about the overwhelming influence of the world market "factor." In the cross-sectional regression reported there, the October index return (not the residual) was related to the institutional zero/one characteristics plus the market-model slope coefficient (or beta) from the time-series regression for each country calculated up through September. This panel differs from the cross-sectional multiple

Table V Local Currency Market Model and Market Characteristics

	Auction	Off. Special.	Forward Trading	Auto. Quot.	Comp. Trading	Options/ Futures	Price Limits	Trans. Tax	Margin Reqs.	Off-Ex. Trading	Beta
	Cont =1 Else = 0	Yes = 1 Else = 0	Yes = 1 Else = 0	Yes = 1 Else = 0	Yes = 1 Else = 0	Yes = 1 Else = 0	None = 0 Else = 0	Non-0 = 1 Else = 0	None = 0 Else = 0	None & Infr. = 0 Else = 1	

Market Model Prediction Errors in October 1987 vs. Market Characteristics

Coeff.	1.688	3.540	8.529	−4.381	1.670	−3.614	−2.201	−5.669	0.551	−0.951	
T-Value	0.361	0.697	1.491	−0.828	0.297	−0.809	−0.376	−1.103	0.141	−0.203	

intercept = 5.89; adjusted R-squared = 0.088

Multiple Regression of October Local-Currency Return on Zero/One Variables and on Typical Response

Coeff.	−1.443	4.010	4.080	−5.460	4.218	−1.476	0.020	−3.088	1.338	0.179	−16.642
T-Value	−0.281	0.786	0.654	−1.046	0.741	−0.326	0.003	−0.571	0.346	0.039	−2.615
TS T-Val	−0.351	1.046	0.779	−1.169	0.945	−0.339	0.004	−0.638	0.387	0.049	−2.251

intercept = 6.42; adjusted R-squared = 0.498

Market Model Betas, January 1981–September 1987 vs. Market Characteristics

Coeff.	0.353	−0.151	0.417	0.036	−0.198	−0.160	−0.097	−0.296	−0.046	−0.077	
T-Value	1.691	−0.665	1.631	0.154	−0.787	−0.803	−0.371	−1.288	−0.266	−0.366	

intercept = 1.21; adjusted R-squared = 0.255

regression in Table IV only by the inclusion of the beta. Comparing the two regressions, we observe that none of the market characteristics remains even marginally significant. In contrast, the beta is highly significant, and its coefficient (−16.6 per cent) is a large fraction of the average world market portfolio return.[15] It is more than four times the magnitude of any other estimated coefficient in the regression.

Because this regression uses total percentage changes during October, it may be subject to cross-sectional dependence. A time-series t-value was computed, using the methods described in the appendix. The results are qualitatively the same: Only the market-model beta is statistically significant in explaining October 1987 returns.

There is one remaining problem: It seems at least conceivable that the typical magnitude of response of a given country to a world market movement is itself a function of the institutional arrangements in that country's stock market. For example, perhaps margin requirements or limits on price movements reduce the market-model beta relative to the level it would otherwise achieve in their absence. If so, the dominance of the beta in the October-return cross-sectional regression in Table V and the absence of a statistically significant market characteristic in the cross-sectional regression for market-model residuals during October may still not entirely remove the suspicion that some of the institutional arrangements had an influence on the crash. Instead of showing up directly, their influence could have been exerted by reducing or increasing the estimated magnitude of response.

To check out this possibility, we computed another cross-sectional regression, this time with the dependent variable being the estimated beta itself and the explanatory variables the zero/one market characteristics. The bottom panel of Table V reports the results.

Two characteristics are marginally significant—continuous auctions and forward trading. Forward trading, however, did not show up as an influence on either the total returns in October or on the October market–model residuals. Although it may be an influence on the typical response of a market to world movements, it does not seem to have played a role in the crash. Continuous trading, however, may be a culprit. Countries whose stock markets conduct continuous auctions did worse during the crash. These markets are also associated with larger betas, hence tend to swing more widely in response to worldwide market influences.

If we were willing to accept this result as evidence of causation, we might go on to speculate on why continuous auctions might be prone to larger price swings. A continuous auction conducts trading throughout the day, as orders are received, while a non-continuous auction collects orders over a 24-hour interval and clears all of them at a given time. The continuous auction is more dynamic, and it certainly offers a larger inducement for a trader to act quickly. Quick decisions are less important in a non-continuous regime, because others may reach similar conclusions before the appointed time for the auction. Acting quickly, in an attempt to beat others to the next trade, could lead to more frequent errors and even to panic. Perhaps haste made waste in October 1987.

Market Liquidity

"Liquidity" may have influenced country responses during the crash. Liquidity is not a well-defined term, but most market observers seem to regard smaller markets as less liquid, hence prone to greater price volatility, susceptible to psychological influences, and probably less "efficient." To examine this idea, we used the aggregate dollar value of stocks traded on each stock exchange as a proxy for liquidity.

On September 30, 1987, the 23 national markets in our database differed widely in aggregate capitalization. The smallest was Norway ($2.65 billion) the largest Japan ($2.03 trillion). The United States market capitalization was $1.85 trillion.

Because market capitalization differs across countries by a factor of almost 100, we used its logarithm in the statistical estimation. Log (Market Cap) was included along with the zero/one institutional characteristics and the estimated market-model beta to explain the cross-sectional differences in return during October 1987. It was completely insignificant, having a t-value of only 0.348, and left all the other coefficients virtually unchanged.[16]

Given the previous information about returns around the crash, the lack of a liquidity effect is probably not all that surprising. Some of the smallest markets (Austria and Denmark) performed relatively well in October, while others (Malaysia and Mexico) did poorly. Similarly, some larger countries (Japan) had small declines, while others (the U.K.) were more severely affected. The relative extent of the October crash was related to characteristics other than sheer size. ■

Footnotes

1. The data source was Goldman, Sachs & Co., "FT-Actuaries World Indices," various monthly editions. The indexes are the most widely followed in each country. A complete list of each country is contained in Goldman, Sachs & Co., "Anatomy of the World's Equity Markets."
2. Between Canada and the U.S. and between Malaysia and Singapore.
3. The previous 76 months go from June 1981 through September 1987.
4. For example, Tokyo is 14 hours ahead of New York, so its observation for October 1, Tokyo time, is plotted as October 0.41666 (i.e., 10/24) New York time. The non-Japanese Asian markets are plotted according to Japanese time, although they are one hour later. Similarly, Mexico is plotted New York time, South Africa is plotted British time, and New Zealand is plotted Australian time. Mexico is one hour behind New York; South Africa and New Zealand are two hours ahead of Britain and Australia, respectively.
5. As Figures G and H show, most other markets did decline even earlier than the U.S. on each day from the 14th through the 16th.
6. Canada's decline from October 22 through October 30 was only 1.62 per cent. Thirteen countries had at least 10 per cent declines in this period.
7. Mexico was excluded from the figure and the regression line because its return during January–September 1987 was 540 per cent in local currency units (although only 271 per cent in dollars); it seems to be an outlier.
8. The data presented in Table III are not easily available. Jim Brandon telephoned every country on the list and interviewed a person knowledgeable about each market. The author thanks Neville Thomas and Michael Crowley, Australia; Robert Schwind, Austria; Mme. Moeremhout, Belgium; Jim Darcel, Canada; Jorgan Brisson, Denmark; M. Douzy, France; Michael Hanke, Germany; Patrick Leong, Hong Kong; Tom Healy, Ireland; Alessandro Wagner, Italy; Moriyuki Iwanaga, Japan; Mr. Izlen, Malaysia; Armando Denegas, Mexico; Paul Koster, The Netherlands; Cathy Gruschow, New Zealand; Melvin Tagen, Norway; Gillian Tam, Singapore; Mrs. De Kock, South Africa; David Jimenez, Spain; Les Vindeyaag, Sweden; Brigette Borsch, Switzerland; and Matthew Hall, United Kingdom.
9. The French market exhibits a unique concept of price limits. They are not enforced if the entire

market seems to be moving in the same direction. According to our informant, enforcement applies only when an individual stock "appears to be manipulated."
10. An explanation of the statistical methods used to obtain the t-value is contained in the appendix.
11. The univariate difference in means across zero/one groups is identical to the slope coefficient in a cross-sectional regression of the October return on a single zero/one variable (for a proof, see the appendix). Thus the effect of multicollinearity can be directly gauged by comparing the slope coefficient in the second panel of Table IV with the corresponding group mean differences in the first.
12. Goldman, Sachs & Co. provided monthly market index levels beginning in January 1981. However, their database does not include Mexico until May 1981. The first month is lost by calculating the monthly percentage change in the index. Thus the index includes 22 countries from February 1981 and 23 countries from June 1981. Dividend yields are available for the latter part of the data period, but dividends have little variability and were thus omitted from the calculations without harm. Because of this omission, the index percentage change for a given month differs slightly from the monthly total return.
13. Indexes were actually constructed both on a common-currency basis and a local-currency basis, and both equally weighted and value-weighted (by the dollar value of total country capitalization). Time-series regressions between individual country returns and the various indexes yielded surprisingly similar slope coefficients (betas). There were differences in R-squares, of course, because the exchange rate adjustment essentially adds a noisy but relatively uncorrelated random variable to the local-currency return. The intercepts also differed, by roughly the difference in mean returns in local currency and in dollars.
14. Note that cross-sectional dependence is probably not material in this regression, simply because the principal source of that dependence, general worldwide market movements, has already been removed.
15. Even this coefficient is probably understated in absolute magnitude because the beta is only an estimated coefficient and is thus an error-contaminated regressor.
16. In particular, the coefficient of beta was about the same (-15.6) and still highly significant (t-value of -2.16). Cross-sectionally, the beta estimated from February 1981 through September 1987 is moderately correlated with the log of market capitalization at the end of September 1987. A cross-sectional regression of beta on log size gives a slope coefficient of -0.147 with a t-value of 1.68. But when both variables compete in a cross-sectional regression predicting the October decline, the beta wins in the sense of being uniquely significant.

Appendix

T-Values for the Univariate Differences

For each institutional characteristic, two portfolios were formed corresponding to whether the group variable was zero or one. As an example, when the institutional characteristic was computer-directed trading, the first portfolio consisted of an equal-weighted combination of the countries with computer–directed trading (Canada, France, Japan, the United Kingdom and the United States, from Table III), and the second portfolio consisted of an equal-weighted combination of the other countries (the 18 without computer-directed trading). There is a total of 20 such portfolios, two for each of 10 institutional characteristics.

The return for each of the 20 portfolios was calculated for all available data periods before October 1987. Except for Mexico, this was February 1981 through September 1987. For Mexico, it was June 1981 through September 1987. Thus, during the first four of 80 months, Mexico was missing from the 10 portfolios to which it later belonged.

For each month and each institutional characteristic, a return difference was formed by subtracting the portfolio return for group 0 from the portfolio return for group 1. This is tantamount to buying long those countries with a "1" and shorting those countries with a "0" *for a particular characteristic*. There were thus 10 time series of return differences, one for each institutional characteristic.

The standard deviation of the return difference was calculated from the 10 time series. Finally, the t-value was calculated as the return difference in October 1987 divided by the calculated time-series standard deviation.

Univariate Regression

The slope coefficient from the regression of y on a zero/one variable x is simply the difference in group means of y. For proof of this, consider the following definitions:

N = total sample size,
n = number of observations, with $x = 1$,
$p = n/N$ and
Y, Y_1, Y_0 = respectively, the sample mean of y, y with $x = 1$, and y with $x = 0$.

Then it is straightforward to show that the ordinary-least-squares bivariate regression slope coefficient of y on x is:

$$b = [p(Y_1 - Y)]/[p(1 - p)],$$
$$= \{Y_1 - [pY_1 + (1 - p)Y_0]\}/(1 - p)$$
$$= Y_1 - Y_0.$$

Time-Series T-Values

The second panels of Tables IV and V present t-values obtained from a time series not including the cross-section month (October 1987). For every month when all countries had available data (June 1981 through September 1987), a cross-sectional multiple regression was calculated between the actual monthly index percentage changes and the explanatory variables, the zero/one variables (corresponding to Table IV), and the zero/one variables plus the country's market model beta (corresponding to Table V). The vector of 10 (11) cross-sectional coefficients corresponding to panel 2 of Table IV (Table V) for month t formed a single time-series observation.

The standard deviation of each element in the vector of coefficients was then computed across all time-series observations. The TS t-value was the estimated cross-sectional coefficient in October 1987 divided by its corresponding standard deviation as computed in steps 1 and 2.

Market–Model Results

Table AI gives means, standard deviations and market–model regression results for local-currency returns, using an equal-weighted, local-currency world market index.

Table AI Local-Currency Index Percentage Changes and Equal-Weighted World Portfolio (Feb.1981–Sept. 1987)

Country	Sample Size (months)	Average % Change (per month)	Standard Deviation (%/month)	Slope (t-values)	Intercept (t-values)	Adjusted R-Squared
Australia	80	1.634	5.896	1.218 (7.208)	−0.563 (−0.938)	0.3921
Austria	80	0.985	5.128	0.563 (3.152)	−0.031 (−0.048)	0.1016
Belgium	80	1.899	5.191	0.808 (4.785)	0.442 (0.736)	0.2170
Canada	80	0.855	4.931	1.116 (8.492)	−1.159 (−2.481)	0.4738
Denmark	80	1.463	5.306	0.579 (3.127)	0.419 (0.637)	0.1000
France	80	1.748	5.602	0.901 (4.995)	0.123 (0.191)	0.2326
Germany	80	1.503	4.923	0.739 (4.567)	0.171 (0.297)	0.2009
Hong Kong	80	1.439	9.248	1.533 (5.201)	−1.326 (−1.266)	0.2480
Ireland	80	1.926	6.445	1.193 (6.074)	−0.226 (−0.324)	0.3124
Italy	80	1.911	7.783	1.192 (4.688)	−0.240 (−0.266)	0.2098
Japan	80	1.989	4.651	0.557 (3.483)	0.983 (1.729)	0.1235
Malaysia	80	0.433	8.108	1.137 (4.197)	−1.618 (−1.681)	0.1738
Mexico	76	6.555	16.110	2.135 (3.914)	2.655 (1.345)	0.1603
Netherlands	80	1.529	4.988	1.050 (7.440)	−0.365 (−0.728)	0.4076
New Zealand	80	2.190	6.609	1.019 (4.726)	0.352 (0.460)	0.2127
Norway	80	1.656	6.381	1.110 (5.553)	−0.346 (−0.487)	0.2742
Singapore	80	0.874	7.858	1.251 (4.930)	−1.383 (−1.534)	0.2278
South Africa	80	2.181	7.247	0.713 (2.790)	0.895 (0.985)	0.0791
Spain	80	2.352	6.443	0.716 (3.196)	1.060 (1.331)	0.1045
Sweden	80	2.513	6.109	0.872 (4.290)	0.940 (1.302)	0.1805
Switzerland	80	1.010	3.876	0.795 (7.117)	−0.424 (−1.068)	0.3860
United Kingdom	80	1.888	4.567	0.950 (7.288)	0.176 (0.379)	0.3975
United States	80	1.221	4.243	0.856 (6.933)	−0.324 (−0.738)	0.3734

The current Southeast Asia financial crisis [1]

Merton H. Miller

The University of Chicago, Graduate School of Business, Chicago, IL 60637, USA

Abstract

The current Southeast Asia financial crisis is not handled easily in a brief speech. Too many countries are involved, each with special features. And worse yet, new developments are occurring almost daily. The crisis, alas, is still very much an ongoing one. What we have all been calling "the" crisis, moreover, is really three separate, closely interrelated crisis, each corresponding to one of the three classic financial risks. These interrelated crisis should be thought of not as natural disasters like the Kobe earthquake, unexpectedly coming out of the blue, nor as divine punishment for our sins, but as man-made, or should I say institution-made disasters. Individuals did indeed make their share of mistakes, but our market-driven institutions should have had enough resilience to keep the damages from compounding. They did not, for reasons I will try to explain; and until some fundamental changes in our financial institutions do occur – and I do not mean mere or more regulation – we will remain vulnerable, I fear, to more of the same in the years ahead. © 1998 Published by Elsevier Science B.V. All rights reserved.

1. The three interrelated risks

The first of my three interrelated risks is interest rate risk, a risk that in principle, affects both lenders and borrowers, but which in the Southeast Asia crises has been falling mainly on borrowers. Borrowers are hit whenever interest rates rise unexpectedly, and the hit is particularly hard when they are borrowing short-term and lending long-term as so many firms and banks throughout Southeast Asia were doing. The rise in interest rates then deals the borrowers a double

---

[1] Earlier versions of this talk were presented at the China Society for Finance, Beijing, China; the Shanghai Social Science Academy, Shanghai, China; and the Asia Society, Hong Kong, China.

0927-538X/98/$ - see front matter © 1998 Published by Elsevier Science B.V. All rights reserved.
PII: S0927-538X(98)00009-2

blow: the value of their fixed rate long-term assets decline, and, at the same time, the cost of rolling over their short-term or floating rate borrowing increases.

The squeeze inflicted on Southeast Asia banks and firms by the rise in interest rates was painful, but hardly unprecedented. Borrowing short and lending long was precisely the source of the U.S. Savings and Loan crisis of the late 1970s and the early 1980s. But while the U.S. is certainly not immune to these maturity mismatches, the Southeast Asia maturity mismatches were magnified by a second risk factor. Many Southeast Asia banks and firms were not simply borrowing short and lending long, but were borrowing short in one currency — typically the dollar or the yen — and lending long in another to wit the local currency. If, therefore, a country's exchange rate falls substantially relative to the dollar, the cost of renewing or rolling over those short-term floating rate, dollar or yen loans can become very high in local, real terms.

Painful as it might be for the borrowers to face higher interest payments on their short-term borrowings, many are wondering why the mere act of rolling over those loans should be causing such havoc. What choice, after all, do the lenders really have than to renegotiate the loans? They either roll over and restructure their loans, or the borrowers will default and the lenders will end up with whatever they can extract from the local bankruptcy courts (which may well be nothing). In our domestic financial markets, these incentives to restructure liabilities after an unexpected shock, normally play out reasonably well. Voluntary workouts between the parties may require much hard bargaining, particularly when there are multiple creditors to a given firm. And, if the firm is considered worth saving, rather than liquidating, new operating funds in the form of DIP (debtor in possession) financing will typically be required. But creditors and debtors reach these accommodations all the time on a company by company basis. Why then, do private initiatives seem unable to do the job currently in the international arena?

Part of the answer is surely the sheer magnitude of the task. Imagine having to do 100,000 pre-packaged bankruptcies simultaneously! And with a one-month deadline. And do not think it can somehow all be left to the IMF. The IMF is tooled to deal, at best, with one or two large debtors, a central bank or a government, as with Mexico, that fabled success tale of bailouts. [2]

Another part of the answer lies in the third, and in some ways, most important of the three risks that underlie the current crises, to wit, credit risk. It is one thing to be borrowing short and buying government bonds, say. But what if they are

---

[2] The IMF, lately, in addition to providing liquid relief to the central banks, has called for major 'reforms' as a condition of its grants. How much lasting effect these conditional programs will have is problematic as the case of Korea suggests. The Korean bailout package arranged by a consortium of bank creditors allows for an automatic extension of maturity for all Korean banks willing to accept 200 basis points over LIBOR, or so of added interest charges, *with these extended loans guaranteed by the Korean government*. So much for the IMF plans for reducing the role of the Korean government in the Korean economy.

borrowing short term dollars to invest in over-built local real estate, as in Thailand; or in steel mills and shipyards with no customers as in Korea? The creditors do not know whether they are dealing with 100,000 Chapter 11's (reorganisations) or Chapter 7's (liquidations).

Still, private negotiating might, in principle, have done the necessary debt restructuring, and done it much earlier except for one thing. The dollar and yen short-term loans to local borrowers are provided mainly by banks. The governments and regulators feared that letting the voluntary restructuring process proceed on a large scale would inevitably have meant a big surge in loan losses and problem loans not just for the local banks, but for the Japanese banks staggering currently under their huge load of bad loans. The overhang of bad loans, especially, but by no means only in Japan is already leading to a virtual freeze-up of normal bank lending operations there and elsewhere in Asia, exactly as their governments feared. Ordinary and necessary commercial letters of credit (to say nothing of DIP loans) are not being provided by the banks even to the still viable firms. This 'credit crunch' emanating to a large extent from Japan is at the heart of the current Southeast Asia Financial crises, crises that cannot be fully resolved until Japan at long last, puts its house in order.

Before turning to the credit quality and banking crises, however, let me digress and say a bit more about the currency and foreign exchange crises which have been receiving so much, perhaps too much, press attention.

2. The foreign exchange crisis

The currency crisis, according to the conventional wisdom, started in Thailand as early as the autumn of 1996. The Thailand baht, which was not rigidly *pegged* to the dollar as in Hong Kong, but merely *linked* to the dollar – actually to a basket of world currencies in which the U.S. dollar was the dominant component – came under increasing pressure from speculators and hedgers. The Bank of Thailand, which had held the value of the baht within a narrow band for 10 years, chose not to abandon that policy, and let the baht float, for fear of spooking foreign investors. But the Bank eventually ran out of foreign currency reserves with which to support the baht, and in July of 1997, had to uncouple the link to the dollar and allow the baht to float. (The word float is a euphemism, of course. Float implies an up-and-down movement, but the baht actually dropped like a stone, losing eventually some 50% or more of its value relative to the U.S. dollar.) With the baht down so dramatically, the contagion quickly spread to Thailand's neighbors and competitors, Malaysia, Indonesia, The Philippines, and most recently to Korea. Singapore and Taiwan were also affected, though, like a strong boxer who takes a blow to the chin, their knees may have buckled a bit, but they did not go down. Their devaluation were minor. Hong Kong was even able to avoid devaluation altogether because Hong Kong has a monetary and foreign exchange system that is fundamentally different from that of the rest of Southeast Asia.

When a currency like the baht loses 50 or 60% of its value virtually overnight, scapegoat-hunting becomes the order of the day. What did the Bank of Thailand do wrong? The Bank had long enjoyed a reputation for technical competence – most of its officials and staff having advanced degrees in economics from the top U.S. universities (other than the University of Chicago, of course) – and for incorruptibility. So if these Thai central bankers were neither incompetent nor corrupt, how and why did they blow away so much of Thailand's hard-earned wealth?

The Bank of Thailand's first mistake was the common one of thinking it could support its currency in the face of strong speculative pressure mainly by raising interest rates and tightening market liquidity (a view, for the most part, shared by the IMF). [3] At first sight, that may indeed seem the obvious way for a country with limited reserves both to attract dollars from abroad and to discourage those pesky speculators. The higher rates would seem to punish speculators by raising the cost of borrowing the currency to sell it short. But even though that cost looks horrendous – sometimes 100% or even 1000% *on an annualized basis* – it comes down to just a pin prick on a *daily* basis compared to what speculators hope to make from even a modest devaluation, let alone one of 50 or 60%. Raising interest not only does not substantially discourage the speculators, but, can be shown, by virtue of the interest rate parity theorem, actually to *enrich* those speculators who have already sold the currency short in the forward exchange market. And, at the same time, raising rates also inflicts great damage on your own citizens, so many of whom, it will be recalled were borrowing short and lending long.

The even more serious, and ultimately fatal, mistake of the Bank of Thailand, however, was the concealment of the facts about the true state of its foreign exchange holdings. Central bankers like to keep things like that secret, ostensibly to keep other traders from learning their strategies, but more likely perhaps, because they think the general public is too panic-prone to be trusted such sensitive information. Lack of transparency is a long tradition of central banks not just in Thailand, of course, but in the U.S. and Japan as well and even, or particularly, by the International Monetary Fund.

In the case of the Bank of Thailand, the deception was over the amount of dollars and foreign currency reserves the Bank had left for fighting off the speculators and maintaining the value of the baht. The Bank said, and the public believed, that those reserves were substantial. But the speculators knew better, because the battles over the value of currency are not fought primarily in the *spot*

---

[3] The IMF seems to believe that most currency problems trace to excessive monetary and budgetary ease. In Latin America, at some times, perhaps so. But not in much of Southeast Asia. Hence the very negative reaction of many observers to IMF's budget and monetary 'austerity' programs.

market, which is a market we can all understand and where dollars spent to support the currency are reflected on the Bank's books immediately. The speculators, however – and that includes, these days, not just the George Soroses, but ordinary commercial firms hedging their foreign currency exposures – are actually operating in the *forward* market, not the spot market. In the forward market, you do not have to put your money up front, but only at maturity of the forward contract, which may be 3 or 6 months or more away, and which can often be rolled forward for a time without posting additional collateral. Thus, the Bank of Thailand, which was fighting the speculators in the forward market by taking long positions to offset the speculator short positions, could, for a while at least, continue to show a substantial amount of foreign currency reserves on its books, even though it had already committed those reserves in the forward market.

Central banks and other traders may not have to mark their position to market daily in the forward market, as they do in futures markets, but they cannot postpone collateral calls indefinitely. The truth must eventually come out. And come out it did, when the Bank finally had to admit its foreign reserves were mostly gone. That admission led, in turn to a massive run against the baht – that is *run* as in bank run – which quickly swamped the modest amount of additional liquidity that the IMF had brought to Thailand's aid. The terms of the Bank's battle changed from one of countering speculators to one of stemming widespread capital fight by the Thai people themselves. With the deception by even the trusted Bank of Thailand revealed, the remaining Thai institutions, financial and political, could not withstand the loss of public confidence. To borrow a phrase from Chinese history, the Thai government and its institutions had lost the mandate of heaven. And in the process what might otherwise have been a minor realignment of 10 or 15% had it been made in 1996 when the Bank still had US$30 billion of reserves, turned into a major disaster.

The collapse of the currency in Thailand was followed by similar collapses and capital flight in Malaysia, Indonesia, the Philippines and most recently Korea, but not, as noted earlier, in Taiwan or Singapore, and especially not in Hong Kong whose currency at least up to the time of this writing, maintains exactly the same value it had before Southeast Asia's financial crisis began. Why had Hong Kong been able to buck the tide? Because, it has a currency board rather than a central bank; and because, so far, at least, the people of Hong Kong have *not* lost confidence in that currency board and its promise to maintain the value of the currency, that is, to maintain the value of so much of their life's savings. As long as the public has this confidence, mere speculators can have little impact in a currency-board system like that of Hong Kong, where nothing is supposed to distract the monetary authorities from their primary task of maintaining the peg. Indeed, the only serious threat to the peg can come when the monetary authorities misunderstand their role and start applying the standard central bank techniques that failed so conspicuously in Thailand, notably raising domestic interest rates. As stressed earlier, that does not hurt the speculators who have already sold short in the forward market, though it hurts *everyone else*. But as long as the people of Hong Kong stay convinced that their peg will hold – and the currency board managers have ample ways other than interest rate increases to signal their determination to hold the peg (for example, by issuing structured notes with embedded puts on Hong Kong dollars) – it *will* hold no matter what the speculators do as the peg continues to hold month after month, the speculators will simply find their wealth steadily being nibbled away by transaction costs of rolling over their short forward positions. They will eventually tire of the game and look for easier targets.

But, enough of foreign exchange problems. Let me turn now to the third of the Southeast Asia crisis, the one, I will argue, that served as the initiation trigger of those Southeast Asia crises in the first place; and the one that until solved, will keep the whole region from returning to its previous state of prosperity and high growth.

3. The credit risk crisis

Credit risk is ever-present in financial markets, and is realized whenever borrowers cannot or will not repay their loans on the original terms. Normally, of course, these bad loans might seem of only local significance. But, in a properly regulated banking system, the rules would require banks to write those bad loans speedily down to market value, taking the losses into income. Recognizing bad loan losses that way, however, erodes the bank's capital ratios; and banks whose capital ratios are impaired, or close to it, cannot make new loans. They can thus no longer play their traditional role of 'greasing the wheels of commerce'.

That scenario caused problems even in the United States, during the years 1988 to 1990. But business firms and consumers in the U.S. for all their complaints about the drying up of bank credit at that time did have plenty of alternatives to bank financing. That, unfortunately is much less true of the firms and consumers in Southeast Asia who remain far more heavily dependent on bank financing. And because they are so dependent, many of the countries of the area have long been reluctant to force their banks to recognize and write off their bad loans. The governments and banking regulators in Southeast Asia feared that recognizing bad loans would impair the capital of their banks and lead to precisely the kind of liquidity freeze-up that is now damaging their economies severely.

Nowhere has this refusal to recognize and write-off bad loans been more obstinate than in Japan, but Thailand, Korea and much of Southeast Asia share essentially the same denial syndrome. Faced with the evidence of mounting bad loans, their regulators kept saying: "Just hang in there. Keep lending the firms with the bad loans enough more money at least to pay the interest due, so the loans can still be considered as 'performing'. The economy will eventually return to rapid growth, and the seemingly bad loans will be repaid." These optimistic views will be recognized, of course, as just the familiar gambler's 'doubling up' strategy, in a new disguise. And the strategy may even seem to work for some time, but over the long run we know it is doomed to fail. And, alas, for much of Southeast Asia, that long run seems to be now.

Economists of the future generations, looking back on the late 1990s, will wonder how the banks and bank regulators of Japan and elsewhere in Asia were able to remain in denial for so long. In the case of countries like Malaysia, Indonesia and Korea, part of the answer is surely that the bad loans were not simply ordinary commercial loans gone sour, but *political* loans reflecting the country's 'industrial' policy. Writing them off would have been a huge embarrassment to the governments involved, to put it mildly. In the case of Japan, the sense of urgency may have been further tempered by the seemingly endless store of bank capital represented by the unrealized capital gains on the stock of Japanese firms held by the banks. As Nikkei 225 Average steadily sank, however, that cushion of capital dried up. And by the time the average was flirting with 14,000, as it did in 1996, the cushion was effectively gone.

To restore Japanese bank capital, the lawyers who run the Japanese Ministry of Finance had a choice of strategies. They could have forced the banks to shrink, but that would have meant calling loans, hardly to be recommended in an economy already in a deep recession. Or they could have insisted that the bank write off the bad loans and raise more outside funds to fill the resulting capital hole. But, that would either have forced out the existing stockholders or, horror of horrors, require them to share their controls with *foreigners*. Instead, MOF adopted another strategy which, among other things, destabilized the rest of Southeast Asia. MOF chose to drive down short-term interest rates; and drive them down, it did, to levels not seen since the depression years of the United States in the 1930s. MOF's hope, of course, was that despite the depression in Japan, the Japanese banks would invest their low-cost short term funds abroad, or at least in higher-yielding, long-term Japanese government securities, earning the carry-spread and adding it to their capital. As the profits from this term-structure play came in, more bad loans could be recognized and written off.

And now, I believe, we can put our fingers on the real culprit for the financial crisis in Southeast Asia: the low and falling value of Japanese interest rates and the reduction that induced in the value of the yen. The low and falling yen was the villain, not because it led to increased Japanese export surpluses in the U.S. For United States trade negotiatiors and automobile manufactures that is indeed an annoyance, but really no more than that given the strength of the U.S. economy. The real trouble, however, was on the other side of the coin of a falling yen, namely a rising dollar. As the yen fell, the dollar rose. Currencies linked to the dollar, therefore, inevitably became overvalued, and as the balance of payments of those countries deteriorated, their currencies became ripe for speculator attack, particularly so after a new Asian Tiger, mainland China, began to enter the export markets in a big way.

4. Conclusion

So much for my three interlinked crises. Where do we go from here? The answers will vary substantially over the region.

For Hong Kong, for example, the answer is simple. The Hong Kong banks unlike the banks in the Japan and Korea are among the strongest, best managed and most honestly regulated in the world. The Hong Kong currency board, moreover, eliminates the need for a central bank, and the mischief such central banks can cause, – always with the best of intentions, of course. The financial community knows that the internal and external value of currency cannot both be held stable at the same time. The United States, under the leadership of Alan Greenspan, has chosen to allow its external value to float, but to maintain the domestic value of the currency. And he has succeeded in that task. Prices in the U.S. have been remarkably stable over the last five years.

Hong Kong, has, in my opinion, wisely adopted the opposite strategy, that is of maintaining a stable foreign exchange value for its currency by firmly pegging into the U.S. dollar with a currency board. Exporters, of course, and in Hong Kong's case that includes the local tourist industry, will always be clamoring for devaluations. But the citizens of Hong Kong should remember that if they do choose to lower their peg, any gains will be temporary. Other countries will match the cuts. Import prices will quickly adjust leaving the exporters no better off competitively in the long run; but with Hong Kong's priceless reputation as an island of financial stability gone forever.

For those countries with weak banking systems, which includes most of Southeast Asia except for Hong Kong, and possibly Singapore and Taiwan, a more rational system of bad-loan recognition must be developed which in turn means huge amounts of new capital must be pumped in to restore capital compliance and to make the banks capable once more of playing their role in the savings/investment process. The countries must recognise, however, that the needed capital can come only from one source: Foreigners. And that those foreigners will be unwilling to put that capital in without substantially more control over the management of that capital than many locals are willing to give up to outsiders. They are still laughing in Wall Street about Thailand's offer to allow foreigners to take major stakes in their banks and businesses – but for no more than five years!

Such steps to shape up the local banks, though urgent, represent short-run solutions at best. Improve banking institutions, yes. But recognize that banking itself is at the root of the problem. Banking is disaster-prone, 19th century technology, not easily tamed. Endowing both bankers *and* regulators with the right incentives to finance industry while avoiding catastrophic collapses is not yet a fully solved problem. Nor will it ever be, given the moral hazards posed by the absurdly high leverage ratios in banking, by deposit insurance, by the doctrine of too big to fail, and by the increasing likelihood that the IMF always stands ready in the wings to bail out bad banks and bad creditors generally.

Southeast Asia and China must look ahead ultimately not just to reforming their banks, but to reducing their dependence on banks as suppliers of capital to industry. They must follow the model of the U.S. in shrinking the banking industry itself, and steadily expanding the number and variety of *market* alternatives to bank loans – everything from leasing to junk bonds, which, after all, are really just liquid, negotiable commercial loans. The biggest deposit-taking institution in the U.S. is not a bank but Merrill Lynch's money market funds (not government insured may I add). The biggest lender to consumers is not a bank, but General Motors Acceptance Corp. The biggest firms, moreover, finance their working capital these days not with bank loans, as in years past, but with marketable commercial paper. Southeast Asia too must come to rely on decentralisation and diversification – in this case diversification of financing alternatives – and not on the presumed superior judgments of large banks, their regulators or their governments for directing society's capital to its most productive uses. If the current crises have done nothing more than to discredit the Japanese and Korean models of bank-driven economic development, then perhaps the whole episode, painful as it has been, and still is to live through, has nevertheless been worthwhile.

The current international financial crisis: how much is new?

Steven B. Kamin*

International Finance Division, Federal Reserve Board, Washington, D.C. 20551, USA

Abstract

This paper surveys a broad array of data to compare the scope and impact of three emerging market financial crises: the debt crisis of the 1980s, the Mexican financial crisis of 1994–95, and the current international financial crisis. While certain conventional views regarding the three episodes are supported by the data examined in this paper, we find that in several respects, the current crisis is more similar to prior emerging market crisis episodes than is commonly believed. © 1999 Elsevier Science Ltd. All rights reserved.

JEL classification: F32; F41

Keywords: Devaluations; Financial crises

1. Introduction

The international financial crisis that began with the devaluation of the Thai baht in July 1997, and which continues to grip world markets as of this writing, represents the third major bout of financial disruption to sweep across the developing countries in recent decades. Compared with the debt crisis of the 1980s and with the Mexican (or so-called 'Tequila') crisis of 1994–95, the current crisis is widely considered to be distinctive in several respects. First, it appears to be the first genuinely global financial crisis to hit the emerging market economies, affecting, as it has, Asia, Russia, South Africa, and Latin America.[1] Second, it appears to be exerting a much

---
* Tel.: + 1-202-452-3339; fax: + 1-202-452-6424; e-mail: steven.kamin@frb.gov
[1] An argument also can be made for including Japan as a participant in this crisis.

greater impact on commodity prices, financial markets, and economic activity throughout the world—including industrialized countries—than was true of the prior two emerging market crises. Finally, the current crisis, particularly as it has taken hold in Asia, appears to be more deeply rooted in financial imbalances in the private sector than in the public sector financial problems that characterized the 1980s debt crisis and the Mexican 1994–95 crisis.

This note represents a broad-brushed survey of selected data to compare salient aspects of the three most recent emerging market crises. In Section 2, we focus on the geographical scope of the crises to compare the extent of the world economy that was affected in each episode. Section 3 addresses the impact of the crises on key macroeconomic performance variables, including exchange rates, inflation, GDP, and the current account. Have these crises grown increasingly severe in their impact on affected countries, or are we merely more aware of their impact than was the case in the past? We find that, notwithstanding certain important differences between recent and previous crises, the basic characteristics of these crises were remarkably similar.

2. The scope of emerging market crises

There is a general perception that the current international financial crisis is more widespread than previous crises. However, precisely gauging the geographical scope of the different crises is less straightforward than it might appear at first glance, since different countries may be affected by financial crises to different degrees. Moreover, at any point in time, there are always countries experiencing difficulties for reasons entirely unrelated to international financial crises. For the purposes of this paper, we have identified—in an admittedly casual and ad hoc manner—the following countries as having been significantly affected by the three recent emerging markets crises:

1980s Debt Crisis:	Argentina, Bolivia, Brazil, Chile, Colombia, Cote D'Ivoire, Ecuador, Mexico, Morocco, Nigeria, Peru, Philippines, Uruguay, Venezuela, Yugoslavia.
1994–95 Tequila Crisis:	Mexico, Argentina.
Current International Financial Crisis:	East Asia (Hong Kong, Indonesia, Korea, Malaysia, Philippines, Singapore, Taiwan, Thailand), Latin America (Argentina, Brazil, Chile, Colombia, Mexico, Peru, Venezuela), Russia, South Africa.

For want of a more definitive list, the countries associated above with the 1980s debt crisis are those identified in 1986 by then-US Treasury Secretary James Baker as particularly affected by external indebtedness, and therefore the focus of attention under the so-called Baker Plan. Mexico and Argentina are the countries identified with the 1994–95 Tequila Crisis. They suffered the most pronounced pressures in financial markets and declines in output, although during that period, many other emerging market countries also either lost their access to international funding or found interest rates too costly to make it worthwhile to issue new liabilities. Finally, we have identified as current crisis countries those that have experienced or are experiencing significant balance-of-payments disruptions and/or reductions in growth.[2]

Based on the groups of countries identified above, Fig. 1 represents a rough cut at portraying the economic weight of the economies affected by the different crises. At the broadest level and consistent with conventional beliefs, the current crisis has involved economies accounting for the greatest share of world activity—measured by GDP, exports, and US exports—while the Mexican 1994–95 crisis has involved the least.

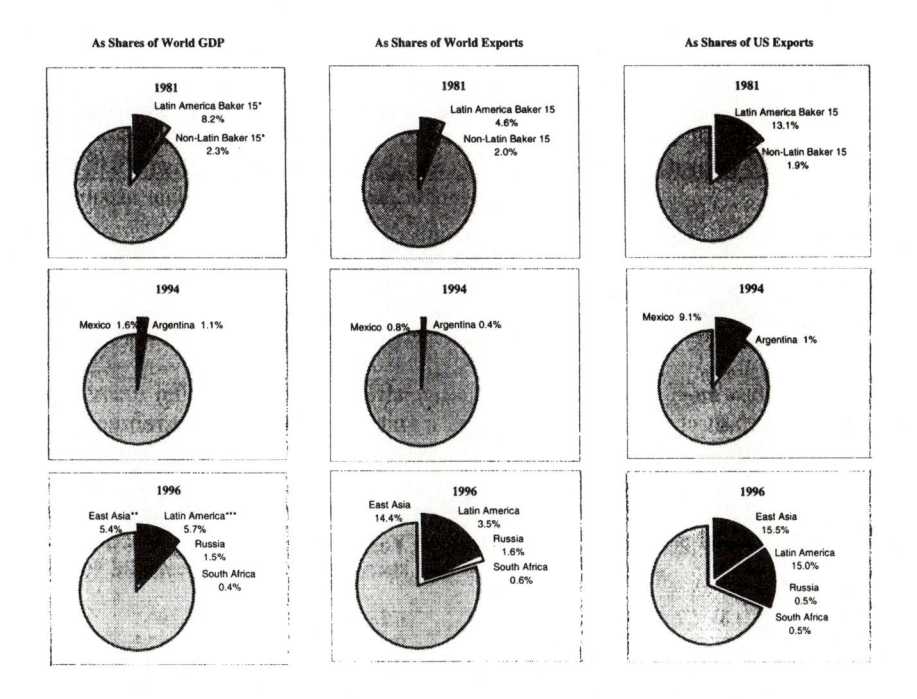

Sources: IMF International Financial Statistics and World Economic Outlook, World Bank World Development Report, and FRB Beatradex data.

Fig. 1. Emerging market crisis countries.

---

[2] For Latin America, we have included seven of the largest economies in the region. Others have been affected as well, in particular Ecuador.

Nonetheless, the scope of the 1980s debt crisis should not be minimized. The countries affected by the 1980s crisis accounted for nearly as high a share of world GDP as those in the current crisis. Because of the less open character of the Latin American economies in the 1980s, their share in world trade was much less than the share of those economies affected by the current crisis, as may be seen in the second column; on the other hand, the third column shows that, as a share of US trade, the Latin American countries in the 1980s were again very prominent.

An alternative means of assessing the scope of the three crises is to compare the amounts of external debt involved, insofar as a central focus of all three emerging market crises has been difficulties in servicing external debt. The first two columns of Table 1 compare the total amount of external debt owed by the affected countries, both in dollar terms and scaled by world GDP. While the dollar value of debt involved in the current crisis certainly is the highest of the three episodes, the differ-

Table 1

	Total external debt		BIS bank claims			
	$billions	% of world GDP	$billions	% of world GPD	US bank claims/US bank capital (%)	non-US bank claims/total BIS bank claims (%)
1982						
Baker 15[a]						
Latin America	301.3	2.8	31.9	0.3	113.0	58.0
Non-Latin America	76.3	0.7	22.8	0.2	16.0	64.5
1994						
Argentina	77.4	0.3	35.3	0.1	4.8	72.0
Mexico	140.0	0.5	64.0	0.2	10.7	65.4
1996						
East Asia[b]	428.1	1.5	283.5	1.0	11.2	89.7
Latin America[c]	549.9	1.9	223.9	0.8	23.7	72.4
Russia	124.8	0.4	57.3	0.2	2.1	90.7
South Africa	23.6	0.1	17.0	0.1	0.8	87.8

[a]The Latin American Baker 15: Argentina, Bolivia, Brazil, Chile, Colombia, Ecuador, Mexico, Peru, Uruguay, and Venezuela. The non-Latin American Baker 15: Cote D'Ivoire, Morocco, Nigeria, Philippines, and Yugoslavia.
[b]East Asia: Indonesia, Korea, Malaysia, Philippines, Taiwan, and Thailand.
[c]Latin America: Argentina, Brazil, Chile, Colombia, Mexico, Peru, and Venezuela.
Sources: Total external debt: World Bank World Debt Tables and Global Development Indicators, IMF World Economic Outlook. BIS bank claims: BIS databases. Country Exposure Lending Survey for US bank capital data and for total claims of US banks in 1982.

ence is much less marked when debt is scaled by world GDP: 3.5% for the Baker 15 countries in 1982 compared with 3.9% for the countries affected by the current crisis.

The next two columns present the claims of industrial country banks on these countries as reported by the BIS. They indicate that bank loans to the countries involved in the emerging market crises, whether measured in dollars or as a share in GDP, have grown more rapidly than total external debt over the past 15 years, perhaps reflecting a fall off in the role of official credits to these countries. Therefore, measured on the basis of bank loans, the current financial crisis appears to be broader in scope than the preceding crises.

A more precise gauge of the exposure, and in particular, the vulnerability of creditor banks to emerging market crises is the share of bank loans to the affected countries in the creditor banks' capital. The fifth column of Table 1 presents these data for US banks. It is clear that the US banking system is far less exposed to the current crisis than it was to the 1980s crisis.

On the other hand, it may well be the case that European and Japanese banks are more exposed to the current emerging market crisis than they were to the previous two episodes. Data on European and Japanese bank capital are not available. However, the final column of Table 1 indicates that the non-US share of BIS bank claims on countries affected by emerging market crises has increased substantially in the current episode compared with the 1980s crisis. Therefore, it is likely that claims on affected emerging market countries represent a much higher share of capital among European and Japanese banks than among US banks.

3. Impact of emerging market crises

Perhaps reflecting the fact that the current financial crisis is more widespread than previous crises, and hence is exerting a greater effect on the industrial countries, the perception has arisen that the current crisis has been more virulent in its impact on the affected economies. In this respect, however, memories of the hardships endured during previous emerging market crises may have been dimmed by the passage of time. Based on several measures of economic performance, the impact of previous crises has been at least as severe as that of the current crisis.

3.1. Exchange rates

Fig. 2 compares movements in nominal exchange rates, inflation, and real exchange rates before and after the start of their respective financial crises for several key countries. The top panel indicates a surprising degree of similarity in the extent of initial nominal exchange rate depreciation experienced in each of the three emerging market crises. Roughly half a year into their respective crises, Mexico (in 1982), Mexico (in 1995), and the East Asian economies affected most severely by the cur-

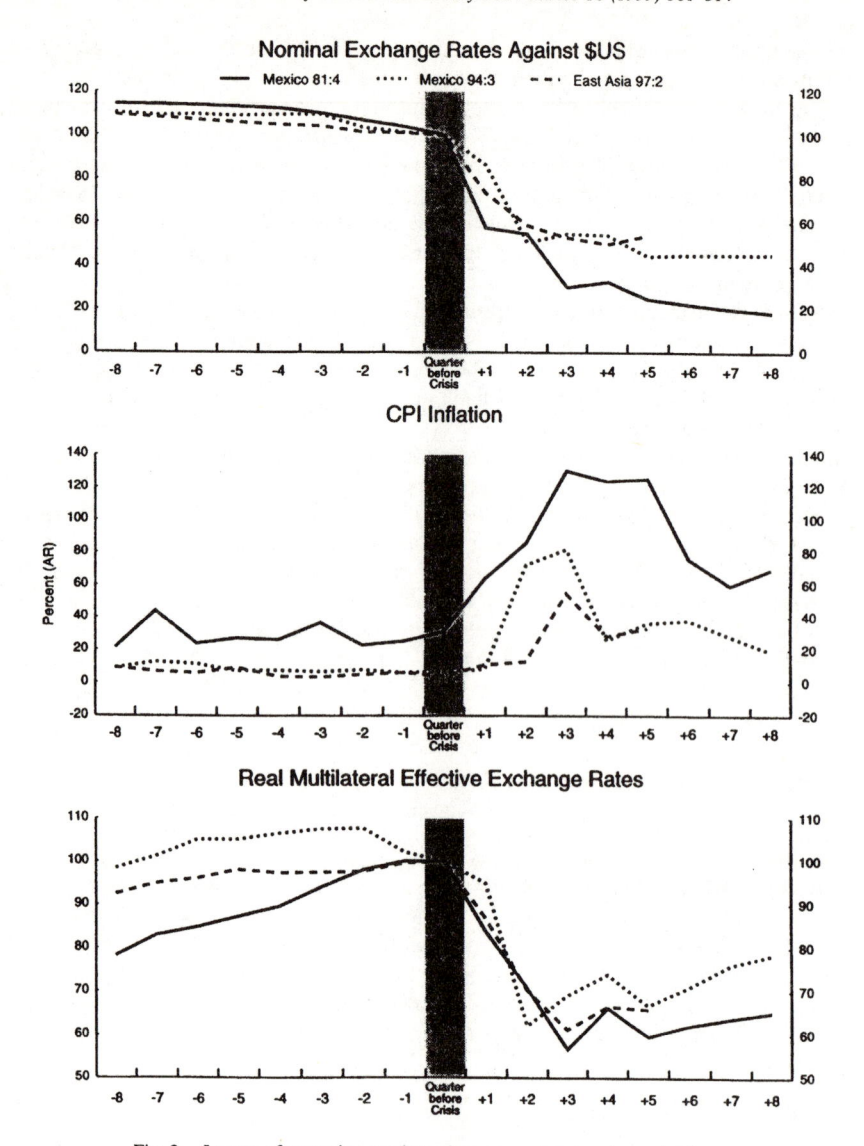

Fig. 2. Impact of emerging market crises on exchange rates and prices.

rent crisis (Indonesia, Korea, Malaysia, Philippines, and Thailand) all experienced declines in nominal currency values on the order of about 40%.[3]

Notwithstanding the initial similarity in depreciations, Fig. 2 indicates that subsequently, the Mexican peso in 1995 and the Asian currencies during the current

---

[3] The East Asia index is a GDP-weighted average of individual country exchange rates, rebased so that their value in the quarter immediately before devaluation—generally 1997 Q2—equals 100. For Korea, the index is constructed so that the quarter before the crisis is 1997 Q3, not 1997 Q2.

crisis largely stabilized, while the Mexican peso in the early 1980s continued to depreciate. This difference may, in part, be attributable to differences in the response of domestic prices to devaluation in the different episodes. As the middle panel makes clear, inflation rates rose substantially in Mexico in 1982 and 1983, while the inflationary response to devaluation during the 1994-95 Mexican crisis and particularly during the current crisis in Asia has been much more muted.[4] This difference in the response of prices to exchange rate changes is consistent with differences in inflationary tendencies between Asia and Latin America even before the current crisis.

The bottom panel of Fig. 2 tracks the movements of multilateral real exchange rates before and after the advent of financial crises. The effect of correcting for changes in prices is to reduce the difference between Mexico in the early 1980s, on the one hand, and Mexico in 1995-96 and the Asian countries in 1997-98. Nevertheless, it is obvious that the real exchange rate for Mexico in the early 1980s recovered more gradually than it did in Mexico after 1995, probably reflecting the much slower and more tentative resolution of that earlier financial crisis.

There are no obvious reasons for why initial depreciations—both real and nominal—were so similar in the three episodes. While it is beyond the scope of this paper to explain the occurrence and severity of these financial crises, Table 2 presents some indicators of vulnerability to external shocks for selected countries (including several not represented in Fig. 2). Interestingly, as shown in the first column, current account deficits were substantial and similar in all three financial crises: about 4-5% of GDP on average. On the other hand, the very rough measure of exchange rate overvaluation shown in the middle column—deviations of real multilateral currency values from their 1980-96 averages—indicates substantial overvaluation in the Latin American economies in the 1980s, but generally appropriate alignments for the East Asian countries immediately before their recent crisis. Finally, ratios of short-term external debt to international reserves were high in all three episodes, but considerably higher on balance among the Latin American countries before the debt Crisis than among the East Asian economies in 1996.

3.2. Output

While all three of the emerging market financial crises started with precipitous exchange rate devaluations, in all cases the crises led subsequently to sharp declines in economic activity. Fig. 3 compares movements in the GDP growth rates of Latin America during the debt crisis of the 1980s, Mexico during its financial crisis in 1994-95, and the most affected East Asian countries during the current crisis. (Data for East Asia in 1999 and 2000 are from the February 1999 Consensus Forecasts.)

---

[4] For the East Asian aggregate, both the depreciation shown in the top panel and the inflationary response shown in the middle panel is exaggerated, to some extent, by the inclusion of Indonesia, where economic difficulties were compounded by political problems. Without Indonesia, the data for East Asia would have indicated a rebound in nominal currency values after two quarters, and a much less pronounced inflationary response to depreciation.

Table 2

	Current account/GDP	Real exchange rate (% of long-term average)	Short-term external debt/reserves (%)
1981			
Argentina	−2.8	131.3	395.4
Brazil	−4.6	104.4	232.0
Chile	−14.5	142.5	93.0
Mexico	−6.5	151.1	613.2
Venezuela	6.0	137.6	207.9
Average	**−4.5**	**133.4**	**308.3**
1993			
Argentina	−3.0	95.6	72.3
Mexico	−5.8	111.2	230.1
Average	**−4.4**	**103.4**	**151.2**
1996			
Indonesia	−3.4	86.0	226.2
Korea	−4.8	91.4	300.2
Malaysia	−4.6	95.5	41.6
Philippines	−4.8	110.0	125.7
Thailand	−8.0	100.4	102.5
Average	**−5.1**	**96.7**	**159.2**

Sources: Current account, GDP and reserves: FRB databases and IMF International Financial Statistics. Short-term debt: World Bank World Debt Tables for 1981; J.P. Morgan for 1993 and 1996. Real exchange rates: J.P. Morgan.

The following observations can be made. First, the reductions in growth experienced in Mexico and Argentina in 1995 and in Asia in 1998 appear to be broadly comparable, although the decline has been more pronounced for the East Asian countries.[5] Second, assuming that the Asian growth performance in 1999 comes close to predictions, East Asia will share Mexico's and Argentina's 1994–95 experience of a sharp rebound after an initial sharp decline. However, Asian growth is projected to rise to a much lower level—about 0%—than was the case during the Tequila Crisis, suggesting that certain aspects of Asia's financial crisis may have much longer-lasting effects than was the case in Mexico and Argentina. Factors that have been cited as likely to retard the recovery of growth in Asia include the dimensions of its financial sector problems, problems of overcapacity relative to world demand for its exports, and flagging economic activity in a key trading partner, Japan. Moreover, since a

---

[5] The comparison is complicated by the fact that 1995 embraces a complete year of the financial crisis in Mexico and Argentina, whereas the Asian crisis started only mid-way through 1997. Hence, 1995 for Mexico–Argentina is best compared with 1998 (that is, year + 1) for East Asia.

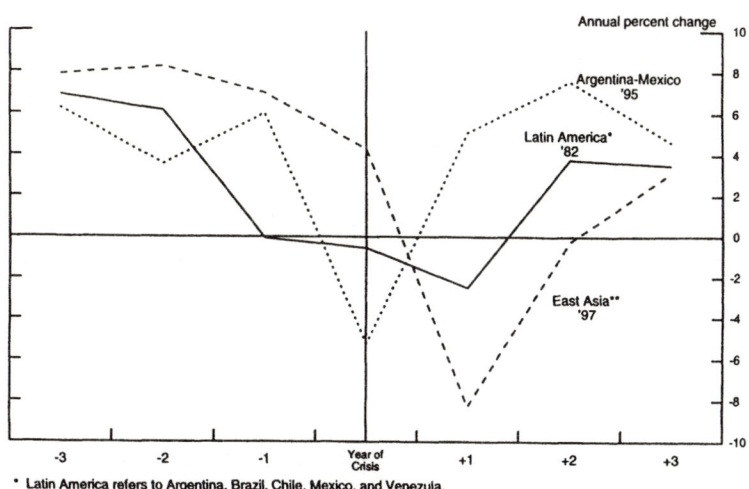

Fig. 3. GDP growth.

significant fraction of the trade of developing East Asian economies is with each other, this makes it more difficult for them to rely on exports as an engine of growth.

Finally, the growth rate of GDP in Latin America during the 1980s debt crisis appears to exhibit less marked upswings and downswings than in the two later episodes. While this could in part reflect differences in the nature of that crisis compared with Mexico and Argentina in 1994–95 and East Asia in 1997–98, it also reflects the fact that the Latin American countries fell into crisis at different times, with Argentina's problems starting in 1981, Chile and Mexico's in 1982, and Brazil's in 1983. In fact, the accumulated loss of GDP growth over the 1981–83 period was comparable to the losses experienced in the first full year of the latter crises. Moreover, output growth in the region remained depressed throughout the remainder of the decade.

3.3. Current accounts

Another important similarity across the three emerging market crises has been the substantial adjustment in current accounts. As indicated in the top panel of Fig. 4, the affected economies in each of the crises started out with substantial current account deficits as a fraction of their GDP. As the crises proceeded, these deficits were sharply reduced, as in Mexico and Argentina in 1995, or swung into surplus, as in Latin America in the 1980s and East Asia currently.

Notwithstanding broad similarities, there also are important differences in the patterns of current account adjustment. Latin American current account deficits continued to widen in 1982 and never moved strongly into surplus. In Mexico and

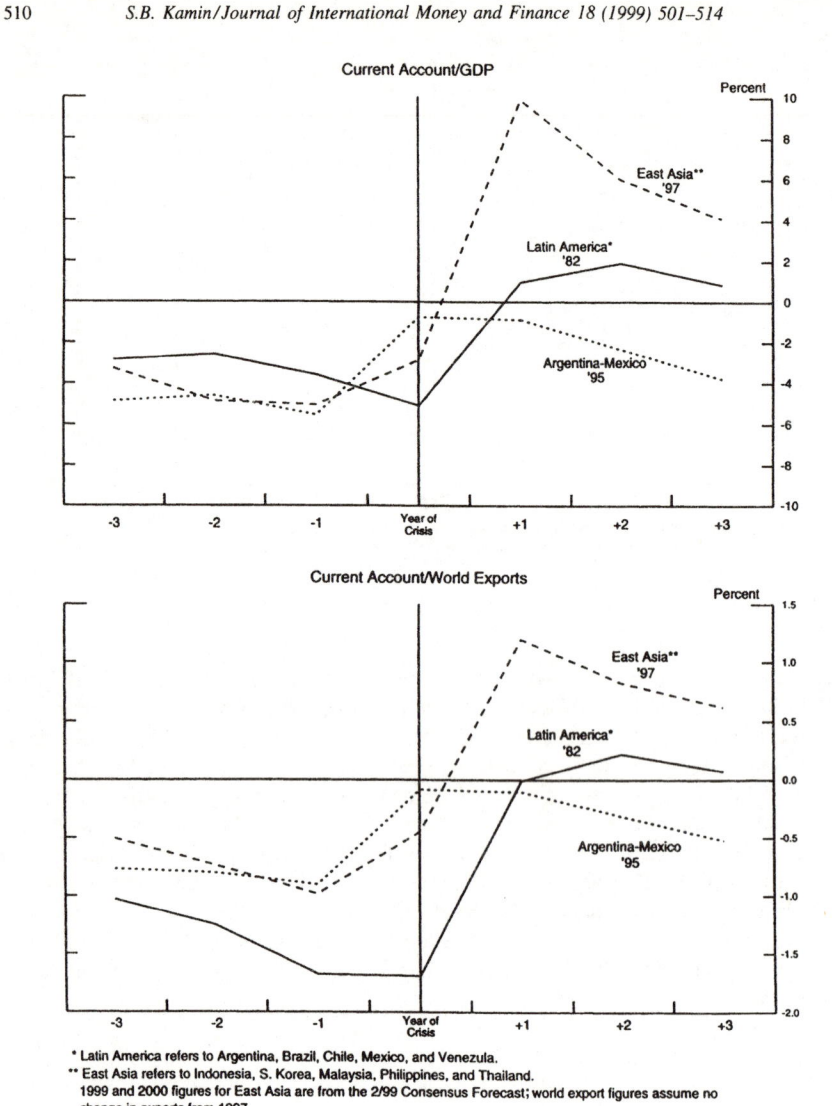

Fig. 4. Current account adjustment.

Argentina in 1995, on the other hand, initial current account adjustment was substantial but access to international capital markets was regained quickly enough so that the countries were not forced to run current account surpluses. Notably, East Asia currently is running very large current account surpluses in spite of sharp apparent declines in dollar export prices, in part because these price declines have been largely offset by increasing export volumes, and also because imports have contracted substantially.

Differences in the international environment explain some of the differences in current account performance across crisis episodes. As shown in Fig. 5, the debt

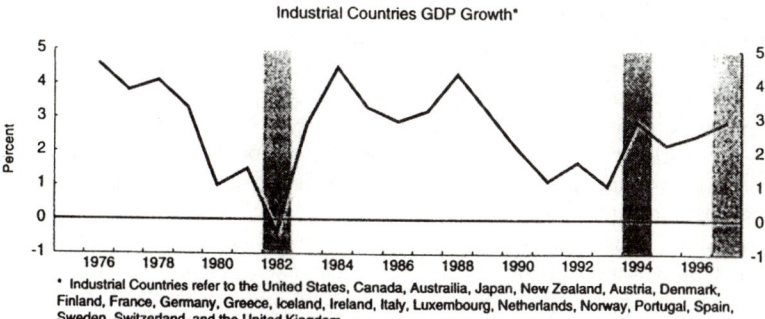

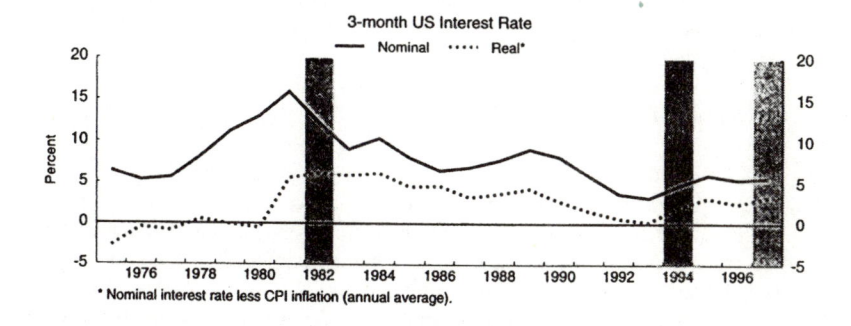

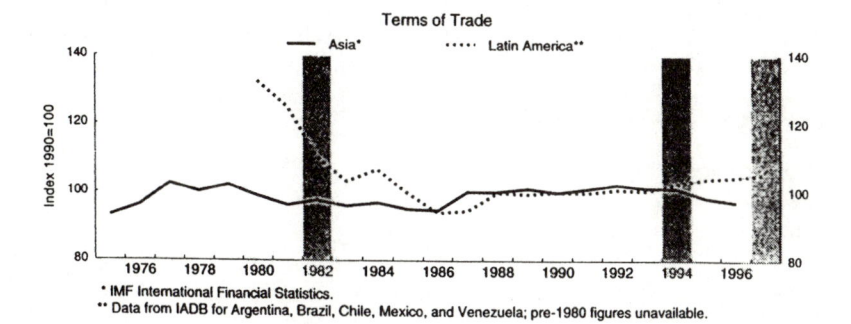

Fig. 5. International environment.

crisis of the 1980s coincided with a deep recession in the industrial countries, high nominal and real international interest rates, and steep declines in the terms of trade. Together, these constrained the extent of current account adjustment. Conversely, international conditions during both the 1994–95 Tequila Crisis and the current international financial crisis have been more favorable for the external balance positions of the affected economies.

Returning to Fig. 4, the bottom panel scales the current account balances of the affected countries by world merchandise exports in order to gauge the importance of current account adjustments to the rest of the world.[6] As might be expected, given the limited geographical scope of the Mexican 1994–95 crisis, it led to a relatively small movement in scaled current account balances. Conversely, the current account adjustments of Latin America in the 1980s and East Asia more recently, relative to total world trade, appear to have been similar in magnitude.

This latter finding appears to contradict the view that the current emerging market crisis is having a more significant impact on global economic activity than was the case during the debt crisis of the 1980s. Two possible explanations for this view arise. First, the industrial countries already were in a very sharp recession in the early 1980s, which may have obscured the marginal impact of the debt crisis in further lowering economic activity. Second, the dollar-value adjustment of East Asian current accounts may obscure an even larger adjustment in real terms, given the decline in their export prices.

3.4. Banking sector problems

As will be discussed further below, the recent financial crises in East Asia are believed to be distinctive in that they were rooted in private financial sector problems. While problems of financial fragility may lead to currency crises in some instances, it also is true that sharp drops in currency values can lead to banking crises by boosting the local currency value of unhedged foreign-currency denominated borrowing. Leaving aside the question of whether banking sector problems led to balance-of-payments crises or vice-versa, it is a fact that banking sector problems have been a feature of all three emerging market crises. Shown below are estimates from various sources of the cost of cleaning up the banking sector in each of the three episodes; costs for the East Asian countries, as well as for Mexico, are based on projections rather than actual outlays.

Banking sector bailout cost/GDP

I. Latin America 1980s:
  Argentina   13%
  Chile   20%

---

[6] The scale is very different in the two panels, since world exports are so much larger than the GDPs of the countries represented in the figure.

II. Mexico 1994–5: 15–20%

III. East Asia 1997–98:
Thailand 42%
Indonesia 36%
Korea 20%
Malaysia 21%

Source: Hausmann and Rojas-Suarez (1996); Deutsche Bank Research (1998) and author's estimates.

The estimates tentatively suggest that the East Asian banking crises may have been larger in magnitude than their predecessors. Explaining why this might be true is beyond the scope of this paper. However, it is worth noting, as shown in the first column of Table 3, that the magnitude of domestic bank loans relative to GDP was much greater in East Asia than in Latin America—this certainly helps to account for the larger prospective cost of the cleanup.

The second column of Table 3 indicates that average loan growth was also higher in East Asia recently than it was among the Latin American countries in the early 1980s, although it was below that in Mexico and Argentina in 1995. It is believed that high loan growth may engender inadequate assessments of borrower creditworthiness by banks, which in turn could lead subsequently to poor loan repayment per-

Table 3

	Bank Loans/GDP (%)	Bank Loans/GDP (3-yr % change)
1981		
Argentina	10.7	17.6
Brazil	9.9	−19.0
Chile	46.4	128.1
Mexico	15.6	3.3
Venezuela	26.5	−21.1
Average	**21.8**	**21.8**
1994		
Argentina	18.2	60.1
Mexico	23.5	93.6
Average	**20.8**	**76.9**
1996		
Indonesia	54.5	14.7
Korea	58.7	14.5
Malaysia	93.1	26.9
Philippines	48.8	89.0
Thailand	99.3	25.1
Average	**70.9**	**34.0**

Sources: FBR databases and IMF International Financial Statistics.

formance and hence financial sector weakness. While there are many reasons why loan growth may be high in emerging market countries, observers have placed considerable weight on the role of deficiencies of supervision and regulation, as well as problems of moral hazard.

4. Conclusion

Our brief and statistical *tour de table* of emerging market crises confirms that the current international financial crisis is the most widespread of the recent emerging market crises. This is true, whether measured by the GDP of the involved countries, their trade, or their external indebtedness.

Nevertheless, the uniqueness of the current crisis should not be exaggerated. First, while its geographical scope exceeds that of the debt crisis of the 1980s, it generally does not do so by a very large margin (depending upon the measure of scope employed). Second, the basic characteristics of the financial crisis—depreciating currencies, sharp declines in output, rapid adjustments in the current account, and (in many cases) banking sector difficulties—were remarkably similar in each of the three episodes. Third, the impact of the current account adjustments of the affected countries on the global economy—as measured by movements in current accounts relative to world trade—were comparable in the debt crisis of the 1980s and in the current international financial crisis.

These similarities suggest that efforts to explain the occurrence of the current emerging market financial crisis, and its impact on the rest of the world, should not be pursued in isolation. Clearly, the current crisis holds much in common with prior crises, although undoubtedly there are important differences as well. Hence, any analysis of recent events in international financial markets will likely be much enhanced by a second look at what took place during the debt crisis of the 1980s and the Tequila Crisis of 1994–95.

Acknowledgements

The author would like to thank Hali Edison and Cornelia McCarthy for their role in organizing the JIMF conference on 'Perspectives on the Financial Crisis in Asia', and Lew Alexander, Tom Connors, Hali Edison, and John Fernald for useful comments. Ollie Babson provided superb research assistance. The views expressed are solely the responsibility of the author's and should not be interpreted as reflecting those of the Board of Governors of the Federal Reserve System nor its staff.

References

Hausmann, R., Rojas-Suarez, L. (Eds.), 1996. Banking Crises in Latin America. Inter-American Development Bank, Washington, D.C.
Deutsche Bank Research, 1998. Global Emerging Markets, December. Deutsche Bank AG, London.

Reforming the Global Economic Architecture: Lessons from Recent Crises

JOSEPH E. STIGLITZ*

RECENT TURMOIL IN INTERNATIONAL financial markets has raised a set of fundamental questions for the global community: Is the set of international financial arrangements, established after the Great Depression and World War II and modified after the abandonment of the gold standard in 1973, up to the challenges of the twenty-first century? Are minor modifications (such as slight changes in the governance of the international financial institutions, increased transparency, or surveillance) all that is required to adapt these institutions to the needs of modern economies, or are more fundamental changes necessary? Today, although much has been proposed, discussed, and argued, no consensus on desirable changes has yet been reached. In the meantime, what can countries, especially the poor, the small, and the less-developed, do to protect themselves from the seeming ravages of storms brought on by international financial instability?

The subject is complicated, and in the time allotted to me, I cannot do it justice. Rather than endeavoring to provide a comprehensive treatment, I shall summarize my views in 10 basic points, followed by three important methodological observations.

We should keep in mind that the success of a development or stabilization program must be assessed by its impact on the livelihood of the concerned individuals, not by whether the exchange rate has stabilized! Our objective should be clear: the welfare of the citizens in the affected country, with due attention to distributional concerns. A program cannot be hailed a success if the exchange rate is stabilized, but the country falls into a deep and prolonged recession. One cannot count a program a success until unemployment has returned to normal levels and growth has resumed. Ascertaining success is made ever more problematic by hypothesizing on the counterfactual—that is, what would have happened in the absence of the program? Perhaps output would have fallen even more, and unemployment risen even more. But since the advent of modern macromanagement, governments in developed countries have been able to shorten downturns and to mitigate their severity by taking strong countercyclical measures.[1] Those advocating contractionary policies, for instance, in the event of a crisis that in any case would have dampened the economy's strength, bear a heavy burden of proof: They must either show that more expansionary

---

*Chief Economist, The World Bank.
[1] See, for example, Stiglitz (1997a, 1997b).

policies were not feasible or that the contractionary policies generated stronger long-term growth. Evidence on growth trajectories in general provides little evidence in favor of the latter hypothesis.

With these caveats in mind, let me turn to 10 key policy points.

1. *The international financial architecture has exhibited enormous fragility over the past quarter century.* Financial and currency crises have hit with increasing frequency, at high budgetary costs to the governments that inevitably try to resurrect their economies. But the cost is high; for years after the crisis, growth is slower and unemployment higher.[2] By one reckoning, 80 to 100 countries have faced a crisis since the mid-1970s.[3]

What inferences can we make from this experience? To introduce one of the two metaphors that I will use frequently in the subsequent discussion: If there is a single accident on a road, one is likely to look for a cause in the driver, his car, or the weather. But if there are hundreds of accidents at the same bend of the road, then questions need to be raised concerning the construction of the road itself. Roads need to be designed not for perfect drivers, nor for drivers trained to drive on race tracks, but for ordinary mortals. If average drivers repeatedly find the curves too difficult to navigate, it is time either to reengineer the design of the road or to impose regulations on the cars that drive on it.

2. *Capital and financial market liberalization are systemically related to this vulnerability.* Both theory and empirical studies confirm this conclusion. Premature financial market liberalization—for instance, before the appropriate regulatory structures are in place—frequently leads to excessively risky lending by banks. Empirical studies show that the probability of a financial crisis is particularly high in the five years following financial market liberalization.[4] The recent crisis in Asia followed this familiar pattern. Given the Asian countries' commitment to continue with financial market liberalization, there was no obvious way in which to manage the macroeconomic consequences of the surge of financial capital, which left even more suddenly than it entered.[5]

Advances in economic theory (e.g., Hellman, Murdock, and Stiglitz (1996)) show that reliance on capital adequacy standards, a common feature in countries that have engaged in financial market liberalization, is not Pareto effi-

---

[2] For the growth result, see Caprio (1997). Economic downturns leave a long-term adverse legacy, among other ways, through the attrition of human capital, which has been emphasized in the literature on the hysteresis effect and may be a factor in the sustained high levels of unemployment in Europe. See Blanchard and Summers (1986).

[3] Caprio and Klingebiel (1996) identify banking crises in 69 countries since the late 1970s, which only includes countries with sufficient data. They estimate that the inclusion of transition economies would add crises in at least 20 more countries.

[4] Kaminsky, Linzondo, and Reinhart (1998). See also the path-breaking study of Chile's 1982 crisis by Diaz-Alejandro (1985). In the context of the Scandinavian crises see Steigum (1992) and Kiander and Vartia (1996).

[5] For a more detailed discussion of the crises, see Furman and Stiglitz (1999).

cient. It is particularly problematic to rely on capital adequacy standards in economies with poor information systems and facing high risks. (Because of their smaller size, most LDCs are less diversified than larger economies and thus face greater risks.) The problems of regulation in the aftermath of liberalization are exacerbated by the drain on trained personnel, as the booming private financial sector is able to outbid the public sector. And the instabilities arising from excessive reliance on collateral lending, an important feature of the Asian economies, have long been known: Such lending practices reinforce a boom, but when collateral values collapse, defaults soar and credit is constrained, furthering the decline in asset prices. These natural instabilities are only reinforced by excessive reliance on capital adequacy standards, without the sophisticated reliance on forbearance-cum-tightened regulatory supervision associated with more advanced economies. The beginning of the downturn leads to a few bankruptcies, putting banks below the required capital adequacy standards. In a pessimistic environment, banks find it impossible to raise additional funds, thus forcing them to cut back on lending. But as they all do this, bankruptcies and the nonperforming loans soar, creating a vicious cycle.

Interestingly, many of the problems might not have arisen in the previous regulatory regimes. Thailand, for instance, before it felt pressure to liberalize, had imposed limitations on bank lending to speculative real estate. It had been aware that such lending is a major source of instability and, moreover, it was still under the impression that investing in employment—creating factories—provided better foundations for a growth strategy than building empty office buildings. But under pressure from those who pushed on it the doctrines of the liberalized market, it succumbed to the judgment of the market with disastrous consequences.[6]

There is a certain irony in this evidence of increased instability: One of the arguments *for* capital market liberalization is that it leads to increased diversification, which in turn makes the country less vulnerable. In fact, what diversification occurred was mainly within East Asia and, as it turned out, the shocks were highly correlated (with the correlation perhaps exacerbated by the policies undertaken). In any case, the increased vulnerability posed by liberalization far outweighed the benefits of diversification, a result also observed elsewhere in the world.

3. Although capital market liberalization clearly portends greater risks, it has not brought commensurate benefits in terms of economic growth. Again, both theory and evidence support this conclusion. Rodrik

---

[6] Another metaphor has become fashionable for small, less developed countries embarking on financial and capital market liberalization. It is likened to a small boat setting sail on a wild and rough ocean—even if well steered and solidly constructed, it is vulnerable to being hit broadside by a wave and capsizing. And if the captain has not had proper training and if holes have not been fully repaired (if capital market liberalization proceeds too fast after financial market regulation), then a speedy and disastrous outcome is even more likely. Indeed, a design to make the boat faster and sleeker at the same time makes it less stable. In Asia, there simply was no time to take advantage of the allegedly improved design before disaster struck.

(1998) shows that neither investment nor growth was associated with capital market liberalization using the same kind of cross country regressions that typically show significant gains from trade liberalization. And of all the regions in the world, East Asia was the least likely to gain from capital account liberalization; with its high savings rate, it was hardly in need of further capital infusions at the margin. The low returns that might be associated with these marginal investments made the expected returns low, and left the risks high.

There are a number of reasons more generally why the view that capital account liberalization gives rise to enhanced growth should be regarded with skepticism. Liberalization has, in general, focused on opening a country to short-term speculative flows; but precisely because of the volatility of such flows, it is hard to base productive long-term investments on these funds.

In assessing the various sources of vulnerability, one factor has received increasing attention: the ratio of short-term foreign debt to reserves. A large fraction of countries in which that variable exceeded unity experienced crises. This variable did not appear in earlier studies of crises because economists had pointed out that any domestic asset could be converted into foreign currency under a regime of complete convertibility, so *existing* short-term foreign liabilities did not really represent the magnitude of the potential "threat."[7] That the variable has recently attained prominence illustrates the potential *negative* effects of short-term borrowing. Consider a poor, small country in which a firm decides to borrow $100 million from an American bank at 18 percent interest. Prudent behavior on the part of the country then implies that it must increase its reserves by $100 million—likely held in the form of U.S. Treasury bills. In effect, the country is then borrowing from the United States at 18 percent and lending at 4 percent—hardly a strategy that is likely to engender domestic growth, though it may resoundingly benefit the United States, among the most ardent advocates of capital account liberalization.

The most important reason that capital and financial market liberalization may not be related to growth is that it enhances instability; instability, as we noted in lesson one, has significant adverse effects on growth.[8]

4. The adverse effects of financial and capital market liberalization can, in turn, be related to the fact that there are marked discrepancies between social and private returns and risks. East Asia's

---

[7] On the other hand, the result is consistent with multiple equilibria sunspot models: If everyone believes that a ratio is believed by everyone else to be associated with a crisis, then when they see the variable pass the threshold, they withdraw their funds, leading to a crisis. For early models of multiple equilibria (including sunspot equilibria), see Stiglitz (1972a) and Shell (1977).

[8] There are a variety of reasons for this: A pattern of instability implies greater riskiness for investment, discouraging one of the main sources of growth. In economic downturns, investments in R&D and other productivity enhancing expenditures, as important as they are for long-term growth, tend to be curtailed. See Greenwald and Stiglitz (1989).

crisis was related to private sector borrowing. Even Thailand's large borrowings should not have been a problem because the borrowing was being used to finance private investment, which presumably yielded a return in excess of the cost of borrowing. Only if one believed that there was a government subsidy (either explicit, or implicit, in the form of a presumed bailout) should one have been worried—that is, *if one believed in the efficiency of market allocations.* But the experience of East Asia has confirmed lessons from experiences elsewhere: There are large systemic risks imposed on the economy by financial sector weaknesses and the surges in capital flows associated with capital account liberalization. The costs of these disruptions are felt not only by the borrowers and lenders who engage in the transactions, but also by workers, small businessmen, and others throughout the economy.

5. *It is intellectually incoherent to argue for bailouts and highlight the importance of contagion and systemic risk but not to try to address the underlying source of the problem.* The previous point argued that there are externalities associated with private, international, short-term borrowing. If there were no such externalities, then it would be hard to defend bailouts, and there would be no worry about contagion. Just as we now recognize that the production of steel may give rise to an important externality—air pollution—and that the externality necessitates an important public role in trying to "force" (through price or other forms of regulation) less pollution, it is imperative to recognize the externalities associated with these short-term private capital flows. The consequence of internalizing this externality in the former case may well be less steel producing—essentially a redeployment of resources to better reflect the social costs and benefits of the activity rather than relying on the distorted market allocations in which important social costs are ignored. This, too, should be the case for the latter example. The widespread worry that interventions might reduce the flow of capital is as misguided as the worry that discouraging air pollution might discourage the production of steel.

6. *The thrust of the interventions should be to stabilize capital flows, for it is the instability of such flows which generates the high costs and which limits their benefits.* Again, let me analogize with a metaphor: Without a dam, the melting of the snows at the top of a mountain may give rise to disastrous floods, resulting in death and destruction. A well-designed dam will temper the flow of water, but it will not stop the movement of water from the mountaintop to the seaside. However, by stabilizing the flow, the dam serves to reduce and perhaps eliminate the deathly and destructive aspects of the torrent—indeed, the dam may convert the water into a powerful, productive force.

This has an important implication: A good dam does not have to stop all flows, even temporarily, to be of considerable value.

7. Frequently, the key to stabilization is a comprehensive program.
Elsewhere, I have outlined a three-pronged program.[9]

1. *Eliminating the government distortions that have encouraged short-term flows.* (Thailand had a facility that had the effect of directly facilitating those flows; Korea's restrictions on long-term flows indirectly encouraged short-term flows.)
2. *Strengthening financial institutions.* This in turn has a number of ingredients such as improved transparency; broad and effective bank regulation, including good, risk-adjusted capital adequacy standards (flexible and adapted to particular circumstances of each country); speed bumps, such as limiting the rate of increase of lending; and exposure limits, both direct and indirect (on the firms to which the banks lend)
3. *Direct interventions to stabilize the flows of capital not mediated through the banking system.*

It is important to recognize that the first two sets of measures, as important as they are, are both difficult—especially for less-developed countries—and are far from sufficient to inoculate countries against the kinds of instabilities that have been so prevalent in the last quarter of a century. Transparency in the form of mark-to-market accounting (requiring banks to record all assets at their current market value), for instance, is resisted today in the United States, even in the aftermath of the S&L crisis (which was in part attributed to poor regulation, including inadequately transparent information systems). There was no reform, even after it was recognized that failing to use marking to market practices not only reduced transparency but led to distorted investment policies that potentially and significantly increased the risk exposure of banks.[10] Even under the best of circumstances, obtaining the relevant data may be difficult—and is becoming increasingly so.

Note that in standard competitive theory (as articulated for instance by Arrow and Debreu (1954)), the basis of the belief in the efficacy of market processes assumes that all the relevant information is conveyed by prices. The kinds of quantitative information being called for would, under standard competitive assumptions, simply be irrelevant—no one is calling for steel firms to release their sales figures. This highlights the difference between markets for commodities such as steel and finance markets, and it undermines the oft-heard argument that free mobility of capital is just as welfare enhancing as free trade in goods. Financial markets are different. Similarly, even countries with advanced institutional structures cannot claim an impressive record in managing their banking systems—witness the recent financial crises in the United States, Scan-

---

[9] See Stiglitz (1998a, 1998b).
[10] Similarly, the well-known—and successful—opposition of U.S. government officials to FASB's proposals for more transparent accounting frameworks for stock options well illustrates the political problems that such proposals frequently encounter. See Stiglitz (1992).

dinavia, and Japan. No country has adequate risk adjustments for capital adequacy standards or deposit insurance premia. Similarly, the fact that the last major set of financial crises occurred in Scandinavia, countries noted for their transparency, suggests that transparency by itself is not sufficient.

The increased use of derivatives—the risk implications of which are often very difficult to assess—and their increasing complexity have further complicated attempts at transparency and improved regulation.[11]

Let me be clear: Improved regulation and increased transparency are clearly desirable. But we should not underestimate the difficulties or overestimate the effectiveness of these measures. Those who think that regulation and transparency are all that are needed are looking for cheap and easy solutions to a complex and serious international problem. Or, alternatively, they seek solutions that are ideologically compatible with the belief in "free markets"—in spite of the evidence of the importance of market failures described above (see point one).

That a comprehensive program needs to go beyond bank regulation is evidenced by the experience of Indonesia, where two-thirds of the domestic borrowing was undertaken by corporates. To return to the dam metaphor, stopping bank borrowing from abroad may be like putting your finger in a dike—it may plug up one hole, but the water will find a way around. If there are economic incentives (or misguided perceptions) that lead to a desire to borrow abroad, corporates that can will do so, even if banks cannot do so on their behalf.[12]

8. Although a comprehensive program is essential, its features need to be adapted to the situation in each country. In particular, the regulatory framework for LDCs may well differ markedly from those of more-developed countries because the risks are greater, the regulatory capacities are weaker, and information is poorer. Developed countries have been moving to monitoring banks' risk management systems, but direct controls should continue to play a more prominent role in LDCs. Thus LDCs may need to impose more stringent regulations on lending—for instance on speculative real estate. They may need to impose speed limits (restrictions on the rate at which loan portfolios can grow). They may need to limit the use of derivatives.

---

[11] In several instances, firms believed that they had a covered position, only to discover that the party providing the cover had gone bankrupt. Thus, bank regulators need not only to look at "exposure" but at the portfolio position of those providing cover, and the correlation between credit and market risks. The difficulties of doing so—and the disadvantaged position of regulators—should be apparent. The recent failure of bank regulators in the United States to prevent a lone hedge fund from borrowing sufficient amounts that its open positions posed systemic risk to the global financial system should make us less than sanguine about a strategy focusing on LDCs improving their transparency or regulatory capacities enough to prevent future crises.

[12] At the same time, strong bank regulation—including restrictions on exposure of firms to which the banks lend—can have a major impact on aggregate exposure. So too could appropriate risk adjustments for capital adequacy standards and deposit insurance, which presumably would induce banks to charge higher interest rates to firms that had high exposure. Current risk adjustments fall markedly short of the mark.

Modern bank regulation recognizes the inefficiencies—and even the dangers—of excessive reliance on capital adequacy standards, and the problems in doing so are particularly acute for LDCs. Matters become even worse if excessively stringent capital adequacy standards are imposed (too rapidly) in an economy in recession, where many banks will naturally fail to meet those standards. The systemic credit contraction to which that can give rise may be self-defeating for as banks contract credit to meet the capital adequacy standards (because in the midst of a recession, they are likely to find it difficult to raise new capital), more firms go bankrupt, only increasing the fraction of loans that are nonperforming. In a dramatic example of the fallacy of composition, a policy designed to ensure strong banks—when an isolated bank has problems—actually undermines the strength of the banking system when there are systemic weaknesses. Countries that have successfully managed financial crises and the accompanying recessions have engaged in "forbearance"—*temporarily* weakening (in effect) capital adequacy standards, while they have increased the intensity of supervision of transactions.

9. *A key part of the reforms to stabilize the international financial system is a fundamental reform of bankruptcy, including what I call a "super chapter 11."* The reform of bankruptcy law needs to recognize the difference between systemic bankruptcy, when a substantial fraction of the firms in an economy are bankrupt, and an individual bankruptcy, when an isolated firm cannot meet its obligations. The inferences that can be drawn concerning managerial competency are dramatically different in the two situations—few firms in any country could survive depreciations of currency and increases in interest rates of the magnitude that occurred in East Asia. The presumption should be that existing management continue in place; the burden of proof should be on creditors to establish that there was a persistent mismanagement of the firm's assets. This is much like chapter 11, in which management typically continues, with a simple rearrangement of claims (with creditors typically taking some equity shares, though the original equity owners are seldom fully wiped out). In a "super chapter 11" there would be an even greater burden of proof on creditors if they seek alternative arrangements, and perhaps even greater clarity in the specification of default options.

It is not only that the information conveyed by the two types of bankruptcy differs. The costs of the standard bankruptcy procedures can also be enormous when applied to systemic bankruptcy. When there is systemic bankruptcy, the frequent delays common in standard bankruptcy proceedings would impose huge social costs. A super chapter 11 should be structured so that corporate reorganizations could occur much faster and at much lower costs than even a standard chapter 11.

The bankruptcy would be a (decentralized, private sector) analogue to a standstill. And the bankruptcy law would act as a circuit breaker in the downward spiral that has characterized East Asia. Now, as the exchange rate falls, more firms become nonperforming in the loans, weakening the banking system, leading to a credit contraction, which reinforces the downward dynamics. With the bankruptcy standstill, the losses of domestic players are limited. (To be sure, a super chapter 11 might lead to higher interest rates—so that the cost of borrowing may more accurately reflect some of the true social costs. See point 4 above.)

But just as bank regulation needs to be adapted to the situation in each country, so too does bankruptcy law. Indeed, there is no single "Pareto dominating" bankruptcy law. There are trade-offs between the interests of lenders and borrowers, and even between domestic lenders and foreign lenders.

I have said nothing so far about grander changes, such as proposals for creating a "lender of last resort." Though this is not the place for a comprehensive treatment of what is, after all, a highly complicated subject, the following points do seem worth making:

- Having a lender of last resort is not sufficient to protect an economy. The Federal Reserve Bank was created as a lender of last resort, considerably prior to the Great Depression. It was only when the lender of last resort was accompanied by deposit insurance and tightened supervision that crises were prevented (and one without the other can actually make a crisis more likely, as the S&L debacle so clearly demonstrated). But in the international context, proposals for a lender of last resort are seldom accompanied by something that would pass as an analogue to deposit insurance, with a tax imposed on lenders to support the "bailout" fund.
- There are, moreover, questions concerning whether a lender of last resort is "necessary," if governments really permit flexible (market-determined) exchange rates and adopt adequate bankruptcy laws. Mutual funds do not need a lender of last resort simply because they do not have a "first-come, first-serve" repayment at "fixed rates." Countries are, in this sense, much more like mutual funds than they are like banks, assuming flexible exchange rates. The funds are needed to support the exchange rate—to give those few extremely wealthy individuals in Russia, for instance, time to take out their money at the high exchange rate. When one recognizes that billions and billions have been misspent by countries in the vain attempt to support their exchange rate—dollars that in the end come out of the pockets of the countries' taxpayers—the small sums lost in Harberger triangles and other forms of microinefficiencies (so often railed against) pale in comparison.
- The essential ingredient of a "lender of last resort" is that there should be a degree of automaticity in access to funds to countries that "qualify." But in our rapidly changing world, can that be assured? A government can gamble and lose its entire reserves overnight with derivatives. Should such a government be entitled to a bailout, simply because it had previously acted in prudential ways? In the end, judgment calls will be necessary. And how different will those judgment calls be from those currently being made?

- Moreover, the signal that a country does not qualify, or has changed from "qualified" to "nonqualified" status could itself set off a crisis. Concern about this has led to a shift from dichotomous policies to more continuous ones: Countries that are "more qualified" get access to funds "more easily" or on better terms. Can such a system be run in a transparent way? The less transparent, the less "rule bound," the less "automaticity" this system has, the less will the lender of last resort function be served. Remember, the principle behind the lender of last resort is that the knowledge that there is a large stock of funds available to support a currency deters an attack. But the greater the discretion, the less assurance there is that there is a large stock of funds available, and hence the greater the incentive for an attack.
- Moreover, we now recognize the central role capital flight plays in currency crises. Given the huge amounts that could leave a country under an open regime, there is a real question of whether any fund that is likely to be amassed will provide sufficient assurance to reduce substantially the likelihood of an attack.
- I noted earlier that central to the success of a lender of last resort is good supervision. Earlier, I detailed the problems LDCs face in bank supervision. How supervision is run is not, however, just a technical matter, which is why governments such as the United States have insisted that, while supervision should remain "independent," it also remain politically accountable. The U.S. Comptroller of the Currency reports directly to the Secretary of the Treasury. Historically, the United States and other countries that have managed their way through cyclical fluctuations well have engaged in a certain degree of forbearance, compensating for the forbearance in capital adequacy standards with tightened supervision of transactions. I doubt that the United States would be willing to delegate supervisory responsibility to a group of international bureaucrats, only remotely politically accountable. Will other countries be willing to do so? Perhaps, if in doing so they can purchase greater credibility for their banking systems and greater "automaticity" of funds in the event of a crisis. But the answer is by no means obvious. Note that financial crises are only one of many stimulants for a currency crisis (and hence the "need" for a bailout). How broad will the reach of supervision need to be? It takes an enormous amount of confidence in international institutions to cede the kind of authority that is required for a lender of last resort to work effectively. It is not clear that we are at that stage yet in the evolution of global economic governance.

10. *Most importantly, there needs to be a congruence between a country's exposure to risks, its ability to reduce (or its tendency to exacerbate) those risks, and the provisions it has made to insulate the most vulnerable from the consequences of those risks (including its safety nets).*

Earlier, I described small, less-developed countries in the international capital markets as small boats in a wild and rough sea: Even if well steered and strongly constructed, they are likely to be capsized by a sufficiently large wave. To be sure, if they are not well steered, and if there are holes in the boat, their survival is even more precarious. This metaphor suggests that strong precautions should be taken before going out to sea. Precisely the opposite has occurred. The boat has been redesigned to make it sleeker and faster (assuming it could survive!), which renders it more unstable, reducing survival chances further still. Worse still, it has been set out to sail in the roughest part of the sea, in the worst conditions, before safety vests have been put on board, and before the skipper has had a chance to be trained for the new design. The consequences have been all too predictable—and at great human costs.

Before concluding, I want to spend a minute on three methodological "lessons."

A. It is imperative that policymakers better integrate financial and real economics. As has been noted repeatedly, at the heart of the East Asia crisis were private capital flows and a worry about bankruptcy and default. If there were not such worries, Western banks would have been more than willing to roll over their loans, especially at the high interest rates being offered. Thus, not only is bankruptcy of a first-order importance, but policymakers need to focus on how policies being pursued affect the likelihood of bankruptcy—it is a key endogenous variable. What is remarkable is that more than 25 years after micromodels began emphasizing the key role that bankruptcy plays in modern capitalism (see, e.g., Stiglitz (1969, 1972b) and Greenwald and Stiglitz (1992)), more than 20 years after the link between interest rates and bankruptcy was clearly articulated (Stiglitz and Weiss (1981)), and 15 years after these ideas were embedded in macromodels (Greenwald and Stiglitz (1984, 1993) and Stiglitz and Weiss (1992)), standard macrotextbooks often do not even mention bankruptcy in the index.

Too often, the financial sector is summarized in a money demand equation. Doing so not only misses the complexity of the financial sector, but can also lead to misguided policies. Indeed, the standard reduced-form relationships between money and aggregate output, summarized in the LM curve, all too often are markedly altered in the event of a financial or currency crisis, even of the mild variety experienced in the U.S. S&L debacle.[13] If this is true for a relatively mild crisis, affecting a small fraction of the financial sector, how much more so is it likely to be the case for the kind of major upheaval experienced, for instance, by Indonesia?

B. One should be wary of anthropomorphizing the market and of the prognostications of armchair market psychologists. The market consists of many players, with different portfolios, risk preferences, and in-

---

[13] This is now recognized to be an important contributor to the Fed's failure to take appropriate actions to stave off the 1991 recession. See Stiglitz (1992).

formation. There is enormous heterogeneity of beliefs, so much so that a piece of information may at the same time make investments in a country more attractive to some and less attractive to others. In particular, economic downturns, while reassuring to foreign investors (though even this is questionable), would normally be expected to generate domestic capital outflows. Increased risk induces domestic residents to diversify. Although they cannot easily diversify their human capital, they can move out more of their physical wealth. Time after time, we have seen domestic capital flight as an important contributor to a crisis and its perpetuation.

One should be suspicious of anyone who says, "The market expects...." I have never met "Mr. Market," and, as a former market participant, I can only say that frequently my expectations differ from those of the armchair market psychologists. Good analyses must take into account the diversity that makes a market, paying due attention to the differences between those in the country and those outside it.

C. We need to reach beyond anecdotes to construct coherent theoretical models and undertake empirical testing. Anecdotes are useful, both as teaching tools and in helping to guide our thinking. Journalists, who have to explain the world in simple terms, can be forgiven for relying on anecdotes in interpreting events. But economists and social scientists more generally should be held to a higher standard. Do higher interest rates lead to a stronger currency? Theoretical models can offer insights into the circumstances in which this might or might not be the case, and empirical work can cast light on whether these predictions are borne out in practice. The evidence is far from overwhelming in support of the "conventional wisdom" that higher interest rates are necessary, if not sufficient, for maintaining the strength of the currency.[14] The theoretical prediction that higher interest rates may so weaken an economy and increase the probability of bankruptcy that rather than attracting capital (net) they may induce capital to leave, seems to have been borne out in the data—and evidenced in the East Asia crisis.

Not only do anecdotes seldom support only one side—adherents of contrary positions can each proffer anecdotes in support of their opinions—but their interpretation is often elusive. In the East Asian context, the Mexican experience is often cited: it "stayed the course" and quickly recovered. But Mexico was smart; it chose as its neighbor and major trading partner a country with a booming economy and a strong financial system, with whom a major trade and investment treaty had just been signed. The countries of East Asia did not show as much wisdom, choosing as their trading partner a country going into its most severe recession in half a century and with a fragile financial system. To what extent should we credit "staying the course" and resolute action for the recovery? And to what extent should we credit "choosing one's neighbor"? My interpretation places a far greater weight on the latter; evidence for this can be gleaned by looking at the source of recovery—exports to U.S. firms. In-

---

[14] See Kraay (1998) and Furman and Stiglitz (1999).

deed, four years after the crisis, the domestic sector remains in weak shape. Considering one of the often reiterated lectures to the East Asian countries reinforces the point: Recovery will require addressing the weaknesses in the financial system. By contrast, there are repeated newspaper reports documenting the continuing deep weaknesses in the Mexican financial system, with nonperforming loans—four years after the crisis—still exceeding those in several of the East Asian crisis countries.

Every cloud has a silver lining, however thin: The disaster in East Asia, like the Great Depression, will prove a rich source of Ph.D. theses for decades to come. By examining such "extreme" events, we gather insights into the workings of the economy in more normal times. The story of East Asia (and the subsequent crises of 1998) is far from over, and it would be premature to reach any final verdicts. I suspect, however, that there will be a growing consensus in support of the basic lessons that I have outlined in this talk.

REFERENCES

Arrow, Kenneth J., and Gerard Debreu, 1954, Existence of an equilibrium for a competitive economy, *Econometrica* 22, 265–290.

Blanchard, Olivier J., and Lawrence H. Summers, 1986, Hysteresis and the European unemployment problem, *National Bureau of Economic Research Macroeconomics Manual* 1, 15–78.

Caprio, Gerard, 1997, Safe and sound banking in developing countries: We're not in Kansas anymore, *Research in Financial Services: Private and Public Policy* 9, 79–97.

Caprio, Gerard, and Daniela Klingebiel, 1996, Bank insolvencies: Cross-country experience, Policy research Working paper 1620, The World Bank.

Diaz-Alejandro, Carlos, 1985, Good-bye financial repression, hello financial crash, *Journal of Development Economics* 19, 1–24.

Furman, Jason, and Joseph E. Stiglitz, 1999, Economic crises: Evidence and insights from East Asia, *Brookings Papers on Economic Activity*, Washington, D.C.

Greenwald, Bruce, and Joseph E. Stiglitz, 1984, Informational imperfections in the capital markets and macroeconomic fluctuations, *American Economic Review* 74, 194–199.

Greenwald, Bruce, and Joseph E. Stiglitz, 1989, Financial market imperfections and productivity growth, National Bureau of Economic Research Working paper 2945.

Greenwald, Bruce, and Joseph E. Stiglitz, 1992, Towards a reformulation of monetary theory: Competitive banking, National Bureau of Economic Research Working paper 4117.

Greenwald, Bruce, and Joseph E. Stiglitz, 1993, Financial market imperfections and business cycles, *Quarterly Journal of Economics* 108, 77–114.

Hellman, Thomas, Kevin Murdock, and Joseph E. Stiglitz, 1996, Deposit mobilization through financial restraint; in Niels Hermes and Robert Lensink, eds.: *Financial Development and Economic Growth: Theory and Experiences from Developing Countries* (Routledge, London and New York).

Kaminsky, Graciela, Saul Linzondo, and Carmen M. Reinhart, 1998, Leading indicators of currency crises, *IMF Staff Papers* 45, 1–48.

Kiander, Jaakko, and Pentti Vartia, 1996, The great depression of the 1990s in Finland, *Finnish Economic Papers* 9, 72–88.

Kraay, Aart, 1998, Do high interest rates defend currencies against speculative attacks?, Unpublished paper, The World Bank.

Rodrik, Dani, 1998, Who needs capital-account convertibility?, *Essays in International Finance*, International Finance Section, Department of Economics, Princeton University, 207, 55–65.

Shell, Karl, 1977, Monnaie et allocation intertemporelle, Mimeo, Centre National de la Recherche Scientifique, Paris.

Steigum, Erling, 1992, Financial, credit boom and the banking crisis: The case of Norway, *Discussion paper 15/92*, Norwegian School of Economics and Business Administration.
Stiglitz, Joseph E., 1969, A re-examination of the Modigliani-Miller Theorem, *American Economic Review* 59, 784–793.
Stiglitz, Joseph E., 1972a, On the optimality of the stock market allocation of investment, *Quarterly Journal of Economics* 86, 25–60.
Stiglitz, Joseph E., 1972b, Some aspects of the pure theory of corporate finance: Bankruptcies and takeovers, *Bell Journal of Economics* 3, 458–482.
Stiglitz, Joseph E., 1992, S&L Bailout; in J. Barth and R. Brumbaugh, Jr., eds.: *The Reform of Federal Deposit Insurance: Disciplining the Government and Protecting Taxpayers* (Harper Collins Publishers, New York).
Stiglitz, Joseph E., 1994, Endogenous growth and cycles; in Y. Shionoya and M. Perlman, eds.: *Innovation in Technology, Industries, and Institution* (University of Michigan Press, Ann Arbor, Michigan).
Stiglitz, Joseph E., 1997a, The economic recovery of the 1990s: Restoring sustainable growth, Paper presented to the Georgetown University Macroeconomics Seminar, September 4, 1997.
Stiglitz, Joseph E., 1997b, The long boom? Business cycles in the 1980s and 1990s, Paper presented to the Center for Economic Policy Research, Stanford University, California, September 5, 1997.
Stiglitz, Joseph E., 1998a, Towards a new paradigm for development: Strategies, policies, and processes, Paper given as the Prebisch Lecture at UNCTAD, Geneva, October 19, 1998.
Stiglitz, Joseph E., 1998b, Beggar-thyself vs. Beggar-thy-neighbor policies: The dangers of intellectual incoherence in addressing the global financial crisis, Address to Annual Meetings of the Southern Economics Association, Baltimore, November 8, 1998 (forthcoming in *Southern Economics Journal*).
Stiglitz, Joseph E., and Andrew Weiss, 1981, Credit rationing in markets with imperfect information, *American Economic Review* 71, 393–410.
Stiglitz, Joseph E., and Andrew Weiss, 1992, Asymmetric information in credit markets and its implications for macroeconomics, *Oxford Economic Papers* 44, 694–724.

Name Index

Abbott, A.B. 58
Adams, T. 127
Agtmael, A.W. 263
Akaike, H. 101, 106
Akgiray, V. 62, 178, 211, 269
Alexander, G. 140, 141, 142, 343
Amihud, Y. 278, 279
Anderson, S.C. 524
Aqmon, T. 96, 223
Arnold, L. 376
Arrow, K.J. 572
Arshanapalli, B. 297
Asquith, P. 145
Atchison, A.D. 213

Bailey, W. 264, 265, 268, 277, 297, 311, 328, 355
Baillie, R.T. 7, 211, 269
Balvers, R.J. 208
Bansal, R. 34
Banz, 51
Bar-Yosef, S. 524
Barth, J.R. 471
Baumol, W.J. 154
Becker, K.G. 57, 174
Beckers, S. 457
Bekaert, G. 33, 272, 278, 317, 319, 328, 336, 337, 338, 354, 360, 361, 365
Benhabib, J. 154
Bernanke, B.S. 467
Berndt, E.K. 60, 77, 178, 212, 270
Bertero, E. 72
Black, F. 58, 174, 265, 271, 281, 289, 343, 375, 392
Blinder, A.S. 467
Bollerslev, T. 60, 62, 75, 76, 80, 81, 177, 183, 211, 212, 264, 267, 269, 270, 281, 284
Booth, G.G. 58, 62, 178, 211, 264, 269, 270, 272, 281, 289
Borio, C. 489
Born, J.A. 524
Borsch, B. 541
Bos, T. 191
Bossaerts, P. 313
Box, G.E.P. 26, 72, 91, 524
Boyle, P.P. 409
Brady, N.F. 19

Brandon, J. 541
Braun, P.A. 34
Breeden, D.T. 208
Breedon, D. 360
Brisson, J. 541
Brock, A.W. 154
Brock, W.A. 160, 170
Brodsky, W.J. 8, 15
Brorsen, W.B. 279, 289
Brown, B. 524
Brown, S.J. 112
Bruner, R.F. 517
Bunov, B. 156

Calomiris, C.W. 467, 473
Campbell, J.Y. 33, 175, 209, 265
Canina, L. 430
Cantor, R. 323
Caprio, G. 568
Carpenter, R.E. 470
Chamberlain, C. 365
Chan, K.C. 297
Chang, E. 362
Chang, R.P. 278
Chen, N.-F. 237
Chernow, R. 318
Cheung, Y.-W. 58, 175, 190, 198
Cho, D.C. 34, 46, 228
Chou, R.Y. 278, 281, 284, 299, 300
Choudhry, T. 278
Chow, V.K. 58
Christie, A.A. 58, 174, 265, 289
Cohen, K.J. 209
Collins, D. 524
Connor, G. 36, 457
Conrad, J. 62, 208, 213, 278
Conze, A. 410
Corhay, A. 58
Cornell, B. 376, 516
Cowles, A. 115, 116
Cox, J.C. 376, 381, 392
Cristofi, A. 297
Cristofi, P. 297
Crowley, M. 541
Culp, C. 449
Curds, R. 457
Cutler, D.M. 208, 209

Dahiya, S. 317
Damodaran, A. 278, 279
Dana, R.A. 154
Darcel, J. 541
Davis, M. 406
Davis, P. 503
Day, R.H. 154
De Jong, F. 58, 524
De Kock 541
De Long, B.J. 210
De Santis, G. 498
Debreu, G. 572
Dechert, W.D. 160, 170
Defusco, R.A. 264, 277
Demigüç-Kunt, A. 479
Denegas, A. 541
Dewynne, J.N. 410
Dickey, D.A. 100, 303
Diebold, F.X. 221, 225
Divecha, A. 261, 264, 277
Domowitz, I. 14, 15
Dornbusch, C.F. 486, 490
Doukas, J. 297
Douzy 541
Drach, J. 261, 277
Drummen, H. 58
Duffee, G.R. 289, 293
Duffie, D. 395, 401, 403
Dullum, K. 141
Dwyer, G.P. 96, 104, 297
Dym, S. 323

Eckbo, B. 313
Edwards, F.R. 20–21
Eichengreen, B. 323, 485
Engle, R.F. 58, 75, 97, 98, 100, 101, 103, 106, 174, 175, 183, 186, 190, 191, 198, 211, 220, 222, 225, 264, 265, 272, 273, 281, 285, 290
Erb, C.B. 317, 323, 457
Errunza, V. 33, 140, 264, 277, 297, 311, 343, 345, 366
Eun, C.S. 46, 57, 96, 97, 103, 108, 140, 141, 142, 174, 190, 191, 228, 297, 362

Fadner, K. 71, 190
Fama, E. 37, 54, 62, 208, 264, 278
Fazzari, S.M. 470
Ferson, W.E. 33, 34, 49
Figlewski, S. 430
Finnerty, J.E. 57
Fischer, K.P. 155
Fisher, L. 213, 278
Fleming, J. 430
Fleming, W.H. 376

Folkerts-Landau, D. 491
Fons, J. 407
Forbes, W.P. 190
Francis, J.C. 6, 10, 11
Frankel, J. 490
French, K.R. 62, 176, 208, 278
Friedman, M. 445
Froland, C. 317
Fuller, W.A. 100, 303, 304
Funaro 524

Gaertner, W. 154
Garber, P. 491
Garman, M. 423
Gennotte, G. 20, 21
Genotte, G. 155
Geppert, J.M. 277
Gertler, M. 469, 470, 479
Giavazzi, F. 486
Gibbons, M.R. 47, 360
Gibson, M. 468
Gielen, C. 116
Gilchrist, S. 469, 470, 479
Giovannini, A. 75
Glenn, D. 343
Glosten, L.R. 272
Goetzmann, W.N. 112, 318
Goldsmith, R. 247, 250–1
Goodhart, C. 492
Goodhart, C.A.E. 96
Gouriéroux, C. 75
Granger, C.W.J. 97, 98, 106
Grassberger, P. 159, 160
Greenspan, A. 446
Greenwald, B. 577
Gros, D. 487, 503
Grossman, S.J. 21
Grubel, H.G. 71, 96, 190, 223
Gruca, E. 437
Grundfest, J.A. 4, 19
Gruschow, C. 541
Gultekin, M.N. 34
Gultekin, N.B. 34
Gup, B.E. 297
Gupta, M. 57
Guy, P. 19

Hafer, R.W. 96, 104
Hall, H.B. 60, 77
Hall, M. 541
Hall, R.E. 60, 77
Hamao, Y. 19, 33, 57, 69, 174, 175, 176, 178, 184, 220
Hanke, M. 541

Hansell, S. 14, 16
Hansen, L.P. 34, 225, 332, 337
Hardouvelis, G.A. 215, 362
Harrison, J.M. 421
Harvey, C.R. 19, 33, 34, 38, 49, 76, 109, 263, 272, 277, 278, 317, 319, 323, 336, 360, 457
Hauser, S. 264, 277
Hausman, J.A. 60, 77
Healy, T. 541
Heimann, J.G. 3
Hellman, T. 568
Hentschel, L. 175
Heston, S.L. 34, 43, 47, 457
Hietala, P.T. 191
Hilliard, J.E. 26, 96, 224
Himmelberg, C.P. 467, 473
Hinchberger, B. 319
Hinich, J.M. 170
Hodrick, R.J. 33, 392
Hoshi, T. 467, 468, 470
Hoshii, I. 127
Howard, B. 12, 14
Hsieh, D.A. 20, 60, 155, 160, 169, 170, 177, 215
Huang, C.F. 437
Huang, R.D. 392
Hubbard, R.G. 470
Huberman, G. 332, 337

Iben, T. 407
Ingersoll, J.E., Jr. 376, 381, 392
Ito, T. 58
Iwanaga, M. 541
Izlen 541

Jaffe, J. 96, 103, 108
Jagannathan, R. 332, 337
Jagtiani, W. 328
Jamshidian, F. 411
Janakiramanan, S. 140, 141, 142
Jarrow, R. 375, 403
Jenkins, G.M. 26
Jenrich, J.I. 72
Jeon, B.N. 72, 87, 220
Jimenez, D. 541
Johansen, S. 296, 299, 304, 305, 307–9, 311, 314
Jorion, P. 33, 75, 112, 318, 332
Joy, O.M. 25, 27, 31, 224, 297
Judge, G.G. 304
Juselius, K. 296, 299, 304, 305, 307–9, 311, 314

Kalay, A. 524
Kandel, S.A. 332, 337
Kaplanis, E.C. 72, 73, 91
Karolyi, G.A. 190

Kasa, K. 190, 264, 297, 298
Kashyap, A.K. 467, 468, 470, 471, 477, 479
Kato, K. 51
Kaufold, H. 516–17, 518
Kaul, G. 62, 208, 213, 278
Kemma, A. 58
Kemna, A.G.Z. 410
Kendall, M.G. 224, 426
Khoury, S.J. 96
King, M.A. 19, 20, 57, 72, 87, 96, 174, 220, 221, 225, 228
Klingebiel, D. 568
Kloek, T. 58
Knif, J. 191
Koch, P.D. 57, 72, 87, 174, 186
Koch, T.W. 57, 72, 87, 174, 186
Kohlhagen, S. 96, 423
Kolb, R.W. 8
Kolodny, R. 362
Korajczyk, R.A. 34, 36, 46, 51
Korwar, A. 145
Koster, P. 541
Koutmos, G. 58, 175, 190, 264, 269, 270, 272, 281, 289
Kozicki, S. 220, 225
Kreps, D. 421
Kroner, K.F. 186, 281, 284

Lamont, O. 470
Lamy 517
Lando, D. 403
Lannoo, K. 503
Laporta, R. 362
Larker, D. 524
Lastrapes, W.D. 67
LeBaron, B. 154, 160, 209, 211, 215–16, 265, 268, 270
Lee, I. 297
Lee, S.B. 264, 265, 278
Lee, U. 58, 59, 174
Leland, H. 20, 21
Leong, P. 541
Lessard, D.R. 71, 96
Lessig, V.P. 25, 27, 31, 224
Levine, R. 479
Levy, H. 27, 71, 96, 223
Lewis, J. 16
Li, W.K. 80
Lim, J. 355
Lin, W.L. 58, 174
Lintner, J. 343
Litterman, R. 407
Litzenberger, R. 360
Liu, J. 313

Lo, A. 425
Lo, A.W. 62, 178, 208, 213, 278
Loewenstein, U. 524
Longin, F. 209
Lorenz, H.W. 154
Losq, E. 33, 140, 343, 345, 366
Lucas, R.E. 208
Ludvigson, S. 467

MacBeth, J. 37, 54
MacKinlay, A.C. 62, 178, 208, 213, 278
Maddala, G. 146
Makridakis, S.G. 26
Maldonado, R. 26, 27, 28, 30, 96
Malkamäki, M. 191
Malliaris, G.A. 156, 170
Mandelbrot, B. 264
Marcus, M. 277
Margrabe, W. 421
Marsh, T. 155
Martikainen, T. 191
Martin, S.A. 297
Mason, R. 139
Masulis, R.W. 19, 57, 69, 145, 220
Mathur, I. 191
Mauer, D.C. 343, 344, 345, 346, 366, 367
Mavroidis, T. 406
May, R.H. 156
Mayer, C. 72
McLeod, A.I. 80
Mehra, R. 111
Mendelson, H. 278, 279
Meric, G. 96, 297
Meric, I. 96, 297
Merton, R.C. 343, 346, 366, 367
Mikkelson, W. 143, 145
Miller, D. 332
Miller, M.H. 15, 20, 215, 445, 449
Milne, A. 470
Minuit, P. 13
Mitchell, B. 129
Mody, A. 323
Moeremhout 541
Monfort, A. 75
Montrucchio, P. 154
Mullin, J. 264, 272, 277
Mullins, D. 145
Murdock, K. 568
Musumeci, J. 517, 520, 525

Nelson, D. 58, 60, 62, 175, 177, 178, 211, 213, 264, 269, 272, 281
Nemerever, W.L. 317
Nerlove, M. 221, 225

Neumark, D. 19
Ng, L.K. 58, 75, 175
Ng, V.K. 19, 57, 69, 75, 174, 186, 220, 264, 265, 272, 273, 278, 285, 290, 299, 300
Nielsen, L.T. 495
Nolle, D.E. 471

Obstfeld 34
Ohk, K.Y. 264, 265, 278
Oldfield, G.S. 375
Osterwald-Lenum, M. 305

Packer, F. 323
Padmanabhan, P. 297, 311
Palasvirta, A.P. 155
Pan, M.-S. 297
Panton, D.B. 25, 27, 31, 96, 224, 297
Park, K.H. 263
Partch, M. 143, 145
Patterson, D.M. 170
Penati, A. 34
Perron, P. 266, 303
Petersen, B.C. 470
Pettway, R. 516
Philippatos, G.C. 97, 155, 156, 297
Phillips, P.C.B. 266, 303
Pilarinu, E. 155
Poon, S.-H. 58, 175, 269
Prescott, E. 111
Procaccia, I. 159, 160
Protter, P. 407
Purcell, J.F.H. 323
Pynnönen, S. 191

Rad, A.R. 58
Rampari, F. 487
Ramsey, J.B. 160
Ratner, M. 72
Reilly, F.K. 297
Reinganum, M.R. 376
Resnik, B. 297
Rice, T.N. 471
Richard, S.F. 376
Rietz, T. 111–12, 124, 125
Ripley, D. 96
Rishel, R.W. 376
Ritchken, P. 437
Rodrick, D. 570
Rogalski, R. 427, 437
Roll, R. 14, 19, 20, 22, 34, 37, 43, 54, 96, 220, 221, 237, 463
Roper, A. 319
Rosenbaum, A. 14, 16
Ross, S.A. 37, 54, 112, 237, 376, 381, 392

Rothschild, M. 220
Rouwenhorst, K.G. 34, 44, 47, 457
Rubinstein, M.E. 343, 430
Rumsey, J. 437

Said, S.E. 303
Saidi, R. 281, 289
Salwen, K.G. 13
Sand, O. 96, 97, 103, 108
Sankarasubramanian, L. 437
Sappenfield, R. 327
Sarnat, M. 27, 71, 96, 223
Sarney 524
Saudagaran, S. 140, 141, 146
Saunders 518
Saunders, A. 26, 27, 28, 30, 96
Scharfstein, D. 467, 468, 470
Scheinkman, J.A. 154, 170
Schoder, S. 516, 518
Schoenmaker, D. 492
Scholes, M. 62, 178, 208, 213, 278, 392
Schollhammer, H. 96, 97, 103, 108
Schwartz, E. 33
Schwert, G.W. 215, 269
Schwind, R. 541
Seber, G.A.F. 44
Senbet, L.W. 46, 228, 343, 344, 345, 346, 366, 367
Sentana, E. 58, 72, 209, 210, 215, 220, 265, 270
Seward, J. 427, 437
Sewell, S. 297
Shaffer, S. 154
Shalheim, J.S. 51
Shanken, J. 36, 37, 47
Shapiro, A.C. 516
Sharpe, S.A. 470
Sharpe, W.F. 337
Sheeline, W.E. 12
Shiller, R.J. 20, 210, 348
Shim, S. 57, 96, 97, 103, 108, 174, 190, 191
Siegel, J. 124, 125
Simms, J.M. 517
Singleton, K. 34, 401, 403, 467, 468, 470
Sinkey, J. 517, 520, 525
Smirlock, M. 516–17, 518
Smith, C. 140, 141, 145, 146
Smith, R. 498
Solnik, B. 33, 35, 71, 76, 96, 141, 209, 264, 277
Sortino, F.A. 288
Speidell, L.S. 327
Stansell, S. 297
Stapleton, R. 140, 141, 142
Stefck, D. 261, 277
Stehle, R. 33
Steil, B. 493, 502, 503

Stein, J.C. 466, 467, 468, 470, 471, 477, 479
Stigler, G. 445
Stiglitz, J.E. 20, 568, 577
Stock, J.H. 298
Stonehill, A. 141
Stuart, A. 224, 439
Stulz, R.M. 49, 190, 264, 277, 297, 311, 343
Subrahmanyam, M. 140, 141, 142, 191
Summers, L.H. 20, 348
Summers, V.P. 20
Sundaresan, M. 376
Susmel, R. 174, 186, 190, 191, 198
Szala, G. 14, 16

Tagen, M. 541
Takens, F. 158
Tam, G. 541
Tang, C. 479
Taylor, B. 116
Taylor, S.J. 58, 175, 269
Tesar, L. 498
Theil, H. 44
Theodossiou, P. 58, 59, 174
Thomas, N. 541
Tiao, G.C. 299, 302, 524
Tinsley, P.A. 19
Tobin 20
Torres, C. 13
Tosini, S. 19
Trzcinka, C.A. 37
Tsay, R.S. 299, 302
Tsetsekos, G.P. 277
Tuckman, B. 341
Tufano, P. 139
Turnbull, S. 403

Uhlaner, R. 36
Urias, M. 337, 338, 354, 361

Van Der Meer, R. 288
Vankudre, P. 516, 518
Viallet, C.J. 34, 46, 51
Vila, J.-L. 341
Vindeyaag, L. 541
Viskanta, T.E. 317, 323, 457
Viswanathan 410
Von Furstenberg, G.M. 72, 87, 220
Von Hagen, J. 487
Vorst, A.C.F. 410
Vorst, T. 410

Wachtel, P. 467, 473
Wadhwani, S. 19, 20, 57, 58, 72, 96, 174, 209, 210, 215, 220, 265, 270

Wagner, A. 541
Wallace, M.S. 297
Watson, J. 26, 28, 31
Watson, M.W. 298
Wei, J. 438
Weiss, A. 577
Weiss, A.A. 98
Weiss, G. 156
Werner, J. 498
Westerfield, R. 96, 103, 108
Wheatley, S. 34, 49, 297
Wheelwright, S.C. 26
White, H. 47
Wilcox, D.W. 467
Wilcox, J. 264, 277

Wilcoxon 145
Willey, T. 155, 163, 169, 170
Williams, J. 62, 178, 208, 213, 278
Wilmott, P. 410
Wizman, T. 362
Wunsch, R.S. 13

Yaari, U. 277
Yen, S. 277
Yoo 100, 101, 103
Yuan, H. 160

Zakoian, J.M. 265, 269
Zhang, P.G. 409
Zimmerman, H. 58